CONTEMPORARY Black Biography

ISSN-1058-1316

CONTEMPORARY
Black
Biography

Profiles from the International Black Community

Volume 48

Detroit • New York • San Francisco • San Diego • New Haven, Conn. • Waterville, Maine • London • Munich

ST. PHILIP'S COLLEGE LIBRARY

Contemporary Black Biography, Volume 48

Sara and Tom Pendergast

Project Editor
Pamela M. Kalte

Image Research and Acquisitions
Robyn V. Young

Editorial Support Services
Nataliya Mikheyeva

Rights and Permissions
Jacqueline Key, William A. Sampson, Shalice Shah-Caldwell

Manufacturing
Dorothy Maki, Rhonda Williams

Composition and Prepress
Mary Beth Trimper, Gary Leach

Imaging
Lezlie Light, Mike Logusz

© 2005 Thomson Gale, a part of the Thomson Corporation.

Thomson and Star Logo are trademarks and Gale is a registered trademark used herein under license.

For more information, contact
Thomson Gale
27500 Drake Rd.
Farmington Hills, MI 48331-3535
Or you can visit our internet site at
http://www.gale.com

ALL RIGHTS RESERVED
No part of this work covered by the copyright hereon may be reproduced or used in any form or by any means—graphic, electronic, or mechanical, including photocopying, recording, taping, Web distribution, or information storage retrieval systems—without the written permission of the publisher.

This publication is a creative work fully protected by all applicable copyright laws, as well as by misappropriation, trade secret, unfair competition, and other applicable laws. The authors and editors of this work have added value to the underlying factual material herein through one or more of the following: unique and original selection, coordination, expression, arrangement, and classification of the information.

For permission to use material from this product, submit your request via the Web at http://www.gale-edit.com/permissions, or you may download our Permissions Request form and submit your request by fax or mail to:

Permissions Department
Thomson Gale
27500 Drake Rd.
Farmington Hills, MI 48331-3535
Permissions Hotline:
248-699-8006 or 800-877-4253, ext. 8006
Fax 248-699-8074 or 800-762-4058

Since this page cannot legibly accommodate all copyright notices, the acknowledgements constitute an extension of the copyright notice.

While every effort has been made to secure permission to reprint material and to ensure the reliability of the information presented in this publication, Thomson Gale neither guarantees the accuracy of the data contained herein nor assumes responsibility for errors, omissions or discrepancies. Thomson Gale accepts no payment for listing; and inclusion in the publication of any organization, agency, institution, publication, service, or individual does not imply endorsement of the editors or publisher. Errors brought to the attention of the publisher and verified to the satisfaction of the publisher will be corrected in future editions.

ISBN 0-7876-6736-6
ISSN 1058-1316

Printed in the United States of America
10 9 8 7 6 5 4 3 2 1

Advisory Board

Emily M. Belcher
General and Humanities Reference Librarian
Firestone Library, Princeton University

Dr. Alton Hornsby, Jr.
Professor of History
Morehouse College

Ernest Kaiser
Editor, Contributor
Retired Librarian, Schomburg Center for Research in Black Culture

Dr. Ronald Woods
Director, Afro-American Studies Program
Eastern Michigan University

Contents

Introduction ix

Cumulative Nationality Index 175

Cumulative Occupation Index 187

Cumulative Subject Index 205

Cumulative Name Index 249

Anderson, Carl 1
    Energetic vocalist and actor
Annan, Kofi Atta 4
    United Nations leader
Baker, Anita 9
    Sophisticated jazz and R&B singer
Berry, Fred "Rerun" 12
    What's Happening!! funnyman
Brimmer, Andrew F. 14
    Authoritative economist
Bully-Cummings, Ella 17
    Distinguished Detroit police chief
Burnim, Mickey 20
    University leader committed to education
Césaire, Aimé 23
    Esteemed politician and writer
Charles, Ray 26
    Legendary American singer
Cole, Lorraine 31
    Devoted women's health advocate
Coleman, Wanda 34
    Uncompromising poet and critic
Coney, PonJola 37
    Motivated college dean and physician
Dabydeen, David 39
    Caribbean-born writer and critic
Davis, Charles T. 42
    Co-editor of The Slave's Narrative

Davis, Ernie 45
    College football hall-of-famer
Delice, Ronald and Rony 49
    Twin designers in the fashion world
Dunston, Georgia 51
    Successful microbiologist and professor
Edley, Christopher 55
    Respected United Negro College Fund leader
Edley, Christopher F., Jr. 58
    UC Berkeley Law School dean
Edmunds, Gladys 61
    Self-starting entrepreneur
Fabio, Sarah Webster 64
    Gifted Black Arts Movement poet
Fax, Elton 67
    Illustrator of black culture
Felix, Allyson 70
    Emerging track and field star
Fleming, Ray 73
    Educated poet and scholar
Foster, Marie 76
    Voting rights pioneer
Foxx, Jamie 79
    Hollywood superstar
Grace, George 82
    Businessman and fraternity leader
Graham, Lorenz 85
    Author of children's literature
Greenlee, Samuel 89
    Forward-thinking writer and broadcaster
Guillaume, Robert 92
    Renowned film and television actor
Jackson, Alphonso 96
    Fighter for fair housing
Jemison, Major L. 99
    Inspirational pastor
Johnson, Levi 102
    Well-liked football player

Johnson, Sheila Crump 104
    Executive and philanthropist
Kenney, John A. 107
    "The Dean of Black Dermatology"
Laraque, Georges 111
    Talented hockey player
Lavizzo-Mourey, Risa 114
    Noted physician and philanthropist
Mensah, Thomas 117
    Ghanaian scientist and entrepreneur
Morton, Azie Taylor 120
    Former U.S. Treasurer
Nelson Meigs, Andrea 122
    Capable talent agent
Oliver, John J., Jr. 124
    Highly regarded newspaper publisher
Owens, Helen 127
    School principal and community activist
Payton, John 130
    Accomplished lawyer
Sanders, Malika 133
    Young civil rights leader

Schmoke, Kurt 135
    Politician and lawyer
Scott, "Little" Jimmy 139
    Unique recording artist
Sims, Howard "Sandman" 141
    Skilled tap dancer
Smith, Vincent D. 144
    Black Arts Movement painter
St. Patrick, Mathew 147
    Actor on HBO series Six Feet Under
Sykes, Wanda 151
    Outspoken comedian
Vandross, Luther 154
    Beloved singer and songwriter
Virgil, Ozzie 158
    Baseball player and coach
White, Bill 161
    Hard-working baseball executive
Wilder, L. Douglas 164
    Virginia's first black governor
Young, Andrew 169
    Politician and champion of civil rights

Introduction

Contemporary Black Biography provides informative biographical profiles of the important and influential persons of African heritage who form the international black community: men and women who have changed today's world and are shaping tomorrow's. *Contemporary Black Biography* covers persons of various nationalities in a wide variety of fields, including architecture, art, business, dance, education, fashion, film, industry, journalism, law, literature, medicine, music, politics and government, publishing, religion, science and technology, social issues, sports, television, theater, and others. In addition to in-depth coverage of names found in today's headlines, *Contemporary Black Biography* provides coverage of selected individuals from earlier in this century whose influence continues to impact on contemporary life. *Contemporary Black Biography* also provides coverage of important and influential persons who are not yet household names and are therefore likely to be ignored by other biographical reference series. Each volume also includes listee updates on names previously appearing in *CBB*.

Designed for Quick Research and Interesting Reading

- **Attractive page design** incorporates textual subheads, making it easy to find the information you're looking for.
- **Easy-to-locate data sections** provide quick access to vital personal statistics, career information, major awards, and mailing addresses, when available.
- **Informative biographical essays** trace the subject's personal and professional life with the kind of in-depth analysis you need.
- **To further enhance your appreciation** of the subject, most entries include photographic portraits.
- **Sources for additional information** direct the user to selected books, magazines, and newspapers where more information on the individuals can be obtained.

Helpful Indexes Make It Easy to Find the Information You Need

Contemporary Black Biography includes cumulative Nationality, Occupation, Subject, and Name indexes that make it easy to locate entries in a variety of useful ways.

Available in Electronic Formats

Diskette/Magnetic Tape. Contemporary Black Biography is available for licensing on magnetic tape or diskette in a fielded format. Either the complete database or a custom selection of entries may be ordered. The database is available for internal data processing and nonpublishing purposes only. For more information, call (800) 877-GALE.

On-line. Contemporary Black Biography is available on-line through Mead Data Central's NEXIS Service in the NEXIS, PEOPLE and SPORTS Libraries in the GALBIO file and Gale's Biography Resource Center.

Disclaimer

Contemporary Black Biography uses and lists websites as sources and these websites may become obsolete.

We Welcome Your Suggestions

The editors welcome your comments and suggestions for enhancing and improving *Contemporary Black Biography*. If you would like to suggest persons for inclusion in the series, please submit these names to the editors. Mail comments or suggestions to:

The Editor

Contemporary Black Biography

Thomson Gale

27500 Drake Rd.

Farmington Hills, MI 48331-3535

Phone: (800) 347-4253

Carl Anderson

1945-2004

Actor, singer

Carlton Earl Anderson, known as Carl to his friends and family, became famous for his portrayal of Judas Iscariot in the stage and screen production of Andrew Lloyd Webber and Tim Rice's 1970s rock opera *Jesus Christ Superstar*. Possessed of high energy and an upbeat attitude, Anderson was also a highly respected jazz vocalist, who released nine solo albums and appeared on countless others. He died in 2004 at the age of 58 from leukemia.

Began Singing with Large Family

Anderson was born on February 27, 1945, in Lynchburg, Virginia, along with his identical twin brother, Charles Edward, who died of bronchitis at the age of 11 months. He grew up in a modest home on Boston Avenue along with his ten surviving siblings. His father, James, was a steelworker, and his mother, Alberta, worked as a seamstress. Anderson first began singing and performing as a child along with his family at the Rivermont Baptist Church.

Anderson attended the racially segregated Dunbar High School during the mid-1960s, where he sang in the school choir. In 1962, as a junior, he served as the choir's student director. Following his junior year, Anderson abandoned school and enlisted in the U.S. Air Force, serving as a communications technician. His experience singing in the World Wide Air Force Talent Contest first prompted Anderson to consider a career in music. After a two-year stint in the military, Anderson returned to Lynchburg and completed high school, graduating in 1965.

In 1969 Anderson moved to Washington, D.C. He simultaneously enrolled in classes at Howard University, took a job as the assistant director of the Columbia Heights Boys Club, and sang in clubs around town. During this time Anderson joined some friends to form a band, which they named The Second Eagle, because their first performance was on the night the Eagle One landed on the moon. With Anderson on lead vocals, the group covered songs at the jazz clubs along M Street in Georgetown to mixed reviews.

Played Judas Iscariot

On Palm Sunday in 1971, The Second Eagle was playing a gig at St. Stephen's Church, and Anderson sang several covers from *Jesus Christ Superstar*, which was released as an album before ever being staged. A talent scout from the William Morris Agency was in the audience and recognized Anderson's potential. As a result, on June 27, 1971, Anderson auditioned in New York City for the stage production of *Jesus Christ Superstar*. He landed the part of Judas Iscariot and started rehearsals two days later.

Five months later Anderson made his Broadway debut, replacing an ailing Ben Vereen. Later, the two would share the role of Judas. Anderson spent six months on stage in New York before moving to Los Angeles to prepare for a West Coast staging of the production. However, while still in rehearsals, he flew to London to audition for the movie version of *Jesus Christ Superstar*. Awarded the role of Judas, he then went to Israel for the shooting of the film.

At a Glance . . .

Born on February 27, 1945, in Lynchburg, VA; died on February 23, 2004, in Los Angeles, CA; son of James and Alberta Anderson; married Kathleen McGhee (divorced); married Verónica Ali; children: (from first marriage) Khalil McGhee-Anderson. *Education:* Attended Howard University. *Military Service:* U.S. Air Force, 1963-64.

Career: Stage and film actor, singer.

Awards: NAACP Image Award.

Already a popular hit on stage both in the United States and the United Kingdom, the movie version of *Jesus Christ Superstar* hit theaters in 1973. This rock opera (all dialogue is sung and there are no spoken words) told the story of the last six days of the life of Jesus Christ through the eyes of Judas, who is portrayed as more sympathetic than sinister. Although the film-as well as the album and stage production-created controversy among some religious groups, it became a huge success. Anderson, who first received press coverage because of the decision to cast an African American as Judas, soon turned the critics' attention to his outstanding, vibrant performance, which was roundly applauded. He received the NAACP Image Award and two Golden Globe nominations for best motion picture actor in a musical/comedy and most promising male newcomer.

Began Recording Career

In the same year, the original motion picture soundtrack from *Jesus Christ Superstar* was released, featuring Anderson as Judas. The 1970s were busy and exciting years in Anderson's life. Not only had he gone from obscurity to fame as Judas Iscariot, he also signed a record deal with Motown Records and worked with the popular musician Stevie Wonder on his seminal album *Songs in the Key of Life,* released in 1976. During this time Anderson married Kathleen McGhee (they later divorced) and had a son, Khalil McGhee-Anderson. He spent much of the early and mid-1970s touring and promoting *Jesus Christ Superstar.* In all, Anderson appeared on stage in the role of Judas more than 1,200 times.

Although Anderson appeared in a Spanish film, *The Black Pearl,* in 1978 (which was never distributed in the United States) and in the made-for-television thriller *Mind Over Murder* in 1979, by the end of the 1970s and early 1980s, he was primarily focusing on his music career. Gaining recognition from his performances in clubs around Los Angeles, he was able to land a record deal with Columbia Records to release four albums on the Epic label. His first two albums, *Absence without Love* and *On and On,* did not garner much attention from the critics or the public. However, Anderson worked with Earth, Wind, and Fire's Al McKay to produce *Protocol* in 1985, which included what is considered one of his best singles, "Can't Stop This Feeling." Despite the improvements in song selection and production, *Protocol* remained basically untouched in the stores.

In 1985 Anderson released the single "Friends and Lovers," a duet with *Days of Our Lives* soap star, Gloria Loring. The duet was a phenomenal success and reached the number-two spot on the charts. Epic hoped that Anderson's fourth album, *Carl Anderson,* would benefit from the popularity of the single, but ultimately found few buyers. With Epic losing interest after completing its four-record deal, Anderson released *Act of Love* in 1988 under RCA's Polydor label. Despite positive critical reviews for its smooth jazz sounds, the album once again failed in stores, and Polydor declined to extend Anderson's contract.

Continued Both Singing and Acting

Eventually Anderson was picked up by the GRP label, known for its jazz offerings. Thus Anderson moved away from the adult contemporary sound to the more decisively jazz style that he loved so dearly. In 1991 he released *Pieces of a Heart,* which became one of his most critically and commercially successful albums. Anderson produced two more albums under the GRP label during the early 1990s, *Fantasy Hotel* and *Heavy Weather/Sunlight Again,* released in 1992 and 1994, respectively. His last album, *Why We Are Here!,* was released in 1997 under the Abu Khalil label, Anderson's own production company named after his son. Although Anderson's solo career never catapulted him into fame as a singer, throughout the years he worked steadily with other artists, including Kenny Loggins, Maynard Ferguson, the Rippingtons, and Peabo Bryson. "Forbidden Lover," his duet with jazz great Nancy Wilson, received a Grammy nomination.

Anderson never completely abandoned acting on stage or screen. During the late 1970s and into the 1980s, he guest-starred on various television series, including *The Rockford Files, Magnum P.I., The Incredible Hulk, Hotel,* and *Starsky and Hutch.* In 1985 he played the part of Rev. Samuel in Steven Spielberg's *The Color Purple,* and in 1990 he was cast as Judge Walter Flynn in ABC's short-lived series *Cop Rocks.* Although for much of the 1980s he shied away from performing, or even mentioning, his defining role as Judas, Anderson reprised the part in 1992 for the production staged in celebration of the movie's twentieth anniversary. Slated for a three-month tour, the show received such attention that it continued for twenty-eight months and grossed over $100 million.

In 1997 Anderson appeared on Broadway as The Duke in the short-run *Play On!*, an adaptation of Shakespeare's *Twelfth Night*. He also appeared on the pre-Broadway soundtrack of *The Civil War—An American Musical*, and in 2002 he played the part of Dr. Klip in the short film *Mello's Kaleidoscope*. During the early 2000s, Anderson continued to work on productions of *Jesus Christ Superstar*. In the summer of 2003, while on tour, Anderson was diagnosed with leukemia. Prior to becoming ill, he was planning a reunion tour with original cast member Ted Neeley as Jesus, which had been slated to perform at the Vatican in the fall of 2004.

He died in Los Angeles on February 23, 2004. He is survived by his wife, Verónica Porche Ali, the former wife of boxing great Muhammad Ali, his son, two stepdaughters, Laila Ali and Hana Yasmeen Ali, as well as three brothers and six sisters. On May 15, 2004, the Dunbar High School Auditorium in Anderson's hometown of Lynchburg, Virginia, was officially renamed the Carl Anderson Performing Arts Auditorium.

Selected works

Albums

Absence without Love, Epic, 1982.
On and On, Epic, 1983.
Protocol, Epic, 1985.
Carl Anderson, Epic, 1986.
Act of Love, Polydor, 1988.
Pieces of a Heart, GRP, 1991.
Fantasy Hotel, GRP, 1992.
Heavy Weather/Sunlight Again, GRP, 1994.
Why We Are Here!, Abu Khalil, 1997.

Films

Jesus Christ Superstar, 1973.
The Black Pearl, 1978.
The Color Purple, 1985.
Mello's Kaleidoscope, 2002.

Sources

Books

Who's Who Among African Americans, 17th ed. Gale Group, 2004.

Periodicals

Daily Variety, March 22, 2004, p. 12.
Essence, January 1991, p. 30.
Jet, March 15, 2004, p. 18.
New York Times, February 27, 2004.
Variety, March 1, 2004, p. 45.
Washington Times, February 15, 2001, p. 3; May 11, 2002, p. D3.

On-line

"Actor Who Played 'Superstar' Judas Dead," *CNN.com*, www.cnn.com/2004/SHOWBIZ/Movies/02/26/obit.anderson.reut/index.html (September 27, 2004).

"Carl Anderson," *The Internet Movie Database*, www.imdb.com/name/nm0026483/ (September 27, 2004).

"Carl Anderson, Known as Judas in Jesus Christ Superstar on Stage and Screen, Dies at 58," *TheaterMania.com*, www.theatermania.com/content/news.cfm?int_news_id=4418 (September 27, 2004).

"Carl Anderson, Star of *Superstar*, Dead at 58," *Broadway.com*, www.broadway.com/template_1.asp?CI=34296&CT=38&qq=1&qs=jesus (September 27, 2004).

"Carl Anderson, Superstar's Judas on Stage and Screen, Dead at 58," *Playbill*, www.playbill.com/news/article/print/84562.html (September 27, 2004).

"Carl Anderson: The Official Website," *Precision Marketing*, www.cstone.net/~dgarlock/carl/ (September 27, 2004).

—Kari Bethel

Kofi Atta Annan

1938—

Secretary General of the United Nations

Annan, Kofi, photograph by Jeff Christensen. Reuters/Archive Photos. Reproduced by permission

On December 18, 1996, the clink of raised champagne glasses rang through the United Nations (UN) headquarters in New York City. The celebration was to honor incoming Secretary General Kofi Annan, the first black African ever to have held the difficult job. His election was greeted with genuine pleasure by UN insiders, who admire him for his unswerving integrity, his cool judgment in the toughest emergencies, and his ability to learn valuable lessons from every situation in which he finds himself. His colleagues had plenty of time to assess Annan's strengths. Other than a two-year period in the mid-1970s when he returned to his native Ghana to run the Tourism Control Board, Annan has devoted his entire career to the international organization.

During Annan's nearly half-century of life in UN service, the number of troubled areas all over the world has soared. Governments have toppled in Africa; blood has stained highly-coveted lands in Europe; Soviet Communism has collapsed, and with it, the grim wall separating East and West Berlin, and the Middle East has exploded in violence. Each change has left in its wake a flood of desperate refugees who depend on the UN for basic humanitarian aid such as food, shelter and medical services.

The huge challenges of assessing these urgent needs, working out suitable strategies for humanitarian aid, and helping to keep peace between warring factions everywhere have taken Annan all over the world. By turns he has visited Iraq, Bosnia, Somalia, Rwanda, Ghana, Ethiopia, Egypt, and Switzerland. Along the way he has gained a comfortable familiarity with English, French, and several African languages. Constant traveling has also taught him a great deal about the ancient traditions by which many people live, and the ways in which they buckle when changes overwhelm them. Well-versed in several ways of life besides his own, he can truly be considered a citizen of the world.

Early Activism

Kofi Annan spent his boyhood years in Africa's Gold Coast, which was then shedding its 70-year-old status as a British crown colony in favor of an up-to-the minute identity as an independent West African country named Ghana. The country's mood about the future

> **At a Glance . . .**
>
> Born April 8, 1938; married (1), divorced; married (2) Nane Cronstedt, 1984; children: one son, one daughter, one stepdaughter. *Education*: Macalester College, St. Paul, Minn, BEcon, 1961; Institut des Institut des Hautes Etudes Internationale, Switzerland, 1961-62; Massachusetts Institute of Technology, Sloan Fellow, MSc Mgmt, 1972.
>
> **Career**: World Health Organization, administrative and budget officer, 1962; Ghana Tourism Control Board, managing director, 1974-76; United Nations Office of Personnel Services, New York, NY, deputy chief of staff services, 1976-80; United Nations High Commissioner for Human Rights (UNHCR), deputy director of administration and head of personnel, Geneva, Switzerland, 1980-83; United Nations Office of Finance, director of budget, 1984-87; United Nations Office of Human Resources Management, assistant secretary general, 1987-90; United Nations assistant secretary general for program planning, 1990-92; United Nations budget and finance controller, 1992-1993; United Nations undersecretary for peacekeeping, 1993-1996; United Nations secretary-general, 1996–.
>
> **Awards**: Nobel Peace Prize, jointly awarded with United Nations, 2001.
>
> **Addresses**: *Office*—United Nations Headquarters, United Nations Plaza, New York, NY 10017.

was optimistic, and young Annan was right in step. A self-confident leader even as a teenager, he undertook his first successful human rights mission while at boarding school, participating in a hunger strike to protest the poor quality of the food there.

That first experience as an activist was so satisfying that Annan continued to take an interest in public service after he entered Ghana's University of Science and Technology, where he studied economics. In 1957, while serving as vice president of the Ghana Students' Union, he happened to visit Sierre Leone for a meeting of student leaders. There he caught the attention of a talent scout from the Ford Foundation's Foreign Students Leadership Project. A scholarship swiftly followed, and Annan was soon on his way to the United States to finish his economics degree at Macalester College in St. Paul, Minnesota.

Annan graduated in 1961, but did not return to his homeland. Instead he became a staff member at the United Nations, embarking upon a series of jobs that gave him valuable experience in the two vitally important areas of finance and human resources management. The first rung of the UN ladder took him to Geneva, Switzerland, where he became a budget administration officer for the World Health Organization. Next, after acquiring a master's degree in management at the Massachusetts Institute of Technology during 1971-72, he spent four years in the UN's Office of Personnel Services in New York. In 1980, he went back to Switzerland, where he spent the following three years as head of personnel for the United Nations' High Commissioner for Human Rights (UNHCR).

Led the UNHCR

The UNHCR is often the only place in which refugees in war-ravaged countries can turn for help with such basic necessities as food and medical care. During 1980 to 1983, the years Annan spent there, its staff members left the Geneva headquarters for Bangladesh, Cambodia, Indonesia, and Hong Kong; they were also sent to Italy, Greece, and Iraq. All in all, UNHCR personnel were able to ease the suffering of more than three million terrified refugees.

While the daily catalog of international anguish was enough to spur Annan to work as hard as possible, even more incentive came from his friendship with Nane Cronstedt, a lawyer who became his second wife in 1984. The inspiration came from Cronstedt's family background. She was a niece of the revered Raoul Wallenberg, a Swedish diplomat who had snatched 5,000 Jews from Adolph Hitler's death camps during World War II. Though a 35-year span separated Wallenberg's mysterious 1945 disappearance in Russia and his niece's friendship with Annan, his wartime bravery was still a matter of breathless awe for Annan.

Annan felt a special message for humanity was present in Wallenberg's selfless heroism. It began, he felt, with the diplomat's pivotal role as a bystander who had been free to choose whether he would turn a blind eye to the Nazis or fight them. Unmoved by his personal danger, Wallenberg had chosen to sacrifice himself rather than turn his back on the agony of Hitler's trapped and helpless human targets. Annan believed the whole wartime saga provided an important example of immortal integrity. "His kind of intervention gives hope to the victims, encourages them to fight and resist, helps them to hang on and bear witness, and hopefully arouses our collective conscience," Annan remarked in 1997, while opening a monument to Wallenberg in London.

Rose through the Ranks at the UN

In January of 1993, after a year as assistant secretary general for Peacekeeping Operations, Annan was promoted to the top post. Now, as under secretary, he held authority over 80,000 troops, dispatching them anywhere they were needed in order to spare lives and restore calm between warring factions. At that time, the UN had 13 peacekeeping missions in progress. Longest-standing was the Middle East operation, which had been monitoring the sporadic Arab-Israeli cease-fires since 1948. Thereafter, in chronological order, came UN observation on the tense India-Pakistan border, dating back to January of 1949; the same kind of operation in Cyprus, Greece (initiated in March of 1964); the Golan Heights (1974) and Lebanon (1978). In the scant two years since the beginning of the 1990s, the UN had also become a formidable presence on the Iraq-Kuwait border, as well as in Angola, El Salvador, Cambodia, and Mozambique. Other urgent missions were appearing on the horizons of Eastern Europe's former Yugoslavia and Somalia, the land that sits directly on the horn of the African continent.

Annan was well-acquainted with the problems of Somalia—a rudderless state that had existed since without a government since the toppling of President Siad Barre in 1991. Somalia had begun to writhe in the grip of power struggles by so many opposition parties that the entire infrastructure of the country had been completely destroyed. In a country with a literacy rate of only 20 percent, the lack of expertise in engineering made replacement impossible, so the loss of the public buildings, bridges, and roads was an inestimable loss. But a far greater tragedy was the smell of death that hung in the air. In just the six months between September of 1991 and March of 1992, the Mogadishu area alone had suffered the injury of 27,000 people and an estimated 14,000 more had been killed.

As if the civil war was not enough for Somalis to bear, their problems were further complicated by a persistent drought. News reports everywhere showed long lines of emaciated people streaming desperately out of the country in search of food. By September of 1992, an estimated 500,000 refugees had poured into neighboring Ethiopia, with an additional 300,000 flooding into Kenya; 65,000 heading for Yemen; and about 115,000 scattered elsewhere.

Dealt with Famine

During the month of August, the UN spearheaded a famine relief operation for the 1.5 million people who were teetering dangerously on the edge of starving to death. By early November, the UNHCR was ready to launch a large-scale rescue operation called UNOSOM, which consisted of setting up camps just outside the country to feed about 65,000 Somalian refugees. Yet even though the UN was quickly flying in the most capacious emergency food stores that could be supplied, the suffering Somalis could not rest easily.

In Mogadishu and other major cities, the unarmed victims were often chased away by looting bandits, who had dusted off the weapons the country had received in the early 1980s to give it greater power in a territorial struggle against Ethiopia. Now, as the coveted grain and flour steadily disappeared into the bandits' hands, the UN saw only one solution—to augment the 500 Pakistani soldiers previously authorized by Secretary-General Boutros Boutros-Ghali. Before long another 3,500 troops were on their way to Africa.

Because the United States was seen by Somalis as the only country capable of staving off the inevitable national tragedy, on November 21, 1992, U.S. president George Bush also sent military units to Somalia. Arriving under the banner of "Operation Restore Hope," the first troops landed on December 9, to be joined for a New Year's Day visit by President Bush himself. By mid-January the number of foreign troops in the country was soaring towards the 18,000 troops from 21 nations, and phase two of the operation called United Nations Operations Somalia, or UNOSOM II, was under way, with the hope that the leaderless country would be turned over to United Nations control by May 4, 1993.

But under the influence of a faction leader named Mohammed Farah Aideed, the gratitude of the Somalis began to turn to resentment and a fear that the foreign troops were heralding a return to the British and Italian colonial influence that the country had experienced in the early years of the century. Seizing the opportunity to consolidate his power, in June of 1993, Aideed attacked and killed 25 UN soldiers. At this point, the United States decided to curtail its interest in Somalia.

UN Acted as Peacemaker

United Nations troops being bound by the United Nations Charter, they had traditionally gone on peacekeeping missions. By these terms, UN troops were usually kept in place by agreement of both conflicting parties and were armed only to an extent that would permit them to defend themselves or their equipment. The situation in Somalia, however, was different. Somalia boasted neither government nor rulers to consult, and no well-defined conflicting parties existed that could be mediated. Therefore, the UN troops had no outside authority to mediate their actions.

For the first time in history, the UN Security Council sent their auxiliary troops into a conflict situation buttressed by a UN Charter mandate. This meant they were allowed to act as peacemakers rather than as mere peacekeepers. By UN decree, they were authorized to force Somalia to accept peace, even if they had to fight to achieve it. The alteration in UN Charter mandate made this present peacekeeping force the most aggressive in the history of the United Nations. Furthermore, since 26 of the organization's 41 missions had been mounted since 1989, controlling the forces and their movements was becoming an ever-mounting challenge that the Peacekeeping Department was not equipped to handle. Annan set out to remedy this situation by instituting a streamlining effort.

First came a situation center to monitor the department's international operations around the clock. In 1993, when it was established, this office consisted of eight military officers and two telephones placed in a Manhattan office. By the end of 1995, however, with 17 peacekeeping missions in progress, it was staffed by 120 officers, serving as ultimate backup to 70,000 peacekeeping soldiers worldwide.

In a second innovation, Annan sought support from member nations who were prepared to contribute troops and equipment for standby duty, in case peacekeeping efforts should be needed for a sudden emergency. The high regard in which he is held was soon obvious, when, by the end of November, 1996, 62 of the 185 members had agreed to provide some 80,000 standby troops between them. Annan also created a "lessons learned" unit within the Department of Peacekeeping Operations to make sure that all phases of each operation are discussed, evaluated and broadened further by interaction with other UN departments. Annan hoped the new departmental wing would improve future operations and minimize avoidable mistakes.

Worked in Bosnia-Herzegovina

Supervising all these innovations made a tight work schedule for Annan. Nevertheless, his workload became greater still in November of 1995, when Secretary-General Boutros Boutros-Ghali appointed him special representative to the former Yugoslavia, a European territory soon to become familiar as Bosnia-Herzegovina. This mission posed a grave responsibility for Annan, who had been asked to coordinate a smooth transition of international peacekeepers from United Nations forces to NATO military units.

Like Somalia, Bosnia-Herzegovina was an international symbol of raw tragedy. Its two principal population groups, the Serbs and the Croats, had been at war over possession of this area ever since the breakup of the Socialist Federated Republic of Yugoslavia in 1991. In the course of a conflict that would eventually cost between 250,000 and 300,000 lives, they had brought such concepts as "ethnic cleansing," back into the limelight from the shadows of World War II, updating them for the 1990s by "rationalizing" the expulsion and wholesale murder of the Bosnian Muslims. The slow torment of Bosnia-Herzegovina led first to an arms embargo from the United Nations Security Council in September of 1991, then, in May of 1992, to the arrival of peacekeeping and humanitarian forces, who brought sanitation, water, and electricity to the city of Sarajevo's residents.

While this desperately-needed aid was offered without reservation, it came at a high cost to the UN itself. When accompanied by the humanitarian aid that is part of the United Nations service, peacekeeping is an exercise so expensive that by 1994 the annual budget had reached a whopping $3.3 billion. And, generous as it seemed, escalating crises all over the world were stretching this money so thin that the organization was sinking dangerously into debt.

A sinking monetary bottom line was one reason that the UN decided to pass the Bosnian peacekeeping burden on to the North Atlantic Treaty Organization (NATO). But this was only part of the story. Equally important was the fact that NATO forces are solely dedicated to defense by military means. This single focus was sorely needed in Bosnia-Herzegovina, where the fragile "peace" could be more accurately described as a sullen cease-fire. In November of 1995, UN Secretary-General Boutros-Ghali asked Annan to go to Bosnia to handle the details of withdrawing UN forces and settling NATO forces in their place. It was a difficult task to accomplish. Nevertheless, with his characteristic energy and efficiency, Annan managed to achieve it within four months and returned to his post at the UN by March of 1996.

Chosen to Lead the UN

Meanwhile, Secretary General Boutros-Ghali was nearing the end of his five-year term of office, and his re-election, though acceptable to many of the UN's 185 members, was far from a done deal with the United States. Though swimming against the tide of public opinion, U.S. ambassador Madeleine Albright quickly made her country's objections known to the UN Security Council, one of the most influential groups of policy-makers in the world.

The Council itself consists of five permanent members, plus ten who are voted onto the body periodically. Each of the permanent five—China, United Kingdom, France, Russia, and the United States—has the power of veto over all other votes, a power Albright was now exercising. Furthermore, she emphasized her feelings by encouraging the United States to withhold $1.4 billion in fees owed to the United Nations. The charges of the United States against Boutros-Ghali were twofold: that he tended to follow his own path rather than the policies laid down by the UN's members, and that he had ignored warnings that the UN and its soaring debt were to be streamlined immediately.

Finding an alternative candidate to fill the difficult post of secretary general became a necessity. As a UN insider with more than 30 years of service under his belt, Annan was a natural choice, easily hurdling France's objection, based incorrectly on the assumption that he was not French-speaking. On December 18, 1996, Annan was welcomed into office to serve, as he modestly put it, "185 masters" and to institute an immediate cost-cutting program at the UN. On his own initiative, Annan also established a public relations program to bring more rapport between the huge organization itself and the international public. As he remarked at his pre-celebration press conference, Annan well understood that he was undertaking a huge challenge. But nobody present doubted his ability to handle whatever the future might bring.

From his first days as Secretary General, Annan has pursued an ambitious plan to renew the UN, maintained an international commitment to Africa, sought to gain Iraqi compliance with security standards, promoted Nigerian civil rule, sought to improve the status of women in the Secretariat, and involved non-state organizations in partnership with the UN. Annan has particularly excelled at involving many different people in debates about world peace and how the UN might best fulfill its mandate. In 1999 Annan published some interesting perspectives on world peace when he served as a guest editor to *Civilization* magazine; he prepared an issue entitled "How to Save the World," with essays from contributors ranging from heads of nations to preeminent scholars. At the turn of the century, Annan published a report called "We the Peoples: The Role of the United Nations in the 21st Century," in which he detailed a plan for UN member states to end poverty and inequality, improve education, reduce the incidence of HIV/AIDS, protect the environment and humanity from violence. The report led to the Millennium Declaration, a plan that has guided the United Nations into the new millennium. For his efforts, Annan was honored with the United Nations in 2001 with a Nobel Peace Prize. Since that time, Annan has continued to push for improvements to the UN's ability to function as a peacemaking body in the world.

Sources

Periodicals

Buffalo News (Buffalo, New York), November 22, 1998.

Chicago Tribune, June 27, 1993, p.10, November 29, 1994; December 18, 1996, p. 30; December 20, 1996, p. 31.

Civilization, June/July 1999.

Commentary, May 2004, p. 15.

Ebony, October 1998, p. 136.

London Times, December 19, 1996, p. 17.

New Republic, May 3, 2004, p. 38.

New York Times, October 6, 1993, p. A17; December 14, 1996, p. 5.

Newsweek, December 23, 1996, p. 30; April 26, 2004, p. 6.

Time, December 3, 1996, p. 51; November 30, 1998, p. 136.

West Africa, December 23, 1996, p. 5; February 3, 1997, p. 181; February 3, 1997, p. 178.

On-line

United Nations Secretary-General, www.un.org/News/ossg/sg/ (November 19, 2004).

Other

Additional information for this profile was obtained from the United Nations Department of Public Information, "The UN in Brief," July 3, 1997; "Press Conference by Secretary-General Elect Kofi Annan," December 18, 1996, Transcript, GA/9212; "Secretary-General warmly congratulates Kofi Annan on Receiving Security Council Recommendation," December 13, 1996, SG/SM/6131; "Secretary-General Says Monument to Raoul Wallenberg Is Inspiration to Act," SG/SM/6169.

—Gillian Wolf and Sara Pendergast

Anita Baker

1957—

Singer

Anita Baker's rich and entirely distinctive alto voice has invited comparisons that range beyond the world of contemporary pop to include mention of such legendary jazz figures as Sarah Vaughan and Nancy Wilson. One of the leading performers in the field of sophisticated black adult pop in the late 1980s and early 1990s, she waged a successful battle to take control of her career and realize her artistic vision. In 1994, with her stardom assured, Baker cut back her activities to focus on home and motherhood—in the process revealing something of the intense difficulties she faced during her own youth. Then, after a ten-year hiatus from the business, she made a triumphal return with a new album that met with critical acclaim.

Baker, Anita, photograph. Jo Hale/Getty Images.

The facts of her early life are far from clear; most have been supplied by Baker herself in interviews that sometimes contradict one another. She was born in 1957 or 1958 in Toledo, Ohio, perhaps on January 26 or December 20, and grew up in Detroit's inner city. Her birth mother, who was only 16 when Anita was born, abandoned her, leaving her in the care of a woman who has been variously described as a friend and as a relative; this woman, Mary Lewis, became her foster mother. When Anita was 13, her foster mother died, and an older sister in her adoptive family told her the truth about her past. This older adoptive sister, Lois Landry, raised Anita.

Combated Feelings of Abandonment

Much later, in an interview with *Essence,* Baker recalled how she tried to cope with this discovery: "That child believed her mother abandoned her," she said (referring to herself), "because there was something bad about her. Something terrible that made her unlovable. And until Walter [Baker's future husband], that is how I felt about me—that I was not good enough. Not good, period." Baker's foster family provided her with a stable environment that emphasized hard work and religion; she joined a church choir and identified with the deep voice of gospel singer Mahalia Jackson. She began to sing secular music with her friends as well, and was performing in Detroit clubs by the time she was 16. Baker attended a community college briefly, but a strong drive toward musical performance asserted itself, and she dropped out of school

At a Glance . . .

Born c. 1957 in Toledo, Ohio; abandoned by birth mother at age two and raised in Detroit, Michigan; married Walter Bridgforth, December 24, 1988; children: Walter and Eddie. *Education:* Attended community college in Detroit. *Religion:* Baptist.

Career: Vocalist. Sang as a teenager in Detroit nightclubs, mid-1970s; joined group Chapter 8, late 1970s; signed with Beverly Glen label, 1983; signed with Elektra, 1986; signed with Atlantic label, 1996 (released on albums); signed with Blue Note, 2004.

Awards: Six Grammy awards, two each for Rapture, Giving You the Best That I Got, and Compositions.

Addresses: *Home*—Grosse Pointe, MI. *Label*—Blue Note, 150 5th Ave., 6th Fl., New York, NY 10011.

---

to front a funk ensemble called Chapter 8, whose bass player had heard her perform in an East Side nightclub.

Chapter 8 toured widely and landed a contract with Los Angeles-based Ariola Records. They had a minor hit with "I Just Want to Be Your Girl" in 1980, but disbanded after being dropped from the label, which was itself in dire financial straits. Label executives offered the assessment that Baker lacked star quality. Later on Baker correctly concluded that their criticism could have masked any number of reasons that might through no fault of their own led to the group's dismissal, but at the time she was shattered by the turn of events. She returned to Detroit, worked as a waitress, and then landed a stable position as a receptionist with a law firm whose members, understandably enough, liked the sound of her voice on the phone.

In 1982 Baker was coaxed back into the music business by a former Ariola executive who started an independent label called Beverly Glen. Promising to make Baker a star, he offered to match her receptionist's salary, and Baker finally agreed to come to Los Angeles. Her first solo album, *The Songstress,* was released in 1983. The album attracted wide industry attention, yielded two R&B hit singles (the sultry "Angel" and the gospel-drenched "No More Tears," which did indeed bring to mind the voice of Mahalia Jackson), and sold a respectable 300,000 copies. But Baker, still unschooled in the frequently unscrupulous ways of the music business, received no royalties from the album and parted ways acrimoniously with Beverly Glen, a much-needed follow-up album still unreleased.

Released Hit Album

Hiring as her manager Sherwin Bash, a Hollywood veteran with the smarts to clear up the resulting legal problems, Baker signed with the Elektra label and threw herself wholeheartedly into her next project, the album *Rapture,* released in 1986. Gaining a reputation as pushy but consistently moving to gain control over her career, Baker supervised every aspect of the record's production. Filling the role of executive producer herself, a nearly unprecedented move for a rising but untested star, Baker chose *Songstress* collaborator Michael Powell as producer, and the two painstakingly selected songs that fit Baker's smooth, ultra-romantic, jazz-inflected vocal stylings. They succeeded brilliantly. The album yielded two massive hit singles in both R&B and pop tabulations, "Sweet Love" and "You Bring Me Joy." Baker's voice—low, intimate, and rounded, yet filled with a gospel-derived intensity that manifested itself in sudden bursts of strong feeling—became familiar to a wide public. The singer was rewarded with two Grammy awards in 1987, and by the end of 1988 *Rapture* had racked up sales of over five million units.

Baker stretched herself with an appearance at Europe's prestigious Montreux Jazz Festival in 1988, but the two albums that followed *Rapture, Giving You the Best That I Got* (1988) and *Compositions* (1990) followed basically the same path as their multi-platinum predecessor. Compositions featured examples of Baker's songwriting, which had gained in technical skill since she had begun to take classes in music theory. The album gained for Baker the respect of jazz musicians, and caused some critics, such as Alex Henderson of the All Music Guide, to suggest that she should record an album of straight jazz. Both recordings again earned Grammy awards for Baker, who kept up a grueling schedule of concerts and personal appearances. After one Detroit nightclub gig, Baker was greeted on her way to her dressing room by a persistent admirer who bought six copies of her album and asked her for a hug and then a date. She and this fan, Walter Bridgforth, were married on Christmas Eve of 1988.

Exhausted from touring and from the pressures of her high-profile career, Baker suffered two miscarriages as she and Bridgforth attempted to start a family. "I sort of came apart," Baker told *Essence.* "All my old negative feelings reemerged. I felt like such a failure." Finally Baker retreated to the sumptuous home she shares with Bridgforth in Grosse Pointe, Michigan, outside Detroit, one of a group of structures originally owned by the Dodge family of automaking fame. She enlisted the help of medical specialists and is now the mother of two sons.

Back on Track After Ten Years

Baker reemerged in 1994 with the *Rhythm of Love* album, which followed up on a series of revelatory interviews in which Baker finally delved into her own painful past. The album received mixed reviews, but sold well. At the time, fans did not know it would be the last Anita Baker album for the next decade. Baker signed a deal to produce an album with Atlantic, but she could never finish the job. It seems that she had more important things on her mind, for Baker had made the decision that she would not repeat the mistakes of her own mother and was giving more and more of her time to taking care of her children. "My grandmother gave up my mother, and my mother gave me up," Baker told *People*. "I just wanted to stop any hint of that cycle." For the next ten years, Baker played the role of mom, joining the local PTA and shuttling her kids to school activities. She also nursed her foster parents, Walter and Lois Landry, through the last years of their lives.

By the early 2000s Baker realized that with her kids needing less attention than before and the Landrys gone, she once again had time to devote to her music. She gave several small concerts in the Detroit area and was overwhelmed by the positive response of her fans. Soon her bookings grew and she signed with Blue Note to record two albums. The first album, *My Everything*, was released in 2004, and its title track soon soared to the top of the charts. To most critics, it appeared that Baker picked up right where she left off, providing soulful R&B in a sultry voice that was unmatched in the business. Ever the perfectionist, Baker insisted on complete control over the album and on not being pressured to tour too much. "I only work two days a week, so I'm not away from the boys and my husband too much," she told *Newsweek*. "And my record company so got it and so understood that. I had to learn to prioritize my life, because I have been the woman who tried to do everything, and I was miserable." With its life-affirming tracks, *My Everything* is a clear indication that Anita Baker is happy to be back.

Selected discography

The Songstress, Beverly Glen, 1983.
Rapture, Elektra, 1986.
Giving You the Best That I Got, Elektra, 1988.
Compositions, Elektra, 1990.
Rhythm of Love, Elektra, 1994.
My Everything, Blue Note, 2004.

Sources

Books

Contemporary Musicians, Volume 9, Gale, 1993.
Erlewine, Michael, et al., eds., *All Music Guide to Rock*, 2nd ed., Miller Freeman, 1997.

Periodicals

Billboard, October 26, 1996; September 4, 2004.
Ebony, September 1994, p. 44.; November 2004.
Essence, December 1994, p. 80; October 1, 2004.
Jet, March 13, 1995, p. 60.
Newsweek, September 13, 2004.
People, October 10, 1994, p. 77; September 13, 2004.

On-line

"Anita Baker," *Blue Note Records*, www.bluenote.com/artistpage.asp?ArtistID=3739&tab=1 (November 18, 2004).
Anita Baker, www.anitabaker.org (November 18, 2004).

—James M. Manheim and Tom Pendergast

Fred "Rerun" Berry

1951-2003

Actor

Fred Berry, the portly actor best known for his comic turn as "Rerun" on the hit ABC sitcom *What's Happening!!* in the late 1970s, died in 2003 at the age of 52 in Los Angeles. Berry never returned to the stardom he attained early in his career, but became a minister and motivational speaker later in his life. One of his last roles was a cameo in the 2003 David Spade movie *Dickie Roberts: Former Child Star.* "He was exactly like he was on TV—a very happy, lovable guy that made everyone laugh," Spade told *People*.

Born on March 13, 1951, Berry grew up in public housing in St. Louis, Missouri. He was a dancer on the long-running dance show *Soul Train* for a number of years, and his fleet-footed moves eventually landed him in a Los Angeles break-dance troupe called the Lockers. The group made a very early appearance on NBC's *Saturday Night Live* during its first season in 1975. But true stardom for Berry came a year later, when he joined the cast of a new ABC sitcom called *What's Happening!!* The show was the brainchild of Eric Monte, who had written the acclaimed 1975 film *Cooley High* about African-American teens in a 1960s Chicago high school. Monte created a television series about a trio of high-school pals in Los Angeles, centered around the studious Roger "Raj" Thomas, played by Ernest Thomas.

Berry was already in his mid-twenties when cast as teenaged Freddie "Rerun" Stubbs, and he managed to win the part over the objections of the show's producers, who originally had a skinny white actor in mind. The heavy-set, easygoing character earned his "Rerun" nickname because he had to repeat all his classes during summer school. His perpetual wisecracking and disco-dance moves quickly stole the show away from Thomas and the third pal, Dwayne (played by Haywood Nelson). Berry usually sported a trademark red beret and suspenders, and his "Rerun" soon became a household name. His typical greeting to Raj and Dwayne—"Hey, hey, hey"—even entered the vernacular for a time. The show's writers began building scripts around Rerun's antics, with the plots carried along by the scrapes in which he found himself—and inadvertently, his friends—enmeshed.

Though *What's Happening!!* was set in the present time, there seemed little evidence of the troubles that plagued many African-American urban communities in the mid- to late 1970s. It was sometimes referred to as the black version of *Happy Days,* a top-rated ABC hit sitcom of the era that was set in the 1950s. *What's Happening!!* aired at a time, wrote *San Francisco Chronicle* writer Peter Hartlaub, "when television executives seemed transfixed with hip urban comedies. While other shows in that decade typecast young black men as street toughs, basketball stars and scratching-and-surviving welfare recipients, 'What's Happening!!' was about three friends who hung out at the soda shop and dealt mostly with the struggles of being a teenager."

Alas, Berry did not handle the fame and fortune well. He later said that in three years he had spent much of his earnings, and then battled substance abuse and health problems for much of his life. "I was empty inside," he told *People* in 1996. "I blew a million dollars on drugs, real estate, an airplane, horses, the

At a Glance . . .

Born on March 13, 1951, in St. Louis, MO; died of diabetes, October 21, 2003, in Los Angeles, CA; married six times to four women; children: Portia Allen, Fred Jr.

Career: *Soul Train,* dancer, 1970s; The Lockers (dance troup), Los Angeles, break-dancer; actor, 1976-2003; ordained a Baptist minister and preached in Madison, AL; motivational speaker.

whole nine yards." The show went off the air in 1979, but became surprisingly popular in syndicated reruns, garnering new fans every year. It returned as *What's Happening Now!!* in 1985, with the nearly all of the original cast, and followed their lives as adults. Rerun was now a used-car salesperson, but Berry appeared only for the first of its three seasons after a contractual dispute with the show's producers. Some of the later comic energy was supplied by a young Martin Lawrence in its final season in 1987-88.

After entering a substance-abuse treatment program, Berry struggled financially for a number of years. Film roles were few and far between. He earned money from shopping-mall appearances, and became a motivational speaker and Baptist minister in Madison, Alabama, at the Little Shiloh Primitive Baptist Church. "Today I live strictly on faith," he said in the 1996 *People* interview. "I have to depend on people calling me to speak." He appeared in the 1998 film *In the Hood,* and in *Big Money Hustlas* two years later, two little-seen projects. But fans everywhere still recognized him from *What's Happening!!* "I'm still called 'Rerun' and I love it!" he once said, according to an article in London's *Guardian* newspaper by Shola Adenekan. "People ask me to dance every day, no matter where I am—in the grocery store or in the bathroom." He even legally changed his middle name to "Rerun."

Berry enjoyed a bit of a comeback in the years just before his death. He appeared on the NBC series *Scrubs* as himself in 2001, took part in *Star Dates* on the cable network E! a year later, and guested on Snoop Dogg's *Doggy Fizzle Televizzle* on MTV. In 2003 he appeared as himself in the *Dickie Roberts* film with Spade. His last television appearance came just weeks before he died, on the syndicated show *Classmates,* which reunites former friends from their school days. Berry appeared with Charles Bradshaw, a beefy football player whom he thanked for defending him when other kids teased him because of his weight.

Berry had lost some of his excess pounds in the 1990s after learning he had diabetes. He suffered a stroke in 2003, and died on October 21 of that year. He was the father of three children, and had been married six times in all, though on two of those occasions he remarried an ex-wife.

Selected works

Films

Vice Squad, 1982.
A Stroke of Genius, 1984.
In the Hood, 1998.
Big Money Hustlas, 2002.
Bum Runner, 2002.
Dickie Roberts: Former Child Star, 2003.

Television

What's Happening!!, 1976-79.
What's Happening Now!, 1985-86.

Sources

Broadcasting & Cable, October 27, 2003, p. 8.
Daily Variety, December 19, 2003, p. 56.
Entertainment Weekly, November 7, 2003, p. 20.
Guardian (London, England), November 7, 2003, p. 31.
Jet, November 10, 2003, p. 17.
New York Post, April 22, 2004, p. 7.
New York Times, October 24, 2003, p. C11.
People, June 24, 1996, p. 87; November 10, 2003, p. 96.
San Francisco Chronicle, October 27, 2003, p. D1.
Time, November 3, 2003, p. 24.
Times (London, England), December 4, 2003, p. 42.

—Carol Brennan

Andrew F. Brimmer

1926—

Economist

Brimmer, Andrew F., photograph. AP/Wide World Photos. Reproduced by permission.

The first black man to be named a governor of the Federal Reserve System, Andrew F. Brimmer is a noted economist who heads his own successful Washington consulting firm, Brimmer & Co., Inc., and is considered a specialist in federal reserve monetary policy. He is also a frequent commentator in newspapers and magazines on economics matters and topics related to the national and international economy, as well as on those especially relevant to the black economic community. For a number of years Brimmer has served on the board of economists of *Black Enterprise,* a monthly magazine devoted to black business in the United States. In his "Economic Perspectives" column Brimmer reports on trends and developments in national economics, and translates them to both individual blacks and the black business community. Brimmer has lent his insight to such topics as the Social Security system, discrimination in black business, black-owned banks, and personal financing.

Excelled in School

Brimmer was born in 1926 in Newellton, Louisiana, the son of Andrew Brimmer, Sr., a sharecropper and warehouse worker. After graduating from high school in 1944 he moved to the state of Washington, and shortly thereafter enlisted in the U.S. Army, serving until 1946 in Hawaii. After his discharge, a federal education grant for servicemen permitted him to attend the University of Washington in Seattle, where he first pursued a degree in journalism. He later switched to the study of economics, convinced that it best allowed him an opportunity to understand the American way of life. Brimmer received his bachelor's degree in 1950, and thereafter was awarded a John Hay Whitney Foundation fellowship with which he pursued his master's degree. One of his early interests, which he explored in several papers, was foreign economies. In 1951 he received a Fulbright fellowship to study in India at the Delhi School of Economics and the University of Bombay, and subsequently published several journal articles on the Indian economy.

After returning to the United States Brimmer began working towards his doctoral degree in economics at Harvard University and at the same time was employed as a research assistant at the Center for International Studies at the Massachusetts Institute of Technology.

At a Glance...

Born Andrew Felton Brimmer on September 13, 1926, in Newellton, LA; son of Andrew (a sharecropper and warehouse worker) and Vellar (Davis) Brimmer; married Doris Millicent Scott, 1953; children: Esther Diane. *Education:* University of Washington, BA, 1950; University of Washington, MA, 1951; Harvard University, Ph.D., 1957. *Politics:* Democrat. Religion: Unitarian. *Military service:* U.S. Army, 1944-46, served in Hawaii.

Career: Federal Reserve Bank, New York City, economist, 1955-58; Michigan State University, East Lansing, assistant professor, 1958-61; University of Pennsylvania, Wharton School of Finance and Commerce, Philadelphia, assistant professor, 1961-63; Securities Exchange Commission, consultant, 1962-63; Department of Commerce, Washington, DC, deputy assistant secretary, 1963-65, assistant secretary for economic affairs, 1965-66; Federal Reserve Board, governor, 1966-74; Harvard University Graduate School of Business Administration, Thomas Henry Carroll Ford Foundation visiting professor, 1974-76; University of Massachusetts at Amherst, professor; Brimmer & Co., Inc. (economic consulting firm), president, 1976–.

Selected memberships: *Black Enterprise* magazine, member of board of economists and contributor of "Economic Perspectives" column; Bank of America, BlackRock Mutual Funds, American Security Bank, UAL-United Air Lines, Du Pont Co., and Gannett Company Inc., member of board of directors for all.

Awards: Named government man of the year by the National Business League, 1963; Arthur S. Flemming Award, Russwurm Award, both 1966; Horatio Alger Award, National Urban League Equal Opportunity Award, both 1974; Fulbright 40th Anniversary Distinguished Lecturer, Ghana and Nigeria, 1986.

Addresses: *Office*—President, Brimmer & Co. Inc., 4400 MacArthur Blvd. NW, Washington, DC 20007.

He married his wife, Doris, a graduate student at nearby Radcliffe College, in 1953. From 1955 through 1958 he gained valuable experience working as an economist for the Federal Reserve Bank of New York, and in 1956 was appointed to the fact-finding Central Banking Mission sent to the developing African country of Sudan. While Brimmer continued to pursue his research interests in foreign economies, he also became a specialist in the monetary practices and investment policies of American life insurance companies. After receiving his Ph.D. in 1957, he worked for five years as an assistant professor of economics at Michigan State University, during which time he published his book, *Life Insurance Companies in the Capital Market*. In 1963 Brimmer began working with the U.S. Commerce Department in Washington, DC, and eventually was promoted to assistant secretary for economic affairs. At the Commerce Department he became further experienced in U.S. foreign investment policies and practice, as he was called upon to encourage American businesses to limit overseas investments as a way to reduce international deficits. In 1966 Brimmer's government service reached its highest level when he was appointed by President Lyndon B. Johnson to fill a vacancy on the seven-member Federal Reserve System Board of Governors. One of the chief functions of the board is to develop federal-reserve policy as well as supervise the budget and operations of the nation's twelve District Reserve Banks. Brimmer served on the Board during the inflationary boom of 1964-65, and was a primary proponent and spokesman for the Board's decision to tighten the money supply by raising interest rates and decreasing the amount of loan funds available to businesses. He also voiced his support for curbing inflation through a tax increase, which occurred in 1968 when President Johnson authorized a ten-percent tax surcharge.

Brimmer's tenure with the Federal Reserve Board lasted until 1974, at which time he became the Thomas Henry Carroll Ford Foundation professor at Harvard University's School of Business Administration. Two years later he founded his own economic consulting firm, Brimmer and Co., Inc., which specializes in federal reserve monetary policy. Combining his interest and experience in foreign economies, Brimmer has also become an authority on the world banking system, especially in the area of foreign debt obligations of Third World countries. In the 1983 Joseph I. Lubin Memorial Lecture at New York University, Brimmer outlined the common circumstances surrounding the crippling, high-interest loans owed by less-developed countries, their roots in the oil crisis of the late 1970s, and the role of U.S. commercial banks and the International Monetary Fund in moderating their resolution. Brimmer warned, however, against viewing the problem in general terms. "Different countries face a variety of particular obstacles which arise from specific circumstances related to their respective economies," he stated in *The World Banking System: Outlook in a Context of Crisis*. "Consequently, it would not only be futile but harmful as well to attempt to mandate a common, universal solution to the debt troubles plaguing developing countries."

Respected for His Economic Expertise

In recent years Brimmer has gained exposure as a leading voice on economic matters relating to blacks and the black business community. In the "Economic Perspectives" articles he contributes to *Black Enterprise,* Brimmer distills national economic topics for a general audience, reports authoritative facts to illustrate his points, and discusses economic topics that specifically pertain to blacks. Among the areas he has discussed are the Social Security system, the soundness of black-owned banks, the implications of free-trade agreements for minority business, and the persistent problems of discrimination toward black businesses. Brimmer's articles serve as an informative voice for the black economic community; regarding the 1990 collapse of New York City's Freedom Bank, the nation's fourth-largest black-owned bank, Brimmer suggested that the Federal Deposit Insurance Corporation (FDIC) engaged in the most severe resolution procedures allowed, thereby limiting the amount of money recouped by depositors—a trend, according to Brimmer, used by the FDIC in resolving the failure of other black-owned banks. He continued to voice his concerns and to propose solutions to the economic life of blacks through magazine articles and his service on the boards of a variety of governmental committees and private businesses.

Over the years Brimmer has decried discrimination against black-owned businesses and in minority hiring processes—yet he cautions against viewing discrimination as the primary culprit behind economic problems faced by black Americans. In a 1985 speech quoted in the *Negro Almanac,* Brimmer warned that deficiencies in both education and marketable skills were likewise to blame, and argued a controversial stance that "certain problems are not a matter of circumstance but a matter of choice for black people." He similarly warned in a 1985 *Ebony* article that by the year 2000 competition for service labor would be particularly intense. "Most jobs will require a much higher degree of skills, and…will be linked much more directly to computers and their operation," Brimmer wrote. When speaking in 1994 specifically about the limited number of black governors at the Federal Reserve Board, Brimmer noted that qualifications are the key to success. "I do not advocate diversity because there is something uniquely related to race, ethnicity or gender which will be brought to the Board," Brimmer told *Black Enterprise.* "The demand is for competent people and if they bring something else, that is a plus." But Brimmer warned in *Black Enterprise* in 1998 that, "Down the road, as competition increases, it will not just be blacks versus whites, it's going to be blacks versus everybody else, and unless conditions change dramatically, we risk dropping out at the bottom."

In addition to his duties as economic consultant and spokesman for the black economic community, Brimmer serves on the board of directors of a number of American corporations and banks. He has received various honors over the years for his work and is also a member of several economic associations. In 1989 he was re-named president of the Association for the Study of Afro-American Life and History and the following year became chairman of the Joint Center for Political and Economic Studies in Washington, DC, a post that he served faithfully until his resignation in 2001. In 1995 President Clinton appointed Brimmer to head a five-person control board, called the District of Columbia Financial Responsibility and Management Assistance Authority, that helped Washington, DC, out of a severe budgetary deficit over the next several years. Brimmer continues his work to encourage black Americans to succeed and prosper.

Selected writings

The Setting of Entrepreneurship in India, Massachusetts Institute of Technology Center for International Studies, c. 1950s.

Some Studies in Monetary Policy, Interest Rates, and the Investment Behavior of Life Insurance Companies, Cambridge, MA, 1957.

Life Insurance Companies in the Capital Market, Michigan State University Bureau of Business and Economic Research, 1962.

The World Banking System: Outlook in a Context of Crisis, New York University Press, 1985.

International Banking and Domestic Economic Policies: Perspectives in Debt and Development, University of California Press, 1986.

"Economic Cost of Discrimination Against Black Americans," in *Economic Perspectives on Affirmative Action,* edited by Margaret C. Simms, Joint Center for Political and Economic Studies, 1995

Sources

Books

Brimmer, Andrew F., *The World Banking System: Outlook in a Context of Crisis,* New York University Press, 1985.

The Negro Almanac: A Reference Work on the African American, 5th edition, Gale, 1989.

Periodicals

Black Enterprise, November 1988; November 1990; March 1991; July 1991; September 1991; December 1991; July 1994; January 1997.

Ebony, August 1985.

Jet, February 27, 1989; November 12, 1990; May 13, 1991; September 3, 2001.

New York Times, April 10, 1988; October 16, 1988.

—Michael E. Mueller and Sara Pendergast

Ella Bully-Cummings

1957(?)—

Police chief

Detroit Police Department veteran Ella Bully-Cummings became the first woman to serve as chief of police in her city, long known for its high crime rate. Bully-Cummings was named to the post in November of 2003 after a spate of recent troubles on the force, and immediately won high marks from civic leaders for her efforts to clean up a problem-plagued department.

Bully-Cummings is of mixed ancestry: her mother is Japanese, and married Daniel Lee Bully, an African American, when he was stationed in Japan with the U.S. military. Born in Japan in the late 1950s, Bully-Cummings barely remembers living in that country, for she was not quite two years old when the family moved to Detroit. She was the second child in a family of eight, and credits her strict disciplinarian father for instilling in her the no-nonsense attitude that helped earn her the post of top cop in her city years later.

Bully-Cummings's family struggled, and at one point, when they numbered seven, shared a one-bedroom apartment. She grew up on Detroit's near-west side, near the intersection of Rosa Parks and West Grand Boulevard. "I never had a room of my own," she told ABC News. "When you sat down for dinner, you had to make sure you were there so that you had food. When you wanted to say something you had to be loud so that everyone could hear you over the other children. But it was also a time of closeness for me."

Bully-Cummings, Ella, photograph. AP/Wide World Photos. Reproduced by permission.

As a teen, Bully-Cummings went to work to help out her family. She was 16 and working at a local movie theater when she saw a female police officer for the first time. Women cops were still a relative rarity in the early 1970s, before federal courts ordered large cities like Detroit to integrate their public-safety ranks with both more minority and more women members. After graduating from the city's top academic high school, Cass Tech, Bully-Cummings sold real estate for a time and worked in the office of another high school. She entered the Detroit Police Department (DPD) academy in 1977.

After making it through the rigorous training, Bully-Cummings was sworn in as a police officer and spent the next ten years as a beat cop. Her first arrest came during a drunk-driving stop, and she and her partner

At a Glance...

Born Ella Mae Bully, c. 1957, in Japan; daughter of Daniel Lee Bully (a television repair technician); married William Cummings (a police commander). *Education:* Earned degree from Madonna University, Detroit, 1993; Detroit College of Law at Michigan State University, J.D. (cum laude), 1998.

Career: Detroit Police Department, police officer, 1977-87, sergeant, 1987-93, lieutenant, 1993-95, inspector, 1995-98; commander, 1998-99, assistant chief, 2002-03, chief of police, 2003– ; Miller, Canfield, Paddock & Stone PLC, associate attorney, and Foley & Lardner, associate attorney, 1999-2002.

Memberships: National Bar Association; Wolverine Bar Association; State Bar of Michigan; International Association of Chiefs of Police; National Organization of Black Law Enforcement Executives; Michigan Association of Chiefs of Police.

Addresses: *Office*—Detroit Police Department, Chief of Police, 1300 Beaubien St., Detroit, MI 48226.

---

began to put the cuffs on a man of immense size who kicked her partner in the groin and knocked him down. "This guy had one cuff on him, and the only thing I could think of is, let me jump on his back...so he wouldn't hit me," she recalled in an interview with *Detroit Free Press* writers Suzette Hackney and Ben Schmitt.

Despite such bravery, Bully-Cummings and her fellow female rookies often encountered hostility from their male colleagues. It was a macho profession, and some tradition-bound DPD veterans resented having to work with women, since the job was an admittedly dangerous one. Some balked at sharing a patrol shift with a woman officer, and would call in sick to avoid duty. Others radioed for backup in the event of a problem, as if a female officer was unqualified to handle a situation. "But I had made up my mind that I wasn't going to let these folks break me," she recalled in the *Detroit Free Press* interview.

Bully-Cummings made sergeant in 1987 and, after helping pay the college tuition of some of her younger siblings, decided to earn her degree as well while still on the job. She took part-time classes at Detroit's Madonna University for a number of years, and earned her degree in public administration in 1993. Five years later, she earned her law degree from the Detroit College of Law at Michigan State University. That same year, after having held several successively higher ranks within the DPD, she was made a precinct commanding officer. Her precinct was a troubled one, however, and Bully-Cummings's tough approach alienated some there. The tires of her car were even slashed. "I came in and I laid down the law, and I don't think they liked it," she told the *Detroit Free Press*.

In 1999, after just a year as the precinct commanding officer, Bully-Cummings decided to retire in order to practice law full-time. She worked for two firms in Detroit, one of them a large, prestigious one, and specialized in labor law for the next three years. By then, rumors of rampant corruption and abuse within the DPD had aroused the attention of the U.S. Department of Justice, and an official investigation was underway. A new chief of police had been brought in from out of state, with the hope that an outsider would be able to fix the internal problems. The new boss, Jerry Oliver, personally asked Bully-Cummings to return to the force. She was made assistant chief in May of 2002, becoming the first woman to hold the office in DPD history.

The Department of Justice investigation found administrative errors, cover-ups, and various civil-rights violations in the handling of detainees, as well as the questionable use of force in arresting suspects. Because of those findings, the DPD came under official monitoring by federal officials, and was obligated to reform itself by implementing new lethal force policies, witness detention procedures, and prisoner care guidelines. But the black mark on the DPD worsened one day in October of 2003, when Chief Oliver tried to board a flight at Detroit Metro Airport with a loaded gun in his luggage. The scandal was a serious one, and Oliver left the job. Detroit Mayor Kwame M. Kilpatrick named Bully-Cummings to serve as interim chief on November 4, and then made the appointment permanent a month later.

Bully-Cummings became head of the tenth largest police force in the United States. But her first year on the job was a tough one: two rookie officers were slain by a single suspect, regular spates of shootings made headlines over the winter and spring, and in June of 2004 several innocent bystanders were shot at the city's annual fireworks festival. But Bully-Cummings won high marks for her visibility and handling of the tragedies under the media spotlight. At the DPD's downtown headquarters, she oversees 4,700 sworn officers and civilian employees, and works with federal monitors to meet compliance standards. "We don't need police officers who are not in control," she told Hackney and Schmitt. "Because they are the only people I know of who can legally take a person's life, and that's a lot of power to put in someone's hands."

Sources

Periodicals

Detroit Free Press, November 8, 2003; November 12, 2003, p. 1A; July 11, 2004, p. 1J.

On-line

"Detroit's Top Cop Sets Out to Fix Ailing Department," *CNN,* www.cnn.com/2003/US/Midwest/11/07/detroit.newchief.ap (September 20, 2004).

"Ella Bully-Cummings, Esq.," *City of Detroit Police Department,* www.ci.detroit.mi.us/police/dept/chief/cop.htm (September 20, 2004).

Leinwand, Donna, "Lawsuits of '70s Shape Current Police Leadership," *USA Today,* www.usatoday.com/news/nation/2004-04-25-female-police_x.htm (September 20, 2004).

"Person of the Week: Ella Bully-Cummings," *ABC News,* http://abcnews.go.com/WNT/PersonOfWeek/story?id=131845&page=1 (September 20, 2004).

—Carol Brennan

Mickey L. Burnim

1949—

Educator, university administrator

When Dr. Mickey L. Burnim was appointed chancellor of North Carolina's Elizabeth City State University, the 105-year-old campus was struggling with auditing problems, slipping enrollment, and an aging infrastructure. Burnim immediately set about turning the historically black university around. He hired three new vice chancellors who helped him balance the books, boost enrollment, launch the school's first graduate programs, and secure funding for new buildings and much needed renovations. Burnim accomplished his goals thanks to hard work, determination, and years of watching other university heads. "I have always tried to learn from the experiences of others," Burnim told *Black Issues in Higher Education*. "...I have learned by observing individual leaders." He learned well, and Elizabeth City State University and its thousands of students will reap the rewards for years to come. He summed up his philosophy in a promise, quoted by *The Virginian Pilot,* to "...treat all of our students like the precious resources with unlimited potential which they are."

Began Academic Career as Economist

Born Michael L. Burnim on January 19, 1949, Burnim was raised by his parents Ruby and A. S. Burnim in the tiny central Texas town of Teague. After graduating from high school he attended the University of North Texas in Denton. He distinguished himself as both an honors student and a campus leader. He was the first African-American student at North Texas to be named to the national Who's Who listing. He also became the first African American to serve on the school's student senate and in 1969 he was elected vice president of the organization. In 1970 he earned his bachelor's degree in economics and, two years later, his master's degree. Burnim next traveled to Wisconsin, where he received a doctorate in economics from the University of Wisconsin-Madison in 1977. His focus of study was public finance and labor economics.

Ph.D. in hand, Burnim began an academic career that would swing between scholarship and administration. From 1976 to 1982 he taught economics as an assistant professor at Florida State University. He then moved to the University of North Carolina (UNC). One of the most respected university systems in the country, UNC is also one of the largest. As the assistant vice president for academic affairs in the general administration office of the 16-campus system, Burnim was in a prime position to move up the ladder of higher education administration. However, he didn't abandon his academic pursuits, and from 1983 to 1986 Burnim also held assistant and associate professorships in the economics department of the university's Chapel Hill campus. In 1986 Burnim moved over to North Carolina Central University in Durham, a Historically Black College and University (HBCU), and became vice-chancellor for academic affairs. In 1990 he was named a provost of the school.

Took Over Top Spot at ECSU

In 1995 the chancellor of Elizabeth City State University (ECSU), another HBCU within the University of

At a Glance...

Born on January 19, 1949, in Teague, TX; married LaVera Levels; children: Cinnamon, Adrian. *Education:* North Texas State University, BA in economics, 1970, MA in economics, 1972; University of Wisconsin-Madison, PhD in economics, 1977.

Career: Florida State University, assistant professor, 1976-82; University of North Carolina, General Administration, assistant vice president for academic affairs, 1982-86; University of North Carolina, Chapel Hill, adjunct assistant professor, 1983-85, adjunct associate professor, 1985-86; North Carolina Central University, Durham, vice chancellor of academic affairs, 1986-95, provost and vice chancellor, 1990-95; Elizabeth City State University, NC, provost, 1995-96, chancellor, 1996–.

Selected memberships: Central Intercollegiate Athletic Association (CIAA), chairman, board of directors; Southern Association of Colleges and Schools' Commission on Colleges, delegate; Council for Adult and Experiential Learning, board member; The Salvation Army, board member; Wachovia Advisory Board, member.

Awards: Brookings Institute, Brookings Economic Policy Fellow, 1980-81.

Addresses: *Office*—Elizabeth City State University, 1704 Weeksville Rd, Elizabeth City, NC, 27909.

North Carolina system, resigned suddenly. Burnim was tapped to serve as interim chancellor and provost until a full-time replacement could be found. The UNC board of governors established a search committee and soon had a pool of 61 candidates. Of those, five were interviewed, two made it to the final round, and one of those was Burnim. Burnim's candidacy was touted by then-UNC president C. D. Spengler, who was quoted by *The Virginian Pilot* as saying, "I firmly believe that Mickey Burnim is the right person to lead Elizabeth City State University into the next century." He continued, "His broad experience and dedicated commitment to scholarship and public service will be forceful and effective for ECSU and the northeastern region of our state."

Burnim had a decided edge. In the year that he had served as interim chancellor his determination and diplomacy had impressed administrators, faculty, and Elizabeth City citizens and community leaders. The previous chancellor had often had a contentious, racially-tinged relationship with the latter. The board of governors agreed with Spengler, unanimously approving Burnim's appointment. According to the university's online transcripts of the meeting, Burnim told the board, "I pledge that I will do my very best to lead the university along a path of continuous progress in providing quality education for its students and support for the ecologically sensitive economic development of Northeastern North Carolina." He then acknowledged, "You are well aware that the university has some problems and challenges. I prefer to view them as opportunities and we will continue our aggressive pursuit of qualitative improvements in management areas as well as academic areas."

On July 1, 1996, Burnim became the third chancellor and eighth CEO of ECSU. His name plaque was barely tacked to his office door when he began to tackle the worst of the university's problems—a 19-year streak of irregular financial audits. "It is obvious that sound financial footing is crucial," Burnim told *Black Issues in Higher Education*. "My first hire was a vice chancellor for financial affairs." Burnim brought his economic background to the table and, along with the new financial chancellor, worked closely with the state auditor to resolve the problem. They did so in under a year. In 1997 the school received its first clean audit in two decades. "The commitment to quality and individual leadership of Chancellor Dr. Mickey L. Burnim, as well as the hard work of the financial staff of the university, cannot be acknowledged enough," the state auditor was quoted in *The Virginian Pilot*. In the same article Burnim was characteristically modest. "We've smiled and congratulated ourselves...but there are no big celebrations. We've got more to do."

Another problem Burnim faced when he became chancellor was a pattern of dwindling enrollment that had begun in 1993. As state and federal support depends on enrollment figures, this posed a serious threat to the future of the school. Burnim did not rely solely on increased recruitment efforts to solve the school's enrollment woes; he attacked the problem on many levels. Even before he assumed the chancellorship he had vowed to focus on educational standards. According to *The Virginian Pilot,* during a 1996 trustees meeting Burnim decried the "large number of teacher absences" and "poorly prepared syllabi." During his inauguration speech the paper quoted him as saying, "The emphasis for faculty and staff will be quality education." He also promised a "staff assessment process" to "see how well we're doing as teachers and administrators."

Burnim also reached out to more students by implementing additional baccalaureate programs in social work and communications studies. He also helped forge a joint pharmacy degree program with the University of North Carolina at Chapel Hill. A new degree program in marine environmental science was augmented with remote sensing technology that allowed researchers at the school to monitor conditions off the nearby Atlantic coast. In addition Burnim was key in launching ECSU's first three master's programs in elementary education, biology, and mathematics. He was also instrumental in the founding of the school's first two endowed professorships, increasing the university's standing in the world of academia. Other moves to improve enrollment included the construction of new facilities, including a state-of-the-art music and arts building, dormitories, and a student center. He also secured approval for a $46 million campus facelift, including tree-lined walkways, fountains, and parking. By 2004 Burnim's efforts had paid off when ECSU broke its enrollment record for the second year in a row with nearly 2,500 students, a six percent increase over the previous year. His goal, set by the UNC board, was 3,000 students by 2008.

Kept Doors Open to Students

The new students stepping onto ECSU's campus found Burnim's door wide open. "My office will always be open," he told *The Virginian Pilot*. "I encourage visitors who have something to say to come in and talk. That doesn't mean they won't ever have to wait a few minutes, but they'll get in." Students could also catch Burnim at football games. For that matter, Burnim informed campus administrators, faculty, and Elizabeth City residents that they could always find him at football games, particularly if his son Adrian—a former ECSU student and varsity player at the University of Virginia—was playing. His enthusiasm for the sport prompted him to work with the Central Intercollegiate Athletic Association (CIAA) to develop a popular tournament in the nearby town of Rocky Mount, the Down East Viking Football Classic. Born in 1998, the game has featured the ECSU Vikings against other teams from the CIAA, an athletic conference consisting of twelve historically African-American institutions of higher education. As the fifth annual game approached Burnim told the *Daily Advance,* "It is wonderful....We had a lot of uncertainty at the beginning. The sponsorship, would people show up. But seeing how everyone has stepped up—all of those pieces were critical in the development to this point." In 2004 Burnim took a more active role in the CIAA when he was appointed chairman of its board of directors.

As the 2004 academic year dawned, Burnim continued to meet the challenges of running a university head on. He faced state and federal budget cuts, ongoing faculty assessments, recruitment goals, and fundraising campaigns, as well as the daily rigors of managing a university campus that plays home to thousands of employees, faculty, and students. He continued to happily and successfully face those challenges, fueled by a commitment he made the day he became chancellor. "This is all about quality education," *The Virginian Pilot* quoted him. "Quality education from top to bottom for quality students. They'll get it. That's my job."

Sources

Periodicals

Black Issues in Higher Education, April 3, 1997.
Ebony, February 2004.
Virginian Pilot, June 15, 1996; October 13, 1996; December 18, 1997; June 13, 1999.

On-line

"Board of Governors Meeting, June 14, 1996," *University of North Carolina,* www.ga.unc.edu/BOG/minutes/1996/1996_0603.html (September 28, 2004).
Hubbard, David, "Buildup for Down East Viking Football Classic Begins," *CIAA,* www.theciaa.com/03-04/features/ecsuf0618.htm (September 28, 2004).
"Chancellor's Biographical Sketch," *Elizabeth City State University,* www.ecsu.edu/fs/chancellorsbio.cfm (September 28, 2004).

—Candace LaBalle

Aimé Césaire

1913—

Writer, politician

The West Indian playwright and politician Aimé Césaire emerged as one of the leading voices in the négritude movement in the 1930s. Searching for a way to unite the peoples of the African diaspora, Césaire and future Senegalese President Léopold Sédar Senghor coined the term "negritude" while studying in Paris in the 1930s. It urged blacks to reject the idea of nationalism as well as that of any white influence upon one's culture, and instead embrace and celebrate one's African heritage. The American poet Langston Hughes was one of the first to adopt it.

Césaire, Aimé, photograph. AP/Wide World Photos. Reproduced by permission

The Martinique-born Césaire wrote a number of plays and poems in his native French, but his best-known work translated for English-speaking audiences may be the epic poem *Return to My Native Land.* Long active in Martinican politics, he served in the French National Assembly as a representative of his island nation for decades; he was also mayor of Fort-de-France, the capital city. In a 1995 *Research in African Literatures* essay, Lilyan Kesteloot called him an "extraordinary man who has profoundly marked two generations of African intellectuals and who continues to stir the students who study him in our schools and universities."

Born on June 25, 1913, in Basse-Pointe, Césaire grew up in a Martinique that had been a colony of France since 1635. It grew sugar and tobacco, and had been the subject of a long battle between the British and the French for hegemony. Once populated by Carib Indians, Martinique was a slave state until 1848, and the descendants of those slaves emerged as a strong political voice on the island nation in the twentieth century. Césaire's political awareness was shaped by his time in Paris, where he arrived in 1931 for further schooling. He fell in with many other black students from other French colonies, especially those from Africa, like Senghor, and was active in the Society for African Culture. Along with Senghor and Léon Damas, he helped found *L'Étudiant noir,* or "The Black Student," a magazine of black culture and politics in 1934.

Césaire studied at the Sorbonne and wrote poetry during his years in Paris. His major work, *Return to My Native Land,* was penned as he planned his return to Martinique. The 1,000-line poem first appeared in an issue of *Volontes* in 1939, in the original French, but it caused a sensation. "Bristling with learned words,

> ### At a Glance...
>
> **B**orn on June 25, 1913, in Basse-Pointe, Martinique, West Indies; married Suzanne Roussy (a teacher), July 10, 1937 (died, 1966); children: Jacques, Jean-Paul, Francis, Ina, Marc, Michelle. *Education:* Attended the École Normale Supérieure, Paris, 1935-39; Sorbonne, University of Paris, licencié és lettres1936. *Politics:* Parti Progressiste Martiniquais.
>
> **Career:** Playwright, poet, and essayist; *L'Étudiant noir*, Paris, founder, with Léopold Senghor and Léon Dames, 1934; Lycée Schoelcher, Fort-de-France, Martinique, teacher, 1939-45; *Tropiques*, Fort-de-France, editor, 1941-45; member of the two French constituent assemblies, 1945-46; Fort-de-France, mayor, 1945-83; French National Assembly, deputy representing Martinique, 1946-83; Parti Progressiste Martiniquais, founding member, later president.
>
> **Memberships:** Conseil régional Martinique, president, 1983-86; Society of African Culture, Paris.
>
> **Awards:** Laporte Prize, 1960; Viareggio-Versilia Prize for Literature, 1968; Grand Prix National de Poésie, 1982; Commander of the Order of Merit of Cote d'Ivoire, 2002.
>
> **Addresses:** *Office*—c/o La Mairie, 97200 Fort-de-France, Martinique, West Indies.

neologisms, and a hypercomplex syntax, it made a direct hit on the African continent as well as on the intellectuals in the Antilles, and even those of anglophone or lusophone [Portuguese-speaking] Africa," noted Kesteloot.

Return to My Native Land contained the first-ever use of the term "négritude," and the idea incited an entire generation of post-colonial writers and minds, in both the Caribbean world and on the African continent. "The West told us that in order to be universal we had to start by denying that we were black," Césaire explained about the concept in an interview with in a *UNESCO Courier* writer Annick Thebia Melsan. "I, on the contrary, said to myself that the more we were black, the more universal we would be. It was a totally different approach. It was not a choice between alternatives, but an effort at reconciliation."

When he returned to Martinique, Césaire taught at a lycée (school) in Fort-de-France for several years, and also served as editor of *Tropiques*, a magazine that was censored by the French authorities on orders of the collaborationist Vichy government at a time when France, still Martinique's master, was occupied by Nazi Germany. After the end of World War II, Césaire emerged as a leading political figure and was elected mayor of Fort-de-France in 1945. The following year, he won a seat representing Martinique in the French National Assembly, and was regularly returned to it by voters.

Initially a member of Martinique's Communist party, Césaire abandoned the party in 1957 to co-found and later head the Parti Progressiste Martiniquais (PPM). The PPM was left-leaning, but did not call for full independence. Instead it advocated maintaining ties to France but with self-rule, a plan that Césaire helped author in the late 1940s. When this plan was adopted, Martinique shed its colonial status and instead became an overseas département of France, equal in the political sphere to storied French areas like Provence-Alpes-Côte-d'Azur and Bretagne, or Brittany. The island is one of four overseas départements, and has a relationship to France similar to that of Puerto Rico to the United States. It is heavily subsidized by France, too, giving it a much higher standard of living than members of some other Caribbean island nations. "The anomaly of modern-day Martinique is hence largely Césaire's creation," declared *Guardian* writer James Ferguson. "A part of France—and by extension the European Union—with identical laws, directives and welfare provisions, it is a subsidised first-world enclave in the Caribbean, eyed enviously yet condescendingly by its poorer but independent neighbours."

Césaire served as mayor of Fort-de-France until 1983, and in addition to his legislative duties in Paris he also continued to write. He turned to playwriting in the late 1950s, and the first of his works for the stage to be translated and performed in English was *The Tragedy of King Christophe*. The work is set in Haiti and follows the true story of King Henri Christophe, a hotel employee who led a rebellion in 1806 and became king of a large portion of Haiti. He ruled as a petty tyrant, and was himself ousted by a rebellion and committed suicide. Césaire's cautionary tale, noted an essay on his career as a playwright in the *International Dictionary of Theatre*, serves as "an account of political failure. Christophe's inability to free his people from the alienation induced by centuries of colonialism sounds a warning to the leaders of newly independent Africa."

Césaire's plays have touched upon other political themes from the history of a post-colonial world. A 1968 work, *A Season in the Congo*, centers around the independence movement and subsequent civil strife involving assassinated Congolese leader Patrice Lumumba. His 1985 play, *A Tempest*, was adapted from the Shakespeare work and features a cast of leading characters who represent the various classes of a post-colonial, African-heritage political atmosphere.

Césaire retired from politics in 1993 at the age of 80. Four years later, interviewed by the *UNESCO Courier*'s Melsan, he remained committed to the ideals he once detailed in his writings as a college student in Paris. "I desire—passionately—that peoples should exist as peoples, that they should prosper and make their contribution to universal civilization, because the world of colonization and its modern manifestations is a world that crushes, a world of awful silence."

Selected writings

Cahier d'un retour au pays natal (poems), 1947; revised edition 1956; published as *Return to My Native Land,* translated by John Berger and Anna Bostock, Penguin, 1969.

Corps perdu (poems), with illustrations by Pablo Picasso, 1950; published as *Lost Body,* translated by Clayton Eshleman and Annette Smith, Braziller, 1986.

Cadastre (poems), 1961; published as *Cadastre,* translated by Emile Snyder and Sanford Upson, Third Press, 1973.

La Tragédie du roi Christophe (play; produced in Salzburg, Austria, 1964), 1963; revised edition, 1970; published as *The Tragedy of King Christophe,* translated by Ralph Manheim, Grove Press, 1970.

Une Saison au Congo (play; produced by the Théâtre Vivant, Brussels, Belgium, 1966), 1966; published as *A Season in the Congo,* translated by Manheim, Grove Press, 1968.

State of the Union (poems), translated by Eshleman and Denis Kelly, distributed by Asphodel Book Shop, 1966.

Une Tempete: Adaptation pour un théâtre nègre, from *The Tempest* by Shakespeare (play; produced in Hammamet, Tunisia, 1969), 1969; published as *A Tempest,* translated by Richard Miller, G. Borchardt, 1985.

Culture and Colonization (nonfiction), University of Yaounde, 1978.

Lyric and Dramatic Poetry 1946-82, translated by Eshleman and Smith, University Press of Virginia, 1990.

Aimé Césaire: The Collected Poetry, translated by Eshleman and Smith, University of California Press, 1983.

Non-Vicious Circle: Twenty Poems, translated by Gregson Davis, Stanford University Press, 1984.

Sources

Books

Arnold, A. James, *Modernism and Négritude: The Poetry and Poetics of Aimé Césaire,* Harvard University Press, 1981.

Davis, Gregson, *Aimé Césaire,* Cambridge University Press, 1997.

Frutkin, Susan, *Aimé Césaire: Black between Worlds,* University of Miami, 1973.

International Dictionary of Theatre, Volume 2: *Playwrights,* St. James Press, 1993.

Pallister, Janis L., *Aimé Césaire,* Twayne, 1991.

Scharfman, Ronnie Leah, *Engagement and the Language of the Subject in the Poetry of Aimé Césaire,* University of Florida Press, 1987.

Suk, Jeannie, *Postcolonial Paradoxes in French Caribbean Writing: Césaire, Glissant, Condé,* Clarendon, 2001.

Periodicals

Guardian (London, England), March 13, 1999, p. 10.

Research in African Literatures, Summer 1995, p. 169, p. 174; Winter 2001, p. 77.

UNESCO Courier, May 1997, p. 4.

On-line

"Aimé Césaire," *Biography Resource Center,* www.galenet.com/servlet/BioRC (October 12, 2004).

—Carol Brennan

Ray Charles

1930-2004

Musician, singer, composer, arranger

Charles, Ray, photograph. Tim Mosenfelder/Getty Images.

Above all his many talents, singing great Ray Charles had the ability to interpret and sing songs in such a way as to fill the words from the depths of his own heart, carrying this emotion to the listener. "I sing the songs for what they mean to me," Charles was quoted in Joe Goldberg's *Jazz Masters of the Fifties*. However, his highly regarded singing long tended to obscure his other considerable accomplishments as a blues pianist, band leader, composer, and arranger. "Jazz musicians speak of a quality called 'the cry,' a quality that echoes the blues no matter what is being played. The cry of blues permeates every Charles performance," wrote Goldberg.

Despite being born into extreme poverty, Ray Charles created a prolific body of work spanning five decades. Proficient in numerous styles, Ray's recordings are rich in blues, jazz, and country, and he was often spoken of as the nation's best rock n' roll singer, best jazz singer, and best pop singer, his preeminence challenged only by Frank Sinatra. Frequently imitated, and honored with countless awards during his career, Charles is best known as the "Father of Soul Music." Charles himself never cared to be pigeonholed into any one category. When told that he had successfully avoided all attempts to be categorized, he replied in Goldberg's book: "I consider that a compliment. I don't want to be branded. I don't want the rhythm-and-blues brand, or the pop brand, or any other. That's why I try all these different things.... I know not everybody likes everything I do. Some like one thing, and some another. But I try to please everybody, while doing what I want. I'm an entertainer."

Lost His Sight at an Early Age

Ray Charles Robinson was born in Albany, Georgia, on September 23, 1930. Charles's absent father, Bailey Robinson, was a migrant railroad worker who never knew his son. Charles and his beloved mother Aretha moved to Greenville, Florida, when Charles was six months old. Times were tough for the young family. In his autobiography, *Brother Ray*, Charles recalled that "Even compared to the other blacks in Greenville, we were at the bottom of the ladder." Tragically, at the age of five, young Ray helplessly watched as his four-year-old brother George drowned in a washtub. Thereafter,

> **At a Glance . . .**
>
> Born Ray Charles Robinson on September 23, 1930, in Albany, GA; died June 10, 2004, in Beverly Hills, CA; son of Bailey and Aretha Robinson; married twice, to Eileen and Della; children: twelve children.
>
> **Career:** Recording artist, 1956-2004. Began touring with dance bands at age 15; recording artist, for Atlantic Records, 1952-59, ABC-Paramount, 1959-65, and his own labels, Tangerine Records 1965-73, and Crossover Records Co., 1973-2004.
>
> **Selected Awards:** 16th International Jazz Critics Poll, named #1 male singer, 1968; NAACP, Image Award, 1983; Rock 'n' Roll Hall of Fame inductee, 1986; Kennedy Center Honors recipient, 1986; 12 Grammy awards, including Lifetime Achievement Award, 1987; National Medal of Arts, 1993; *Ebony* magazine, Lifetime Achievement Award, 1994.

Charles's eyesight worsened considerably from glaucoma, leaving him completely blind by the age of seven. Charles then attended a state school in St. Augustine for the deaf and blind.

While in St. Augustine, Charles learned to read, compose, and write music in braille, as well as to play the clarinet, trumpet, saxophone, and keyboards. Though Charles became familiar with classical music there, it was at the upright piano of Wylie Pittman, a local grocer, where Charles first experienced playing the piano. Robert Palmer writes that Charles fondly recalls visiting Wylie's after school, where "… he'd let me sit on the piano stool or in the chair next to him and bang on the piano with him." Charles credits four pianists as influencing him the most as a child: Art Tatum, Bud Powell, King Cole, and Oscar Peterson. Ray's excellence as a blues pianist is evident on his instrumental albums, including *The Great Ray Charles*. Arranger Quincy Jones credits Chalres's piano abilities as a major factor in the success of his recordings. Young Charles possessed a natural talent for music and, by age twelve, was reportedly able to arrange and score all parts of big band or orchestral music. As a child, Charles listened to a wide variety of blues and swing along with the weekly Grand Ole Opry and gospel music of his Baptist church.

While in St. Augustine at age 15, Charles learned of his mother's death. Ray's father had also died several years earlier. With no immediate family left, Charles moved to Jacksonville, Florida, in search of work. Charles recalled those days as being rough times, however, he felt that his youth provided him with a certain resilience. Soon, Charles was playing in numerous small bands across the state of Florida. By 1948, now 18 years old, Charles was a seasoned road musician. By this time, however, Charles had become acquainted with heroin, which he continued using for many years to come. However, the ambitious Charles was determined to make his way in music and he purchased an early wire recorder, recording some demo tapes in Tampa, Florida.

Seasoned on the Road

Once he had saved around $600 from performances, Charles traveled to the West Coast, settling for a time in Seattle. Out west, Charles met Quincy Jones and Bumps Blackwell, producer of the original Little Richard hits. Charles also successfully assembled a trio of guitar, bass, and piano, dropping his last name Robinson so as not to be confused with then popular boxer, Sugar Ray Robinson. Charles's trio came to the attention of Jack Lauderdale of Downbeat and later Swingtime records. By 1950, Charles had moved to Los Angeles and was cutting records for Swingtime. One of Charles's daughters was also born during this year by a woman named Louise. (He would ultimately father twelve children.)

In 1951, Charles recorded a hit popular with the black community known as "Baby Let Me Hold Your Hand," which reached the Top 10 on the rhythm-and-blues charts. This, along with other Swingtime singles, were in the style of Nat King Cole and Charles Brown, as young Charles had not yet mastered his own style. Charles tried to sound like them in order to get work, especially club work.

During this same period, Charles toured with blues singer Lowell Fulsom and became the pianist for Fulsom's band. Near the end of 1951, Swingtime records opted to drop Charles, and Atlantic Records partners Ahmet Ertegun, Herb Abramson, and Jerry Wexler snatched Charles up without ever having seen him, paying around $2,500 for his contract. For his beginning sessions with Atlantic, Charles was teamed with an extraordinarily talented group of New York studio players under the direction of Jesse Stone, including guitarist Mickey Baker, drummer Connie Kay, and bassist Lloyd Trotman. For Atlantic, Charles was never considered as just another artist. To them, Charles was a musical genius with a lot more to offer than writing and singing songs.

Charles worked out of New Orleans for much of 1953, the final period of his formative years. However, the Louisiana rhythm had less effect on his overall work than some have speculated. By this time, Charles was well on his way to a comfortable, innovative style. Actually, his mid-fifties band arrangements more closely resembled the style of James Brown than New

Orleans rhythm-and-blues. Charles's original style also emerged as a result of his work with "Guitar Slim," whose crude gospel blues greatly influenced him. Charles even arranged Slim's million-selling single, "Things That I Used to Do." Early recordings are based on blues and gospel forms, including the soulful, "A Fool For You," "What Would I Do Without You?," "It's Allright," and "Drown In My Own Tears." During this time, Charles divorced his wife of approximately 16 months, a beautician named Eileen, and subsequently remarried a woman by the name of Della.

Developed Unique Sound

By 1954, Charles began to create songs which differed radically from his expert imitations of Nat King Cole, Charles Brown, and Louis Jordan. Charles united gospel and blues music to help form a sound known as soul music. Once Charles's new music caught on, he became known as "The Genius" and "The Bishop." From New Orleans, Charles moved on to Dallas, where he put together his first true band, with bandleader Renald Richard. The band began performing with Ruth Brown from El Paso throughout Florida. During this time, saxophonist David "Fathead" Newman joined the band, and Charles and Richard developed the song, "I Got a Woman," which marked the turning point in Charles's music from rhythm-and-blues to soul, exuding the fervor of the Baptist Church. In November of 1954 Charles extended an invitation to Atlantic executives Ahmet Ertegun and Jerry Wexler to come hear his new music at the Peacock Club in Atlanta. It was there that Wexler first realized the overall change in Charles's music. However, Nesuhi Ertegun, Ahmet's brother, acknowledged that Charles's style was not necessarily unique, as noted by author Robert Palmer, "Ray was not the first to do this, combine gospel and blues. He is the best of a long tradition, but there were people singing this way twenty years ago. But Ray was able to bring so much of his own to it."

Early Atlantic recordings were made with Charles while he performed in Atlanta, Florida, and New York. Nesuhi Ertegun viewed this as an advantage for recording purposes, as it gave Charles a chance to work out his arrangements on the road. Upon Charles's return to Atlanta, Wexler and Ertegun managed to produce his first number one hit album, *Ray Charles*, a confirmation of the greatness of Ray Charles. The single "I Got a Woman" also soared to number one on the rhythm-and-blues charts. The extraordinary success of his new style, both commercially and artistically, spurred similar hit songs to follow, including, "This Little Girl of Mine" (1955), "Talkin' 'Bout You" (1957), and "Don't Let The Sun Catch You Crying" (1959), whose call-and-response style was fully realized with Charles's mega-hit, "What'd I Say?" in 1959. This song remains a favorite closing number among performing soul singers worldwide.

It was during this period that America's white youth discovered recordings by black artists. Elvis Presley had helped to erode racial barriers and, in fact, was somewhat of a Ray Charles fan. However, despite the fact that Atlantic executives wished to pursue sales in the white pop marketplace, Charles refused to compromise his musical style with the simpler beat, adolescent lyrics, and smoother singing. Charles continued with his soulful music, and his recordings continued to sell, albeit largely among the black community. Atlantic continued to support Charles in his endeavors, hence, his soul music was undiluted and some of his landmark songs from this time were even more soulful than his earlier recordings, including "Come Back Baby," "Drown In My Own Tears," and "Hallelujah I Love Her So."

Became "Father of Soul"

Despite his early success in soul music, Charles never fully accepted the accolade of "father of soul." Said Charles to Robert Palmer: "When people ask me what I think about soul music…. I think all these terms are names that the media give the music in order to try to describe what they mean. I don't know the difference between rhythm-and-blues, soul music, and the black version of disco; the rhythm patterns are the same." Charles also shied away from taking credit for the creation of rock 'n' roll, feeling that his music was more adult and filled with despair, considering rhythm-and-blues as genuine down-to-earth Negro music. Of all Charles's tunes from the mid-fifties, only "Swanee River Rock" remotely resembles rock 'n' roll, and it became Charles's first significant pop hit, reaching number 34 on the Billboard chart. In *Jazz Masters of the Fifties*, Charles spoke of his work in this way: "The things I write and sing about concern the general Joe and his general problems. There are four basic things: love, somebody runnin' his mouth too much, having fun, and jobs are hard to get…. When I put myself in the place of the…general Joe I'm singing about,… I sing with all the feeling I can put into it, so that I can feel it myself."

Luckily for Charles his band was both flexible and talented enough to accommodate his sense of musical perfection. Until 1959, Charles's band had two saxophonists, with Charles playing a third, alto sax. He realized a stroke of luck when, around this time, baritone saxophonist Leroy "Hog" Cooper joined the band. The band now consisted of Hank Crawford on alto, Newman on tenor, and Cooper on baritone sax. There were also two trumpeters, Joe Bridgewater and Marcus Belgrave, with William Peoples as the primary drummer and Roosevelt Sheffield as bassist. Between 1957 and 1959, with the expansion of his band, Charles delved into greater musical forays, including an extended interest in country and western music. From here, Charles recruited three female singers to contrast against his voice, reminiscent of traditional call-and-response gospel singing. The female singers included Mary Ann Fisher, Darlene McRae, and Margie Hendrix. Thereafter, the chorus became known as the

"Raeletts." The hit single, "What Kind of Man Are You" is a splendid example of the intense, spiritual feel added by the Raeletts. "What'd I Say?" his first million-seller song, was one of the finest renderings of the call-and-response pattern between Ray Charles and his new girls. The suggestion of sex in this particular song, however, resulted in its first being played only by black radio stations until it was played by Elvis Presley, at which time the white radio stations also picked it up.

Despite past inconsistencies in terms of concert arrival times, drug abuse, and temperamental ways, Charles was always a superb musician and gracious performer who captivated his audience. Fortunately, Atlantic records took advantage of Charles's live audience appeal, recording two in-person appearances, *Ray Charles at Newport* and *Ray Charles in Person*, where the live vocals take on a quality not easily captured in the studio. It was the Atlantic executives who first recognized Charles as a genius, not hesitating to call him such, as they considered Charles's whole approach to music as very different from anybody else's. During his final days with Atlantic, Charles experimented with a passion, leaving Atlantic with his final recording, *The Genius of Ray Charles*, which freed him from the stereotype of rock 'n' roll singer and sealing him firmly as "Mr. Soul." Charles had a large hand in the arrangement of this album, resulting in three triumphant singles, "Don't Let the Sun Catch You Cryin'," "Am I Blue," and "Come Rain or Come Shine." When Charles's Atlantic contract expired in late 1959, ABC-Paramount made him a rare and generous offer and he moved on.

Experienced Highs and Lows

In 1961 Ray Charles and Betty Carter collaborated on an album that produced the hit, "Baby It's Cold Outside." While Atlantic felt a terrible loss when Charles left, ABC was well satisfied as Charles churned out one mega-hit after another, including, "Georgia on My Mind" in 1960 and "Hit the Road Jack" in 1961, thereby establishing himself as an international artist. In 1962, *Modern Sounds in Country and Western Music* was released to massive sales. A single from this album, "I Can't Stop Loving You," sold three million copies. Though Charles's crossover into country music caused significant controversy, the popularity of his recording spawned a second volume under the same name with several more hits. Charles did not become mainstream, like most black country artists, but rather, retained his gospel-blues sound. Charles changed stylistically somewhat, though, in 1961, as he moved from a blues shouter to a crooner of soul, achieving a phenomenal sweep of four Grammy awards in 1961 for Best Vocal Performer (male), Best Single ("Georgia on My Mind"), Best Album (*The Genius of Ray Charles*), and Best Song ("Let the Good Times Roll").

While Charles was an unquestioned musical success, he was also a long-term drug user. On November 14, 1961, Charles was arrested on a narcotics charge in an Indiana hotel room, where he waited to perform. The detectives seized heroin, marijuana, and other items. Charles, then 31 years old, stated that he had been a drug addict since the age of 16. While the case was dismissed because of the manner in which the evidence was obtained, Charles's situation did not improve until a few years later. Individuals who cared for Charles, such as Quincy Jones and Reverend Henry Griffin, felt that those around Charles were responsible for his drug use, as he was unable to obtain or administer drugs to himself, given his blindness. By 1964 Charles's drug addiction caught up with him and he was arrested for possession of marijuana and heroin. Following a self-imposed stay at St. Francis Hospital in Lynwood, California, where he kicked his drug habit in 96 hours, Charles received five years probation. Charles responded to the saga of his drug abuse and reform with the songs "I Don't Need No Doctor," "Let's Go Get Stoned," and the release of his first album since kicking his heroin habit in 1966, the impassioned *Crying Time*.

From the late 1960s onward, Charles was no longer at the forefront of musical innovation, but that did not mean that he wasn't producing excellent music. His musical releases had shifted from strong gospel and R&B to softer pop, jazz, and country songs, and he recorded many popular songs. In 1973, Charles left ABC to form Crossover Records with Atlantic, his original company. He continued to influence other musicians such as Otis Redding, Stevie Wonder, Steve Winwood, and Joe Cocker, earning numerous awards and countless hits along the way. By the late 1970s, however, Charles's 20-year marriage to Della Robinson had ended. His lengthy absences and womanizing were contributing factors to the breakdown of the marriage.

A Lifetime of Achievement

From the 1970s onward, Ray Charles was a major celebrity, recording numerous albums, accumulating awards, and making several film and television appearances. He composed songs for films and television shows, including the theme song for the sitcom *Three's Company* and "Beers to You" for the Clint Eastwood film *Any Which Way You Can*. He appeared in the film *The Blues Brothers* as well as television's *Moonlighting*. In 1979, his rendition of "Georgia on My Mind" was officially named Georgia's state song. Charles was one of the first musicians to be inducted into the Rock and Roll Hall of Fame in 1986, and in 1988 he was awarded the National Academy of Recording Arts and Sciences Lifetime Achievement Award. In 1991 Charles's selection by Pepsi-Cola to act as their spokesman with a catchy "Uh-Huh" theme introduced his music to a new generation of listeners. In 1994, Charles was honored with a twelfth Grammy Award for his rendition of "Song for You." A 1997 collection of his hits, *Genius and Soul: The 50th*

Anniversary Collection, had critics and fans taking a trip down memory lane.

Charles continued to tour and to make music until the very end of his life. His last tour, in 2003, was cut short by illness, yet despite his illness he worked that year to produce an album of duets, *Genius Loves Company,* which featured Charles performing with such greats as Norah Jones, Elton John, Bonnie Raitt, and B.B. King. When Charles died in his Beverly Hills, California, home on June 10, 2004, the music world mourned the passing of a legend. Performers and executives from across the industry celebrated his great career, and *Newsweek* commented that "Generations of singers have wanted to sound like him. No one comes close." A movie celebrating Charles's life, *Ray,* was already in the works, and its release in October of 2004 was greeted with critical accolades, especially the performance of Jamie Foxx in the lead role.

Selected discography

Ray Charles, Atlantic, 1957; re-released as *Hallelujah, I Love Her So,* WEA International, 2003.
What'd I Say, Atlantic, 1958.
Ray Charles at Newport, Atlantic, 1958.
What'd I Say, Atlantic, 1959.
The Genius of Ray Charles, Atlantic, 1959.
The Genius Sings the Blues, Atlantic, 1960.
Ray Charles in Person, Atlantic, 1960.
The Genius Hits the Road, ABC, 1960.
Genius + Soul = Jazz, ABC, 1961.
Modern Sounds in Country and Western, ABC, 1961.
Modern Sounds in Country and Western Volume 2, ABC, 1962.
Crying Time, ABC, 1966.
Ray's Moods, ABC/Paramount, 1966.
Doing His Thing, ABC/Tangerine, 1969.
Volcanic Action of My Soul, ABC/Tangerine, 1971.
Brother Ray Is at It Again, Atlantic, 1980.
The Spirit of Christmas, Rhino, 1985.
My World, Warner Brothers, 1993.
Genius and Soul: The 50th Anniversary Collection, Rhino, 1997.
Thanks for Bringing Love Around Again, Crossover, 2002.
Genius Loves Company, Concord/Hear Music, 2004.

Sources

Books

Charles, Ray, with David Ritz, *Brother Ray: Ray Charles' Own Story,* Dial Press, 1978, revised, 1992.
Goldberg, Joe, *Jazz Masters of the Fifties,* Macmillan, 1965.
Lydon, Michael, *Ray Charles: Man and Music,* Routledge, 2004.
Palmer, Robert, *The Birth of Soul* (discography booklet insert), Atlantic Records, 1991.
White, Timothy, *Rock Lives,* Henry Holt, 1990.
Winski, Norman, *Ray Charles,* Melrose Square, 1994.

Periodicals

Newsweek, June 21, 2004.
Time, June 21, 2004.

On-line

Ray Charles, www.raycharles.com (November 4, 2004).

—Marilyn Williams and Tom Pendergast

Lorraine Cole

195(?)—

Women's health advocate, association executive

Much of Lorraine Cole's professional life has been devoted to the service of people, causes, and not-for-profit organizations. Inspired by the strength, integrity, and creativity of her mother and father, she not only became the first in her family to finish college, but she also earned her doctorate and went on to hold high positions in several important professional organizations. As President and Chief Executive Officer of the Black Women's Health Imperative, Cole has combined her skill at managing organizations with her passion about the importance of health issues for African-American women.

Cole was born in Chicago, Illinois, the daughter of Sherman and Eleanor Cole. Her father was a World War II veteran and served in the Naval Air Force until he died when Lorraine was only six. Eleanor Cole raised her family on her own, working as a fashion designer and seamstress. In spite of this early grief, Lorraine had a secure and happy childhood, enjoying both school and play in her mostly black middle-class neighborhood on Chicago's south side. She was an excellent student and spent many of her leisure hours practicing the piano, taught by her great aunt, who was a concert pianist.

Broke Barriers to Attend College

Before the mid-1950s, many schools in the United States were racially segregated. This meant that schools intended for white students did not allow students of color to attend. Instead, African-American students attended schools that were largely black. These black schools often did not receive as much funding or supplies as white schools, which were usually placed in more affluent neighborhoods. This practice officially ended in 1954, when the Supreme Court ruled that public schools must admit all students equally. Even though segregation in schools became illegal, blacks and whites still often lived in different neighborhoods. Schools served their local neighborhoods, so white and black schools continued to exist, even after legal segregation ended. This continued unofficial segregation often kept black students in underfunded schools which did not tend to encourage them to aim high in their career goals.

During the late 1960s, a counselor at Lorraine Cole's largely black high school told students at an assembly that they could not succeed in college because they would not be able to compete with white students. Because of such attitudes, Cole did not at first view college as a possibility, even though she always had been an excellent student. She began to think that following her father into the Navy would be her best chance for higher education. However, her mother encouraged her to apply to college, and Cole's grades and hard work earned her a scholarship for tuition to the largely white Northern Illinois University, located within the small farm town of DeKalb.

As she was adjusting to life away from the fairly sheltered and familiar world of her family and completing her first year of college, Cole suffered another deep loss. Her mother died of breast cancer at the age of 44. Lorraine Cole was 18, in college, and suddenly on her own. Her mother's support had given her the

At a Glance...

Born in 195(?) in Chicago, Illinois; married Vincent Stovall; children: one daughter. *Education:* Northern Illinois University, BS, 1971, MA, 1972; Northwestern University, Ph.D., 1980.

Career: American Speech-Language-Hearing Association, Director of Office of Minority Concerns, 1979-92; Minority Health Professions Foundation, Executive Director, 1993-95; National Medical Association, Executive Director, 1995-2001; Black Women's Health Imperative, President and Chief Executive Officer, 2001–.

Selected Memberships: Congressional Black Caucus Foundation, congressional fellow; Avery Institute for Social Change, health advocacy fellow; American Society of Association Executives, board of directors; U.S. Department of Health and Human Services Office of Women's Health, panel of experts; U.S. Department of Health and Human Services Office of Minority Health, African-American work group.

Selected Awards: Northern Illinois University, Outstanding Young Alumni Award, 1990; American Speech-Language-Hearing Association Outstanding Service Award, 1992; McDonald's Corporation Black History Makers of Today and Tomorrow Award, 2001; Southern Connecticut State University, honorary doctorate, 2004.

Addresses: *Office*—Black Women's Health Imperative, 600 Pennsylvania Avenue S.E., Suite 310, Washington, D.C. 20003.

---

confidence to enroll in college, but her own determination and work would keep her there. She paid the expenses not covered by her scholarship by working in the dormitories as a resident assistant and modeling for local fashion boutiques.

Studied Communication Disorders

Cole had chosen NIU because it was close to home, and because it had a strong program in physical therapy, which is the treatment of injuries and disabilities by using physical methods like heat, cold, or exercise. Cole had written a high school paper on physical therapy and thought she would like to make it her career. However, after taking a speech pathology class, where she learned about the various problems that can make it hard for people to speak, she changed her focus to speech-language pathology and the larger field of communication disorders. Communication disorders include both speaking and hearing problems that make it difficult for people to express themselves or understand others. Cole had always been fascinated by the ways people learn and use language, and she earned both bachelor's and master's degrees in communication disorders.

For several years, Cole worked as a speech-language pathologist, helping those with speech and language difficulties, especially children through the national Head Start program and the University of Illinois Division of Services for Crippled Children. She also continued her education, earning her doctorate in communication disorders from Northwestern University in suburban Chicago.

After she received her Ph.D., Cole moved to the Washington, D.C., area to take a job with the American Speech-Language-Hearing Association (ASHA) as Director of the Office of Minority Concerns. ASHA is the organization that certifies and offers support to speech and hearing professionals. During her thirteen years as Director of the Office of Minority Concerns, Cole started many programs to help increase understanding of cultural and linguistic differences in the speech-language pathology and audiology professions, as well as creating a minority scholarship fund. She also began to develop new skills in managing organizations.

Built a Career as Association Executive

Cole's success in her role at ASHA led to even more responsible jobs. She became Executive Director of the Minority Health Professions Foundation (MHPF), an organization that provides funds for biomedical research conducted in historically black medical, dental, pharmacy, and veterinary schools. She worked there for three years, supervising large research projects at eleven different colleges and universities.

Cole left the MHPF to take another very responsible job, as Executive Director of the National Medical Association (NMA). The NMA is a professional organization of black physicians. It was founded in 1895 to offer connections and support to African-American doctors, who were not permitted to join white professional organizations like the American Medical Association. The modern NMA is a complex organization with more than 25,000 members, and it prospered under Cole's leadership.

Became a Health Advocate

In 2001, Cole left the NMA and moved on to another challenge. She took a job heading the National Black

Women's Health Project (NBWHP), an organization that had been formed in 1983 by Byllye Avery. Avery was an African-American woman who had been an activist in the movement for women's health that had been borne out of the women's liberation movement. Avery saw that the health issues facing black women were different from those of white women. Partly, this was due to cultural and lifestyle differences between the races, but mostly it was due to the stress that racism and poverty causes in the lives of many black women. Avery started the NBWHP in order to empower African-American women to take steps to improve their physical, mental, and spiritual health.

The goals of the NBWHP struck a deep chord with Lorraine Cole. Not only had she lost her mother to breast cancer while she was still a teenager, but by her mid twenties all of the other women in her family who she was close to had died from various health-related causes. Cole believed that the poor health and early deaths of many black women were due in large part to the fact that the medical and political establishments paid little attention to black women's health. She also believed that the first step toward changing this was to get more African-American women involved in their own health issues. One of her first acts as head of NBWHP was to work towards increasing membership of the organization by abolishing membership dues and publicizing the group's goals nationwide. Between 2001 and 2004, the membership of the organization grew from 6,000 to over 150,000, and Cole has continued to work to attract even more members.

In 2003, the name of NBWHP was changed to the Black Women's Health Imperative. Imperative means something that is important and urgent, requiring action, which expresses well Lorraine Cole's attitude toward the health of African-American women. Cole had become an advocate for black women's health, speaking out about a causes and ideas as a service to others. Along with publicizing health issues, Cole has devoted herself to promoting the importance of advocacy among black women, because legislation about health care and other health issues will directly affect their lives. She has also been a part of organizing history-making events, such as the April 2004 March for Women's Lives, where she spoke to a crowd of over a million people who had gathered in Washington, D.C., to demonstrate about women's rights and health issues.

As head of the Imperative, Cole writes and speaks frequently about women's health issues. She addresses government groups, the medical establishment, professional societies, and black women themselves in order to publicize the importance of these issues. Because of her work as a health advocate, she holds a place on various advisory boards of corporations, government agencies, foundations, and national magazines.

Though much of Cole's job at the Imperative has been to sound an alarm about African-American women's health issues, she has remained hopeful and positive. She expressed both of these positions from the rally stage at the March for Women's Lives when she said, "The health of black women is in a state of crisis. Black women are suffering and dying too often, too soon, and needlessly. …When we leave here today, let's turn pain into promise, let's turn promise into partnership, and let's turn partnership into power."

Sources

Periodicals

Network News, May-June 1995, p. 1.
Ebony, October, 2001, p. 56; October 2002, p. 43; October 2003, p. 84; October 2004. p. 26.

On-line

American Speech-Language-Hearing Association, www.asha.org (October 8, 2004).
Black Women's Health Imperative, www.blackwomenshealth.org (September 27, 2004).
"Lorraine Cole, Ph.D.," *The Office on Women's Health,* www.4woman.gov/owh/MinorityPanel/l cole.htm (September 27, 2004).
"About NMA," *National Medical Association,* www.nmanet.org/about_nma.htm (October 8, 2004).
"1,150,000 March on Washington, D.C.," *March for Women's Lives,* www.marchforwomen.org/content/index.php?pid=119 (September 27, 2004).

Other

Information for this profile was obtained through an interview with Lorraine Cole on October 8, 2004.

—Tina Gianoulis

Wanda Coleman

1946—

Poet, critic

"Others often use the word 'uncompromising' to describe my work," poet Wanda Coleman told Contemporary Poets. "I find that quite pleasing." Coleman, who has claimed to be the most prolific African-American poet of all time, has written thousands of poems and has read her poetry in public more than 500 times. The thread that ties all her work together is a refusal to accept racism in America; she writes about the shattered landscapes of African-American life that racism has left in its wake. Coleman's long career has illustrated the difficulties African-American writers face in making an independent living, but she has left several strong impressions on the literary map, and she is no stranger to controversy.

A native of Los Angeles who has never left Southern California for long, Wanda Coleman was born Wanda Evans on November 13, 1946. The family was poor. Her father was an ex-boxer whose career had ended with injuries; he later worked for an advertising agency. Her mother was a seamstress and housecleaner who sometimes found work in the homes of Hollywood film stars. Coleman found no enjoyment in school, but she was fascinated by books and writing from the time she

Coleman, Wanda, photograph. © Christopher Felver/Corbis.

was a young girl. She had some poems published in a local newspaper when she was 13.

Held a Wide Variety of Jobs

Coleman attended Valley Junior College in Van Nuys, California, and California State University at Los Angeles, but did not finish degree programs at these schools. She married young and had two children by the time she was 20. Struggling to support her children after divorcing her first husband in 1969, Coleman worked in an amazing variety of jobs from the late 1960s through the early 1980s, working all the while toward the goal of becoming a professional writer. She was, at various times, the editorial coordinator of an arts newsletter (for the Studio Watts organization), a medical secretary, a journalist, a proofreader, a waitress, and a Peace Corps/Vista recruiter.

Working in various creative media during this period, Coleman experimented with fiction, screenwriting, and even dance. Her first short story, "Watching the Sunset," appeared in Negro Digest in 1970, and an early hint of her major talent came when she won an Emmy

At a Glance . . .

Born Wanda Evans on November 13, 1946, in Los Angeles, CA; daughter of George and Lewana Evans; married and divorced twice before marrying Austin Straus, a poet; children: Anthony, Tunisia, Ian Wayne Grant. *Education:* Attended Valley Junior College, Van Nuys, CA; California State University at Los Angeles.

Career: Peace Corps/Vista, production editor, proofreader, magazine editor, waitress, and assistant recruiter, 1968-75; *Days of Our Lives,* NBC television, staff writer, 1975-76; medical transcriber and billing clerk, 1979-84; Pacifica Radio network, co-host of poetry program, 1981-1990s; UCLA extension program, fiction instructor, 1989; *Los Angeles Times Magazine,* columnist, 1992-95; Loyola Marymount University, Fletcher Jones endowed chair in literature and writing, 1994-97; California State University at Long Beach, lecturer in black studies, 1997; *Los Angeles Times,* contributor, 1990s; City of Los Angeles Department of Cultural Affairs, fellow, 2003-04.

Memberships: PEN international writers' organization.

Selected awards: Emmy, best writing in daytime drama, *Days of Our Lives,* 1976; National Endowment for the Arts fellowship, 1981-82; Guggenheim fellowship, 1984; California Arts Council fellowship, 1989; Harriette Simpson Arrow prize, 1990; Djerassi Foundation, writer's residence, 1990-91; Lenore Marshall National Poetry Prize, for *Bathwater Wine,* 1999.

Addresses: *Home*—Marina Del Rey, CA.

---

award for her work as a staff writer on the NBC television soap opera *Days of Our Lives* for the 1975-76 season. A pamphlet-like chapbook of Coleman's poems was issued by Black Sparrow Press in 1977.

That publishing house, which also issued the works of the unconventional white writer Charles Bukowski (whose works influenced Coleman's own, as did Walt Whitman's poetry), was a good fit for Coleman's energetic, ambitious, sprawling poetry. Black Sparrow continued to issue Coleman's poetry in publications such as *Mad Dog Black Lady* (1979) and *Imagoes* (1983). Those works brought Coleman national attention, and she benefited from a National Endowment for the Arts grant in 1981 and a Guggenheim Fellowship for Poetry in 1984. *Imagoes* was a very personal work that Coleman regarded as a watershed in her career. Coleman had married and divorced a second time before marrying her third husband, the poet Austin Straus, in 1981.

Collaborated with Musicians

Coleman's street reputation was strengthened during the 1980s. She was a tireless reader of her own poetry at public events, and she made a series of recordings for the Freeway and BarKubCo labels that saw her collaborating with progressive musicians such as Exene Cervenka, former lead vocalist of the punk rock band X. Although the term hadn't yet been coined during the rise of Coleman's career, she was a definite forerunner to the "poetry slam" movement that invigorated African-American literary communities with live poetry contests in the 1990s and 2000s. *Heavy Daughter Blues,* a collection of Coleman's writings from the late 1960s through the mid-1980s, was published by Black Sparrow in 1987.

That book gave many readers a good sampling of Coleman's poetry, which won widespread praise from reviewers for its unquenchable imagination but was sometimes deemed hard to swallow for its grim portrayals of the down-on-their-luck characters who populate Los Angeles's streets. Coleman's poems about love seethed with sexual and violent themes. She continued to produce new work at an astonishing rate—in addition to her many published works she accumulated a collection of over 4,500 rejection slips—and in 1990 the strongly autobiographical *African Sleeping Sickness* was published; it included short stories and prose poems. One story from that volume, "Where the Sun Don't Shine," won the 1990 Harriette Simpson Arrow Prize for fiction; another, "Today I Am a Homicide in the North of the City," was often reprinted and gave an example of the poet's drawn-from-the-streets subject matter.

Hand Dance (1993) was Coleman's seventh thick book of poetry in 14 years. In addition to this prodigious output of poems, Coleman was also active as a critic and essayist. *Native in a Strange Land: Trials and Tremors* (1996) collected many of her prose writings. *Publishers Weekly* noted Coleman's "Swiftian" sense of humor as Coleman asked, "How about a school that teaches the well-heeled the ins and outs of hard-core urban warfare?" Coleman taught writing at a variety of Los Angeles institutions in the 1990s. She also worked as a columnist for the *Los Angeles Times Magazine* from 1992 to 1995 and occasionally wrote book reviews for the *Los Angeles Times,* and her reviews were as uncompromising as her poetry.

Stirred Controversy with Angelou Review

A mixed review Coleman wrote in 1997 of Audre Lord's collected works raised some eyebrows, but it was an acid Coleman review of iconic black poet Maya Angelou's *A Song Flung Up to Heaven* in 2002 that generated a firestorm of controversy. Coleman was banned from a bookstore that had scheduled a reading of poetry from an anthology to which she had contributed, and the *Times* was flooded with letters. The uproar had the effect of introducing Coleman's name to many readers who hadn't encountered her before, for she had always worked along the fringes of the literary mainstream. "Anyone whose assumes that I derive any satisfaction from [that new attention], other than that of a job well done professionally," Coleman wrote in the on-line magazine *Konch*, "is grossly mistaken."

None of this slowed Coleman down in the least. Her vast 1998 poetry volume *Bathwater Wine*, which loosely chronicled the growth of a young black woman to adulthood against a backdrop of poverty and urban violence, won the important Lenore Marshall National Poetry Prize in 1999, and Coleman returned with two more books, *Mercurochrome: New Poems* (2001) and *Ostinato Vamps* (2003), the latter published by the University of Pittsburgh Press after the demise of Black Sparrow. She is also the author of a novel, *Mambo Hips & Make Believe*.

In 2003 and 2004, Coleman became the first literary fellow of the City of Los Angeles Department of Cultural Affairs. Asked at about that time by the Poetry Society of America whether gender, sexual preference, or ethnicity figured more prominently than being an American in her self-identity as a poet, Coleman responded this way: "As a Usually Het Interracially Married Los Angeles-based African American Womonist Matrilinear Working Class Poor Pink/White Collar College Drop-out Baby Boomer Earth Mother and Closet Smoker Unmolested-by-her-father, I am unable to separate these and, as time progresses, resent having to fit into every niggling PC pigeon hole some retard trendoid academic with a grant or hidden agenda barfs up." Readers looked forward to many more years of words laid on the line by Wanda Coleman.

Selected works

Poetry

Art in the Court of the Blue Fag, Black Sparrow, 1977.
Mad Dog Black Lady, Black Sparrow, 1979.
Imagoes, Black Sparrow, 1983.
Heavy Daughter Blues: Poems & Stories, Black Sparrow, 1987.
The Dicksboro Hotel & Other Travels, Ambrosia, 1989.
African Sleeping Sickness: Stories & Poems, Black Sparrow, 1990.
Hand Dance, Black Sparrow, 1993.
American Sonnets, Woodland Pattern/Light and Dark Press, 1994.
Native in a Strange Land: Trials and Tremors, Black Sparrow, 1996.
Bathwater Wine, Black Sparrow, 1998.
Mercurochrome: New Poems, Black Sparrow, 2001.
Ostinato Vamps, University of Pittsburgh, 2003.

Other

(with Jeff Spurrier) *24 Hours in the Life of Los Angeles* (photo essay), Alfred Van Der Marck Editions, 1984.
A War of Eyes & Other Stories (short stories), Black Sparrow, 1988.
Mambo Hips & Make Believe (novel), 1999.
Also made 11 recordings for the Freeway, New Alliance, and BarKubCo labels, reissued by Rhino label.

Sources

Books

Contemporary Poets, 7th ed., St. James Press, 2001.

Periodicals

African American Review, Fall 2000, p. 554; Winter 2002, p. 695.
Library Journal, November 15, 2003, p. 70.
Publishers Weekly, March 29, 1993, p. 46; October 28, 1996, p. 73; June 29, 1998, p. 54.
Village Voice, September 4, 2002.

On-line

"Black on Black: Fear & Reviewing in Los Angeles," *Ishmael Reed's KONCH Magazine,* www.ishmaelreedpub.com/ (September 22, 2004).
"Wanda Coleman," *Biography Resource Center,* www.galenet.galegroup.com/servlet/BioRC (September 22, 2004).
"Wanda Coleman," *Mi Poesias,* www.mipoesias.com/April2004/coleman.htm (September 22, 2004).
"What Is American about American Poetry?" *Poetry Society of America,* www.poetrysociety.org/coleman.html (September 22, 2004).

—James M. Manheim

PonJola Coney

1951—

College dean, physician

Dr. PonJola Coney serves as the dean of the School of Medicine at Meharry Medical College in Nashville, Tennessee. Meharry is a respected professional training ground among historically black colleges in America, and Coney is one of just a handful of women to head a medical school in the United States.

Born on New Year's Eve in 1951, Coney was one of seven children born to Lethell and Dorothy Williams, a farm family in rural Pike County, Mississippi. She attended all-black schools in the community, during an era when public schools were still segregated. Her high school was located in nearby Magnolia, and during her senior year she began driving the school bus for the 30-mile round trip. "I actively sought that job," she laughed in an interview with *Contemporary Black Biography* (*CBB*). "It was a way to make some money that didn't interfere with any of the class schedule." Her science teacher, Charles Andrews, was an important early influence in her life, Coney recalled to *CBB*, and "actually identified me early on, and decided that I could have a career in medicine, in the sciences.... He ultimately served as the superintendent of the school district there, and his wife, who also taught me—I'm her namesake, they served as my godparents—and actually helped to direct and support my career."

After graduating from high school in 1969, Coney went on to Xavier University of Louisiana, a Roman Catholic institution in New Orleans with a largely black student body. "I grew up Southern Baptist," she explained to *CBB*. "They didn't convert me! But I went to school there because it was a great school and it had an excellent program in what I chose to major in college, which is medical technology." After she graduated, Coney returned to Mississippi, and took a job at the University Medical Center in Jackson. "I was a medical technologist in one of the acute-care laboratories there, and had the opportunity to interact with a lot of the medical students and residents and interns in training," she told *CBB*. "I became very close to one of the black medical students who, after several months said to me that I really should attend medical school. And I asked him why, and he said, because you're intelligent, and you can do it. And that was the first time anybody'd ever said that to me."

Coney was accepted into medical school at the University of Mississippi in Jackson, which was her first real experience at an integrated educational institution. She was one of just 15 black students out of her class of 150. "I had a very good experience in medical school," she told *CBB*. "I think everyone was a little bit tentative in the first few months, but the students in the class were very gracious, and were very kind and considerate toward us, and it actually ended up being a good experience.... We had one or two instructors who were derogatory and denigrating, but that was responded to by the students as well as the administration, and it sort of cleared up. Those incidences were very far [between] and few."

Coney graduated from medical school in 1978, and decided to specialize in obstetrics and gynecology. She completed her residency at the University of North Carolina, and did a research fellowship in her chosen area of expertise, reproductive endocrinology, at historic Pennsylvania Hospital in Philadelphia. Intrigued

At a Glance...

Born on December 31, 1951, in McComb, MS; daughter of Lethell (a farmer) and Dorothy (a homemaker) Williams. *Education:* Xavier University of Louisiana, BS, 1973; University of Mississippi Medical School, MD, 1978. *Religion:* Southern Baptist.

Career: Worked as a medical technologist, c. 1973-74; completed residency in obstetrics and gynecology at the University of North Carolina—Chapel Hill Hospital; fellowship at Pennsylvania Hospital, Philadelphia; University of Oklahoma, researcher, professor, physician, and head of its first reproductive fertility program, 1984-87; University of Nebraska, researcher, professor, physician, and head of its first reproductive fertility program, 1987-90; University of Arizona, researcher, professor, physician, and head of its first reproductive fertility program, 1990-95; Southern Illinois University School of Medicine, department chair, obstetrics and gynecology; Meharry Medical College, dean of the School of Medicine, and senior vice president for health affairs, 2002–.

Addresses: *Office*—Dean's Office, Meharry Medical College, 1005 Dr. D.B. Todd, Jr. Blvd., Nashville, TN 37208-3599.

by recent advances in reproductive medicine, Coney became an infertility specialist and was hired by the University of Oklahoma in Oklahoma City as a reproductive endocrinologist. She set up the school's first infertility program in 1984. This was just six years after the world's first test-tube baby had been born in the United Kingdom, in a process known as in vitro fertilization. At the time, this and other new scientific advances were helping couples conceive children. Coney went on to set up the infertility program at the University of Nebraska, and her facility helped to pave the way for that state's first in vitro birth. She then spent time at the University of Arizona, also launching its advanced fertility clinic. "It was very interesting, very exciting, and really encompassed the major part of gynecology," she told *CBB*. "It also had a strong research component to it, so that's what attracted me."

In 1995 Coney became department chair for obstetrics and gynecology at Southern Illinois University School of Medicine in Springfield. She left after seven years to head Meharry Medical College's School of Medicine.

Founded in 1876 as the Medical Department of Central Tennessee College of Nashville, Meharry had a long and illustrious history in training African-American physicians, dentists, and other health care professionals. It is a leading research facility for medical issues that disproportionately affect the African-American community, such as sickle cell anemia, and strives to send its graduates into areas, both rural and urban, that have been traditionally underserved by health care professionals.

Coney is the dean of the medical school and also holds the title of senior vice president for health affairs at Meharry. Despite her busy schedule, she continues to teach classes and maintain a small practice. "I still see patients every week," she told *CBB*. "I stopped delivering babies a couple of years ago...but I still work with infertility patients. I work with a lot of menopausal patients, and I still teach. And I probably won't ever stop doing that." In her spare time, she enjoys outdoor activities, woodworking, and golf.

In 2003 Coney returned to her alma mater at the University of Mississippi to deliver the commencement address for the Medical Center graduates that year. She is its first alumnus to head a U.S. medical school, and she is proud that it is a historically black institution she leads. "Meharry has a very distinguished history, in that it has for a long time had a single mission that it has adhered to—and that's training minority health professionals," she told *CBB*. "I wanted to be a part of doing that, which I think is critical in shaping the future of medicine, particularly for minority populations in this country. And this gave me an opportunity to do that, one that I didn't have in majority institutions. So that's really what attracted me here. And that's what keeps me here."

Sources

Periodicals

Ebony, October 2003.
Tennessee Tribune, June 6, 2003.

On-line

"UMC Commencement Features Alum Coney, Thanks Conerly," *Mississippi Hospital Association,* www.mhanet.org/i4a/pages/headlinedetails.cfm?id=364&archive=1 (July 7, 2004).

Other

Additional information for this profile was obtained through an interview with Dr. PonJola Coney on October 5, 2004.

—Carol Brennan

David Dabydeen

1956—

Poet, novelist, and critic

Award-winning poet, novelist, and critic David Dabydeen writes about his native Guyana and the experiences of colonialism and migration. He makes particular use of Guyanese Creole, a dialect that blends African, French, Spanish, and Indian languages with English and contributes a great deal to the rhythms, rhymes, and emotional power of his work. The language itself is revealed as an area of dispute between colonial power and individuals themselves. Dabydeen was awarded the Commonwealth Poetry Prize in 1984 for his book *Slave Song*. His novels have attracted critical acclaim and his critical works, many of which explore the status of black writers and their work in the English literary tradition, have also been influential; he claims Shakespeare's famous colonial play *The Tempest* as among his major influences. He is a professor at the Centre for Caribbean Studies at the University of Warwick, England.

David Dabydeen was born in Berbice, Guyana, on December 9, 1956; his family was Indo-Guyanese, tracing their heritage back to East Indian indentured workers brought to Guyana between 1838 and 1917. A British colony until 1966, Guyana was in a state of political turmoil during Dabydeen's childhood, and his family moved often to avoid what the British called the "disturbances." In 1969, as the country moved closer to becoming a republic under Forbes Burnham and his People's National Congress party, attacks on the Indo-Guyanese became more common. Dabydeen moved with his parents to London, England, where they believed life would be better, but their sense of disappointment and displacement later became a common thread in Dabydeen's work. After being told by a teacher that he would be lucky even to get into university, Dabydeen won a rare scholarship to Cambridge University and graduated in 1978 with a Bachelor of Arts degree in English. He studied for his doctorate in English literature at London University, graduating in 1982.

Dabydeen began writing the poems that would form his first book, *Slave Song* (1984), while he was an undergraduate at Cambridge. Surprised at the lack of poetry written in creole, he set about recreating the authentic voice of enslaved laborers on the Guyanese sugar cane plantations. The poems explore all aspects of the workers' lives, from their backbreaking, dangerous work, to their leisure-time drinking and singing. But Dabydeen is also interested in exploring the experience of colonization. He uses the conflict between the slaves' patois and the language of the colonial masters to express the physical, political, and cultural conflicts in their lives. In *Coolie Odyssey* (1988), his second book of poetry, this tension between place, language, and identity comes to the surface in the form of an immigrant's journey from the Caribbean to England. This book is written almost entirely in standard English, perhaps reflecting the way immigrants find themselves swamped by the language and culture of their adopted country. Nevertheless the rhythms are markedly Caribbean, as if retaining some identity at least in the face of an alien mode of speech.

The way in which language is used to control and dominate is a central theme in many of Dabydeen's works. In his first two novels, Dabydeen creates char-

At a Glance...

Born on December 9, 1956, in Berbice, British Guyana; son of Krishna Prasad and Vera Dabydeen; immigrated to the United Kingdom, 1969; married Rachel (an occupational therapist), 2003. *Education:* Cambridge University, BA (Honors) in English literature, 1978; London University, PhD in English literature, 1982; postdoctoral study at Wolfson College, Oxford, 1983-87.

Career: Community education officer, Wolverhampton, 1982-84; Centre for Caribbean Studies, Warwick University, Coventry, lecturer, then professor and director, 1984–; Association for the Teaching of Caribbean, African, and Asian Literature, president, 1985-87.

Awards: Cambridge University Quiller-Couch prize, 1978; Yale University Center for British Art resident fellowship, 1982; Commonwealth Poetry Prize, 1984; Guyana Literature Prize, for *The Intended*, 1992; James Tait Black Memorial Prize for Fiction (shortlist), for *A Harlot's Progress*, 1999; Samvad India Foundation, Raja Rao Award for Literature, 2004.

Addresses: *Office*—Centre for Caribbean Studies, University of Warwick, Coventry CV4 7AL, England. *Agent*—Curtis Brown Ltd., Haymarket House, 28/29 Haymarket, London SW1Y 4SP.

---

acters whose narration in creole grates against the language of those around them. Somehow his characters have to negotiate an identity that remembers its origins, yet avoids descending into mimicry or parody. Above all, Dabydeen's characters struggle to assimilate many identities, a state that he applies to the wider context of Britain itself. In an interview with Wolfgang Binder in *The Art of David Dabydeen,* he said: "Over the centuries our cultures have become so interwoven that you can't be a Guyanese without being a Brit, and you can't be a Brit without being a Guyanese, or a Caribbean."

Dabydeen's work as an historian and critic explores similar themes. In the 1990s he wrote and edited several books exploring the importance of black writers and of blacks in English literature. His third poetry book, *Turner: New and Selected Poems,* includes a long poem, from which the book gets its title, on the subject of the representation of blacks in the paintings of J. W. Turner. His book *Hogarth's Blacks: Images of Blacks in Eighteenth-Century English Art* is a major study of race and identity in the eighteenth century and received much praise for its central argument, that artist William Hogarth includes black characters in his paintings as a subversive or unsettling presence.

In 2004 Dabydeen published his fourth novel, called *Our Lady of Demerara* and set in 1990s Coventry, England, and Guyana. Writing in the *Daily Telegraph,* Sukhdev Sandhu described it as "a murder-mystery of sorts...a brooding, powerful novel of unusual ambition." The novel develops many of the themes for which Dabydeen has become known—cultural loss, the problem of poverty and failed ambition, colonialism—but it does so with perhaps a lighter touch than before. Sukhdev Sandhu explains: "Yet such themes...are explored with wit and fire. Not for Dabydeen the hand-wringing dolours and communal uplift of a certain strain of postcolonial literature. He prefers intellectual bawdy."

Dabydeen's diverse work has generally been admired by reviewers and he holds a distinguished position in the British literary establishment, making many television, radio, and live appearances to read his work and speak as a cultural commentator. He is Professor and director of the Department of Caribbean Studies at Warwick University and is the Guyanese ambassador to the United Nations Education, Scientific, and Cultural Organisation (UNESCO).

Selected writings

Novels

The Intended, Minerva, 1992.
Disappearance, Secker & Warburg, 1993.
The Counting House, Jonathan Cape, 1996.
A Harlot's Progress, Jonathan Cape, 1999.
Our Lady of Demerara, Dido Press, 2004.

Poetry

Slave Song, Dangaroo, 1984.
Coolie Odyssey, Hansib, 1988.
Turner: New and Selected Poems, Cape Poetry, 1994.

Other

Hogarth's Blacks: Images of Blacks in Eighteenth-Century English Art, Dangaroo, 1985; University of Georgia Press, 1987.
Caribbean Literature: A Teacher's Handbook, Heinemann, 1986.
Hogarth, Walpole, and Commercial Britain, Hansib, 1987.
(With Nana Wilson-Tagoe) *A Reader's Guide to West Indian and Black British Literature*, Dangaroo, 1987.
Handbook for Teaching Caribbean Literature, Heinemann, 1988.

Editor (with Paul Edwards), *Black Writers in Britain, 1760-1890*, Edinburgh University Press, 1991.

Editor, *Cheddi Jagan: Selected Speeches 1992-1994*, introduction by John Gaffar LaGuerre, Hansib, 1995.

Editor (with Brinsley Samaroo), *Across the Dark Waters: Ethnicity and Indian Identity in the Caribbean*, Macmillan Caribbean, 1996.

Sources

Books

Grant, Kevin, ed., *The Art of David Dabydeen*, Peepal Tree, 1997.

Periodicals

African American Review, Spring 1997, p. 134.
Daily Telegraph (London), July 17, 2004.
History Today, June 1993, p. 57.
Poetry Review (London), vol. 78, no. 2, 1988.
The Guardian (London), March 13, 2004, p.11.
World Literature in Review, Fall 1999, p. 795.

On-line

"David Dabydeen," *Biography Resource Center*, www.galenet.com/servlet/BioRC (October 4, 2004).

"David Dabydeen," *British Council Contemporary Writers*, www.contemporarywriters.com/authors/?p=auth113 (October 4, 2004).

"David Dabydeen," *Poetry International Web*, www.poetryinternational.org/cwolk/view/15897 (October 4, 2004).

Shepler, William, "David Dabydeen," *Postcolonial Studies at Emory*, www.emory.edu/ENGLISH/Bahri/Dabydeen.html (October 4, 2004)

—Chris Routledge

Charles T. Davis

1918-1981

Literary critic, scholar

Charles T. Davis made a name for himself as an influential literary critic and scholar. His early work was on American poetry of the nineteenth and early twentieth centuries, but later in his career Davis began to focus more on black literature, culture, and history. His work boosted the study of black American literature and helped bring it to the fore as a significant part of the American literary tradition. In his role as leader of the African-American studies program at Yale University he was also an important figure in the development of African-American studies in American universities. Davis's most important books are generally considered to be *Black is the Color of the Cosmos* (1982) and *The Slave's Narrative* (1985), but his work from the 1950s onwards, covering authors such as Richard Wright and Walt Whitman, as well as his literary histories of African-American writing, rank among the most important literary scholarship of the late twentieth century.

Charles Twitchell Davis was born on April 29, 1918, in Hampton, Virginia, into a middle-class family. He attended Dartmouth College, where he was awarded a bachelor's degree in 1939. He went on to the University of Chicago, graduating with a master's degree in 1942, and became an instructor in American civilizations at New York University (NYU) in 1948. While working at NYU, Davis earned his doctorate in 1951 before moving to Princeton as an assistant professor in 1955, a post he held until 1961. He became associate professor and later full professor at Pennsylvania State University, where he founded the African American Studies program. After six years as professor of English at the University of Iowa, Davis became professor of English at Yale in 1976, where he was the first African American to be awarded tenure, and the first black master of John C. Calhoun College, eventually rising to become chair of the Afro-American studies program at the university. Eminent black scholar Henry Louis Gates Jr., who worked extensively with Davis and who regards him as his mentor, told *Contemporary Black Biography* (*CBB*) that Davis landed him his first job at Yale—as a typist—while he supervised his dissertation. Davis later helped appoint Gates to the faculty.

Although he is known for his work on African-American writing, for most of his career Davis concentrated on British and American Romanticism, in particular Walt Whitman and the late nineteenth-century poet E. A. Robinson, who has been compared with Robert Frost. Reviewing *Black Is the Color of the Cosmos*, R. Baxter Miller wrote in *Black American Literature Forum* in 1984 that Davis is "among the foremost American literary scholars who happened to be black." The quality of his work and the high regard for it among the literary establishment is reflected in his rapid rise through the academic ranks at a time when blacks were still barred from studying at many American universities. Davis's passion for literature was based on his faith in literary tradition. But while he was praised by writer Ishmael Reed for his ability to be comfortable with black and white cultures, critics such as Miller worried that he was too deeply immersed in white Western culture.

At a Glance . . .

Born on April 29, 1918, in Hampton, VA; died in 1981; married; children: Christopher and Anthony. *Education:* Dartmouth College, AB, 1939; University of Chicago, AM, 1942; New York University, PhD, 1951.

Career: New York University, 1948-55; Princeton University, assistant professor, 1955-61; Pennsylvania State University, associate professor, then professor, 1961-70; University of Iowa, professor of English, 1970-76; Yale University, professor of English and chair of Afro-American studies, 1972-81, Calhoun College, master, 1973-81.

Memberships: Senate Committee on Student Affairs, Pennsylvania State University, chair, during the 1960s; English Institute, member of supervisory committee, 1962-65; Center for Advanced Study in Behavioral Science, Stanford, CA, fellow, 1976-77; Center of Independent Study in New Haven, member of advisory council, 1977-81; National Humanities Center in Research, Triangle Park, NC, member of board of trustees, 1978-81; State of Connecticut's academic awards, member of board, 1979-81; Modern Language Association of America; American Studies Association; Society for the Study of Southern Literature.

Awards: Fulbright professorship at the University of Turin, Italy, 1966-67; Rockefeller Humanities Fellowship.

In the last decade or so of his career, Davis turned increasingly towards black literature but his most important work was published after his death in 1981. *Black Is the Color of the Cosmos* is a collection of essays on black literature and culture spanning his entire career, from his 1942 Master's thesis to the late 1970s. Interestingly the book contains essays from the 1960s challenging the idea of the Black Power movement that art and politics should go together. Sticking to his view that literature and art should not be driven by politics Davis reaffirms his belief that they should be seen as part of a tradition, not for a political purpose. In studying black literature and culture, Davis was always interested in discussing the aspects of a piece of work that made it specifically African American, but he was also careful to acknowledge the influence of the wider American culture.

While some of the essays in *Black Is the Color of the Cosmos* might explain why Davis was not always popular with some members of the black intellectual community in the 1960s and 1970s, his most famous book, co-edited with Henry Louis Gates Jr., *The Slave's Narrative*, was more influential. Slave narratives were written in the nineteenth century by runaway or released black slaves and were used by abolitionists to highlight the plight of black slaves in the southern states. They were a key part of the American literary tradition even before the book appeared, but what Davis and Gates achieved was a re-evaluation of the whole genre. Organized in three parts, the book includes contemporary reviews of slave narratives, essays considering slave narratives as historical documents, and essays considering their literary value. What made the book so significant was partly the breadth of its scope, but mainly that it tested the narratives against late twentieth century ideas of history and literature, rather than as a "special case" or literary curiosity.

Davis is remembered as a perceptive and sensitive literary critic; through his later work, which was published after his death in 1981, he became a key figure in the expanding discipline of African-American studies. He was also a major influence on younger high-profile scholars such as Henry Louis Gates, Jr. who told *CBB* "I cannot imagine a better mentor or advisor for a young academic in training: Professor Davis was unfailingly generous with his time and unerringly incisive in his comments and criticism. Professor Davis was a demanding reader and critic, and he certainly made me want to work to earn his praise. He was a model scholar and gentleman, and I am indebted to him for any success I have enjoyed."

Selected works

Books

(With Gay Wilson Allen), *Walt Whitman's Poems: Selections with Critical Aids*, New York University Press, 1955.
(Editor, with E. A. Robinson), *Selected Early Poems and Letters*, Holt, 1960.
(Editor, with Lucy Larcom), *A New England Girlhood*, Corinth Books, 1961.
(Editor, with Daniel Walden), *On Being Black: Writings by Afro-Americans From Frederick Douglass to the Present*, Fawcett, 1970.
(With Michel Fabre) *Richard Wright: A Primary Bibliography*, G. K. Hall, 1982.
Black Is the Color of the Cosmos: Essays on Afro-American Literature and Culture, 1942-1981, edited by Henry Louis Gates, Jr., foreword by A. Barlett Giamatti, Garland Publishing, 1982.
(Editor, with Henry Louis Gates Jr.), *The Slave's Narrative*, Oxford University Press, 1985.

Sources

Periodicals

Black American Literature Forum, Winter 1984, pp. 178-181.
New York Times Book Review, July 7, 1985, p. BR17.

On-line

"Charles T(witchell) Davis," *Biography Resource Center*, http://galenet.galegroup.com/servlet/BioRC (September 27, 2004).

Other

Additional information and commentary for this profile was generously supplied by Henry Louis Gates Jr.

—Chris Routledge

Ernie Davis

1939-1963

Professional football player

Ernest R. Davis, commonly known as Ernie, was one of the best running backs ever to play college football. He followed the legendary Jim Brown to Syracuse University, where he led the Orangemen to a national championship in 1959, and in 1961 he became the first African American to be awarded the Heisman Trophy, given to the college game's best player. On the precipice of a promising career with the Cleveland Browns of the National Football League (NFL), Davis was struck with leukemia. He never played in a single NFL game and died on May 18, 1963, at the age of 23. He is remembered as a superior athlete and a young man who lived and died with dignity, grace, and compassion.

Davis, Ernie, photograph. AP/Wide World Photos. Reproduced by permission.

The Young Athlete

Davis was born on December 14, 1939, in New Salem, Pennsylvania, to Marie Davis. His parents were separated, and his father was killed in an auto accident before Davis was born. Young and needing a job, Davis's mother sent him to live with his maternal grandparents in Uniontown, Pennsylvania, when he was fourteen months old. Willie, a coalminer, and Elizabeth Davis already had twelve children but welcomed their young grandson into their home. Davis spent his early years playing sports with his older uncles.

When he was eleven years old, Davis's mother remarried and summoned her only child to Elmira, New York, to live with her. For Davis, who was quiet and shy, the transition was tough, but his athletic abilities, already apparent at a young age, helped earn him the respect of the kids at the local community center. Also, even in his youth, others noticed the special quality of Davis's character that radiated sincerity, enthusiasm, and friendliness. He played tackle on Small Fry football for the Superior Buick team. Although he was big for his age, he never delivered punishing blows and often would simply pick the smaller kids up and wait for the whistle to blow rather than slam them to the ground.

As a freshman at Elmira Free Academy, Ernie joined the junior varsity football team, but broke his wrist in the first game and was out for the rest of the season. However, it did not stop him from playing basketball. Having made the varsity team, Davis, with his wrist still

> **At a Glance . . .**
>
> Born on December 14, 1939, in New Salem, PA; died on May 18, 1963, in Cleveland, OH; son of Marie Davis Fleming. *Education:* Syracuse University, BA, economics, 1962.
>
> **Career:** Professional football player, 1962-63 (died before playing in first game).
>
> **Selected awards:** First Team All-American, 1960, 1961; Heisman Trophy, 1961; *Sports Magazine* Player of the Year, 1961; Walter Camp Trophy (college player of the year), 1961; College Football Hall of Fame, 1979.

in a splint, came off the bench in his first game to score 22 points. He also played first base and pitched for the baseball team. Although baseball was the weakest of his three sports, several professional scouts kept an eye on him.

In 1955, during his sophomore year, Davis played defensive end on the football team, and they went undefeated on the season and won the conference championship. The following year his coach moved him to halfback, and the Blue Devils won another league title. In 1957, Davis's senior year, they suffered some losses due to a bout of the Asian flu that weakened the team, but Davis earned all-conference for the third consecutive year. In the thirteen games he played in the halfback position, he carried the ball 179 times for 1,314 yards, averaging 7.4 yards per carry, and he scored a school-record 138 career points on 21 touchdowns and 12 place kicks.

Davis also continued to excel on the basketball court. He led his team to 52 straight wins during his junior and senior years, averaged 18.4 points per game, and set a conference record of 1,065 points. He could jump, rebound, and shoot. If the game was close, his point total would go up; if the Blue Devils had a padded lead, Davis would back off and his point total would fall. It was simply his style to never try to play to the crowds or embarrass an opponent. A career in professional basketball was well within Davis's reach, but, in the end, football was his first love.

College Career

More than thirty colleges and universities, including football superpowers the University of Michigan and Notre Dame, actively sought to add Davis to their football programs. He was also heavily recruited by Syracuse University, another football powerhouse, who sent Jim Brown, their All-American running back and one of the team's first African Americans players, to convince Davis. Based on Brown's influence, his own coach's friendship with Syracuse coach Ben Schwartzwalder, and its close proximity to his home (90 miles), Davis chose Syracuse.

Davis's freshman team in 1958 went undefeated. At 6-foot, 2-inches and 210 pounds, he was a fast, strong, and smart player. He was a skilled running back, compiling 100-plus yards in eleven games during his college career. He could also return kicks, block, catch passes, and even kick the team's extra points. In the days when players freely switched between offense and defense, he also was an effective defensive back. Not only did Davis impress those around him with his athletic skills, he also earned their respect for his kind and generous nature. "Ernie was just like a puppy dog, friendly and warm and kind," Schwartzwalder told *Sports Illustrated*. "He had that spontaneous goodness about him. He radiated enthusiasm. His enthusiasm rubbed off on the kids. Oh, he'd knock you down, but then he'd run back and pick you up. We never had a kid so thoughtful and polite."

In 1959 Davis, now a sophomore, rushed for 686 yards and led the Syracuse Orangemen to an 11-0 record. Davis individually outscored Syracuse's opponents 80-73. On January 1, 1960, the Orangemen faced second-ranked University of Texas in the Cotton Bowl for the national title. While practicing place kicks prior to the game, Davis strained his hamstring and played the game hurt, but it did little to slow him down. On the third play from scrimmage, the Orangemen ran a halfback pitch in which Gerhard Schwedes took the handoff and then flung the ball down the field to Davis who caught the pass and ran for an 87-yard touchdown, setting a Cotton Bowl record. Davis later caught a 4-yard touchdown pass, scored a 2-point conversion, and intercepted a pass while playing defensive back.

Tensions flared during the game when Syracuse players accused the University of Texas players of directing racial slurs at one of their black players, and a bench-clearing brawl broke out just before the end of the first half. Although Texas managed to get on the board in the second half, Syracuse won the game 23-14. Davis was named player of the game, but when he was informed that he would have to leave the banquet after receiving his award and that he and his two black teammates would not be allowed attend the dinner, the entire Syracuse team boycotted the event.

During his junior year Davis rushed for 877 yards and was named an All-American. Although his senior year of 1961 was not his best all-round performance, Davis was once again named an All-American. He also had a stellar performance in Syracuse's 15-14 win over the University of Miami (Florida) in the Liberty Bowl, with 140 total yards and a touchdown, and was named the game's most valuable player. Over his college career, Davis broke numerous records previously set by

Brown, including 2,386 yards rushing, 6.6 yards per carry, 35 touchdowns, and 220 points. At the end of the season he edged out Ohio State halfback Bob Ferguson by 53 votes to become the first African-American player to be awarded the Heisman Trophy, college football's highest honor.

NFL Career Cut Short

After graduating from Syracuse with a bachelor's degree in economics in 1962, Davis prepared to enter the NFL. The Buffalo Bills of the fledging American Football League reportedly offered Davis a three-year contract, but Davis wanted to play in the NFL so he turned down the offer. The Washington Redskins took Davis as the overall number-one pick and then traded him to the Cleveland Browns for the Browns' running back Bobby Mitchell and their number-one pick. Cleveland gave Davis a three-year contract worth $200,000 (initially reported at $80,000). Jim Brown was already a member of the Cleveland organization, and Browns' owner Art Modell was looking forward to having the most explosive backfield in the history of the NFL.

Looking back, those who knew Davis first remember seeing a change in him at the Coaches All-Star Game on June 29, 1962. He looked tired and sluggish. Davis blamed it on the scorching heat out on the field, but after the game he continued to complain of fatigue and mentioned to a friend that his gums were bleeding. In late July Davis flew out to Chicago to begin practice for the College All-Stars match-up with the Chicago Bears, and others began to notice his lackluster behavior on the field. On July 28, 1962, Davis felt swelling in his neck and was admitted to Evanston Hospital. It was suspected that he had the mumps or mononucleosis, but the tests brought back much more dire results: Davis had acute monocytic leukemia.

The doctors did not disclose Davis's condition to him but rather called Modell and broke the news to the team's owner. Modell immediately traveled to Evanston, where he conferred with doctors and checked Davis out of the hospital. Told he had some type of blood disorder, Davis flew back to Cleveland and was admitted to Marymount Hospital, where Modell insisted the lab work be redone. The results were clear: Davis had less than a year to live.

After undergoing a round of chemotherapy and spending almost two months in and out of hospitals, Davis's leukemia went into remission, and on October 4, 1962, Davis's doctor, with Modell present, finally explained the extent of his illness to him. Although Modell's doctor told Davis he could continue to play football as long as the disease was in remission, the Browns' head coach Paul Brown refused to allow Davis to suit up on the advice of his own team doctor. It became a point of contention between Modell and Brown, but Davis never complained. He remained hopeful that he could beat the disease and refused any pity offered by others.

While the disease was in remission, Davis reported that he felt fine. He even participated in some exhibition basketball games with some Browns' players. According to *ESPN Classic*'s Bob Carter, Davis wrote an article for the *Saturday Evening Post* in March of 1963, in which he said, "Some people say that I am unlucky. I don't believe it. And I don't want to sound as if I am particularly brave or unusual. Sometimes I still get down, and sometimes I feel sorry for myself. Nobody is just one thing all the time. But when I look back I can't call myself unlucky. My 23rd birthday was December 14. In these years I have had more than most people get in a lifetime."

Died at Age 23

Shortly after the article appeared, the leukemia reoccurred, and Davis once again became a regular at the hospital. The Browns paid his salary and all his medical bills. "He used to come in to my office," recalled Modell, according to *Newsline*, "and apologize for taking the money. He knew he was dying but he never lost his poise. Knowing him taught me a lot about life. You could not know him without suffering for him which was exactly what he didn't want you to do."

On Thursday, May 16, 1963, Davis wrote Coach Brown a note that said, "Going to the hospital for a few days. Don't tell anybody. See you around." He then went to Modell's office to say that he was once again entering the hospital. Although at the time Modell wondered why Davis had not simply called, later he understood that Davis was coming to say goodbye. Davis then checked into the hospital for the last time. On Friday night he fell into a coma. At 2 a.m. on Saturday, May 18, 1963, he coughed once and died.

Thousands turned out to mourn his passing. Nearly thirty Browns players and staff flew in to Elmira for the funeral service. President John F. Kennedy sent a telegram, and more than 10,000 people filed past his coffin in one day. The Browns retired Davis's number 45, even though he had never played an NFL game. He was elected into the College Football Hall of Fame in 1979. According to *ESPN.com*, Jim Brown said of his friend: "The way he carried himself, the way he did not drown in his own tears, the way that he did not hang on his sickness, the way that he functioned as a human being under all of those conditions was tremendous courage."

Sources

Books

Dictionary of American Biography, Supplement 7: 1961-1965, American Council of Learned Societies, 1981.

Gallagher, Robert C., *Ernie Davis, the Elmira Express: The Story of a Heisman Trophy Winner,* Bartleby Press, 1983.

Periodicals

Jet, December 4, 2000, p. 19; December 1, 2003, p. 22.
Knight Ridder/Tribune News Service, November 16, 2003.
Newsline, Spring 1993, pp. 4-5.
Sports Illustrated, September 4, 1989, p. 136.
Star-Gazette (Elmira, NY), December 8, 2001.
Washington Times, July 15, 2003, p. B8.

On-line

"Davis Won Heisman, Respect," *ESPN Classic,* www.espn.go.com/classic/biography/s/Davis_Ernie.html (September 27, 2004).
"Ernie Davis, Elmira Express," *Star-Gazette* (Elmira, NY), www.stargazettesports.com/ErnieDavis/ (September 27, 2004).
"Ernie Davis: The Elmira Express," *City of Elmira* (NY), www.ci.elmira.ny.us/history/ernie_davis.html (October 14, 2004).
"More Info on Ernie Davis," *ESPN Classic,* www.espn.go.com/classic/s/000801erniedavisadd.html (September 27, 2004).
"1961, 27th Award: Ernest Davis," *The Heisman Memorial Trophy Winners,* www.heisman.com/years/1961.html (September 27, 2004).

—Kari Bethel

Ronald and Rony Delice

1966—

Fashion designers, entrepreneurs

On the cutting edge of men's fashion design since the late 1990s, twin brothers Ronald and Rony Delice have become known for creating fine suits that incorporate bold color combinations with edgy styling. Their Ron & Ron menswear label, worn by such celebrities as Will Smith and Samuel L. Jackson, has brought the brothers both critical acclaim and financial success, and has earned them a respected place among what *Daily News Record* writer Stan Gellers called "a hip new breed of 30-something tailors with a real passion for clothing."

The brothers, born in 1966 in Haiti, were the two surviving siblings among a set of quadruplets. They are fraternal twins: Ronald is older than Rony by ten seconds. With their five other siblings, the brothers grew up in a family of modest means in Haiti. They wore uniforms to their Catholic school, but enjoyed dressing up in their "Sunday best" clothes for church. Their father was a tailor and their mother, who worked as a seamstress, taught the brothers the importance of presenting a good appearance even though they could not afford elegant clothing. As Ronald observed to Kathryn Wexler of the *Miami Herald*, their mother used to tell them, "When you have no money in your pocket...the way you present yourself as far as your clothes, your demeanor, makes a whole big difference. They don't categorize you if you're always well presented."

The brothers moved to New York City at age 11, and during their high school years they enjoyed visiting upscale Manhattan department stores to look at the latest clothing. They went on to attend the prestigious Fashion Institute of Technology, and after graduating went to Europe for a year, where Ronald trained with expert tailors in France and Rony studied fine tailoring in Italy. As Ronald commented to *Black Enterprise* writer Demetria Lucas, "Fashion is in our blood. It just comes naturally."

Ronald and Rony began working at Beau Brummel, a men's boutique in the Soho district of Manhattan, in the 1980s. "They were the best dressed guys in the store from the day they started working," the boutique's former owner told Wexler. Indeed, customers often liked what the brothers wore more than what was available in the store. "Everyone kept asking us where we had our suits made," Ronald told *Daily News Record* contributor Stan Gellers. After customers began asking to buy the same suits that the brothers themselves were wearing, Beau Brummel's owners asked the Delices to create a signature line for the boutique. The brothers' designs matched vibrant colors with striking details such as multiple buttons and top stitching—elements that Ronald and Rony link to their roots in Haiti, where even the poorest people wear their clothes with inimitable flair. "Our style was totally different from the stuff that the store carried," Rony told Lucas. "We have always just done our own thing."

In 1998 the brothers launched their own clothing and accessories label, Ron & Ron. The business has performed extraordinarily well. "Our first year went smoothly," Ronald told Lucas. "Usually, even if you know what you're doing, it's terrible. But we were very focused." With an initial investment of $35,000 from

At a Glance . . .

Born in 1966 in Haiti; sons of a tailor and taxi driver and a seamstress. Ronald: married Shelly Meridith, 2001 (second marriage); children: Maude, Ioan, Zinedine. Rony: married; two children. *Education*: Attended Fashion Institute of Technology.

Career: Beau Brummel men's boutique, New York, NY, sales staff, late 1980s-1998; Ron & Ron, New York, founders and owners, 1998–.

Awards: Gen Art International Design Award, 2002; Fashion Group International, Rising Star Award, 2002.

Addresses: *Office*—Ron & Ron, 55 Mercer St., Fourth Floor, New York, NY 10013.

---

their savings and those of Ronald's wife, a toy designer and graphic artist, the brothers built Ron & Ron into a major force in the men's fashion industry. By 2003 the company saw annual sales of more than $500,000.

The Delices' fashion sense, which according to *Hardbeatnews* "combines class with a hint of rogue," quickly attracted fans among the celebrity world. The brothers have dressed such well-known figures as actors, athletes including Latrell Sprewell and Steve Francis, and the musician Andre 3000 of Outkast, and have designed the men's suits worn on the TV series *Law & Order: Criminal Intent*. Their designs have also been seen in major fashion publications, such as *Vogue* (France), *Cosmopolitan* (Italy), and *Elle* (Italy). Critics have admired Ron & Ron clothing for its intricate tailoring and its original combinations of texture and color. The look was described by Stan Gellars in *Daily News Record* as "rock & roll meets Milan" with shorter jacket lengths and unexpected details such as patch pockets and topstitching in red and blue, the colors of the Haitian flag. With suits ranging in price from $1,750 to as much as $8,500, Ron & Ron has clearly found a niche in the luxury market. But the brothers also keep more humble elements in their collections as well; they always feature a denim piece, according to the *Miami Herald*, because the fabric is so popular among poorer people in Haiti.

In 2002 the Delice brothers won an international menswear design award from Gen Art, which showcases emerging talent. That same year Ronald and Rony also won Fashion Group International's Rising Star award. Though their showroom features made-to-measure designs, the brothers have recently increased their wholesale division. Ronald, who owns an apartment with his wife in Paris and spends every other month in that city, hopes to bring a Ron & Ron boutique there in the near future. Plans are also in the works to open Ron & Ron stores in New York, Los Angeles, and Atlanta. At the same time, however, the brothers insist that custom-made designs will always be their primary focus because they enjoy the close interaction with customers.

Their success, the brothers have noted, is rooted in their creative drive. "We're artists more than business people," Ronald told Lucas in *Black Enterprise*. Their work, Ronald commented in *Hardbeatnews*, "is in our blood. And when you love something from the heart, there's no holding back." Indeed, the brothers' impact on the fashion world suggests that their designs will grow ever more popular. As *New York Times* writer Penelope Green pointed out in a feature on the Delice brothers, "In Haitian culture, the loa, or spirit, of the twins is a force to be reckoned with."

Sources

Periodicals

Black Enterprise, April, 2003, p. 47.
Daily News Record, June 28, 2004, p. 33.
Miami Herald, June 23, 2004.
New York Times, October 5, 2003.

On-line

"Spotlight on Haitian-Born Designer Ronald and Rony Delice," *Hardbeatnews*, http://www.hardbeatnews.com/newsdetails.php?aaad=2008 (September 15, 2003).

—E. Shostak

Georgia Mae Dunston

1944—

Professor of microbiology, research scientist

Born into a working class African-American family in the segregated southern United States, Georgia Dunston had little reason to believe that her life and career would be very different from those of her parents or grandparents. She was motivated to pursue higher learning, however, by the inspiration of encouraging teachers at every level of her education and by her own burning curiosity about the human condition. In search of the answers to her early childhood question, "Why are people different?," she has not only continued to study human biology throughout her life, but she has initiated various studies into the much-neglected field of African-American genetics.

Georgia Mae Dunston was born in the summer of 1944 in the small port city of Norfolk, Virginia. Her father, Ulyses, worked for many years as a cook at a commercial barbecue wholesaler, and her mother, Rosa, had various working-class jobs as a restaurant dishwasher, a laundry presser, and a commercial cleaner. Though the Dunstons worked hard at fairly low-paying jobs, they did not consider themselves poor. Their lives were similar to those of the other families in their tight-knit black community, centered on family, community, and the church. Young Georgia went to the local Baptist church every week with her family, attending Sunday school and singing in the choir. As she looked at the unfairness in the world around her, she began to come up with some big questions for God.

Began to Look for Answers

Dunston was only ten years old when the Supreme Court ruled that segregation in the nation's schools was illegal. In the South of the 1950s, segregation—or separation by race—was enforced by white people to keep blacks out of white institutions. In schools this meant that black students were not allowed to attend school with white students. After the Supreme Court's ruling in 1954, some of Dunston's classmates were among the first sent to white schools. This was called integration, and many racist whites continued to resist integration long after it had been required by law.

Though Dunston herself was not bussed to a white school, she was aware of the tension between whites and blacks, and of the unfair treatment many blacks received. She tried hard to fit in this knowledge with the lessons she learned in church, but she could not. Over and over, the same questions arose in her mind. If God created everyone, then why did God make people different from each other? In addition, she wondered, if everyone is equal in the sight of God, why do white people seem so much better off?

Dunston liked going to school and did well there. One of her elementary school teachers, Eleanor Williams, was an especially strong influence, both praising and encouraging Dunston and inspiring her to work harder so that she could live up to Ms. Williams' high opinion of her.

When a junior high school science teacher sparked an interest in biology, Dunston brought her old question to God into her study of science. "Why are people different?" seemed as much at the root of biology as of religion. In high school, her thirst to understand the human experience led her to philosophy, and she read

At a Glance . . .

Born in 1944 in Norfolk, Virginia. *Education:* Norfolk State University, BA in Biology, 1965; Tuskegee University, MS in Biology, 1967; University of Michigan, PhD in Human Genetics, 1972; National Cancer Institute, Postdoctoral work in Tumor Immunology, 1975.

Career: Department of Microbiology, Howard University College of Medicine, Washington, D.C., assistant professor, 1972-78; Department of Microbiology, Howard University College of Medicine, associate professor, 1978-1993; Department of Genetics and Human Genetics, Howard University, associate professor, 1978–; Department of Dermatology, Howard University College of Medicine, associate professor, 1993–; Department of Microbiology, Howard University College of Medicine, professor, 1993– (also served as interim chair, 1994-98, and chair, 1998-2004); National Human Genome Center at Howard University, founding director, 1998–.

Selected Memberships: North American Committee of the Human Genome Diversity Project; Howard University Chapter of Sigma Xi, Research Society of North America; National Academies of Sciences Committee on Emerging Issues and Data on Environmental Contaminants, External Advisory Board; National Institutes of Health National Institute of Environmental Health Sciences Scientific Advisory Board for the Sister Study.

Selected Awards: Howard University, College of Medicine Student Council, Excellence in Teaching Award, 1978; New Millennium Foundation, Excellence in Technology Award, 2001; International Black Women's Congress, Oni Award, 2001; NAACP Science Achievement Award, Montgomery County Chapter, 1990; *AARP Magazine,* Impact Award, 2004

Address: *Office*—Department of Microbiology, Howard University, College of Medicine, 520 W St. NW, Washington, DC 20059.

Jean-Paul Sartre and other philosophers who wrote about the nature of society. However, she soon focused again on science when a teacher suggested that science offered a better chance of getting a job, pointing out: "There are no black philosophers."

Studied Human Biology

As her high school graduation grew near, Dunston had thought little about going to college. No one in her family had ever graduated from college, and her parents assumed that she would go to work once she was out of high school. However, she was one of the top five students in her graduating class and received a full scholarship to Norfolk State University, a traditionally black college close to home. Dunston thus began her work toward a college degree.

At Norfolk State, Dunston continued her study of biology. As in elementary and high school, she developed good relationships with her teachers. She was especially impressed with the dedication of Professor Louis Austin. Austin was so determined to give his biology majors a wide variety of courses equal to that available at a large university that he taught a large number of classes himself. Though he worked tirelessly to encourage blacks to go into scientific fields, Austin was also demanding. Shocked to receive her first C grade on work she knew she had done well, Dunston approached Austin to ask him why. "Because you can do better," he told her. Inspired by his confidence, she continued to work harder and do better.

After her college graduation, Dunston went to stay with her aunt in New York City and look for a job. She had a biology degree and thought she would easily get a job as a medical technician. Medical technicians work in laboratories performing tests that help doctors diagnose and treat diseases. She went to an employment agency and saw that there were many such jobs available. Hopefully, she began to go out for interviews. However, once employers saw that she was a black woman, they claimed that they did not have any job openings for technicians. The only jobs she was offered were unskilled cleaning jobs.

Determined not to take a job which would not use any of her scientific knowledge or skills, and discouraged by the racist attitudes she had encountered, Dunston returned home to Norfolk. Professor Austin, her old professor and biology mentor at Norfolk State, suggested that she should go back to school for a graduate degree. He told her that there was an advertisement in the journal *Science* seeking applications for a George Washington Carver research fellowship at Tuskegee University, a well-known historically black university in Alabama. Dunston applied for and received the fellowship and began to work toward her master's degree at Tuskegee.

Discovered Genetics

Still fascinated by the mysteries and variety of human biology, Dunston began to study genetics at Tuskegee. Genetics is the study of how characteristics are passed from one generation of living things to another. During the 1950s scientists had discovered that genetic information is encoded in a certain kind of molecule, called deoxyribonucleic acid, or DNA. This DNA is carried in living cells in units called genes. When living things reproduce, they pass their DNA on to their offspring and this causes their offspring to have some of the same characteristics as the parents. The study of DNA was a new and exciting field when Dunston began her work on it in the early 1970s.

Away from home for the first time and recovering from the breakup of an important romantic relationship, Dunston threw all of her energy into her studies and laboratory work at Tuskegee. David Aminoff, an exchange professor from the University of Michigan who taught Dunston biochemistry at Tuskegee, was so impressed with her academic performance and dedication that he offered to help her get a training grant so that she could continue studying toward her doctorate in human genetics.

During the early 1970s, a group of African-American students at the University of Michigan had organized demonstrations and other actions about several political issues on campus. This group was called the Black Action Movement, and one result of their work was that the university launched a program for admitting more black students. Georgia Dunston was accepted into the Rackham Graduate School of the University of Michigan as one of the African-American students admitted during this time. She was the first black student in the university's Human Genetics department and likely the first black to earn her Ph.D. in that field. Though the work was hard, Dunston was still propelled by the same basic question that had driven her quest for knowledge as a child: Why are people different from each other?

Returned to the Black Community

As Dunston was finishing her studies at the University of Michigan, she met Dr. Willie Turner, an African-American scientist who wanted to build a scientific research facility in microbiology at Howard University in Washington, D.C. He was visiting colleges around the country looking for black Ph.D.'s who were interested in careers in scientific research. If Dunston would join his effort at Howard, he told her, he would help her get a grant to do post-doctoral studies at the National Institutes of Health (NIH), the nation's major center for medical research, also located near Washington, D.C. Studying at the NIH appealed to Dunston. The idea of helping to create a research department intrigued her, as did the idea of taking her skills and knowledge back to serve the black community. She decided to take the job at Howard, joining the faculty of the Microbiology department in the College of Medicine.

Founded in 1867, Howard is one of the most respected historically black colleges in the world, though the university has always admitted all qualified applicants. Starting with a graduating class of four in 1870, by 2003 Howard had 10,500 students enrolled in twelve different colleges. It is considered by some to be one of the hundred best colleges in the United States. Nonetheless, because it was an historically black college, Dunston's professors at the University of Michigan were disappointed that she chose to take a job at Howard rather than seeking a position at a more prestigious (and largely white) institution.

Dunston, however, did not regret her choice. Once told, "There are no black philosophers," she set about to combat the notion that there were no black research scientists. During an exciting period of growth for the Microbiology Department, she helped create a Ph.D. program for medical microbiology research at Howard and completed her post-doctoral work at the NIH National Cancer Institute.

As the research facility at Howard grew, so did Dunston's career as a research scientist. Still following her childhood quest for "what made people different," she began investigating the particular biology of African and African-American people. Very little previous research had focused on the health issues of black people, and Dunston obtained grants to establish her research at Howard. Through these grants she was able to investigate such important questions as why black people frequently had difficulties with organ transplants. Dunston's research uncovered the fact that, since the tests for organ matches had been created using cells from white people, they often did not work when used to test organ matches for blacks. Other Dunston research projects involved studying the genetics of type II diabetes among both African-American and West African people, asthma in African Americans, breast cancer in black women, and prostate cancer in black men.

As she began to study the health issues of black people, Dunston quickly realized that studies done on people of European descent were of limited use when investigating the genetic basis of disease in African Americans. Much of her study of disease had led her back to her fascination with human variation, and it was soon apparent to her that too little research had been done in African and African-American genetics.

Worked to Uncover the Secrets of the Gene

In 1990 a group of international scientists had begun the Human Genome Project, an attempt to discover and study all of the approximately 30,000 human genes and to map out the structure of the human DNA molecule. Dunston correctly suspected that without the influence of African-American researchers, little of the project's work would focus on black populations. She applied for and received a grant to study the genetics of African Americans in order to build a body of reference material that would help apply future gene research to black people.

Dunston's work resulted in the founding of the National Human Genome Center at Howard University in 2001. She raised funds to build labs and recruit other investigators to head various genetic research departments focusing on African Americans, Africans, and other African diaspora populations. Dunston saw the genetic heritage of the African disapora as especially rich for many reasons.

First, many scientists believe that Africa is the birthplace of humankind and of the human genome itself. Because it is the place of human origin, with the oldest continuous history of human populations, the continent is home to the widest range of human genetic variation. The fossil record indicates that modern humans migrated out of east Africa around 100,000 years ago and settled in all parts of the world. Today, most scientists accept that all human populations today are descendents of founding groups out of Africa which have changed in biological characteristics as they have adapted over time to new geographical environments. In more recent history, many African people were forcibly taken across the Atlantic Ocean by the slave trade. Because they were slaves, they did not intermingle with their new society in the same way voluntary immigrants do, and the broad base of genetic variation in the African gene pool has stayed together and remained characteristic of populations of African descent, whether in the Caribbean, Europe, or the United States.

Though Dunston's research into genetics at the National Human Genome Center has provided some important answers to why people from different parts of the world look different, it has also opened a whole new world of questions. For a research scientist these new questions are the most exciting form of success. One of the most interesting findings of the researchers of the Human Genome Project is that in the human genome, 99.9 percent of the genetic material is identical for every human. "And yet each of us is unique," Dunston has said. "We are literally part of one big human family, the genome bears that out. Now the question is how we're going to reflect that knowledge in how we live."

When Georgia Dunston first formed her childhood question about the variations in human beings, she could not have predicted where her search would lead her, or the number of lives that would be affected by her search for the answer. However, digging into the deepest mysteries of the living and studying how different cells work together in the human body to express life, she discovered that research science is not so far from philosophy after all.

Selected writings

(With others) "Organ Donation and Blacks: A Critical Frontier," *The New England Journal of Medicine,* Vol. 325, No. 6, August 8, 1991, pp. 442-46.
(With others) "Breast Cancer Genetics in African Americans," *Cancer,* Vol. 96, No. 1, January 1, 2003, pp. 236-46.

Sources

Periodicals

Ebony, May 2003, pp. 60-68.
Emerge, September 1997. p. 30.
Health, March 1995, pp. 19-22.

On-line

"History of the Human Genome Project," *National Genome Project Information,* www.ornl.gov/sci/techresources/Human_Genome/project/hgp.shtml (October 18, 2004).
"NHGRI Cosponsors a Conference about the Human Genome Project for Local Minority Communities," *National Human Genome Research Institute,* www.genome.gov/pfv.cfm?pageid=10003008 (October 1, 2004).
"Scientist at Work," *Annenberg/CPB Learner,* www.learner.org/channel/courses/essential/life/session5/scientist.html (October 1, 2004)

Other

Information for this profile was obtained through an interview with Georgia Dunston on October 12, 2004.

—Tina Gianoulis

Christopher Edley

1928-2003

Organization president, advocate, lawyer

"All of my adult life has been heavily laden with the things and the kind of work that would advance Black life," recounted Christopher Edley, former president and chief executive officer of the United Negro College Fund (UNCF), in *Jet* magazine. Under Edley's tutelage, the UNCF became one of the most widely recognized charitable organizations in America. He joined the UNCF in 1973, a year after the organization enacted one of the first national advertising campaigns to raise money for black higher education. Edley assumed guidance of the campaign with the slogan "A Mind is a Terrible Thing to Waste" for 17 successful years. Poor health forced him to retire in 1991, after helping to solicit the largest individual donation in the history of black philanthropy. Instituting a strong organization was Edley's "greatest gift," related Fisk University president Henry Ponder to Matthew Scott in *Black Enterprise*. "He has set a well-defined management style into motion that will ensure that our institution moves forward, continuing the mission of raising money for our schools, to provide the best quality education for our students."

Born on January 1, 1928, in Charleston, West Virginia, Edley graduated magna cum laude from Howard University in Washington, D.C., in 1949. He was one of a handful of black students studying law at Harvard University, and he received his law degree in 1953. He then moved to Philadelphia, where he practiced law both as an assistant district attorney and in private practice with Moore, Lightfoot & Edley. In 1960 he became the chief administrator for the United States Commission on Civil Rights. In 1963 he joined the Ford Foundation, becoming the organizations first black officer. Edley worked for ten years at the Ford Foundation before moving to the UNCF. He married Zaida Coles in 1950, and the couple had two children: daughter Judith and son Christopher F. Edley Jr., a prominent educator and dean of the University of California-Berkeley School of Law.

When Edley was hired to direct the UNCF, it was "like a mom and pop kind of store that was getting bigger," he confessed to Leon E. Wynter in the *Wall Street Journal*. "People were so busy waiting on customers that no strategic thoughts were being given." During his tenure, Edley provided the UNCF with future goals and fund-raising ideas, including the only national higher education telethon, the "Lou Rawls Parade of Stars." Noted for aggressive maneuvers, Edley actively promoted increased giving by individuals, engineered UNCF's entry into the Combined Federal Campaign, and implemented state and municipal payroll deduction campaigns. His use of television to advertise not only made the needs of black colleges highly visible, but also set new standards in public service advertising. The UNCF's award-winning college fund ads were some of the most eminent in public service advertising history. While he headed the organization, Edley used advertising "to soften people up," he told Wynter. To provide the public with an immediate opportunity to give money after viewing an ad, he created yearly telethons and special events featuring sports and entertainment celebrities.

Based in an office in New York City, Edley employed his successful tactics for nearly two decades. The fund

At a Glance . . .

Born Christopher Fairfield Edley on January 1, 1928, in Charleston, WV; son of Phillip and Helen (Penn) Edley; died May 5, 2003, in New Rochelle, NY; married Zaida Coles, September 2, 1950; children: Christopher, Jr., Judith Coles Edley. *Education:* Howard University, AB (magna cum laude), 1949; Harvard Law School, LLB, 1953; Swarthmore College, LLD, 1976. *Military service:* U.S. Army, 1946-47 and 1950-51; became sergeant.

Career: Lewis, Tanner, Moore (law firm), Philadelphia, law clerk, 1953-54; Philadelphia, PA, assistant district attorney, 1954-56; Moore, Lightfoot & Edley (law firm), partner, 1956-60 and 1960-61; U.S. Commission on Civil Rights, chief administrator, justice division, 1960; Federal Housing & Home Finance Region 3 (later HUD), regional counsel, 1961-63; Ford Foundation, government and law program officer, 1963-73; United Negro College Fund, Inc., president and chief executive officer, 1973-91, president emeritus, 1991-2003.

Selected memberships: Allstate Insurance Co., board of directors, 1993-97; Student Loan Corp, board of directors, 1993-98; American Airlines, board of directors, 1977-98; American Bar Association; New York Bar Assocation; Harvard Law School, trustee, 1972-78; National Partnership to Prevent Drug and Alcohol Abuse, trustee; NAACP.

Selected awards: Philadelphia Commission on Human Relations, Distinguished Service Award, 1966; Humanitarian Father of the Year Award, 1974; Ohio State University, Outstanding Achievement Award, 1977; Howard University, Distinguished Alumni Award, 1979; New York Urban League, Whitney M. Young Jr. Memorial Award, 1987; Martin Luther King Center, Salute to Greatness Award, 1991; OIC Humanitarian Award, 1992; Congressional Black Caucus George W. Collins Award, 1991; also recipient of numerous honorary doctoral degrees.

received more than $700 million during his tenure to support 41 private black colleges and universities. When Edley began office in 1973, the UNCF received annual donations of about $9.5 million. By the end of his time in office in 1990, the annual average had risen to $48.6 million. Enrollment in historically black colleges rose to 48,233 students in the late 1980s, a 13-percent increase over mid-decade figures. Colleagues credited the financial triumph of the UNCF to Edley's business savvy. "Mr. Edley has made tremendous strides," Ponder informed Scott. "His ability to raise funds is a significant feat when you consider that during his tenure, the country was in and out of recession, large corporations were merging and there were fewer dollars available." Cathy Mitchell, handler of the Advertising Council Fund's campaign, told Wynter, "I think that Chris is quite a leader. He's directly involved with the advertising and he knows his organization. He knows his market and what he wants to convey."

"If I have succeeded in doing something wonderful, it is because of the leadership, the volunteers and the staff who have supported me," Edley told Scott. "We have implemented all of the modern techniques of business to help our favorite cause." During his last year as head of the UNCF, Edley initiated "Campaign 2000: An Investment in America's Future." Under his direction, the UNCF obtained a $50 million challenge grant—the largest single donation to a black charity to date—from former ambassador to Britain and founder of *TV Guide* magazine, Walter H. Annenberg. "You can't reduce tension and run the fund," Edley divulged to Don Wycliff of the *New York Times* in the year of his retirement. Edley, who had a heart bypass operation seven years earlier, was motivated to leave his position upon the advice of his doctors to reduce stress.

"Dad's whole career has been public service in one form or another," Edley, Jr., revealed in *Ebony* about his distinguished father, "so the uplifting memories are kitchen-table discussions about helping people, about civil rights, about economic opportunity, about housing and the Emancipation Proclamation, about loaning money to poor clients and, later, about planting and nurturing the seeds that became the public-interest-law movement across the nation." "The gift of giving will be the lasting legacy of Christopher F. Edley," assessed Scott, describing one of America's most illustrious public servants. "He will always be remembered for his ability to inspire others to give." Edley passed away on May 5, 2003, after experiencing a heart attack at his home in New Rochelle, New York.

Sources

Periodicals

Black Enterprise, December 1990.
Black Issues in Higher Education, June 5, 2003, p. 12.
Ebony, June 1988; August 1988.
Jet, August 20, 1990; May 26, 2003, p. 27.
New York Times, August 2, 1990.

Non-Profit Times, November 1990, p. 10.
Wall Street Journal, August 1, 1990.

—Marjorie Burgess and Tom Pendergast

Christopher F. Edley, Jr.

1953—

Law school dean

Christopher F. Edley Jr., a longtime Harvard law professor and public-policy expert on affirmative action, became dean of the renowned Boalt Hall School of Law at the University of California at Berkeley in 2004. His appointment made him the first African American to head a major U.S. law school. "I chose him because he is absolutely outstanding," a *Black Issues in Higher Education* article quoted the UC-Berkeley chancellor, Robert Berdahl, as saying. "He is a leader in issues related to social justice and has written some magnificent books on issues related to affirmative action and is concerned about civil rights and immigration, all of the issues that are important in California and nationally."

Edley was born in 1953 in Boston, Massachusetts, the same year his father and namesake graduated from Harvard Law School. The senior Edley would go on to an illustrious career, serving as a consultant for the U.S. Civil Rights Commission in the early 1960s and taking over the leadership of the United Negro College Fund in 1973. Edley's father did much to publicize the memorable UNCF slogan, "A mind is a terrible thing to waste," and brought in an estimated $700 million for the program, which provides scholarship funds to African American students, before he retired in 1990.

Edley spent part of his childhood in Philadelphia, and went on to Pennsylvania's Swarthmore College, where he studied math and economics. After graduating in 1973, he followed in his father's footsteps and gained a place at Harvard Law School, but took a break in 1976 to work for the Democratic Party presidential candidate Jimmy Carter, working in the campaign's situation room. He returned to Harvard and graduated in 1978 with a dual degree—a J.D. from the Law School and a master's degree in public policy from the John F. Kennedy School of Government at Harvard. Attaining his professional degree 25 years after his father had done so gave Edley a historic "first" at Harvard: he was the first second-generation African-American graduate of the prestigious law school.

Edley went to work for the Carter administration, serving as assistant director on the White House domestic policy staff for two years, and then moving on to a stint as special assistant to the U.S. Secretary of Housing, Education, and Welfare. Three subsequent Republican presidential administrations hampered his future political prospects, however, and so Edley returned to Harvard Law School once again, in 1981, this time to teach. He became only the fourth African American in the law school's history to receive tenure. Over the next several years, he would take time off from his teaching duties to commit himself to other projects: he became national issues director for another Democratic hopeful, Michael Dukakis, in 1987, and served on the transition team when Bill Clinton was elected to the White House in 1992. Between 1993 and 1995, he worked in the U.S. Office of Management and Budget as associate director of economics and government.

Searching for a way to solve the divisive battles over affirmative action in the United States, President Clinton established the White House Review of Affirmative

At a Glance . . .

Born on January 13, 1953, in Boston, MA; son of Christopher Sr. (an attorney) and Zaida Coles Edley; married Tana Pesso, September 23, 1983 (divorced); married Maria Echaveste; children: (first marriage) Christopher Edley III; (second marriage) Zara and Elias;. *Education:* Swarthmore College, BA, 1973; Harvard University Law School, JD, 1978; Harvard University, John F. Kennedy School of Government, MPP, 1978. *Politics:* Democrat.

Career: White House Domestic Policy Staff, Washington, DC, assistant director, 1978-80; special assistant to U.S. Secretary of Housing, Education, and Welfare, 1980; Harvard Law School, Cambridge, MA, professor, 1981-2004; *Washington Post*, Washington, part-time editorial page staff, 1982-84; Dukakis for President, national issues director, 1987-88; U.S. Office of Management and Budget, Washington, DC, associate director of economics and government, 1993-95; special counsel to President Bill Clinton, 1995; University of California at Berkeley, Berkeley, CA, Boalt Hall School of Law, dean, 2004–. Also board of managers, Swarthmore College, since 1980; founding trustee, Working Assets Money fund, 1982-84; member on Commission on Policy for Racial Justice, 1984–; consultant, Joint Center for Political Studies, 1988-; and U.S. Civil Rights Commission member since 1999.

Memberships: American Bar Association; National Bar Association; Council of Foreign Relations.

Addresses: *Office*–Dean's Office, University of California-Berkeley, School of Law, 215 Boalt Hall, Berkeley, CA 94720-7200.

Action commission, and named Edley its director in 1995. In this role Edley was charged with trying to shape White House policy on the matter and provide some new federal guidelines. There were some in the Clinton White House who believed that such programs might be retooled as class-based, not race-based, but Edley argued in favor of maintaining rules based on race, and that policy continued. The reviews and suggestions were collated in Clinton's official "Mend It, Don't End It" policy.

His experiences in Washington convinced Edley that a more substantial effort was needed in academia, and back in Cambridge, Massachusetts, in 1996 he co-founded the Civil Rights Project (CRP) at Harvard University. The CRP conducts and publishes research on civil rights issues, and works to shape public policy for a truly multicultural future in America. Edley's intense involvement led him to write *Not All Black and White: Affirmative Action, Race and American Values* in 1996. *Civil Rights Journal* writer Alicia Bond asked him his personal predictions on the future of race relations in America. "It depends on my mood," he replied. "Some days I'm very optimistic and other days I feel as though there are substantial majorities that are indifferent to the moral shortcomings of the nation."

Edley's high profile brought him another presidential appointment in 1999, this one to the U.S. Civil Rights Commission. Still active in Democratic politics, he served as a senior adviser for the 2000 presidential campaign of Democratic Party nominee Al Gore, and continued a longtime side career penning newspaper editorial pieces. In one that appeared in the Milwaukee *Journal Sentinel* in 2002, he voiced concerns about potential civil-rights violations in new detention policies in the post-9/11 world. He suggested that an Office of Rights and Liberties should be established within the Department of Homeland Security to prevent abuses of authority. "Over time, the tension between security and liberty will create corrosive doubts about the war's home-front legitimacy," Edley wrote. "This is because, even more than in conventional crime-fighting, we cynically see a political agenda behind every move, and many moves are altogether secret."

Edley's distinguished teaching career and leadership in public-policy matters brought him to the attention of the University of California at Berkeley, which undertook a lengthy search for a new dean of its Boalt Hall School of Law. Edley beat out 200 other candidates and his appointment was announced in December of 2003. The campus, long known for its political activism and liberal-minded spirit, would also become home to a new Civil Rights Project there, which Edley planned to establish in tandem with the Harvard Center. In fact, he told *New York Times* journalist Dean E. Murphy, he had been leery about leaving Harvard in the first place. "I tried to withdraw from this dean search, citing my deep commitment to the Harvard Civil Rights Project," he said. "And the committee's response was that I should come to Berkeley and build a West Coast Civil Rights Project, because California is ground zero on issues of race and ethnicity. That was an extremely persuasive argument."

Edley's wife, Maria Echaveste, a Clinton administration alumnus herself, joined the Berkeley faculty as well. He has two children with her as well as a son, Christopher Edley III, from a previous marriage. His own father and namesake passed away in 2003. Reflecting upon the legacy he inherited, he once commented in the *Civil Rights Journal* about his own generation's civil-rights work: "We grew up watching the successes of the older generation in knocking down barriers and advancing justice, but mistakenly concluded that progress is inevitable. We went about our own personal agendas and just assumed that justice would move forward as inevitably as the years rolled by. That was wrong—every generation has to decide how to pick up the burden and carry it forward."

Selected writings

Administrative Law: Rethinking Judicial Control of Bureaucracy, Yale University Press, 1990.
Not All Black and White: Affirmative Action, Race and American Values, Hill & Wang, 1996.

Sources

Periodicals

Black Issues in Higher Education, January 1, 2004, p. 18; July 29, 2004, p. 22.
Buffalo News, August 24, 1996, p. B3.
Civil Rights Journal, Fall 1999, p. 5.
Milwaukee Sentinel, July 21, 2002, p. 3.
New Republic, March 22, 1999, p. 12.
New York Times, December 11, 2003, p. A39.
San Francisco Chronicle, October 23, 1996, p. A23; December 11, 2003, p. A21.
Washington Monthly, December 1996, p. 48.

On-line

"Christopher Edley, Jr.," *Boalt Hall,* www.law.berkeley.edu/faculty/profiles/facultyProfile.php?facID=4954 (November 4, 2004).

—Carol Brennan

Gladys Edmunds

1951(?)—

Entrepreneur

It was the early 1960s and society had her pegged as another sad statistic: a poor African-American teenager from the inner city, a high school dropout, and, at the age of 16, an unwed mother. But Gladys Edmunds didn't believe in statistics. "I was shocked the day I heard someone say 'Inner-city teen-age mothers have become an epidemic.' I didn't know that, I was busy managing myself. I wasn't trying to live what others had decided for me," she told the *Boomer Career* Web site. Determined to provide for her child, Edmunds started up a travel business from a card table in her tiny Pittsburgh apartment. Thirty years later the card table has given way to a multi-million dollar business. Looking back on her life, Edmunds realized that anyone could achieve what she had. "Everyone is an entrepreneur," she told *Boomer Career*. "Your life is your enterprise and your assets and net profit are your well-being; everyone has something to manage and grow." So Edmunds wrote a book on entrepreneurship, founded a motivational speaking firm, and began penning a column for *USAToday*. Soon the press was clamoring for interviews. Everyone wanted to know how a teenaged mother from the wrong side of the tracks made her way up the corporate ladder of success. Edmunds graciously complied, but modestly rejected the accolades. "Am I successful? Success means something different for everyone. If longevity equates success, then maybe. But the way I see it, everyday above ground is a success," she told the *E-Magnify* Web site. "You just do what you have to do, and that's what I've done all my life."

Founded First Business at Age 12

Born Gladys Baynes in the early 1950s, Edmunds was the first of nine children of Peter and Jeanne Baynes. While her mother raised the children, pinching pennies and saving spare change to be able to afford the down payment on a suburban home, her father often worked two jobs as a laborer to provide for the family. Peter Baynes was used to the task. He had left school as a teenager to help raise his 12 brothers and sisters after his father died. His mother had dropped out of school when she got pregnant. Edmunds recalled to *Boomer Career* that her parents often reminded her of the sacrifices they had made and hoped that she would become the first in the family to go to college. However the young Edmunds had other things to think about—mainly money.

"I equated working and making money, from way back," Edmunds told *USAToday*. After a brief stint selling candy at a neighbor's store when she was barely six, Edmunds took to fantasizing about having her own store. Soon her fantasies shifted to a pair of Buster Brown shoes. She had seen them in television commercials and had to have them. Begging her mother did no good, as the family was struggling as it was without worrying about over-priced black and white lace-up oxfords. So Edmunds did what came natural to her—she started a business. Just 12 years old at the time, Edmunds disguised her voice and cold-called several office buildings to sell them her cleaning services. She

At a Glance...

Born in 1951(?) in Pittsburgh, PA; married, Arthur Edmunds; children: Sharon Jackson.

Career: Edmunds Travel Consultants, Pittsburgh, PA, owner, 1963–; Gladys Edmunds Programs, Pittsburgh, PA, owner, 2000–.

Selected memberships: Pennsylvania Public Television, commissioner; Port Authority Transit of Allegheny County, board member; I Have a Dream Foundation, founding member; White House Conference on Small Business, Pennsylvania delegate; White House Conference on Travel and Tourism, Pennsylvania delegate.

Selected awards: Alpha Kappa Alpha Sorority, Outstanding Businesswoman, 1988; Pennsylvania Department of Commerce, One of the Top 25 Women-owned Businesses, 1992; Avon, Women of Enterprise Award, 1993; Carlow University, Woman of Spirit Award, 1994; State of Pennsylvania, Pennsylvania Honor Roll of Distinguished Women.

Addresses: *Office*—PO Box 144, Monroeville, PA, 15146.

---

told *USAToday* that within hours, "I had tons of [jobs]." She cajoled family and friends into helping her out and shared the profits with them. When school started two weeks later, Edmunds showed up for the first day of class with a brand new pair of Buster Browns on her feet.

Edmunds future looked bright until, at the age of 15, she wound up pregnant. "My father said I had ruined my life," she recalled to *Boomer Career*. Though her parents insisted that she marry her boyfriend, Edmunds refused. Despite the social stigma attached to being an unwed teenaged mother, Edmunds wanted to take on the challenge of motherhood by herself. Doing that would require money and Edmunds wasted no time getting to work. "I never thought in terms of labels, whether I could or could not do something," she told *E-Magnify*. "I just did it, and I didn't have any great vision. I just needed to make some money [for me and my baby]—legally." She sold fire extinguishers and Bibles door-to-door. She made home-cooked meals for taxi drivers. She ironed clothes. After her daughter, Sharon, was born, Edmunds moved into her own apartment and began to think of other ways to make money. A bus trip to a horse track in West Virginia provided the answer.

Launched Travel Business from Card Table

Edmunds paid five dollars for the bus ticket, then looked around and counted 40 seats on the bus. When she learned that she could rent the entire bus herself for $49, she recalled to *USAToday*, "My antenna went way up." Within days she set up shop on a card table in her living room. Again disguising her voice to seem older, she chartered the bus then hit the phones to sell the seats. She sold out in two days. The following week, she chartered two buses. She quickly proved herself an expert at customer service, arranging special charters and different destinations for clients. The business began to grow and Edmunds hired other single mothers on commission.

Two years after chartering her first bus, Edmunds moved into new territory. "Some women approached me and said that instead of taking a bus, they wanted to fly to New York," Edmunds told *Good Housekeeping*. "I came from a working-class family and had never been on a plane before. What did I know about airlines? But I made it happen, and business really exploded after that." Over the next several years Edmunds began to take on several corporate clients and decided it was time to get a real office. With a $70,000 bank loan Edmunds moved into a commercial space. She then almost lost the business.

The economy was souring and vacation sales were down. Edmunds watched helplessly as her loan interest rates soared and capital dwindled. By cutting staff and briefly taking on a partner, Edmunds just barely survived the recession. In 1985 she re-launched the business as Edmunds Travel Consultants. (She had married retired Pittsburgh Union League CEO Arthur Edmunds in 1982.) Her brush with financial ruin provided her with what she has called one of the most important lessons of her career—not letting fear take control. "There are things that occur in the overall scheme of things that are totally and completely out of your control," she told *USAToday*.

Over the next decade Edmunds's business grew until, in 1999, she had revenues of $6 million a year and a staff of eight. Along the way she became one of the most-respected business leaders in the state of Pennsylvania. The governor twice named her to White House delegations on travel and small business. She won awards with titles like "Woman of Spirit," "Honor Roll of Distinguished Women," and "Outstanding Businesswoman." In 1993 she won the prestigious "Woman of Enterprise" award from the Avon Corporation. She also made herself very visible in Pittsburgh charitable and civic circles. She became an active member of the local Rotary Club. She joined the boards of a hospital and the Port Authority. She donated time and money to several charities. Impressed with her business savvy, a public television executive nominated Edmunds to be a commissioner of the Pennsylvania

Public Television Network. He told *USAToday*, "She gets right to the heart of issues."

Developed Holistic Business Philosophy

Edmunds has long demonstrated a practical modesty when describing her rags-to-riches story. "Society said I couldn't succeed because I was a young black female with a baby and no high school diploma," she told *Good Housekeeping*. "Those were handicaps, but I refused to let them cripple me. I didn't care what other people thought. I had a baby to feed—and I couldn't do that earning $1.25 an hour bagging groceries." As far as Edmunds was concerned every bit of her success is nothing more than a result of a mother's love for her child. "My whole life evolved because I wanted to be a darn good mother," she told *USAToday*. She succeeded—not only with her daughter, but also in business and life. As she reflected on this over the years, Edmunds began to develop a philosophy based on holism in work, family, and home.

"What I had to learn to do in my life is understand that one hat blends into another instead of being fragmented," she told *Boomer Career*. "I couldn't compartmentalize. The whole reason for me being in business was because I was a mother. I talk whole-ism. It starts with that in order to bring balance to your world and success to your business." She has augmented that balance by practicing yoga and meditation but, above all, by listening to herself. "People today accept being dictated to; they turn on the television to find out who they are and what they should think," she told *Boomer Career*. "The same thing you need to be an effective business person, is what you need to do to simply be an effective person, and that is manage yourself. Do an inventory, see what you have and what you need, and then create a system for yourself. And don't listen to anyone's voice but your own."

Edmunds compiled her philosophy in the book *There's No Business Like Your Own Business: Six Practical and Holistic Steps to Entrepreneurial Success*, published by Viking/Penguin in 2000. It met popular success and put Edmunds in the national spotlight. She appeared on *Oprah!, Good Morning America,* and *CNN*. She was profiled in *Money Magazine, Entrepreneur, Ebony,* and *Good Housekeeping*. *USAToday* hired her to write a weekly column, "Entrepreneurial Tightrope," which appeared every Wednesday. She also launched Gladys Edmunds Programs and began a very successful second career as a public speaker, appearing at conferences, conventions, civic, and corporate events. With sponsor Mellon Bank she developed a series of Holistic Business Conferences that taught business owners that financial success and personal health and well-being are integral components of one whole. "When we apply holistic thinking to how we do business, a magic happens, everything works well, and everyone wins because you rise above the thinking that everything is about the 'bottom line,'" she told the *New Pittsburgh Courier*. "This new elevated thinking transcends race, age, and gender."

Edmunds told *E-Magnify* that she hoped to write more books in the coming decades. There was little doubt she would accomplish that goal. "If you have big dreams, then do them, and get on with the real important things in life. Don't listen to labels and external expectations, just listen to yourself."

Selected writings

There's No Business Like Your Own Business: Six Practical and Holistic Steps to Entrepreneurial Success, Viking Penguin, 2000.

Sources

Periodicals

Good Housekeeping, September 1, 2002.
New Pittsburgh Courier, June 20, 2001.
USAToday, May 24, 2000.

On-line

"Buster Browns Stoke the Entrepreneurial Fire in Gladys Edmunds," *E-Magnify,* www.e-magnify.com/gladys_edmunds.asp (September 28, 2004).
"From Zero to Millions: She Did It and Says You Can, Too," *Boomer Career,* www.boomercareer.com/public/169.cfm?sd=41 (September 28, 2004).
Gladys Edmunds, www.gladysedmunds.com (September 28, 2004).
"Success for Women a Matter of Balance, Author Says," *Pittsburgh Post-Gazette,* www.post-gazette.com/yourbiz/20010618edmunds0618bnp2.asp (September 28, 2004).
"Travel Career Began with Her Journey on a Bus," *Pittsburgh Post-Gazette,* www.post-gazette.com/blackhistorymonth/19980205kids.asp (September 28, 2004).

—Candace LaBalle

Sarah Webster Fabio

1928-1979

Poet

Well ahead of the connections that grew between music and poetry during the hip-hop era, several generations of African-American poets drew on musical influences in their works. The writers associated with the politically oriented Black Arts Movement in the 1960s and 1970s were especially active in this regard, joining spoken words with blues and jazz in an attempt to create a distinctively African-American form of poetic expression. Sarah Webster Fabio, active later in her life in the movement's San Francisco Bay Area epicenter, gained attention during that era. But she had formed her own style well in advance of these developments, doggedly pursuing chances to express herself while she dealt with the responsibilities of marriage and family.

Fabio was born Sarah Webster in Nashville, Tennessee, on January 20, 1928. She was one of six children. Her father, Thomas Jefferson Webster, took one of the most important paths that led African Americans out of poverty: he worked as a Pullman porter for the Southern Illinois Railroad. Between that job and a real estate business he operated on the side, the family had enough money to send their academically talented daughter to Atlanta's Spelman College. She had graduated from high school in 1943, when she was only 15.

Finished College by Age 18

At Spelman, Sarah Webster majored in English and history. She moved back to Nashville in the summer of 1945, however, possibly because she had met her future husband Cyril Fabio II, a dental student at Nashville's Meharry Medical College. She enrolled at Nashville's Fisk University and graduated in 1946, after just three years of college. In June of 1946, soon after her graduation, she and Cyril Fabio were married.

Cyril Fabio put his dentistry skills to work in the United States military, and he was soon stationed in Florida. The Fabio family grew quickly: one son, Cyril Leslie Fabio III, was born on January 30, 1947, and another son, Thomas Albert Fabio, was born in January of 1948. By that time the family had been able to move back to Nashville, but they shuttled between Tennessee and Florida for the next several years. When she could, Sarah Webster Fabio took classes at Nashville's Tennessee Agricultural and Industrial College (now Tennessee State University). A daughter, Cheryl Elisa Louse Fabio, was born in 1949, and the 21-year-old Fabio found herself juggling classwork, the needs of three children under five, and the demands of being the spouse of a military medical officer.

Higher education became an even more distant goal after the Fabios moved to West Germany, again as a result of Cyril's military career, in 1953. All through the family's travels, however, Sarah was writing poetry. Once she was back in the United States, she took graduate English classes at Wichita State University in Kansas. Two more children were born, daughter Renee Angela in 1955 and a third son, Ronald Eric, in 1956.

Taught at Community College

After Cyril Fabio left the military, the family moved to California and settled in Palo Alto, near San Francisco. After getting her five children into school and involved

At a Glance...

Born on January 20, 1928, in Nashville, TN; died November 7, 1979, in Pinole, CA; married Cyril L. Fabio II, 1946 (divorced 1972); children: Cheryl, Ronnie, Renee Angela, Leslie, Thomas. *Education:* Attended Spelman College, Atlanta, GA; Fisk University, Nashville, BA, 1946; San Francisco State College (now University), master's degree, 1965; pursued graduate studies at University of Wisconsin.

Career: Merritt College, Oakland, CA, faculty member, 1965-68; lectured and gave readings, University of California, Berkeley, and California College of Arts and Crafts, Oakland, 1968-71; Oberlin College, faculty member, 1972-74.

in activities outside the home, Sarah Webster Fabio was finally able to return to her own education. She enrolled at San Francisco State College (now University) in 1963, completing a master's degree two years later. From 1965 to 1968 she taught at Merritt College, a community college in downtown Oakland. She also served as an instructor at the East Bay Skills Center, teaching language skills to inner-city young people, and in 1966 she attended the First World Festival of Negro Art in Dakar, Senegal.

The flowering of Fabio's teaching career coincided with tremendous growth in African-American literary creativity in the late 1960s. The Black Arts Movement was a loosely connected group of creative figures with ties to political organizations, ranging from progressive to militant, that arose within the larger counterculture scene. Fabio's tenure at Merritt College has been credited with helping to introduce the ideas of the Black Arts Movement to Bay Area students. Her first book of poetry, *Saga of a Black Man*, was published in 1968.

Soon Fabio's poetry was being published in the most vigorous and widely read African-American literary journals of the day: *Black World*, the *Journal of Black Renaissance*, and *Negro Digest*. More prestigious teaching appointments came her way; she taught, lectured, and read her poetry often from 1968 to 1971 at the University of California at Berkeley and at Oakland's California College of Arts and Crafts. Her next two books, *A Mirror, A Soul* (1971) and *Black Talk: Shield and Sword* (1973) were issued by the nationally prominent Doubleday publishing company.

Poems Featured Musical Influences

Fabio's poems were collected in a host of anthologies of the early 1970s, including *The Black Aesthetic* (1971) and *Understanding the New Black Poetry* (1973). She also collected many of her own poems in a self-published seven-volume set entitled *Rainbow Signs*. The works in that collection included "Of Puddles, Worms, Slimy Things," which ran through its basic text twice: once in standard English ("Pity the poor worm who dares go it alone," read one line) and once in truncated, telegraphic words that suggested black speech ("Hv merci on d po wrm who dares go it alone"). Many of Fabio's poems dealt with music or were inspired by it. One of her best-known poems, "Tribute to Duke," paid homage to jazz composer and bandleader Duke Ellington.

Fabio taught at Oberlin College in Ohio from 1972 (the year she and Cyril Fabio divorced) to 1974. She recorded two albums in 1972 on the Folkways label, *Boss Soul* and *Soul Ain't, Soul Is*. After enrolling once again in graduate school at the University of Wisconsin in 1975 she began to exhibit symptoms of colon cancer. She moved to live with her daughter Cheryl in Pinole, California, and mother and daughter collaborated on the 1976 film *Rainbow Black*, which featured many of Fabio's poems in musical settings. Fabio died in Pinole on November 7, 1979.

Although she was not the first poet to record with musical accompaniment (Nikki Giovanni's *Truth Is On Its Way* gained wide success in 1971), it is perhaps for her musical efforts that Fabio is best remembered. In 1975 she recorded one volume of *Rainbow Black* with musical accompaniment as *Jujus: Alchemy of the Blues*, and in the late 1990s that recording became one of three counterculture jazz classics reissued by Britain's BGP record label. The recording included Fabio's tribute to jazz great John Coltrane, who himself died young in 1967. "Sweet songs, you said, were gonna come again, My Man/and didn't they?" Fabio wrote. "I mean they jetted in on a ray of radiance like the sun/to shine on those in our midst and/the still unborn in this hour of our great need."

Selected works

Poetry

Race Results, U.S.A., 1966 (pamphlet), 1967.
Saga of the Black Man, Turn Over Book Stores, 1968.
A Mirror, A Soul, Julian Richardson, 1969; Doubleday, 1971.
Black Talk: Shield, and Sword, Doubleday, 1973.
Jujus & Jubilees: Critical Essays in Rhyme about Poets, Musicians, Black Heroes, with Introductory Notes, 1973.
The Rainbow Sign, 7 vols., self-published, 1973.

Recordings

Boss Soul, Folkways, 1972.
Soul Ain't, Soul Is, Folkways, 1972.
Jujus: Alchemy of the Blues, BGP, 1998.

Other

Rainbow Black (film), privately distributed, 1976.

Sources

Books

Page, James A., compiler, *Selected Black American Authors: An Illustrated Bio-Bibliography,* G.K. Hall, 1977.

Smith, Jessie Carney, ed., *Notable Black American Women,* Book 1, Gale, 1992.

Periodicals

African American Review, Spring 1993, p. 125.

Guardian (London, England), November 21, 1997, p. 23.

On-line

"Sarah Webster Fabio," *Biography Resource Center,* www.galenet.com/servlet/BioRC (October 13, 2004).

—James M. Manheim

Elton Fax

1909-1993

Cartoonist, illustrator, writer

Award-winning cartoonist, illustrator, and writer Elton Fax enjoyed a 60-year career as one of America's most celebrated black artists. He taught in colleges and universities, gave one-off lectures around the world, and became famous as a "chalk-talk" artist, illustrating his stories with spontaneous sketches; he was especially successful in his talks for children. Fax illustrated over 30 books and many magazine articles; his weekly cartoon strip "Suzabelle" was a favorite in several black newspapers of the 1940s. He was also a successful writer, traveling widely to collect material for his books on black culture and life, and earning praise for his sensitive word and picture illustrations of the people and places he visited. Fax was the recipient of many awards, including a Rockefeller Foundation fellowship in 1976 and a Chancellor's Medal from Syracuse University in 1990.

Elton Clay Fax was born on October 9, 1909, in Baltimore, Maryland, the son of Mark Oakland, a clerk, and Willie Estelle Fax. He attended Claflin College and then Syracuse University's College of Fine Arts, graduating in 1931 with a BFA. He married Grace Elizabeth Turner on March 12, 1929, and they had three children. Fax started out as an art teacher and lecturer at Claflin College, in Orangeburg, South Carolina, before becoming an artist and teacher with the Depression-era Works Progress Administration (WPA) in New York City between 1936 and 1940. He turned freelance in 1940 and concentrated on producing illustrations for the pulp magazines and children's books, but he also gave public talks and quickly developed his trademark "chalk-talk" style. He also began a weekly cartoon based on black history that appeared in several black newspapers.

Between 1953 and 1956 Fax and his young family lived in Mexico, where he sketched scenes and tried to represent the conditions for working Mexicans. He later toured Bolivia, Argentina, Uruguay, and other parts of South America. He notes in his article "It's Been a Beautiful but Rugged Journey" that he was troubled by being asked by United States embassy officials whether he had witnessed any communist activity. Fax, whose sympathy for the poor and exploited people of the countries he visited is evident in his drawings of the time, was invited to attend the 1959 Rome conference of the newly-formed American Society of African Culture (AMSAC) and afterwards toured Africa, providing sketches that were published in his first book, *West African Vignettes*.

In the following decades Fax continued to travel around the world, giving his illustrated talks and recording the plight of people in third-world countries such as Nigeria, Northern Sudan, Ethiopia, and elsewhere. The subject matter for his talks was often the civil rights struggle going on in the United States, yet he managed to remain on good terms with the State Department observers who monitored his visits to politically sensitive countries such as the U.S.S.R. By the 1970s Fax was able to begin publishing books on black history in the United States. The most celebrated of these is *Garvey*, a biography of the black nationalist Marcus Garvey, best know for his declaration: "Africa for the Africans."

At a Glance...

Born Elton Clay Fax on October 9, 1909, in Baltimore, MD; married Grace Elizabeth Turner, March 12, 1929 (deceased); children: Betty Louise, Virginia Mae, Leon. *Education:* Syracuse University, BFA, painting, 1931. *Religion:* Protestant.

Career: Claflin College, Orangeburg, SC, teacher of art, art history, and history, 1935-36; Harlem Art Center, New York City, teacher of life drawing, 1936-41; City College (now of the City University of New York), New York City, teacher of watercolor painting and art history, 1957-58. Lecturer in high schools and community centers; held residencies at Purdue University, Princeton University, Fisk University, Western Michigan University, University of Hartford, and Texas Southern University. Specialist-grantee for U.S. Department of State in international cultural exchange program to South America and the Caribbean, 1955; delegate to Second International Congress of Society of African Culture in Rome, Italy, 1959; State Department lecturer in East Africa, 1963; guest writer of Soviet Writers Union, 1971, 1973; participant in Union of Bulgarian Writers Conference in Sofia, Bulgaria, 1977. Notable exhibitions include: National Gallery of Art and Corcoran Gallery of Art, Washington, DC; Kerlan Collection, University of Minnesota; and National Museum, Tashkent, Uzbekistan.

Awards: Women's Civic League Contest, gold medal, 1932; MacDowell Colony fellow, 1968; Coretta Scott King Award, American Library Association, for *Seventeen Black Artists*, 1972; Louis E. Seley NACAL gold medal for painting, 1972; Rockefeller Foundation fellow, 1976; Syracuse University, Chancellor's Medal, 1990.

Fax travelled widely in Asia, the Soviet Union, and Africa. He was a guest of the Soviet Writers' Union in 1971 and 1973 and continued to sketch scenes of working people around the world. As a guest of the Bulgarian Writers' Conference in 1982 he shared a platform with such luminaries as John Cheever, William Saroyan, and Gore Vidal. In the same period he continued to exhibit his work at important galleries, including the National Gallery of Art in Washington, D.C. His work sometimes makes for uncomfortable viewing, though it is always more interested in dignity than degradation. Fax never faltered in his efforts to expose injustice and exploitation. He justified his efforts in direct terms: "[E]xclude a small number of high-salaried and widely-publicized athletes and entertainers; exclude also the few Blacks occupying highly visible and lucrative places in government and private industry; and what is left is a great mass struggling to attain and thereby fully realize the Great American Dream."

Selected writings

Books

West Africa Vignettes (self-illustrated), American Society of African Culture, 1960, enlarged edition, 1963.
Contemporary Black Leaders, Dodd, 1970.
Seventeen Black Artists, Dodd, 1971.
Garvey: The Story of a Pioneer Black Nationalist, Dodd, 1972.
Through Black Eyes: Journeys of a Black Artist in East Africa and Russia (self-illustrated), Dodd, 1974.
Black Artists of the New Generation, Dodd, 1977.
Hashar (self-illustrated), Progress Publishers, 1980.
Elyuchin, Progress Publishers, 1983.
Soviet People as I Knew Them, Progress Publishers, 1988.

Illustrated Works

Tommy Two Wheels, Friendship Press, 1943.
Dr. George Washington Carver: Scientist, Messner, 1944.
Melindy's Medal, Messner, 1945.
Upton Arithmetic–Grade 4, American Book Co., 1945.
Sitting Bull: Champion of His People, Messner, 1946.
Story Parade Treasure Book, John C. Winston, 1946.
Skid, Houghton, 1948.
Buffalo Bill, Messner, 1948.
Melindy's Happy Summer, Messner, 1949.
Avalanche Patrol, Random House, 1951.
A Present from Rosita, Messner, 1952.
Rustlers on the High Range, Random House, 1952.
Famous Harbors of the World, Random House, 1953.
Almena's Dogs, Farrar, Strauss, 1954.
Cotton for Jim, Abingdon, 1954.
Genghis Khan and the Mongol Horde, Random House, 1954.
Trumpeter's Tale: The Story of Young Louis Armstrong, Morrow, 1955.
Love of This Land, Christian Education Press, 1956.
Terrapin's Pot of Sense, Holt, 1957.
Mateo of Mexico, Friendship Press, 1958.
Otwe, Coward, 1960.
The Na of Wa, Coward, 1960.
The Sky God Stories, Coward, 1960.
Tales from the Story Hat, Coward, 1960.
Taiwo and Her Twin, McGraw-Hill, 1964.

More Tales from the Story Hat, Coward, 1966.
Paul Cuffee: America's First Black Captain, Dodd, 1970.
The Seven Wishes of Joanna Peabody, Lothrop, 1972.
Take a Walk in Their Shoes, Cobblehill Books, 1989.

Periodicals

"It's Been a Beautiful but Rugged Journey," *Black American Literature Forum*, Autumn 1986, pp. 273-288.

Sources

Books

Driskell, David C., *Elton Fax: Drawings from Africa*, Fisk University Press, 1968.

Periodicals

New York Times Book Review, August 20, 1972, pp. 5, 18.

On-line

"Elton Fax Papers," *New York Public Library Digital Library Collections*, http://digilib.nypl.org/dynaweb/ead/scm/scmgfaxe/@Generic__Bookview (October 8, 2004).

"From 'Under Cork' to Overcoming: Black Images in the Comics," *Jim Crow Museum of Racist Memorabilia,* www.ferris.edu/news/jimcrow/links/comics/ (October 8, 2004).

—Chris Routledge

Allyson Felix

1985—

Track athlete

Felix, Allyson, photograph. © 2004 Landov LLC. All rights reserved. Reproduced by permission.

American sprinter Allyson Felix became one of the star athletes of the 2004 Summer Olympics in Athens, Greece. A record-breaking sprinter in the 200-meter event, Felix is also the first American track athlete to enter professional ranks straight out of high school. She has been hailed as the new savior for an American track-and-field team blighted by rumors of doping, and she has found the sudden celebrity a bit intense. "You could say it's been a little busy, but it's all been good fun," she told Richard Luscombe of the London *Observer*. "Everything that's happened has been a blessing, something new and different, although all the attention takes a little adjusting to."

Born on November 18, 1985, Felix grew up in Santa Clarita, California. Her father, Paul, is a Baptist minister who had once been an excellent sprinter as a teen, and from her schoolteacher mother, Marlean, she inherited her long legs. Felix followed her older brother, Wes, into the sport, though she did not try out for a track team until her ninth-grade year at Los Angeles Baptist High School in North Hills. That March of 2000 date proved an apocryphal one: she was the first to make a run when the coach, Jonathan Patton, lined up the possible sprinting stars during tryout week. She ran it so fast that he thought he had mismeasured the distance, but then the other runners who came after her clocked in normal times. She ran it again at his request, and with the same result.

Felix went on to an impressive high school career almost immediately. Just ten weeks after that tryout, she qualified for a state meet, and among the notoriously competitive California high-school ranks—rife with outstanding athletes—managed to finish seventh in the 200-meter event. She was also the only freshman to compete at the state meet that year. She was such an early phenomenon that the Los Angeles *Daily News* ran an article on her that summer, and she went on to set records and take titles over the next three of her high-school years. She became the first sophomore to win the 100-meter state title since Marion Jones had done it in 1990, and won two other state titles in short distances. Each year, she shaved four-tenths of a second off her 200-meter time, and broke Jones's high-school record in April of 2003 at the Mount San Antonio College Relays

At a Glance . . .

Born on November 18, 1985; daughter of Paul (a minister) and Marlean (a teacher) Felix. *Education:* University of Southern California. *Religion:* Baptist.

Career: Professional track athlete, sponsored by Adidas, 2003–.

Awards: Silver medal, 2004 Olympic Games, Athens, Greece, for 200-meter dash.

Addresses: *Home*—Santa Clarita, CA. *Office*—Allyson Felix, c/o USA Track & Field, One RCA Dome, Suite 140, Indianapolis, IN 46225.

---

in Walnut, California, running the 200-meter in 22.51 seconds.

Just weeks later, however, Felix turned in an even more impressive performance when she competed in the Banamex Grand Prix in Mexico City's Olympic Stadium. She broke her own record in the 200-meter, clocking a time of 22.11 seconds, which was a new world record in the under-20 category. The world record has stood since 1980, when Natalya Bochina of the Soviet Union ran it in 22.19 seconds. At the Banamex, Felix also matched Jones's best time in the 200-meter from the previous year, and beat Inger Miller as well, the 1999 world champion. Some of the speed was due in small part to the Mexico City's high altitude, and many of the runners achieved personal bests.

Felix emerged as the new American female runner to watch, just as Jones was taking some time off to have a baby. Both women were African Americans from California and had emerged as top sprinters while still in high school. But Felix—whom friends, acquaintances, and fellow competitors describe as both modest and a gracious winner—tried to avoid taking part in the "next" game. "I understand where people are coming from when they make the comparison, and I take that as a compliment," she told *Knight Ridder/Tribune News Service* reporter Mark Gomez about the comparisons with Jones. "But I also want to be something different. I'm my own person."

Some weeks after her dazzling Mexico City run, Felix learned that her 22.11 was a U.S. national record time, but would not be posted as the new world junior record in the 200-meter because she didn't take a drug test within an hour after finishing. She learned this only in July of 2003, when she traveled to Paris for an international meet. "It does bother me a little bit, but not too much," she said in an interview with *Daily News* journalist Matthew Kredell. "I still ran the same time. It's unfortunate that I've been drug-tested so many times and, for whatever reason, it didn't happen at this meet."

After graduating from Los Angeles Baptist High School in 2003, Felix decided to turn professional. She began attending the University of Southern California, but did not run for its team. Instead she signed with Adidas, a deal that made her ineligible to compete in college events. The six-figure, six-year endorsement contract, negotiated by her father, also included her USC tuition. She continued to train and work with coach Pat Connolly, a former Olympic runner who coached Evelyn Ashford to an Olympic gold medal in 1984. At five feet, six inches, Felix weighed 125 pounds, but could leg-press 700 pounds. She noted that being the daughter of a Baptist minister also gave her an inner boost. "Prayer helps me. I pray before big meets," she told *Sports Illustrated* writer Tim Layden. Laughing, she added, "I pray a little more before really hard workouts."

In June of 2004, while training for the Olympics, Felix found herself short of breath, and was diagnosed with exercise-induced asthma. She was allowed to use an inhaler, which is permitted under competition rules with a doctor's prescription. Athletes must undergo regular tests for banned substances, and there was a growing controversy over Marion Jones's involvement with a questionable nutritionist and nutritional-supplement company. The controversy put a cloud over Jones's 2000 Sydney Games achievement, when she won gold medals in the 100- and 200-meter events and a relay event, and two bronze as well. Her outstanding performance had made Jones the first woman in Olympic history to win five medals in a single Games, but now detractors were wondering if she had somehow eluded regulations to achieve it.

Because of the whiff of scandal, the 2004 Games were heralded as a chance for several new up-and-coming runners and jumpers to shine and, in the process, revive the American reputation in the sport. Jones qualified only for the long jump, and many predicted that Allyson Felix would win a medal in the 200-meter dash. True to form, she took the silver, coming in second after Veronica Campbell of Jamaica, but Felix did set a new junior world record of 22.18 seconds. "Her Olympics are Beijing" in 2008, Felix's sports agent, Renaldo Nehemiah, told *Houston Chronicle* reporter John P. Lopez. "She's just scratching the surface."

Both Felix and her brother are University of Southern California students. An outstanding runner as well, he was the U.S. junior men's champion in 200-meter in 2002 and a world junior champion that same year in the 400-meter. "Wes and I help each other; he's a huge inspiration," Felix told Luscombe in the *Observer* article. "And I've got a life away from the track as well, which is also important. I like hanging out with my friends and watching movies."

Sources

Periodicals

Daily News (Los Angeles, CA), August 17, 2000, p. AV2; April 20, 2002, p. S1; July 10, 2003, p. N1.
Houston Chronicle, August 26, 2004, p. 4.
Knight Ridder/Tribune News Service, June 19, 2003.
New York Times, May 28, 2003, p. D6; July 6, 2004, p. D1.
Observer (London, England), June 15, 2003, p. 7.
Sports Illustrated, June 9, 2003, p. 52.
Time, August 9, 2004, p. 78.

On-line

"Allyson Felix," *USA Track & Field,* http://www.usatf.org/athletes/bios/Felix_Allyson.asp (October 13, 2004).

—Carol Brennan

Raymond Fleming

1945—

Poet, scholar

"Much like Tennyson's Ulysses I would like to think that I am a part of all that I have met," Raymond Fleming told *Contemporary Authors Online.* The remark was a revealing one, for Fleming has been a border-crossing figure in many ways, comfortable in many realms but at the same time not quite at home in any of them. As an African-American scholar who has specialized in European literary subjects he is unusual; as a poet who has succeeded in the high-pressure world of academic literary studies he is perhaps even more of a solitary figure. Nevertheless, Fleming has gained wide recognition for his many and various endeavors.

Born in Cleveland, Ohio, on February 27, 1945, Fleming enjoyed the benefits of a top-notch education at the University of Notre Dame, from which he graduated with a bachelor's degree in 1967. He spent one summer before graduation working at the Department of State in Washington, D.C., at a time when African Americans were finding new opportunities in the world of diplomacy. But another, more unusual interest proved stronger: the language and literature of Italy. With support from a Ford Foundation fellowship and a Fulbright grant, the promising young student spent the 1967-68 academic year studying at the University of Florence in Italy.

After returning to the United States, Fleming spent a year as assistant director of an Upward Bound program at St. Mary's College and studied comparative literature—the investigation of literature and literary theory from an international perspective—at Harvard University on a Woodrow Wilson fellowship. That experience would lead to his admission to Harvard's doctoral program in comparative literature, but for the next three years after that, from 1969 to 1972, Fleming worked as an Italian instructor at Notre Dame. He recalled that experience in his poem "Young Black Man Teaching Italian to Middle-Class White Students," a work that typified many of his poems in its mixture of personal themes, a serious outlook on the American racial divide, and a certain wry humor. "May your lives not always be/sad polemics like your fathers' lives," Fleming addressed his students in verse. "Next year the intrepid will discover/that Dante, too, was a nigger."

Fleming's poems began to find publication in a wide variety of journals, and he won the Ingram-Merrill Poetry Award in 1971. A partial list of the publications in which his poetry appeared in the 1970s includes: *Midwest Quarterly, America, Texas Quarterly,* the *Black American Literary Forum, Kansas Quarterly, Black Opinion, Forum Italicum,* and *Roadwork.* Fleming taught literature at the University of California at San Diego from 1973 to 1980, and his reputation as a poet increased. He received his Ph.D. degree from Harvard in 1976. The only detour from this literary career came when Fleming, a sports enthusiast since childhood who described himself in his book *Diplomatic Relations* as "a frustrated jock," had a tryout with the San Diego Chargers professional football team in 1977.

Fleming's first book, *Ice and Honey,* was published in 1979. It revealed a writer who addressed specifically African-American themes and drew strongly on

> **At a Glance . . .**
>
> **B**orn on February 27, 1945, in Cleveland, OH; son of Ethel Dorsey Fleming and Theodore Robert Fleming; married Nancy Runge, 1969; children: John, Peter, Stephen. *Education:* University of Notre Dame, BA, 1967; University of Florence, Italy, 1967-68; Harvard University, Ph.D., 1976.
>
> **Career:** University of Notre Dame, Italian instructor, 1969-72; University of California at San Diego, assistant professor, 1973-80; Miami University, Oxford, OH, associate professor of Italian, 1980-87; Miami University, Oxford, OH, assistant graduate school dean, 1985-87; Pennsylvania State University, professor of Italian, 1987-95; Florida State University, distinguished professor of Italian, 1995–.
>
> **Selected memberships:** Dante Society of America; American Council of Learned Societies; American Conference on Romanticism, president, 1998-2000; International Association for the Study of Italian Language and Literature, member of executive board, 1998-2002.
>
> **Selected awards:** Ford Foundation fellowships, 1966, 1972; Fulbright grant, 1967; Woodrow Wilson fellowship, 1968; Ingram-Merrill Poetry Award, 1971; Alexander von Humboldt fellowship (Germany), 1978; National Endowment for the Humanities grant, 1989; Teaching Excellence Award, Florida State University, 1998-99; Florida Poetry Award, 2000; Djerassi Artist Residency, Woodside, CA, 2003.
>
> **Addresses:** *Office*—Department of Modern Languages, Florida State University, 362 Diffenbaugh Bldg., Tallahassee, FL 32306.

memories of his own childhood in Cleveland, yet also touched on evocations of the other places he had traveled and lived, from Italy, Germany (where Fleming spent the 1978-79 academic year on an Alexander von Humboldt fellowship), England, and Norway to California. "The Hough Ghetto of Cleveland" spoke of storefront churchgoers: "from a midsummer to midsummer they prayed/to the black God for a year without/a layoff, without rats, without cops...." Some of the poems in the book reflected Fleming's love of sports; they were short, fleeting images of African-American sports heroes. And in the poem "Aretha" he praised singer Aretha Franklin as "the moving/sister of my soul/plunging deep down, darkly/into melodious shadows of my heart...."

The follow-up to *Ice and Honey*, entitled *Diplomatic Relations*, was published in 1982 by Lotus Press, a Detroit publishing house long associated with African-American writers. It included the long serious poem "Diplomatic Relations with America," an examination of the ambiguous position of African-American soldiers who have given their lives for a country that has long denied them full citizenship. Fleming also turned to international themes and included several translations of works by the Italian poet Diego Valeri. In "Pragmatic Sanction" he offered a wry look at the poet's life: "The poet is/a cop-out artist/and a bit of a fool,/but sometimes he writes down/good excuses."

Quoted in *Contemporary Authors Online*, Fleming linked the academic and creative sides of his writing life. "My training as a comparatist has enabled me to be at home within the contexts of both European and Afro-American poetry, and my reference seeks to combine those traditions when possible and to point out the contradictory assumptions of these cultures with humor and compassion." Fleming was hired as associate professor of Italian by Miami University of Ohio in 1980, becoming assistant graduate school dean in 1985. With the help of a 1981 fellowship from Northwestern University's School of Criticism and Theory and a 1984 stint as a visiting professor of literary theory at the Centre Universitaire in the small European nation of Luxembourg in 1984, he began to delve more deeply into literary studies.

In 1987 Fleming published a full-length work of literary criticism comparing Romantic-era poets of three different nationalities: *Keats, Leopardi, and Hölderlin: The Poet as Priest of the Absolute*. He also wrote shorter articles on a variety of writers, mostly poets, from Dante and Boccaccio of the Medieval Era through John Milton, John Keats, Daniel Defoe, and writers of the modern era such as Thomas Mann and Rainer Maria Rilke. Fleming became a professor at Penn State University in 1987. He attended National Institute for the Humanities summer seminars from 1985 to 1989, and his academic reputation grew. However, Fleming told the *Journal of Blacks in Higher Education* that "prestige, as a matter of course, continues to be attached to scholarship that excludes the contributions, experiences, and perspectives of women and people of color."

Fleming left Penn State for the post of distinguished university professor at Florida State University in 1995. Fleming won Florida State's Teaching Excellence

Award for the 1998-99 school year and the Florida Poetry Award in 2000. His activities in the early 2000s included the delivery of the Britsch Lectures at Brigham Young University in 2002 and a stint as Djerassi Artist Residency in Woodside, California, in 2003. He was president of the American Conference on Romanticism from 1998 to 2000 and an executive board member of the International Association for the Study of Italian Language and Literature from 1999 to 2002.

Selected works

Ice and Honey (poetry), Dorrance, 1979.
Diplomatic Relations (poetry), Lotus, 1982.
Keats, Leopardi, and Hölderlin: The Poet as Priest of the Absolute (literary criticism), Garland, 1987.

Sources

Periodicals

Journal of Blacks in Higher Education, December 31, 1993, p. 40.
Richmond Times-Dispatch, April 11, 1987, p. A29.

On-line

"Ray Fleming," *Contemporary Authors Online,* the Gale Group, 2001. Reproduced in *Biography Resource Center,* The Gale Group, 2004, www.galenet.com/servlet/BioRC (October 13, 2004).
"Fleming, Raymond," *Florida State University,* www.fsu.edu/~modlang/divisions/italian/rfleming.html (September 30, 2004).

—James M. Manheim

Marie Foster

1917–2003

Voting rights activist

Foster, Marie, photograph. © Flip Schulke/Corbis.

The civil rights movement is known for its great leaders more than for its foot soldiers. The movement came to national attention through a series of dramatic events, but those events emerged out of pressures that had been building for years, thanks to the work of large numbers of generally unheralded individuals. Selma, Alabama's Marie Foster suffered white violence at one of the most shameful occurrences in the civil rights chronology: the Bloody Sunday attack on voting rights marchers by Alabama state troopers and local law enforcement officers at Selma's Edmund Pettus Bridge on March 7, 1965. Yet Foster had begun her personal struggle against the suppression of black voting rights several years before that, gaining support from just a few fellow activists at first. Some organizers, according to the New York Times, called her "the mother of the voting rights movement."

Difficult Early Years

Although she faced the same kinds of harassment and the same threats of violence as her better-known male colleagues, Marie Foster's life is touched on only briefly in histories of the civil rights era. She was born Marie Priscilla Martin on October 24, 1917, near Alberta, Alabama, in Wilcox County. Foster's early years were spent in the countryside, but her mother dreamed of an education for her children. When Foster's father refused to move to a town where the children could be enrolled in school, her mother responded by spiriting them away to Selma and doing just that.

Foster didn't pursue her education to the fullest extent at first. She dropped out of high school, got married, raised three children, and worked at low-level jobs for some years after her husband's death. Eventually she completed high school, graduating after her daughter Rose, and then went on to junior college and studied to become a dental hygienist. After she finished her studies, she was hired by her brother, Dr. Sullivan Jackson.

In the early 1960s, Foster became inspired by the spirit of resistance that was spreading among African Americans across the South. "I decided to become involved in the Civil Rights Movement because the race relations were so bad in Selma," she recalled in a statement quoted on the Web site of Selma's Voting Rights

At a Glance . . .

Born on October 24, 1917, in Wilcox County, near Alberta, AL; died on September 6, 2003, in Selma, AL; married (widowed); children: three. *Education:* Attended junior college and studied dental hygiene.

Career: Dr. Sullivan Jackson (her brother), Selma, AL, dental technician; political activist, 1960s-2003; Selma, African-American voter registration efforts, instructor of literacy and citizenship classes, 1963-65.

Memberships: Dallas County Voters League, founding member; Southern Christian Leadership Conference.

Museum. "I had a vision that we could do something about the bias conditions in Selma, the state, and someday the world." The movement, which took off in larger cities and on historically black college campuses, was just beginning to make an impact in Selma. Voter registration figures told the story: in 1961, out of about 15,000 eligible black voters in Selma and surrounding Dallas County, only 156 were registered. Only 14 new black voters had been added to the rolls since 1954.

Registration Efforts Frustrated for Eight Years

Foster herself attempted to register to vote on numerous occasions, but each time officials found a new reason to turn her registration down. Black applicants had to pass literacy tests and perform outlandishly difficult feats, such as knowing the number of words in the United States Constitution, and the final decision lay with an individual and invariably white registrar. "They were not registering teachers, doctors, or any professionals," Foster told the *Atlanta Journal and Constitution* in 1991. After eight years, Foster received the treasured postcard informing her that she was a registered voter, and she resolved to pass her knowledge on to others. Early in 1963, she began offering literacy and citizenship classes in Selma.

It was tough going at first. Even though she had advertised the classes in mailings sent to Selma's black churches, she had a grand total of one student enrolled in her first class, a 70-year-old man whom she taught to write his own name. But two people came to the next class, and four to the one after that. Soon, drawn by the chance to meet voting rights organizer Bernard "Little Gandhi" Lafayette, a crowd of 14 showed up. Before long, Foster's classes were incubators for activism beyond Selma; she sent graduates to a Southern Christian Leadership Conference (SCLC) training site near Savannah, Georgia. She found copies of old tests that had been used to frustrate blacks' voting ambitions, and she turned them into study guides.

Foster was one of the creators of the Dallas County Voters League, a group of black citizens who demanded improvements in the voter registration process. This group's central steering committee of eight members became known as the "Courageous Eight," a term that Foster herself may have coined. Others, however, sometimes referred to them as the "Crazy Eight," and indeed they seemed to be up against formidable odds. One member of the group was fired from his job and faced false embezzlement charges. Foster, employed by her brother, enjoyed some insulation from such pressures. But Selma's white power structure soon began to sit up and take notice of what was happening. Foster's life was threatened more than once by the Ku Klux Klan. In July of 1964, Dallas County Circuit Court Judge James Hare issued an order that prohibited blacks from meeting in groups of three or more to discuss civil rights. Foster and her cohorts, including Student Nonviolent Coordinating Committee (SNCC) organizer and future U.S. Representative John Lewis, were the direct target of the injunction, for their meetings over the past year had drawn as many as 350 people.

Stood Her Ground during Historic March

After demonstrations began and grew in Selma in 1963 and 1964, Foster became one of the key local contacts for the SCLC and SNCC. She worked on various fronts as she and the Dallas County Voters League pondered how to respond to Hare's order. Foster and another activist met with *Selma Times-Journal* publisher Roswell Falkenberry to try to persuade him to discontinue the paper's separate "colored" edition and instead integrate news of African Americans into its usual run. Finally, Foster and the rest of the Courageous Eight, in December of 1964, invited the Rev. Martin Luther King Jr. to come to Selma to support the cause of voting rights there—a direct violation of the court's injunction, and a decisive step that in the opinion of many historians led ultimately to the passage of the epochal Voting Rights Act of 1965.

King, who may have been thinking along the same lines himself, responded with a concerted effort to make Selma the next front in the civil rights battle. Foster dismissed any fear that local activists might lose control over what was happening now that Selma had been thrust into the national spotlight, telling author Stephen L. Longenecker that she "was just so glad to have 'em [the SCLC]." King's effort culminated on the March 7, 1965, Bloody Sunday march, planned to extend from Selma to Montgomery, 50 miles away. At the foot of the Edmund Pettus Bridge, Foster was clubbed, leaving her hobbled with swollen knees. "It was a trooper who hit me," she recalled in a United Press International interview quoted in the New York Times. "I lay on the pavement with my eyes closed. I didn't move. I stood my ground." Despite her injuries, Foster returned to the streets with other demonstrators on March 9. That march was also stopped by police, but without violence.

The forces of white recalcitrance won that skirmish against the power of King's nonviolent resistance, but they were fast losing the war. Public opinion became galvanized against the segregationists as Americans watched Southern police brutality unfold on their television screens, and on March 11, President Lyndon Johnson announced his support for what became the Voting Rights Act of 1965, an omnibus measure outlawing many of the practices that Foster had spent years fighting against. Fittingly, it was in Foster's living room that King watched Johnson's speech on television.

The twice-delayed march from Selma to Montgomery was finally allowed to begin on March 21, and Foster, still suffering from her injuries, became one of only two women to complete it. The vest she wore on the march, bearing autographs from prominent civil rights leaders, later became part of the displays of Selma's National Voting Rights Institute and Museum, which she helped to found. "Oooh, I would be so tired by the end of everyday," she told the Christian Science Monitor. "We stayed in tents. It rained every day, and there was lots of mud."

Remained Active in Selma

Foster remained active in the years after the Selma marches. She continued to work toward the goal of equal opportunity, confronting longtime Selma mayor Joe Smitherman on issues ranging from public housing, to the conduct of white bus drivers, to the removal of a park statue commemorating a Ku Klux Klan member. And she continued to work to register black voters, first as a deputy registrar. During one of several campaigns in which black candidates unsuccessfully attempted to dislodge Smitherman (he was finally defeated by black candidate James Perkins Jr. in 2000), Foster was temporarily removed from her post after unspecified registration irregularities occurred; she believed that the action was taken merely because she had been so successful in registering new voters. In the end, she was appointed to the Dallas County Board of Registrars—the same entity that had worked for so long to frustrate the civic aspirations of Foster and other African Americans. In 1984 Foster worked on the presidential campaign of Rev. Jesse Jackson.

Until the end, Foster taught children to read in a classroom near her home, and she volunteered to drive underprivileged children to Sunday school. She met President Bill Clinton at the Voting Rights Museum in the year 2000. On September 6, 2003, at the age of 85, she died in Selma after a short illness. "Even in her old age, she could still outwork the young activists of today," Mayor Perkins was quoted by the Associated Press. Selma attorney J. L Chestnut Jr. added, "It was lost on the public…that prior to Bloody Sunday, Mother Marie Foster—through her citizenship classes and her fiery stances at the courthouse—had actually added more black voters than all the marching and demonstrations together had produced."

Sources

Books

Branch, Taylor, *Pillar of Fire: America in the King Years, 1963-65*, Simon & Schuster, 1998.
Longenecker, Stephen, *Selma's Peacemaker: Ralph Smeltzer and Civil Rights Mediation*, Temple University Press, 1987.

Periodicals

Associated Press, September 10, 2003.
Atlanta Journal and Constitution, October 16, 1991, p. A3.
Christian Science Monitor, March 13, 1995, p. 1.
Demopolis Times, September 27, 2004.
Jet, September 29, 2003, p. 56.
New York Times, September 12, 2003, p. B11.
Selma Times-Journal, March 5, 2000.
Washington Informer, January 22, 1997, p. 19.
Washington Post, February 8, 1984, p. A2; September 13, 2003, p. B6.

On-line

"Selma civil rights icon dies at 85," *Ledger-Enquirer*, http://www.ledger-enquirer.com/mld/ledgerenquirer/2003/08/13/news/local/6737929.htm (September 10, 2003).

—James M. Manheim

Jamie Foxx

1967—

Comedian, actor, singer

In the ever-shifting, multimedia world of Hollywood entertainment, the art of juggling talents has always paid off. Comedian, actor, singer, and producer Jamie Foxx has helped to affirm this, scoring successes on the stage, the screen, on television, and in the recording studio. A dynamic and easily likable performer, Foxx has rapidly moved from obscurity to the helm of a highly rated television series for the WB network, and shows no signs of decreasing his activity. "As a comedian, as an actor, you've got to make things happen," Foxx told *People* magazine. "I want to have a lot of things in the air," he added.

Foxx, Jamie, photograph. © 2004 Landov LLC. All rights reserved. Reproduced by permission.

Prepared for the Stage

Jamie Foxx was born Eric Bishop on December 13, 1967, in Terrell, Texas, to stockbroker Shaheed Abdullah and Louise Annette Talley—now surnamed Dixon through remarriage—in the small town of Terrell, Texas. Foxx's parents quickly found themselves overwhelmed by the demands of child rearing, and at the age of seven months, he was adopted by his maternal grandparents, Mark and Esther Talley. Foxx rarely saw his biological parents throughout his childhood, so he felt no affect from their divorce when he was six years old. Fortunately, his new family, including two half sisters and a stepbrother, provided a loving, supportive environment, and his childhood was a trauma-free one.

At a very young age, Foxx showed evidence of his flair for performing and entertaining. At five years old, he started piano lessons, immersing himself both in the language of music and in the often-shocking experience of facing an audience—crucial skills for his future career. While performing in a talent competition at Terrell High School, his peers noticed Foxx's magnetic stage presence. "He was singing, and the women just moved to the front to be near him," ex-classmate Chris Barron recalled to *People*. Although the teenage Foxx was a standout in his local church choir who embarked on an academic pursuit of music at the U.S. International University in San Diego, California, it was comedy, not music, that gave Foxx his break.

Like many small-town celebrities in waiting, Foxx dropped out of college and moved to Los Angeles in 1990 to enter directly, working from the very bottom

At a Glance . . .

Born Eric Bishop on December 13, 1967, in Terrell, TX; son of Shaheed Abdullah and Louise Annette Dixon; adopted by grandparents Mark and Esther Talley. *Education:* Attended U.S. International University, San Diego, CA, 1986-88.

Career: Comedian, 1990–; actor, director, and producer, 1991–; musician, 1994–.

Awards: Black Bay Area Comedy Competition, 1991; Image Award, for *The Jamie Foxx Show,* 1998; Image Award, for *Ali,* 2002; Black Reel Award, for *Ali,* 2002.

Addresses: *Agent*—The Gersh Agency, 232 N. Canon Dr., Beverly Hills, CA 90210.

---

up. With no formal experience and no connections, the struggling Foxx soon ended up peddling shoes in a Thom McAn shoe store outlet, and sat in at local comedy clubs on amateur nights in hopes of performing himself. He quickly noticed a pattern of gender in the roster of comedians which he decided to use to his advantage. As he confessed to *Jet* magazine, "[t]hree girls would show up and 22 guys would show up. They had to put all the girls on who were on the list to break up the monotony." Foxx, still named Eric Bishop, began signing unisex monikers on audition lists in hopes of being taken for a woman. The ploy soon worked. On his twenty-first birthday, Foxx and his friends were attending a San Francisco nightclub, and the young comedian flooded the entry list with fabricated, ambiguous names. When the master of ceremonies called out, "Jamie Foxx...Is she here?," Foxx responded in a resonant, masculine tone, to everyone's surprise, and stepped to the microphone.

Made a Name for Himself

From this first comedy performance, which garnered a standing ovation from the audience, it was evident that Foxx could rely on talent, not gimmicks, to sustain a career in entertainment. Nonetheless, he retained the assumed name that had helped finagle his comedy debut, perhaps in part as an acknowledgement of a new life. "I loved my old name," he told *People*. "But Eric Bishop was Clark Kent. And Jamie Foxx is Superman." With a new name, a boosted level of confidence, and one auspicious stage outing, the newly dubbed Foxx stormed the Los Angeles comedy circuit, winning the Black Bay Area Comedy Competition in 1991, and quitting his job as a shoe clerk to perform up to seven nights per week. On stage, he began to develop a sassy, outrageous persona, as well as a repertoire of characters he would use later in his career, including "Wanda, the Ugly Woman." In addition, his impersonations of celebrities such as fellow comedian/actor Bill Cosby and prizefighter Mike Tyson were marked by a perfect balance of mimicry and exaggeration. Foxx had elevated his entertainment with rehearsed artistry and contagious energy. And yet while he had become a hero within the Southern California comedy scene, Foxx was quickly becoming a television "Superman."

Aspiring to expand beyond a local audience, Foxx auditioned alongside several hundred other comedians for a part in an ensemble cast of a new television comedy for the Fox television network entitled *In Living Color*. Foxx landed the role, and in 1991 joined the cast of the highly rated show that would last several seasons and help elevate the careers of future stars' Jim Carrey, Tommy Davidson, and the Wayans Brothers. The show followed a short sketch comedy format, with an exuberant, outrageous attitude perfect for Foxx's style of comedy. Adapting his material for television, Foxx was able to translate his stand-up characters into favorites of television comedy, and quickly developed a nation-wide fan base. Not only was *In Living Color* a kindling fire for Foxx's popularity, it also provided the growing funnyman an opportunity to hone his comic skills among his contemporaries. "Damon [Wayans] taught me the importance of having a little attitude," he remarked to *People* about one of his co-stars. "And Jim [Carrey] taught me goofiness," he added.

In Living Color proved to be a gateway of opportunity for Foxx, catapulting him into numerous engagements in both television and film. During the show's run, Foxx managed to portray a recurring character on the series *Roc*, also on the Fox network, in addition to making guest appearances on stand-up specials. In 1993, HBO invited him to create a one-man concert program, and the result was *Jamie Foxx: Straight from the Foxxhole*. The uncensored nature of cable television allowed him to return to the style of his earliest material, and the program fared well. Foxx even juggled his motion picture debut into his demanding television schedule, acting alongside veteran comedian Robin Williams in the family feature *Toys*.

By the time *In Living Color* ran its final season in 1994, Foxx's resume was impressive enough to establish himself securely in the comedy world. However, in the following year Foxx took a brief vacation from comedy and made an impressive return to his performing roots—music. Still under the Fox studios banner, he released a full- length album of 12 R&B tracks, all of which he wrote, sang, and produced. The record climbed to #12 on *Billboard* magazine's sales charts, and received warm reviews from music critics. Easily slipping back into the vocal training of his youth, Foxx had successfully given life to yet another branch of his career.

Continued Success in Film and Music

After a brief period of respite, Foxx plunged back into film and television with full force. In 1996, he played supporting roles in the films *The Truth About Cats and Dogs* and *The Great White Hype*, the latter gaining Foxx critical merit for his portrayal of a small-time boxing manager. But once again, it was television comedy that helped push his popularity. Moving from the Fox network to the WB (Warner Brothers) network, Foxx helped create and produce a program that was different from most of his work to date. With *The Jamie Foxx Show*, WB launched a family-oriented situation comedy, starring a decidedly adult comedian. The combination worked.

Prior to *The Jamie Foxx Show*, the comedian attracted backlash from critics who objected to Foxx's sometimes shocking comic arsenal, especially for his negative discussion of women. Taking this into consideration, Foxx decided to create a show "[l]ike *I Love Lucy* or *The Dick Van Dyke Show*," he explained to *Mediaweek* magazine. "They were clean and still funny. If you try to be on the edge you cut lots of people out," he continued. His efforts were received as planned, and the series became the WB network's highest-rated series, scoring heavily among younger audiences and women. The show, in which Foxx essays the semi-autobiographical portrait of a struggling actor eking out a living as a worker at a shady hotel, is the product of a diverse creative team, made up of men and women, blacks and whites, which strives for a fresh, universal appeal. "You don't have to be gimmicky, you don't have to fall back on stereotypes," Foxx told *Mediaweek*. "It's not a conveyor belt. We try to handcraft the show," he added. Alongside many programs that thrive on a barrage of sexual innuendos alone, *The Jamie Foxx Show* was a refreshing surprise and a marked sign of growth for its star. *The Jamie Foxx Show* aired for five seasons on the WB Network and won Foxx an Image Award in 1998. The reruns of the comedy show are played in syndication and remain popular with fans.

His work on *The Jamie Foxx Show* led to a variety of roles that proved Foxx was more than just a comedic actor. But acting continued to be the mainstay of his professional life. His part in *Any Given Sunday* in 1999 featured Foxx's true talent: versatility. In his role as Willie Beamen, a third-string quarterback, Foxx deftly switches from being uncertain to cocky, and back again. Foxx also wrote and performed two songs for the movie's soundtrack. Foxx had made a name for himself among producers as a serious actor and won the critics' attention in 2002 with his role in *Ali*. For his part as Muhammad Ali's trainer, the director Taylor Hackford told *Newsweek* that "Jamie was the best thing about that movie." Hackford directed Foxx in the 2004 movie *Ray*. Foxx played the title role of Ray Charles. In preparation for his role, Foxx spent hours with Charles before his death, learning his unique mannerisms and speech patterns. He used his talent as a comic to mimic Charles, but did so with such sympathy and understanding that his characterization of Charles stunned viewers. Foxx told *Ebony* that Charles' children saw him acting in some scenes and said, "Man, that's my daddy." Charles' long-time friend Quincy Jones told *Newsweek* that Foxx "nailed" his depiction of Charles. "It's interesting that Jamie started out as a comic, because that's not where his career is going," Hackford told *Newsweek*. "He's not going to be the next Eddie Murphy—he's going to be the next Denzel [Washington]."

Selected works

Films

Toys, 1992.
The Great White Hype, 1996.
The Truth About Cats and Dogs, 1996.
Booty Call, 1997.
The Players Club, 1998.
Any Given Sunday, 1999.
Held Up, 1999.
Bait, 2000.
Ali, 2001.
Date from Hell, 2001.
Shade, 2003.
Breakin' All the Rules, 2004.
Collateral, 2004.
Ray, 2004.

Television

In Living Color, 1991-94.
C-Bear and Jamal, 1996.
The Jamie Foxx Show, 1996-2001.
Redemption: The Stan Tookie Williams Story, 2004.

Sources

Periodicals

Ebony, November 1, 2004, p. 96.
Jet, March 24, 1997, pp. 32-35.
Mediaweek, October 21, 1996, pp. 9.
Newsweek, August 2, 2004.
People, January 13, 1997; November 29, 2004.

On-line

"Jamie Foxx," *The Gersh Agency*, www.gershcomedy.com/JamieFoxx.aspx (November 23, 2004).

—Shaun Frentner and Sara Pendergast

George H. Grace

1948—

Grand Basileus, Omega Psi Phi; corporate executive

Having learned hard work and teamwork as a young man, George H. Grace, Grand Basileus (or chief executive) of the Omega Psi Phi Fraternity, understands well what a brotherhood of African Americans can accomplish. "To succeed you need a team," Grace told *Contemporary Black Biography* (*CBB*), "with everyone committed to the same objectives." Likewise the men of Omega Psi Phi live and work by four shared principles: manhood, scholarship, perseverance, and uplift, and with an organization of 200,000 initiates these men do succeed. Grace counts many great African Americans among his membership, men like Michael Jordan, Bill Cosby, Count Basie, Carter G. Woodson, and many others. Known for their activism and their excellence, some members enjoy world recognition and are viewed with pride and admiration by the black community.

This black fraternity was founded in 1911, on the Washington, D.C., campus of Howard University, and today has 762 chapters located on college campuses throughout the United States, in Japan, Korea, Germany, the Virgin Islands, and the Bahamas. Local Omega Psi Phi chapters have donated thousands of dollars over the years to organizations like the NAACP, the Urban League, and the Negro College Fund, and members have rolled up their sleeves for Habitat for Humanity in an effort to provide decent housing to families in need. In addition, the organization gives year awards to members for scholarships. Grace and the brotherhood are a team working together to build a better life for minorities and to serve as a source of guidance for young African Americans.

Learned from Early Examples

George H. Grace was born on May 20, 1948, in Bartow, Florida, to Lillie Mae and DeeCee Grace. Grace was raised with four brothers and a cousin; they all learned life skills at an early age. Their father and grandfather taught them never to fear hard work. "They said I could achieve anything if I worked hard enough," Grace told *CBB*. "My father worked two jobs for 30 years without taking a day off until he broke his arm. He returned to work the following day." Grace learned many handy skills, such as electrical work and plumbing. "My first regular job was at a plant nursery and later I worked on a cattle ranch. I was only eight years old," he said.

Later, at Union Academy High School, his teachers reinforced these lessons and left a lasting impression on Grace. "I admired my junior high school principal, James Stephens," said Grace. "He ran a tight ship and had complete control of the school. He was like Jesus walking on the Red Sea. The hallways would part when he walked through them. Forrest McKinney and Jordan J. Corbett were coaches who instilled in me the importance of education and athletics. Corbett was a great motivator and taught you to never give up."

Grace entered Tuskegee University in 1967 with the idea of later becoming a commissioned officer in the military. Having entered school on a football scholarship, he also considered becoming a professional athlete. At Tuskegee his hard work paid off on the football field. As captain from 1967 to 1970, Tuskegee's team

At a Glance...

Born George H. Grace on May 20, 1948, in Bartow, FL; married Regina Mobley, 1991 (divorced); married Barbara Milton, 1992; children: Jerhonda, Gregory, Keenyn. *Education:* Tuskegee University, BS, 1971; University of Miami, MS, 1978. *Religion:* Baptist.

Career: General Motors, Pontiac, MI, production supervisor, 1972-73; BellSouth, Florida, regional manager, 1974–. Omega Psi Phi fraternity, worked in various district and state offices, 1978-98; Omega Psi Phi, Grand Keeper of Records and Seals, 1998; Omega Psi Phi, Grand Basileus, 2002–.

Selected memberships: NAACP; Urban League; Hialeah (Florida) Chamber of Commerce.

Selected awards: Ebony Magazine 100+ Most Influential Black Americans, 2004.

Address: *Office*—Omega Psi Phi Fraternity, 3951 Snapfinger Parkway, Decatur, GA 30035.

lost only six games in four years. Following his graduation Grace decided against both the military and sports, and in 1972 began work as a production supervisor for General Motors in Pontiac, Michigan.

Admired Omega Psi Phi Brotherhood

Grace joined the Omega Psi Phi fraternity in 1973 when he began graduate school at the University of Miami. He admired a neighbor and fraternity bother, Dr. Herbert Green, who seemed to take pride in helping in the community. After researching the work of fraternity brothers like Rev. Jesse Jackson, Benjamin Hooks of the NAACP, and Vernon Jordan of the Urban League, Grace wanted to get more involved; a few years later he took his first position as an officer at the local chapter of Omega Psi Phi. There he sat on every committee and moved readily from Chapter Basileus into district and state offices.

Grace became Grand Keeper of Records and Seals in 1998 and was then elected Grand Basileus of Omega Psi Phi in 2002. "I never sought to be an officer," he told *CBB*. "It was a course of events and I was in the right place at the right time." But he added: "I was asked because of my track record." Grace believes his ability to surround himself with accomplished supporters has been central to his success. "They wanted the same things that I wanted and the record showed that."

Offering a glimpse of life in an all male fraternity, Grace remarked: "It's hard work and it can be very political. It's that way because there are so many members and no set path for anyone to follow."

Focused on Empowerment and the Vote

As Grand Basileus, Grace has focused on changing the economic plight of minorities in America through better education, greater involvement in the political process, and early training in economics and money management. "We blame others for our own shortcomings," Grace explained to *CBB*. "We can change a lot of things ourselves; no one is going to do it for us."

With Grace's vision the fraternity adopted as its theme: *Economic Empowerment, Leading to Social and Political Change.* "I believe the way to economic empowerment is to look at how you spend your dollar, where you spend it, and what you are spending it for; we can make a difference if we use our buying power in a different way."

Teaching underprivileged kids about home ownership and credit is a key component of this initiative. Each year the fraternity holds a Youth Economic Summit in Washington, D.C., offering seminars on topics like first-time home purchasing and managing credit. "We need to talk about these things before it's too late, to make sure African-American youth never get credit problems," Grace says. "Home ownership is a key to success. Our members take this message to the community. We go into high schools, and it has paid off. The kids learn about buying habits and investing; then they take it home to the parents. Not everything is found in a book. It's about being exposed to people like our fraternity members." Through these seminars young African Americans are able to hear brothers like Earl Graves, Sr., president and CEO of Black Enterprise, share his expertise in creating wealth and controlling one's own destiny.

In this effort to empower minorities, which included a big push by black fraternities and sororities to register 1.5 million unregistered and uncommitted voters for the 2004 U.S. presidential election, Grace said: "We've got to get out and vote. To the victor goes the spoils; that's how this country works." Omega Psi Phi members are reaching out to urge citizens to vote and advise them on their rights as voters, including offering transportation to ensure that anyone who wants to get to the polls can.

Positioned for the Future

Grace has guided the organization through its purchase of the first black fraternity house at the University of

South Carolina and has led discussions with Hilton Hotels for the construction of the first black conference center and resort in the United States. Located in Zenia, Ohio, near Wilberforce and Central States College, two of the oldest historically black colleges in the country, this 59-acre parcel of landmark property is the former homestead of Colonel Charles Young, one of the nation's first black military officers.

In 2004 Grace was re-elected to his position as Grand Basileus and began the Undergraduate Economic Summit initiative with the Minority Business Office of the Department of Commerce, whose director is a fraternity member. The plan is to spread their lessons in money management into historically black college campuses.

In addition to his many duties at Omega Psi Phi, Grace is employed by BellSouth and has earned several executive promotions since starting there as a management trainee in 1974. As regional manager he is responsible for phone service for all city government municipalities in Palm Beach, Dade, Broward, and Monroe counties, and for several of their emergency 911 systems. Considering conventional images of employment in this sunny locale we could view his work there as a day at the beach. Grace disagrees. "It's not a vacation," he told *CBB*. "It's a lot of hard work."

Sources

Periodicals

Miami Times, September 2, 2003, p. 1.

On-line

Omega Psi Phi Fraternity, Incorporated, www.oppf.org (October 15, 2004).

Other

Additional information for this profile was obtained through an interview with George H. Grace on October 1, 2004.

—Sharon Melson Fletcher

Lorenz Graham

1902-1989

Author

In the 1930s, when Lorenz Graham began writing stories, black characters in children's literature were typically portrayed in negative stereotypes. Graham changed that. In a writing career that spanned more than 50 years, Graham introduced authentic black characters into literature for children and young adults. His collection of biblical tales, *How God Fix Jonah*, written in West-African English, has become a classic of the genre. His "Town" series of novels for young adults—among the first in this genre to confront racism when they were published beginning in the late 1950s—have been rediscovered by a new generation of students and educators. Graham's dual careers as a social worker and educator inspired his writings on racial issues, black adolescents, and parent-child relationships.

Grew Up amidst Racial Prejudice

Lorenz Bell Graham was born on January 27, 1902, in New Orleans, Louisiana, the son of David Andrew and Etta (Bell) Graham. David Graham was an African-Methodist-Episcopal (AME) minister who moved his family north soon after Lorenz was born. Lorenz's sister Shirley taught him to read and he entered the Doolittle School in Chicago as a six-year-old second-grader.

Soon the family moved to Nashville, Tennessee. It was Graham's first experience in a segregated city and school, and he was astonished to find that his new black friends were afraid of whites. Then a gang of white boys hit Graham in the head with a rock. When his father reported the attack, the police responded with their own racial epithets. Graham learned to be afraid.

The Grahams always assumed that their children would attend college. However their next move was to a town in which the black schools ended with the ninth grade. This, in addition to Graham's poor grades and his new-found fear of whites, convinced David Graham to move his family out of the South, first to Colorado Springs, Colorado, and then to Spokane, Washington. Graham's schoolwork improved significantly and he discovered the public library.

Sailed for Africa

As a student at the University of Washington in Seattle, Graham heard from an AME bishop about the need for teacher-missionaries in West Africa. In 1924, during his junior year at the University of California, Los Angeles, Graham left college to teach at a boys' missionary school in Monrovia, Liberia. In 1973 he told *Elementary English* that he went there "believing that I would be able to help the poor benighted Africans, that I could bring light to the dark land, and that I could open the door to a new life for the ignorant people. I was due for a rude awakening." His four years in Liberia were life-changing. He decided to "write books which would make Americans know that Africans were people."

After acquiring malaria in Liberia, Graham spent several months recuperating in France, where he quickly learned to speak the language. Graham found that in

At a Glance...

Born Lorenz Bell Graham on January 27, 1902, in New Orleans, LA; died September 11, 1989, in West Covina, CA; married Ruth Morris, 1929; children: Lorenz, Jr., Jean, Joyce, Ruth, Charles. *Education:* Attended the University of Washington, Seattle, the University of California, Los Angeles, City University, New York, and Columbia University; Virginia Union University, BA, 1936; Columbia University, MSW, 1954. *Religion:* Disciples of Christ. *Politics:* Democrat.

Career: Monrovia College, Liberia, teacher/missionary, 1924-28; Foreign Mission Board, National Baptist Convention, lecturer and fund-raiser, 1929-32; Richmond, VA, teacher, 1930-35; U. S. Civilian Conservation Corps, camp educational adviser, 1936-42; Housing Authority, Newport News, VA, manager of public housing, 1942-46; Long Island, NY, realtor and building contractor, 1946-49; writer, 1946-80; Queens (NY) Federation of Churches, social worker, 1950-57; Los Angeles County, probation officer, 1957-67; California State Polytechnic College (now University), Pomona, lecturer, 1970-78.

Selected Memberships: P.E.N. International; Authors League of America; National Association for the Advancement of Colored People; U.S./China Peoples Friendship Association; U.S.A./Soviet Friendship Society.

Selected awards: Association for Study of Negro Life and History Award, 1959; Los Angeles City Council Award, 1966; Southern California Council on Literature for Children and Young People, award for significant contribution to the field of literature for young people, 1968; California Association of Teachers of English, citation, 1973; honorary Doctor of Humane Letters, Virginia Union University, 1983.

France, unlike Liberia or the United States, his race was of no significance.

When his commitment in Liberia ended, Graham moved to New York City, where his sister Shirley was studying and writing for children. The black literary and artistic movement known as the Harlem Renaissance was at its height. Graham took classes at Columbia University and the City College of New York, lectured about his African experiences, and immersed himself in the literary life. He appeared in the play *Harlem*, which enjoyed a 20-week run on Broadway.

Graham had met fellow missionary and teacher Ruth Morris in Liberia. They married on August 20, 1929, and subsequently had five children. The family settled in Richmond, Virginia, where Graham finally completed his bachelor's degree in social studies at Virginia Union University.

Publishers Reject His African Stories

Numerous publishers rejected Graham's African-based stories, telling him that the American public was not interested in Africans who were portrayed as intelligent human beings. They thought that his African and black American characters were too much like white people.

It took Graham more than 15 years to find a publisher for *How God Fix Jonah*. This collection of 21 biblical stories was written in the style of African story-telling and in the English dialect spoken in Liberia. The stories were intended to be read aloud: "Long time past // Before you papa live // Before him papa live // Before him pa's papa live— // Long time past // Before them big tree live // before them big tree's papa live— // That time God live."

The title story opens with: "Jonah was a prophet. // God put Him hand on Jonah // But Jonah head be hard. // Jonah head be hard too much. // Lord God Almighty can fix the thing. // Hear how He fix Jonah." In the story of David and Goliath, Goliath asks David "Do you mommy know you out?" Shirley Graham's husband, noted historian W. E. B. Du Bois, wrote the introduction and the book became a favorite in black churches and Sunday schools around the country.

Some of these stories—including *David He No Fear*; a retelling of the Christmas story called *Every Man Heart Lay Down*; the story of Noah told in *God Wash the World and Start Again*; and the story of the prodigal son, *Hongry Catch the Foolish Boy*—were published as individual editions during the 1970s. A 2000 edition of *How God Fix Jonah* included two previously unpublished stories. It was an American Library Association Notable Children's Book for 2001 and *Booklist* named it one of the top ten religion books for youth. *How God Fix Jonah* had become a classic, aimed at adults and scholars, as well as young people.

Graham's first volume of African coming-of-age stories—*Tales of Momolu*—also was published in 1946. As a teacher in Liberia, Graham had encouraged a group of African students to become doctors and nurses. He was chastised by his superiors for "overstimulating" the children. Twenty years later in Norfolk, Virginia, Graham was treated for malaria by one of those children, Dr. Momolu Tugbah, who lent his name to the title character. One of these stories, "Song of the Boat," was republished in its own edition in 1975.

During the 1950s Graham was hired to write adaptations for *Classics Illustrated* comic books. *The Story of Jesus* was the first *Classics Illustrated* special edition. *The Ten Commandments* was promoted along with the film starring Charlton Heston and it earned Graham a special citation from the Thomas Alva Edison Foundation.

"Town" Series Became a Popular Success

Graham's graduate studies in sociology at Columbia University and New York University influenced his young adult novels. However, it took 12 years to find a publisher for *South Town*. Graham's characters did not conform to black stereotypes. One editor wrote that Graham had failed to distinguish between the lifestyles of Southern blacks and whites. Nevertheless, *South Town* earned Graham the Charles W. Follett Award when it was published in 1958, the Child Study Association of America Award in 1959, and the *Boston Globe-Horn Book* and Children's Book Showcase awards in 1976. The "Town" series became Graham's best-known work. These four novels focus on the courage and determination of black Americans struggling to overcome violence and racial oppression. Graham's message was that all people should be judged as individuals fighting against hatred and evil and working toward racial reconciliation.

At the age of 16, lead character David Williams is an ambitious young man who wants to become a doctor to help right the wrongs of South Town society. However racial oppression and terrorism force the Williams family to move to North Town. In the second novel, titled *North Town*, David is isolated in a mostly-white high school and becomes cynical about his own future and his dreams of racial justice. *Whose Town?*, published in 1969, deals with the racial unrest of the 1960s. Like Graham himself, David is listening to both militant black leaders and the more moderate voices of family and church. *Whose Town?* earned first prize from *Book World* in 1969. *Return to South Town* documents the successes and failures of the civil rights movement in the South. David says: "You know I used to be afraid of what white folks could do, but if I've learned anything, I've learned that even the meanest of them, the most rebbish, are people too. They aren't giants and they aren't great brains. Most of them are small and weak. I know I've got what it takes to deal with them. They can't hurt me."

Poet Maya Angelou praised the "Town" series on Dr. Ruth Graham Siegrist's Web site, *Graham Books*: "*South Town* and *North Town* were the bookends to a small library which I used to raise a teenage African American boy.... The Graham books were so accessible that I noticed those were the only two books my son refused to lend out and in fact kept privately secreted under his bed."

Wrote Novelettes, Stories, and Plays

Graham also wrote in a number of other genres. His four novelettes for adolescents were influenced by his careers as a social worker and a Los Angeles probation officer. The publisher of *Runaway* objected to Graham's depiction of a black ghetto girl writing beautiful poetry. As always, Graham refused to make any changes. A number of his short stories were included in the four *Directions* textbooks that he helped to compile.

John Brown: A Cry for Freedom became one of Graham's best-known works. In this well-documented biography—as well as in his earlier text for a picture book recounting Brown's historic attack on the arsenal at Harper's Ferry—Graham presented the white abolitionist martyr, not as a fanatic, but as a major force in American history. In 1969 Graham sang an accompaniment in sound recordings of excerpts from John Brown's last speech and from the *Dred Scott* U. S. Supreme Court decision.

Graham wrote plays for schools, colleges, and amateur theater groups. During the 1970s he lectured at California State Polytechnic College in Pomona. Ruth Morris Graham wrote several children's stories herself and the Grahams remained active in the civil rights movement. One of Graham's last public appearances was at a symposium on children's literature in South Africa in 1987. Lorenz Graham died of cancer on September 11, 1989, in West Covina, California. His manuscripts are deposited in the Kerlan Collection of the University of Minnesota, Minneapolis, and the North Carolina Central University Library in Durham.

Selected writings

Fiction

How God Fix Jonah, Reynal and Hitchcock, 1946; rev. ed., Boyds Mills Press, 2000.
Tales of Momolu, Reynal and Hitchcock, 1946.
(Adapter) *The Story of Jesus*, Gilberton, 1955.
(Adapter) *The Ten Commandments*, Gilberton, 1956.
Every Man Heart Lay Down, Crowell, 1970; Boyds Mills Press, 1993.
David He No Fear, Crowell, 1971.
God Wash the World and Start Again, Crowell, 1971.
Carolina Cracker, Houghton Mifflin, 1972.
Detention Center, Houghton Mifflin, 1972.
John Brown's Raid: A Picture History of the Attack on Harpers Ferry, Virginia, Scholastic, 1972.
Runaway, Houghton Mifflin, 1972.
Hongry Catch the Foolish Boy, Crowell, 1973.
John Brown: A Cry for Freedom, Crowell, 1980.

"Town" Series

South Town, Follett, 1958; Boyds Mills Press, 2003.
North Town, Crowell, 1965; Boyds Mills Press, 2003.

Whose Town? Crowell, 1969; Boyds Mills Press, 2003.

Return to South Town, Crowell, 1976; Boyds Mills Press, 2003.

Nonfiction

(Contributor and co-compiler) *Directions 1-4*, Houghton Mifflin, 1972.

Sources

Books

"Lorenz (Bell) Graham," in *St. James Guide to Young Adult Writers*, 2nd ed. St. James Press, 1999.

"Lorenz (Bell) Graham," in *Major Authors and Illustrators for Children and Young Adults*, 2nd ed., Gale, 2002.

Williams, Ora, "Lorenz Graham," in *Dictionary of Literary Biography*, vol. 76, Gale Group, 1988. pp. 57-66.

Periodicals

Booklist, October 1, 2000, p. 353; October 1, 2001, p. 333.
Connections, Winter 2004, p. 2.
Elementary English, February 1973, pp. 185-88.
Publishers Weekly, June 14, 2003, p. 78.

On-line

Graham Books, www.grahambooks.com (October 21, 2004).

"Lorenz B. Graham Papers, 1947-1980," *University of Minnesota Libraries*, http://special.lib.umn.edu/findaid/html/clrc/clrc0135.html (October 21, 2004).

"Lorenz (Bell) Graham," *Biography Resource Center*, www.galenet.com/servlet/BioRC (October 21, 2004).

"Writer Continues Literary Legacy," *Sacramento Observer*, www.sacobserver.com/soul/poetry_literature/061504/ruth_graham_siegrist.shtml (October 21, 2004).

—Margaret Alic

Sam Greenlee

1930—

Writer, broadcaster

Best known for his novels *The Spook Who Sat by the Door* (1969) and *Baghdad Blues* (1976), Sam Greenlee is a controversial writer and political activist. His work has always faced opposition because of its confrontational style and troubling imagery, but it has also attracted a large audience of activists, rebels, and radicals. Greenlee makes commercial publishers nervous; in fact *The Spook Who Sat by the Door* was first published in England when if failed to find an American publisher, but it went on to sell over one million copies and was printed in six languages. A film adaptation of the novel—about a black CIA operative who decides to use his training to organize race riots—was withdrawn without explanation after a promising opening at the box office in 1973. His 1976 novel *Baghdad Blues*, set in Iraq in 1958, the year of the Ba'athist takeover of the country, is based on his own experiences and has acquired a new audience since the overthrow of Saddam Hussein in 2003. *Black Issues Book Review* listed Greenlee's two novels as among the bestselling books by a black author in that year. Greenlee is also a poet, a journalist, and since 1988 a radio talk show host in his home town of Chicago.

Sam Greenlee was born on July 13, 1930, in Chicago and was educated in public schools before attending the University of Wisconsin, Madison, graduating in 1952 with a bachelor's degree in political science. After graduation he joined the United States Army, serving for two years as a first lieutenant, then studied international relations at the University of Chicago between 1954 and 1957. Greenlee claims that he was politically active from an early age, participating in his first sit-in at the age of 15. But his early career with the United States Information Agency put him at the heart of the government propaganda machine, placing artists and writers on assignments to promote American culture overseas. Greenlee became one of the first black foreign service officers, holding assignments in Iraq, Pakistan, Indonesia, and Greece between 1957 and 1965. He finally left the service after becoming disillusioned about his role as a government propagandist. He told *Echo* magazine: "Essentially I was an overseas public relations representative for the United States. Our job was to sell the best image of the United States overseas—basically I lied a lot."

Novel Became Cult Favorite

After leaving the U.S. Information Agency, Greenlee lived for a while on the Greek island of Mykonos in the Aegean Sea and wrote *The Spook Who Sat by the Door* in four months during his stay there. The novel centers on a black CIA operative hired by the agency to demonstrate its multiracial outlook. Tiring of doing menial office tasks and showing white visitors around the facility, agent Dan Freeman quits his job and uses his training and experience as a spy to set up a black revolutionary protest movement in Chicago. Greenlee himself lived on Chicago's South Side, the backdrop to some of the most destructive rioting of the 1960s. In 1968 his novel provided a frightening reminder of the events of that year. More threateningly, the novel

At a Glance . . .

Born Samuel Greenlee on July 13, 1930, in Chicago, IL; married Nienke Greenlee (divorced); children: one daughter. *Education:* University of Wisconsin, BS, political science, 1952; University of Chicago, studied international relations, 1954-57. *Military service:* United States Army, 1952-54.

Career: United States Information Agency, Washington, DC, served in Iraq, Pakistan, Indonesia, and Greece, 1957-65; Leadership Council for Metropolitan Communities, Chicago deputy director, 1965-69; WVON-AM radio, talk show host, 1988–; Columbia College, screenwriting tutor, 1990–.

Awards: United States Information Agency, meritorious service award for bravery during the 1958 Baghdad revolution; *Sunday Times* (London) Book of the Year award, for *The Spook Who Sat by the Door*, 1969; Ragdale Foundation fellowship, 1989; Illinois Arts Council fellowship, 1990; Illinois Poet Laureate award, 1990.

Addresses: *Office*—c/o WVON 1450 AM, 3350 South Kedzie, Chicago IL, 60623.

---

actually depicted the revolutionaries as capable of winning. It was submitted to 40 publishers before finally being accepted by Allison and Busby in London.

Spook soon became a cult favorite, selling well in black and radical bookshops around the United States. It is regarded as the first black-nationalist novel and is credited with inspiring the "blaxploitation" movie genre of the 1970s. Most importantly it attacked the real-life rioters for making no attempt to channel their anger and energy into anything more significant than violence and destruction; in the character of Dan Freeman, Greenlee created a true revolutionary leader, which made him far more dangerous to the white establishment than a mere rioter. The novel suggests that the outcome of the rioting might have been very different had the real-life rioters been led by someone as well organized and rational as Dan Freeman.

In presenting black protest groups with techniques that might be used for the violent overthrow of white-run organizations and government, Greelee's novel was always going to be controversial. But the novel made Greenlee's life harder in unexpected ways. His telephone was apparently tapped, his mail intercepted, and he began to suspect that the FBI was working to damage his career and silence him. Perhaps because of this Greenlee has earned a reputation for bitterness and a tendency to view his relative lack of mainstream success as part of a conspiracy against him. There is no denying the political power of the novel and its potential to frighten powerful whites. That power is emphasized by a story Greenlee told *Echo*. Befriending an ex-FBI agent Aubrey Lewis in a bar near the San Francisco airport, Greenlee was flattered to hear that not only had Lewis read *Spook*, but it was "required reading in the FBI academy."

More trouble followed when Ivan Dixon attempted to get permission to film an adaptation of *Spook* in Chicago. The city authorities tried to stop the film being made, refusing to allow the filmmakers access to Chicago streets and making it difficult for them to hire personnel and acquire the large numbers of firearms demanded by Greenlee's script. In the end the film was shot in Gary, Indiana, aided by that city's black mayor, Richard Hatcher, though one or two clandestine shots of Chicago did make it into the final cut. After a long struggle to raise money to make the film, it was eventually released by United Artists in September 1973, only to be withdrawn after a few weeks despite a good start at the box office. It was re-released in 2004 and toured film festivals around the United States to great acclaim.

Despite their violent plotlines, both the novel and the film of *Spook* come down on the side of freedom rather than race hatred. A reviewer in *The Christian Century* noted that "the film makes it clear that the revolution arose not out of hatred toward whites, but out of love for the black people and their liberation." This is in keeping with Greenlee's own literary stance, favoring diversity rather than domination or conflict. He told *Echo* of his dismay when he discovered that his creative writing tutor at the University of Wisconsin was "addicted to Hemingway and Faulkner," because for Greenlee writing and literature should be inclusive and diverse.

Enjoyed Brief Revival

Despite his brushes with the authorities, Greenlee continued to write, producing two books of poetry, including *Blues for an African* Princess (1971), and in 1976 his second novel, *Baghdad Blues*. Based on his experiences in Iraq during the Ba'athist takeover in 1958, when Saddam Hussein's party came to power, the novel did not have the immediate impact of his first. But it nevertheless offers some insights into that period in Iraq's history. Although it did little at the time to revive Greenlee's fortunes as a writer, the political climate of the early twenty-first century helped make his novels relevant for a new generation. Both *Spook* and *Baghdad Blues* speak of political struggle, oppression, and opposition.

Although he has not published a novel-length prose work since the 1970s, Greenlee has published stories, poems, and articles in small magazines and journals, as well as stage plays and screenplays; he has stuck to the routine of writing for four hours a day that he established early in his career and completed a third novel, *Djakarta Blues,* in 2002. Greenlee spent much of the 1980s living in Spain and West Africa, but in 1988 he became a talk show host on Chicago's WVON-AM radio station; in 1990 he won the Illinois Poet Laureate Award. Since 1990 he has also taught screenwriting at Columbia College in Chicago, read his poetry at recitals, and since the re-release of the film *The Spook Who Sat by the Door* in 2004, has introduced the film at many festivals and one-off showings.

Selected writings

Novels

The Spook Who Sat by the Door, Baron, 1969.
Baghdad Blues, Bantam, 1976.

Poetry

Blues for an African Princess, Third World Press, 1971.
Ammunition!: Poetry and Other Raps, Bogle L'Ouverture, 1975.

Sources

Periodicals

The Times (London), Saturday March 1, 1969, p. 20.
The Christian Century, October 3, 1973.
Echo. A Student Magazine of Columbia College, Chicago, Winter 2002.
Black Issues Book Review, May-June, 2003.

On-line

"How the Riots Might Have Turned Out," *Chicken Bones: A Journal for Literary and Artistic African American Themes* (first published in *The Christian Century*, October 3, 1973), www.nathanielturner.com/spookbythedoor.htm (October 26, 2004).
"Sam Greenlee," *Biography resource Center*, www.galenet.com/servlet/BioRC (November 1, 2004).
"Sam Greenlee's Book Is Still Making a Statement," *Chicken Bones: A Journal for Literary and Artistic African American Themes*, www.nathanielturner.com/spookbythedoor2.htm (October 26, 2004).

Other

Interview with Sam Greenlee on the DVD edition of *The Spook Who Sat by the Door*, Monarch Home Video, January 2004.

—Chris Routledge

Robert Guillaume

1927—

Actor, singer, producer

Before Robert Guillaume became a popular television actor and Broadway musical star, he was Robert Williams from St. Louis, Missouri: a young man with a golden voice and a future in the accounting field. Fortunately for all his fans, the young man threw caution to the wind and opted for show business. He chose a new name, Guillaume, the French translation of Williams, for its sophisticated image, but it was a decision he soon came to regret because so many people tripped on the pronunciation. That concern has long since dissolved. Guillaume, an Emmy Award winner for his roles in the television sitcoms, *Soap* and *Benson,* and a star in theater's smash hit musical *Phantom of the Opera*, is now one of the most respected and recognized talents in the business. And his name—tricky pronunciation and all—has become a household word.

Family "Pulled Together,"

Guillaume was born in 1927 and grew up during a difficult era in U.S. history. America suffered through the Great Depression in the 1930s. World War II began in 1939, and after the Japanese attack on Pearl Harbor in 1941, the United States entered the war that was supposed to end all wars. Meanwhile Guillaume's family was facing a much more personal crisis: it was disintegrating. Guillaume's life began in St. Louis, Missouri, just a few miles south of where the Missouri River outflows from the Mississippi. When he was only a toddler his alcoholic mother turned over the care of her four young children to their grandmother. The father had abandoned them early on. The kids grew up in a poor black section of the city under the protective wing of a strong-willed and altruistic woman; Guillaume's grandmother provided for the youngsters as best she could on the wages she earned as a laundress at a Catholic rectory. "The sum total of my grandmother," Guillaume told the *Boston Globe,* "can be measured in the fact that she took me and three of my sisters and brothers into her family in the middle of the Great Depression. She taught us that we could pull together. It was an enormous task of love, dedication, and devotion."

Guillaume, Robert, photograph. © Trapper Frank/Corbis Sygma.

Early on, Guillaume learned how to use his voice, but not only as a fine instrument in school musicals. By his own admission he was an outspoken boy with an

At a Glance . . .

Born Robert Peter Williams on November 30, 1927, St. Louis, MO; name legally changed to Robert Guillaume (pronounced "gee-yome"); married Marlene, 1955 (marriage ended); married Fay Hauser, 1978 (divorced); married Donna Brown (a freelance television producer), 1985; children: Patricia, Kevin, Jacques (deceased), Melissa, Rachel. *Education:* Attended St. Louis University and Washington University. *Military service:* U.S. Army, 1945-46.

Career: Theatrical singer, actor, and producer, 1957–; Confetti Entertainment, co-founder, 1991–.

Awards: Tony nomination, for *Guys and Dolls,* 1976; Emmy Award, for *Soap,* 1979; Emmy Award for best actor in a comedy series, for *Benson,* 1985; Massachusetts Association for Mental Health, award for "projection of a positive image of blacks on television," 1985; named honorary Lt. Governor for the day by Massachusetts governor Michael Dukakis, 1985; St. Louis Walk of Fame, inductee, 1999; Daytime Emmy Award nomination for outstanding performer in an animated program, for *Happily Every After: Fairy Tales for Every Child,* 2000; National Association for the Advancement of Colored People (NAACP) Image Award nomination for outstanding lead actor in a comedy series, for *Sports Night,* 1999 and 2001; Image Award nomination for outstanding supporting actor in a comedy series, for *Sports Night,* 2000; Screen Actors Guild Award nomination (with others) for outstanding performance by an ensemble in a comedy series, for *Sports Night,* 2000; Golden Satellite Award nomination for best performance by an actor in a series or musical, for *Sports Night,* 2001; received four NAACP Image Awards.

Addresses: *Office*—Confetti Entertainment, 15250 Ventura Blvd., Sherman Oaks, CA 91403; *Agent*—Metropolitan Talent Agency, 4526, Wilshire Blvd., Los Angeles, CA 90010-3801.

explosive temper—talents that got him suspended from grammar school and then expelled from parochial school in the ninth grade. His dual nature became apparent before he reached his teens: the well-behaved child was a choir boy and an altar boy, while the restless one hung out in the pool halls of St. Louis.

The U.S. Army and Robert Guillaume were not a combination that was meant to be. He joined in 1945, but after 15 months Guillaume resigned with an honorable discharge. "I have a big mouth and I had a Southern captain who hated my guts," he explained in *US* magazine. "One day he called me into his office and announced, 'This army isn't big enough for the both of us.'" So the captain stayed, and Guillaume left.

After his brief stint in the army, Guillaume finished high school and tried a number of odd jobs to save money for college. He ran a women's clothing store, worked in the post office and as a candy cook, washed dishes, and tried his hand at sales. But his most interesting short-term career was driving a St. Louis street car. His route took him down the same tracks that Judy Garland's "Trolley Song" made famous in the musical *Meet Me in St. Louis.* "I used to sing as I was barreling along, drowning out customers' screams," he told *People* magazine. "I was always crashing into the back of a Packard or Dodge. Then everyone would fall down on the floor screaming 'whiplash!'"

Possible exaggerations aside, the story illustrates Guillaume's enduring dream of becoming a professional singer. But in those times of extreme financial hardship, Guillaume, then in his mid-twenties, was sensitive to his grandmother's influence and tried to think practically. He enrolled in night classes at St. Louis University and chose business administration as his major. But it wasn't long before the dream of being a singer resurfaced, and he transferred to the music school at St. Louis's Washington University.

A Dream Becomes a Career

It was there that his talent captured the attention of Hungarian opera tenor and artist-in-residence Laslo Chabay. "Chabay," Guillaume told the *Washington Post,* "was the first person to say I had potential to sing the classics." With well over 140 hours of credits in liberal arts, Guillaume forgot about business administration and graduating and decided he could make a living with his voice.

It was not a misguided decision. Chabay helped Guillaume obtain a scholarship to the 1957 Aspen Music Festival in Colorado where he caught the attention of Russell and Rowena Jelliffe. The Jelliffes were founders of one of the oldest interracial theaters in America, the Karamu Theater in Cleveland, Ohio, and they offered Guillaume an apprenticeship. Guillaume, then already 31 years old, had his professional debut in the Karamu's production of *Carousel.* "When I started out," Guillaume told *US* magazine, "I had pretentious notions and I was somewhat hypocritical. I told myself I didn't care about fame; I just wanted to be an artist.

That was a lie. Becoming famous was always important to me."

His debut performance was witnessed and applauded by a very special member of the audience: renowned dramatist Oscar Hammerstein. Guillaume was recruited from *Carousel* for a Broadway revue called *Free and Easy*. The musical was a reworking of *The St. Louis Blues*. Though it soon folded, it had given him the experience of touring Europe.

Guillaume did not spend long between jobs. He toured with *Finian's Rainbow*, *Golden Boy*, *Kwamina*, and *Porgy and Bess*. In 1970, he appeared in *Some Place to Be Somebody*, a job he considered to be his first real acting role. In 1972, he was picked for the lead in *Purlie*, a musical adaption of the Ossie Davis play *Purlie Victorious*. The *St. Louis Post-Dispatch* described his character as "a resourceful young black preacher who returns home to the Georgia plantation to rally Uncle Toms against oppressive paternalism." To this day, it is one of the roles with which Guillaume is most identified.

Guillaume also had the opportunity to get a taste of the television medium. He performed in the special *S' Wonderful, S' Gershwin* and took bit acting roles in the shows *Marcus Welby, M.D.*, *The Jeffersons*, *Sanford and Son*, and *All in the Family*.

From Tony Award to Television

It was during one of his 750 performances in the play *Jacques Brel Is Alive and Well and Living in Paris* that Guillaume received his biggest break yet. Once again he was recruited, this time for the role of Nathan Detroit in the 1976 all-black revival of the hit *Guys and Dolls*. Guillaume's impressive performance as the street-smart owner of "the oldest established permanent floating crap game in New York" won him a Tony nomination. He had finally arrived. And then he left—for television. Guillaume explained the circumstances in the *Christian Science Monitor*: "I was doing *Guys and Dolls* in New York and we'd been notified we were going to close shortly. We were on pins and needles." Panicked, Guillaume called his agent who informed him that the industry had dried up and chances of finding anything were nil.

"A half hour later my agent called back and told me about plans for a prime time soap opera," Guillaume continued. *Soap*, the ABC nighttime satire of daytime soaps that became controversial for its brazen storylines riddled with infidelities, murders, and sexual orientations, was searching for a butler. Even after Guillaume successfully progressed through several auditions for the part, he was forced to wait while the producers went back and forth on the decision of the character's ethnicity. But he got the part and became Benson DuBois from the West Indies: the cantankerous, irreverent, and condescending butler who did not suffer fools gladly.

Guillaume received an Emmy for his role in *Soap* in 1979. His character became so popular that the network decided to create *Benson*, a spin-off show. *Soap*'s butler turned in his resignation, and the character of Benson DuBois was hired as the head of household at the governor's mansion in the same fictitious town. Benson quickly made his way to state budget director and finally lieutenant governor. Guillaume was given the opportunity to transform Benson into a three-dimensional character, one that symbolized the changing role of black Americans in society. He told the *Washington Post*, "I wanted the character to have that kind of upward mobility because it mirrored the American dream." At the time, such a dream had rarely been attained by minorities on television.

Actor and Advocate

Benson had a successful run for seven years, earning Guillaume his second Emmy in 1985, before it was canceled a year later. In 1989, Guillaume co-created and was executive co-producer of *The Robert Guillaume Show*, a short-lived interracial romantic comedy. After his stint with television, Guillaume began pursuing different directions. He hit the nightclub circuits, singing in places like Las Vegas, Lake Tahoe, and Atlantic City; he added movies to his acting experience with *Lean on Me*; he formed his own production company, Longridge Enterprises, to develop acting projects; and he returned to the theater.

Guillaume's greatest theatrical achievement came in May of 1990, when he was hand-picked as the new star of Andrew Lloyd Webber's spectacular musical *The Phantom of the Opera*. There was much skepticism that any actor could successfully fill the mask of the wildly popular Michael Crawford—especially, a black actor in a traditionally white role. But Guillaume triumphed. He did not attempt to imitate his predecessor's original version of the lonely, disfigured, mad, and love-sick phantom. Instead, Guillaume gave life to his own monster. And the loyal audience loved it. The fact that the phantom was now being performed by a black actor became irrelevant. But this high point in Guillaume's professional life coincided with a tragic time in his personal life. His 33-year-old son, Jacques, died on December 23, 1990, following a two-year fight against AIDS (acquired immune deficiency syndrome). Jacques and his brother Kevin had grown up with their mother, Guillaume's first wife, while the actor pursued his career. "I felt guilty," Guillaume revealed in a *Parade* interview, " because what I call the 'long arm of the ghetto,' where he spent his childhood, had gotten to him and programmed him for defeat…. I think he interpreted my urging to put his brain and talents to use as snobbishness and disapproval. He didn't seem to understand that, at the same time I loved him without qualification and accepted his homosexuality, I still hoped he'd find direction for his life."

Guillaume is an introspective man. He is also an extremely private and sensitive artist who has held a long-lived struggle with self-esteem and the fear of failure. "As a black man I'd been in a kind of wilderness," he told the *Chicago Tribune* in 1972. "I did not know I did not like being black. I though I had the whole thing together." He continued, "It was only this emergence, this black thing that happened in the sixties, particularly to black males—becoming aware and appreciating themselves.... I'd lived a whole lifetime and...always felt ugly."

Since then, Guillaume has risen to become one of America's most appreciated and successful black actors and a powerful voice in the fight for fair and equal treatment of African Americans. "It outraged me then, it outrages me now," he asserted in *Parade*. "It gets me crazy, the assumption that being black and poor is our own fault.... I'll never forget where I came from and how I got here."

For his part, Guillaume has tried to serve as a positive role model. With his wife Donna he co-founded Confetti Entertainment in 1991. The company, that's mission is to combat illiteracy, produces multicultural educational books and teacher resources, as well as the "Happily Ever After: Fairy Tales for Every Child" videos that show children of a variety of ethnicities in classic fairy tales. In 1994, Guillaume lent his voice to the character of Rafiki in Disney's animated film *The Lion King*. While acting in the sitcom *Sports Night* in 1999, Guillaume took yet another opportunity to serve as a role model, but this time for older folks. He suffered a debilitating stroke on the set. But within three weeks, he returned to his job, weakened and walking with a cane, but positive about his recovery. He told *People Weekly* that "I hope that people who have had strokes will see me and take a positive approach toward their own recoveries." He added that "I see the stroke as something that God laid on me as a way of saying, 'This guy has been thinking he's in charge a little too much.' To me, my whole life has been spent trying to overcome limitations, to take what I have and make it better. This stroke has given me the same kind of chance to improve." Guillaume has indeed continued to improve, paving the way for others to follow. After discovering he also had diabetes, Guillaume began speaking out about health issues to alert people that "your health really does matter," as he told *Jet*. Dividing his time between acting and health advocacy, Guillaume also found time to write his autobiography. Published in 2003, *Guillaume: A Life*, traces his struggles and triumphs from his early years.

Selected works

Books

(With David Ritz) *Guillaume: A Life*, Missouri Press, 2003.

Plays

Carousel, 1957.
Some Place to Be Somebody, 1970.
Purlie, 1972.
Guys and Dolls, 1976.
Cabaret, 1987.
Phantom of the Opera, 1990.
Cyrano–The Musical, 1994.

Films

Super Fly T.N.T., 1973.
Seems like Old Times, 1980.
Prince Jack, 1985.
They Still Call Me Bruce, 1987.
Wanted: Dead or Alive, 1987.
Lean on Me, 1989.
Death Warrant, 1990.
The Meteor Man, 1993.
The Lion King (animated), 1994.
Spy Hard, 1996.
First Kid, 1996.
The Lion King II: Simba's Pride (animated), 1998.
The Adventures of Tom Thumb and Thumbelina (animated), 2000.

Television

Soap, 1977-79.
Benson, 1979-86.
The Robert Guillaume Show, 1989.
Pacific Station, 1991.
Fish Police (animated), 1992.
The Lion King's Timon and Pumbaa (animated), 1995.
Sports Night, 1998-2000.

Sources

Periodicals

Boston Globe, July 13, 1981.
Chicago Tribune, June 18, 1972.
Christian Science Monitor, September 12, 1979.
Jet, November 3, 2003.
New York Daily News, August 20, 1976.
New York Times, December 18, 1977.
Parade, May 24, 1992.
People, January 23, 1978.
People Weekly, October 11, 1999.
St. Louis Post-Dispatch, September 25, 1972.
US, August 15, 1983.
Washington Post, May 6, 1976; September 15, 1979; September 24, 1985.

—Iva Sipal and Sara Pendergast

Alphonso R. Jackson

1946—

Government official

Alphonso R. Jackson heads the U.S. Department of Housing and Urban Development (HUD). Appointed to the job by President George W. Bush in 2004, Jackson is the nation's top housing chief and one of the few African Americans in Bush's cabinet. "When the president asks you to serve your country, I think it's an honor that you really can't refuse," Jackson told *St. Louis Post-Dispatch* journalist Karen Branch-Brioso. "It's even more difficult when the president happens to have been your friend for a long time."

Jackson, Alphonso, photograph. © 2003 Landov LLC. All rights reserved. Reproduced by permission.

but articulate proponent for more minority enrollment at the law school, at a time when civil-rights consciousness was helping usher in a new era in America. "I was not very well-liked by most of the professors," he joked in the *St. Louis Post-Dispatch* interview.

Jackson began his professional career in St. Louis, and in 1977 he was named the city's director of public safety. He became executive director of the St. Louis Housing Authority four years later, a job he held until 1983. He left it to work as a consultant to a St. Louis accounting firm and intensified his political activities. Active in both Democratic and Republican circles in the city for many years, he even ran for a spot as St. Louis's municipal revenue collector. He also worked for the U.S. Senate campaign of Jack Danforth, a Republican. His rising profile earned him the attention of officials in Washington, and in 1987 he was made the director of the U.S. Department of Public and Assisted Housing for Washington, D.C.

Jackson was born on September 9, 1946, in Marshall, Texas, and grew up in South Dallas as the youngest of twelve children in the family. His mother was a midwife, while his father sometimes worked as many as three jobs—as a foundry worker, janitor, and landscaper—to make ends meet. Jackson attended Northeast Missouri State University (now called Truman State University) and studied political science there; he also went on to earn a master's degree in education administration from the school in 1969. But instead of taking a teaching job, Jackson enrolled in Washington University School of Law in St. Louis, where he quickly became known as a firebrand. He was an outspoken

In 1989 Jackson was tapped to take over the Housing Authority of the City of Dallas as its president and chief executive officer. He was the first African American to

At a Glance . . .

Born on September 9, 1946, in Marshall, TX; son of a foundry worker, janitor, and landscaper, and a midwife; married Marcia A. Clark; children: Annette, Lesley. *Education:* Northeast Missouri State University, Kirksville, BA, political science, 1968, MEd, 1969; Washington University School of Law, St. Louis, Missouri, JD, 1972; also attended the University of Pennsylvania. *Politics:* Republican.

Career: City of St. Louis, Missouri, director of public safety, 1977-81; St. Louis Housing Authority, executive director, 1981-83; worked as a consultant for a St. Louis accounting firm, 1983-87; U.S. Department of Public and Assisted Housing, Washington, DC, director, 1987-89; Dallas Housing Authority, president and chief executive officer, 1989-96; American Electric Power-TEXAS, president, 1996-2001; U.S. Department of Housing and Urban Development (HUD), deputy secretary, 2001-2004, secretary, 2004–.

Selected memberships: JP Morgan Chase & Co.-Texas, board of directors; Nature Conservancy of Texas, board of directors; Truman State University, board of directors; U.S. Chamber of Commerce, board of directors.

Awards: Fellow, Aspen Institute, 1995; National Boys and Girls Clubs of America, Chairman's Award, 1997; AFLAC, Lifetime Achievement Award, 2001.

Addresses: *Office*—U.S. Department of Housing and Urban Development (HUD), 451 7th S. SW, Washington, DC 20410-1047.

---

lead the formerly troubled agency, which had become the target of discrimination lawsuits. In his seven years on the job, Jackson was credited with fixing the problems within the Dallas Housing Authority (DHA) and improving conditions for the city's poorest residents, who turned to it for help in a time of need. He worked to improve the run-down buildings and unsafe conditions that had become standard in the city's aging public-housing units, and also arranged deals that improved neighborhood conditions. He managed to find funds for a commercial development project, for example, that brought the first supermarket back to a struggling West Dallas neighborhood in several years.

Jackson's seven-year stint in Dallas was not without its challenges. In 1995 the DHA began implementing a U.S. District Court order that came about after a mid-1980s challenge to desegregate the city's public-housing units. The court order called for 3,200 low-income families to be placed in neighborhoods that were predominantly white, and the agency drew up a plan for new units to be built in a section of North Dallas that was predominantly white. The townhouses or duplexes would house just 75 families, but some 2,000 local homeowners organized to fight it. Jackson fought back with the characteristic mettle that had emerged during those law-school days, targeting one committee organizer from the neighborhood in particular. "I'm not going to accept this nonsense anymore," he asserted in an interview with the *Austin American-Statesman*'s Stefani G. Kopenec, "so tell him to come with something that's substantive and not the subterfuge for race, because that's what it's coming down to.... They don't want people of color out there. It's simple."

Jackson even received threatening phone calls and letters for his stance, and found himself at odds occasionally with the Dallas City Council, some of whom called for his resignation. In the end, Jackson left the public sector when American Electric Power-TEXAS offered him the president's job in 1996. He ran the Austin-based utility, a company worth $13 billion, for the next five years. With a new Republican administration in the White House, Jackson was a likely contender for a federal appointment, especially since he had known George W. Bush, the Texas governor declared the winner of the 2000 presidential election, since 1989, when both lived in the same Dallas neighborhood. In early 2001 Jackson's name was approved by Congress to serve as the deputy secretary of the Department of Housing and Urban Development (HUD), a post that essentially made him second-in-command and chief operating officer of the cabinet department, working under HUD Secretary Mel Martinez.

As deputy secretary, Jackson oversaw a budget of $32 billion and 9,300 employees, and encountered a bit of trouble with HUD regional office employees in Los Angeles, where a union-organizing effort was underway. Jackson visited the office and made remarks interpreted by some as intimidating. Jackson had told the poorly-run regional office to shape up, noting that when he was as a youngster, "it took my father three whuppings to get the message through to me, and that's what I am prepared to do," he said, according to an article in *American Banker* by Michele Heller. Jackson was investigated and later cleared on charges of making intimidating statements in the workplace, an issue that came up when Martinez decided to step down and Bush nominated Jackson to replace him. "Alphonso is a friend, and one of the most experienced and respected authorities on housing policy in America," Bush said on the day of the announcement, according to a report in *Mortgage Banking*.

Jackson was approved by Congress on March 31, 2004, and sworn into office as the thirteenth Secretary of Housing and Urban Development the following day. He became the third African American in the Bush cabinet, after Secretary of State Colin Powell and Rod Paige, the Education secretary. Almost immediately, Jackson found himself on the frontlines of a furor over Section 8, a HUD program in existence since 1975 that allows low-income families to search for rental properties on the private market; HUD then covers up to 70 percent of the rent for the program's enrollees, with the tenants responsible for the rest. The program is crucially dependant on something called the "fair-market value," which sets the guidelines for the amount that HUD will cover. The fair-market values are determined after surveys from the rental market in the area.

Drastic cuts had been made to the Section 8 program in the past few years, and housing activists and advocates for the poor believed the Bush Administration was determined to dismantle the program. Jackson even authored a *New York Times* editorial piece that appeared in August of 2004 in which he pointed out that since its inception, "Section 8 has grown into an overly prescriptive and unwieldy program. It has separate rules for more than a dozen different types of housing vouchers, along with 120 pages of regulations. Costs have spiraled out of control, without a corresponding gain in benefits." He argued that the changes HUD was proposing—to include suburban-rent statistics in determining urban fair-market value—would mean that HUD would not find itself paying a slightly over-market price in some areas. "If Congress passes the flexible voucher program we have proposed," wrote Jackson in the Op-Ed piece, "President Bush and I are convinced that we can better serve the two million families who depend on Section 8—and help even more Americans find affordable housing in the process." Jackson's characteristic method of attacking problems head-on is likely to keep him in the headlines as he proceeds in his important assignment.

Sources

Periodicals

American Banker, December 15, 2003, p. 21; January 13, 2004, p. 4; February 23, 2004, p. 14; March 31, 2004, p. 3; June 3, 2004, p. 3.
Austin American-Statesman, July 23, 1995, p. B3.
Community Banker, May 2004, p. 16.
Connecticut Law Tribune, August 30, 2004.
Ebony, June 2004, p. 12.
Economic Opportunity Report, January 19, 2004, p. 18; April 26, 2004, p. 91.
Houston Chronicle, December 13, 2003, p. 14.
Knight Ridder/Tribune Business News, December 11, 2003; April 15, 2004.
Knight Ridder/Tribune News Service, December 12, 2003.
Mortgage Banking, February 2004, p. 10; May 2004, p. 10.
New York Times, May 21, 2004, p. A16; August 6, 2004, p. A19.
Origination News, January 2004, p. 1.
St. Louis Post-Dispatch, June 24, 2001, p. A12.

On-line

"The Honorable Alphonso Jackson," *Homes and Communities: U.S. Department of Housing and Urban Development,* www.hud.gov/about/secretary/jacksonbio.cfm (October 13, 2004).

—Carol Brennan

Major L. Jemison

1955(?)–

Pastor, denominational leader

The Rev. Major Lewis Jemison, Senior Pastor of Oklahoma City, Oklahoma's St. John Missionary Baptist Church, has emerged as one of the key religious leaders of recent years. A political activist, an innovative church leader, and a bridge-builder between African-American denominations, he has addressed a great variety of issues that are central to the development of the modern black church. President of the Progressive National Baptist Convention since 2002, he stepped into a position once held by Rev. Martin Luther King Jr. In 2003 Jemison was recognized by *Ebony* magazine as one of the 100-plus most influential figures in black America.

Major L. Jemison was born in Birmingham, Alabama, around 1955. He attended Bishop College in Dallas, receiving a bachelor's degree in religion and philosophy with an emphasis on church ministries and pastoral care in 1977. By that time he had already been licensed as a Baptist minister. He served on the staff of Dallas's Greater Bethlehem Baptist Church, and went on to earn a master's degree at the city's Perkins School of Theology. He received his degree in 1982, the same year he became an ordained minister at Concord Baptist Church, where he would become Associate Pastor.

Jemison's move to St. John in Oklahoma City came in January of 1984. He was an assistant to Pastor W. K. Jackson at first, becoming co-pastor in 1988 as he was groomed to succeed Jackson. Jemison continued to round out his theological and practical education, earning a Doctorate of Ministry from the Midwestern Baptist Theological Seminary in Kansas City, Missouri in 1990 and also attaining the status of Certified Psychiatric Counselor from Timberlawn Psychiatric Hospital.

St. John Missionary Baptist Church experienced impressive growth as Jemison moved into positions of day-to-day leadership. With a membership approaching 2,500 as of the early 2000s, St. John was something of an African-American "megachurch"—a large institution offering numerous educational, social, and recreational opportunities under the church umbrella. The church boasted a Physical Fitness Ministry (complete with aerobics, judo instruction, and a bowling league), a drama department and dance corps, a decoration ministry, an Optimists' Club chapter, a museum, several choirs, and a 25-piece orchestra, among other enterprises. St. John's range of activities was recognized with an Innovative Church Award from *Church Business* magazine in 2004.

Jemison also assumed positions of leadership beyond the church, in the Oklahoma City community. He has been a longtime member of the executive board of the Oklahoma City branch of the Urban League and is a life member of the National Association for the Advancement of Colored People (NAACP). A member of both the Rotary Club and the Masons, Jemison chaired the Oklahoma City Christian Relief Fund, which delivered aid to families of victims of the 1995 terrorist bombing of the Alfred P. Murrah federal office building. He has served on several civic boards and is a member of the Oklahoma City Parks & Recreation Commission.

At a Glance . . .

Born c. 1955 in Birmingham, AL; married Jacqueline; children: one son, Master MaKinsley. *Education:* Bishop College, Dallas, TX, BA, 1977; Perkins School of Theology, Dallas, Master of Theology, 1982; Midwestern Baptist Theological Seminary, Doctor of Ministry, 1990. *Religion:* Baptist (Progressive National Baptist Convention).

Career: Greater Bethlehem Baptist Church, Dallas, served on staff, 1970s; Concord Baptist Church, Dallas, associate pastor, early 1980s; St. John Missionary Baptist Church, Oklahoma City, OK, assistant-to-the-pastor, 1984-88, co-pastor, 1988-2002, senior pastor, 2002–; Progressive National Baptist Convention, first local vice president, president of Southwest Region, second and first vice president, and president, 2002–.

Selected memberships: Urban League; Northeast Homeownership Consortium, board member; Coalition of Civic Leadership; NAACP; Ambassadors' Concert Choir, board member; Oklahoma City Parks and Recreation Commission.

Address: *Office*—St. John Missionary Baptist Church, 5700 N. Kelley Ave., Oklahoma City, OK 73111.

Jemison became Senior Pastor at St. John in April of 2002. By that time he had taken on several high-profile preaching assignments, including a guest slot at Washington's National Cathedral in January of 2002. Even in the face of large new projects, such as the construction of a building for the St. John Christian Heritage Academy church school, Jemison led the congregation in a mortgage burning ceremony celebrating the payoff of all debt incurred on the church's landmark building in northeast Oklahoma City, nestled in a natural setting on a 35-acre campus.

Like several of his contemporaries among the top ranks of African-American church leaders, Jemison realized the role the black church could play in encouraging home ownership among African Americans. St. John partnered with the federal Department of Housing and Urban Development (HUD) to offer an Oklahoma African-American Homeownership Initiative Housing Fair, offering financial counseling and putting prospective homeowners in contact with private and governmental lending institutions. Jemison spearheaded the event, which grew from an internal St. John program to include representatives from 35 or more area churches.

Jemison's all-around success fitted him for national leadership. Serving successively as first local vice president, Southwest Region president, and second and then first vice president of the nationwide Progressive National Baptist Convention (PNBC), he was elected president of that organization in 2002. The election put Jemison at the helm of more than 1,100 churches nationwide. The post was a historic one, with a long lineage of civil rights activism dating back to Martin Luther King Jr.'s presidency. Jemison was the group's youngest president in more than two decades, and he called for a variety of new initiatives, including an effort to reach prison inmates. "I think that we have surrendered so much of that ministry area to the Muslims, and they are to be commended for their work in that area," Jemison pointed out to the *Daily Oklahoman*.

Jemison exhorted PNBC member churches to voter registration efforts, and in 2004 he promoted an appearance by minister and Democratic primary presidential candidate the Rev. Al Sharpton, although he did not formally endorse the fiery New Yorker. Jemison also led calls for the withdrawal of U.S. troops from Iraq. "Our nation is still burdened with the spoils and rough tirades from the smell of a war that was presented to us under false pretenses," he was quoted as saying by the *Houston Chronicle*. "Our boys and girls are being upended as we send them out to defend a war that is seemingly pointless and endless."

Many of Jemison's efforts on the national stage were directed toward reconciliation between the PNBC and the larger National Baptist Convention, from which the PNBC had split in the early 1960s. Jemison gave the keynote address at a banquet at the National Baptist Convention's annual meeting and worked to bring about closer relations between the two groups. In 2004 he also was one of the leaders who planned an unprecedented meeting among the boards of all four splintered national black Baptist groups. It was a fitting task for the man Oklahoma City mayor Kirk Humphreys had called a servant leader and a peacemaker. Jemison is married to his college sweetheart, Jacqueline, and the couple has one son, Master MaKinsley.

Sources

Periodicals

Atlanta Journal-Constitution, June 26, 2004, p. B2.
Charlotte Observer, August 6, 2003.
Christian Century, August 28, 2002, p. 17.
Daily Oklahoman, August 9, 2002, p. A2; December 7, 2002, p. D1.
Ebony, May 2003.
Houston Chronicle, August 5, 2004, p. B5.
Times-Picayune (New Orleans, LA), September 28, 2002, p. 16.

On-line

"Innovative Church Awards 2004," *Church Business*, www.churchbusiness.com/articles/481cover1.html (October 7, 2004).

"Major Lewis Jemison," *St. John Missionary Baptist Church*, www.stjohnokc.org/data/bio.html (October 7, 2004).

"Sowing for the Homeownership Harvest," *U.S. Department of Housing and Urban Development*, www.hud.gov/local/ok/library/archives/2004-03-04.cfm (October 7, 2004).

—James M. Manheim

Levi Johnson

1950—

Professional football player

A key member of the powerful Detroit Lions squads of the 1970s, Levi Johnson delighted National Football League (NFL) fans with his agile feats at the defensive positions of cornerback and safety. Johnson's career was prematurely ended by injury in the late 1970s. Since he had been named the Lions' most valuable player in 1974 and had followed that up with his strongest season two years later, however, some wondered how far he might have gone in a full-length career.

One of three children, Levi Johnson was born in Corpus Christi, Texas, on October 23, 1950. Athletics seemed to run in the family, for Johnson's brother entered major league baseball straight out of high school. Johnson himself, attending Corpus Christi's Roy Miller High School, where he "basically played every sport there was except for golf and tennis," he told Contemporary Black Biography (CBB). He could have gone on to play one of several sports in college, but a coach pressed him to make a decision after telling him that several different college coaches had come calling to inquire about his talents. Johnson decided on football after noticing how much bigger typical football crowds were than those for other sports.

Even so, Johnson briefly played basketball and ran track at Texas A&M University at Kingsville in addition to playing football. And he was all over the field on offense and defense as a football player as well, taking to the gridiron initially as a quarterback, wide receiver, and running back in addition to his eventual specialty in the defensive backfield. It was a single play that converted Johnson permanently to defense. "I ran a 7 or 8 yard out, and the defensive back read it to a T," Johnson told CBB. The guy folded me up like a jackknife, busted my pancreas." Suffering from internal injuries, Johnson was hospitalized. "I told the coach that's the last time I'm going to be the hittee."

The decision worked out well, however, as Johnson became a defensive star at Texas A&M Kingsville. He set a team record for interceptions, and with his size and speed—he stood six feet, three inches and weighed close to 200 pounds—he had no problem attracting the attention of NFL scouts. He won postseason All-America honors from one magazine. In the 1973 draft, Johnson was drafted in the third round by the Detroit Lions.

Johnson got into every game as a rookie, grabbing five interceptions for 82 yards and taking three kickoff returns for an impressive 51 total yards. Legendary Lions defensive back Lem Barney served as a mentor to Johnson, helping him fit in amidst the pressures of coming to big-time sports for the first time. Johnson credited Barney with "just basically making me realize football is a team game. What you do and what you say and how you act has a direct reflection on your teammates and your organization and you and your family," Johnson told CBB.

Benefiting from Barney's guidance as he played opposite Barney at the position of right cornerback, Johnson flourished from the start with the Lions. After leading the Lions squad with five pass interceptions, he was named to All-Rookie teams by several publications. He did even better over the 1974 season, once again

At a Glance . . .

Born on October 23, 1950, in Corpus Christi, TX; married and divorced; children: two daughters. *Education:* Texas A&M University, Kingsville, BA.

Career: Detroit Lions, professional football player, 1973-79; Mel Farr Ford & Lincoln Mercury, Oak Park, MI, salesman, 1980s and 1990s; Stu Evans Lincoln Mercury, salesman.

Awards: Detroit Lions, Most Valuable Defensive Player, 1974; named to several All-Rookie teams, 1973.

Addresses: *Home*—Westland, MI.

---

notching five interceptions, returning two of them for touchdowns, and amassing a total of 139 yards in interception returns. He was the sixth Lions player in history to score two interception-return touchdowns in the same season. Grabbing an opposition fumble gave Johnson another touchdown for a total of three, and with all these achievements on the field, Johnson was named the Lions' defensive Most Valuable Player for 1974.

Johnson intercepted three passes in 1975, scoring one touchdown on a fumble recovery. In 1976 he had his best year yet, with six interceptions for 206 yards (sixth-best in Lion team history) and one touchdown. Between 1973 and 1976 Johnson didn't miss a single game, and he seemed to be hitting his stride on the way to a top-flight NFL career. In addition to his role in the defensive backfield he was a threat in the special-teams department, with five blocked punts over the course of his career.

Then, in the third game of the 1977 season, against the Philadelphia Eagles, disaster struck. With two interceptions by halftime, Johnson was already a candidate for a spot in the next morning's newspaper headlines. But he injured his knee in the second half and spent the rest of the season on injured reserve. The knee healed, but in training camp before the 1978 season he ruptured an Achilles tendon. He sat that season out as well. As the 1979 season approached, Johnson told *CBB*, he found that he had "lost a step." Doctors advised him to quit if he valued his future health, and, newly married as of 1978, he agreed.

With two daughters (and eventually a grandchild) to support, Johnson spent 19 years working for Mel Farr Ford and Lincoln Mercury in Oak Park, Michigan, near Detroit, a dealership founded by a former Lions running back that for many years was the largest African-American-owned business in the United States. He later signed on with another dealership, Stu Evans Lincoln Mercury, where he was working as of 2004. But he never completely lost touch with the game of football, and he became a familiar figure of the Detroit-area sports scene.

Working with kids at football camps and taking such community-oriented posts as spokesman for the Police Athletic League, Johnson made many appearances on behalf of charities associated with the Lions. He appeared on a program called *Football Sunday* on the Fox television network's Detroit affiliate in the 1990s, and several times in the early 2000s he served as Alumni Honorary Captain at Lions' home football games. "It's always been about people, you know, I want to be around people," Johnson told *CBB* by way of summarizing his post-NFL career. On the field in the 1970s, however, this people person and natural salesman was something else again: a figure who struck fear into the hearts of opposing quarterbacks.

Sources

Books

Carroll, Bob, et al., *Total Football: The Official Encyclopedia of the National Football League,* HarperCollins, 2004.

On-line

"Levi Johnson," *Lions History: Top 100,* www.lions-fans.com/history/journal/journal_comments.asp?JournalID=79 (October 7, 2004).

Other

Additional information for this profile was obtained from an interview with Levi Johnson, October 5, 2004, and from Detroit Lions press releases, December 19, 2001 and October 15, 2003.

—James M. Manheim

Sheila Crump Johnson

1949(?)—

Executive, philanthropist, musician, horse farmer

Those who never took the trouble to find out more might have heard of Sheila Crump Johnson as the former wife of longtime Black Entertainment Television (BET) chief executive Robert L. Johnson. That designation, however, ignores Sheila Crump Johnson's long and varied record of accomplishments of her own, before, during, and after her marriage. One of those accomplishments was the co-founding of BET itself, which the two Johnson spouses created together and expanded into a broadcasting empire. After the couple's divorce in 2002, Johnson became the first African-American female billionaire in the United States. She then gained recognition for giving large amounts of her money away.

Johnson was born Sheila Crump around 1949 in the Chicago, Illinois, suburb of Maywood. Her father was a neurosurgeon. Johnson attended Irving School in Maywood and graduated from Proviso High School in 1966. She was a member of the cheerleading squad at Proviso, but her heart was in music. She aspired to a career as a concert violinist, and she would sometimes get up at midnight, after the rest of the family had gone to sleep, to practice her violin for hours in the kitchen of her home. "I realized that after I graduated from high school, I always had a drive in me that desired to be the best that I could be," Johnson said in a 2002 speech at the State University of New York at Morrisville, as quoted by the *New York Times*. "But still, I believed you should do unto others as you would have them do unto you."

Concentrated on Music

Majoring in music at the University of Illinois, she rose to the rank of concertmaster in the Illinois All-State Orchestra. It was at Illinois that she met Robert L. Johnson. The romance flowered, and the two were married in 1969 after Robert abandoned a graduate scholarship at Princeton University to move back to Illinois so they could be closer to each other. After Sheila's graduation in 1970, the couple moved to Washington, D.C.

At first, Johnson worked as a researcher in the office of New York Republican Senator Jacob K. Javits, but she soon got a job teaching music at a private school, the Sidwell Friends School. As her husband became involved with the then-minuscule world of cable television, she sometimes helped the family make ends meet by giving music lessons at their home.

It was in the field of classical music, before she ever became involved with BET, that Johnson's ability to think big first showed itself. In 1975 she founded a 140-member youth orchestra, Youth Strings in Action. The group was invited to perform in the Middle Eastern nation of Jordan, and the trip went off well enough that Johnson won an appointment as cultural liaison to Jordan for the United States Information Agency, a governmental entity that worked to foster cultural exchanges and display American culture around the world. Johnson helped set up Jordan's first national music conservatory, and she was given the country's

At a Glance . . .

Born Sheila Crump in 1949(?) in Maywood, IL; daughter of a neurosurgeon; married Robert L. Johnson (a cable television executive) (divorced, 2002); children: Paige, Brett. *Education:* University of Illinois, BA, music, 1970.

Career: Sidwell Friends School, Washington, DC, instructor, 1970s; Youth Strings in Action orchestra, founder, 1975; United States Information Agency, cultural liaison to Jordan, 1970s; Black Entertainment Television, co-founder (with Robert L. Johnson), executive vice president for corporate affairs, early 1980s-1999; Salamander Farm, Loudoun County, VA, owner, 2002–; Washington International Horse Show, administrator, 2002–.

Selected awards: Honorary doctorate, Bennett College, 2004; honorary doctorate, State University of New York at Morrisville.

Addresses: *Office*—Salamander Inn & Spa, 3074 Zulla Rd., The Plains, VA 20198.

top educational award by Jordan's King Hussein. Johnson later authored a music textbook for student violinists, and for a time she served on the board of trustees of New York's Carnegie Hall.

Co-founded BET

By the early 1980s, the BET cable network had taken shape and was beginning its meteoric growth. Its founding was a joint enterprise on the part of both Johnsons, and when BET was sold to cable giant Viacom in 2002, even as both their personal and business relationships had become acrimonious, they split the proceeds of the sale equally. In the early years, BET was noted for a variety of programs showcasing the best of African-American culture. Sheila Johnson had a hand in several of those, forming an in-house hip-hop chorus and personally creating the weekly "Teen Summit" talk show, featuring up-front discussion of problems such as the threat of AIDS.

Johnson's official title at BET was executive vice president for corporate affairs, but she was an equal partner with her husband in many respects. Family friend Susan Starrett told the *Washington Post* that the billion-dollar Johnson fortune couldn't have been built without her work, and Johnson herself, asked by the *Post* whether she had played a supportive role in her husband's career, answered "Why, yes I did. I always put him first. I knew who he was. I know who he is. I was his best friend and his biggest supporter. I believed in him before he believed in himself."

Yet Johnson was dissatisfied with her role. "I detested that, living up under the cloud of Wife Of. I could not stand going to places, and everything was focused on the man, and the wives were sitting around, like they don't exist. Don't. Exist," she told the *Post*. Too, she felt alienated by the increasingly raunchy direction of BET's programming in the late 1990s. Some felt she played the role of the conscience of the company, and on a day-to-day basis she was more likely to be found listening to the music of classical composer Maurice Ravel than taking in one of BET's bump-and-grind musical productions. As the Johnsons' marriage deteriorated amidst rumors of Robert Johnson's affair with one or more subordinates, Sheila Johnson (who later lamented to the *Post* that her husband "had a body count") was fired by her husband in 1999.

The marriage itself ended in 2002. "I consider it a tragedy, and very painful," she told the *Post*. "But we move on. That's the way it is. I'm not going to sit down and shrivel up and disappear." And indeed she didn't. Johnson's divorce marked not only the end of one career but the beginning of several others.

Turned to Equestrian Lifestyle

Johnson purchased (for over $7 million) and took up residence on a 349-acre farm, formerly owned by Washington socialite and mover-and-shaker Pamela Harriman, near Middleburg in Loudoun County, Virginia. This was horse-farm country, extremely wealthy and almost all-white in its population. Johnson had to hire a hairstylist to make weekly trips from Washington, but she fit in quickly with her new community. "We have real neighbors who come over and bring warm breads and jams that they have made," Johnson enthused in the *Washington Post*. A few locals who had made veiled racial comments were won over when Johnson invited them to a letter-perfect hunt breakfast. Soon Johnson had the elaborate rituals of aristocratic Virginia country life down to a science.

Her massive fundraisers for local charities became legendary. To raise money for the Piedmont Environmental Council she organized a holiday ball that transformed an indoor horse track into a meticulously detailed winter scene, complete with falling snow, a performance by R&B greats Ashford & Simpson, and a snow queen gown for Johnson herself. A frequent guest at such events and at Johnson's Salamander Farm was her friend, Washington-based television weather personality Willard Scott.

One thing that drew Johnson to Loudoun County was the budding equestrian career of her daughter Paige, who trained six days a week on horseback and was considered a strong contender for a spot on the United States Olympic equestrian team. "I started to accumulate horses, then decided we needed our own place," Johnson told *Ebony*. Paige's involvement in the sport cost Johnson an estimated $1 million annually. Johnson became involved in horse show administration herself, and as president of the Washington International Horse Show she guided the event to its first-ever profit. Her younger son, Brett, also showed promise as an athlete.

Generously Gave Away Millions

Johnson's fundraising experiences had begun during her marriage, as she and her husband helped build the campaign war chests of President Bill Clinton. She gave $3 million to Middleburg's Hill School, a private institution her son attended, but she quickly expanded her philanthropic efforts beyond their local scope. She was invited to give a commencement speech at the State University of New York at Morrisville, a school with both a strong equestrian program and a large minority enrollment; after her highly motivational speech proved a rousing success, Johnson offered a $1 million gift. She followed that up with a $2 million gift to the financially struggling Bennett College, a historically black school in Greensboro, North Carolina, and in 2003 she gave $7 million to New York's Parsons School of Design; it was by far the largest gift the school had ever received.

Typically, Johnson had still bigger things in mind. She planned to create a foundation with $100 million in assets, and she met with Microsoft founder Bill Gates to discuss the administration of his multibillion-dollar Bill and Melinda Gates Foundation. On the income side of the ledger, Johnson announced plans for the Salamander Inn & Spa, a luxury resort to be built on a portion of her Loudoun County property. The only hint of conflict with her new neighbors came when local residents resisted the project even though Johnson had herself rescued Salamander Farm from tract development plans a few years earlier. Johnson won some people over with plans to serve local products at the resort's restaurant and at a planned Salamander Market in Middleburg.

Winning approval for the inn was an exacting process, with county officials questioning details right down to the thread count of the sheets to be used in guest rooms. But by mid-2004 the final hurdles in the path of the project seemed to have been cleared, and Sheila Crump Johnson was ready to add another item to her list of "firsts": she was the first African-American woman to build a luxury hotel. She continued to shape her children's educations and careers, exhibited and sold her photographs of Europe in local galleries, and supervised the staff of 25 who attended to the 13 buildings on Salamander Farm. And sometimes, when she staged or attended a fundraising event, she provided the music herself by bringing along her violin.

Sources

Periodicals

Chicago Sun-Times, June 9, 1999, p. 27.
Ebony, September 2003, p. 166.
Greensboro News Record (North Carolina), May 12, 2004, p. B1.
Jet, June 14, 2004, p. 24.
New York Times, May 8, 2003, p. B1.
Post-Standard (Syracuse, NY), November 3, 2003, p. B1.
Washington Post, May 26, 2002, p. F10; December 4, 2002, p. B1; February 2, 2004, p. E1; May 30, 2004, p. D3; September 26, 2004, Loudoun Extra, p. T3.

—James M. Manheim

John A. Kenney, Jr.

1914-2003

Dermatologist

John A. "Jack" Kenney Jr. was a distinguished dermatologist and pioneer in the study of skin diseases afflicting non-white populations. One of the first black doctors trained in dermatology, he was a prominent member of the dermatology department at Howard University's medical school for more than 40 years. Kenney became an inspirational figure to several generations of black medical professionals. His obituary in the *Washington Post* estimated that Kenney mentored or trained about a third of the 300 black dermatologists currently practicing in the United States.

Raised by Successful Parents

John Andrew Kenney, Jr. was born on October 8, 1914 in Tuskegee, Alabama, the eldest of four children born to Dr. John A. Kenney, Sr. and Frieda Armstrong Kenney. His father was also an extremely important figure in black medicine, an advocate both for black patients and medical professionals. The author of the groundbreaking 1912 book, *The Negro in Medicine*, he served as medical director and chief surgeon at the general hospital at the Tuskegee Institute. Kenney's mother, one of the first black women to graduate from Boston University, also taught at the Institute.

Kenney's father joined the Tuskegee Institute staff at the personal invitation of Booker T. Washington, the Institute's founder, and was the personal physician to both Washington and agricultural scientist George Washington Carver who, according to Kenney's obituary in the *Washington Post*, took the Kenney children on Sunday nature walks.

The family was forced to leave Tuskegee in 1923 as a result of Dr. Kenney Sr.'s attempts to get black doctors hired at the Tuskegee Veterans Administration Hospital, an institution built to serve black veterans of World War I. When the Ku Klux Klan threatened his life and burned a cross on the family's lawn: the Kenney family fled within 24 hours, moving north to Montclair, New Jersey. There they encountered the same lack of medical services for black patients and professional opportunities for black medical professionals. Kenney's father founded the first hospital for blacks in nearby Newark. Kenney Memorial Hospital opened in 1927, and Kenney donated the small private hospital to the black community of New Jersey on Christmas Eve, 1934.

Followed in Father's Footsteps

After graduating from Montclair High School, Kenney attended Bates College, a college founded in 1855 by Maine abolitionists. Kenney earned a double major in chemistry and biology, and was also president of his class during his senior year, and a frequent contributor to the *Garnet*, the Bates College literary magazine. Illness meant he had to withdraw from college for a period, graduating in 1942 instead of with the class of 1938 as anticipated. At Bates he won the William F. Manuel Award for the graduate who made the most significant progress in biology.

In 1945, Kenney received his medical degree from Howard University, a private black university founded

At a Glance . . .

Born on October 8, 1914, in Tuskegee, Alabama; died of heart failure on November 29, 2003, in Washington, DC; married Larcenia Ferne Wood, 1943 (died 2000); children: Frances, John Andrew, and Anne. *Education*: Bates College, BS, 1942; Howard University, MD, 1945.

Career: Howard Medical School, instructor in biochemistry, 1946-48; University of Pennsylvania School of Medicine, graduate training in dermatology and syphilology, 1949-50; University of Michigan Hospital, resident physician, dermatology, 1950-52; University of Michigan Medical School, research associate, 1952-53; Cleveland, Ohio, private practice, dermatology and syphilology, 1953-61; Case Western Reserve School of Medicine, assistant clinical professor in dermatology, 1956-61; Howard University College of Medicine, professor, chairman of department in dermatology, 1961-2001; U.S. Department of State, consultant; Washington D.C. Department of Corrections, consultant.

Selected memberships: American Academy of Dermatology; American Dermatological Association; Society for Investigative Dermatology; American Association for the Advancement of Science; Dermatology Foundation; Washington Dermatology Association; Social Hygiene Society of Metropolitan Washington.

Selected awards: William F. Manuel Award, 1942; Dermatology Foundation, Finnerwood Award, 1988; Master of Dermatology, 1995; Gold Medal of American Academy of Dermatology, 2001; Benjamin Elijah Mays Award, 2001.

---

in 1867, where he was inducted into the Alpha Omega Alpha and Kappa Pi honor societies. From 1947 to 1952, while completing his professional training, Kenney served as assistant editor of the *Journal of the National Medical Association*. Kenney's father had co-founded the association of black physicians at the end of the nineteenth century.

His younger brother, Howard, graduated from Bates in 1940 and ultimately became the medical director of Tuskegee's John A. Andrew Hospital. Another brother, Oscar, was one of the famous Tuskegee Airmen pilots, the group of volunteers who became America's first black military airmen. He was killed on active duty in 1943.

Specialized in the Study of Skin

It was at the Cleveland City Hospital, where Kenney interned from 1948 to 1949, that he was urged to train as a dermatologist, according to his Bates College obituary. "At that time," he said, in a 1975 interview in *Black Enterprise*, "dermatology was considered a 'Society' specialty area, with only well-to-do whites going for treatments. When blacks sought service from a dermatologist, they were usually not treated well or not treated at all."

He continued his professional training in dermatology at the University of Pennsylvania and at the University of Michigan, where, according to *African American Firsts in Science and Technology*, he was the first black resident in dermatology. His Bates College obituary recalls that, at Michigan, Kenney often encountered problems acquiring sufficient samples of black skin for his experiments, and was forced to drive into Detroit to retrieve amputated limbs. Once he even resorted to using his own skin for research.

After working for five years on the faculty of Case Western Reserve University as an assistant clinical professor of dermatology, he returned to the faculty of medicine at Howard University in 1961. He was to remain part of the Howard University faculty for 40 years, chairing the dermatology department for almost half that time and overseeing the university's development into a major research center.

Founded Discipline of Ethnic Dermatology

When Kenney arrived at Howard, he discovered the department was extremely underfunded: it was a year before he got his own telephone line, according to the Bates College Web site. Kenney established the Department of Dermatology Postgraduate Training in 1963. Initially the program comprised two years of training, but by 1968 Kenney received approval for a fully accredited three-year residency program. When he began work at Howard, the department was still a division of internal medicine. By 1973, Kenney had managed to create a separate department of dermatology.

Kenney soon established a reputation as a leading researcher, publishing numerous academic articles on conditions such as vitiligo, a pigmentation disease that causes white blotches on skin, and establishing black dermatology as a medical specialty. "He was known nationally as a founder of the discipline known as ethnic dermatology, which is the study of skin diseases in nonwhite populations," said Dr. Rebat Halder, chairman of Howard's dermatology department, as quoted in the *New York Times*. "The manifestations, symptoms and treatments of many skin disorders are different in black populations, and his career was devoted to research and clinical efforts in those areas."

In recognition of his achievements, Kenney was offered prominent positions in a number of organizations, including the presidency of the National Medical Association from 1962 to 1963. Kenney was the first black member of the American Dermatology Association, to which he was admitted in 1970. From 1971 to 1973 he served as the first black board member of the American Academy of Dermatology. He was also a trustee of the Dermatology Foundation, president of the Washington Dermatology Association from 1969 to 1970, and president of the Social Hygiene Society of Metropolitan Washington from 1971 to 1972.

Advised Author of Soul Sister

In 1968, white journalist Grace Halsell approached Kenney for medical advice. Inspired by John Howard Griffin's *Black Like Me*, Halsell wanted to turn herself black with medication in order to experience life as a black person. Dr. Aaron Lerner at the Yale University Medical Center, referred her to John A. Kenney for advice. "It was one of my most unusual medical requests," he told *Black Enterprise*. In her book, *Soul Sister*, which describes her experiences living as a black woman in Mississippi and Harlem, Halsell recalled Kenney as "a fair-skinned Negro, intensely serious, with a kind expression in his eyes." He agreed to help her "both as your doctor and your friend," providing Halsell with emergency medical treatment on one occasion early in the experiment when she suffered severe burns to her feet.

When Halsell died in 2000, she left a gift of $800,000 gift to Howard University's School of Communications for scholarships to journalism students. Her estate's representative, Robert Norberg, told the university that Halsell never forgot Dr. Kenney's kind guidance when she was writing *Soul Sister*. He told *HBCU News* that the "association [with Kenney] was one of the major factors in her mind when she decided during the final year of her life to leave the bulk of her estate to Howard University."

Kenney received honorary degrees from Howard in 1987 and from Bates in 1988. He also maintained close ties with his first college, Bates, serving twenty-three years as a Bates Trustee and winning, in 2001, the Benjamin Elijah Mays Award for extraordinary contributions to society and the college. Jamie P. Merisotis, a Past President of Bates' Alumni Council, described Kenney as an "example of the Hippocratic Oath, the highest standards associated with being a role model, steadfast, a real teacher, authoritative yet compassionate." Kenney's colleagues and students, he said, used "a word seldom heard these days in describing an individual: 'noble.'"

Numerous honors distinguished Kenney's last years, including the Finnerwood Award of the Dermatology Foundation in 1988, of which he was the first black recipient. He became a director of the American Academy of Dermatology, which named him a master of dermatology, one of the highest honors in the field, in 1995 and awarded him its gold medal in 2001.

He continued to practice medicine until he was 85. A sought-after lecturer on international circuits, he also served as a consultant to the U.S. State Department and the Washington D.C. Department of Corrections, holding weekly clinics for 29 years. He died after heart failure at the age of 89 on November 29, 2003, at his home in Washington. His wife, Larcenia Ferne Wood, whom he married in 1943, died in 2000. John Kenney was survived by his two daughters, Frances Wood Kenney Moseley and Anne Kenney, and his son, John A. Kenney III. The numerous doctors and researchers he mentored remember him by the nickname—"the dean of black dermatology"—that suggests the stature he achieved in his profession.

Selected writings

Books

(Editor, with William Montagna and Giuseppe Prota) *Black Skin: Structure and Function*, Academic Press, 1993.

Periodicals

"Vitiligo Treated by Psoralen: a Long-Term Follow-Up Study of the Permanency of Repigmentation," *Archives of Dermatology,* No. 103, 1971.
(With others) "Determination of Trimethylpsoralen in Blood, Ophthalmic Fluids, and Skin," *Journal of Investigative Dermatology,* Vol. 79, No. 6, December 1982.
"Black Dermatology," *Cutis*, 32, 1983.
(With P.E. Grimes) "Should Vitiligo Be Treated?" *Cutis*, 32, 1983.
"Experiences of a Black in Dermatology," *Journal of the American Academy of Dermatology,* 2, 1986.
"Pigmentary Disorders in Black Skin," *Clinical Dermatology*, Vol. 7, 1989.

Sources

Books

Halsell, Grace, *Soul Sister*, World Publishing Company, 1969.
Webster, Raymond B., *African American Firsts in Science and Technology*, Gale Group, 1999.

Periodicals

Black Enterprise, February 1975, pp. 26-27.
Jet, January 5, 2004, p. 16.
New York Times, December 6, 2003, Sec. C, p. 16.
Washington Post, Sunday, December 7, 2003, Sec. C, p. 12.

On-line

"Bates Reunion 2001," *Bates College*, www.bates.edu/x13979.xml (October 23, 2004).

"The Benjamin Elijah Mays Award," *Bates College*, www.bates.edu/alumni-reunion-awards.xml (October 25, 2004).

"Department of Dermatology," *Howard University*, www.howard.edu/huh-gme/programs/Dermatology.htm (October 20, 2004).

"Howard Receives Journalism Bequest," *HBCU News*, www.facultyvoice.com/News/news2001/10-October/October%20829.html, (October 14, 2004).

"John A. Kenney, Jr.," *Bates College*, http://abacus.bates.edu/pubs/mag/96-Summer/kenney.html (October 8, 2004).

"Old Newark Hospitals, Homes and Orphanages," *Old Newark*, www.oldnewark.com/hospitals/kenney.htm (October 8, 2004).

"The Stories of Alumni Lives," *Bates College*, www.bates.edu/x57002.xml (October 25, 2004).

—Paula J.K. Morris

Georges Laraque

1976—

Professional hockey player

Georges Laraque is the first black hockey player from French Canada to play in the National Hockey League (NHL). From Montreal, Quebec, he was drafted in 1995 by the Edmonton Oilers. Working as his team's enforcer, Laraque is charged with retaliating against anyone who tries to intimidate with his teammates, which sometimes leads to him dropping his gloves to brawl with opponents. Such actions naturally lead Laraque to a significant amount of time in the penalty box. But his ability to take on opponents on the ice, combined with his gregarious personality off the ice, has made him a crowd favorite.

Laraque, Georges, photograph. Jeff Vinnick/Getty Images.

Refused to Quit

Laraque was born on December 7, 1976, in Montreal, Quebec. He grew up in Tracy, a small community outside Montreal. His family included his parents and his brother and sister. Laraque began skating when he was five years old and grew up idolizing Mario Lemieux and Wayne Gretzky. While playing minor hockey as a youngster, Laraque was continually besieged with racist remarks from both players and spectators. Although his parents begged him to give up the game because the environment was so hostile, Laraque refused to quit. "I loved hockey so much," he told the *National Hockey League* Web site. "I couldn't quit even though the kids would say the N-word and tell me this wasn't my sport so I couldn't play. It wasn't right so I used it as motivation. I kept playing to show them they were wrong. In my mind, if I had quit, that would have proved they were right."

Finally, when he was fourteen, his father moved the family into the more racially diverse city of Montreal, which became a turning point for Laraque's game. First, he found a more open and accepting environment in which to play, and second, he began to mature into one of the biggest players on the ice. He was drafted into the junior ranks. Although his size worked to his advantage in some instances, it didn't make him the most agile player on the ice. In 1993 he began skating for the St.-Jean Lynx, and when he realized the gap in his abilities compared to the other players on the ice, he briefly considered giving up hockey to pursue a football scholarship in the United States. However, his love of hockey prevailed, and his footwork improved

> **At a Glance . . .**
>
> Born on December 7, 1976, in Montreal, Quebec. Religion: Catholic.
>
> **Career:** Professional hockey player, 1995–.
>
> **Address:** *Office*—Edmonton Oilers, 11230-110 Street, Edmonton, Alberta T5G 3H7, Canada.

after he spent the summer of 1994 working on power skating under the direction of Montreal Canadiens coach Claude Ruel.

During his first season with the St.-Jean Lynx, Laraque scored 22 goals. In 1994 he logged 19 goals and 22 assists in 62 games—as well as 259 minutes in penalties. Growing to six-foot, three-inches and 230 pounds, with good hockey skills, Laraque became a serious prospect for professional hockey teams, especially as an enforcer-type player who could create offensive opportunities for other players and punish opponents on the boards. In 1995 Laraque was drafted into the NHL, selected in the second round as the thirty-first pick overall by the Edmonton Oilers.

Joined the Edmonton Oilers

Laraque joined Oilers training camp in September of 1995. His first practices on the ice with "all the guys I used to watch on TV," Laraque admitted to *SportsLine,* made him feel "intimidated." Because Laraque was just nineteen years old, the Oilers decided to season him in the junior leagues for another year, and for the following two seasons he played in the minor leagues for the Hamilton Bulldogs in the American Hockey League. During the 1997-98 he was called up to the Oilers for 11 games, which gave him a taste for the majors and motivation to work hard to earn a permanent place on the team. During his stint with the Oilers, Laraque took four shots on goal, scored no points, and logged 59 penalty minutes.

When Laraque, who expected to be called up by the Oilers for the 1998-99 season, got cut before the season even started, he became even more determined to prove himself in the minors. The team's management took notice and just after Christmas in 1998, he joined the Oilers, where he has remained. Almost immediately Laraque began forming his reputation as the league's new enforcer. "It took all of 30 seconds for the towering 6-foot-3, 230 pound winger to stake his claim as the Edmonton Oilers' newest regulator," the *Oilers Zone* reported after Laraque's appearance on March 4, 1999. "He rained down about 30 punches on [Buffalo's Rob] Ray, finally ending the one-sided pummeling by body slamming his Buffalo counterpart to the ice."

In the second half of the 1998-99 season Laraque appeared in 39 games, scoring three goals and two assists. During the 1999-2000 season, his first full season with the Oilers, he appeared in 75 games, in which he scored eight goals and had eight assists, and his reputation as a fighter continued to grow. Known off the ice for his outgoing, friendly personality, on the ice, Laraque refused to back down from any challenge. "As soon as the puck drops, you get so much focus. It's like I change," he told the *Globe and Mail* in 2000, "I become more mean. And then when the game is over, I love everybody. That's the way I am."

Re-signed with Oilers

The 2000-01 season got off to a rocky start when Laraque found himself in the midst of stalled contract negotiations. Laraque wanted a big bump up in salary, and the Oilers wanted him to sign a three-year, rather than two-year, contract. Eventually, in midnight talks, Laraque agreed to the longer contract and the Oilers agreed to more money. The result was a three-year deal worth $2.7 million, and Laraque was given more playing time to prove his worth. He responded by scoring 13 goals and handing out 16 assists in 82 games for a career-high 29 points.

At the beginning of the 2001-02 season Laraque predicted that he would have 20-20-20 (goals, assists, and fights) season. However, instead he hit a scoring drought and struggled to meet the weight limit of 255 pounds set by his coach Craig MacTavish, who once sent the winger home from practice for being too heavy. "I gain 20 pounds just looking at a steak," Laraque told the *Edmonton Journal.* "My metabolism is bad." Despite his bold predictions, he held to just five goals for the season. He did, however, manage to get into 25 fights. Although he remained one of the most popular players among fans, Laraque longed to be more than a fighter. "You're not involved," he explained to the *Edmonton Sun.* "You're just watching everybody else. And when you lose a game you know there's nothing you could have done. All you do is fight."

Despite dropping 20 pounds in the off season, Laraque's season started off shaky in the fall of 2002. After suffering several injuries that hampered his play early in the season, in late November he wrecked his BMW in a collision with another car. Although he was not badly injured, the traumatic event added to a litany of things that had gone wrong that year. In December Laraque lacerated his elbow, requiring 15 stitches, and just after returning to the ice from that injury, he was hurt again when his face met up with an opponent's skate, requiring another 16 stitches in his lip and nose. Then, in January, Laraque was sidelined once more, this time with a knee injury requiring arthroscopic surgery. At the end of the season, Laraque had played in 64 games, scored six goals and seven assists, had 14 fights, and spent a total of 110 minutes in the penalty box.

At the beginning of the 2003-04 season, Laraque re-signed with the Oilers, putting ink to a three-year contract worth $4.1 million. However, once again hampered by injuries, Laraque was unable to break through as a highly productive offensive player, scoring just 6 goals with 11 assists in 66 games. He did, however, lead his team in penalty minutes with 99 minutes in the box. With two years remaining on his contract, Laraque still has plenty of punch in his game and his fists.

In 2003 Laraque began hosting his own radio program, "The Georges Laraque Biggest Hits Radio Show" on Edmonton's Power 92.5 FM. Airing on Saturday mornings, the show features a weekly countdown and entertainment news. Laraque also enjoys being involved in the community, volunteers for numerous charities, and hopes to serve as a role model to young people. He explained to the *Edmonton Sun,* "I know that because of the position I'm in, people, especially kids, will listen to me.... So if I made all the right decisions, then they'll want to make the same decisions that I made." After years of honing his tough-guy reputation on the ice, off the ice Laraque is anything but the rough-and-tumble type. Charismatic and outgoing, he is one of the most popular athletes in Edmonton.

Sources

Periodicals

Alberta Report, April 5, 1999.
Globe and Mail (Toronto), April 18, 2000.
Edmonton Journal, May 13, 2000; December 27, 2001; December 28, 2001; February 4, 2002; April 4, 2002; October 24, 2002; November 11, 2002; November 30, 2002; December 12, 2002; August 7, 2003.
Edmonton Sun, September 9, 2000; January 14, 2002; October 10, 2002; October 12, 2002; January 15, 2002; February 28, 2002; April 15, 2003; August 7, 2003; September 20, 2003; October, 2, 2003.
Oilers Zone, March 24, 1999; March 19, 2001.
Sports Illustrated for Kids, March 1, 2001.
Vancouver Sun, September 25, 2002.

On-line

"The Edmonton Oilers' Right-Winger on Playing and Web Surfing," *National Hockey League,* www.nhl.com/kids/futures02.html (October 20, 2004).
"Georges Laraque," *SportsLine,* http://cbs.sportsline.com/nhl/players/playerpage/19972 (October 20, 2004).
"Georges Laraque," *National Hockey League,* www.nhl.com/lineups/player/8462060.html (October 20, 2004).
Georges Laraque, www.georgeslaraque.com (October 20, 2004).

—Kari Bethel

Risa Lavizzo-Mourey

1954—

Physician

A specialist in geriatrics, Dr. Risa Lavizzo-Mourey has made significant contributions to health care policy in the United States. In addition to maintaining a clinical practice and a teaching career, she has served on numerous committees and has advised the federal government on health care reform. In 2003 she assumed leadership of the country's largest health care philanthropy, the Robert Wood Johnson Foundation, which distributes more than $500 million annually to agencies and programs that focus on public health issues. In 2003 *Modern Physician* named Lavizzo-Mourey one of 25 "visionary doctors...who rattle the status quo by flexing their experience and reputations in a variety of disciplines—politics, quality, information technology, public health, philanthropy and business."

Parents Sparked Interest in Medical Career

Lavizzo-Mourey, who grew up in Seattle, credits her parents with nurturing her interest in becoming a doctor. "I was blessed to have two parents who were physicians," she told *Chronicle of Philanthropy* writer Domenica Marchetti, "so I grew up seeing what an incredible opportunity it is to be a physician." She also learned that there is a "tremendous need" for health care among underserved populations, including uninsured and low-income groups. "I saw that very clearly in my parents' practice," she recalled to Marchetti, "when they were practicing in fairly poor neighborhoods in the time before Medicare."

After one year at the University of Washington, Lavizzo-Mourey attended the State University of New York at Stony Brook. She was admitted to Harvard Medical School after completing her junior year of college, and received her M.D. in 1979. After completing her internship and residency in internal medicine at Brigham and Women's Hospital in Boston, she did additional training in geriatrics at the University of Pennsylvania School of Medicine. There she also completed postgraduate research as a Robert Wood Johnson Clinical Scholar. She joined the university's medical school faculty in 1986. While pursuing an ambitious academic career, Lavizzo-Mourey also earned an M.B.A. in health care administration from the University of Pennsylvania's Wharton School.

Lavizzo-Mourey held several distinguished positions at the University of Pennsylvania. She began as an assistant professor, rose to associate professor, and was later named the Sylvan Eisman Professor of Medicine and Health Care Systems. She also served as director of the university's Institute on Aging, and was chief of geriatric medicine at the medical school.

Advised Government on Health Care Policies

In 1992 Lavizzo-Mourey took a leave of absence from the University of Pennsylvania to join the Federal Agency for Health Care Policy and Research (now the Agency for Health Care Quality), where she served as deputy director until 1994. She also served on other federal advisory committees, including the Task Force of Aging Research, the National Committee for Vital and Health Statistics, and the Institute of Medicine's Panel on Disease and Disability Prevention among

At a Glance...

Born on September 25, 1954, in Seattle, WA; daughter of Philip V. Lavizzo and Blanche Sellers Lavizzo, both physicians; married Robert J. Mourey, a physician, June 21, 1975; children: Rel, Max. *Education:* University of Washington, 1972-73; State University of New York-Stony Brook, 1973-75; Harvard Medical School, MD, 1979; Wharton School, University of Pennsylvania, MBA, 1986.

Career: Brigham and Women's Hospital, Boston, MA, medical resident, 1979-82; Temple University Medical School, Philadelphia, PA, clinical instructor, 1982-84; University of Pennsylvania School of Medicine, assistant professor of medicine, 1986-92, associate professor, 1992-97, Sylvan Eisman Professor of Medicine, 1997-2001, director of the Institute of Aging, chief of Division of Geriatric Medicine, 1984-1992, 1994-2001; Philadelphia Veterans Administration Medical Center, associate chief of staff; Agency for Health Care Policy and Research, Rockville, MD, deputy administrator, 1992-94; Robert Wood Johnson Foundation, Princeton, NJ, senior vice president and director, Health Care Group, 2001-2002, president and chief executive officer, 2003–.

Memberships: Association of Academic Minority Physicians; National Medical Association.

Awards: University of Pennsylvania, Class of 1970 Term Professor, 1992; American College of Physicians, fellowship; American Geriatric Society, fellowship; Alonzo Smythe Yerby Award, 2002.

Addresses: *Office*—P.O. Box 2316, College Road East and Route 1, Princeton, NJ 0853-2316.

Older Adults. As a member of the White House Task Force on Health Care Reform, Lavizzo-Mourey chaired the working group on Quality of Care.

Among her particular concerns is the delivery of quality medical care to minority populations. In 2002 she coauthored an Institute of Medicine report, "Unequal Treatment: Confronting Racial and Ethnic Disparities in Health Care," that found that minorities are likely to receive lower-quality medical care than whites, regardless of income. In fact, evidence showed that this tendency occurs even when medical insurance, age, and the extent of the disease were comparable across race and ethnicities. According to *Harvard Public Health Now*, the report showed that "evidence suggests that bias, prejudice, and stereotyping by health care providers may contribute to differences in care."

Indeed, Lavizzo-Mourey herself had been treated dismissively when she brought her daughter, then aged two, to a hospital emergency room in Philadelphia. Though the child had symptoms that Lavizzo-Mourey knew to be serious, the resident physician who examined her said that the child was not ill. Only after Lavizzo-Mourey asserted her own medical training and demanded more tests did it become evident that the child had pneumonia. Such treatment, Lavizzo-Mourey stated in remarks quoted in *Health Leaders*, "is really very troubling" and must be addressed.

Became Head of Nation's Largest Health Philanthropy

In 2001 Lavizzo-Mourey became senior vice president of the Robert Wood Johnson Foundation. This organization had funded her earlier postgraduate research and, according to a *Health Leaders* article, had watched her career with increasing respect. As vice president, Lavizzo-Mourey took charge of the foundation's grant making in health care, much of which focused on treating and preventing substance abuse and improving care for patients with chronic illnesses. Upon the retirement of foundation head Steven Schroeder, Lavizzo-Mourey became president and chief executive officer of the foundation in January of 2003. She is the first woman to hold this position.

In an interview in the *Journal of the American Medical Association (JAMA)*, Lavizzo-Mourey noted that she has been interested in the "interface between public policy, clinical medicine, and business" since her days as a medical student. The expertise in this area that she gained while earning her Wharton School M.B.A. in health care administration, she observed, positioned her to become an effective consultant on public health policy. As an advisor to both the first Bush administration and the Clinton administration, she learned how to create effective cooperation across different agencies and how to set realistic expectations.

Lavizzo-Mourey told *JAMA* that the Robert Wood Johnson Foundation would continue to focus on its four "bedrock goals—ensuring access to quality care; improving the quality of care and support of people with chronic health conditions; reducing the harm caused by substance abuse; and promoting healthy communities and lifestyles." She outlined a plan to distribute funds through a portfolio system that would allow the foundation to evaluate programs more effectively, and also noted that the foundation's efforts to improve public health systems would help to strengthen their ability to respond to possible biological or chemical weapons attacks.

While continuing with the foundation's basic work, Lavizzo-Mourey also hopes to expand efforts in several areas, including programs to meet needs of elderly patients; programs to address obesity; and measures to eliminate unequal treatment due to race or ethnicity. Her vision, she told *JAMA*, is that "everyone in this country has access to safe, effective, equitable health care when they need it, and that everyone gets a good start in life with a nurturing relationship that protects them from harm, including things like tobacco, alcohol, and drugs. That everyone has an opportunity for lifelong vitality, an opportunity for treatment if they are addicted, and that we promote a caring society and we keep our attention focused on the possible."

Sources

Periodicals

Chronicle of Philanthropy, August 8, 2002.
Journal of the American Medical Association (JAMA), April 16, 2003, pp. 1909-1911.
Modern Healthcare, August 5, 2002, p. 33.
Modern Physician, May 1, 2003, p. 26.

On-line

"Profile: Giving Spirit," *Health Leaders,* www.healthleaders.com (September 14, 2004).

"Risa Lavizzo-Mourey Named Head of the Robert Wood Johnson Foundation," *Wharton Health Care Management Alumni*, www.whartonhealthcare.org (September 14, 2004).

"Risa Lavizzo-Mourey: President and CEO," *Robert Wood Johnson Foundation,* www.rwjf.org (September 14, 2004).

"Lavizzo-Mourey Receives 2002 Yerby Award," *Harvard Public Health Now*, www.hsph.harvard.edu (September 14, 2004).

—E. Shostak

Thomas Mensah

1950—

Scientist, entrepreneur

Ghanaian-born materials scientist Thomas Mensah has had a high-flying career, first as a scientist and then as an entrepreneur. Mensah has at least 14 patents to his name, has edited two books and authored several articles, and has been involved with several of the fastest-growing fields in engineering, notably fiber optics and superconductor technology. Late in his career Mensah attempted to turn his theoretical knowledge into moneymaking enterprises, but his efforts ran up against some of the obstacles that face scholars who plunge into the hard world of finance facts and figures. He has an impressive record of accomplishment as one of the few blacks, and even fewer Africans, to excel at the highest levels of science.

Thomas O. Mensah was born in Kumasi, Ghana, in 1950. He attended school in his home country up to the undergraduate level, receiving a degree in chemical engineering from the University of Science and Technology, Kumasi (now known as the Kwame Nkrumah University of Science and Technology) in 1974. In addition to his scientific prowess, his facility with foreign languages helped set him on the path to international prominence. In the Ghanaian capital of Accra, he won the country's national French-language competition twice, at two different levels, in 1968 and 1970.

Studied in France and the United States

Those awards helped Mensah win a French government fellowship in 1974 for studies in chemical engineering at Montpellier University in France. He received a Ph.D. there in 1978. Equally fluent in English, he had already completed a program at the prestigious Massachusetts Institute of Technology and received a Certificate in Modeling of Chemical Processes in 1977. Settling in the United States, Mensah took a job at Air Products and Chemicals in Allentown, Pennsylvania, from 1980 to 1983.

Mensah's jobs in the 1980s were well suited to his strengths in basic research. From 1983 to 1986 he worked for Corning Glass Works in its fiber optics research division in Sullivan Park, New York. There he devised a new and faster method of accomplishing a fiber optics manufacturing procedure, the draw and coating process, that brought him four patents. In 1986 he joined AT&T Bell Laboratories in Georgia, part of a group of facilities that had long been one of the leading research enterprises in the United States. His work there centered on fiber optic reels that could be used at supersonic speeds in the U.S. military's guided missile program. Mensah realized several more patents from his work in the field of missile technology.

Fiber optics, the transmission of light through materials configured as cables, was a key technology of the 1980s and 1990s, underlying many of the revolutions in communications and computer technology that led to the rise of personal computing and the Internet. In 1987 Mensah edited *Fiber Optics Engineering: Processing and Applications,* a collection of cutting-edge articles detailing the latest research in the field. The second collection of articles Mensah edited,

At a Glance...

Born 1950 in Kumasi, Ghana. *Education:* University of Science and Technology, Kumasi, undergraduate degree, 1974; Massachusetts Institute of Technology, Certificate in Modeling of Chemical Processes, 1977; University of Montpellier, France, PhD, 1978.

Career: Air Products and Chemicals, Allentown, PA, engineer, 1980-83; Corning Glass Works, Sullivan Park, NY, engineer, 1983-86; AT&T Bell Laboratories, Atlanta, engineer, 1986-early 1990s; Supercond Technology, Norcross, GA, founder and president; Georgia Aerospace Systems Manufacturing, Atlanta, GA, president, early 2000s-.

Awards: Featured in 100 Black Achievers in Science and Technology and Black Inventors traveling exhibits.

Memberships: American Institute of Chemical Engineers.

Address: *Office*—Georgia Aerospace Systems Manufacturing, Suite 340, 75 Piedmont Ave., Atlanta, GA 30303.

Superconductor Engineering (1992), also pertained to a hot scientific area; superconductors are materials that exhibit no resistance to electricity when placed in extreme temperature environments. "The application of superconductivity in modern society can revolutionize everything from high-speed computing to magnetically levitated high-speed trains," Mensah wrote in his introduction to the book.

Pioneered Technology Applied During Gulf War

Mensah's fiber optics innovations played a role in the successful use of new missile technology that helped the United States to a quick victory in the 1991 Gulf War. He continued to add to his professional reputation as the first African American to become the national chairman of the Materials and Engineering Sciences Division of the American Institute of Chemical Engineers (AIChE) and as a member of an MIT advisory board. He was also a founding member of the AIChE's Emerging Technologies area. With these impressive credentials, Mensah had no problem finding investors when he moved to set up a company of his own, Supercond Technologies of Norcross, Georgia, in 1992.

The company had discussions with Lockheed, an aircraft manufacturer, about supplying materials for the company's new F-22 fighter bomber. But Mensah aimed at non-defense products as well. As U.S. defense spending dropped following the end of the Cold War in the early 1990s, a host of companies, including Supercond, vied for opportunities to apply military technology to civilian enterprises, with what they hoped would be lucrative results. The company promoted an extra-strong composite material it had developed, hoping to interest manufacturers of such items as stadium seats and waste containers. "I think that many companies, even small ones, should be able to come up with dual-purpose ideas that served a defense need but have a market elsewhere," Mensah told the *Atlanta Journal and Constitution*.

The approaching 1996 Atlanta Olympics helped get Supercond off to a good start. The company partnered with the Oak Ridge National Laboratory in Tennessee to try to develop "smart" materials for roadway design that would allow traffic monitoring during the Games, and Mensah also hoped to use fiber-optic technology to develop new video devices that could be used in the massive Olympic logistics enterprise. "Lots of ideas are floating about out there, but what I found impressive about Supercond was that it already has assembled seed capital and is now at work on a sequence of products to provide working capital," commented *Atlanta Journal and Constitution* writer Ernest Holsendolph.

Featured in Traveling Exhibitions

Mensah won several public honors for his work. He was featured in a traveling exhibit showcasing the accomplishments of 100 black scientists and engineers, as well as in an internationally exhibited display called *Black Inventors*. Black-oriented websites began to mention the African-born black scientist who had helped the United States win the Gulf War. By the early 2000s, however, financial troubles had driven Supercond from business.

Mensah bounced back as president of a new company, Georgia Aerospace Systems Manufacturing, which was headquartered in Atlanta. Georgia Aerospace announced plans to purchase a vacant building in Warner Robins, Georgia, and to hire 200 people trained in cooperation with local educational institutions. By late 2003, however, the deal had not yet been completed, and Georgia Aerospace had missed a deadline for the use of local bond money in financing the project. As of 2004, Mensah was listed as a contributor to the Robins Air Force Base 21st Century Partnership fund, and Georgia Aerospace was continuing to solicit clients as U.S. defense spending once again ramped up. It is yet to be seen whether Mensah will manage to place himself with a company capable of utilizing his ample talents in science and engineering.

Selected writings

(Editor, with Pundi L. Narasimham) *Fiber Optics Engineering: Processing and Applications,* American Institute of Chemical Engineers, 1987.

(Editor) *Superconductor Engineering,* American Institute of Chemical Engineers, 1992.

Sources

Periodicals

Atlanta Journal and Constitution, August 7, 1992, p. F1; February 16, 1994, p. F1.

Macon Telegraph, April 16, 2002; July 11, 2002; September 13, 2003, Houston/Peach ed., p. A1.

On-line

"ORNL Joins Supercond to Develop a Traffic Monitoring System for 1996 Olympics," *Oak Ridge National Laboratory Press Release,* http://www.ornl.gov/press_releases/get_press_release.cfm?ReleaseNumber=olympics (October 10, 2004).

"Thomas Mensah," *GhanaWeb,* http://www.ghanaweb.com/GhanaHomePage/people/pop-up.php?ID=165 (October 10, 2004).

—James M. Manheim

Azie Taylor Morton

1936-2003

Treasurer of the United States, civil servant

Azie Taylor Morton is distinguished as the only African American ever to hold the post of Treasurer of the United States. Appointed by President Jimmy Carter on September 12, 1977, Morton served as the United States' 36th Treasurer until January 20, 1981. Along with the Secretary of the Treasury, the Treasurer must sign Federal Reserve notes before they can become legal tender, thus Morton's signature was on U.S. currency for three years. Her work as U.S. Treasurer was preceded by many years of public service, and her upstanding character and giving spirit are well known in her Texas community. In spite of an underprivileged childhood, Morton's amazing accomplishments along with her gracious spirit give hope to those less fortunate. "It isn't luck, and it isn't circumstances, and it isn't being born a certain way that causes a person's future to become what it becomes," Morton said in the book *Chicken Soup for the Soul at Work*. Her life's work is a strong testimony to her belief that a person can accomplish anything they set their mind to.

Azie Taylor was born on February 1, 1936, in Dale, Texas, to Fleta Hazel Taylor. Morton said in a speech to the student body of a small college in South Carolina (as quoted in *Chicken Soup for the Soul at Work*), "I was born to a mother who was deaf and could not speak. I do not know who my father is or was. The first job I ever had was in a cotton field." Morton was raised by her maternal grandparents, and because there was no high school for African Americans in Dale, she attended high school at a charity-sponsored school for black children in Austin called the Texas Blind, Deaf, and Orphan School. She graduated there at the age of 16 with high grades, and enrolled at Huston-Tillotson, an all-black college in Austin, where she graduated cum laude with a Bachelor of Science degree in commercial education in 1956. Although she applied to graduate school at the University of Texas, her admission was denied on the grounds that she did not have enough undergraduate courses. Her admission was then denied for the undergraduate courses she needed based on Texas University's policy of not allowing African Americans into its undergraduate programs. In spite of this emotional setback, Azie began a fulfilling and successful forty-five year career. "Nothing has to remain the way it is if that's not the way a person wants it to be," Morton was quoted in *Chicken Soup for the Soul at Work*.

Morton spent a short time teaching at a state-supported school for delinquent girls after she graduated from college in 1956. After this, she returned to her alma mater to serve as assistant to the president of the college for a short time. In 1957 she applied and was hired as a staff member for the new Texas AFL-CIO, a major labor union. She later moved to Washington to serve on President John F. Kennedy's Committee on Equal Employment Opportunity, beginning twenty years of service in the public sector that culminated with her appointment in 1977 as Treasurer of the United States. As Treasurer, Morton was responsible for the receipt and custody of government funds.

Morton also served on several important foreign affairs committees during her political career. She was a member of the American Delegation to Rome for the

At a Glance . . .

Born Azie Taylor on February 1, 1936, in Dale, TX; died December 7, 2003; married James Homer Morton, 1956; children: Virgie Floyd and Stacey Hurst. *Education:* Huston-Tillotson College, Austin, TX, BS, commercial education, 1956.

Career: Huston-Tillotson College, Austin, TX, assistant to the president, 1957; Texas AFL-CIO, staff, 1957; Committee on Equal Employment Opportunity, Washington, D.C., various positions, 1957-77; Treasurer of the United States 1977-1981.

Selected Memberships: American Delegation to Rome, Italy, for the Enthronement of Pope John Paul II; People to People Mission to the Soviet Union and China, chair; First African-American Conference in Africa, representative; National Democratic Institute, board member; Citizens Fund, board of trustees, 1991-2001; Austin Housing Authority, board of commissioners, 1999-2001.

Enthronement of Pope John Paul II, and chair of a People to People Mission to the Soviet Union and China. She was also an Election Observer for the Presidential elections in Haiti, Senegal, and the Dominican Republic, and a representative to the first African/African American Conference held in Africa.

At home, Morton served on the Austin Housing Authority Board of Commissioners (HACA) from 1999 to 2001. On the PRWeb Web site, James L. Hargrove, Executive Director of HACA said that Morton "was a leading voice in the push for awarding scholarships to low-income residents." Consequently, the HACA set up the Azie Taylor Morton Scholarship Fund after her death, donating $5,000 in her name to provide scholarships for low-income students attending Huston-Tillotson College. Through this scholarship Morton will be remembered as a person who worked across racial, religious, and ethnic lines, and loved working with young people. In the *Austin American-Statesman* newspaper, Lavon Marshall, friend and colleague of Morton, said, "She tried to share with them her hardships growing up and tried to encourage them to do better."

In addition to her political career, Morton was one of the directors for a company called HIV-VAC, a Nevada corporation that conducts HIV research. She also served on the Citizens Fund Board of trustees for ten years, from 1991-2001, including five years as chair. At the time of her death, she was manager of Ram Bookstore, an independent store that served Huston-Tillotson students. She was president of Exeter Capital Asset Management Co., and a member of Schlotzsky's Deli board of directors. She had also previously served on the boards of Wendy's Old Fashioned Hamburgers, St. Edward's University, the National Democratic Institute, and Austin Children's Museum. "She was a no-nonsense kind of woman but at the same time a caring woman," said Texas state representative Dawnna Dukes in the *Austin American-Statesman*. "She taught you that you could be a woman and an African American and succeed regardless of the obstacles before you."

Azie Taylor married James Homer Morton on May 29, 1965. The couple had two daughters, Virgie Floyd and Stacey Hurst, who later brought them two granddaughters and three great-grandchildren. James Homer Morton died in January of 2003. Morton's daughter Stacey recalled in a prize-winning essay posted on the Soulciti Web site that her mother used to invite students into their home who were unable to spend holidays with their families, and to provide furniture, clothing, and gifts to students who could not afford them. She did all of these good deeds, and "asks for nothing in return," her daughter wrote. "My father passed away in January 2003," Stacey says, "and she has suffered the loss of her life companion of 37 years. In the midst of the mourning, she is managing to financially support the weddings of both my sister and myself—within the same year—despite the loss of financial support provided from my father." Azie Taylor Morton passed away only months after her husband, on December 7, 2003 from complications of a stroke.

Sources

Books

Chicken Soup for the Soul at Work, Health Communications, 1996.

Periodicals

Austin American-Statesman, December 9, 2003.

On-line

"Azie Taylor Morton, 1936-2003," *soulciti*, http://soulciti.com/morton (September 25, 2004).

"The Housing Authority of the City of Austin Dedicates Scholarship for Low-Income Students to Azie Taylor Morton," *PRWeb*, www.prweb.com/releases/2004/7/prweb145217.htm (September 26, 2004).

—Cheryl Dudley

Andrea Nelson Meigs

1968—

Motion picture talent agent

Nelson Meigs, Andrea, photograph. Courtesy of Andrea Nelson Meigs.

Named in 2003 to *Black Enterprise* magazine's "Hot List" as one of its "fifty under forty" members of "generation exceptional," Andrea Nelson Meigs is a talent agent at the Creative Artists Agency (CAA), arguably the largest and most influential agency in the entertainment and corporate world. Nelson Meigs joined CAA in 1995 and became only the second black talent agent in the history of the company to rise through the ranks from the mailroom. She has worked with some of the biggest stars in music and film, including Christina Applegate, Halle Berry, Ellen Burstyn, Beyoncé Knowles, and John Voight, and enjoys brokering deals for artists moving from one area of the entertainment industry to another.

Andrea Nelson Meigs was born on October 30, 1968, in Bellflower, California, the daughter of David Nelson Jr. and Dorothy Nelson. Her father is a retired school principal in the Los Angeles Unified School District; her mother, also retired, was a college professor specializing in health information technology. She has one brother, Byron, and is married to John Meigs Jr., an entertainment attorney. Nelson Meigs spent her early childhood in the Compton area of Los Angeles. She attended a private Christian school, then entered the public school system in the fifth grade. She spent her teen years in Palos Verdes before moving to Boston to attend Tufts University. She received her bachelor's degree in English and Spanish in 1990 after studying as an exchange student at the celebrated African-American women's college, Spelman, in Atlanta, Georgia, and at the Universidad Autónoma de Madrid, Spain. She then studied law at Duke University, receiving her Juris Doctorate in 1994.

Nelson Meigs had her first taste of show business as a child actor. From the age of six she appeared in several internationally aired commercials for products such as Mattel Toys, Burger King, and Kellogg's Sugar Smacks. She also appeared in television sitcoms and was a child model. Her experiences in acting made her realize that she preferred to be in a decision-making position, and this in turn led her to attend law school with an eye to entertainment law. Nelson Meigs enjoyed law and joined the Los Angeles District Attorney's office after graduating, but she was still drawn to the fast pace, the people, and the sheer variety of work involved in a career in the entertainment industry. She applied to CAA, where

At a Glance . . .

Born Andrea Nelson on October 30, 1968, in Bellflower, California; married John Meigs Jr. *Education:* Tufts University, Medford, Massachusetts, BA, 1990; also attended Spelman College, Atlanta, Georgia, and Universidad Autónoma de Madrid, Spain; Duke University, North Carolina, JD, 1994.

Career: Los Angeles District Attorney's office, 1994-95; Creative Artists Agency, Los Angeles, 1995–.

Memberships: California Bar Association; Los Angeles County Bar Association; Delta Sigma Theta Sorority Inc.; American Black Film Festival, steering committee member, 2003—.

Awards: *Black Enterprise* magazine, named to "Hot List," 2003; *Honey* magazine, named one of the "25 Hottest Women in Entertainment."

Address: *Office*—Creative Artists Agency, 9830 Wilshire Boulevard, Beverly Hills, CA 90212-1825.

she was given a job working in the mail room, delivering packages to clients and studio executives around Los Angeles. The transition from lawyer to mailroom attendant was difficult, but Nelson Meigs told *Contemporary Black Biography* (*CBB*) that she decided to "check her ego at the door" in order to achieve her goals. Having expected to become an entertainment lawyer, she realized that her legal background would be invaluable as a talent agent, a job that is contracts-based, demands acute negotiation skills, and is also highly creative. She spent four years learning the business at CAA before becoming an agent in 2000.

Nelson Meigs's first client was Cedric the Entertainer, co-star of the "Steve Harvey Show," who at the time was trying to break out of television comedy into film. By 2004 Cedric the Entertainer had starred in several hit movies as well as taking credits as a producer and creating his own TV series. Nelson Meigs is proud of the fact that she helped his career take off. Watching a career develop in that way and knowing she was part of it is what she says she most enjoys about her work. She believes the movie industry often struggles to take advantage of the versatility of actors and other artists and sees part of her role as being to offer artists new opportunities to explore their talents.

Deeply committed to the future of the movie industry and passionate about using her influence to change it for the better, Nelson Meigs told *CBB* that her job would not be done until "I know that I have left a mark on the industry." She represents and admires artists such as Beyoncé Knowles, of the vocal group Destiny's Child, who show that it is possible to be successful in more than one area. With a team of other agents she helped Beyoncé and the other members of the group develop successful acting careers alongside their music. She said that it is "very gratifying" to see artists break out of categories the industry places on them to be celebrated as artists first and foremost.

Nelson Meigs explained that the movie industry is difficult to get into and difficult to stay in, but that there are more opportunities now than there used to be. She thrives on the combination of business, contract law, script appraisal, and contact with clients that her career involves, and she tries to use her position to "educate college-bound students of other job opportunities in this close-knit industry" and to make it more open. She pointed out that while she was only the second black talent agent to work her way up at CAA, by 2004 the agency had five black trainees. When asked where she hopes to go with her career, Nelson Meigs said that she wants to play a part in allowing "people to enjoy actors as themselves—not as Latin, or black, or as just a comedian, or just a singer—and to be celebrated in all areas by everyone."

Sources

Periodicals

Black Enterprise, December 2003.

On-line

"Black Enterprise Presents the Best and Brightest under 40," *Black Enterprise,* www.blackenterprise.com/AboutUsOpen.asp?Source=AboutBE/1203pr.html (September 13, 2004).

Other

Additional material for this profile was obtained through interviews with Andrea Nelson Meigs on September 10, 2004 and October 1, 2004.

—Chris Routledge

John J. Oliver, Jr.

1945–

Newspaper publisher

In the world of African-American newspaper publishing, John J. Oliver Jr. is both a figure rooted in tradition and an innovator who has revitalized a vital strand of black community discourse. The publisher and chief executive of Baltimore, Maryland's *Afro-American* newspapers, Oliver inherited the mantle of family tradition: his great-grandfather, a former slave, founded the publication in 1892, and his father served with the company for 47 years. Over two terms as president of the National Newspaper Publishers Association (NNPA), however, he moved decisively to modernize the world of African-American journalism and to bring it into the age of electronics and the Internet.

Born in Baltimore on July 20, 1945, Oliver grew up in a family that helped bring about the golden age of African-American newspaper publishing. His father, John J. Oliver Sr., presided over an *Afro-American* staff that boasted correspondents in London and Paris, producing a paper with a print run of 150,000 copies that circulated in a dozen cities. Black-oriented newspapers were crucial incubators of the civil rights movement, and the young Oliver became a civil rights pioneer himself: he entered sixth grade as the first black student at Baltimore's John E. Howard Elementary School.

Took Helm at Family Paper

After graduating from Baltimore City College High School in 1963, Oliver started college at the University of Maryland but transferred to Fisk University in Nashville after two years. His teachers at Fisk included the poet and historian Arna Bontemps. Becoming a student leader at Fisk, he received a bachelor's degree there in 1969. He moved on to law school at Columbia University, finishing his degree in 1972 and passing bar exams in both New York and Maryland.

For a decade, Oliver was a corporate lawyer. From 1972 to 1978 he worked for the firm of Davis Polk & Wardwell in New York; the partner named Davis in that firm, ironically enough, had been the losing lawyer in the 1954 Brown v. Board of Education Supreme Court case that demolished racial segregation in American schools. In 1978 he moved back to Baltimore and became a staff lawyer for a Rockville, Maryland, arm of the General Electric corporation. He also did work for the family *Afro-American* newspaper, and in 1982 he took over the business. At first, in May of that year, he was named vice chairman; by the end of the year he had assumed the position of publisher, and in March of 1983 he added chairman of the board of directors to his portfolio of positions.

At the time, the *Afro-American* empire still maintained offices in Baltimore, Washington, D.C., Richmond, Virginia, and Newark, New Jersey, publishing twice-weekly editions in several cities as well as a weekly national newspaper. But circulation was dropping; by 1992 it was a third of its peak in the 1940s, and black readers were abandoning the traditional black press for large, white-owned metropolitan dailies. The Baltimore paper limped along on an old-fashioned typesetting machine that had been purchased in the 1930s. It was readers of his own generation, Oliver pointed out to the *Houston Chronicle,* that had been responsible for the

At a Glance . . .

Born on July 20, 1945, in Baltimore, Maryland; son of newspaper publisher John J. Oliver Sr. *Education:* Attended University of Maryland, College Park; Fisk University, Nashville, TN, BA, 1969; Columbia University, New York, JD, 1972.

Career: Davis Polk & Wardwell, New York, corporate attorney, 1972-78; General Electric, Rockville, MD, staff counsel, 1978-82; *Afro-American* newspapers, Baltimore, vice chairman, 1982; *Afro-American* newspapers, publisher, 1982–, and chairman of board of directors, 1983–; National Newspaper Publishers Association, president, 1999-2003.

Selected memberships: Maryland Higher Education Commission, chairman; First Mariner Bank, Board of Directors; has served on diversity oversight committees for Coors and Texaco corporations.

Address: *Office*—Afro-American Newspapers, 2519 N. Charles St., Baltimore, MD 21218.

---

decline, "because we felt the world held greater promise than was evident on the pages of the Afro."

Pioneered Black Press Web Presence

By 1992, celebrating its centennial as the second-oldest continuously published black newspaper in the United States, the *Afro-American* was down to papers in Baltimore, Washington, and Richmond. Later in the 1990s the Richmond operation, too, was shuttered. Despite these discouraging trends, Oliver was putting in place the seeds of a renaissance as many African-American readers began to turn back to their own communities for information. Equipment was modernized and the paper was produced by an outside printer, linked by computer with the *Afro-American*'s Baltimore offices. In 1994 the *Afro-American* became the first black-oriented newspaper in the United States, and one of the few newspapers of any kind, to go online when its www.afro.com Web site made its debut.

In 1996 Oliver penned for *Afro-American* readers a vivid account of a personal experience that showed why a paper that reported firsthand on racial discrimination in the community was still a vital need. After running a red light, Oliver was pulled over by Baltimore police. With that infraction compounded by several other minor ones (Oliver's license had expired, and he wasn't wearing a seat belt), Oliver was placed under arrest and spent eight hours in Baltimore's central lockup.

In his alternately funny and horrifying article, Oliver likened the actions of the white officers who jailed him to the robot officers in Isaac Asimov's *I, Robot*. He described his cell as: "small, uncomfortable (all steel, no mattress), and covered with dry puke, dried blood, and partially dried urine." Some men who were being released asked him what he was doing there. "As they shook their heads in amazement while continuing on their way," Oliver wrote, "the profoundness of this encounter and the absurdity of my situation began to sink in as I realized that these high-spirited alleged drug offenders were all on their way out—while I, with my traffic violation, was on my way in!"

Elected NNPA President

The *Afro-American* newspapers under Oliver's leadership began to gain readers after years of decline, and in 1999 Oliver got the chance to put his innovative ideas to a national test when he was elected president of the National Newspaper Publishers Association. This national trade group boasted 210 member newspapers with a combined 15 million readers. Oliver launched several initiatives designed to help black-oriented newspapers compete in the electronic age, including an effort to help member papers publish online editions. He warned of the threat online newspapers posed to traditional publications. Oliver also launched a collective news service (dubbed a black Associated Press) and, in partnership with the Howard University School of Journalism, established a new Black Press Institute. A new media service helped advertisers reach member papers' combined audiences. For the first time in 40 years, the NNPA sent reporters to cover the 2000 political conventions.

Yet Oliver also stressed the traditional roots of the black press in highlighting racial discrimination. "[R]ecent events including the dragging death of James Byrd in Texas, the murder of Tyisha Miller in California, and the assault on Abner Louima at the hands of New York City police officers remind us that there is still much work to be done and the Black press must be diligent in our role as champions for justice, equality, and human rights," he was quoted as saying by the *New York Amsterdam News*. "The NNPA has an important place at the table of national debate as we enter a new century."

A satisfied NNPA membership reelected Oliver to its presidency in 2001; it was the first time an incumbent president of the organization had run unopposed. "I would like to institutionalize these programs and the benefit these programs bring the members, so that regardless of who my successor is, it will be something that future publishers will benefit from," he told the *Afro-American*. After finally stepping down in 2003, Oliver kept busy with a host of community responsibilities. He served as chairman of the Maryland Higher Education Commission, and in 2003 he led a panel of journalists who examined the role that race played in coverage of the U.S.-led Iraq War. He remained at the helm of the *Afro-American* and could point to a resurgence of interest in the African-American press that he himself had helped create.

Sources

Periodicals

Afro-American Red Star, February 19, 1994, p. A1; March 2, 1996, p. A1, A5; July 6, 2001, p. A1.
Houston Chronicle, August 23, 1992, p. A13.
Jacksonville Free Press, February 23, 2000, p. 2.
New York Amsterdam News, June 24, 1999, p. 11.
Washington Post, March 7, 1983, p. 19; August 15, 1992, p. D1; May 10, 2001, p. E13.

On-line

The Afro-American Newspapers, www.afro.com (October 28, 2004).
"The Black Press: Future Tense," *We Wish to Plead Our Own Cause: The Black Press: Past, Present, Future,* www.huarchivesnet.howard.edu/0002huarnet/nnpa1.htm (October 28, 2004).

—James Manheim

Helen Owens

1937—

Principal, educational consultant, community activist

Although Helen Owens spent her first 12 years of life as the child of sharecroppers in Tennessee, she has since become an educated, caring, and committed professional well known for her devoted community service. The long list of honors and awards Owens has received indicate not only her achievements, but also her passion for improving life for her fellow man. As the nineteenth Grand Basileus for Sigma Gamma Rho Sorority, Inc., she is committed to public service, leadership development, and the education of youth. She has also been a teacher, and is principal of Rose Hill Middle School in Jackson, Tennessee. Additionally, she owns an educational consulting firm, and is a common radio talk show host on Tennessee stations. Through her community activism and dedication to serving and improving the lives of youth, Owens has proven that a humble beginning need not lead to a humble life. Rising above her situation and striving to better herself and her community, Helen Owens has become a powerful example of professional and humanitarian success.

Born on March 10, 1937, Helen Louise Johnson was the fifth and youngest child of Womack Neville Johnson and Edna Newbern Johnson of Jackson, Tennessee. As sharecroppers, the Johnson family worked a farm owned by a landowner who provided the seed, tools, and living accommodations in exchange for a share of the crops produced on the farm. Although sharecropping was a part of life for many after the Civil War, it often produced more poverty for the workers because of unfair practices by powerful landowners. The majority of Owens' childhood was spent in this environment.

The will to rise above her situation and her desire to learn soon became evident in young Owens. She overcame her underprivileged childhood, graduated from Denmark High School, and then enrolled in Lane College, where she earned a Bachelor of Arts degree. She continued on to graduate school and earned a Masters of Education degree from Memphis University. Because of her love for learning, she then attended Trenton State University in New Jersey and North Carolina State University, and in 2004 was enrolled in a doctoral program at Memphis University.

While pursuing higher education, Helen found time to marry Robert G. Owens. The couple has since had four children: Robert Jr., born in 1959, Casandra, born in 1961, Roger, born in 1963, and Roderick, born in 1966. They also have two grandchildren.

Professionally, Owens has had a wide range of experiences, including public school teacher, principal, program coordinator, and consultant. Once she moved into higher education, Owens worked as an administrative assistant for the directors of several programs at Fayetteville State University and Lane College. She also helped the Tennessee State Department of Education develop the goals and strategies for the Career Ladder Program, which offered pay incentives for educators.

Once Owens became principal of the Jackson Rose Hill Middle School, her passion for ensuring student

At a Glance...

Born Helen Louise Johnson on March 10, 1937, in Jackson, TN; married Robert G. Owens; children: Robert Jr., Roger Fitzgerald, Roderick, and Casandra. *Education:* Lane College; TN, BA; University of Memphis, TN, MEd; enrolled in the doctoral program at the University of Memphis, 2004. *Religion:* Church of God in Christ.

Career: Fayetteville State University and Lane College, administrative assistant; Rose Hill Middle School, Jackson, TN, principal; Grand Basileus, Sigma Gamma Rho Sorority, Inc.; Owens and Associates (education consulting), founder.

Selected Memberships: Jackson, TN, Chamber of Commerce; Jackson-Madison County General Hospital Foundation, board member; United Way, board member; Salvation Army, board member; YMCA, board member; National Association of Secondary School Principals.

Selected Awards: Lane College, Meritorious Service and Alumni of the Year Award; National Association for Higher Education Organization, Outstanding Alumni Award; Omega Psi Phi Fraternity, Inc., Educator of the Year, 1999; Sigma Gamma Rho Sorority, Inc., Leadership Award; United Methodist Church, Leadership Award.

Addresses: *Office*—Rose Hill Middle School, 2233 Beech Bluff Road, Jackson, TN 38301.

---

success became evident. As principal, she has been able to provide a service to the children of her community by managing the quality of their education. According to the *Jackson-Madison County School System* Web site where Owens is principal, the mission of the school is "to develop students who will graduate with the skills and attitudes to succeed in secondary education, post-secondary education, and the world of work, and who demonstrate the attributes of socially responsible citizens." Owens is an example of someone who has accomplished this mission. The National Association for the Advancement of Colored People website claims that "Owens has a deep sense of commitment for the care and welfare of all children because of the extent to which programs and community played roles in her life."

In addition to her educational work, Owens served as the nineteenth Grand Basileus for the Sigma Gamma Rho Sorority, Inc. The mission of this organization is to enhance the quality of life within the community through public service, leadership development, as well as education of youth. As Grand Basileus, or leader, of the organization, Owens shared in these goals. Sigma Gamma Rho addresses concerns that impact society educationally, civically, and economically, such as its 2004 campaign to increase the number of registered voters nationwide and mobilize voter turnout on election day. "Our goal is to add a minimum of 1.5 million new registered voters," said Owens on the *National Coalition on Black Civic Participation* Web site. "This may not seem like a significant number in a country as large as the United States. However, one need only reflect on the last presidential election to realize the importance of each and every vote."

Owens became the first black woman to serve on the Madison County Commission, where she was a member of the highway committee and liaison for the Juvenile Protective Services, the Madison County School Board, and the Jackson Symphony Association. She also owns a motivational speaking and consulting firm called Owens and Associates, through which she provides professional education services in the areas of human resources, diversity training, and motivational speaking. As an eloquent orator, she is also well known as a radio and television talk show host on local Tennessee stations.

A further indication of her interest in and concern for her community is her membership in numerous organizations. Some of these memberships include the United Way Board, the YMCA Board, Phi Delta Kappa, the Mayor's Committee on Diversity, the Jackson-Madison County General Hospital Foundation Board, the Salvation Army Board, and the National Pan Hellenic Council. As a member of the education profession, Owens is also a member of the National Association of Secondary School Principals, the National Association of Curriculum Development, the National Education Association, and the Jackson Education Association.

Because of her deep commitment and service, Owens has a long list of honors and awards, indicating her community's appreciation for her sacrifices and hard work. She has received the Meritorious Service Award and Alumni of the Year Award from Lane College; the National Association for Higher Education Organization (NAFEO) Outstanding Alumni Award; the Leadership Jackson Service Award; the Kiwanis Club of Jackson Leadership Award; the Sigma Gamma Rho Sorority, Inc. Leadership Award; the Omega Psi Phi Fraternity, Inc. Educator of the Year award in 1999; the Boys and Girls Club Service Award; the United Methodist Church Leadership Award; and is listed in Outstanding Women of the Southeast for 1998.

Helen Owens is a powerful example of enduring dedication and commitment to improving the lives of those around her. She has proven that success is a choice, and her ongoing service to her community has undoubtedly enhanced the lives of numerous individuals on many different levels.

Sources

On-line

"Black Greek-letter Organizations Unify and Collaborate for a Nationwide Voter Mobilization Campaign," *National Coalition on Black Civic Participation*, www.bigvote.org/content2004/pan_hellenic.html (September 23, 2004).

"Brown 50th Anniversary Education Equity Commission," *NAACP,* www.naacp.org/BvBE/helen-owens.shtml (September 29, 2004).

"Rose Hill Middle School," *Jackson-Madison County School System*, www.jmcss.net/rosehill (October 19, 2004).

Nancy Womack Johnson Family, www.womackfamily.com/nancy_johnson.htm (October 1, 2004).

Sigma Gamma Rho Sorority, Inc., www.sgrho1922.org (September 29, 2004).

—Cheryl Dudley

John Payton

1946—

Lawyer

Attorney John Payton has defended some of the most important civil rights cases in the United States in recent years. He has also served on several professional boards and committees. According to a profile from Wilmer, Cutler, Pickering, Hale and Dorr, the prestigious Washington, D.C., law firm where Payton is a partner, he "has been recognized as one of the premier litigators in the country and has handled complex civil matters from the trial court to the United States Supreme Court."

Payton was born on December 27, 1946. Growing up in Los Angeles, he thought at first of pursuing a career in science. But once he arrived at Pomona College, he recalled in an interview on the *D.C. Bar* Web site, he was quickly attracted to the social activism that was prevalent on campuses during the 1960s. "Everybody was worried about the draft and the Vietnam war," he observed. "We were all worried about civil rights and issues of equality and justice." Payton became a leader on campus, co-founding the Black Student Association and organizing protest events. "During those years," he added, "I became interested in pursuing something that would have the possibility of helping to create social change, and that was how I became interested in becoming a lawyer."

After graduating from Pomona in 1973, he took a job as an admissions officer at the Claremont Colleges, of which Pomona is a member school. He had helped to create this position, the black admissions office, and held this post for three years. He then traveled to West Africa for a year on a Watson fellowship, studying West Africa literature—an experience he described as "fabulous." Upon returning from Africa, he attended Harvard Law School.

During his first year at Harvard, Payton joined a group of students who wrote briefs for a civil rights lawyer. Among these projects were defenses for activists charged with crimes related to the events at Wounded Knee, South Dakota, where members of the American Indian Movement (AIM) had engaged in armed conflict with federal marshals in 1973. AIM activists took over the reservation town of Wounded Knee on February 27 to protest the government's Indian policy. A siege ensued which led to two Indian deaths and the wounding of a U.S. marshal before AIM surrendered on May 8. Wounded Knee became one of the most high-profile civil rights cases of the 1970s. Payton also started working on a case that had been brought by white merchants in Mississippi against the National Association for the Advancement of Colored People (NAACP) in 1966. This case, which Payton continued to work on for years after completing law school, was eventually decided in the NAACP's favor by the U.S. Supreme Court.

In addition to working on briefs as a student, Payton also served as comments editor for the *Harvard Civil Rights and Civil Liberties Law Review*. "There was always some part of my legal education where I was involved with civil rights," he noted in *D.C. Bar*. After earning his law degree from Harvard in 1977, Payton served as a law clerk to U.S. District Court Judge Cecil Poole in San Francisco.

Upon completing his clerkship, Payton moved to Washington, D.C., in hopes of finding a job that

At a Glance...

Born December 27, 1946; married Gay McDougall, a lawyer, in 1991. *Education:* Pomona College, BA, 1973; Harvard University, JD, 1977.

Career: U.S. District Court, San Francisco, CA, law clerk to Judge Cecil Poole, 1977-78; Wilmer, Cutler, and Pickering (now known as Wilmer, Cutler, Pickering, Hale and Dorr) Washington, D.C, general litigator, 1978-91, partner, 1994–; District of Columbia, corporation counsel, 1991-94.

Memberships: D.C. Bar, president, 2001-2002; American Bar Association; American Law Institute; National Lawyers Committee for Civil Rights Under Law; Washington Lawyers Committee for Civil Rights and Urban Affairs; International Human Rights Law Group; D.C. Appleseed Center; D.C. Public Defender Service; People for the American Way.

Addresses: *Office*—Wilmer Cutler Pickering Hale and Dorr, 2445 M St. NW, Washington, DC 20037.

matched his interest in social change. Wilmer, Cutler, and Pickering (now Wilmer, Cutler, Pickering, Hale and Dorr), a firm that was then working on the NAACP case, hired him as a general litigator. He handled a broad range of cases, and did *pro bono* work (that is, worked without payment) on a case that challenged discrimination in the construction industry.

In 1991 Payton left the firm to become corporation counsel for the District of Columbia. In this position, he supervised all the legal business of the District and represented it in any lawsuits. During his three years in this job, he also streamlined management to create an office "that could operate in a much more professional and engaged way," as he commented in *D.C. Bar*.

Payton attracted national attention in 1993 when he became President Bill Clinton's top choice to head the U.S. Department of Justice's Civil Rights Division. But Clinton did not officially nominate him because of objections from the Congressional Black Caucus. They cited Payton's lack of knowledge about a major Supreme Court voting rights decision, as well as the fact that Payton was unregistered to vote from 1984 until October of 1988 and did not vote in the 1990 D.C. election, as reasons against his candidacy. "It was a mistake not to vote," he said in an interview quoted in the *Washington Post*. "I wish I had voted.... People did sacrifice to get that right. I should have voted." Though some prominent African Americans supported Payton, many black lawmakers were shocked and disappointed by his poor voting record. Acknowledging the lack of political support for his nomination, Payton withdrew his name for consideration on December 17.

Payton left the corporation counsel job in 1994. He then accompanied his wife, attorney Gay McDougall, to South Africa, where she had been appointed to the Independent Electoral Commission in charge of supervising the 1994 election that made Nelson Mandela the country's first post-apartheid president. Payton became part of the international team of observers to ensure an honest election. Upon returning to Washington later that year, he went back to his litigation practice at Wilmer, Cutler, Pickering, Hale and Dorr.

From 1998 to 2000, Payton headed the firm's litigation practice. He has worked on several recent landmark cases, most notably the controversial lawsuit challenging affirmative action admissions practices at the University of Michigan. Payton led the legal team that defended the university in its use of race-based admissions criteria in its undergraduate school and its law school. He successfully defended the undergraduate case, *Gratz, et al. v. Bollinger*, before the U.S. Supreme Court in 2003. The decision was hailed as a huge victory for advocates of affirmative action. As Payton said in remarks quoted in the *University of Michigan Record*, "All selective higher education institutions will be affected" by this result.

Payton also headed the legal team representing the American Legacy Foundation, which was formed in the aftermath of states' lawsuits against the tobacco industry and which in 2004 was embroiled in a lawsuit about truthful advertising of tobacco products (*American Legacy Foundation v. Lorillard Tobacco Co.*). He also directed the defense of the Federal National Mortgage Association (Fannie Mae) in a major class-action suit.

From June of 2001 to June of 2002, Payton served as President of the District of Columbia Bar. He has been active in many professional organizations, including the American Bar Association, where he is a member of the Council of the Section on Individual Rights and Responsibilities and of the Commission on Immigration Policy. He is also a board member of the International Human Rights Law Group and is the vice chair of the D.C. Public Defender Service.

Sources

Periodicals

Washington Post, November 5, 1993, p. A10; November 6, 1993, p. A11; December 18, 1993, p. A1.

On-line

"A Conversation with D.C. Bar President John Payton," *D.C. Bar*, www.dcbar.org/for_lawyers/washington_lawyer/june_2001/payton.cfm June, 2001 (September 14, 2004).

"John Payton," *William Cutler Pickering Hale and Dorr,* http://www.wilmerhale.com/john_payton (September 14, 2004).

"The Legal Team: John Payton," *The University Record Online,* www.umich.edu/~urecord/0203/June16_03/07_payton.shtml (accessed September 14, 2004).

—E. Shostak

Malika Sanders

1973—

Political activist

The civil rights movement of the 1960s spawned great social changes and the emergence of a large group of African-American political leaders, put in power as a direct result of newly safeguarded black participation in the electoral process. For many years, though, no new generation of activists materialized to take the place of the heroic figures who initiated the civil rights struggle. That began to change in the 1990s as young people like Malika Sanders began to make their voices heard on a wide variety of issues that contributed to the world's ongoing cycles of poverty and oppression.

Malika Asha Sanders drew in her activist career on roots that extended into the very center of the early civil rights movement. She was born in 1973 in Selma, Alabama—several years after the tumultuous events that shook that segregated Southern town in the 1960s, but still close enough to them that Sanders could remember the power of people working together on a common cause. "I was born in a time of protest, when civil rights leaders would sleep in our house—as many as 50 or 100 curled up right there on the floor," she told *Marie Claire*.

Her parents were Harvard-educated lawyers who played major roles in the civil rights movement; her father, Hank Sanders, went on to become an Alabama state senator, and her mother, Rose, was a judge, a partner in Alabama's largest black-owned law firm, and author of the play, *Follow the Path,* which depicted a series of women struggling to overcome great odds. Malika Sanders also remembered her father's mother, a housekeeper with an eighth-grade education, as an influence. "She had an amazing way of standing up to people," Sanders told the *My Hero* Web site. "People in the community would come to her to have her settle problems."

When she was 12, Sanders decided to dedicate her life to fighting injustice and inequality. She later described the decision as a spiritual one, but it didn't take her long to put her ideas into practice. As a 15-year-old high school student in Selma, she realized that African-American students were routinely being tracked into lower-level classes rather than college-preparatory programs, regardless of their grades or test scores. The result was a new form of segregation. Sanders led a student walkout that began with just a few participants but grew into a series of marches and protest meetings that drew more than 100 students. The students formed an organization dubbed SMART—the Student Movement Against Racial Tracking.

The group staged a five-day sit-in, facing down FBI and National Guard forces called in by Selma mayor Joe Smitherman. The Ku Klux Klan erected a sign atop the school building where the students were ensconced. Sanders herself was arrested for the questionable crime of passing out leaflets. But in the end the students were victorious; impartial testing programs were implemented, and the Selma school board's white majority, which had terminated a black superintendent who had tried to take the students' side, was soon eliminated.

Sanders attended Spelman College in Atlanta, graduating with a degree in psychology. While she was there, she participated in protests including a shantytown, built on the campus of nearby Morehouse College, that

At a Glance . . .

Born in 1973 in Selma, AL; daughter of Hank and Rose Sanders, both lawyers, activists, and political leaders. *Education:* Spelman College, Atlanta, GA, BA, psychology.

Career: Political activist, 1980s–; 21st Century Youth Leadership Movement, Selma, AL, executive director.

Awards: Reebok Human Rights Award, 2002.

Addresses: *Office*—21st Century Youth Leadership Movement, P.O. Box 2516, Selma, AL 36702.

---

hoped to persuade the United Nations to withdraw from the troubled African nation of Somalia. She also called for the elimination of the Confederate battle flag element in the design of Georgia's state flag, and she organized student protests against police brutality in the wake of the beating of black motorist Rodney King at the hands of Los Angeles police. The normal path for Sanders might have involved a job in a large city, but she returned instead to Selma. "I wasn't sure if I ever wanted to go back," she told *Marie Claire*. "And yet, I felt a responsibility to Selma and the South; I wanted to develop a new generation of leaders who understood and continued the legacy of civil rights."

Soon Sanders became involved with an organization her mother had founded in 1985, the 21st Century Youth Leadership Movement. The goal of the group was to involve young blacks in the political process and to register them to vote. Sanders had attended the group's summer camps when she was younger, and now she became its executive director. At the time, the group consisted of a small band of volunteers, but under Sanders it grew to a membership of 1,500 young people, organized into 32 chapters in the United States and three in Africa.

The newly empowered organization faced one of its first major challenges in Selma itself. The city's 2000 mayoral election featured a new attempt to dislodge Mayor Joe Smitherman, a former segregationist who had been in office since Selma's infamous Bloody Sunday in 1965 but had, through a combination of political compromise and efforts to minimize black voter turnout, remained in office even as Selma's black majority elected other black officeholders. Sanders and her fellow activists organized a massive "Joe Gotta Go" campaign, persisting in the face of tactics of intimidation on the part of Selma police.

"At first, people were too scared to honk" when the group held up signs along local roadways, Sanders told *Marie Claire*. "So we went to football games, to churches, door-to-door. We began to see change, a hope in people's eyes. For the first time ever, we forced a runoff." On Election Day, Selma saw a record 80 percent voter turnout as Smitherman went down to defeat at the hands of African-American candidate James Perkins Jr. For these and other efforts, Sanders was chosen to receive a Reebok Human Rights Award in 2002. The award carried a $50,000 grant, which Sanders plowed back into the 21st Century Youth Movement.

Sanders was ambivalent about the award. "It put me in the spotlight, instead of my organization, and my generation of activists believe we are all leaders," Sanders told the *My Hero* Web site. Nevertheless, it gave Sanders a new national platform. She gave a speech at the 2003 re-enactment of the 1963 March on Washington, leading 21st Century Youth members in a chant of "I must prepare my mind, body, and spirit; we are 21st-century leaders, so let's act like it," as quoted in the *Washington Times*.

Sanders has often been asked to address national meetings like the State of the Black World conference and the rapidly growing National Hip-Hop Political Convention, where she appeared in 2004. In a time of transition, Malika Sanders seemed a leader who could deepen and extend the idea of civil rights. "I want my child to walk in a world guided by love," she told *Marie Claire*. "This means that everybody will have a job, or the resources to take care of basic needs. A world where families are not oppressed and are connected to their neighbors and their communities, where the best in humanity is honored. That's when we will truly be at peace."

Sources

Periodicals

Atlanta Journal and Constitution, October 29, 1993, p. F5.
Bay State Banner, November 17, 1994, p. A2.
Essence, April 2002, p. 25.
Los Angeles Sentinel, December 12, 2001, p. A7.
Marie Claire, February 2002, p. 40.
Washington Post, August 22, 2003, p. C1.

On-line

"Community Hero: Malika Sanders," *MyHero*, http://myhero.com/myhero/hero.asp?hero=M_sanders (October 6, 2004).
"Malika Asha Sanders," *Forefront*, www.forefrontleaders.org/partners/north-america/malika-asha-sanders/ (October 6, 2004).

—James M. Manheim

Kurt Schmoke

1949—

Mayor, lawyer

Schmoke, Kurt, photograph. AP/Wide World Photos. Reproduced by permission.

Kurt L. Schmoke made history in 1987 when he became the first black man elected mayor of Baltimore, Maryland. At that time he was considered a rising star in American politics, with some mentioning him as a potential Senate or even vice-presidential candidate. The promise of his early career, however, ran aground on the difficulties of running America's eleventh largest city. In his three terms as mayor of the city, Schmoke earned a reputation for developing innovative approaches to urban problems. Yet the failure of those approaches to address Baltimore's persistent problems, including poverty, crime, and urban decay, eventually diminished Schmoke's reputation, and he chose not to seek reelection in 1999. However, Schmoke's impressive academic credentials, his studious, professional demeanor, and his skill at solving problems have contributed to his continuing career as a lawyer and, since 2003, as Dean of the Howard University School of Law.

Started Strong

Schmoke's rise to the Baltimore mayor's office was both swift and unique. His relative youth and inexperience notwithstanding, he beat an older and highly popular candidate (also black) who had the backing of the city's former mayor and a circle of powerful friends. Schmoke won the race by appealing to young and liberal voters—and by addressing the many problems still facing Baltimore despite the city's well-publicized cosmetic improvements. Schmoke's agenda was not nearly as flamboyant as that of his predecessor, William Donald Schaefer, but it was certainly more pragmatic. The new mayor of Baltimore wanted to improve the city's school system, fight illiteracy and teenage pregnancy, and prepare Baltimore's citizens for a job market that required high-tech skills. "There comes a time when people feel it's time for a change," Schmoke told the *Washington Post* in 1987. "To a great extent, people [are] looking for a fresh start."

Kurt Schmoke was not born into poverty or illiteracy. His parents were both college graduates with good jobs, and he was their only child. Growing up in Baltimore, Schmoke was encouraged to excel in school not only by his parents but also by Marion Bascom, the pastor of the Douglas Memorial Community Church. Everyone assumed Schmoke would attend college too,

At a Glance...

Born Kurt Lidell Schmoke on December 1, 1949, in Baltimore, MD; son of Murray (a chemist) and Irene Schmoke; married Patricia Locks (an ophthalmologist); children: Katherine, Gregory. *Education:* Yale University, BA, 1971; studied at Oxford University under Rhodes Scholarship; Harvard University, JD, 1978.

Career: Piper & Marbury, Baltimore, MD, associate, 1978-79; member of White House Domestic Policy Staff, 1977-78, and employed in the Department of Transportation, Washington, DC, 1979-81; City of Baltimore, state's attorney, 1982-87; City of Baltimore, mayor, 1987-99; Wilmer, Cutler & Pickering, Baltimore, partner, 1999-2002; Howard University, Washington, DC, Dean of the School of Law, 2003–.

Memberships: Legg Mason Inc., board of directors; Baltimore Life, board of directors; Yale Corporation, Senior Fellow; Just Democracy, advisory board; Council on Foreign Relations; American Bar Association.

Awards: National Literacy Award, 1992.

Addresses: *Office*—Dean of the Law School, Howard University, 112 Charles Hamilton Houston Hall, Washington, DC 20008.

preferably his father's alma mater, Morehouse University in Atlanta. In the *Washington Post,* Bascom remembered the young Kurt Schmoke as "a quiet, unassuming boy, but always a boy whom you felt had great depth of mind and spirit."

Schmoke is the first to admit that he profited from the controversial Supreme Court decision that mandated integration of all public schools. Because he became a student shortly after the landmark *Brown* vs. *Board of Education* ruling, he was given the opportunity to attend predominantly white schools, where he earned good grades while participating in a variety of sports. Schmoke attended Baltimore's City College (a public high school), serving as both school president and starting quarterback in his senior year. Even before he turned eighteen he was a minor celebrity in Baltimore for leading City College to a state championship in football.

Wise Beyond His Years

Schmoke's poise and maturity as a teenager caught the attention of Robert Hammerman, a white Baltimore city judge who devoted his spare time to running a club for boys. Hammerman invited Schmoke to join the club, known as the Lancers, and the two quickly became close friends. It was Hammerman who suggested that Schmoke aim high in his choice of a college, and it was also Hammerman who told Schmoke about the Rhodes Scholarship for study at Oxford University in England. Schmoke had already decided upon a career in politics and law, so Hammerman introduced him to a number of influential Baltimore lawyers and legislators. Some observers feel it may have been Hammerman who suggested that Schmoke aim for the mayor's office, but others claim that Schmoke had wanted to be mayor of Baltimore from the time he was a small boy.

At any rate, failure was almost unknown to Kurt Schmoke as a youth. After graduating from City College he enrolled in Yale University, continuing to distinguish himself as an athlete and a student leader. Schmoke found himself in college in the late 1960s, when anti-war sentiment turned many campuses into near battlegrounds. In the spring of 1970 tensions erupted at Yale during the New Haven murder trial of Black Panther activist Bobby Seale. As Seale's trial progressed downtown, a group of Yale students massed outside the campus administration building, quickly becoming an angry mob. Inside the building, as faculty members predicted the university's imminent destruction, Yale president Kingman Brewster agreed to hear one representative from the students outside. Kurt Schmoke was chosen to be that representative.

If the assembled Yale faculty expected an avalanche of abuse that day, it was only because they did not know Kurt Schmoke. Not yet 20, Schmoke calmly took the podium and merely said: "The students on this campus are confused, they're frightened. They don't know what to think. You are older than we are, and more experienced. We want guidance from you, moral leadership. On behalf of my fellow students, I beg you to give it to us." Schmoke was awarded a standing ovation as he left the hall, and order was restored on the Yale campus.

The Rhodes scholarship is one of academia's most prestigious awards. Rhodes scholars win the opportunity to study for two years at Oxford University; competition is intense for the few available positions. After graduating from Yale, Schmoke was chosen for the Rhodes scholarship by a committee from his home state of Maryland. He spent two years in England and traveled through Europe and Africa when he was out of class. Upon his return to America he enrolled in Harvard Law School, earning his law degree in 1978. Elsewhere Schmoke might have been an unknown, but many eyes in Baltimore were already on him, and expectations for his success in local politics were growing day by day.

A Successful Lawyer

Schmoke passed the Maryland bar and joined Piper & Marbury, one of Baltimore's most influential law firms. He did not work there long, however—he was recruited by the Carter Administration in Washington, D.C., to work in the Department of Transportation under Stuart Eizenstat. *Washington Post* writer Timothy Noah wrote: "It was the kind of job hordes of bright Ivy Leaguers would give their eye teeth for, but Schmoke was restless." Even though he met regularly with President Carter's cabinet members and even Carter himself, even though he had a high-paid and high-visibility position, Schmoke had other aspirations for himself. He wanted to be mayor of Baltimore. He returned to his hometown and threw himself into the political arena.

While in law school Schmoke had married Patricia Locks, a Baltimore native who was studying ophthalmology. Schmoke's father-in-law had been a member of the Maryland General Assembly and was full of advice for the young would-be candidate. Schmoke rejected most of the advice, centered as it was on the traditional step-by-step system that had long been part of Baltimore politics. Noah noted: "Times had changed, and the city's once-powerful [neighborhood] clubhouses were no longer the gateways to political power. Instead, Schmoke would work as a prosecutor for the U.S. attorney, involve himself in assorted civic activities, and begin scouting political opportunities. The opening came in 1982, in the race for Baltimore district attorney, a position known somewhat confusingly as 'state's attorney.'

In order to win as state's attorney, Schmoke had to defeat a white incumbent whose law-and-order rhetoric was very popular among the citizenry. Schmoke did not attack his opponent for racial insensitivity, as many of his predecessors had, but instead presented himself as an able young professional who would be more aggressive on drug prosecutions. He won by a landslide, carrying almost all of the black vote and a good many white votes besides. Schmoke served as state's attorney for four years—heading an office of 133 lawyers—and he sought the death penalty in several cases where narcotics policemen were shot by drug dealers. His years as a district attorney gave Schmoke an insider's awareness of the scope of the illegal narcotics industry, and that awareness has shaped his attitude toward illegal drugs to this day.

Strong Start as Mayor of Baltimore

It seemed unlikely that Schmoke—or anyone else—could have beaten William Donald Schaefer in a race for mayor of Baltimore. In the fifteen years that Schaefer ran Baltimore (1972-87), the city had experienced a transformation. Whole regions around the harbor that once housed rotting warehouses and abandoned homes bloomed into tourist attractions and upscale neighborhoods. Many Baltimoreans felt that Schaefer was solely responsible for the city's renaissance, and when the popular mayor moved on to become governor of Maryland, it was widely assumed that his hand-picked successor, Clarence "Du" Burns, would fill his shoes.

Schaefer was flamboyant and perennially optimistic. From the outset of his campaign Schmoke presented an entirely different picture. He was quiet, deliberate, and anything but optimistic about Baltimore's future. The civic improvements, he pointed out, were laudable but completely inadequate for solving the many problems still besetting the city. Schmoke called for immediate attention to the soaring teen pregnancy rate and the numbers of high school dropouts. Claiming that Baltimore had become "prettier but poorer," Schmoke struck a chord among those who had not benefited from the city's so-called recovery. At the age of thirty-eight he was elected mayor in a very close race.

Mayor Schmoke became controversial almost immediately. Only four months after he was elected he stunned the audience at the National Conference of Mayors by suggesting that at least some drug use should be made legal. Schmoke told the *Washington Post:* "I started to think, maybe we ought to consider this drug problem a public health problem rather than a criminal justice problem." Schmoke took bold and innovative stands on other issues as well. Decrying the poor performance of the city's public schools, he instituted the privatization of several schools and introduced private school curriculum in other schools—over the objections of teachers and school administrators. Hoping to solve the problem of soaring crime rates in urban housing projects, Schmoke okayed the hiring of a Nation of Islam security force in one project. Within a short time, crime rates fell dramatically. "Right or wrong," the *Post* reporter noted, "it's hard not to give Schmoke points for political bravery."

Faced Difficulties of Running a Big City

Schmoke won reelection in 1991 with over 70 percent of the vote, and he won a third term in 1995. During his tenure in office, he was able to claim many successes. He promoted a citywide reading program, instituted a needle-exchange program among drug users, kept tax rates stable, and attracted a new football team, the Baltimore Ravens, to the city. Though he was never a charismatic, inspirational leader, Schmoke also maintained his personal popularity in the city. Chi Chi Sileo wrote in *Insight on the News:* "He shies from the media, insulates himself against special-interest influences, has a background free of either flash or scandal and lives quietly in his hometown with his wife and two children. The biggest complaint people have about Schmoke is that he's boring—and even his critics agree that he is likable and honest."

By the end of his third term, however, neither his real accomplishments nor his personal popularity could mask the fact that Baltimore remained plagued by crime, poverty, and illiteracy—the very problems Schmoke had hoped to address. Critics charged that Schmoke had delegated power over important programs to poor administrators, that he stuck with failing programs for too long, and that he lacked the charisma to motivate people to pursue real change. Others accused Schmoke of resorting to racial politics when the difficulties of improving the city proved insurmountable. More charitable analysts believe that Schmoke should not take the blame for the problems of urban decay that continue to plague many formerly industrial American cities. The *Washington Post*'s Timothy Noah wrote: "Even with the best of intentions and a long-term strategy for change, success can be maddeningly elusive. Tough urban problems do not easily yield to even the most innovative solutions...." By 1998 Schmoke had evidently come to the same conclusion, for he announced at that time that he would not seek a fourth term in office.

After leaving office as the mayor of Baltimore in 1999 Schmoke became a partner in the Baltimore Office of the international law firm of Wilmer, Cutler & Pickering. With his extensive network of contacts Schmoke was a valuable addition to the firm, and he also was asked to serve on the board of directors of several major companies, including the insurance company Baltimore Life and the finance firm Legg Mason. In 2002 Schmoke left the law firm to take the position of Dean of the Howard University School of Law. Howard University president H. Patrick Swygert announced in a university press release: "We are extremely fortunate to have someone with the depth of his intellect and the breadth of his talents and experiences." Whether the man once hailed as the next great black politician will return to the public arena or will use his immense talents to train the next generation of African-American leaders is a question that remains open.

Sources

Periodicals

Black Issues in Higher Education, November 7, 2002.
Economist, September 10, 1994, p. A27-28.
Insight on the News, November 28, 1994.
Jet, October 18, 1993, p. 13; November 27, 1995, p. 8; December 21, 1998.
New Republic, January 29, 1996; August 10, 1998.
Phi Delta Kappan, November 1995.
Washington Post, August 25, 1985; September 16, 1987; December 8, 1987; December 20, 1988; May 27, 1990.

On-line

"Kurt L. Schmoke Named New Dean of Howard University School of Law," *School of Law, Howard University,* www.law.howard.edu/publicaffairs/stories/newlawdean.htm (September 1, 2004).

—Mark Kram and Tom Pendergast

"Little" Jimmy Scott

1925—

Jazz and rhythm-and-blues singer

A jazz and rhythm-and-blues (R&B) singer with a distinctive high-pitched voice, Jimmy Scott is admired by singing stars as diverse as Madonna and Lou Reed. His heyday was the 1950s and 1960s, when he was known among jazz fans as a vocalist with the Lionel Hampton Orchestra, and his most acclaimed album is 1962's *Falling in Love Is Wonderful*, which he made with Ray Charles. His pretty, girlish voice was well suited to the sad, lonely songs that were his specialty in the 1960s and he was a major influence on singers like Charles, Marvin Gaye, and Nancy Wilson. Though his career faltered in the 1970s and 1980s, Scott made a highly successful comeback in the 1990s. Since then he has recorded several albums and performs to sell-out audiences. Madonna has been reported as saying that "Jimmy Scott is the only singer who makes me cry."

James Victor Scott was born on July 17, 1925, in Cleveland, Ohio, one of ten children. When Scott was 13 his mother was hit by a car and killed. His father, who worked as an asphalt layer on road gangs, left soon after and the children were raised in foster homes. Scott's late childhood was also blighted by a rare inherited hormone deficiency known as Kallmann's Syndrome, which meant he never went through puberty and forever carried the nickname "Little" Jimmy. His celebrated high-pitched voice is the result, but Scott had a difficult time growing up in his teens, growing to only four feet eleven inches until his mid-thirties, when he inexplicably grew a little more. Throughout his early adult life Scott was accused of being a woman in disguise and subjected to humiliating abuse and police searches. He began singing in church and at first hoped to record gospel songs—he names Paul Robeson, Ivey James, and Bessie Smith as his early influences—but his voice and the way he uses it make him ideally suited for the cool, slow-paced jazz for which he has become famous. His private life, including four turbulent marriages—one of his wives stabbed him with a kitchen knife—and bouts of heavy drinking, have also proved more in line with the jazz lifestyle than the gospel scene. He married his fifth wife, Jeanie, on December 31, 2003.

Scott's professional career began with Estelle Young, touring the Midwest and performing in black theaters and bars. He seemed about to break into the big time in 1949 when he joined Lionel Hampton's band. Scott made some of his most influential recordings in the following few years, including "Everybody's Somebody's Fool," and "I Wish I Knew," but the records were credited as "Lionel Hampton and vocalists," so the singer's name did not appear on them. Even so, his voice was so distinctive that it was well known among Hampton's followers. Scott left Hampton's band and joined Paul Gayten's group, but despite having recorded "Embraceable You" with Charlie Parker, Scott felt he was struggling to break out from the limited coverage and sales offered by the audiences in the small clubs.

During the late 1950s and early 1960s he recorded with the Savoy label under various smaller labels, and thus came under the control of Savoy's owner, Herman Lubinsky. Lubinsky was well known for having his artists sign very restrictive contracts and when Scott left

At a Glance...

Born James Victor Scott on July 17, 1925, in Cleveland, Ohio; married five times, most recently to Jeanie, 2003. *Religion:* Baptist.

Career: Recording artist, 1940s–; toured with Estelle Young, 1940s; joined the Lionel Hampton Orchestra, 1949; joined Paul Gayten's band, 1951; recorded with Charlie Parker, Ray Charles, and others until late 1960s; worked as an elevator operator, waiter, shipping clerk, and other jobs, 1970s and 1980s; signed by Sire Records, 1991.

Addresses: *Label*—c/o Milestone Records, Tenth and Parker, Berkeley CA, 94710.

---

to record with Ray Charles under Charles's Tangerine record label, Lubinsky blocked him. *Falling in Love Is Wonderful* is probably Scott's most important record, yet it was on sale for only a few weeks. For this reason it is one of the most collectable jazz records on the market. After several failed deals in the late 1960s Scott started drinking heavily and gave up on his singing career. In the 1970s he worked as a helper in a nursing home and as a clerk. He started singing again in 1984, but it was the death of his friend songwriter Doc Pomus in 1991 that really began his comeback. Singing at Pomus's funeral, Scott was spotted by Sire Records president Seymour Stein and received a five-album contract the next day.

Since then Scott has toured with Lou Reed and sung backing vocals on his *Magic and Loss* album; he has since appeared with Bruce Springsteen and Madonna, as well as having one of his songs featured on *The Cosby Show* and singing "Under the Sycamore Tree" on the cult favorite TV show *Twin Peaks*. In the 1990s a cure was found for Kallmann's Syndrome, but Scott refused it on the basis that it would rob him of his gift. Listing entertainment business luminaries such as Quincy Jones, Robert DeNiro, and Tony Bennett among his friends, Jimmy Scott achieved stardom over 40 years after his career began. Writing in the *New York Times Magazine,* Joseph Hooper attributes the revival in Scott's fortunes at least partly to the singer's strange, feminine voice and a growing acceptance of sexual ambiguity in entertainment: "Scott's aging androgyny undoubtedly helped him secure his cult status," he argues, but it is only with age that his voice and approach to music have matured. He describes Scott as "perhaps the most unjustly ignored American singer of the twentieth century." In 2003 Scott toured in Asia and Europe and in 2004 he continues to perform, enjoying a career that ended so abruptly in the late 1960s that many fans thought he was dead.

Selected discography

Little Jimmy Scott/The Paul Gayten Band: Regal Records: Live in New Orleans!, Specialty, 1951; re-released, 1991.
If You Only Knew, Savoy, 1956; re-released, 2001.
The Fabulous Songs of Jimmy Scott, Savoy, 1960; re-released, 2003.
Falling in Love is Wonderful, Tangerine, 1963; re-released by Rhino, 2002.
The Source, Atlantic, 1969; re-released, 2001.
All the Way, Warner Brothers, 1992.
Lost and Found, (recorded in 1969 and 1972) Atlantic, 1993.
Heaven, Sire, 1996.
Holding Back the Years, Artists Only!, 1998.
Everybody's Somebody's Fool, Universal Music, 1999.
The Savoy Years and More, Atlantic, 1999.
Mood Indigo, Milestone, 2000.
Over the Rainbow, Milestone, 2001.
But Beautiful, Milestone, 2002.
Moon Glow, Milestone, 2003.

Sources

Books

Ritz, David, *Faith in Time: The Jazz Life of Jimmy Scott,* Da Capo, 2002.

Periodicals

New York Times Magazine, August 27, 2000.
Jet, March 17, 2003, p.34.

On-line

"Interview with Little Jimmy Scott," *All About Jazz,* www.allaboutjazz.com/iviews/jscott.htm (October 15, 2004).
"Jimmy Scott Biography," *Fantasy Jazz,* www.fantasyjazz.com/html/scott_j_bio.html (October 15, 2004).

Other

Little Jimmy Scott: Why Was I Born? (documentary biography), Bravo Profiles, Bravo, 1998.
Jimmy Scott: If You Only Knew (documentary biography), PBS, 2004.

—Chris Routledge

Howard "Sandman" Sims

1917-2003

Tap dancer

Howard "Sandman" Sims was a tap dancer, a practitioner of a style of dance in which a beat is loudly, clearly tapped out by a dancer sporting specially-made hard-soled shoes with metal plates, or taps, on their heels or toes. He developed his own distinctive dance style, in which he tapped on sand, and he was among the legendary black American entertainers whose careers linked nineteenth-century slave and minstrel-show dancing first to the glory years of vaudeville and then to the popularity of such contemporary tap dance stars as Gregory Hines and Savion Glover.

Sims was born on January 24, 1917, in Fort Smith, Arkansas, but he grew up in Los Angeles. He first tap-danced at age three—and never formally studied tap or any other dancing style. "I was born dancing," Sims told the *New York Times's* Jennifer Dunning in 1977. Of his childhood, he recalled, "It was just a whole big dancing family." He added, "When I got up off the ground, I danced. I was just full of rhythm. I used to wear the toes out of my shoes, so my mother put steel taps on them, and that really did it. My sister and I were doing Buck and Bubbles (a celebrated black-American rhythmic tap dancing/piano playing duo who earned acclaim during the 1920s) before they ever arrived."

Developed Unique Dance Style

Sims earned the nickname "Sandman" because of his specialty: dancing on a board covered with sand, or dancing on sand sprinkled on the floor of the stage. By moving his feet on the sand, he produced a variety of distinctive brushing, grinding sounds. His sand dancing dates from his adolescence in the 1930s, when he aspired to become a boxer. "I broke my hand," he explained to Dunning, "so I went to play around, moving my feet in the rosin box instead. People got so that they'd rather see me in the rosin box than in the ring." Consequently, he was inspired to duplicate the technique in his dance moves. "First I glued sandpaper on my shoes, and I wore my mat out. Then I glued sandpaper on the mat and wore my shoes out. Then I put loose sand in a box with a sounding board that can be miked, and on that board I am the world's greatest sand dancer." He added, "The hoofer uses the whole foot…. In tap, you use the toe and the heel…. The steps are not taught: You create them as you go along. You never do the same thing twice. It's not the steps, but the sounds."

After toiling in obscurity as a dancer on the West Coast and in Latin America, Sims arrived in Harlem, New York's renowned African-American community, in 1947. He soon established himself as a local personality, primarily performing at the famed Apollo Theater. Starting in the mid-1950s, he served as the theater's stage manager. One of his duties was as the "executioner" during the Apollo's renowned Wednesday night amateur competitions, during which a gaudily-dressed Sims would comically chase unpopular performers off the stage. He continued in this capacity semi-regularly through the 1980s. He liked to joke that he himself was booted off the stage during his first ten

> **At a Glance . . .**
>
> **B**orn on January 24, 1917, in Fort Smith, AK; died on May 20, 2003, in The Bronx, NY; married Solange; children: Howard, Jr., Mercedes White, Diane Jones.
>
> **Career:** Tap dancer, 1930s-2003; Apollo Theater, Harlem, regular performer from 1947; worked as a dance teacher, mechanic, and carpenter, and operated a café, 1950s-60s; toured the world as a representative of the U.S. State Department, 1980s; appeared in movies, film, and television as a tap dancer, 1980s and early 1990s.
>
> **Awards:** National Heritage Fellowship, 1984; honoree, Fourth Annual Young People's Tap Conference, 1998.

Apollo appearances. He persisted, however, and eventually won a record 25-straight amateur contests.

Despite his Harlem success, Sims never became a nationally acclaimed dance headliner of the caliber of Bill "Bojangles" Robinson, Fred Astaire, Gene Kelly, Ray Bolger, Buck and Bubbles, or the Nicholas Brothers. During the 1950s and 1960s, as tap dancing went out of vogue, Sims struggled professionally. He supplemented his work at the Apollo by teaching dance, operating a café, and toiling as a mechanic and carpenter. Most significantly, he tutored future dancing stars Gregory Hines and Ben Vereen, and taught boxers Sugar Ray Robinson and Muhammad Ali how to deftly move their feet in the ring.

Rediscovered by Tap Aficionados

Beginning in the late 1960s, a nostalgia for traditional tap dancing flourished among dance enthusiasts, and Sims became cherished as a practitioner of a beloved American art form. He regularly performed solo or on programs with other dancers in New York and elsewhere. In 1969 he and several veteran tap dancers opened in *Tap Happening*, a revue which played Off-Broadway for several years. Each show featured a "challenge," in which the performers would endeavor to outshine one another in a street corner-style dance contest.

During the 1980s, Sims was at the center of what had become a full-scale tap dance revival. Throughout the decade, he toured the world as a representative of the U.S. State Department, becoming an unofficial ambassador of tap dance. He was featured in various documentaries on tap dancing, most significantly George T. Nierenberg's *No Maps on My Taps* (1979) and *Tap Dance in America* (1989), a PBS special. He appeared as a hoofer in Francis Coppola's *The Cotton Club* (1984), but his most significant screen role was in *Tap* (1989), a fictionalized homage to tap dancing starring Gregory Hines, Sammy Davis Jr., and Savion Glover. Sims' character was called "Sandman," and was based on himself. In once sequence, he partook in a memorable tap dance "competition" with several peers. In a similar vein, he played a tap dance teacher in "Mr. Sandman," a 1990 episode of *The Cosby Show*.

Sims's career was paid homage in *The Sand Dancer*, a verse play written by Sandra Hochman, which combined dialogue, dance, music, and filmed images. The play, in which Hochman equated Sims to a poet, was presented in New York in 1986, and featured Sims in a cameo appearance. In her *New York Times* review, Anna Kisselgoff noted Sims' "brief solo" in which he "delights us when he suddenly springs out to dance upon his traylike box covered with sand."

Cited as an Innovator

In his senior years, Sims' expertise as a tap dance artist was acknowledged by critics. In her review of *The Sand Dancer*, Kisselgoff described Sims as "a virtuoso among virtuosos—in a class by himself" and "an innovator in a traditional art." Also in 1986, the *Times's* Jack Anderson dubbed Sims "one of our finest tap dancers." Reviewing a program, titled "The Tap Tradition" and presented at New York's Symphony Space, Anderson observed, "Mr. Sims moved deftly. Often, he let his feet just whisper to the floor. Then his taps started chattering and at times he punctuated his phrases with bright bursts of sound." Anderson reported that, after his performance, Sims conversed with the audience and declared, "Anyone can dance. Dancing is nothing but walking." Sims added that "everything in nature dances," and offered impersonations of dancing frogs, camels, ducks, and elephants.

Sims felt a responsibility for passing on his knowledge and love of tap dancing to others, and to young people in particular. In 1984 he received a National Heritage Fellowship, a $5,000 prize presented by the Folk Arts Program of the National Endowment for the Arts. He employed his winnings to transform part of a Harlem parking lot into an outdoor dancing school for children. "Hoofing is not a dying art form," he told the *New York Times's* Dunning. "Some people have lost the art, but we have never quit dancing."

Sims died in The Bronx, New York, on May 20, 2003 at age 86; he suffered from Alzheimer's disease, diabetes, and an ulcer. Twenty-six years earlier, he told Dunning, "I'm in show business not for a season, but a reason.... I want to just dance my way away at the end."

Selected works

Films

No Maps on My Taps, 1979.
The Cotton Club, 1984.
Harlem Nights, 1989.
Tap, 1989.

Television

Uptown: A Tribute to the Apollo Theatre (also known as *Uptown: A Musical Comedy History of Harlem's Apollo Theatre*), 1980.
It's Showtime at the Apollo, 1983.
Motown Returns to the Apollo, 1985.
Tap Dance in America, 1989.
"Mr. Sandman," *The Cosby Show,* 1990.

Other

The Sand Dancer (verse play), 1986.

Sources

Periodicals

Jet, June 23, 2003.
New York Times, September 9, 1977, p. 50; September 8, 1985, p. 78; March 2, 1986, p.64; July 2, 1986, p. C29.
Washington Post, October 8, 1976, p. B6; June 25, 1984, p. B4.
Variety, June 2003.

On-line

"Taps for the Legendary Sandman Sims," *Amsterdam News,* www.amsterdamnews.org/News/article/article.asp?NewsID=27030&sID=4 (October 13, 2004).
History of Tap Dance, http://www.offjazz.com/tp-hist.htm

—Rob Edelman

Vincent D. Smith

1929-2003

Artist

In a career that spanned half a century, painter Vincent Smith documented in brilliant color some of the most compelling events in twentieth-century America. From the be-bop-fueled improvisation of 1940s Harlem jazz clubs, to the visceral tug of civil rights workers confronting deep-seated hate with soul-clearing hope, to the creative militancy of the Black Arts Movement, Smith was there, brush in hand, bearing witness. "A figurative painter with an often subtle, social thrust, he placed his subjects in a stylized way against geometric, textured and intricately colored backgrounds," noted the *New York Times*. "I always knew that I was either going to do something or do nothing," he told *American Visions*. "And when I thought of myself as a painter, I dreamed of myself as a great painter." He succeeded.

From Hobo to Artist

Vincent Dacosta Smith was born on December 12, 1929, in New York and raised in Brooklyn by his parents, Louise and Beresford Smith. As a high school student he preferred sketching to studying and at fifteen he dropped out. "I was a good student, but I got into trouble," he admitted to *American Visions*. Soon he and a friend began hanging around the Bowery district of Manhattan. "There were hundreds of bars. There were guys sleeping all over the street, people sleeping in the back of the bars," Smith told *American Visions*. "We used to go down there and hang out and drink with those guys and sit around and talk." Many of those men worked on the railroads and filled Smith's head with visions of life on the road. "They hopped on a train, and then when they got where they're going, they hopped off. My friend and I thought that sounded exciting, so we went to the office and signed up." At the age of 16 Smith began life as a hobo. He also began to open his eyes. "My first social awareness came about in 1947 while I was working on the Lackawanna Railroad—repairing the tracks, listening to the chants, visiting bars and roadhouses, and looking into the faces of the people who lived near the tracks in rural communities," *American Visions* quoted him as writing.

After hopping off his last train, Smith signed up for a one-year stint in the Army. In 1949 he returned to Brooklyn and landed a job in the post office. He was not thrilled, however; something was missing in his life. When a friend invited him to the Museum of Modern Art to see a Cezanne retrospective, he found out what it was. "Something told me when I walked into the museum that this was where I belonged," he told *American Visions*. "I always knew that I would do art, but you know how you carry something around with you, and you know that one day it will surface, but you don't know when." With that insight, Smith set about becoming an artist. "I came away so moved with a feeling that I had been in touch with something sacred," he was quoted in a profile on the *Afro American Newspapers* Web site. "For a year afterward I haunted the libraries reading everything I could get my hands on about art, literature, philosophy, religion, existentialism—you name it—I touched on it somewhere."

In 1953 Smith left his postal job to become a full-time artist. He took classes at the Brooklyn Museum of Art

At a Glance . . .

Born on December 12, 1929 in New York, NY; died on December 27, 2003 in New York, NY; married Cynthia Linton, 1972. *Education:* Arts Students League, New York, NY; Empire State College, Saratoga, NY, 1953-56; Brooklyn Museum Art School, Brooklyn, NY, 1954-56; Skowhegan School of Painting and Sculpture, Skowhegan, ME, 1955; State University of New York, Saratoga, 1980. *Military:* United States Army, 1948-49.

Career: Painter, 1953-2003. Whitney Museum Art Resources Center, New York, NY, instructor, 1967; Smithsonian Conference Center, Elkridge, MD, artist-in-residence, 1967; Cite des Arts International, Paris, France, artist-in-residence, 1978; WPAI-FM, New York, NY, host, *Vincent Smith Dialogues with Contemporary Artists,* 1986-88.

Selected memberships: National Conference of Artists; African-American Museum Association; Audubon Society; National Society of Painters in Casein and Acrylics.

Selected awards: Skowhegan School of Painting and Sculpture, scholarship, 1955; John Hay Whitney Foundation, fellowship, 1959-60; National Institute of Arts and Letters, grant, 1968; American Academy of Arts and Letters, Childe Hassam Purchase Prize, 1973, 1974; National Academy of Design, Thomas B. Clark Prize, 1974.

School and New York City's Art Students League. He traveled to Maine to study on scholarship at the prestigious Skowhegan School of Painting and Sculpture. He learned about technique and style, history and form. Yet some of his greatest insights came from the other black artists he met. "Most people I came in contact with never knew a black painter nor had they hardly ever heard of one," he is quoted by *Afro American Newspapers.* "We went through the hallowed halls of these museums...and we didn't see anything reflect the black experience or black contribution to American culture. We knew that we were going to be scorned and ridiculed. We also knew that our achievements were going to have to take, not rage, but knowledge and skill and scholarship and long years of dedication." He continued: "There were no black art historians, blacks with PhD's were unheard of. Few blacks taught art in colleges in the North; there were no publications about black visual arts. There were only about four or five galleries open to us.... Yet we painted up a storm!"

Documented Struggles of Black America

Smith's first solo show, held at the Brooklyn Museum Art School Gallery in 1955, debuted without him. "I never even showed up...," he told *American Visions.* "It was like revealing your soul for the first time. You have to develop a tough hide to get through that early period; it is very rough." His work reflected the world he moved in—New York's avant garde music scene. "During the day I painted and at night I went to the jazz clubs," the *New York Amsterdam News* quoted Smith as saying. For a while he lived in an apartment next door to a jazz musician who introduced him to famed saxophonist Charlie "Bird" Parker. The musical legend took a look at Smith's work and told him to "stick to his vision," wrote the *New York Amsterdam News.* Smith named a 1950s series of paintings *Saturday Night in Harlem.* In the 1980s and 1990s he completed another jazz series, *Riding on a Blue Note.* One work from that group, "Rootin Tootin Blues," was given to President and Mrs. Bill Clinton during Clinton's first inauguration ceremony.

Smith's work took a political turn in the mid-1950s as the civil rights movement exploded. In 1954 the Supreme Court case "Brown vs. the Board of Education" ordered all public schools to integrate. After watching mobs of angry white adults taunting black school children, Smith made "First Day of School." The *Afro American Newspapers* Web site wrote of the black and white etching: "In this picture we see that a mob of furious people is lashing out at the seven black schoolchildren who have arrived for their first day at school.... We see a Klansman in his Ku Klux Klan hood and a man wielding a billy club. Other men carry a knife, a gun, a Corn liquor bottle. There is no kindness in any of their faces."

In the late 1960s and 1970s, Smith became a fixture in the Black Arts Movement. Spearheaded by poets such as Amiri Baraka and Larry Neal, the movement celebrated both black power and black creativity. Poetry and music poured from the movement. Smith documented it all with swashes of bright, illuminated color, sand-thickened canvasses, geometry, symbolism, and movement. Baraka, quoted in *American Visions,* wrote of Smith's work, "Sisters smile a little, buildings hang stiff in Smithspace, flowers glow indelibly, into the consciousness, civil rights leaders and militants are caught in paint like fixed artifacts of the black creative aesthetic, their politics collected forever in colors and forms." One painting from that era, "Coal Duck," featured a single black man looming large on the canvas. The surface is thick with grit like dirt stuck under fingernails after a long day's labor. The symbolism sticks thickly too. Coal is black, like the man. Duck is short for "sitting duck"—a black man caught in a white man's world.

Orchestrated Work with Color and Spontaneity

Though different themes snaked their way through his work over the decades, tight composition was always a constant. "When I paint, I'm always aware of composition because I've always felt that the tighter the composition, the more interesting the work," he told *American Visions*. Color was also a driving element in his art, though it altered over time. "It changes in very subtle ways. You're not conscious of it, but it's reflected in the work," Smith told *American Visions*. "When I was in Maryland, I did some landscapes, which I normally don't do. But the green was so strong that at night, when I got into bed to read, the pages on the book would turn green." He continued, "Then, when I went to Africa, the landscape was all over the place, and so the yellow started coming into the painting—all those yellows. It was coming from the sun, from all that sky."

Smith was also very conscious of how his paintings came to be, how he willed them from his head onto canvas. "My approach has always been very spontaneous and sort of inventive, instinctive, intuitive," he told *American Visions*. "I tend to refer to whatever I am doing as an orchestration." He continued, "I may be working with seven or eight ingredients at the same time—oil and sand, dry pigment and collage and pebbles and dirt and so forth. To control all of these elements, all of these things have to work together in certain way so that when the finished product is presented, it makes sense. When I hit, I'm like a conductor."

Once he decided to be a painter, Smith immersed himself in art, not only as a student but as a working artist. His work was featured in over 25 one-man shows and more than 30 group shows. He received dozens of awards, grants, and fellowships. In the 1970s he was awarded a fellowship to paint and travel in Africa. He was an instructor at the Whitney Museum Art Resource Center and artist-in-residence at the Smithsonian Conference Center in Maryland and Cité des Arts International in Paris. Dozens of prominent museums added his works to their permanent collections, including the Art Institute of Chicago, the Detroit Institute of Arts, the Museum of Fine Arts in Boston, and the Library of Congress in Washington, D.C. Coming around full circle, the Museum of Modern Art in New York, where Smith was first inspired to paint, also added his work to its collection. Smith was also commissioned to create several public murals, including two that stand today in the West 116th Street station of the New York City subway system.

Even when Smith was not in his studio, paint-spattered and working, he was steeped in the art world in one form or another. He worked as an illustrator for a book on jazz by Amiri Baraka and for a line of greeting cards. From 1986 to 1988 he hosted *Vincent Smith Dialogues with Contemporary Artists,* a bi-weekly New York radio show. He and his wife Cynthia Linton—they married in 1972—traveled extensively through Africa, the Caribbean, and Latin America. They filled their Lower East Side apartment with artifacts from their trips, as well as art, books, poetry, photographs, and mementos documenting Smith's five decades as an artist. In October of 2003, during a show of his work at New York's Alexandre Gallery, Smith told the *New York Amsterdam News*, "I'm busy these days assembling my papers," referring to the task of writing his memoirs. It was a task he would not finish. On December 27, 2003, Smith died from lymphoma complicated by pneumonia. He was 74. He told *American Visions*, "You have to titillate your public in a sense. You have to wind up saying what you want to say, but you also like to take them on a journey." Art historians, collectors, students, and anyone lucky enough to stand before one of his vibrant, evocative works will be thankful for the ride.

Sources

Books

In This Particular Gumbo...Jazz in Art and Literature, Smithsonian Institution, 1994.
Lenten Meditations, Trinity Church, 1989.
Morgan, Norman, ed., *The Lower East Side, Literary and Arts Movement of the 1960s,* African American Review, 1993.
St. James Guide to Black Artists, St. James Press, 1997.

Periodicals

American Visions, June 1999.
Art in America, April 2004.
New York Amsterdam News, October 8, 2003.
The New York Times, January 3, 2004.

On-line

"Vincent DaCosta Smith," *Biography Resource Center,* www.galenet.com/servlet/BioRC (October 11, 2004).
"Vincent Smith," *Afro American Newspapers,* www.afro.com/culture/artgallery/archive9/art4.html (September 28, 2004).

—Candace LaBalle

Mathew St. Patrick

1969—

Actor

St. Patrick, Mathew, photograph. Jon Kopaloff/Getty Images.

When Mathew St. Patrick was a boy, he escaped from the rough streets of his neighborhood by watching film after film in the all-night theater near his home. Watching the actors on the screen, he often thought, "I can do that." Although all too often he felt that no one else had confidence in his abilities, St. Patrick held on to his belief in himself. He weathered hard work and violence during his childhood, homelessness and poverty at the start of his career, and criticism and rejection from casting agents. Though he was finally rewarded with an important and groundbreaking role in an award-winning television series, St. Patrick has continued to reach for new goals. Laughingly describing actors as "professional rejects," he has continued to take risks by seeking new acting projects, as well as beginning to write scripts himself.

St. Patrick was born on March 17, 1969, in Philadelphia, Pennsylvania, and grew up with two brothers and one sister. His mother, Brenda, was an elementary school teacher, while his father, Curtis, was a salesman and entrepreneur. St. Patrick's father started several different businesses, and, from the age of nine, young Mathew began to work with him, doing such jobs as selling hot dogs from vending carts.

Grew Up in the City

Though Mathew spent much of his free time with friends playing tackle football or stickball in the city streets of his neighborhood, he also valued the time he spent with his family, especially getting to know his mother's grandparents. He loved to sit and talk with his tiny, frail great-grandmother and his quiet, affectionate great-grandfather. Though his great-grandmother called Mathew her favorite, she never hesitated to correct him and teach him manners. From his gentle great-grandfather he learned the value of a positive attitude, and from his great-grandmother he acquired his stern look, which masks a spirited sense of humor and fondness for laughter.

His mother's father, Charlie Queen, owned a pool hall in the Germantown neighborhood of Philadelphia. A much-loved longtime resident of the area, Queen was dubbed "the mayor of Germantown" by his friends and neighbors. Young Mathew spent many hours in Queen's Pool Hall, first learning how to shoot pool, then winning against men much older than himself.

At a Glance...

Born March 17, 1969, in Philadelphia, Pennsylvania; married; children: one son, Tommy.

Career: West Coast Theater Ensemble, cast member, 1996; actor, 1996–.

Selected Memberships: Elizabeth Glaser Pediatric AIDS Foundation; Best Buddies Organization; Screen Actors Guild.

Awards: Named one of *People Magazine*'s Sexiest Men Alive, 2001; National Gay and Lesbian Task Force, National Leadership Award, 2002.

Addresses: *Office*—c/o HBO, 120 E 23rd St., Ste. A, New York, NY 10010. *Agent*—9200 Sunset Blvd. Suite 620, Los Angeles, CA 90069.

While St. Patrick was developing his skill at pool and sports, he had little confidence in his abilities in school. Though his experience working in his father's businesses had helped teach him math, he did not read well and his teachers did not offer him a great deal of help. When his seventh-grade geography teacher criticized him and his family in front of the class, St. Patrick began to forge a determination to prove him wrong.

Escaped Harsh Realities

Young Mathew's view of the world outside the bleak streets of his neighborhood came from the films he saw at the all-night movie theater and from the magazines he read. He spent many nights at the movies, watching black men like himself acting in films like *Mother, Jugs and Speed* (1976) and *Cornbread, Earl and Me* (1975). As he watched actors like Bill Cosby, Laurence Fishburne, and Keith Wilkes, he began to see a way out of the neighborhood streets that too often proved to be a dead end for young black men.

Often uncomfortable in school, St. Patrick had never learned to read well, so at first he just looked at the sports and fashion magazines that he enjoyed. He admired the successful players, many of whom had come from similar working-class backgrounds, and he admired the sophisticated people pictured in the fashion magazines whose stylish clothes seemed to symbolize their success. Their stories interested him, so he painstakingly taught himself to read, hoping that he could learn more about worlds different from the one he lived in.

Though St. Patrick tried to stay uninvolved in hoodlum activities, it was hard to stay out of trouble in his neighborhood. He was beaten up regularly, often just because he was not involved with local gangs. By the time he graduated from high school, most of his friends were in jail and others had already been killed. St. Patrick began to fear for his own life if he did not get away.

His father had an old Air Force friend who lived in the suburbs of Chicago. In 1987, shortly after his graduation from high school, Mathew St. Patrick left his home in Philadelphia and headed for Chicago. Seeking a career either in sports or fashion, he rented a room from his father's old friend and began to look for work. The results of his search were disappointing. Though he got some runway modeling work, he was turned down by a major modeling agent because he did not have the standard look required for modeling. While he attended a few college classes and worked as a carpenter, weight trainer, and Coca-Cola salesman to pay the rent, he continued to look for a way to break into a more creative and profitable field.

Sought the Actor's Life

In 1994 St. Patrick was cast in a small role in a local independent film. Though he eventually ended up playing the lead in the film, he had differences with the filmmaker, making it a difficult work experience. The film was never completed but St. Patrick had finally found the work he wanted to do. Within a week he headed for Los Angeles, a major center for film and television work, determined to prove to himself that he could make it as an actor.

St. Patrick's introduction to Los Angeles was not easy. For the first year-and-a-half he was often homeless, sleeping in friends' porches and garages while he took jobs as a bartender or personal trainer and tried to find acting work. He took acting classes and conquered his fear of improvisation, that is, acting without a script by making up actions and words on the spot. He "crashed" auditions to which he had no appointment. Once, when he heard about casting for a film called *Eddie*, starring Whoopie Goldberg, he went back to see the producers three times in an effort to get even a small part. He had little success, though he did develop a good relationship with a commercial casting agent who cast him in several commercials.

St. Patrick was beginning to doubt that he would ever succeed when a friend suggested that he try working in live theater, both to develop his acting skills and to appear onstage where his abilities could be seen by those who could cast him in films or television. He had recently had a very discouraging experience in an acting class when a visiting casting agent had told him that, with his muscular body, bald head, and black skin, he could only ever expect to be cast as a criminal. Angered at being seen only as a stereotype rather than a full human being, St. Patrick determined to take no more acting classes. Instead, he wrote a monologue casting himself as an attorney, arguing a case for a mother who was in danger of losing her children. Taking his friend's advice, he took this powerful monologue and auditioned for the West Coast Theater Ensemble.

Appeared on Stage and Screen

Founded in 1986, the West Coast Theater Ensemble is a respected, multi-ethnic theater company which has produced many award-winning plays. Before St. Patrick performed his audition monologue, he made a secret decision that if he got into the company he would quit his non-acting jobs and concentrate all his energies on his acting career. He was accepted into the troupe and two days later auditioned for his first play, a basketball drama called *Full Court Press* by Chicago playwright Donald Lewis.

St. Patrick won the lead role in *Full Court Press*. A talent agent who saw his opening night performance agreed to represent him, and sent him to audition for a role in the film *Steel Sharks*. St. Patrick was cast in the film as a Navy Seal sniper, already proving wrong the casting director who had been so sure he would only play gang members and bank robbers.

Once he had his first film role, St. Patrick's career seemed to take off. He was cast in another film, a military drama called *Surface to Air,* and won the role of police lieutenant Marcus Taggart on the ABC soap opera *General Hospital*. In 1998 he moved to New York City to play another soap opera law enforcement official, Adrian Sword, an FBI agent, on *All My Children*. St. Patrick's determination not to play only negative stereotypes like criminal roles drew notice from those watching him on television. In both 1998 and 1999, he was nominated for an Image Award by the National Association for the Advancement of Colored People (NAACP).

While working on *General Hospital* and *All My Children,* St. Patrick continued to audition for new roles. He performed in a number of episodes on major television shows, including *Moesha, NYPD Blue,* and *Diagnosis Murder*. In 2000 he had the opportunity to audition for the role of Keith Charles, a gay police officer on a new HBO series called *Six Feet Under*. The series was to be a quirky, gothic drama about a family-run funeral home. Keith Charles would be the partner of David, one of the mortician sons in the Fisher family. St. Patrick was cast in the role of Keith and returned to Los Angeles to begin work on the new project.

Broke Stereotypes

Six Feet Under captured the public imagination immediately. Funny and offbeat, it also had a grim and slightly gruesome side, as it showed the nuts and bolts of the funeral parlor business. Along with being a look at an unusual line of work, *Six Feet Under* was also a family drama, and viewers were captivated by the day-to-day lives of the Fisher family and their friends and lovers. Michael St. Patrick immediately drew notice for his work portraying Keith Charles. Along with a Golden Globe Award for Best Television Series, the show won an award for Outstanding Drama Series from the Gay & Lesbian Alliance Against Defamation (GLAAD) Media Awards during its first season in 2001.

The GLAAD award was a testimony to St. Patrick's sensitive portrayal of a complex gay character. St. Patrick is not gay himself, and at first had misgivings about identifying himself so closely with a gay character. Mainstream society, and especially mainstream African-American society, has been slow to accept gay and lesbian lifestyles, and St. Patrick was apprehensive that these homophobic attitudes would affect his career. However, he remembered the black actors he had watched in films during his childhood. Some had made difficult choices in order to play socially important roles, as Sidney Poitier did in *Guess Who's Coming to Dinner* (1967). Inspired by those who had gone before him, St. Patrick decided that if he was to play a gay character, it was important not to play a gay stereotype. Having been stereotyped himself by those who made assumptions about him based on his black skin and muscular good looks, he did not want to participate in stereotyping another group of people.

The success of *Six Feet Under* has continued through four seasons. Among the awards that the show and its cast have won every season was a National Leadership Award from the National Gay and Lesbian Task Force, presented to Mathew St. Patrick in 2002 for his development of the role of Keith Charles.

Never one to stop after a single success, St. Patrick continues to expand his career. Along with continuing to seek out acting roles that interest him, he is involved in charity work. He is an active member of the Elizabeth Glaser Pediatric AIDS Foundation and the Best Buddies Organization, which promotes friendship between those with developmental disabilities and those without such disabilities. He has also begun to work on creating his own film projects. Through his own hard work, the young boy who taught himself to read with magazines is becoming a writer.

Though somewhat uncomfortable with the public attention thrust upon him by his sudden fame, St. Patrick takes his position as a role model seriously, viewing his success not with self-satisfaction, but with a sense of responsibility. Not only is he a parent, guiding the growth of his young son, but he has also kept in touch with many of his old friends from the neighborhood, offering support and encouragement to those who did not escape from the damaging effects of the poverty, violence, and racism of the inner city. "My advice is to not get sidetracked by things that don't matter," St. Patrick said to *Back Stage West* writer Pamely Bock. "Keep your focus, be very open to possibilities, and set some concrete goals."

Selected works

Films

Steel Sharks, 1996.
Surface to Air, 1997.

Plays

Full Court Press, 1996.

Television

General Hospital, ABC, 1997.
All My Children, ABC, 1998-2000.
Six Feet Under, HBO, 2001–.

Sources

Periodicals

Back Stage West, August 29, 2002. p. 6.

On-line

"Mathew St. Patrick, as Keith Charles," *Six Feet Under*, www.hbo.com/sixfeetunder/cast/actors/mathew_stpatrick.shtml (September 7, 2004).
"Mathew St. Patrick," *IMDb,* www.imdb.com/name/nm0820783/ (September 7, 2004).

Other

Information for this profile was obtained through an interview with Mathew St. Patrick on October 14, 2004.

—Tina Gianoulis

Wanda Sykes

1964—

Comedian, actor

Wanda Sykes has been doing standup comedy since the late 1980s. Known for her sharp, edgy wit, she has become a regular on Comedy Central and HBO as both a writer and a performer. In 2003 she starred in Fox Television's short-lived *Wanda at Large,* and in 2004 she debuted in *Wanda Does It* on Comedy Central. A book, a standup tour, and various appearances in film and on television also keep Sykes busy as one of the more popular female comics on the comedy circuit.

Sykes, Wanda, photograph. Frederick M. Brown/Getty Images.

Funny Girl

Sykes was born on March 7, 1964, in Portsmouth, Virginia. She grew up in Anne Arundel County, Maryland, in the Washington, D.C. area, with her parents and an older brother. Her father was a colonel in the U.S. Army, and her mother was a journalist. Sykes was opinionated and unrestrained even as a child. "I remember in the first grade telling some woman her wig was crooked," she told *Newsweek*. "I thought I was doing her a favor." She joked her way through school, and as a result her high school yearbook is filled with personal notes from classmates who comment on how comical she was.

After graduating from Arundel High School in 1982, Sykes enrolled at Hampton University in Hampton, Virginia, where she earned a bachelor of science degree in marketing in 1986. Fresh out of college she took a job with the National Security Agency, the government's high-tech communications and intelligence-gathering arm, where she eventually served as a contract specialist dealing with the procurement of spy equipment. Initially she dove into the government bureaucracy with her trademark enthusiasm and energy, but her excitement soon gave way to boredom. In 1987 a local radio station staged a talent show, with comedy as one of the categories, and Sykes decided to enter. Armed with a few jokes she had written while sitting at her desk, she walked onto the stage for the first time.

Although she did not win the talent contest, she received plenty of positive feedback and was exhilarated by the experience of performing. "It was great. It was a rush," she told *Complex Magazine*. "I didn't think about the downside—the rejection. I just got onstage, did it, and fell in love with it. When I finally got into the comedy clubs and found out all the things that could go wrong, that was when the fear hit. I was like,

At a Glance...

Born on March 7, 1964, in Portsmouth, VA; married 1992 (divorced 1998). *Education:* Hampton University, BS, marketing, 1986.

Career: National Security Agency, contract specialist, 1986-91; standup comedian, 1987–; television writer and actress, 1997–.

Awards: Emmy Award, Outstanding Writing for a Variety, Music, or Comedy Special, 1999; American Comedy Award, Outstanding Female Stand Up Comic, 2001; Comedy Central's Commie Award, Funniest TV Actress, 2004.

Address: *Agent*—William Morris, 1325 Avenue of the Americas, New York, NY 10019.

Oh my God. What have I subjected myself to?" Fear of rejection was not enough to dissuade Sykes from pursuing her newfound passion, however. After five years at the National Security Agency, she quit her day job. She moved to New Jersey so she could travel the comedy club circuits around the Washington, D.C., and Baltimore areas.

Became Writer and Comedian

In 1995 Sykes opened for Chris Rock, who was duly impressed with her sharp and edgy style. As a result, when Rock began production of his own critically acclaimed HBO series, *The Chris Rock Show*, in 1997, he invited Sykes to join the show as a writer and performer. As a member of the cast and writing team, Sykes received three Primetime Emmy nominations and in 1999 won for "Outstanding Writing for a Variety, Music, or Comedy Special." Sykes honed her skills on *The Chris Rock Show* for five years, until that show was cancelled in 2002.

During that time she continued to pursue other outlets for her comedy. She was first invited to perform on *The Tonight Show with Jay Leno* in 2001, and in that year her no-holds-barred standup act earned her the American Comedy Award for "Outstanding Female Stand Up Comic." She also appeared in several television series, including *The Drew Carey Show*, *Dr. Katz: Professional Therapist*, and *MADtv*. Sykes also had a regular role on Larry David's *Curb Your Enthusiasm*, produced by HBO. She played the part of the sarcastic, sometimes caustic, friend and neighbor of Larry David's television wife. In 2001 Sykes appeared on *The Downer Channel*, a short-lived sitcom on NBC that was quickly panned by the critics and ignored by viewers, and in 2002 she hosted a 12-episode season of Comedy Central's standup series *Premium Blend* and starred in a half-hour special "Comedy Central Presents Wanda Sykes." She also has a reoccurring role on Comedy Central's *Crank Yankers*, in which she provides voice-over crank phone calls for the puppet-based show.

Sykes landed an ongoing gig as a correspondent for HBO's *Inside the NFL* after an HBO executive witnessed her comical evaluation, or heckling, of sportscaster Bob Costas during an after-production party. "He couldn't avoid hearing me," she told *The Washington Post*, "I was pretty loud. I'm a Bob Costas fan, but after a half-hour conversation with Bob, you find out Bob knows everything. Every now and then, he should just shrug, mix it up. That would amaze people." As a correspondent, Sykes contributes comedy bits and banter as well as light-hearted, comical player interviews.

Turned to Movies

In 1998 Sykes had a small part in the independent film *Tomorrow Night*. Her first role in a film by a major studio was *Nutty Professor II: The Klumps*, released in 2000 and starring Eddie Murphy, and in 2001 she appeared in *Down to Earth*, starring Chris Rock. In that same year, Sykes also appeared in the comedy *Pootie Tang* as Pootie's (played by Lance Crouthers) girlfriend Biggie Shorty. Although the film, which was based on a *Saturday Night Live* sketch, was panned by critics, it did find something of a niche following that earned Sykes expanded recognition.

Eventually Fox Television offered Sykes her own sitcom. *Wanda at Large*, which first aired on March 26, 2003, as a midseason replacement show, cast Sykes as a Washington, D.C.-based comedian who becomes a correspondent and host of a Sunday morning political talk show and subsequently butts heads with her conservative co-host, played by Phil Morris. Sykes served as the show's star, writer, and executive producer. "She has her feet firmly planted in her own ego," Nancy Franklin wrote in *The New Yorker*, "and you couldn't knock her down, though you might want to.... [She] has an oversized and combative personality: she's not just in the house; she's in your room and she's in your face." Most critics gave a nod to Sykes's comedic strength, and the first episodes showed strong ratings. However, after the summer hiatus, the show returned to the air in the new season with poor ratings, and in early November of 2003, with just 3.8 million viewers, it was cancelled.

Despite the failure of the show, Sykes's career has continued to progress. In 2003 Comedy Central aired a one-hour comedy special "Wanda Sykes: Tongue Untied." She also signed a deal with Atria to publish a book. *Yeah, I Said It*, released in October of 2004, is a collection of humorous commentaries and witticisms on a wide variety of issues, including relationships, transsexuals, vanity license plates, and the death penalty. "Writing a book is one of the great American dreams," Sykes told *Essence*. "It's right up there with finding your soul mate, or buying a home, or raising nonsociopathic kids." In October 2004, Sykes began her traveling to promote her book with her "Cotton T-Shirt Tour."

Early in 2004 Sykes signed a six-show deal with Comedy Central for the series *Wanda Does It*, a half-hour show in which Sykes takes on the duties of various service providers. For example, in the pilot, she decides to learn how to fly after suffering through a turbulent flight. In other episodes she becomes a professional repossessor, a prostitute, and a casino employee. Her efforts in front of the small screen earned her Comedy Central's 2004 Commie Award for "Funniest TV Actress."

Sykes, who was divorced in 1998 after a six-year marriage to a pharmaceutical salesman, maintains households on both coasts and continues to juggle a very busy calendar. Along with her standup and book promotion tours, she also has several upcoming movie roles, including *Monster-in-Law*, starring Jennifer Lopez, and *The Barnyard*, an animated comedy in which Sykes lends her voice to the character Bessy the Cow. Both films are schedule for release in 2005. "I work all the time, I really do," she told *Jet*. "But I don't mind, it's fulfilling. I love what I'm doing and I don't think I'd be happy doing it any other way."

Selected works

Films

Tomorrow Night (independent film), 1998.
Nutty Professor II: The Klumps, Universal Studios, 2000.
Down to Earth, Paramount Home Entertainment, 2001.
Pootie Tang, Paramount Home Entertainment, 2001.
Monster-in-Law, New Line Cinema, 2005.
The Barnyard, Paramount Pictures, 2005.

Television

The Chris Rock Show, HBO, 1997-2002.
Curb Your Enthusiasm, HBO, 1999.
The Downer Channel, NBC, 2001.
Crank Yankers, Comedy Central, 2002.
Premium Blend, Comedy Central, 2002.
Wanda at Large, Fox, 2003.
Wanda Does It, Comedy Central 2004.

Books

Yeah, I Said It, Atria, 2004.

Sources

Periodicals

Black Issue Book Review, May-June 2003, p. 8.
Daily Variety, August 21, 2002, p. 3; September 22, 2003, p. 1; April 26, 2004, p. 6.
Ebony, October 2003, p. 118.
Entertainment Weekly, March 21, 2003, p. 23; December 19, 2003, p. 62.
Essence, December 2000, p. 60; December 2003, p. 228; October 2004, p. 146.
Jet, October 13, 2003, p. 58-62.
Newsweek, April 7, 2003, p. 62.
New Yorker, May 5, 2003, p. 102.
People Weekly, March 31, 2003, p. 25; April 7, 2003, p. 197.
Publisher's Weekly, August 16, 2004, p. 56.
Washington Post, February 16, 2001, p. 5; August 12, 2003, p. B06; March 26, 2003, p. B05; December 10, 2003, p. B06; February 9, 2004, p. B06.

On-line

"Wanda Does It," *Comedy Central*, www.comedycentral.com/tv_shows/wandadoesit (October 20, 2004).
"Wanda Sykes," *Biography Resource Center*, www.galenet.com/servlet/BioRC (October 20, 2004).
Wanda Sykes, www.wandasykes.com (October 20, 2004).

—Kari Bethel

Luther Vandross

1951—

Singer, songwriter, producer

Vandross, Luther, photograph. © 2002 Landov LLC. All rights reserved. Reproduced by permission.

For many years, Luther Vandross was the vintage Cadillac among the banged-up jalopies in the used car lot of male pop singers. With a sound that echoed the smooth soul stylings of the 1960s, Vandross was a fixture on the rhythm and blues charts from his solo recording debut in 1981 until his tragic stroke in 2003. Over the course of his career he has released a string of platinum albums and established himself as one of the leading romantic singers of his generation. Much of his appeal comes from his emotional approach to music, which is modeled after great female vocalists such as his friends Aretha Franklin and Dionne Warwick.

Came from Musical Family

Born in New York City in 1951, Vandross was the youngest of four children. His father, an upholsterer, died when Luther was only eight years old, leaving his mother, Mary Ida Vandross, to support the family through her job as a licensed practical nurse. They lived in the Alfred E. Smith housing project in lower Manhattan. The Vandross family was a musical one, and from an early age Luther was exposed to the black pop music of the day. His first piano lessons came at the age of three. His sister Pat was a member of a doo-wop group called the Crests, whose song "Sixteen Candles" was a fairly big hit when it came out.

By the time he was 13, Vandross was the only child still living at home. He and his mother moved to the Bronx. As a senior at William Howard Taft High School, Vandross became obsessed with the girl groups of the Motown label, as well as the gospel-based soul sounds being produced by the likes of Aretha Franklin and Cissy Houston. He was part of a crowd that liked to hang out in the school hallways and sing doo-wop. As he immersed himself more deeply in music, his interest in school waned. His grades plummeted, and he became increasingly certain that his future was in the music industry.

After high school, Vandross enrolled at Western Michigan University in Kalamazoo. He quit after two miserable semesters, more determined than ever to pursue his dream of becoming a professional singer. In 1972 a song written by Vandross, "Everybody Rejoice," was chosen for the Broadway musical *The Wiz*. Although he received substantial royalties for the composition,

> ### At a Glance . . .
>
> Born Luther Ronzoni Vandross on April 20, 1951, in New York, NY; son of Mary Ida (a licensed practical nurse) Vandross. *Education*: Attended Western Michigan University, 1970.
>
> **Career**: Professional singer and songwriter, 1972–. Wrote the song "Everybody Rejoice" for the Broadway musical The Wiz, 1972; toured with David Bowie, 1974; sang and arranged on albums by numerous performers, including Chaka Khan, Bette Midler, Average White Band, and Roberta Flack, 1974–; sang commercial jingles, c. 1970s-1981; solo performer and record producer, 1981–.
>
> **Selected awards**: National Academy of Recording Arts & Sciences, Most Valuable Player–Best Male Vocalist, 1979; Grammy Awards, 1979, 1990, 1991 (2), 1996, 2003 (4); NAACP Image Awards, 1990, 2003.
>
> **Address**: *Office*—c/o J-Records, 745 Fifth Ave., New York, NY 10151.

the money was not enough to support him completely, and Vandross continued to work at a variety of "day jobs" while he continued in his pursuit of fame.

Entered the Music Industry through the Back Door

In 1974, Vandross received his first real professional break. A childhood friend, guitarist Carlos Alomar, had landed a job backing British singer David Bowie, and he invited Vandross to accompany him to a recording session during the making of Bowie's album *Young Americans*. During the session, Bowie overheard Vandross mentioning some background vocal arrangement suggestions to Alomar. Bowie loved the ideas, and he immediately hired Vandross to sing and arrange backup vocals for the album. He also recorded a Vandross-penned song, "Fascination." When the album was finished, Vandross joined the Bowie tour as a backup singer. Through Bowie, Vandross made many important connections in the music industry, laying the groundwork for his own budding career.

One of the musicians to whom Bowie introduced Vandross was Bette Midler. Impressed with his voice and ideas, she hired Vandross to sing backup vocals on her next two albums. Vandross soon became much sought after for singing and arranging work, and was finally able to concentrate on music full-time. Among the artists whose recordings his voice appeared on during the next few years were Chaka Khan, Carly Simon, Ringo Starr, the Average White Band, Barbra Streisand, and Donna Summer. He also became one of Madison Avenue's favorite voices for commercial jingles. During the late 1970s, Vandross's anonymous voice was used to sell everything from fried chicken to long-distance telephone service, not to mention as a recruiting tool for the U.S. Army.

Through this combination of commercial and backup work, Vandross was earning a more-than-comfortable living from music by the end of the 1970s. Artistically, however, those jobs did not satisfy him, and he continued to try to break out as a solo act. He formed or joined several groups, with such names as Luther, Bionic Boogie, and Change, but none proved commercially viable. He also sang the lead vocal on Chic's song "Dance, Dance, Dance."

Hit the Big Time

Part of the problem in landing a solo recording contract was Vandross's insistence on total creative control of the recording process. Another problem was the prevalence of disco, a musical form antithetical to Vandross's lyrical approach. Finally, in 1980, Vandross used his own money to rent a studio and began recording. He took the resulting handful of songs to Epic Records, and he was immediately given a contract. Epic released Vandross's first solo album, *Never Too Much*, in 1981. The album sold more than one million copies, cracked the top ten on black pop charts, and effectively launched Vandross's career as a solo superstar.

Vandross released his follow-up album, *For Ever, For Always, For Love*, one year later. It, too, sold more than one million copies and cemented Vandross's growing reputation as a first class love balladeer. His third LP, *Busy Body*, likewise sold more a million copies. All three of those albums, and the next three as well, reached number one on the R&B charts. In fact, it was not until 1989, with *The Best of Luther, The Best of Love*, that a Vandross LP failed to make it to the top of the R&B charts. Each of those albums also included at least one single that made it into the R&B top ten. Meanwhile, his talent as a producer was also gaining recognition. In 1982, Vandross produced Cheryl Lynn's hit album *Instant Love*, and over the years, he has produced songs and/or albums for such stars as Diana Ross, Aretha Franklin, and Whitney Houston.

As Vandross's career expanded, so did his waistline. At times his weight soared to well over 300 pounds. Angered by the constant mention of his size in the press, where he was tagged with such nicknames as the "heavyweight of soul," Vandross shed 120 pounds, only to seesaw back and forth between weight extremes for the next several years. In a number of interviews, Vandross has attributed this yo-yoing to his love life. When things are going well, he loses weight; when he is heartsick, he overcompensates with food.

Achieved Crossover Stardom

In spite of the success of his first several albums, by the late 1980s Vandross was vexed by his failure to produce a major crossover hit—one that would be as popular among white audiences as it was with black buyers. He finally cracked the pop top ten in 1989, with the single "Here and Now." From that point on, Vandross became the kind of fixture on the pop charts that he had been on the R&B lists for nearly a decade. In 1991, his gospel medley "Power of Love/Love Power" reached number four on the pop charts. In addition to his own albums, Vandross continued to produce recordings for other artists on occasion, and, in 1993, he made his motion picture acting debut in Robert Townsend's *Meteor Man*.

In 1994 Vandross released the album Songs, which consisted of remakes of hits from the past. "Endless Love," a duet with pop star Mariah Carey from the album, soared to number two on the pop charts. That same year he was spotlighted in a PBS television special, *In the Spotlight,* recorded at the Royal Albert Hall in London. He released a Christmas album in 1995, featuring seven new co-written songs, along with a variety of classic carols. And in 1997 Vandross sang the national anthem at the 1997 NFL Super Bowl, a sure sign of his crossover success.

Vandross's string of successes and his high public profile allowed him to experiment musically, and to seek new freedom with a new label. In 1998 ended his 16-year partnership with the Epic label, a partnership that had produced 12 hit albums and sent 22 singles onto the R&B charts. Vandross soon signed with Virgin Records, and in 1998 he released *I Know*, featuring such stars as Stevie Wonder, Cassandra Wilson, and Bob James. The album received generally excellent reviews, but Vandross soon left Virgin. He released *Smooth Love* on the AMW label in 2000, then found a more stable home with J-Records, where released three albums between 2001 and 2003, including *Luther Vandross, Dance with My Father,* and *Live 2003 at Radio City Music Hall.* Each of the albums was well received by fans and critics alike, and Vandross continued to attract adoring fans at his concert. Explaining his success to *Jet,* Vandross said: "It's a really good feat at this point in my career. That's what makes it so special. I don't even try to figure it out or analyze it. I just go ahead and do what feels good and that seems to work."

By 2003 Vandross was at the peak of his career. Though considered one of the enduring artists of the late twentieth century, he continued to release vibrant, meaningful music. Sadly, in April of 2003 Vandross suffered a debilitating stroke that left him temporarily in a coma; the stroke was likely caused by a combination of his recent weight gain and his ongoing struggle with diabetes. Vandross's recovery has been slow and difficult. Six months after his stroke he was just regaining the ability to speak and sing, yet he was still confined to a wheelchair and remained weak. As a result of the stroke Vandross was unable to attend the 2003 Grammy Awards (held in early 2004), where *Dance with My Father* was honored with four Grammys, including the award for Song of the Year. The Grammy ceremony included a tribute to Vandross performed by Alicia Keys and Celine Dion. In a taped appearance, Vandross made his first public statement, telling fans: "I wish I could be with you there tonight. I want to thank everyone for your love and support. And remember, when I say goodbye it's never for long, because I believe in the power of love."

Selected discography

Never Too Much, Epic, 1981.
Forever, For Always, For Love, Epic, 1982.
Busy Body, Epic, 1983.
The Night I Fell in Love, Epic, 1985.
Give Me The Reason, Epic, 1986.
Any Love, Epic, 1988.
The Best of Luther Vandross, The Best of Love, Epic, 1989.
Power of Love (includes "Power of Love"/"Love Power"), Epic, 1991.
Never Let Me Go, Epic, 1993.
Songs (includes "Endless Love"), Epic, 1994.
This Is Christmas, Epic, 1995.
Your Secret Love, Sony, 1996.
I Know, Virgin, 1998.
Greatest Hits, Epic, 1999.
Smooth Love, AMW, 2000.
Luther Vandross, J-Records, 2001.
The Ultimate Luther Vandross, Epic, 2001.
The Very Best of Luther Vandross, Sony, 2002.
Dance with My Father, J-Records, 2003.
Live 2003 at Radio City Music Hall, J-Records, 2003.
The Essential Luther Vandross, Epic/Legacy, 2003.

Sources

Periodicals

Ebony, December 1985, pp. 83-87; December 1991, pp. 93-98; December 18, 1995, pp. 32-37.
Entertainment Weekly, October 17, 2003, p. 34.
Jet, June 28, 1993, pp. 34-36; October 24, 1994, pp. 36-39; July 16, 2001, p. 12; January 19, 2004, p. 58.

New York, February 15, 1982, pp. 45-49.
New York Times Magazine, September 22, 1991, pp. 53-63.
People, February 28, 1983, pp. 101-102; September 7, 1998, p. 121; June 16, 2003, p. 101; October 20, 2003, p. 95.
Rolling Stone, September 6, 1990, pp. 76-81.

On-line

"Luther Vandross," *Biography Resource Center,* www.galenet.com/servlet/BioRC (October 28, 2004).
Luther Vandross, www.luthervandross.com/ (January 24, 2004).

—Robert R. Jacobson and Tom Pendergast

Ozzie Virgil

1933—

Baseball player, coach

There will be no plaque for Ozzie Virgil in the Baseball Hall of Fame. The statistics he compiled during his nine-year major league career simply do not qualify him for baseball's great honor. But there is no doubt that Virgil deserves acknowledgement for the firsts that he achieved, even if it is just an asterisk next to his name in the baseball record book. In 1956, he became the first native Dominican to play in the major leagues. Then in 1958—eleven seasons after Jackie Robinson integrated the big leagues with the Brooklyn Dodgers—he became the first person of color to play for the Detroit Tigers.

Virgil was born Osvaldo Jose Virgil in Montecristi, Dominican Republic, on May 17, 1933. His family moved to The Bronx, New York, when he was thirteen, and he attended DeWitt Clinton High School. "I did not make the baseball team in high school but did play sandlot ball," he recalled in a 1997 interview with William M. Anderson in *Michigan History Magazine*. "I played in a Puerto Rican league, which had eight or nine teams." After graduating from high school in 1950, Virgil joined the U.S. Marine Corps Reserves. "They called me up to active duty. I played baseball with the Marine Corps team at Camp LeJeune, North Carolina. When I got out, the (New York) Giants gave me a tryout and signed me."

Played in the Minor Leagues

Virgil made his minor league debut in 1953 with St. Cloud, Minnesota, in the Northern League, where he hit .259. In 1954, he upped his average to .291 at Danville, North Carolina, in the Piedmont League. By 1955, Virgil had developed into a highly-touted prospect. Past midseason, he was hitting .309 for Dallas in the Texas League. "It's too early to bring him up, but the Giant front office suspects it has a major league third baseman in the making in Ossie (sic) Virgil...," wrote sportswriter Zander Hollander in 1955 in the *New York World-Telegram and Sun*. That season, Virgil led Texas League third sackers with a .975 fielding percentage and was named to the All-Star team. He further honed his skills by playing winter ball in Puerto Rico.

After spending the 1956 season with Minneapolis, where he hit .278 with ten home-runs and 73 runs-batted-in, Virgil made his major league debut with the New York Giants on September 23. He appeared in three games, collecting 5 hits in 12 at-bats. More importantly, he was the first Dominican to play for any major league team, predating players from Hall-of-Famer Juan Marichal to Sammy Sosa, Vladimir Guerrero, Albert Pujols, Pedro Martinez, Manny Ramirez, and Miguel Tejada. "The Dominican Republic likely could have sent several players to the major leagues before Ozzie Virgil made his debut in 1956," observed Kathleen O'Brien, writing in the *Fort Worth Star-Telegram* in 2004, "but racial discrimination was still the norm."

Virgil spent the 1957 season with the Giants. During the campaign, *New York World-Telegram and Sun* sportswriter Bill Roeder described him as soft-spoken,

At a Glance . . .

Born Osvaldo Jose Virgil on May 17, 1933, in Montecristi, Dominican Republic; married Maria Lopez, January 29, 1955; children: three (including Ozzie Virgil, Jr., who played in the major leagues between 1980-1990).

Career: Professional baseball player, 1953-68; played in the major leagues for the New York Giants, 1956-57, the Detroit Tigers, 1958-61, the Kansas City Athletics, 1961, the Baltimore Orioles, 1962, the Pittsburgh Pirates, 1965, and the San Francisco Giants, 1966, 1969; Phoenix (San Francisco Giants' AAA affiliate), player-coach, 1968; San Francisco Giants, coach, 1969-72; held numerous jobs in professional baseball, among them managing winter league teams in the Dominican Republic, Venezuela, and Mexico, coaching for the Montreal Expos, San Diego Padres, and Seattle Mariners, and coaching, scouting, working in player development, and managing in the minor leagues for the San Francisco Giants, 1971–.

Awards: American Association All-Star Team, 1959; voted "Smartest Player" in a poll of International League managers, 1964; voted the Phoenix Giants' most popular player, 1967; Pacific Coast League All-Star Team, 1967.

"a polite, good-looking chap." By then, it had become clear that Virgil was not star material. Roeder added, "As far as we can tell, it's neither Ossie's (sic) fault nor anyone else's that he has such a hard time attracting attention. He seems to be a good ballplayer, but not the kind that makes a big impression."

Before the 1958 season, Virgil was dealt to the Detroit Tigers along with first baseman Gail Harris for infielder Jim Finigan and $25,000. "I was very disappointed when traded to Detroit," Virgil told *Michigan History Magazine* in 1997. "I thought the Giants needed a third baseman at that particular time. I knew that the Tigers did not have any black players on their roster or had never invited one to spring training. I wondered what they were going to do with me."

Recalled to the Majors

Virgil began the season with the Tigers' Charleston farm club, where he hit .293 and led the American Association with 34 runs-batted-in. On June 5, he was promoted back to the big leagues. The following day, he made his debut against the Washington Senators in the nation's capitol. "I never expected to play in the major leagues this year," Virgil told the *Detroit Free Press* after his promotion. "I had resigned myself to another year in the minors. Frankly, I'm completely surprised."

The Tigers' front office downplayed Virgil's advancement. "He was the best player available at [third base] in our farm system," team publicity director Neal (Doc) Fenkell told Lawrence Casey of the *Michigan Chronicle*. "Virgil was promoted on merit alone. As far as we are concerned he will be just another ball player." Nonetheless, his call-up was of utmost significance to Detroit's black community, some of whose leaders were threatening to organize a boycott of Tigers' games because of the team's reluctance to integrate. The *Detroit News* reported that Virgil's promotion was "received with satisfaction by Negro leaders and fans...." Virgil's own version of his promotion is more ambiguous. In 1997—almost four decades after integrating the Tigers—Virgil told *Detroit Free Press* reporter Jodie Valade, that, although warmly received by most Tigers' fans, he was not acknowledged as a "true representative" by the city's black community. "The only thing I didn't like was that the black people in Detroit didn't accept me," he explained. "They thought of me more as a Dominican Republic player instead of a Negro. "If they called me black, fine. If they called me white, fine. If they called me Latino, fine. I didn't care what they called me—I just wanted to play."

Virgil had earned his opportunity with the Tigers, and his Briggs Stadium debut was triumphant. In his first game in the Detroit ballpark, on June 17, he went five-for-five, doubling and singling off Washington Senators' hurler Pedro Ramos and adding three singles off Al Cicotte. After his final hit, the crowd of 29,794 serenaded him with a standing ovation. "In the locker room Virgil accepted congratulations from teammates and visitors with inherent modesty," reported *Detroit News* sportswriter Sam Greene, who added that the ballplayer "dismissed his effort as a 'good night' and voiced gratitude for his reception by the Detroit public." Virgil often has cited this game as his foremost baseball thrill.

During the 1961 season, the Tigers traded Virgil to the Kansas City Athletics. He eventually served brief stints with the Baltimore Orioles (for one game), Pittsburgh Pirates, and San Francisco Giants while shuttling between the major and minor leagues. Virgil retired as an active player after the 1968 campaign; he never appeared in more than 96 major league games a season (which he accomplished with the 1957 New York Giants). His big league career lasted 324 games as an infielder, outfielder, and catcher. He collected 174 hits in 753 at-bats for a lifetime batting average of .231.

Began His Coaching Career

Virgil's expertise at teaching the game was acknowledged in 1968 when he became the player-coach of Phoenix, the Giants' AAA affiliate. After that year's campaign, Clyde King, the Giants manager, named him a coach. At the time, he was one of four black coaches in the major league; the others were Elston Howard (New York Yankees), Jim Gilliam (Los Angeles Dodgers), and Luke Easter (Cleveland Indians). There were no black managers or general managers, and few persons of color in major league front offices.

Virgil's hiring was a testament to the high esteem in which he was held by the Giants. "His tutoring of young players and all-round savvy helped the Giants take the West Division championship in 1971," observed Pat Frizzell in *The Sporting News* in 1974. Charlie Fox, by then the Giants manager, told Frizzell, "We won a lot of games with Ozzie coaching at third." Virgil himself added, "I enjoy managing and I enjoy coaching at third base. You're right in the game there.... I like to work with young players, too, and help them if I can."

Virgil remained with the Giants through 1972. During subsequent decades, he led a nomadic existence as a major league coach, scout, and winter league manager. His early successes included winning pennants managing Aguilas in the Dominican League during 1971-72 and Caracas in the Venezuelan League in 1972-73. He coached for the San Diego Padres against the Detroit Tigers in the 1984 World Series. He also coached in Montreal and Seattle, and managed various teams in the Dominican Republic, Venezuela, and Mexico. Virgil's son, Ozzie, Jr., a catcher, played in the major leagues from 1980-1990 and, in 2004, his grandson, Oklahoma State outfielder Jose Virgil, was selected by the St. Louis Cardinals in the 18th round of the baseball draft.

With typical modesty, Virgil has downplayed his breaking the color line in Detroit while expressing dismay that so many younger players are unfamiliar with Jackie Robinson. "He gave me the opportunity to make a living in baseball," Virgil told the *Detroit Free Press* in 1997. "If these kids don't know Jackie Robinson, they're crazy. He opened the game to all of us."

Sources

Periodicals

Detroit Free Press, June 6, 1958; June 9, 1958; July 5, 1997.
Detroit News, June 6, 1958; June 18, 1958.
Michigan Chronicle, June 14, 1958.
Michigan History Magazine, September-October 1997, pp. 47-53.
New York Times, April 6, 1969, p. S3; April 15, 1997, p. B15.
New York World- Telegram and Sun, July 26, 1955; September 22, 1956; May 2, 1957.
Sporting News, February 23, 1974.

On-line

"Ozzie Virgil," *The Ballplayers Historical Biographies,* www.baseball-almanac.com/players/player.php?p=virgioz01 (October 13, 2004).
"Ozzie Virgil," *Baseball Reference,* baseballreference.com/v/virgioz01.shtml (October 13, 2004).
"Ozzie Virgil," *MLB,* mlb.mlb.com/NASApp/mlb/mlb/stats_historical/mlb_individual_stats_player.jsp?playerID=123736 (October 13, 2004).

—Rob Edelman

Bill White

1933?—

Baseball player, broadcaster, league executive

When Bill White was named president of baseball's National League in 1989, he became the highest-ranking black executive in all of professional sports. With a salary of $250,000 per year in a demanding administrative position that requires resolution, judgment, and a thorough grounding in the game of baseball, White was not only expected to bring a new wave of integration to the all-white halls of baseball management, he was also expected to do a very good job. As Rich Ashburn put it in the *Philadelphia Daily News,* "The National League should be in pretty good hands.... Bill White is intelligent, articulate, firm and fair. And he's determined." By 1994, however, White had left the office, openly noting his frustration at working with baseball owners.

At the time of White's appointment, blacks were well represented on teams in virtually every American sport, but they remained rare in managerial and executive positions. But White did not necessarily see his appointment as a means to correct that imbalance. Both he and the baseball team owners who chose him agreed that it was his experience, his maturity, and his love of the game that made him the man for the job.

White, Bill, photograph. AP/Wide World Photos. Reproduced by permission.

Peter O'Malley, chairman of the search committee and owner of the Los Angeles Dodgers, remarked to the *New York Times:* "Bill White was selected because he was the best man for the job. He was the only man who was offered the job and, fortunately, he was the only man who accepted. Race was not a factor."

For his own part, White had this to say about the position. "I've been in the game since 1952," he told the *Boston Globe.* "It wasn't integrated. When I came into baseball, spring training wasn't integrated. The country wasn't integrated. I think we've both come along. I'm here now, and there have been quite a few improvements in hiring at certain levels. I feel that will continue, and the people here feel the same way.... I've told people the most important thing that has happened in baseball history was Jackie Robinson getting a chance to play. It gave a lot of people before who had no hope a lot of hope. I'm glad for the opportunity, and I will do the best that I can. If I didn't think I could do this job, I'd be foolish to take it."

Born in Lakewood, Florida, in 1933(?), White attended Warren G. Harding High School in Warren, Ohio,

At a Glance ...

Born William DeKova White in Lakewood, FL, c. 1933; divorced; five children. *Education:* Attended Hiram College.

Career: New York Giants (later San Francisco Giants), professional baseball player, 1956-59; St. Louis Cardinals, professional baseball player, 1959-65, 1969; Philadelphia Phillies, professional baseball player, 1966-68. St. Louis Cardinals and Philadelpia Phillies, radio commentator, 1970-71; New York Yankees, television commentator, 1971-89; National League, president, 1989-1994.

Memberships: National Baseball Hall of Fame, committee on baseball veterans, 1994–, and board of directors, 2000–;

Awards: National League All-Star Team selection, 1959, 1960, 1961, 1963, 1964; Gold Glove for first base, 1960-66.

---

before attending college at Hiram College, near Cleveland. White earned a reputation as an outspoken player almost from the moment he signed with his first major league team in 1953. Perhaps because he came to professional baseball after several years in college, he was quicker to address injustices than others, and more forceful in demanding that changes be made. As *New York Times* correspondent Claire Smith wrote: "Bill White has long prided himself on being a person who cannot be easily fitted into any mold. In the early 1960s, when it was safer for one's career as well as health to acquiesce quietly to the nation's Jim Crow laws, White was among a vocal minority of black players who spoke out vociferously against inadequacies at Florida spring-training sites and in minor league cities throughout the South." White originally agreed to play baseball with the New York Giants merely as a means to earn college tuition (he was enrolled in pre-med courses). He made the Giants' roster in 1956, however, and moved with the team to San Francisco, embarking on a fine 13-year career.

White hit 22 home runs as a rookie with the Giants. In 1959 he was traded to the St. Louis Cardinals, where he batted .286 and played first base. The beginning of the 1965 season found White with the Philadelphia Phillies, where he played until the end of 1968. For his last season he returned to the Cardinals, performing well despite severe injuries to his Achilles tendon. His career statistics are far above the average for a sport that uses players like fodder: in 1,673 games he had 5,972 at bats, with 1,706 hits, 202 home runs, and 870 runs batted in. Six times he was named to the National League All-Star team, and seven times he brought home the Gold Glove for first base.

After retiring from baseball, White found work as a radio and television announcer in St. Louis and then in Philadelphia. Howard Cosell happened to catch White doing play-by-play for a college basketball game and recommended him to the New York Yankees. In 1971 White entered the broadcast booth with Phil Rizzuto and began an 18-year tenure as the Yankees' play-by-play man for televised games. White carried his strong opinions on affirmative action with him into the booth, but he resisted using his power to become a spokesman for special interest groups. Instead he concentrated on baseball and became immensely popular with the hard-to-please Yankee fans.

White never made any bones about it: he loved being an announcer for the Yankees. The job paid a princely salary of $300,000 per year for about 60 days' work each summer, allowing him to purchase a stately home in Bucks County, Pennsylvania, for his family of five children. In 1989, White told the *Philadelphia Daily News:* "The Yankees took a trip to the West Coast last summer. I worked a game in Seattle and then I flew to Alaska and fished for five days. I flew back to Oakland for a game and then fished another four days in northern California. That's the kind of thing I'm going to miss."

His years of experience with baseball notwithstanding, White was surprised when he was approached about taking the presidency of the National League. White told the *New York Times:* "My first comment was, 'Are you serious?' But in meeting with people, I found out they were dead serious. Once I knew that, we proceeded from there." White was the unanimous choice of the National League team owners to succeed A. Bartlett Giamatti, who was named Baseball Commissioner. As president of the league, White arbitrated disputes between players and umpires and supervised contracts for the league's professional players. He also determined the rules under which the teams play. Most importantly, he presided over a major expansion of major league teams, expected to bring baseball into a number of new American cities.

What White did not do as league president was actively champion the recruiting of more minorities in managerial positions within baseball. When he took the job, White told the *Boston Globe:* "My goal is to be the best president I can be. I hope that in the opinion of the committee, I met those qualifications. I know my hiring will be symbolic and important to some people. To me, it's getting on with my life and doing something that I enjoy." As president, he told *Ebony* that "I haven't used my position to try and be visible to do anything except do my job here." But he was very clear that he hoped that his example of effective management would make it evident to everyone that blacks could handle positions of responsibility.

By 1993, however, White had grown increasingly frustrated with the difficulties of his position. Team owners were not interested in following the guidance of a strong league president, and backstage political gamesmanship meant that White was often thwarted in his efforts to institute new practices or overruled by the more powerful commissioner of baseball. Most frustrating of all was the aborted search for a new commissioner. Though White was asked by the owners to lead the highly-publicized search, in fact the owners fully intended to renew the contract of the current commissioner, Bud Selig. Unwilling to be a pawn in the owners' games, White announced his intention to leave office in March of 1993. When the owners had taken little action to replace him nearly a year later, he stepped down in March of 1994. Asked by Frank Dolson of the *Knight Ridder/Tribune News Service* to describe his feelings about his job, White said "it's been a great experience, gave me a lot of insight. It gave me a chance…to evaluate the owners and form opinions of them." Prompted to describe his opinions of the owners, White—who always strived to uphold the honor of the game— replied diplomatically: "they vary."

Since his retirement White has largely disappeared from the public eye, though he does serve on several committees for the Baseball Hall of Fame.

Sources

Periodicals

Boston Globe, February 4, 1989; February 13, 1989.
Ebony, August 1992, p. 52.
Knight Ridder/Tribune News Service, January 22, 1994.
Philadelphia Daily News, February 16, 1989.
Philadelphia Inquirer, February 4, 1989.
New York Times, February 4, 1989; February 5, 1989; September 17, 1990.
Sports Illustrated, September 17, 1990, p. 81.
Washington Post, February 4, 1989.

—Mark Kram and Tom Pendergast

L. Douglas Wilder

1931—

Politician, lawyer

Wilder, L. Douglas, photograph. © Tim Wright/Corbis.

On January 14, 1990, L. Douglas Wilder was sworn in as governor of Virginia, joining a line that includes Patrick Henry, Thomas Jefferson, and Harry F. Byrd. Wilder became Virginia's 66th governor and the nation's first elected black governor. In 2004, Wilder became the first mayor of the city of Richmond, Virginia. The grandson of slaves, Wilder is a moderate who immediately became a major influence in the U.S. political arena, announcing—but eventually repealing—his decision to run for the Democratic nomination in the 1992 U.S. presidential election. As a *Washington Post* correspondent wrote shortly before Wilder's gubernatorial inauguration, "Willingly or not, Wilder becomes a symbol of the changing climate of politics in the South and the nation as a whole, the aspirations of American blacks to assume an equal place in society, and the uncertainties that confront any public leader as a new century looms."

Wilder himself appeared aware of the significance of his victory in Virginia, noting in the *Richmond News Leader* that his office would be housed just blocks from the old White House of the Confederacy and just miles from the segregated neighborhood where he grew up. "As a boy," he recalled in the *News Leader,* "I read the writings of [former U.S. President] Abraham Lincoln about freedom and equality, and I knew they were referring to me. My victory fulfills all of the dreams that could be dreamed by any person."

Surprisingly, race was hardly an issue in the campaign leading to Wilder's November 1989 election. Rather, abortion became the pivotal controversy, and Wilder benefited from his highly publicized pro-choice stance. His media campaign cast the issue in terms of government intervention and personal privacy, and it invoked such symbols as the American flag and Thomas Jefferson's Monticello to illustrate Wilder's abortion-rights views. In the end, one exit-polling sample indicated that single-issue voters concerned about abortion were 62 percent to 38 percent for him. After the elections, analysts predicted that abortion would be one of the litmus tests for candidates in the early 1990s and that politicians favoring a woman's right to an abortion would most often benefit.

At a Glance . . .

Born Lawrence Douglas Wilder, January 17, 1931, in Richmond, VA; son of Robert Wilder (in insurance sales) and Beulah (Richards) Wilder; married Eunice (divorced, 1978); children: Loren, Lynn, Lawrence, Jr. *Education:* Virginia Union University, BS, 1952; Howard University, JD, 1959. *Military service:* U.S. Army, served in Korea; received Bronze Star.

Career: Attorney, 1959–; Virginia state senator, 1969-86; lieutenant governor of Virginia, 1986-90; governor of Virginia, 1990-94; Richmond, Virginia, mayor, 2004–. Hosted radio talk show, 1994-95; headed state commission, 2002.

Selected memberships: American Bar Association; American Trial Lawyers Association; National Association for the Advancement of Colored People (NAACP); United Negro College Fund.

Selected awards: NAACP, Spingarn Medal, 1990.

Addresses: *Office*—Office of the Mayor, 900 E. Broad St., Richmond, VA 23219.

Grandson of Slaves

Wilder was born on January 17, 1931, in the poor and strictly segregated Richmond neighborhood of Church Hill, a few miles and a world away from the state capitol. His father's parents—James Wilder and Agnes Johnson Wilder—had been slaves in nearby Goochland County. The two were sold to separate owners after their wedding, and James Wilder needed a pass to visit his wife on Sundays. Douglas Wilder was the seventh of eight children born to Robert Wilder, a salesman and supervisor of agents for a black-owned insurance company, and Beulah Wilder, a woman who loved books and kept house full time for her large family.

According to the *Atlanta Constitution,* Wilder described his family's financial situation as "gentle poverty;" his parents never had spare money, but were always able to provide hot meals and warm beds for their children. He remarked in the *Washington Post:* "It was stressed that however things are, they can be better if you make them better. We were never told there were limitations. Our parents acted as if we had great opportunities compared to what they had. We were never afraid of challenge." As a youth, Wilder shined shoes, delivered papers, and waited tables at clubs and hotels in Richmond while attending the all-black Armstrong High School, where he acted in plays, was a sergeant in the cadet corps, and earned good grades.

During his early years, Wilder explained, he was hardly aware of racism because he rarely encountered white people. But as he began riding streetcars he noticed that black people were always seated in the rear. After high school, he was barred from even considering the state's all-white public colleges, so he enrolled in Virginia Union University, a private all-black school in Richmond. There, he studied chemistry, waiting tables to pay his tuition money and learning about racism firsthand.

"I read Ralph Ellison's *Invisible Man,* and I didn't understand it at first," Wilder told the *Washington Post.* "But then I realized, I'm experiencing this. I'm invisible. Here I am serving the coffee, pouring the tea, and guys are telling all these kinds of [racial] jokes around me." *Washington Post* reporter Donald P. Baker wrote that Wilder eventually became so outraged that he half-seriously considered "sprinkling poison in the salads" of white diners. Wilder himself told the *Philadelphia Inquirer* that he instead sought more peaceful solutions. "I won't mislead you and say I was not angry, but I didn't react to anger."

After graduating from college in 1952, Wilder was drafted into the army and served in the Korean War; the experience changed his life dramatically. The army, which had been desegregated by presidential order, was Wilder's first experience in an integrated environment. It also gave him his first opportunity for leadership: he was promoted to sergeant and won the Bronze Star for heroism at Pork Chop Hill in 1953. While dodging enemy fire, he and another soldier had captured 19 North Korean soldiers by hurling smoke grenades in their bunkers.

Back from Korea and armed with a degree in chemistry, Wilder answered an advertisement run by the state of Virginia for a chemist-technician. Upon applying, he was told that the job was not available but that he could become a cook at a state school for troubled boys. He called the experience "humiliating." Around the same time, the U.S. Supreme Court issued its 1954 *Brown v. Board of Education* decision outlawing segregation of public schools. Wilder said the ruling prompted him to attend law school. "It restored my faith," he acknowledged in the *Philadelphia Inquirer.* "It had a very startling effect on me because nine white men wrote the decision. Whether it was because of political expediency, I don't care, but it was something that was cathartic [for me]."

Since there were no Virginia law schools open to blacks, Wilder soon enrolled at Howard University in Washington, D.C. His roommate, Henry Marsh, who later became Richmond's mayor, told the *Washington Post,* "Doug was one of the more outstanding members of the class. He was articulate and intelligent. He had a lot of skills." Upon obtaining his degree, Wilder returned to Church Hill in 1959 to open a law practice. He quickly developed a reputation for flamboyance, driving convertibles and wearing trendy clothes, but also for competence, taking on difficult criminal defense cases. He ran a one-man firm specializing in lucrative personal injury cases and eventually became wealthy.

Entered Politics

After establishing himself as one of Richmond's up-and-coming criminal lawyers, Wilder entered politics in 1969. He announced his bid for a vacant state senate seat, fully aware that no black had ever been elected to that body. Wilder, a Democrat, won a three-way race with less than 50 percent of the vote. Over the next 16 years, however, he was never opposed in a reelection bid for the seat.

In the Virginia state senate Wilder immediately attracted attention. In his first speech, in February of 1970, he called for dropping the state song, "Carry Me Back to Old Virginia," because its lyrics glorified slavery and were offensive to blacks. Wilder told his fellow legislators that he and his wife had walked out of an official dinner when the song was played, with its warm words about "old massa" and the state where "this old darky's heart am long'd to go." His bill never passed and "Carry Me Back" remains Virginia's official, if rarely sung, anthem. His protest, however, immediately established Wilder as the senate's angry young man. Though he had never attended a civil rights demonstration, he was now seen as a spokesperson for black Virginians.

"I was perceived as the fair housing guy, the Martin Luther King guy, the 'Carry Me Back' guy," he pointed out in the *Atlanta Constitution.* "All the pictures of me showed the Afro [haircut], and I was always frowning or snarling. But my record was working with people, too." In fact, Wilder de-emphasized civil rights issues during his 16 years in the legislature, instead focusing on becoming a power among established leaders in the senate. He did, however, launch a nine-year campaign for a state holiday honoring the slain civil rights leader Dr. Martin Luther King, Jr., with the effort ending in a compromise; the day was combined with a long-standing state holiday in January honoring Robert E. Lee and Stonewall Jackson, resulting in a "Lee-Jackson-King Day."

Over the years, noted the *Washington Post,* "Wilder earned a reputation as a shrewd, pragmatic politician who used his engaging personality and deft sense of humor, as well as his clout with black voters, to maneuver into the inner circles of power in Virginia's clubby legislature." Wilder's close friend and political ally, Jay Shropshire, told the *Washington Post,* "He was the black kingpin. They all called on Doug Wilder either up front or out back." The extent of this power was made clear in 1982 when he managed almost single-handedly to block the nomination of the man chosen by Democratic Governor Charles Robb to run for the U.S. Senate. The aspiring nominee, Owen Pickett, then a member of the state House of Delegates, was too conservative to suit Wilder, so Wilder announced plans to run against Pickett as an independent. The threat scuttled Pickett's nomination.

A Power in the Senate

As Wilder's seniority grew in the senate so did his power. By 1985 he was a committee chairman and was rated among the five most influential senators. And while his early legislative record could be considered liberal—particularly on law-and-order issues—he grew more conservative over the years. He began to sponsor fewer anti-discrimination bills and became increasingly interested in stiffening jail sentences.

Republican opponents contended that Wilder changed his views to more conservative positions when he started to think about seeking statewide office. Wilder disagreed, telling a *Philadelphia Inquirer* correspondent, "When you increase your seniority, you don't have to fight as hard to be seen and heard. I started growing politically." Regardless, he was given little chance of success when he ran for lieutenant governor of Virginia in 1985. Prominent Democrats openly feared that public resistance to a black candidate would not only mean defeat for Wilder, but for Democrats on the rest of the statewide ticket as well. But Wilder refused to accept the conventional wisdom, renting a station wagon and, over a period of two months, visiting each of the state's 95 counties and hundreds of its towns. The personal approach worked, and in a state where blacks constitute 19 percent of the voting population, Wilder beat his Republican opponent, 52 to 48 percent, becoming the first black candidate ever elected to statewide office.

As lieutenant governor, a job with limited duties, Wilder concentrated on politics. He made a number of highly publicized speeches urging blacks to assume more responsibility for eliminating social problems in the black community. Such addresses drew praise from conservatives who, in the past, had rarely sided with Wilder. By 1989, Wilder was in such a strong position to run for governor that only one Democrat, state senator Daniel W. Bird, Jr., of Wytheville, offered a challenge for the party's nomination. Bird withdrew early, and Wilder was nominated unanimously.

In the general election, Wilder faced Republican J. Marshall Coleman, a surprise winner of a divisive Republican primary. Coleman tried to paint Wilder as a liberal while presenting himself as the conservative alternative, a stance more in line with Virginia's political tradition. He pledged to make the war on drugs a central goal of his administration and ran hard-hitting television commercials accusing Wilder of being soft on crime. Wilder, meanwhile, focused on positive themes, including his own rise from poverty to a prominent political standing and his ability to form coalitions. The underlying message was clear: he wanted to reassure independent and Republican-leaning whites that he was an approachable politician. Abortion, however, became the overriding issue of the campaign. Coleman's staff included activists from anti-abortion organizations, while Wilder's media consultant had previously worked for a national abortion-rights group. Polls indicated that Wilder benefited more from the issue than Coleman did because most Virginians favored at least some degree of abortion rights. Coleman opposed abortion in nearly all cases.

And while abortion was the most visible issue, race was regarded as a significant force underlying the election. Although Wilder made few direct appeals to the black community, support for him there was close to unanimous. He campaigned hard in white neighborhoods, especially the rural regions of southern Virginia. Spending a record $7 million on the campaign, Wilder was, according to polls, comfortably in the lead going into election day. When the votes were counted, however, he won by the slimmest of margins, beating Coleman by only 6,741 votes.

Became Virginia's First Black Governor

Wilder was inaugurated as governor in January of 1990. "As we salute the idea of freedom today, let us pledge to extend that same freedom to others tomorrow," he told a huge crowd of spectators gathered at Capitol Square. "For we know that freedom is but a word for the man or woman who needs and cannot find a job." Quoting black playwright Lorraine Hansberry, he added, "Freedom is a dream deferred when it dries up like a raisin in the sun."

As governor, Wilder became known for conducting matters in Richmond secretively and earned a reputation for being vengeful toward his adversaries and inconstant in his political agenda. Though he has maintained his pro-choice position and continues to stress the importance of enacting civil rights legislation, he has eschewed his liberal views on the death penalty and taxation. He also gained the attention of the national media in what was referred to as a feud with a former governor of Virginia, U.S. Senator Charles Robb. A years-long rivalry between the two Democrats culminated in allegations by Wilder of phone tapping, and a criminal investigation was initiated. Commenting that the Wilder-Robb dissension may have "irreparably hurt" Robb's career and "[raised] new questions about the Democrats' image," *Newsweek* correspondent Bill Turque noted in 1991, "For Wilder, the feud is likely to burn much of the historic luster from his national reputation."

Wilder has, however, received praise from financial analysts as well as his constituents for maintaining his firm views on fiscal matters, trimming Virginia's budget and cutting government staff during the recession of the early 1990s. "My vision is of a government that is prioritizing the spending of the taxpayer's money," he explained to Range. "We should spend for needed services, not for nonsense." Virginia, an especially hard-hit state during the economic downturn, was faced with a budget deficit of $2.2 billion upon Wilder's inauguration. "Instead of raising taxes," observed *Time* correspondent Laurence I. Barrett, "[Wilder] deftly shaved expenses without cutting major arteries. He also created a $200 million contingency fund as a buffer against a 1992 deficit."

After only two years in the governor's mansion, Wilder announced on September 13, 1991, his intentions to seek the 1992 Democratic presidential nomination. Taking his moderate credo to the national arena, Wilder rose as a viable candidate who offered black voters an alternative to the more liberal aspirant of past elections, Jesse Jackson. The governor drew criticism early in his underfunded campaign, though, for such vague policy proposals as his Put America First Initiative, which entailed a "$50 billion spending cut, $35 billion in breaks for middle-class families and $15 billion in 'reduce bureaucracy grants' to states," according to *Time'* s Barrett. "How this game of musical dollars would lessen the deficit is murky," the reporter remarked.

Pointing to the financial straits of the state of Virginia, Wilder withdrew his candidacy in January of 1992. "I said that if it became too difficult for me to govern the Commonwealth and conduct a presidential campaign, I would terminate one endeavor," Wilder announced in his State of the Commonwealth address to the Virginia General Assembly, as quoted in the *New York Times*. "I was left with a choice: either to devote all of my energies to delivering the message or to guiding Virginia through these difficult times. I have chosen the latter." Ayres also cited lack of voter confidence and Wilder's less than one million-dollar store of campaign funds as reasons for his withdrawal. With his term as governor ending in 1994, Wilder, a man who, according to Barrett, "is in love with public life," will no doubt remain an influential figure in American politics. "I am concerned about the direction this country is headed," he declared, according to Ayres. "I have the vision, experience and fortitude that is necessary to help reverse this dangerous trend and put this great nation of ours on the right track again."

Back to Politics

Wilder left office in 1994, obeying a Virginia law that does not allow governors to hold consecutive terms. For nearly ten years, Wilder engaged in the types of activities befitting an ex-governor: he briefly hosted a morning radio show that was broadcast in Virginia, Baltimore, Maryland, Washington, D.C.; he taught political science at Virginia Commonwealth University; he practiced law; and in 2002 he served as chairman of a commission to study efficiency in Virginia's state government. He was honored to be considered for the presidency of his alma mater, Virginia Union University, though he declined the offer, and he has consistently backed efforts to create a National Slavery Museum in Fredericksburg, Virginia.

By 2004, however, the call of politics had pulled him back into public life. The city of Richmond, Viriginia, had been in decline for years, with poverty and crime plaguing the once-proud city. Citizens approved a new form of government headed by a strong mayor, and many in the city called for the experienced ex-governor to join the race. Explaining to *Jet* why he was willing to run, Wilder said: "I'm not entitled to rest when I look and see little kids being shot up and maimed and crippled, and people are afraid to go on their streets and walk and to be educated in their schools. I began to look around and see the reason." In November of 2004 Wilder easily won the mayoral election, trouncing opponents who were outmatched against such a seasoned politician. In his acceptance speech, quoted in the *Washington Post,* Wilder told the citizens of Richmond: "This is a new beginning." In truth, it was a new beginning for Wilder as well.

Sources

Periodicals

Atlanta Constitution, November 5, 1989.
Black Enterprise, January 1985; February 1986; January 1989; January 1990; June 1991; January 1992.
Business Week, November 20, 1989; December 9, 1991.
Detroit News and Free Press, September 14, 1991.
Ebony, April 1986; November 1989; February 1990; February 1991.
Jet, May 6, 1985; November 25, 1985; February 3, 1986; June 26, 1989; November 6, 1989; November 27, 1989; April 9, 1990; December 30, 1990; February 25, 1991; September 23, 1991; September 11, 1995; March 17, 1997; February 11, 2002; June 21, 2004; October 18, 2004.
Maclean's, November 20, 1989; December 9, 1991; January 20, 1992.
Newark Star-Ledger, November 8, 1989.
Newsweek, February 18, 1985; November 18, 1985; November 6, 1989; November 20, 1989; May 14, 1990; November 12, 1990; March 4, 1991; June 24, 1991; October 14, 1991; November 25, 1991.
New York Times, November 8, 1991; December 9, 1991; December 23, 1991; January 9, 1992; January 10, 1992; January 11, 1992.
New York Times Magazine, January 12, 1992.
People, December 9, 1985; November 6, 1989; July 23, 1990.
Philadelphia Inquirer, November 5, 1989.
Playboy, September 1991.
Richmond News Leader, April 10, 1989; October 21, 1989; January 13, 1990.
Richmond Times-Dispatch, October 8, 1989; January 14, 1990; November 7, 2004.
Sacramento Bee, October 29, 1989.
Time, April 17, 1989; November 20, 1989; September 17, 1990; November 26, 1990; March 4, 1991; November 11, 1991; November 25, 1991; January 20, 1992.
U.S. News & World Report, November 18, 1985; December 26, 1988; November 20, 1989; January 22, 1990; May 13, 1991; December 30, 1991.
Wall Street Journal, November 26, 1991; December 23, 1991; January 6, 1992; January 9, 1992.
Washington Post, October 22, 1989; November 8, 1989; January 7, 1990; November 3, 2004.

—Glen Macnow and Tom Pendergast

Andrew Young

1932—

Politician, civil rights activist

Young, Andrew, photograph. © 1989 Landov LLC. All rights reserved. Reproduced by permission.

As a civil rights activist in the turbulent 1960s and one of Martin Luther King Jr.'s most trusted lieutenants, Andrew Young earned a reputation for tact and diplomacy. As an outspoken ambassador to the United Nations (UN) under the administration of U.S. President Jimmy Carter, he often stirred controversy. Young's dynamic style of balancing principle and pragmatism has confused and angered some, but has won the respect of opponents as well as allies, rendering him one of the most effective and influential African-American political leaders of the twentieth century.

The son of a dentist and a teacher, Young grew up in a predominantly Italian and Irish neighborhood in New Orleans, which, like other southern cities, was generally segregated. His parents tried to shield him from racism but, Young recalled in *Time* in 1979, "I was taught to fight when people called me 'Nigger.'" He continued, "That's when I learned that negotiating was better than fighting."

Young had learned to read and write before he started school and graduated from high school at the age of 15. In the fall of 1947 he entered Howard University, where he majored in biology, preparing to follow his father into dentistry. As he later acknowledged, though, he was more interested in the social side of college life. Still, Young was inspired by Howard's president, Mordecai Johnson, an admirer of Mahatma Gandhi who did much to spread the Indian activist's principles of nonviolent resistance among young African-Americans. In his senior year, Young became disillusioned with the superficiality and snobbery he felt was common among his classmates, and an encounter with a young white man who was on his way to Africa to do missionary work brought him to a point of decision: he abandoned his plans for dental school and decided to become a minister.

Learned from King

Young went north to study at Hartford Theological Seminary in Connecticut and, upon his ordination as a minister of the United Church of Christ in 1955, was sent south to be a pastor in the small towns of Marion, Alabama, and Thomasville and Beachton, Georgia. The civil rights movement, under the leadership of Martin Luther King Jr. and Ralph Abernathy, was

At a Glance . . .

Born Andrew Jackson Young Jr. on March 12, 1932, in New Orleans, LA; son of Andrew Jackson (a dentist) and Daisy (maiden name, Fuller; a teacher) Young; married Jean Childs, 1954 (died 1994); married Carolyn McClain, 1996; children: Andrea, Lisa, Paula, Andrew III. *Education:* Howard University, BS, 1951; Hartford Theological Seminary, BDiv, 1955.

Career: United Church of Christ, Marion, AL, and Thomasville and Beachton, GA, pastor, 1955-57; National Council of Churches, New York City, associate director for youth work, 1957-61; United Church of Christ Christian Education Program, Atlanta, GA, administrator, 1961-64; Southern Christian Leadership Conference (SCLC), administrative assistant, 1962-64, executive director, 1964-68, executive vice-president, 1968-70; Atlanta Community Relations Commission, chair, 1970-72; U.S. House of Representatives, congressman from Georgia's fifth district, 1972-76; U.S. Ambassador to the United Nations, 1977-79; Atlanta, Georgia, mayor, 1982-90; Atlanta Committee for the Olympic Games, chair, 1990; National Council of Churches, president, 2000-2001. Founder and head of Young Ideas, a consulting firm; chairman, GoodWorks International.

Selected Memberships: Member of board of directors of Delta Air Lines, Argus, Host Marriott Corp., Archer Daniels Midland, Cox Communications, Thomas Nelson Publishing, Martin Luther King Jr. Center for Non-Violent Social Change, and the Atlanta Symphony Orchestra.

Selected Awards: Pax-Christi Award, St. Johns University, 1970; Spingarn Medal, National Association for the Advancement of Colored People (NAACP), 1978; Presidential Medal of Freedom from U.S. President Jimmy Carter, 1980; numerous honorary degrees.

Addresses: *Office*—Andrew Young School of Policy Studies, Georgia State University, Atlanta, GA 30303-3084.

entering a new phase: the strategy of legal action initiated by the National Association for the Advancement of Colored People (NAACP) was being supplemented by Gandhian tactics of civil disobedience, boycotts, and other direct action. Inspired by the example of the Montgomery, Alabama, bus boycott, Young began organizing his parishioners into community action groups and leading voter registration drives, in spite of threats from the white supremacist Ku Klux Klan.

In 1957 Young went north again, this time to serve as associate director of the Department of Youth Work of the National Council of Churches. In his four years in the council's New York office, he developed the administrative and political skills that he would later put to good use in the civil rights movement, Congress, and the United Nations. In 1961, the United Church of Christ began a voter education program aimed at southern blacks, and Young was chosen to lead it. Back in Atlanta, he became involved with King's organization, the Southern Christian Leadership Conference (SCLC), and in 1962 became King's administrative assistant. It was a difficult role that Young handled deftly. As fellow activist and later Georgia State Senator Julian Bond put it in the *New York Times* in 1976, "King was the spear thrower, and Andy came behind and put it all together. He could be the man on the tightrope and he never slipped."

Young took over as SCLC's executive director in 1964 and remained at King's side during campaigns throughout the South and in Chicago, accompanying King and the SCLC in the antiwar movement and movements for economic justice. Young, like most of the other SCLC leaders, opposed King's decision to go to Memphis, Tennessee, to support the sanitation workers' strike in 1968, but eventually joined the effort. He was standing in the courtyard of the Lorraine Motel on April 4, 1968, when he heard the gunshot that ended King's life.

In the aftermath of King's assassination, Young, Abernathy, and the other SCLC ministers carried on the leader's work. But in the late 1960s support for the discipline of nonviolence ebbed, and without its charismatic leader the SCLC was less effective. After a series of exhausting battles in support of black workers and the poor, Young decided to change his own direction. In 1970 he announced that he would run for the U.S. House of Representatives as a Democrat from Georgia's fifth district.

Joined Political Process

Southern politics had changed during Young's years in Atlanta. A black man, Maynard Jackson, had recently been elected vice-mayor, and blacks and liberals were contesting elections throughout the state. In the fifth district, which was 40 percent black, Young found himself opposed in the primary by two white candidates and one black. He won the primary but lost the general election, in part due to low turnout by black voters.

In the aftermath of the election, Young was appointed chair of the Community Relations Commission (CRC). Though the CRC was an advisory group with no enforcement powers, Young took an activist role, pressing the city government on many issues, from sanitation and open housing to mass transit, consumer affairs, and Atlanta's drug problem. By the time the 1972 election approached, he had a higher public profile as well as an answer to critics who had called him inexperienced in government.

The election of 1972 was a hard-fought campaign waged against the background of the Richard Nixon-George McGovern contest for the presidency. In November of 1972, in spite of the Republican landslide in the presidential race, Young won with nearly 53 percent of the vote in a district that was 62 percent white, without the benefit of an exceptionally large black turnout. He was the first black representative to be elected from the South in 70 years as well as the first from Georgia since the post-Civil War Reconstruction period.

Young believed in the "New South" and the potential of the coalition of blacks, white liberals, and labor voters who had elected him. Though he upheld his vocal stand on racial issues, he told an *Ebony* correspondent, "I've never been given to a lot of blacker-than-thou rhetoric and that will not be the style that I'll adopt in Washington. You cannot serve a black issue by approaching it as such—or not in *this* Congress. Instead you must plug for jobs...or a day-care program, or some similar goal." As Young had said during the campaign, "The main role of a congressman is to bring together a variety of opinions that a lot of people can support."

Young quickly proved himself adept at the negotiating and committee work that make legislation pass. His biographer, Carl Gardner, quoted Congressman Morris Udall as saying that Young "could make public statements and play to public opinion and get attention. But he doesn't. He plays the inside game, works within the Congress, and does it very effectively." Fellow Democratic Representative Shirley Chisholm praised his leadership qualities, noting his skill in mediating within the Congressional Black Caucus. Young also became known his willingness to take a public stand on principle, appearing before a U.S. House of Representatives subcommittee to defend the principle of affirmative action and publicly criticize President Nixon for slowing progress on civil rights.

Young easily won re-election in 1974 and 1976. In 1976 he was also deeply involved in the presidential campaign of Jimmy Carter, whom he had known since 1970 when they were both newcomers to Georgia politics. Young was the first prominent black politician to endorse Carter and was given much of the credit for Carter's good showing among black voters in the primaries and the general election.

Became UN Ambassador

It was no surprise when Young resigned his congressional seat to take the post of ambassador to the United Nations. Though the UN ambassador had traditionally been little more than a mouthpiece for the State Department, Young immediately made it known that he would not be confined by tradition. "I wanted [Secretary of State] Cyrus Vance to understand my kind of independent style," he told a *New York Times* reporter. "There is a sense in which the United States Ambassador speaks to the United States, as well as for the United States. I have always seen my role as a thermostat, rather than a thermometer. So I'm going to be actively working...for my own concerns. I have always had people advise me on what to say, but never on what not to say."

During the two and a half years of his tenure at the UN, Young frequently expressed his opinions. Many of his statements were controversial, and several conflicted with official U.S. policy, as when he stated the day after he was sworn in that Cuban troops had brought "a certain stability and order" to Angola. He was particularly outspoken on African issues, in which he had taken a strong interest since his election to Congress. He visited the continent several times and took an active role in trying to resolve disputes there. His attacks on apartheid—a racially segregated form of government—in South Africa, including his questioning of the legitimacy of the South African government, outraged American conservatives, as did his attacks on human rights violations and racism in the United States and throughout the world.

Though there were periodic calls for his resignation and the State Department was occasionally forced to issue statements denying that Andrew Young spoke for the government of the United States, he kept Carter's support. This was in large part due to the fact that he was the first American official in years—perhaps ever—to achieve real credibility in the Third World.

Many wondered why Young, previously known for his tact, had begun delivering statements that were seen as outrageous, especially since he had become a diplomat. But Young, Gardner wrote, saw himself as a "point man," the lead soldier in an infantry patrol, the one who scouts out dangerous territory and is most likely to draw enemy fire. Young said he had told Secretary of State Vance "that there were a number of things the American people were thinking about. I told him that if he did not mind, I would raise controversial points and talk about them."

Ironically, Young's downfall came in August of 1979, not because of a public statement, but because of an attempt at quiet diplomacy. Trying to forestall a UN Security Council debate on Palestinian rights that he believed would be detrimental to U.S. efforts to advance peace negotiations in the Middle East, he met with Zehdi Labib Terzi, the UN observer for the Palestine Liberation Organization (PLO). This was a violation of explicit State Department rules prohibiting official contact with the PLO, and when news of the meeting was leaked to the press, Young was forced to resign. He did so without any sign of anger or repentance: "It is very difficult to do the things that I think are in the interest of the country and maintain the standards of protocol and diplomacy," a *Time* correspondent quoted him as saying. "I really don't feel a bit sorry for anything that I have done. And I could not say to anybody that given the same situation I wouldn't do it again almost exactly the same way."

Elected Mayor of Atlanta

Young returned to private life for two years, devoting himself to his consulting firm, Young Ideas. In 1981, at the urging of Coretta Scott King, the widow of Martin Luther King Jr., and other black Atlantans, he decided to run for mayor. "I'm a public person," he explained in the *New Republic,* "and there's nothing more exciting than America's cities." After a bitterly fought campaign and an election tainted by racial overtones, Young won with 55 percent of the vote. *U.S. News & World Report* predicted that "whatever skills Andrew Young had as a diplomat will be needed to curb racial divisions and a host of other troubles that boiled up in his election." The "other troubles" included a massive budget deficit, widespread poverty, a rising crime rate, and the flight of white residents to the suburbs.

Some critics doubted Young's ability to deal with the Atlanta's problems. He was seen as antibusiness, a weak administrator, and too much of an activist to "bridge the racial gap," as one Georgia politician put it in the *New Republic.* Young quickly proved his critics wrong. By 1984, *Ebony* reported, the city had been so successful at attracting new businesses that it was experiencing "a major growth spurt," and by 1988, *U.S. News & World Report* noted, a survey of 385 executives showed that Atlanta was "their overwhelming first choice to locate a business." In addition, the crime rate dropped sharply, and racial harmony seemed an established fact.

Though African-Americans dominated the city's politics and whites dominated its economy, both groups seemed willing to work together. "My job," Young told *Esquire'* s Art Harris in 1985, "is to see that whites get some of the power and blacks get some of the money." Some black leaders accused Young of catering exclusively to the white business establishment and neglecting the black poor, but he garnered the support of Atlanta's growing black middle class and was reelected decisively in 1985.

Limited by law to two terms as mayor, Young decided to run for governor of Georgia in 1990. "It's something I have to do," he told Robin Toner of the *New York Times.* "If I don't get elected I think I'd probably say 'Free at last.' But I have to give it my best possible shot." Young ran primarily on his record of presiding over Atlanta's economic boom; he was criticized, however, for not being a "hands-on" mayor, and was blamed for Atlanta's crime rate, which had risen again after falling during the early years of his administration.

There was also the issue of race. Though Young was popular with younger, suburban whites, many rural and small-town white Georgians still hesitated to vote for a black man. Young made it through the first stage of the primary, but was defeated by Lieutenant Governor Zell Miller in a runoff that featured a low black turnout.

Played Role of Elder Statesman

The loss left Young free to concentrate on another project—preparing Atlanta to host the 1996 Olympic games. As chairman of the Atlanta Organizing Committee, he was, according to *Black Enterprise'* s Alfred Edmond, Jr., "the reason Atlanta was able to capture and hold the attention of the IOC [International Olympic Committee]." Young's diplomatic experience was important in Atlanta's winning the bid over such contenders as Athens, Greece and Melbourne, Australia: "I knew government officials and business people in almost every country represented in the IOC," he told Edmond. "Our approach was intensely personal." The Atlanta Olympics were a major success, yet another feather in the cap of one of America's most effective political leaders.

On a personal level, the 1990s offered a number of challenges for Young. In 1991, his wife, Jean, learned that she had cancer of the colon that had metastasized to her liver. Following a long battle with the cancer, Jean died on September 16, 1994. Also in 1991, Young's son Bo, a freshman at Howard University, was stopped by police a block from campus and beaten in full view of witnesses, for no apparent reason. An investigation later cleared the Washington, D.C., police from any wrongdoing. And in 1999, Young waged a successful battle of his own against prostate cancer.

Young's work with the Olympics was characteristic of the many ventures he took on as a senior statesman. Young served for a time as chairman of the Metro Atlanta Chamber of Commerce and as vice chairman of Law Companies Group, a consulting firm. Young also served as chairman of GoodWorks International, a consulting group for global economics, and held a public affairs professorship at Georgia State University's Andrew Young School of Policy Studies. He was asked to serve on the board of directors of numerous companies and organizations, including Delta Air Lines, Argus, Host Marriott Corp., Archer Daniels Midland, Cox Communications, Thomas Nelson Publishing, the Martin Luther King Jr. Center for Non-Violent Social Change, and the Atlanta Symphony

Orchestra. In April 1996, Young remarried Carolyn McClain, a longtime family friend, in Cape Town, South Africa. The couple lives in Atlanta.

No matter the position, Young has remained "a preacher and a moralist," observed Joseph Lelyveld in the *New York Times*. Nowhere was this more true than when he accepted the presidency of the National Council of Churches (NCC) for 2000-2001. On taking that position, Young said he would be talking more about poverty and less and less about racism because "racism is one of the symptoms of poverty and insecurity." He added, "most of the problems we face in America, whether crime or education problems or hate groups, are derived from what Martin Luther King used to call 'the lonely islands of poverty in the midst of this ocean of material wealth.'" Though he was withdrawing from more active roles in the 2000s, Young remained a powerful voice for progressive political change in America.

Selected writings

A Way Out of No Way: The Spiritual Memoirs of Andrew Young, T. Nelson, 1994.

An Easy Burden: The Civil Rights Movement and the Transformation of America, HarperCollins, 1996.

Sources

Books

DeRoche, Andrew, *Andrew Young: Civil Rights Ambassador,* Scholarly Resources, 2003.

Gardner, Carl, *Andrew Young: A Biography,* Drake, 1978.

Jones, Bartlett C. *Flawed Triumphs: Andy Young at the United Nations,* University Press of America, 1996.

Periodicals

Black Enterprise, January 1991.
Ebony, February 1973; August 1984.
Esquire, June 1985.
Jet, August 20, 2001.
New Republic, September 23, 1981.
New York Times, December 17, 1976; February 6, 1977; August 16, 1979; May 22, 1990.
Time, August 27, 1979.
U.S. News & World Report, November 9, 1981; July 25, 1988.

On-line

"Andrew Young," *Andrew Young School of Policy Studies, Georgia State University,* www.gsu.edu/~wwwsps/people/YoungA.htm (September 14, 2004).

"NCC President 2000-2001: Ambassador Andrew Young," *National Council of Churches USA,* www.ncccusa.org/about/young.html (September 14, 2004).

—Tim Connor and Tom Pendergast

Cumulative Nationality Index

American
Aaron, Hank **5**
Abbott, Robert Sengstacke **27**
Abdul-Jabbar, Kareem **8**
Abdur-Rahim, Shareef **28**
Abernathy, Ralph David **1**
Abu-Jamal, Mumia **15**
Ace, Johnny **36**
Adams Earley, Charity **13, 34**
Adams, Eula L. **39**
Adams, Floyd, Jr. **12**
Adams, Johnny **39**
Adams, Leslie **39**
Adams, Oleta **18**
Adams, Osceola Macarthy **31**
Adams, Sheila J. **25**
Adams, Yolanda **17**
Adams-Ender, Clara **40**
Adderley, Julian "Cannonball" **30**
Adderley, Nat **29**
Adkins, Rod **41**
Adkins, Rutherford H. **21**
Agyeman, Jaramogi Abebe **10**
Ailey, Alvin **8**
Al-Amin, Jamil Abdullah **6**
Albright, Gerald **23**
Alert, Kool DJ Red **33**
Alexander, Archie Alphonso **14**
Alexander, Clifford **26**
Alexander, Joyce London **18**
Alexander, Khandi **43**
Alexander, Margaret Walker **22**
Alexander, Sadie Tanner Mossell **22**
Ali, Laila **27**
Ali, Muhammad **2, 16**
Allen, Byron **3, 24**
Allen, Debbie **13, 42**
Allen, Ethel D. **13**
Allen, Marcus **20**
Allen, Robert L. **38**
Allen, Samuel W. **38**
Allen, Tina **22**
Alston, Charles **33**
Ames, Wilmer **27**
Amos, John **8**
Amos, Wally **9**
Anderson, Carl **48**
Anderson, Charles Edward **37**
Anderson, Eddie "Rochester" **30**
Anderson, Elmer **25**
Anderson, Jamal **22**
Anderson, Marian **2, 33**

Anderson, Michael P. **40**
Anderson, Norman B. **45**
Andrews, Benny **22**
Andrews, Bert **13**
Andrews, Raymond **4**
Angelou, Maya **1, 15**
Ansa, Tina McElroy **14**
Anthony, Carmelo **46**
Anthony, Wendell **25**
Archer, Dennis **7, 36**
Archie-Hudson, Marguerite **44**
Arkadie, Kevin **17**
Armstrong, Louis **2**
Armstrong, Robb **15**
Armstrong, Vanessa Bell **24**
Arnwine, Barbara **28**
Arroyo, Martina **30**
Arrington, Richard **24**
Asante, Molefi Kete **3**
Ashanti **37**
Ashe, Arthur **1, 18**
Ashford, Emmett **22**
Ashford, Nickolas **21**
Ashley-Ward, Amelia **23**
Atkins, Cholly **40**
Atkins, Erica **34**
Atkins, Russell **45**
Atkins, Tina **34**
Aubert, Alvin **41**
Auguste, Donna **29**
Austin, Junius C. **44**
Austin, Lovie **40**
Austin, Patti **24**
Avant, Clarence **19**
Ayers, Roy **16**
Babatunde, Obba **35**
Bacon-Bercey, June **38**
Badu, Erykah **22**
Bailey, Buster **38**
Bailey, Clyde **45**
Bailey, DeFord **33**
Bailey, Radcliffe **19**
Bailey, Xenobia **11**
Baines, Harold **32**
Baiocchi, Regina Harris **41**
Baisden, Michael **25**
Baker, Anita **21, 48**
Baker, Augusta **38**
Baker, Dusty **8, 43**
Baker, Ella **5**
Baker, Gwendolyn Calvert **9**
Baker, Houston A., Jr. **6**
Baker, Josephine **3**

Baker, LaVern **26**
Baker, Maxine B. **28**
Baker, Thurbert **22**
Baldwin, James **1**
Ballance, Frank W. **41**
Ballard, Allen Butler, Jr. **40**
Ballard, Hank **41**
Bambaataa, Afrika **34**
Bambara, Toni Cade **10**
Bandele, Asha **36**
Banks, Ernie **33**
Banks, Jeffrey **17**
Banks, Tyra **11**
Banks, William **11**
Baraka, Amiri **1, 38**
Barber, Ronde **41**
Barboza, Anthony **10**
Barclay, Paris **37**
Barden, Don H. **9, 20**
Barker, Danny **32**
Barkley, Charles **5**
Barnes, Roosevelt "Booba" **33**
Barnett, Amy Du Bois **46**
Barnett, Marguerite **46**
Barney, Lem **26**
Barnhill, David **30**
Barrax, Gerald William **45**
Barrett, Andrew C. **12**
Barrett, Jacquelyn **28**
Barry, Marion S(hepilov, Jr.) **7, 44**
Barthe, Richmond **15**
Basie, Count **23**
Basquiat, Jean-Michel **5**
Bass, Charlotta Spears **40**
Bassett, Angela **6, 23**
Bates, Daisy **13**
Bates, Karen Grigsby **40**
Bates, Peg Leg **14**
Bath, Patricia E. **37**
Baugh, David **23**
Baylor, Don **6**
Baylor, Helen **36**
Beach, Michael **26**
Beal, Bernard B. **46**
Beals, Jennifer **12**
Beals, Melba Patillo **15**
Bearden, Romare **2**
Beasley, Jamar **29**
Beasley, Phoebe **34**
Beatty, Talley **35**
Bechet, Sidney **18**
Beckford, Tyson **11**
Beckham, Barry **41**

Belafonte, Harry **4**
Bell, Derrick **6**
Bell, James "Cool Papa" **36**
Bell, James Madison **40**
Bell, Michael **40**
Bell, Robert Mack **22**
Bellamy, Bill **12**
Belle, Albert **10**
Belle, Regina **1**
Belton, Sharon Sayles **9, 16**
Benét, Eric **28**
Ben-Israel, Ben Ami **11**
Benjamin, Andre **45**
Benjamin, Regina **20**
Bennett, George Harold "Hal" **45**
Bennett, Lerone, Jr. **5**
Benson, Angela **34**
Berry, Bertice **8**
Berry, Chuck **29**
Berry, Fred "Rerun" **48**
Berry, Halle **4, 19**
Berry, Mary Frances **7**
Berry, Theodore **31**
Bethune, Mary McLeod **4**
Betsch, MaVynee **28**
Beverly, Frankie **25**
Bickerstaff, Bernie **21**
Biggers, John **20, 33**
Bing, Dave **3**
Bishop, Sanford D. Jr. **24**
Black, Barry C. **47**
Black, Keith Lanier **18**
Blackburn, Robert **28**
Blackwell, Unita **17**
Blair, Paul **36**
Blake, Asha **26**
Blake, Eubie **29**
Blake, James **43**
Blakey, Art **37**
Blanchard, Terence **43**
Bland, Bobby "Blue" **36**
Bland, Eleanor Taylor **39**
Blanks, Billy **22**
Blanton, Dain **29**
Blassingame, John Wesley **40**
Blige, Mary J. **20, 34**
Blockson, Charles L. **42**
Blow, Kurtis **31**
Bluford, Guy **2, 35**
Bluitt, Juliann S. **14**
Bogle, Donald **34**
Bolden, Buddy **39**
Bolden, Charles F., Jr. **7**

Bolden, Frank E. **44**
Bolden, Tonya **32**
Bolin, Jane **22**
Bolton, Terrell D. **25**
Bolton-Holifield, Ruthie **28**
Bond, Julian **2, 35**
Bonds, Barry **6, 34**
Bonds, Bobby **43**
Bonds, Margaret **39**
Bontemps, Arna **8**
Booker, Simeon **23**
Borders, James **9**
Bosley, Freeman, Jr. **7**
Boston, Kelvin E. **25**
Boston, Lloyd **24**
Bowe, Riddick **6**
Bowser, Yvette Lee **17**
Boyd, Gerald M. **32**
Boyd, John W., Jr. **20**
Boyd, T. B. III **6**
Boykin, Keith **14**
Bradley, David Henry, Jr. **39**
Bradley, Ed **2**
Bradley, Jennette B. **40**
Bradley, Thomas **2, 20**
Brady, Wayne **32**
Branch, William Blackwell **39**
Brand, Elton **31**
Brandon, Barbara **3**
Brandon, Terrell **16**
Brandy **14, 34**
Brashear, Carl **29**
Brashear, Donald **39**
Braugher, Andre **13**
Braun, Carol Moseley **4, 42**
Brawley, Benjamin **44**
Braxton, Toni **15**
Brazile, Donna **25**
Bridges, Sheila **36**
Bridges, Todd **37**
Bridgewater, Dee Dee **32**
Bridgforth, Glinda **36**
Brimmer, Andrew F. **2, 48**
Briscoe, Connie **15**
Briscoe, Marlin **37**
Britt, Donna **28**
Broadbent, Hydeia **36**
Brock, Lou **18**
Bronner, Nathaniel H., Sr. **32**
Brooke, Edward **8**
Brooks, Aaron **33**
Brooks, Avery **9**
Brooks, Derrick **43**
Brooks, Gwendolyn **1, 28**
Brooks, Hadda **40**
Brown, Cecil M. **46**
Brown, Charles **23**
Brown, Claude **38**
Brown, Cora **33**
Brown, Corrine **24**
Brown, Donald **19**
Brown, Eddie C. **35**
Brown, Elaine **8**
Brown, Erroll M. **23**
Brown, Foxy **25**
Brown, Homer S. **47**
Brown, James **22**
Brown, Janice Rogers **43**
Brown, Jesse **6, 41**
Brown, Jesse Leroy **31**
Brown, Jim **11**
Brown, Joe **29**
Brown, Joyce F. **25**

Brown, Lee Patrick **1, 24**
Brown, Les **5**
Brown, Llyod Louis **42**
Brown, Marie Dutton **12**
Brown, Ron **5**
Brown, Sterling **10**
Brown, Tony **3**
Brown, Uzee **42**
Brown, Vivian **27**
Brown, Wesley **23**
Brown, Willa **40**
Brown, Willard **36**
Brown, Willie L., Jr. **7**
Brown, Zora Kramer **12**
Bruce, Blanche Kelso **33**
Bruce, Isaac **26**
Brunson, Dorothy **1**
Bryan, Ashley F. **41**
Bryant, John **26**
Bryant, John R. **45**
Bryant, Kobe **15, 31**
Bryant, Wayne R. **6**
Buchanan, Ray **32**
Buckley, Gail Lumet **39**
Buckley, Victoria (Vikki) **24**
Bullard, Eugene **12**
Bullins, Ed **25**
Bullock, Steve **22**
Bully-Cummings, Ella **48**
Bumbry, Grace **5**
Bunche, Ralph J. **5**
Bunkley, Anita Richmond **39**
Burgess, John **46**
Burke, Selma **16**
Burke, Solomon **31**
Burke, Yvonne Braithwaite **42**
Burks, Mary Fair **40**
Burnett, Charles **16**
Burnim, Mickey L. **48**
Burns, Eddie **44**
Burrell, Thomas J. **21**
Burris, Chuck **21**
Burris, Roland W. **25**
Burroughs, Margaret Taylor **9**
Burrows, Stephen **31**
Burrus, William Henry "Bill" **45**
Burton, LeVar **8**
Busby, Jheryl **3**
Butler, Jerry **26**
Butler, Leroy III **17**
Butler, Octavia **8, 43**
Butler, Paul D. **17**
Butts, Calvin O., III **9**
Bynoe, Peter C.B. **40**
Bynum, Juanita **31**
Byrd, Donald **10**
Byrd, Michelle **19**
Byrd, Robert **11**
Cadoria, Sherian Grace **14**
Caesar, Shirley **19**
Cain, Herman **15**
Caldwell, Benjamin **46**
Callender, Clive O. **3**
Calloway, Cab **14**
Camp, Kimberly **19**
Campanella, Roy **25**
Campbell, Bebe Moore **6, 24**
Campbell, Bill **9**
Campbell, E. Simms **13**
Campbell, Mary Schmidt **43**
Campbell-Martin, Tisha **8, 42**
Canada, Geoffrey **23**
Canady, Alexa **28**

Cannon, Katie **10**
Cannon, Nick **47**
Cardozo, Francis L. **33**
Carew, Rod **20**
Carey, Mariah **32**
Cargill, Victoria A. **43**
Carroll, Diahann **9**
Carroll, L. Natalie **44**
Carruthers, George R. **40**
Carson, Benjamin **1, 35**
Carson, Julia **23**
Carson, Lisa Nicole **21**
Cartíer, Xam Wilson **41**
Carter, Anson **24**
Carter, Benny **46**
Carter, Betty **19**
Carter, Butch **27**
Carter, Cris **21**
Carter, Joe **30**
Carter, Joye Maureen **41**
Carter, Mandy **11**
Carter, Nell **39**
Carter, Regina **23**
Carter, Rubin **26**
Carter, Stephen L. **4**
Carter, Vince **26**
Carter, Warrick L. **27**
Cartey, Wilfred 1992 **47**
Carver, George Washington **4**
Cary, Lorene **3**
Cary, Mary Ann Shadd **30**
Cash, Rosalind **28**
CasSelle, Malcolm **11**
Catchings, Tamika **43**
Catlett, Elizabeth **2**
Cayton, Horace **26**
Cedric the Entertainer **29**
Chamberlain, Wilt **18, 47**
Chambers, Julius **3**
Chapman, Nathan A. Jr. **21**
Chapman, Tracy **26**
Chappell, Emma **18**
Charles, Ray **16, 48**
Charleston, Oscar **39**
Chase-Riboud, Barbara **20, 46**
Chatard, Peter **44**
Chavis, Benjamin **6**
Cheadle, Don **19**
Checker, Chubby **28**
Cheeks, Maurice **47**
Chenault, John **40**
Chenault, Kenneth I. **4, 36**
Cherry, Deron **40**
Chesnutt, Charles **29**
Chestnut, Morris **31**
Chideya, Farai **14**
Childress, Alice **15**
Chinn, May Edward **26**
Chisholm, Samuel **32**
Chisholm, Shirley **2**
Christian, Barbara T. **44**
Christian, Spencer **15**
Christian-Green, Donna M. **17**
Christie, Angella **36**
Chuck D **9**
Claiborne, Loretta **34**
Clark, Celeste **15**
Clark, Joe **1**
Clark, Kenneth B. **5**
Clark, Patrick **14**
Clark, Septima **7**
Clarke, Cheryl **32**
Clarke, Hope **14**

Clarke, John Henrik **20**
Clarke, Kenny **27**
Clark-Sheard, Karen **22**
Clash, Kevin **14**
Clay, William Lacy **8**
Clayton, Constance **1**
Clayton, Eva M. **20**
Clayton, Xernona **3, 45**
Claytor, Helen **14**
Cleage, Pearl **17**
Cleaver, Eldridge **5**
Cleaver, Emanuel **4, 45**
Cleaver, Kathleen **29**
Clements, George **2**
Clemmons, Reginal G. **41**
Clemons, Clarence **41**
Clendenon, Donn **26**
Cleveland, James **19**
Cliff, Michelle **42**
Clifton, Lucille **14**
Clifton, Nathaniel "Sweetwater" **47**
Clinton, George **9**
Clyburn, James **21**
Coachman, Alice **18**
Cobb, Jewel Plummer **42**
Cobb, W. Montague **39**
Cobbs, Price M. **9**
Cochran, Johnnie L., Jr. **11, 39**
Cohen, Anthony **15**
Colbert, Virgis William **17**
Cole, Johnnetta B. **5, 43**
Cole, Lorraine **48**
Cole, Nat King **17**
Cole, Natalie Maria **17**
Cole, Rebecca **38**
Coleman, Bessie **9**
Coleman, Donald A. **24**
Coleman, Gary **35**
Coleman, Leonard S., Jr. **12**
Coleman, Mary **46**
Coleman, Michael B. **28**
Coleman, Ornette **39**
Coleman, Wanda **48**
Colemon, Johnnie **11**
Collins, Albert **12**
Collins, Barbara-Rose **7**
Collins, Bootsy **31**
Collins, Cardiss **10**
Collins, Janet **33**
Collins, Marva **3**
Colter, Cyrus J. **36**
Coltrane, John **19**
Combs, Sean "Puffy" **17, 43**
Comer, James P. **6**
Common **31**
Cone, James H. **3**
Coney, PonJola **48**
Connerly, Ward **14**
Conyers, John, Jr. **4**
Conyers, Nathan G. **24, 45**
Cook, (Will) Mercer **40**
Cook, Charles "Doc" **44**
Cook, Samuel DuBois **14**
Cook, Suzan D. Johnson **22**
Cook, Toni **23**
Cook, Will Marion **40**
Cooke, Marvel **31**
Cooper Cafritz, Peggy **43**
Cooper, Andrew W. **36**
Cooper, Anna Julia **20**
Cooper, Barry **33**
Cooper, Charles "Chuck" **47**
Cooper, Cynthia **17**

Cooper, Edward S. 6
Cooper, Evern 40
Cooper, J. California 12
Cooper, Margaret J. 46
Cooper, Michael 31
Copeland, Michael 47
Corbi, Lana 42
Cornelius, Don 4
Cortez, Jayne 43
Corthron, Kia 43
Cortor, Eldzier 42
Cosby, Bill 7, 26
Cosby, Camille 14
Cose, Ellis 5
Cotter, Joseph Seamon, Sr. 40
Cottrell, Comer 11
Cowans, Adger W. 20
Cox, Ida 42
Craig, Carl 31
Craig-Jones, Ellen Walker 44
Crawford, Randy 19
Cray, Robert 30
Creagh, Milton 27
Crew, Rudolph F. 16
Crite, Alan Rohan 29
Crocker, Frankie 29
Crockett, George Jr. 10
Cross, Dolores E. 23
Crothers, Scatman 19
Crouch, Andraé 27
Crouch, Stanley 11
Crowder, Henry 16
Cullen, Countee 8
Culpepper, Daunte 32
Cummings, Elijah E. 24
Cuney, William Waring 44
Cunningham, Evelyn 23
Cunningham, Randall 23
Currie, Betty 21
Curry, George E. 23
Curry, Mark 17
Curtis, Christopher Paul 26
Curtis-Hall, Vondie 17
D'Angelo 27
Daly, Marie Maynard 37
Dandridge, Dorothy 3
Dandridge, Ray 36
Dandridge, Raymond Garfield 45
Daniels, Lee Louis 36
Daniels-Carter, Valerie 23
Darden, Calvin 38
Darden, Christopher 13
Dash, Damon 31
Dash, Julie 4
Dash, Leon 47
David, Keith 27
Davidson, Jaye 5
Davidson, Tommy 21
Davis, Allison 12
Davis, Angela 5
Davis, Anthony 11
Davis, Arthur P. 41
Davis, Artur 41
Davis, Benjamin O., Jr. 2, 43
Davis, Benjamin O., Sr. 4
Davis, Charles T. 48
Davis, Chuck 33
Davis, Danny K. 24
Davis, Ed 24
Davis, Ernie 48
Davis, Frank Marshall 47
Davis, Gary 41
Davis, George 36

Davis, Guy 36
Davis, Mike 41
Davis, Miles 4
Davis, Nolan 45
Davis, Ossie 5
Davis, Piper 19
Davis, Ruth 37
Davis, Terrell 20
Davis, Viola 34
Dawes, Dominique 11
Dawkins, Wayne 20
Dawson, Matel "Mat," Jr. 39
Dawson, William Levi 39
Day, Leon 39
Days, Drew S., III 10
de Passe, Suzanne 25
De Veaux, Alexis 44
Dean, Mark E. 35
DeBaptiste, George 32
DeCarava, Roy 42
Dee, Ruby 8
DeFrantz, Anita 37
Delaney, Beauford 19
Delaney, Joseph 30
Delany, Bessie 12
Delany, Martin R. 27
Delany, Sadie 12
Delany, Samuel R., Jr. 9
Delco, Wilhemina 33
DeLille, Henriette 30
Dellums, Ronald 2
DeLoach, Nora 30
Delsarte, Louis 34
Dennard, Brazeal 37
DePriest, James 37
Devers, Gail 7
Devine, Loretta 24
Dickens, Helen Octavia 14
Dickenson, Vic 38
Dickerson, Eric 27
Dickerson, Ernest R. 6, 17
Dickey, Eric Jerome 21
Diddley, Bo 39
Diesel, Vin 29
Diggs, Charles C. 21
Diggs, Taye 25
Diggs-Taylor, Anna 20
Dillard, Godfrey J. 45
Dinkins, David 4
Divine, Father 7
Dixon, Julian C. 24
Dixon, Margaret 14
Dixon, Sharon Pratt 1
Dixon, Willie 4
DMX 28
Dobbs, Mattiwilda 34
Doby, Lawrence Eugene, Sr. 16, 41
Dodson, Howard, Jr. 7
Dodson, Owen Vincent 38
Doley, Harold, Jr. 26
Donald, Arnold Wayne 36
Donaldson, Jeff 46
Donegan, Dorothy 19
Dorsey, Thomas 15
Dortch, Thomas W., Jr. 45
Dougherty, Mary Pearl 47
Douglas, Aaron 7
Dourdan, Gary 37
Dove, Rita 6
Dove, Ulysses 5
Downing, Will 19
Dr. Dre 10
Draper, Sharon Mills 16, 43

Dre, Dr. 14, 30
Drew, Charles Richard 7
Drexler, Clyde 4
Driskell, David C. 7
Driver, David E. 11
Drummond, William J. 40
Du Bois, David Graham 45
DuBois, Shirley Graham 21
DuBois, W. E. B. 3
Ducksworth, Marilyn 12
Due, Tananarive 30
Duke, Bill 3
Duke, George 21
Dumars, Joe 16
Dumas, Henry 41
Dunbar, Paul Laurence 8
Dunbar-Nelson, Alice Ruth Moore 44
Duncan, Michael Clarke 26
Duncan, Tim 20
Dungy, Tony 17, 42
Dunham, Katherine 4
Dunn, Jerry 27
Dunner, Leslie B. 45
Dunnigan, Alice Allison 41
Dunston, Georgia Mae 48
Dupri, Jermaine 13, 46
Dutton, Charles S. 4, 22
Dyson, Michael Eric 11, 40
Early, Gerald 15
Eckstine, Billy 28
Edelin, Ramona Hoage 19
Edelman, Marian Wright 5, 42
Edley, Christopher 2, 48
Edley, Christopher F., Jr. 48
Edmonds, Kenneth "Babyface" 10, 31
Edmonds, Terry 17
Edmonds, Tracey 16
Edmunds, Gladys 48
Edwards, Esther Gordy 43
Edwards, Harry 2
Edwards, Melvin 22
Edwards, Teresa 14
El Wilson, Barbara 35
Elder, Larry 25
Elder, Lee 6
Elder, Lonne, III 38
Elders, Joycelyn 6
Eldridge, Roy 37
Elise, Kimberly 32
Ellerbe, Brian 22
Ellington, Duke 5
Ellington, E. David 11
Ellington, Mercedes 34
Elliott, Missy "Misdemeanor" 31
Elliott, Sean 26
Ellis, Clarence A. 38
Ellis, Jimmy 44
Ellison, Ralph 7
Elmore, Ronn 21
Emanuel, James A. 46
Emeagwali, Dale 31
Ephriam, Mablean 29
Epps, Archie C., III 45
Epps, Omar 23
Ericsson-Jackson, Aprille 28
Erving, Julius 18, 47
Esposito, Giancarlo 9
Espy, Mike 6
Estes, Rufus 29
Estes, Simon 28
Estes, Sleepy John 33

Eubanks, Kevin 15
Europe, James Reese 10
Evans, Darryl 22
Evans, Faith 22
Evans, Harry 25
Evans, Mari 26
Eve 29
Everett, Francine 23
Evers, Medgar 3
Evers, Myrlie 8
Fabio, Sarah Webster 48
Fair, Ronald L. 47
Faison, George 16
Falana, Lola 42
Farmer, Art 38
Farmer, Forest J. 1
Farmer, James 2
Farmer-Paellmann, Deadria 43
Farr, Mel, Sr. 24
Farrakhan, Louis 2, 15
Fats Domino 20
Fattah, Chaka 11
Faulk, Marshall 35
Fauntroy, Walter E. 11
Fauset, Jessie 7
Favors, Steve 23
Fax, Elton 48
Feelings, Muriel 44
Feelings, Tom 11, 47
Felix, Allyson 48
Ferguson, Roger W. 25
Ferrell, Rachelle 29
Fetchit, Stepin 32
Fielder, Cecil 2
Fields, C. Virginia 25
Fields, Cleo 13
Fields, Evelyn J. 27
Fields, Julia 45
Fields, Kim 36
50 Cent 46
Files, Lolita 35
Fishburne, Larry 4, 22
Fisher, Antwone 40
Fitzgerald, Ella 1, 18
Flack, Roberta 19
Fleming, Raymond 48
Fletcher, Bill, Jr. 41
Flowers, Vonetta 35
Floyd, Elson S. 41
Forbes, Calvin 46
Ford, Cheryl 45
Ford, Clyde W. 40
Ford, Harold Eugene 42
Ford, Harold Eugene, Jr. 16
Ford, Jack 39
Ford, Nick Aaron 44
Forrest, Leon 44
Forrest, Vernon 40
Foster, Ezola 28
Foster, George "Pops" 40
Foster, Henry W., Jr. 26
Foster, Jylla Moore 45
Foster, Marie 48
Foxx, Jamie 15, 48
Franklin, Aretha 11, 44
Franklin, J.E. 44
Franklin, Shirley 34
Frazier, E. Franklin 10
Frazier, Joe 19
Frazier-Lyde, Jacqui 31
Freelon, Nnenna 32
Freeman, Al, Jr. 11
Freeman, Charles 19

Freeman, Harold P. 23
Freeman, Leonard 27
Freeman, Marianna 23
Freeman, Morgan 2, 20
Freeman, Paul 39
Freeman, Yvette 27
French, Albert 18
Friday, Jeff 24
Fudge, Ann 11
Fulani, Lenora 11
Fuller, A. Oveta 43
Fuller, Arthur 27
Fuller, Charles 8
Fuller, Howard L. 37
Fuller, Hoyt 44
Fuller, Meta Vaux Warrick 27
Fuller, S. B. 13
Fuller, Solomon Carter, Jr. 15
Fuller, Vivian 33
Funderburg, I. Owen 38
Fuqua, Antoine 35
Futch, Eddie 33
Gaines, Brenda 41
Gaines, Ernest J. 7
Gaines, Grady 38
Gaither, Alonzo Smith (Jake) 14
Gantt, Harvey 1
Gardner, Edward G. 45
Garnett, Kevin 14
Garrison, Zina 2
Gary, Willie E. 12
Gaston, Arthur G. 4
Gates, Henry Louis, Jr. 3, 38
Gates, Sylvester James, Jr. 15
Gaye, Marvin 2
Gayle, Addison, Jr. 41
Gayle, Helene D. 3, 46
Gaynor, Gloria 36
Gentry, Alvin 23
George, Nelson 12
George, Zelma Watson 42
Gibson, Althea 8, 43
Gibson, Bob 33
Gibson, Donald Bernard 40
Gibson, Johnnie Mae 23
Gibson, Josh 22
Gibson, Kenneth Allen 6
Gibson, William F. 6
Giddings, Paula 11
Gillespie, Dizzy 1
Gilliam, Frank 23
Gilliam, Joe 31
Gilliam, Sam 16
Gilmore, Marshall 46
Ginuwine 35
Giovanni, Nikki 9, 39
Gist, Carole 1
Givens, Robin 4, 25
Glover, Corey 34
Glover, Danny 1, 24
Glover, Nathaniel, Jr. 12
Glover, Savion 14
Goines, Donald 19
Goldberg, Whoopi 4, 33
Golden, Marita 19
Golden, Thelma 10
Goldsberry, Ronald 18
Golson, Benny 37
Gomes, Peter J. 15
Gomez, Jewelle 30
Gomez-Preston, Cheryl 9
Goode, Mal 13
Goode, W. Wilson 4

Gooden, Dwight 20
Gooding, Cuba 16
Goodnight, Paul 32
Gordon, Bruce S. 41
Gordon, Dexter 25
Gordon, Ed 10
Gordone, Charles 15
Gordy, Berry, Jr. 1
Goss, Tom 23
Gossett, Louis, Jr. 7
Gotti, Irv 39
Gourdine, Meredith 33
Gourdine, Simon 11
Grace, George H. 48
Graham, Lawrence Otis 12
Graham, Lorenz 48
Graham, Stedman 13
Grant, Gwendolyn Goldsby 28
Granville, Evelyn Boyd 36
Gravely, Samuel L., Jr. 5
Graves, Denyce 19
Graves, Earl G. 1, 35
Gray, F. Gary 14
Gray, Fred 37
Gray, Ida 41
Gray, Macy 29
Gray, William H. III 3
Gray, Willie 46
Greaves, William 38
Greely, M. Gasby 27
Green, A. C. 32
Green, Al 13, 47
Green, Darrell 39
Green, Dennis 5, 45
Greene, Joe 10
Greene, Maurice 27
Greenfield, Eloise 9
Greenlee, Sam 48
Greenwood, Monique 38
Gregory, Dick 1
Gregory, Frederick D. 8
Gregory, Wilton 37
Grier, David Alan 28
Grier, Mike 43
Grier, Pam 9, 31
Grier, Roosevelt 13
Griffey, Ken, Jr. 12
Griffin, Bessie Blout 43
Griffith, Mark Winston 8
Griffith, Yolanda 25
Griffith-Joyner, Florence 28
Grimké, Archibald H. 9
Guillaume, Robert 3, 48
Guinier, Lani 7, 30
Gumbel, Bryant 14
Gumbel, Greg 8
Gunn, Moses 10
Guy, George "Buddy" 31
Guy, Jasmine 2
Guy, Rosa 5
Guy-Sheftall, Beverly 13
Guyton, Tyree 9
Gwynn, Tony 18
Hageman, Hans 36
Hageman, Ivan 36
Hailey, JoJo 22
Hailey, K-Ci 22
Hale, Clara 16
Hale, Lorraine 8
Haley, Alex 4
Haley, George Williford Boyce 21
Hall, Arthur 39
Hall, Elliott S. 24

Hall, Lloyd A. 8
Hamblin, Ken 10
Hamer, Fannie Lou 6
Hamilton, Samuel C. 47
Hamilton, Virginia 10
Hammer, M. C. 20
Hammond, Fred 23
Hampton, Fred 18
Hampton, Henry 6
Hampton, Lionel 17, 41
Hancock, Herbie 20
Handy, W. C. 8
Hannah, Marc 10
Hansberry, Lorraine 6
Hansberry, William Leo 11
Hardaway, Anfernee (Penny) 13
Hardaway, Tim 35
Hardin Armstrong, Lil 39
Hardison, Bethann 12
Hardison, Kadeem 22
Hare, Nathan 44
Harkless, Necia Desiree 19
Harmon, Clarence 26
Harper, Ben 34
Harper, Frances Ellen Watkins 11
Harper, Hill 32
Harper, Michael S. 34
Harrell, Andre 9, 30
Harrington, Oliver W. 9
Harris, Alice 7
Harris, Barbara 12
Harris, Corey 39
Harris, E. Lynn 12, 33
Harris, Eddy L. 18
Harris, Jay T. 19
Harris, Leslie 6
Harris, Marcelite Jordon 16
Harris, Mary Styles 31
Harris, Monica 18
Harris, Patricia Roberts 2
Harris, Robin 7
Harrison, Alvin 28
Harrison, Calvin 28
Harsh, Vivian Gordon 14
Harvard, Beverly 11
Harvey, Steve 18
Harvey, William R. 42
Haskins, Clem 23
Haskins, James 36
Hassell, Leroy Rountree, Sr. 41
Hastie, William H. 8
Hastings, Alcee L. 16
Hatchett, Glenda 32
Hathaway, Donny 18
Hathaway, Isaac Scott 33
Hawkins, Coleman 9
Hawkins, Erskine 14
Hawkins, La-Van 17
Hawkins, Screamin' Jay 30
Hawkins, Steven 14
Hawkins, Tramaine 16
Hayden, Carla D. 47
Hayden, Palmer 13
Hayden, Robert 12
Hayes, Cecil N. 46
Hayes, Isaac 20
Hayes, James C. 10
Hayes, Roland 4
Hayes, Teddy 40
Haynes, George Edmund 8
Haynes, Marques 22
Haynes, Trudy 44
Haysbert, Dennis 42

Haywood, Gar Anthony 43
Haywood, Margaret A. 24
Healy, James Augustine 30
Heard, Gar 25
Heard, Nathan C. 45
Hearns, Thomas 29
Hedgeman, Anna Arnold 22
Height, Dorothy I. 2, 23
Hemphill, Essex 10
Hemphill, Jessie Mae 33
Hemsley, Sherman 19
Henderson, Cornelius Langston 26
Henderson, Fletcher 32
Henderson, Gordon 5
Henderson, Rickey 28
Henderson, Stephen E. 45
Henderson, Wade J. 14
Hendricks, Barbara 3
Hendrix, Jimi 10
Hendy, Francis 47
Henries, A. Doris Banks 44
Henry, Aaron 19
Henry, Clarence "Frogman" 46
Henson, Darrin 33
Henson, Matthew 2
Hercules, Frank 44
Herenton, Willie W. 24
Herman, Alexis M. 15
Hernandez, Aileen Clarke 13
Hickman, Fred 11
Higginbotham, A. Leon, Jr. 13, 25
Higginbotham, Jay C. 37
Hightower, Dennis F. 13
Hill, Anita 5
Hill, Bonnie Guiton 20
Hill, Calvin 19
Hill, Donna 32
Hill, Dulé 29
Hill, Grant 13
Hill, Janet 19
Hill, Jessie, Jr. 13
Hill, Lauryn 20
Hill, Leslie Pinckney 44
Hill, Oliver W. 24
Hillard, Terry 25
Hilliard, David 7
Hilliard, Earl F. 24
Himes, Chester 8
Hinderas, Natalie 5
Hine, Darlene Clark 24
Hines, Earl "Fatha" 39
Hines, Garrett 35
Hines, Gregory 1, 42
Hinton, Milt 30
Hinton, William Augustus 8
Hoagland, Everett H. 45
Hobson, Julius W. 44
Hobson, Mellody 40
Holder, Eric H., Jr. 9
Holder, Laurence 34
Holdsclaw, Chamique 24
Holiday, Billie 1
Holland, Endesha Ida Mae 3
Holland, Robert, Jr. 11
Holland-Dozier-Holland 36
Holmes, Larry 20
Holt, Nora 38
Holton, Hugh, Jr. 39
Holyfield, Evander 6
Hooker, John Lee 30
hooks, bell 5
Hooks, Benjamin L. 2
Hope, John 8

Hopkins, Bernard 35
Horn, Shirley 32
Horne, Frank 44
Horne, Lena 5
Horton, Andre 33
Horton, Suki 33
House, Son 8
Houston, Charles Hamilton 4
Houston, Cissy 20
Houston, Whitney 7, 28
Howard, Desmond 16
Howard, Juwan 15
Howard, M. William, Jr. 26
Howard, Michelle 28
Howard, Sherri 36
Howlin' Wolf 9
Howroyd, Janice Bryant 42
Hrabowski, Freeman A. III 22
Hubbard, Arnette Rhinehart 38
Hudlin, Reginald 9
Hudlin, Warrington 9
Hudson, Cheryl 15
Hudson, Wade 15
Huggins, Larry 21
Hughes, Albert 7
Hughes, Allen 7
Hughes, Cathy 27
Hughes, Langston 4
Hughley, D.L. 23
Hull, Akasha Gloria 45
Humphrey, Bobbi 20
Humphries, Frederick 20
Hunt, Richard 6
Hunter, Alberta 42
Hunter, Clementine 45
Hunter, Torii 43
Hunter-Gault, Charlayne 6, 31
Hurston, Zora Neale 3
Hurtt, Harold 46
Hutchinson, Earl Ofari 24
Hutson, Jean Blackwell 16
Hyde, Cowan F. "Bubba" 47
Hyman, Earle 25
Hyman, Phyllis 19
Ice Cube 8, 30
Iceberg Slim 11
Ice-T 6, 31
Ifill, Gwen 28
Imes, Elmer Samuel 39
India.Arie 34
Ingram, Rex 5
Innis, Roy 5
Irvin, Monford Merrill 31
Irving, Larry, Jr. 12
Isley, Ronald 25
Iverson, Allen 24, 46
Ja Rule 35
Jackson Lee, Sheila 20
Jackson, Alexine Clement 22
Jackson, Alphonso R. 48
Jackson, Earl 31
Jackson, Fred James 25
Jackson, George 14
Jackson, George 19
Jackson, Hal 41
Jackson, Isaiah 3
Jackson, Janet 6, 30
Jackson, Jesse 1, 27
Jackson, Jesse, Jr. 14, 45
Jackson, John 36
Jackson, Mahalia 5
Jackson, Mannie 14
Jackson, Maynard 2, 41

Jackson, Michael 19
Jackson, Millie 25
Jackson, Milt 26
Jackson, Randy 40
Jackson, Reggie 15
Jackson, Samuel L. 8, 19
Jackson, Sheneska 18
Jackson, Shirley Ann 12
Jackson, Vera 40
Jacob, John E. 2
Jacobs, Regina 38
Jakes, Thomas "T.D." 17, 43
James, Daniel Jr. 16
James, Etta 13
James, Juanita 13
James, LeBron 46
James, Rick 19
James, Sharpe 23
James, Skip 38
Jamison, Judith 7
Jarreau, Al 21
Jarret, Vernon D. 42
Jarvis, Charlene Drew 21
Jasper, Kenji 39
Jay-Z 27
Jazzy Jeff 32
Jefferson, William J. 25
Jeffries, Leonard 8
Jemison, Mae C. 1, 35
Jemison, Major L. 48
Jenifer, Franklyn G. 2
Jenkins, Beverly 14
Jenkins, Ella 15
Jerkins, Rodney 31
Jeter, Derek 27
Jimmy Jam 13
Joe, Yolanda 21
John, Daymond 23
Johns, Vernon 38
Johnson Buddy 36
Johnson, Beverly 2
Johnson, Charles 1
Johnson, Charles S. 12
Johnson, Dwayne "The Rock" 29
Johnson, Earvin "Magic" 3, 39
Johnson, Eddie Bernice 8
Johnson, George E. 29
Johnson, Georgia Douglas 41
Johnson, Harvey Jr. 24
Johnson, J. J. 37
Johnson, Jack 8
Johnson, James Weldon 5
Johnson, Jeh Vincent 44
Johnson, John H. 3
Johnson, Larry 28
Johnson, Levi 48
Johnson, Lonnie 32
Johnson, Mamie "Peanut" 40
Johnson, Mat 31
Johnson, Michael 13
Johnson, Norma L. Holloway 17
Johnson, R.M. 36
Johnson, Rafer 33
Johnson, Robert 2
Johnson, Robert L. 3, 39
Johnson, Robert T. 17
Johnson, Rodney Van 28
Johnson, Sheila Crump 48
Johnson, Shoshana 47
Johnson, Virginia 9
Johnson, William Henry 3
Jolley, Willie 28
Jones, Bill T. 1, 46

Jones, Bobby 20
Jones, Carl 7
Jones, Caroline 29
Jones, Cobi N'Gai 18
Jones, Donell 29
Jones, E. Edward, Sr. 45
Jones, Ed "Too Tall" 46
Jones, Edward P. 43
Jones, Elaine R. 7, 45
Jones, Elvin 14
Jones, Etta 35
Jones, Gayl 37
Jones, Ingrid Saunders 18
Jones, James Earl 3
Jones, Jonah 39
Jones, Lois Mailou 13
Jones, Marion 21
Jones, Merlakia 34
Jones, Orlando 30
Jones, Quincy 8, 30
Jones, Randy 35
Jones, Sarah 39
Jones, Star 10, 27
Jones, Thomas W. 41
Joplin, Scott 6
Jordan, Barbara 4
Jordan, June 7, 35
Jordan, Michael 6, 21
Jordan, Montell 23
Jordan, Vernon E. 3, 35
Josey, E. J. 10
Joyner, Marjorie Stewart 26
Joyner, Matilda Sissieretta 15
Joyner, Tom 19
Joyner-Kersee, Jackie 5
Julian, Percy Lavon 6
July, William 27
Just, Ernest Everett 3
Justice, David 18
Kaiser, Cecil 42
Kani, Karl 10
Karenga, Maulana 10
Kay, Ulysses 37
Kearse, Amalya Lyle 12
Kee, John P. 43
Keith, Damon J. 16
Kelly, Patrick 3
Kelly, R. 18, 44
Kem 47
Kendricks, Eddie 22
Kennedy, Adrienne 11
Kennedy, Florynce 12, 33
Kennedy, Randall 40
Kennedy-Overton, Jayne Harris 46
Kenney, John A., Jr. 48
Kenoly, Ron 45
Kerry, Leon G. 46
Keyes, Alan L. 11
Keys, Alicia 32
Khan, Chaka 12
Khanga, Yelena 6
Kidd, Mae Street 39
Kilpatrick, Carolyn Cheeks 16
Kilpatrick, Kwame 34
Kimbro, Dennis 10
Kimbro, Henry A. 25
Kincaid, Bernard 28
Kincaid, Jamaica 4
King, Alonzo 38
King, B. B. 7
King, Barbara 22
King, Bernice 4
King, Coretta Scott 3

King, Dexter 10
King, Don 14
King, Gayle 19
King, Martin Luther, III 20
King, Martin Luther, Jr. 1
King, Preston 28
King, Regina 22, 45
King, Woodie, Jr. 27
King, Yolanda 6
Kirby, George 14
Kirk, Ron 11
Kitt, Eartha 16
Kitt, Sandra 23
Knight, Etheridge 37
Knight, Gladys 16
Knight, Suge 11, 30
Knowles, Beyoncé 39
Knowling, Robert E., Jr. 38
Knuckles, Frankie 42
Komunyakaa, Yusef 9
Kool Moe Dee 37
Kotto, Yaphet 7
Kountz, Samuel L. 10
Kravitz, Lenny 10, 34
KRS-One 34
Kunjufu, Jawanza 3
L.L. Cool J 16
La Salle, Eriq 12
LaBelle, Patti 13, 30
Lacy, Sam 30, 46
Ladner, Joyce A. 42
Lafontant, Jewel Stradford 3
Lampkin, Daisy 19
Lampley, Oni Faida 43
Lane, Charles 3
Lane, Vincent 5
Langhart, Janet 19
Lanier, Bob 47
Lanier, Willie 33
Lankford, Ray 23
Larkin, Barry 24
Lars, Byron 32
Larsen, Nella 10
Lassiter, Roy 24
Lathan, Sanaa 27
Latimer, Lewis H. 4
Lattimore, Kenny 35
Lavizzo-Mourey, Risa 48
Lawless, Theodore K. 8
Lawrence, Jacob 4, 28
Lawrence, Martin 6, 27
Lawrence, Robert H., Jr. 16
Lawrence-Lightfoot, Sara 10
Lawson, Jennifer 1
Leary, Kathryn D. 10
Leavell, Dorothy R. 17
Lee, Annie Francis 22
Lee, Barbara 25
Lee, Canada 8
Lee, Joe A. 45
Lee, Joie 1
Lee, Spike 5, 19
Lee, Sr., Bertram M. 46
Lee-Smith, Hughie 5, 22
Leevy, Carrol M. 42
Leffall, LaSalle, Jr. 3
Leland, Mickey 2
Lemmons, Kasi 20
Lennox, Betty 31
LeNoire, Rosetta 37
Leon, Kenny 10
Leonard, Sugar Ray 15
Lester, Bill 42

Lester, Julius 9
Letson, Al 39
Levert, Gerald 22
Lewellyn, J. Bruce 13
Lewis, Ananda 28
Lewis, Byron E. 13
Lewis, Carl 4
Lewis, David Levering 9
Lewis, Delano 7
Lewis, Edmonia 10
Lewis, Edward T. 21
Lewis, Emmanuel 36
Lewis, Henry 38
Lewis, John 2, 46
Lewis, Norman 39
Lewis, Ramsey 35
Lewis, Ray 33
Lewis, Reginald F. 6
Lewis, Samella 25
Lewis, Shirley A. R. 14
Lewis, Terry 13
Lewis, Thomas 19
Lewis, William M., Jr. 40
Lewis-Thornton, Rae 32
Ligging, Alfred III 43
(Lil') Bow Wow 35
Lil' Kim 28
Liles, Kevin 42
Lincoln, Abbey 3
Lincoln, C. Eric 38
LisaRaye 27
Liston, Sonny 33
Little Milton 36
Little Richard 15
Little Walter 36
Little, Benilde 21
Little, Robert L. 2
Littlepage, Craig 35
Lloyd, Earl 26
Lloyd, John Henry "Pop" 30
Locke, Alain 10
Locke, Eddie 44
Lofton, James 42
Lofton, Kenny 12
Logan, Onnie Lee 14
Logan, Rayford W. 40
Long, Eddie L. 29
Long, Nia 17
Lopes, Lisa "Left Eye" 36
Lorde, Audre 6
Lott, Ronnie 9
Louis, Errol T. 8
Louis, Joe 5
Loury, Glenn 36
Love, Darlene 23
Love, Nat 9
Lover, Ed 10
Loving, Alvin 35
Lowery, Joseph 2
Lucas, John 7
Lucy Foster, Autherine 35
Ludacris 37
Lumbly, Carl 47
Lyles, Lester Lawrence 31
Lymon, Frankie 22
Lyons, Henry 12
Lyttle, Hulda Margaret 14
Mabley, Moms 15
Mabrey, Vicki 26
Mac, Bernie 29
Madhubuti, Haki R. 7
Madison, Joseph E. 17
Madison, Paula 37

Madison, Romell 45
Mahal, Taj 39
Majette, Denise 41
Major, Clarence 9
Majors, Jeff 41
Mallett, Conrad Jr. 16
Malone, Annie 13
Malone, Karl A. 18
Malone, Maurice 32
Malveaux, Julianne 32
Manigault, Earl "The Goat" 15
Manley, Audrey Forbes 16
Marable, Manning 10
Mariner, Jonathan 41
Marino, Eugene Antonio 30
Marrow, Queen Esther 24
Marsalis, Branford 34
Marsalis, Delfeayo 41
Marsalis, Wynton 16
Marsh, Henry, III 32
Marshall, Bella 22
Marshall, Paule 7
Marshall, Thurgood 1, 44
Martin, Darnell 43
Martin, Helen 31
Martin, Jesse L. 31
Martin, Louis E. 16
Martin, Sara 38
Mase 24
Mason, Felicia 31
Mason, Ronald 27
Massaquoi, Hans J. 30
Massenburg, Kedar 23
Massey, Brandon 40
Massey, Walter E. 5, 45
Massie, Samuel Proctor Jr. 29
Master P 21
Mathis, Greg 26
Mathis, Johnny 20
Maxey, Randall 46
Maxwell 20
May, Derrick 41
Mayfield, Curtis 2, 43
Mayhew, Richard 39
Maynard, Robert C. 7
Maynor, Dorothy 19
Mayo, Whitman 32
Mays, Benjamin E. 7
Mays, Leslie A. 41
Mays, William G. 34
Mays, Willie 3
MC Lyte 34
McBride, Bryant 18
McBride, James C. 35
McCabe, Jewell Jackson 10
McCall, H. Carl 27
McCall, Nathan 8
McCann, Renetta 44
McCarty, Osceola 16
McClurkin, Donnie 25
McCoy, Elijah 8
McCray, Nikki 18
McDaniel, Hattie 5
McDonald, Audra 20
McDonald, Erroll 1
McDonald, Gabrielle Kirk 20
McDougall, Gay J. 11, 43
McEwen, Mark 5
McFadden, Bernice L. 39
McGee, Charles 10
McGee, James Madison 46
McGriff, Fred 24
McGruder, Aaron Vincent 28

McGruder, Robert 22, 35
McKay, Claude 6
McKay, Nellie Yvonne 17
Mckee, Lonette 12
McKenzie, Vashti M. 29
McKinney, Cynthia Ann 11
McKinney, Nina Mae 40
McKinney-Whetstone, Diane 27
McKinnon, Isaiah 9
McKissick, Floyd B. 3
McKnight, Brian 18, 34
McLeod, Gus 27
McMillan, Rosaylnn A. 36
McMillan, Terry 4, 17
McMurray, Georgia L. 36
McNabb, Donovan 29
McNair, Ronald 3
McNair, Steve 22, 47
McNeil, Lori 1
McPhail, Sharon 2
McPherson, David 32
McQueen, Butterfly 6
McWhorter, John 35
Meadows, Tim 30
Meek, Carrie 6, 36
Meek, Kendrick 41
Meeks, Gregory 25
Memphis Minnie 33
Mercado-Valdes, Frank 43
Meredith, James H. 11
Merkerson, S. Epatha 47
Metcalfe, Ralph 26
Mfume, Kweisi 6, 41
Micheaux, Oscar 7
Michele, Michael 31
Mickelbury, Penny 28
Millender-McDonald, Juanita 21
Miller, Bebe 3
Miller, Cheryl 10
Miller, Dorie 29
Miller, Reggie 33
Millines Dziko, Trish 28
Mills, Florence 22
Mills, Sam 33
Mills, Stephanie 36
Mills, Steve 47
Milner, Ron 39
Milton, DeLisha 31
Mingo, Frank 32
Mingus, Charles 15
Minor, DeWayne 32
Mitchell, Arthur 2, 47
Mitchell, Brian Stokes 21
Mitchell, Corinne 8
Mitchell, Leona 42
Mitchell, Loften 31
Mitchell, Parren J. 42
Mitchell, Russ 21
Mitchell, Stephanie 36
Mo', Keb' 36
Mo'Nique 35
Mohammed, W. Deen 27
Monica 21
Monk, Art 38
Monk, Thelonious 1
Monroe, Mary 35
Montgomery, Tim 41
Moon, Warren 8
Mooney, Paul 37
Moore, Chante 26
Moore, Dorothy Rudd 46
Moore, Harry T. 29
Moore, Jessica Care 30

Moore, Johnny B. 38
Moore, Melba 21
Moore, Minyon 45
Moore, Shemar 21
Moore, Undine Smith 28
Moorer, Michael 19
Moose, Charles 40
Morgan, Garrett 1
Morgan, Joe Leonard 9
Morgan, Rose 11
Morial, Ernest "Dutch" 26
Morial, Marc 20
Morris, Garrett 31
Morris, Greg 28
Morrison, Toni 2, 15
Morton, Azie Taylor 48
Morton, Jelly Roll 29
Morton, Joe 18
Mos Def 30
Moses, Edwin 8
Moses, Gilbert 12
Moses, Robert Parris 11
Mosley, Shane 32
Mosley, Walter 5, 25
Moss, Carlton 17
Moss, Randy 23
Mossell, Gertrude Bustill 40
Moten, Etta 18
Motley, Archibald Jr. 30
Motley, Constance Baker 10
Motley, Marion 26
Mourning, Alonzo 17, 44
Moutoussamy-Ashe, Jeanne 7
Mowry, Jess 7
Moyo, Karega Kofi 36
Moyo, Yvette Jackson 36
Muhammad, Ava 31
Muhammad, Elijah 4
Muhammad, Khallid Abdul 10, 31
Mullen, Harryette 34
Mullen, Nicole C. 45
Murphy, Eddie 4, 20
Murphy, John H. 42
Murphy, Laura M. 43
Murray, Albert L. 33
Murray, Cecil 12, 47
Murray, Eddie 12
Murray, Lenda 10
Murray, Pauli 38
Murray, Tai 47
Muse, Clarence Edouard 21
Musiq 37
Mya 35
Myers, Walter Dean 8
N'Namdi, George R. 17
Nabrit, Samuel Milton 47
Nagin, Ray 42
Nanula, Richard D. 20
Napoleon, Benny N. 23
Nas 33
Nash, Johnny 40
Naylor, Gloria 10, 42
Ndegéocello, Me'Shell 15
Neal, Elise 29
Neal, Larry 38
Neal, Raful 44
Nelly 32
Nelson Meigs, Andrea 48
Nelson, Jill 6
Neville, Aaron 21
Newcombe, Don 24
Newsome, Ozzie 26
Newton, Huey 2

Nicholas, Fayard 20
Nicholas, Harold 20
Nichols, Nichelle 11
Nissel, Angela 42
Noble, Ronald 46
Norman, Christina 47
Norman, Jessye 5
Norman, Maidie 20
Norman, Pat 10
Norton, Eleanor Holmes 7
Notorious B.I.G. 20
Nugent, Richard Bruce 39
Nunn, Annetta 43
O'Leary, Hazel 6
O'Neal, Ron 46
O'Neal, Shaquille 8, 30
O'Neal, Stanley 38
O'Neil, Buck 19
Odetta 37
Oglesby, Zena 12
Ogletree, Charles, Jr. 12, 47
Olden, Georg(e) 44
Oliver, Jerry 37
Oliver, Joe "King" 42
Oliver, John J., Jr. 48
Orlandersmith, Dael 42
Osborne, Jeffrey 26
Owens, Helen 48
Owens, Jack 38
Owens, Jesse 2
Owens, Major 6
Pace, Orlando 21
Page, Alan 7
Page, Clarence 4
Paige, Rod 29
Paige, Satchel 7
Painter, Nell Irvin 24
Parish, Robert 43
Parker, Charlie 20
Parker, Kellis E. 30
Parker, Pat 19
Parks, Bernard C. 17
Parks, Gordon 1, 35
Parks, Rosa 1, 35
Parks, Suzan-Lori 34
Parsons, James 14
Parsons, Richard Dean 11, 33
Patrick, Deval 12
Patterson, Floyd 19
Patterson, Frederick Douglass 12
Patterson, Gilbert Earl 41
Patterson, Louise 25
Patton, Antwan 45
Payne, Allen 13
Payne, Donald M. 2
Payne, Ethel L. 28
Payne, Ulice 42
Payton, Benjamin F. 23
Payton, John 48
Payton, Walter 11, 25
Peck, Carolyn 23
Peete, Calvin 11
Peete, Holly Robinson 20
Pendergrass, Teddy 22
Peoples, Dottie 22
Perez, Anna 1
Perkins, Edward 5
Perkins, Marion 38
Perkins, Tony 24
Perrot, Kim 23
Perry, Lowell 30
Perry, Tyler 40
Person, Waverly 9

Peters, Margaret and Matilda 43
Petersen, Frank E. 31
Peterson, James 38
Peterson, Marvin "Hannibal" 27
Petry, Ann 19
Phifer, Mekhi 25
Phillips, Teresa L. 42
Pickett, Bill 11
Pickett, Cecil 39
Pierre, Percy Anthony 46
Pinchback, P. B. S. 9
Pinckney, Bill 42
Pinderhughes, John 47
Pinkett Smith, Jada 10, 41
Pinkney, Jerry 15
Pinkston, W. Randall 24
Pippen, Scottie 15
Pippin, Horace 9
Player, Willa B. 43
Pleasant, Mary Ellen 9
Plessy, Homer Adolph 31
Poitier, Sidney 11, 36
Porter, James A. 11
Potter, Myrtle 40
Poussaint, Alvin F. 5
Powell, Adam Clayton, Jr. 3
Powell, Bud 24
Powell, Colin 1, 28
Powell, Debra A. 23
Powell, Kevin 31
Powell, Maxine 8
Powell, Michael 32
Powell, Mike 7
Powell, Renee 34
Pratt, Awadagin 31
Pratt, Geronimo 18
Premice, Josephine 41
Pressley, Condace L. 41
Preston, Billy 39
Price, Florence 37
Price, Frederick K.C. 21
Price, Glenda 22
Price, Hugh B. 9
Price, Kelly 23
Price, Leontyne 1
Pride, Charley 26
Primus, Pearl 6
Prince 18
Prince-Bythewood, Gina 31
Pritchard, Robert Starling 21
Procope, Ernesta 23
Prophet, Nancy Elizabeth 42
Prothrow-Stith, Deborah 10
Pryor, Richard 3, 24
Puckett, Kirby 4
Puryear, Martin 42
Quarles, Benjamin Arthur 18
Quarles, Norma 25
Quarterman, Lloyd Albert 4
Queen Latifah 1, 16
Rahman, Aishah 37
Raines, Franklin Delano 14
Rainey, Ma 33
Ralph, Sheryl Lee 18
Ramsey, Charles H. 21
Rand, A. Barry 6
Randall, Alice 38
Randall, Dudley 8
Randle, Theresa 16
Randolph, A. Philip 3
Rangel, Charles 3
Rashad, Ahmad 18
Rashad, Phylicia 21

Raspberry, William 2
Raven, 44
Rawls, Lou 17
Ray, Gene Anthony 47
Razaf, Andy 19
Reagon, Bernice Johnson 7
Reason, J. Paul 19
Reddick, Lawrence Dunbar 20
Redding, J. Saunders 26
Redding, Louis L. 26
Redding, Otis 16
Redman, Joshua 30
Redmond, Eugene 23
Reed, A. C. 36
Reed, Ishmael 8
Reed, Jimmy 38
Reems, Ernestine Cleveland 27
Reese, Della 6, 20
Reese, Pokey 28
Reeves, Dianne 32
Reeves, Rachel J. 23
Reeves, Triette Lipsey 27
Reid, Antonio "L.A." 28
Reid, Irvin D. 20
Reid, Vernon 34
Rhames, Ving 14
Rhoden, Dwight 40
Rhodes, Ray 14
Rhone, Sylvia 2
Rhymes, Busta 31
Ribbs, Willy T. 2
Ribeiro, Alfonso 17
Rice, Condoleezza 3, 28
Rice, Jerry 5
Rice, Linda Johnson 9, 41
Rice, Norm 8
Richards, Beah 30
Richardson, Desmond 39
Richardson, Donna 39
Richardson, Nolan 9
Richie, Leroy C. 18
Richie, Lionel 27
Richmond, Mitch 19
Rideau, Iris 46
Riggs, Marlon 5, 44
Riley, Helen Caldwell Day 13
Ringgold, Faith 4
Riperton, Minnie 32
Rivers, Glenn "Doc" 25
Roach, Max 21
Roberts, Deborah 35
Roberts, Marcus 19
Roberts, Robin 16
Roberts, Roy S. 14
Robertson, Oscar 26
Robeson, Eslanda Goode 13
Robeson, Paul 2
Robinson, Bill "Bojangles" 11
Robinson, Cleo Parker 38
Robinson, David 24
Robinson, Eddie G. 10
Robinson, Fatima 34
Robinson, Fenton 38
Robinson, Frank 9
Robinson, Jackie 6
Robinson, Malcolm S. 44
Robinson, Max 3
Robinson, Patrick 19
Robinson, Rachel 16
Robinson, Randall 7, 46
Robinson, Sharon 22
Robinson, Shaun 36
Robinson, Smokey 3

Robinson, Spottswood W. III 22
Robinson, Sugar Ray 18
Roche, Joyce M. 17
Rochon, Lela 16
Rock, Chris 3, 22
Rodgers, Johnathan 6
Rodgers, Rod 36
Rodman, Dennis 12, 44
Rodriguez, Jimmy 47
Rogers, Jimmy 38
Rogers, Joe 27
Rogers, Joel Augustus 30
Rogers, John W., Jr. 5
Roker, Al 12
Rolle, Esther 13, 21
Rollins, Charlemae Hill 27
Rollins, Howard E., Jr. 16
Rollins, Sonny 37
Ross, Charles 27
Ross, Diana 8, 27
Ross, Don 27
Ross, Isaiah "Doc" 40
Ross, Tracee Ellis 35
Roundtree, Richard 27
Rowan, Carl T. 1, 30
Rowell, Victoria 13
Roxanne Shante 33
Rubin, Chanda 37
Rucker, Darius 34
Rudolph, Maya 46
Rudolph, Wilma 4
Ruley, Ellis 38
Rupaul 17
Rush, Bobby 26
Rush, Otis 38
Rushen, Patrice 12
Rushing, Jimmy 37
Russell, Bill 8
Russell, Herman Jerome 17
Russell-McCloud, Patricia A. 17
Rustin, Bayard 4
Saar, Alison 16
Saint James, Synthia 12
Sallee, Charles 38
Samara, Noah 15
Sampson, Charles 13
Sanchez, Sonia 17
Sanders, Deion 4, 31
Sanders, Joseph R., Jr. 11
Sanders, Malika 48
Sapp, Warren 38
Sapphire 14
Savage, Augusta 12
Sayers, Gale 28
Sayles Belton, Sharon, 9, 16
Schmoke, Kurt 1, 48
Schuyler, George Samuel 40
Scott, "Little" Jimmy 48
Scott, C(ornelius) A(dolphus) 29
Scott, David 41
Scott, Jill 29
Scott, Robert C. 23
Scott, Stuart 34
Scott, Wendell Oliver, Sr. 19
Scurry, Briana 27
Sebree, Charles 40
Seele, Pernessa 46
Sengstacke, John 18
Serrano, Andres 3
Shabazz, Attallah 6
Shabazz, Betty 7, 26
Shabazz, Ilyasah 36
Shakur, Assata 6

Shakur, Tupac 14
Shange, Ntozake 8
Sharper, Darren 32
Sharpton, Al 21
Shavers, Cheryl 31
Shaw, Bernard 2, 28
Shaw, William J. 30
Sheffield, Gary 16
Shell, Art 1
Sherrod, Clayton 17
Shinhoster, Earl 32
Shipp, E. R. 15
Shippen, John 43
Shirley, George 33
Showers, Reggie 30
Shuttlesworth, Fred 47
Sifford, Charlie 4
Sigur, Wanda 44
Silas, Paul 24
Silver, Horace 26
Simmons, Bob 29
Simmons, Russell 1, 30
Simmons, Ruth J. 13, 38
Simone, Nina 15, 41
Simpson, Carole 6, 30
Simpson, Lorna 4, 36
Simpson, O. J. 15
Simpson, Valerie 21
Sims, Howard "Sandman" 48
Sims, Lowery Stokes 27
Sims, Naomi 29
Sinbad, 1, 16
Singletary, Mike 4
Singleton, John 2, 30
Sinkford, Jeanne C. 13
Sisqo 30
Sissle, Noble 29
Sister Souljah 11
Sizemore, Barbara A. 26
Sklarek, Norma Merrick 25
Slater, Rodney E. 15
Sledge, Percy 39
Sleet, Moneta, Jr. 5
Smaltz, Audrey 12
Smiley, Tavis 20
Smith, Anna Deavere 6, 44
Smith, Barbara 11
Smith, Barbara 28
Smith, Bessie 3
Smith, Cladys "Jabbo" 32
Smith, Clarence O. 21
Smith, Danyel 40
Smith, Emmitt 7
Smith, Greg 28
Smith, Hilton 29
Smith, Jane E. 24
Smith, Jessie Carney 35
Smith, John L. 22
Smith, Joshua 10
Smith, Mamie 32
Smith, Marvin 46
Smith, Mary Carter 26
Smith, Morgan 46
Smith, Roger Guenveur 12
Smith, Stuff 37
Smith, Trixie 34
Smith, Tubby 18
Smith, Vincent D. 48
Smith, Will 8, 18
Smith, Willi 8
Sneed, Paula A. 18
Snipes, Wesley 3, 24
Snoop Dogg 35

Solomon, Jimmie Lee 38
Sowell, Thomas 2
Spaulding, Charles Clinton 9
Spencer, Anne 27
Spikes, Dolores 18
Sprewell, Latrell 23
St. Jacques, Raymond 8
St. John, Kristoff 25
St. Julien, Marlon 29
St. Patrick, Mathew 48
Stackhouse, Jerry 30
Stallings, George A., Jr. 6
Stanford, John 20
Stanton, Robert 20
Staples, "Pops" 32
Staples, Brent 8
Stargell, Willie 29
Staton, Candi 27
Staupers, Mabel K. 7
Stearnes, Norman "Turkey" 31
Steele, Claude Mason 13
Steele, Lawrence 28
Steele, Michael 38
Steele, Shelby 13
Steinberg, Martha Jean "The Queen" 28
Stephens, Charlotte Andrews 14
Steward, David L. 36
Steward, Emanuel 18
Stewart, Alison 13
Stewart, Ella 39
Stewart, Kordell 21
Stewart, Maria W. Miller 19
Stewart, Paul Wilbur 12
Still, William Grant 37
Stokes, Carl B. 10
Stokes, Louis 3
Stone, Angie 31
Stone, Chuck 9
Stone, Toni 15
Stout, Juanita Kidd 24
Stoute, Steve 38
Strahan, Michael 35
Strawberry, Darryl 22
Strayhorn, Billy 31
Street, John F. 24
Streeter, Sarah 45
Stringer, C. Vivian 13
Stringer, Korey 35
Studdard, Ruben 46
Sudarkasa, Niara 4
Sullivan, Leon H. 3, 30
Sullivan, Louis 8
Sullivan, Maxine 37
Summer, Donna 25
Sutton, Percy E. 42
Swann, Lynn 28
Sweat, Keith 19
Swoopes, Sheryl 12
Swygert, H. Patrick 22
Sykes, Roosevelt 20
Sykes, Wanda 48
Tademy, Lalita 36
Talbert, David 34
Tamia 24
Tanksley, Ann 37
Tanner, Henry Ossawa 1
Tate, Eleanora E. 20
Tate, Larenz 15
Tatum, Art 28
Tatum, Beverly Daniel 42
Taulbert, Clifton Lemoure 19
Taylor, Billy 23

Taylor, Charles 20
Taylor, Helen (Lavon Hollingshed) 30
Taylor, Koko 40
Taylor, Kristin Clark 8
Taylor, Lawrence 25
Taylor, Meshach 4
Taylor, Mildred D. 26
Taylor, Natalie 47
Taylor, Regina 9, 46
Taylor, Ron 35
Taylor, Susan L. 10
Taylor, Susie King 13
Terrell, Dorothy A. 24
Terrell, Mary Church 9
Terrell, Tammi 32
Terry, Clark 39
Thigpen, Lynne 17, 41
Thomas, Alma 14
Thomas, Clarence 2, 39
Thomas, Debi 26
Thomas, Derrick 25
Thomas, Frank 12
Thomas, Franklin A. 5
Thomas, Irma 29
Thomas, Isiah 7, 26
Thomas, Rozonda "Chilli" 34
Thomas, Rufus 20
Thomas, Sean Patrick 35
Thomas, Vivien 9
Thomas-Graham, Pamela 29
Thompson, Bennie G. 26
Thompson, John W. 26
Thompson, Larry D. 39
Thompson, Tazewell 13
Thompson, Tina 25
Thompson, William C. 35
Thornton, Big Mama 33
Thrash, Dox 35
Thrower, Willie 35
Thurman, Howard 3
Thurman, Wallace 16
Till, Emmett 7
Tillard, Conrad 47
Tillis, Frederick 40
Tillman, George, Jr. 20
Timbaland 32
Tolliver, William 9
Tolson, Melvin 37
Toomer, Jean 6
Torry, Guy 31
Touré, Askia (Muhammad Abu Bakr el) 47
Towns, Edolphus 19
Townsend, Robert 4, 23
Tribble, Israel, Jr. 8
Trotter, Donne E. 28
Trotter, Monroe 9
Tubbs Jones, Stephanie 24
Tubman, Harriet 9
Tucker, C. DeLores 12
Tucker, Chris 13, 23
Tucker, Cynthia 15
Tucker, Rosina 14
Turnbull, Walter 13
Turner, Henry McNeal 5
Turner, Tina 6, 27
Tyler, Aisha N. 36
Tyree, Omar Rashad 21
Tyrese 27
Tyson, Andre 40
Tyson, Asha 39
Tyson, Cicely 7

Tyson, Mike 28, 44
Tyson, Neil de Grasse 15
Uggams, Leslie 23
Underwood, Blair 7, 27
Union, Gabrielle 31
Unseld, Wes 23
Upshaw, Gene 18, 47
Usher 23
Usry, James L. 23
Ussery, Terdema II 29
Utendahl, John 23
Van Peebles, Mario 2
Van Peebles, Melvin 7
Vance, Courtney B. 15
VanDerZee, James 6
Vandross, Luther 13, 48
Vanzant, Iyanla 17, 47
Vaughan, Sarah 13
Vaughn, Gladys Gary 47
Vaughn, Mo 16
Vaughns, Cleopatra 46
Verdelle, A. J. 26
Vereen, Ben 4
Vick, Michael 39
Vincent, Marjorie Judith 2
Von Lipsey, Roderick K. 11
Waddles, Charleszetta (Mother) 10
Wade-Gayles, Gloria Jean 41
Wagner, Annice 22
Wainwright, Joscelyn 46
Walker, A'lelia 14
Walker, Albertina 10
Walker, Alice 1, 43
Walker, Cedric "Ricky" 19
Walker, George 37
Walker, Herschel 1
Walker, Hezekiah 34
Walker, Madame C. J. 7
Walker, Maggie Lena 17
Walker, Margaret 29
Walker, T. J. 7
Wallace, Michele Faith 13
Wallace, Perry E. 47
Wallace, Phyllis A. 9
Wallace, Sippie 1
Waller, Fats 29
Ward, Douglas Turner 42
Ward, Lloyd 21, 46
Ware, Andre 37
Ware, Carl H. 30
Warfield, Marsha 2
Warner, Malcolm-Jamal 22, 36
Warren, Michael 27
Warwick, Dionne 18
Washington, Alonzo 29
Washington, Booker T. 4
Washington, Denzel 1, 16
Washington, Dinah 22
Washington, Fredi 10
Washington, Grover, Jr. 17, 44
Washington, Harold 6
Washington, James, Jr. 38
Washington, Kerry 46
Washington, Laura S. 18
Washington, MaliVai 8
Washington, Patrice Clarke 12
Washington, Regynald G. 44
Washington, Val 12
Washington, Walter 45
Wasow, Omar 15
Waters, Benny 26
Waters, Ethel 7
Waters, Maxine 3

Waters, Muddy 34
Watkins, Donald 35
Watkins, Levi, Jr. 9
Watkins, Perry 12
Watkins, Shirley R. 17
Watkins, Tionne "T-Boz" 34
Watkins, Walter C. 24
Watson, Bob 25
Watson, Diane 41
Watson, Johnny "Guitar" 18
Watt, Melvin 26
Wattleton, Faye 9
Watts, J. C., Jr. 14, 38
Watts, Rolonda 9
Wayans, Damon 8, 41
Wayans, Keenen Ivory 18
Wayans, Marlon 29
Wayans, Shawn 29
Weathers, Carl 10
Weaver, Afaa Michael 37
Weaver, Robert C. 8, 46
Webb, Veronica 10
Webb, Wellington 3
Webber, Chris 15, 30
Webster, Katie 29
Wedgeworth, Robert W. 42
Weems, Renita J. 44
Wells, James Lesesne 10
Wells, Mary 28
Wells-Barnett, Ida B. 8
Welsing, Frances Cress 5
Wesley, Dorothy Porter 19
Wesley, Valerie Wilson 18
West, Cornel 5, 33
West, Dorothy 12
West, Togo D., Jr. 16
Westbrook, Peter 20
Whack, Rita Coburn 36
Whalum, Kirk 37
Wharton, Clifton R., Jr. 7
Wharton, Clifton Reginald, Sr. 36
Wheat, Alan 14
Whitaker, Forest 2
Whitaker, Mark 21, 47
Whitaker, Pernell 10
White, Barry 13, 41
White, Bill 1, 48
White, Charles 39
White, Dondi 34
White, Jesse 22
White, John H. 27
White, Linda M. 45
White, Lois Jean 20
White, Maurice 29
White, Michael R. 5
White, Reggie 6
White, Walter F. 4
Whitfield, Fred 23
Whitfield, Lynn 18
Whitfield, Van 34
Wideman, John Edgar 5
Wilder, L. Douglas 3, 48
Wiley, Ralph 8
Wilkens, J. Ernest, Jr. 43
Wilkens, Lenny 11
Wilkins, Ray 47
Wilkins, Roger 2
Wilkins, Roy 4
Williams, Anthony 21
Williams, Armstrong 29
Williams, Bert 18
Williams, Billy Dee 8
Williams, Clarence 33

Williams, Clarence, III 26
Williams, Daniel Hale 2
Williams, Deniece 36
Williams, Doug 22
Williams, Eddie N. 44
Aaliyah 30
Williams, Evelyn 10
Williams, Fannie Barrier 27
Williams, George Washington 18
Williams, Gregory 11
Williams, Hosea Lorenzo 15, 31
Williams, Joe 5, 25
Williams, John A. 27
Williams, Maggie 7
Williams, Mary Lou 15
Williams, Montel 4
Williams, Natalie 31
Williams, O. S. 13
Williams, Patricia J. 11
Williams, Paul R. 9
Williams, Pharrell 47
Williams, Robert F. 11
Williams, Samm-Art 21
Williams, Saul 31
Williams, Serena 20, 41
Williams, Sherley Anne 25
Williams, Stanley "Tookie" 29
Williams, Terrie M. 35
Williams, Vanessa 32
Williams, Vanessa L. 4, 17
Williams, Venus 17, 34
Williams, Walter E. 4
Williams, William T. 11
Williams, Willie L. 4
Williamson, Mykelti 22
Willingham, Tyrone 43
Wilson, August 7, 33
Wilson, Cassandra 16
Wilson, Charlie 31
Wilson, Debra 38
Wilson, Ellis 39
Wilson, Flip 21
Wilson, Jimmy 45
Wilson, Mary 28
Wilson, Nancy 10
Wilson, Natalie 38
Wilson, Phill 9
Wilson, Sunnie 7
Wilson, William Julius 20
Winans, Angie 36
Winans, BeBe 14
Winans, CeCe 14, 43
Winans, Debbie 36
Winans, Marvin L. 17
Winans, Vickie 24
Winfield, Dave 5
Winfield, Paul 2, 45
Winfrey, Oprah 2, 15
Winkfield, Jimmy 42
Witherspoon, John 38
Witt, Edwin T. 26
Wolfe, George C. 6, 43
Wonder, Stevie 11
Woodard, Alfre 9
Woodruff, Hale 9
Woods, Granville T. 5
Woods, Sylvia 34
Woods, Tiger 14, 31
Woodson, Carter G. 2
Woodson, Robert L. 10
Worrill, Conrad 12
Wright, Bruce McMarion 3
Wright, Charles H. 35

Wright, Deborah C. 25
Wright, Jeremiah A., Jr. 45
Wright, Lewin 43
Wright, Louis Tompkins 4
Wright, Richard 5
Wynn, Albert R. 25
X, Malcolm 1
X, Marvin 45
Yancy, Dorothy Cowser 42
Yarbrough, Camille 40
Yoba, Malik 11
York, Vincent 40
Young, Andrew 3, 48
Young, Coleman 1, 20
Young, Jean Childs 14
Young, Lester 37
Young, Roger Arliner 29
Young, Whitney M., Jr. 4
Youngblood, Johnny Ray 8
Youngblood, Shay 32
Zollar, Alfred 40
Zollar, Jawole Willa Jo 28

Angolan
Bonga, Kuenda 13
dos Santos, José Eduardo 43
Neto, António Agostinho 43
Savimbi, Jonas 2, 34

Antiguan
Williams, Denise 40

Australian
Freeman, Cathy 29

Austrian
Kodjoe, Boris 34

Bahamian
Ingraham, Hubert A. 19

Barbadian
Arthur, Owen 33
Brathwaite, Kamau 36
Clarke, Austin C. 32
Flash, Grandmaster 33
Foster, Cecil 32
Kamau, Kwadwo Agymah 28
Lamming, George 35

Batswana
Masire, Quett 5

Belizian
Jones, Marion 21

Beninois
Hounsou, Djimon 19, 45
Joachim, Paulin 34
Kerekou, Ahmed (Mathieu) 1
Mogae, Festus Gontebanye 19
Soglo, Nicéphore 15

Bermudian
Cameron, Earl 44
Gordon, Pamela 17
Smith, Jennifer 21

Brazilian
da Silva, Benedita 5
Nascimento, Milton 2
Pelé 7
Pitta, Celso 17

British
Abbott, Diane 9
Adjaye, David 38

Akomfrah, John 37
Amos, Valerie 41
Armatrading, Joan 32
Bassey, Shirley 25
Berry, James 41
Blackwood, Maureen 37
Boateng, Ozwald 35
Breeze, Jean "Binta" 37
Campbell, Naomi 1, 31
Carby, Hazel 27
Christie, Linford 8
David, Craig 31
Davidson, Jaye 5
Emmanuel, Alphonsia 38
Henriques, Julian 37
Henry, Lenny 9
Holmes, Kelly 47
Jean-Baptiste, Marianne 17, 46
Jordan, Ronny 26
Julien, Isaac 3
Kay, Jackie 37
King, Oona 27
Lester, Adrian 46
Lewis, Denise 33
Lewis, Lennox 27
Lindo, Delroy 18, 45
Markham, E.A. 37
Newton, Thandie 26
Pitt, David Thomas 10
Scantlebury, Janna 47
Seal 14
Smith, Anjela Lauren 44
Taylor, John (David Beckett) 16
Thomason, Marsha 47
Walker, Eamonn 37

Burkinabé
Somé, Malidoma Patrice 10

Burundian
Ndadaye, Melchior 7
Ntaryamira, Cyprien 8

Cameroonian
Bebey, Francis 45
Beti, Mongo 36
Biya, Paul 28
Kotto, Yaphet 7
Milla, Roger 2
Oyono, Ferdinand 38

Canadian
Auguste, Arnold A. 47
Bell, Ralph S. 5
Brand, Dionne 32
Brathwaite, Fred 35
Carnegie, Herbert 25
Clarke, Austin 32
Clarke, George 32
Cox, Deborah 28
Curling, Alvin 34
Doig, Jason 45
Elliot, Lorris 37
Foster, Cecil 32
Fox, Rick 27
Fuhr, Grant 1
Grand-Pierre, Jean-Luc 46
Hammond, Lenn 34
Harris, Claire 25
Iginla, Jarome 35
Isaac, Julius 34
Jenkins, Fergie 46
Johnson, Ben 1
Laraque, Georges 48

Mayers, Jamal **39**
McKegney, Tony **3**
Mollel, Tololwa **38**
O'Ree, Willie **5**
Philip, Marlene Nourbese **32**
Reuben, Gloria **15**
Richards, Lloyd **2**
Senior, Olive **37**
Williams, Denise **40**

Cape Verdean
Evora, Cesaria **12**
Pereira, Aristides **30**

Chadian
Déby, Idriss **30**
Habré, Hissène **6**

Congolese
Kabila, Joseph **30**
Lumumba, Patrice **33**

Costa Rican
McDonald, Erroll **1**

Cuban
Ferrer, Ibrahim **41**
León, Tania **13**
Quirot, Ana **13**

Dominican
Charles, Mary Eugenia **10**
Sosa, Sammy **21, 44**
Virgil, Ozzie **48**

Dutch
Liberia-Peters, Maria Philomena **12**

Ethiopian
Gerima, Haile **38**
Haile Selassie **7**
Meles Zenawi **3**

French
Baker, Josephine **3**
Baldwin, James **1**
Bebey, Francis **45**
Bonaly, Surya **7**
Chase-Riboud, Barbara **20, 46**
Fanon, Frantz **44**
Noah, Yannick **4**
Tanner, Henry Ossawa **1**

Gabonese
Bongo, Omar **1**

Gambian
Jammeh, Yahya **23**
Peters, Lenrie **43**

German
Massaquoi, Hans J. **30**

Ghanaian
Aidoo, Ama Ata **38**
Annan, Kofi Atta **15, 48**
Awoonor, Kofi **37**
DuBois, Shirley Graham **21**
Jawara, Sir Dawda Kairaba **11**
Mensah, Thomas **48**
Nkrumah, Kwame **3**
Rawlings, Jerry **9**
Rawlings, Nana Konadu Agyeman **13**

Grenadian
Bishop, Maurice **39**
Isaac, Julius **34**

Guinea-Bissauan
Vieira, Joao **14**

Guinean
Conté, Lansana **7**
Diallo, Amadou **27**
Touré, Sekou **6**

Guyanese
Amos, Valerie **41**
Beaton, Norman **14**
Dabydeen, David **48**
Damas, Léon-Gontran **46**
Jagan, Cheddi **16**
Lefel, Edith **41**
van Sertima, Ivan **25**

Haitian
Aristide, Jean-Bertrand **6, 45**
Auguste, Rose-Anne **13**
Beauvais, Garcelle **29**
Charlemagne, Manno **11**
Christophe, Henri **9**
Danticat, Edwidge **15**
Delice, Ronald **48**
Delice, Rony **48**
Jean, Wyclef **20**
Laferriere, Dany **33**
Pascal-Trouillot, Ertha **3**
Peck, Raoul **32**
Pierre, Andre **17**
Siméus, Dumas M. **25**

Irish
Mumba, Samantha **29**

Italian
Esposito, Giancarlo **9**

Ivorian
Bedie, Henri Konan **21**
Blondy, Alpha **30**
Dadié, Bernard **34**
Gbagbo, Laurent **43**
Houphouët-Boigny, Félix **4**
Ouattara **43**

Jamaican
Ashley, Maurice **15, 47**
Barrett, Lindsay **43**
Beenie Man **32**
Belafonte, Harry **4**
Berry, James **41**
Channer, Colin **36**
Cliff, Jimmy **28**
Cliff, Michelle **42**
Curling, Alvin **34**
Dunbar, Sly **34**
Ewing, Patrick A. **17**
Fagan, Garth **18**
Figueroa, John J. **40**
Garvey, Marcus **1**
Griffiths, Marcia **29**
Hammond, Lenn **34**
Hearne, John Edgar Caulwell **45**
Johnson, Ben **1**
Johnson, Linton Kwesi **37**
Manley, Edna **26**
Manley, Ruth **34**
Marley, Bob **5**
Marley, Rita **32**

Marley, Ziggy **41**
McKay, Claude **6**
Moody, Ronald **30**
Morrison, Keith **13**
Mowatt, Judy **38**
Palmer, Everard **37**
Patterson, Orlando **4**
Patterson, P. J. **6, 20**
Perry, Ruth **19**
Rogers, Joel Augustus **30**
Senior, Olive **37**
Shaggy **31**
Shakespeare, Robbie **34**
Taylor, Karin **34**
Tosh, Peter **9**

Kenyan
Kenyatta, Jomo **5**
Kobia, Rev. Dr. Samuel **43**
Maathai, Wangari **43**
Mazrui, Ali A. **12**
Moi, Daniel **1, 35**
Mutu, Wangechi **19(?) 44**
Mwangi, Meja **40**
wa Thiong'o, Ngugi **29**
Wambugu, Florence **42**

Lesothoian
Mofolo, Thomas **37**

Liberian
Fuller, Solomon Carter, Jr. **15**
Perry, Ruth **15**
Sawyer, Amos **2**
Taylor, Charles **20**

Malawian
Banda, Hastings Kamuzu **6**
Kayira, Legson **40**
Muluzi, Bakili **14**

Malian
Touré, Amadou Toumani **18**

Mozambican
Chissano, Joaquim **7**
Couto, Mia **45**
Machel, Graca Simbine **16**
Machel, Samora Moises **8**
Mutola, Maria **12**

Namibian
Mbuende, Kaire **12**
Nujoma, Samuel **10**

Nigerian
Abacha, Sani **11**
Achebe, Chinua **6**
Ade, King Sunny **41**
Ake, Claude **30**
Amadi, Elechi **40**
Arinze, Francis Cardinal **19**
Azikiwe, Nnamdi **13**
Babangida, Ibrahim **4**
Clark-Bekedermo, J. P. **44**
Ekwensi, Cyprian **37**
Emeagwali, Philip **30**
Emecheta, Buchi **30**
Fela **1, 42**
Kuti, Femi **47**
Lawal, Kase L. **45**
Obasanjo, Olusegun **5, 22**
Obasanjo, Stella **32**
Ogunlesi, Adebayo O. **37**
Okara, Gabriel **37**

Olajuwon, Hakeem **2**
Olatunji, Babatunde **36**
Onwueme, Tess Osonye **23**
Onwurah, Ngozi **38**
Rotimi, Ola **1**
Sade **15**
Saro-Wiwa, Kenule **39**
Sowande, Fela **39**
Soyinka, Wole **4**
Tutuola, Amos **30**

Nigerien
Mamadou, Tandja **33**

Panamanian
Williams, Juan **35**

Puerto Rican
Schomburg, Arthur Alfonso **9**

Rhodesian
Brutus, Dennis **38**

Russian
Khanga, Yelena **6**

Rwandan
Bizimungu, Pasteur **19**
Habyarimana, Juvenal **8**

Senegalese
Ba, Mariama **30**
Boye, Madior **30**
Diop, Cheikh Anta **4**
Diouf, Abdou **3**
Mbaye, Mariétou **31**
Mboup, Souleymane **10**
N'Dour, Youssou **1**
Sané, Pierre Gabriel **21**
Sembène, Ousmane **13**
Senghor, Léopold Sédar **12**

Sierra Leonean
Cheney-Coker, Syl **43**
Kabbah, Ahmad Tejan **23**

Somali
Ali Mahdi Mohamed **5**
Farah, Nuruddin **27**
Iman **4, 33**

South African
Abrahams, Peter **39**
Biko, Steven **4**
Brutus, Dennis **38**
Buthelezi, Mangosuthu Gatsha **9**
Butler, Jonathan **28**
Hani, Chris **6**
Head, Bessie **28**
Ka Dinizulu, Mcwayizeni **29**
LaGuma, Alex **30**
Luthuli, Albert **13**
Mabuza, Lindiwe **18**
Mabuza-Suttle, Felicia **43**
Makeba, Miriam **2**
Mandela, Nelson **1, 14**
Mandela, Winnie **2, 35**
Masekela, Barbara **18**
Masekela, Hugh **1**
Mathabane, Mark **5**
Mbeki, Thabo Mvuyelwa **14**
Mphalele, Es'kia (Ezekiel) **40**
Ngubane, Ben **33**
Nkosi, Lewis **46**
Nyanda, Siphiwe **21**
Nzo, Alfred **15**

Ramaphosa, Cyril **3**
Ramphele, Mamphela **29**
Sisulu, Sheila Violet Makate **24**
Sisulu, Walter **47**
Thugwane, Josia **21**
Tutu, Desmond (Mpilo) **6, 44**
Zuma, Jacob **33**
Zuma, Nkosazana Dlamini **34**

Sudanese
Bol, Manute **1**
Salih, Al-Tayyib **37**
Wek, Alek **18**

Tanzanian
Mkapa, Benjamin **16**
Mongella, Gertrude **11**
Mollel, Tololwa **38**
Mwinyi, Ali Hassan **1**
Nyerere, Julius **5**
Rugambwa, Laurean **20**

Togolese
Eyadéma, Gnassingbé **7**
Soglo, Nicéphore **15**

Trinidadian
Anthony, Michael **29**
Auguste, Arnold A. **47**
Brand, Dionne **32**
Carmichael, Stokely **5, 26**
Cartey, Wilfred 1992 **47**
Dymally, Mervyn **42**
Harris, Claire **34**
Hendy, Francis **47**
Hercules, Frank **44**
Guy, Rosa **5**
Hill, Errol **40**
Nakhid, David **25**
Primus, Pearl **6**
Shorty I, Ras **47**
Toussaint, Lorraine **32**

Tunisian
Memmi, Albert **37**

Ugandan
Amin, Idi **42**
Museveni, Yoweri **4**
Mutebi, Ronald **25**

Upper Voltan
Sankara, Thomas **17**

West Indian
Césaire, Aimé **48**
Coombs, Orde M. **44**
Innis, Roy **5**
Kincaid, Jamaica **4**
Rojas, Don **33**
Staupers, Mabel K. **7**
Pitt, David Thomas **10**
Taylor, Susan L. **10**
Walcott, Derek **5**

Zairean
Kabila, Laurent **20**
Mobutu Sese Seko **1**
Mutombo, Dikembe **7**
Ongala, Remmy **9**

Zambian
Kaunda, Kenneth **2**

Zimbabwean
Chideya, Farai **14**
Marechera, Dambudzo **39**
Mugabe, Robert Gabriel **10**
Nkomo, Joshua, **4**
Tsvangirai, Morgan **26**
Vera, Yvonne **32**

Cumulative Occupation Index

Art and design
Adjaye, David **38**
Allen, Tina **22**
Alston, Charles **33**
Andrews, Benny **22**
Andrews, Bert **13**
Armstrong, Robb **15**
Bailey, Radcliffe **19**
Bailey, Xenobia **11**
Barboza, Anthony **10**
Barnes, Ernie **16**
Barthe, Richmond **15**
Basquiat, Jean-Michel **5**
Bearden, Romare **2**
Beasley, Phoebe **34**
Biggers, John **20, 33**
Blacknurn, Robert **28**
Brandon, Barbara **3**
Brown, Donald **19**
Burke, Selma **16**
Burroughs, Margaret Taylor **9**
Camp, Kimberly **19**
Campbell, E. Simms **13**
Campbell, Mary Schmidt **43**
Catlett, Elizabeth **2**
Chase-Riboud, Barbara **20, 46**
Cortor, Eldzier **42**
Cowans, Adger W. **20**
Crite, Alan Rohan **29**
De Veaux, Alexis **44**
DeCarava, Roy **42**
Delaney, Beauford **19**
Delaney, Joseph **30**
Delsarte, Louis **34**
Donaldson, Jeff **46**
Douglas, Aaron **7**
Driskell, David C. **7**
Edwards, Melvin **22**
El Wilson, Barbara **35**
Ewing, Patrick A. **17**
Fax, Elton **48**
Feelings, Tom **11, 47**
Freeman, Leonard **27**
Fuller, Meta Vaux Warrick **27**
Gantt, Harvey **1**
Gilliam, Sam **16**
Golden, Thelma **10**
Goodnight, Paul **32**
Guyton, Tyree **9**
Harkless, Necia Desiree **19**
Harrington, Oliver W. **9**
Hathaway, Isaac Scott **33**
Hayden, Palmer **13**

Hayes, Cecil N. **46**
Hope, John **8**
Hudson, Cheryl **15**
Hudson, Wade **15**
Hunt, Richard **6**
Hunter, Clementine **45**
Hutson, Jean Blackwell **16**
Jackson, Earl **31**
Jackson, Vera **40**
John, Daymond **23**
Johnson, Jeh Vincent **44**
Johnson, William Henry **3**
Jones, Lois Mailou **13**
Kitt, Sandra **23**
Lawrence, Jacob **4, 28**
Lee, Annie Francis **22**
Lee-Smith, Hughie **5, 22**
Lewis, Edmonia **10**
Lewis, Norman **39**
Lewis, Samella **25**
Loving, Alvin **35**
Manley, Edna **26**
Mayhew, Richard **39**
McGee, Charles **10**
McGruder, Aaron **28**
Mitchell, Corinne **8**
Moody, Ronald **30**
Morrison, Keith **13**
Motley, Archibald Jr. **30**
Moutoussamy-Ashe, Jeanne **7**
Mutu, Wangechi **44**
N'Namdi, George R. **17**
Nugent, Richard Bruce **39**
Olden, Georg(e) **44**
Ouattara **43**
Perkins, Marion **38**
Pierre, Andre **17**
Pinderhughes, John **47**
Pinkney, Jerry **15**
Pippin, Horace **9**
Porter, James A. **11**
Prophet, Nancy Elizabeth **42**
Puryear, Martin **42**
Ringgold, Faith **4**
Ruley, Ellis **38**
Saar, Alison **16**
Saint James, Synthia **12**
Sallee, Charles **38**
Sanders, Joseph R., Jr. **11**
Savage, Augusta **12**
Sebree, Charles **40**
Serrano, Andres **3**
Shabazz, Attallah **6**

Simpson, Lorna **4, 36**
Sims, Lowery Stokes **27**
Sklarek, Norma Merrick **25**
Sleet, Moneta, Jr. **5**
Smith, Marvin **46**
Smith, Morgan **46**
Smith, Vincent D. **48**
Tanksley, Ann **37**
Tanner, Henry Ossawa **1**
Thomas, Alma **14**
Thrash, Dox **35**
Tolliver, William **9**
VanDerZee, James **6**
Wainwright, Joscelyn **46**
Walker, A'lelia **14**
Walker, Kara **16**
Washington, Alonzo **29**
Washington, James, Jr. **38**
Wells, James Lesesne **10**
White, Charles **39**
White, Dondi **34**
White, John H. **27**
Williams, Billy Dee **8**
Williams, O. S. **13**
Williams, Paul R. **9**
Williams, William T. **11**
Wilson, Ellis **39**
Woodruff, Hale **9**

Business
Abbot, Robert Sengstacke **27**
Abdul-Jabbar, Kareem **8**
Adams, Eula L. **39**
Adkins, Rod **41**
Ailey, Alvin **8**
Al-Amin, Jamil Abdullah **6**
Alexander, Archie Alphonso **14**
Allen, Byron **24**
Ames, Wilmer **27**
Amos, Wally **9**
Auguste, Donna **29**
Avant, Clarence **19**
Beal, Bernard B. **46**
Beamon, Bob **30**
Baker, Dusty **8, 43**
Baker, Ella **5**
Baker, Gwendolyn Calvert **9**
Baker, Maxine **28**
Banks, Jeffrey **17**
Banks, William **11**
Barden, Don H. **9, 20**
Barrett, Andrew C. **12**
Beasley, Phoebe **34**
Bennett, Lerone, Jr. **5**

Bing, Dave **3**
Bolden, Frank E. **44**
Borders, James **9**
Boston, Kelvin E. **25**
Boston, Lloyd **24**
Boyd, John W., Jr. **20**
Boyd, T. B., III **6**
Bradley, Jennette B. **40**
Bridges, Shelia **36**
Bridgforth, Glinda **36**
Brimmer, Andrew F. **2, 48**
Bronner, Nathaniel H., Sr. **32**
Brown, Eddie C. **35**
Brown, Les **5**
Brown, Marie Dutton **12**
Brunson, Dorothy **1**
Bryant, John **26**
Burrell, Thomas J. **21**
Burroughs, Margaret Taylor **9**
Burrus, William Henry "Bill" **45**
Busby, Jheryl **3**
Cain, Herman **15**
CasSelle, Malcolm **11**
Chamberlain, Wilt **18, 47**
Chapman, Nathan A. Jr. **21**
Chappell, Emma **18**
Chenault, Kenneth I. **4, 36**
Cherry, Deron **40**
Chisholm, Samuel J. **32**
Clark, Celeste **15**
Clark, Patrick **14**
Clay, William Lacy **8**
Clayton, Xernona **3, 45**
Cobbs, Price M. **9**
Colbert, Virgis William **17**
Coleman, Donald A. **24**
Combs, Sean "Puffy" **17, 43**
Connerly, Ward **14**
Conyers, Nathan G. **24**
Cooper, Barry **33**
Cooper, Evern **40**
Corbi, Lana **42**
Cornelius, Don **4**
Cosby, Bill **7, 26**
Cottrell, Comer **11**
Creagh, Milton **27**
Daniels-Carter, Valerie **23**
Darden, Calvin **38**
Dash, Darien **29**
Davis, Ed **24**
Dawson, Matel "Mat," Jr. **39**
de Passe, Suzanne **25**
Dean, Mark **35**

Delany, Bessie **12**
Delany, Martin R. **27**
Delany, Sadie **12**
Diallo, Amadou **27**
Divine, Father **7**
Doley, Harold Jr. **26**
Donald, Arnold Wayne **36**
Dre, Dr. **14, 30**
Driver, David E. **11**
Ducksworth, Marilyn **12**
Edelin, Ramona Hoage **19**
Edmonds, Tracey **16**
Edmunds, Gladys **48**
El Wilson, Barbara **35**
Elder, Lee **6**
Ellington, E. David **11**
Evans, Darryl **22**
Evers, Myrlie **8**
Farmer, Forest J. **1**
Farr, Mel Sr. **24**
Farrakhan, Louis **15**
Fauntroy, Walter E. **11**
Fletcher, Alphonse, Jr. **16**
Foster, Jylla Moore **45**
Franklin, Hardy R. **9**
Friday, Jeff **24**
Fudge, Ann **11**
Fuller, S. B. **13**
Funderburg, I. Owen **38**
Gaines, Brenda **41**
Gardner, Edward G. **45**
Gaston, Arthur G. **4**
Gibson, Kenneth Allen **6**
Goldsberry, Ronald **18**
Gordon, Bruce S. **41**
Gordon, Pamela **17**
Gordy, Berry, Jr. **1**
Goss, Tom **23**
Grace, George H. **48**
Graham, Stedman **13**
Graves, Earl G. **1, 35**
Greely, M. Gasby **27**
Greenwood, Monique **38**
Griffith, Mark Winston **8**
Hale, Lorraine **8**
Hamer, Fannie Lou **6**
Hamilton, Samuel C. **47**
Hammer, M. C. **20**
Handy, W. C. **8**
Hannah, Marc **10**
Hardison, Bethann **12**
Harrell, Andre **9, 30**
Harris, Alice **7**
Harris, E. Lynn **12, 33**
Harris, Monica **18**
Harvey, Steve **18**
Harvey, William R. **42**
Hawkins, La-Van **17**
Hayden, Carla D. **47**
Henderson, Gordon **5**
Henry, Lenny **9**
Hightower, Dennis F. **13**
Hill, Bonnie Guiton **20**
Hill, Calvin **19**
Hill, Janet **19**
Hill, Jessie, Jr. **13**
Hobson, Mellody **40**
Holland, Robert, Jr. **11**
Holmes, Larry **20**
Houston, Whitney **7**
Howroyd, Janice Bryant **42**
Hudlin, Reginald **9**
Hudlin, Warrington **9**
Hudson, Cheryl **15**
Hudson, Wade **15**
Huggins, Larry **21**
Hughes, Cathy **27**
Ice Cube **8, 30**
Jackson, George **19**
Jackson, Mannie **14**
Jackson, Michael **19**
Jakes, Thomas "T.D." **17, 43**
James, Juanita **13**
John, Daymond **23**
Johnson, Eddie Bernice **8**
Johnson, Earvin "Magic" **3, 39**
Johnson, George E. **29**
Johnson, John H. **3**
Johnson, Robert L. **3, 39**
Johnson, Sheila Crump **48**
Jolley, Willie **28**
Jones, Bobby **20**
Jones, Carl **7**
Jones, Caroline **29**
Jones, Ingrid Saunders **18**
Jones, Quincy **8, 30**
Jones, Thomas W. **41**
Jordan, Michael **6, 21**
Jordan, Montell **23**
Joyner, Marjorie Stewart **26**
Julian, Percy Lavon **6**
Kelly, Patrick **3**
Kidd, Mae Street **39**
Kimbro, Dennis **10**
King, Dexter **10**
King, Don **14**
Knight, Suge **11, 30**
Knowling, Robert E., Jr. **38**
Lane, Vincent **5**
Langhart, Janet **19**
Lanier, Willie **33**
Lawal, Kase L. **45**
Lawless, Theodore K. **8**
Lawson, Jennifer **1**
Leary, Kathryn D. **10**
Leavell, Dorothy R. **17**
Lee, Annie Francis **22**
Lee, Sr., Bertram M. **46**
Leonard, Sugar Ray **15**
Lewellyn, J. Bruce **13**
Lewis, Byron E. **13**
Lewis, Delano **7**
Lewis, Edward T. **21**
Lewis, Reginald F. **6**
Lewis, William M., Jr. **40**
Ligging, Alfred III **43**
Long, Eddie L. **29**
Lott, Ronnie **9**
Louis, Errol T. **8**
Lucas, John **7**
Madhubuti, Haki R. **7**
Madison, Paula **37**
Malone, Annie **13**
Marshall, Bella **22**
Massenburg, Kedar **23**
Master P **21**
Maynard, Robert C. **7**
Mays, Leslie A. **41**
Mays, William G. **34**
McCabe, Jewell Jackson **10**
McCann, Renetta **44**
McCoy, Elijah **8**
McDonald, Erroll **1**
McGee, James Madison **46**
McLeod, Gus **27**
McPherson, David **32**
Micheaux, Oscar **7**
Millines Dziko, Trish **28**
Mills, Steve **47**
Mingo, Frank **32**
Monk, Art **38**
Morgan, Garrett **1**
Morgan, Joe Leonard **9**
Morgan, Rose **11**
Moyo, Karega Kofi **36**
Moyo, Yvette Jackson **36**
Nanula, Richard D. **20**
Nelson Meigs, Andrea **48**
Nichols, Nichelle **11**
Norman, Christina **47**
O'Neal, Stanley **38**
Ogunlesi, Adebayo O. **37**
Parks, Gordon **1, 35**
Parsons, Richard Dean **11, 33**
Payton, Walter **11, 25**
Peck, Carolyn **23**
Perez, Anna **1**
Perry, Lowell **30**
Pleasant, Mary Ellen **9**
Pinckney, Bill **42**
Potter, Myrtle **40**
Powell, Maxine **8**
Price, Frederick K.C. **21**
Price, Hugh B. **9**
Procope, Ernesta **23**
Queen Latifah **1, 16**
Ralph, Sheryl Lee **18**
Rand, A. Barry **6**
Reid, Antonio "L.A." **28**
Reeves, Rachel J. **23**
Rhone, Sylvia **2**
Rice, Linda Johnson **9, 41**
Rice, Norm **8**
Richardson, Donna **39**
Richie, Leroy C. **18**
Rideau, Iris **46**
Roberts, Roy S. **14**
Robertson, Oscar **26**
Robeson, Eslanda Goode **13**
Robinson, Jackie **6**
Robinson, Rachel **16**
Robinson, Randall **7, 46**
Roche, Joyce M. **17**
Rodgers, Johnathan **6**
Rodriguez, Jimmy **47**
Rogers, John W., Jr. **5**
Rojas, Don **33**
Ross, Diana **8, 27**
Ross, Charles **27**
Russell, Bill **8**
Russell, Herman Jerome **17**
Russell-McCloud, Patricia **17**
Saint James, Synthia **12**
Samara, Noah **15**
Sanders, Dori **8**
Scott, C. A. **29**
Sengstacke, John **18**
Siméus, Dumas M. **25**
Simmons, Russell **1, 30**
Sims, Naomi **29**
Sinbad **1, 16**
Smith, B(arbara) **11**
Smith, Clarence O. **21**
Smith, Jane E. **24**
Smith, Joshua **10**
Smith, Willi **8**
Sneed, Paula A. **18**
Spaulding, Charles Clinton **9**
Steinberg, Martha Jean "The Queen" **28**
Steward, David L. **36**
Stewart, Ella **39**
Stewart, Paul Wilbur **12**
Sullivan, Leon H. **3, 30**
Sutton, Percy E. **42**
Taylor, Karin **34**
Taylor, Kristin Clark **8**
Taylor, Natalie **47**
Taylor, Susan L. **10**
Terrell, Dorothy A. **24**
Thomas, Franklin A. **5**
Thomas, Isiah **7, 26**
Thomas-Graham, Pamela **29**
Thompson, John W. **26**
Tribble, Israel, Jr. **8**
Trotter, Monroe **9**
Tyson, Asha **39**
Ussery, Terdema, II **29**
Utendahl, John **23**
Van Peebles, Melvin **7**
VanDerZee, James **6**
Vaughn, Gladys Gary **47**
Vaughns, Cleopatra **46**
Walker, A'lelia **14**
Walker, Cedric "Ricky" **19**
Walker, Madame C. J. **7**
Walker, Maggie Lena **17**
Walker, T. J. **7**
Ward, Lloyd **21, 46**
Ware, Carl H. **30**
Washington, Alonzo **29**
Washington, Regynald G. **44**
Washington, Val **12**
Wasow, Omar **15**
Watkins, Donald **35**
Watkins, Walter C. Jr. **24**
Wattleton, Faye **9**
Wek, Alek **18**
Wells-Barnett, Ida B. **8**
Wharton, Clifton R., Jr. **7**
White, Linda M. **45**
White, Walter F. **4**
Wiley, Ralph **8**
Wilkins, Ray **47**
Williams, Armstrong **29**
Williams, O. S. **13**
Williams, Paul R. **9**
Williams, Terrie **35**
Williams, Walter E. **4**
Wilson, Phill **9**
Wilson, Sunnie **7**
Winfrey, Oprah **2, 15**
Woods, Sylvia **34**
Woodson, Robert L. **10**
Wright, Charles H. **35**
Wright, Deborah C. **25**
Yoba, Malik **11**
Zollar, Alfred **40**

Dance

Ailey, Alvin **8**
Alexander, Khandi **43**
Allen, Debbie **13, 42**
Atkins, Cholly **40**
Babatunde, Obba **35**
Baker, Josephine **3**
Bates, Peg Leg **14**
Beals, Jennifer **12**
Beatty, Talley **35**
Byrd, Donald **10**
Clarke, Hope **14**

Collins, Janet **33**
Davis, Chuck **33**
Davis, Sammy Jr. **18**
Dove, Ulysses **5**
Dunham, Katherine **4**
Ellington, Mercedes **34**
Fagan, Garth **18**
Falana, Lola **42**
Glover, Savion **14**
Guy, Jasmine **2**
Hall, Arthur **39**
Hammer, M. C. **20**
Henson, Darrin **33**
Hines, Gregory **1, 42**
Horne, Lena **5**
Jackson, Michael **19**
Jamison, Judith **7**
Johnson, Virginia **9**
Jones, Bill T. **1, 46**
King, Alonzo **38**
McQueen, Butterfly **6**
Miller, Bebe **3**
Mills, Florence **22**
Mitchell, Arthur **2, 47**
Moten, Etta **18**
Muse, Clarence Edouard **21**
Nicholas, Fayard **20**
Nicholas, Harold **20**
Nichols, Nichelle **11**
Powell, Maxine **8**
Premice, Josephine **41**
Primus, Pearl **6**
Ray, Gene Anthony **47**
Rhoden, Dwight **40**
Ribeiro, Alfonso **17**
Richardson, Desmond **39**
Robinson, Bill "Bojangles" **11**
Robinson, Cleo Parker **38**
Robinson, Fatima **34**
Rodgers, Rod **36**
Rolle, Esther **13, 21**
Sims, Howard "Sandman" **48**
Tyson, Andre **40**
Vereen, Ben **4**
Walker, Cedric "Ricky" **19**
Washington, Fredi **10**
Williams, Vanessa L. **4, 17**
Zollar, Jawole Willa Jo **28**

Education
Achebe, Chinua **6**
Adams, Leslie **39**
Adams-Ender, Clara **40**
Adkins, Rutherford H. **21**
Aidoo, Ama Ata **38**
Ake, Claude **30**
Alexander, Margaret Walker **22**
Allen, Robert L. **38**
Allen, Samuel W. **38**
Alston, Charles **33**
Amadi, Elechi **40**
Anderson, Charles Edward **37**
Archer, Dennis **7**
Archie-Hudson, Marguerite **44**
Aristide, Jean-Bertrand **6, 45**
Asante, Molefi Kete **3**
Aubert, Alvin **41**
Awoonor, Kofi **37**
Bacon-Bercey, June **38**
Baiocchi, Regina Harris **41**
Baker, Augusta **38**
Baker, Gwendolyn Calvert **9**
Baker, Houston A., Jr. **6**
Ballard, Allen Butler, Jr. **40**
Bambara, Toni Cade **10**
Baraka, Amiri **1, 38**
Barboza, Anthony **10**
Barnett, Marguerite **46**
Bath, Patricia E. **37**
Beckham, Barry **41**
Boll, Derrick **6**
Berry, Bertice **8**
Berry, Mary Frances **7**
Bethune, Mary McLeod **4**
Biggers, John **20, 33**
Black, Keith Lanier **18**
Blassingame, John Wesley **40**
Blockson, Charles L. **42**
Bluitt, Juliann S. **14**
Bogle, Donald **34**
Bolden, Tonya **32**
Bosley, Freeman, Jr. **7**
Boyd, T. B., III **6**
Bradley, David Henry, Jr. **39**
Branch, William Blackwell **39**
Brathwaite, Kamau **36**
Braun, Carol Moseley **4, 42**
Briscoe, Marlin **37**
Brooks, Avery **9**
Brown, Claude **38**
Brown, Joyce F. **25**
Brown, Sterling **10**
Brown, Uzee **42**
Brown, Wesley **23**
Brown, Willa **40**
Bruce, Blanche Kelso **33**
Brutus, Dennis **38**
Bryan, Ashley F. **41**
Burke, Selma **16**
Burke, Yvonne Braithwaite **42**
Burks, Mary Fair **40**
Burnim, Mickey L. **48**
Burroughs, Margaret Taylor **9**
Burton, LeVar **8**
Butler, Paul D. **17**
Callender, Clive O. **3**
Campbell, Bebe Moore **6, 24**
Campbell, Mary Schmidt **43**
Cannon, Katie **10**
Carby, Hazel **27**
Cardozo, Francis L. **33**
Carnegie, Herbert **25**
Carruthers, George R. **40**
Carter, Joye Maureen **41**
Carter, Warrick L. **27**
Cartey, Wilfred **47**
Carver, George Washington **4**
Cary, Lorene **3**
Cary, Mary Ann Shadd **30**
Catlett, Elizabeth **2**
Cayton, Horace **26**
Cheney-Coker, Syl **43**
Clark, Joe **1**
Clark, Kenneth B. **5**
Clark, Septima **7**
Clarke, Cheryl **32**
Clarke, George **32**
Clarke, John Henrik **20**
Clayton, Constance **1**
Cleaver, Kathleen Neal **29**
Clements, George **2**
Clemmons, Reginal G. **41**
Clifton, Lucille **14**
Cobb, Jewel Plummer **42**
Cobb, W. Montague **39**
Cobbs, Price M. **9**
Cohen, Anthony **15**
Cole, Johnnetta B. **5, 43**
Collins, Janet **33**
Collins, Marva **3**
Comer, James P. **6**
Cone, James H. **3**
Coney, PonJola **48**
Cook, Mercer **40**
Cook, Samuel DuBois **14**
Cook, Toni **23**
Cooper Cafritz, Peggy **43**
Cooper, Anna Julia **20**
Cooper, Edward S. **6**
Copeland, Michael **47**
Cortez, Jayne **43**
Cosby, Bill **7, 26**
Cotter, Joseph Seamon, Sr. **40**
Cottrell, Comer **11**
Creagh, Milton **27**
Crew, Rudolph F. **16**
Cross, Dolores E. **23**
Crouch, Stanley **11**
Cullen, Countee **8**
Daly, Marie Maynard **37**
Davis, Allison **12**
Davis, Angela **5**
Davis, Arthur P. **41**
Davis, Charles T. **48**
Davis, George **36**
Dawson, William Levi **39**
Days, Drew S., III **10**
Delany, Sadie **12**
Delany, Samuel R., Jr. **9**
Delco, Wilhemina R. **33**
Delsarte, Louis **34**
Dennard, Brazeal **37**
DePriest, James **37**
Dickens, Helen Octavia **14**
Diop, Cheikh Anta **4**
Dixon, Margaret **14**
Dodson, Howard, Jr. **7**
Dodson, Owen Vincent **38**
Donaldson, Jeff **46**
Douglas, Aaron **7**
Dove, Rita **6**
Dove, Ulysses **5**
Draper, Sharon Mills **16, 43**
Driskell, David C. **7**
Drummond, William J. **40**
Du Bois, David Graham **45**
Dumas, Henry **41**
Dunbar-Nelson, Alice Ruth Moore **44**
Dunnigan, Alice Allison **41**
Dunston, Georgia Mae **48**
Dymally, Mervyn **42**
Dyson, Michael Eric **11, 40**
Early, Gerald **15**
Edelin, Ramona Hoage **19**
Edelman, Marian Wright **5, 42**
Edley, Christopher **2, 48**
Edley, Christopher F., Jr. **48**
Edwards, Harry **2**
Elders, Joycelyn **6**
Elliot, Lorris **37**
Ellis, Clarence A. **38**
Ellison, Ralph **7**
Epps, Archie C., III **45**
Evans, Mari **26**
Fauset, Jessie **7**
Favors, Steve **23**
Feelings, Muriel **44**
Figueroa, John J. **40**
Fleming, Raymond **48**
Fletcher, Bill, Jr. **41**
Floyd, Elson S. **41**
Ford, Jack **39**
Foster, Ezola **28**
Foster, Henry W., Jr. **26**
Franklin, John Hope **5**
Franklin, Robert M. **13**
Frazier, E. Franklin **10**
Freeman, Al, Jr. **11**
Fuller, A. Oveta **43**
Fuller, Arthur **27**
Fuller, Howard L. **37**
Fuller, Solomon Carter, Jr. **15**
Futrell, Mary Hatwood **33**
Gaines, Ernest J. **7**
Gates, Henry Louis, Jr. **3, 38**
Gates, Sylvester James, Jr. **15**
Gayle, Addison, Jr. **41**
George, Zelma Watson **42**
Gerima, Haile **38**
Gibson, Donald Bernard **40**
Giddings, Paula **11**
Giovanni, Nikki **9, 39**
Golden, Marita **19**
Gomes, Peter J. **15**
Gomez, Jewelle **30**
Granville, Evelyn Boyd **36**
Greenfield, Eloise **9**
Guinier, Lani **7, 30**
Guy-Sheftall, Beverly **13**
Hageman, Hans and Ivan **36**
Hale, Lorraine **8**
Handy, W. C. **8**
Hansberry, William Leo **11**
Harkless, Necia Desiree **19**
Harper, Michael S. **34**
Harris, Alice **7**
Harris, Jay T. **19**
Harris, Patricia Roberts **2**
Harsh, Vivian Gordon **14**
Harvey, William R. **42**
Haskins, James **36**
Hathaway, Isaac Scott **33**
Hayden, Carla D. **47**
Hayden, Robert **12**
Haynes, George Edmund **8**
Henderson, Stephen E. **45**
Henries, A. Doris Banks **44**
Herenton, Willie W. **24**
Hill, Anita **5**
Hill, Bonnie Guiton **20**
Hill, Errol **40**
Hill, Leslie Pinckney **44**
Hine, Darlene Clark **24**
Hinton, William Augustus **8**
Hoagland, Everett H. **45**
Holland, Endesha Ida Mae **3**
Holt, Nora **38**
Hooks, Bell **5**
Hope, John **8**
Houston, Charles Hamilton **4**
Hrabowski, Freeman A. III **22**
Hull, Akasha Gloria **45**
Humphries, Frederick **20**
Hunt, Richard **6**
Hutson, Jean Blackwell **16**
Imes, Elmer Samuel **39**
Jackson, Fred James **25**
Jackson, Vera **40**
Jarret, Vernon D. **42**
Jarvis, Charlene Drew **21**
Jeffries, Leonard **8**

Jenifer, Franklyn G. 2
Jenkins, Ella 15
Johns, Vernon 38
Johnson, Hazel 22
Johnson, James Weldon 5
Jones, Bobby 20
Jones, Edward P. 43
Jones, Gayl 37
Jones, Ingrid Saunders 18
Jones, Lois Mailou 13
Joplin, Scott 6
Jordan, Barbara 4
Jordan, June 7, 35
Josey, E. J. 10
Just, Ernest Everett 3
Karenga, Maulana 10
Kay, Ulysses 37
Keith, Damon J. 16
Kennedy, Florynce 12, 33
Kennedy, Randall 40
Kilpatrick, Carolyn Cheeks 16
Kimbro, Dennis 10
King, Preston 28
Komunyakaa, Yusef 9
Kunjufu, Jawanza 3
Ladner, Joyce A. 42
Lawrence, Jacob 4, 28
Lawrence-Lightfoot, Sara 10
Lee, Annie Francis 22
Lee, Joe A. 45
Leevy, Carrol M. 42
Leffall, LaSalle, Jr. 3
Lester, Julius 9
Lewis, David Levering 9
Lewis, Norman 39
Lewis, Samella 25
Lewis, Shirley A. R. 14
Lewis, Thomas 19
Liberia-Peters, Maria Philomena 12
Lincoln, C. Eric 38
Locke, Alain 10
Logan, Rayford W. 40
Lorde, Audre 6
Loury, Glenn 36
Loving, Alvin 35
Lucy Foster, Autherine 35
Lyttle, Hulda Margaret 14
Madhubuti, Haki R. 7
Major, Clarence 9
Manley, Audrey Forbes 16
Marable, Manning 10
Markham, E.A. 37
Marsalis, Wynton 16
Marshall, Paule 7
Masekela, Barbara 18
Mason, Ronald 27
Massey, Walter E. 5, 45
Massie, Samuel P., Jr. 29
Mayhew, Richard 39
Maynard, Robert C. 7
Maynor, Dorothy 19
Mayo, Whitman 32
Mays, Benjamin E. 7
McCarty, Osceola 16
McKay, Nellie Yvonne 17
McMillan, Terry 4, 17
McMurray, Georgia L. 36
McWhorter, John 35
Meek, Carrie 6
Memmi, Albert 37
Meredith, James H. 11
Millender-McDonald, Juanita 21
Mitchell, Corinne 8

Mitchell, Sharon 36
Mofolo, Thomas Mokopu 37
Mollel, Tololwa 38
Mongella, Gertrude 11
Mooney, Paul 37
Moore, Harry T. 29
Moore, Melba 21
Morrison, Keith 13
Morrison, Toni 15
Moses, Robert Parris 11
Mphalele, Es'kia (Ezekiel) 40
Mullen, Harryette 34
Murray, Pauli 38
Nabrit, Samuel Milton 47
N'Namdi, George R. 17
Naylor, Gloria 10, 42
Neal, Larry 38
N'Namdi, George R. 17
Norman, Maidie 20
Norton, Eleanor Holmes 7
Ogletree, Charles, Jr. 12, 47
Onwueme, Tess Osonye 23
Onwurah, Ngozi 38
Owens, Helen 48
Owens, Major 6
Page, Alan 7
Paige, Rod 29
Painter, Nell Irvin 24
Palmer, Everard 37
Parker, Kellis E. 30
Parks, Suzan-Lori 34
Patterson, Frederick Douglass 12
Patterson, Orlando 4
Payton, Benjamin F. 23
Peters, Margaret and Matilda 43
Pickett, Cecil 39
Pinckney, Bill 42
Player, Willa B. 43
Porter, James A. 11
Poussaint, Alvin F. 5
Price, Florence 37
Price, Glenda 22
Primus, Pearl 6
Prophet, Nancy Elizabeth 42
Puryear, Martin 42
Quarles, Benjamin Arthur 18
Rahman, Aishah 37
Ramphele, Mamphela 29
Reagon, Bernice Johnson 7
Reddick, Lawrence Dunbar 20
Redding, J. Saunders 26
Redmond, Eugene 23
Reid, Irvin D. 20
Ringgold, Faith 4
Robinson, Sharon 22
Robinson, Spottswood 22
Rogers, Joel Augustus 30
Rollins, Charlemae Hill 27
Russell-McCloud, Patricia 17
Salih, Al-Tayyib 37
Sallee, Charles Louis, Jr. 38
Satcher, David 7
Schomburg, Arthur Alfonso 9
Senior, Olive 37
Shabazz, Betty 7, 26
Shange, Ntozake 8
Shipp, E. R. 15
Shirley, George 33
Simmons, Ruth J. 13, 38
Sinkford, Jeanne C. 13
Sisulu, Sheila Violet Makate 24
Sizemore, Barbara A. 26
Smith, Anna Deavere 6

Smith, Barbara 28
Smith, Jessie Carney 35
Smith, John L. 22
Smith, Mary Carter 26
Smith, Tubby 18
Sowande, Fela 39
Soyinka, Wole 4
Spikes, Dolores 18
Stanford, John 20
Steele, Claude Mason 13
Steele, Shelby 13
Stephens, Charlotte Andrews 14
Stewart, Maria W. Miller 19
Stone, Chuck 9
Sudarkasa, Niara 4
Sullivan, Louis 8
Swygert, H. Patrick 22
Tanksley, Ann 37
Tatum, Beverly Daniel 42
Taylor, Helen (Lavon Hollingshed) 30
Taylor, Susie King 13
Terrell, Mary Church 9
Thomas, Alma 14
Thurman, Howard 3
Tillis, Frederick 40
Tolson, Melvin 37
Tribble, Israel, Jr. 8
Tucker, Rosina 14
Turnbull, Walter 13
Tutu, Desmond 6
Tutuola, Amos 30
Tyson, Andre 40
Tyson, Asha 39
Tyson, Neil de Grasse 15
Usry, James L. 23
van Sertima, Ivan 25
Wade-Gayles, Gloria Jean 41
Walcott, Derek 5
Walker, George 37
Wallace, Michele Faith 13
Wallace, Perry E. 47
Wallace, Phyllis A. 9
Washington, Booker T. 4
Watkins, Shirley R. 17
Wattleton, Faye 9
Weaver, Afaa Michael 37
Wedgeworth, Robert W. 42
Wells, James Lesesne 10
Wells-Barnett, Ida B. 8
Welsing, Frances Cress 5
Wesley, Dorothy Porter 19
West, Cornel 5, 33
Wharton, Clifton R., Jr. 7
White, Charles 39
White, Lois Jean 20
Wilkens, J. Ernest, Jr. 43
Wilkins, Roger 2
Williams, Fannie Barrier 27
Williams, Gregory 11
Williams, Patricia J. 11
Williams, Sherley Anne 25
Williams, Walter E. 4
Wilson, William Julius 22
Woodruff, Hale 9
Woodson, Carter G. 2
Worrill, Conrad 12
Yancy, Dorothy Cowser 42
Young, Jean Childs 14

Fashion

Bailey, Xenobia 11
Banks, Jeffrey 17

Banks, Tyra 11
Barboza, Anthony 10
Beals, Jennifer 12
Beckford, Tyson 11
Berry, Halle 4, 19
Boateng, Ozwald 35
Bridges, Sheila 36
Brown, Joyce F. 25
Burrows, Stephen 31
Campbell, Naomi 1, 31
Dash, Damon 31
Davidson, Jaye 5
Delice, Ronald 48
Delice, Rony 48
Henderson, Gordon 5
Hendy, Francis 47
Iman 4, 33
Jay-Z 27
John, Daymond 23
Johnson, Beverly 2
Jones, Carl 7
Kodjoe, Boris 34
Kani, Karl 10
Kelly, Patrick 3
Lars, Byron 32
Malone, Maurice 32
Michele, Michael 31
Onwurah, Ngozi 38
Powell, Maxine 8
Rhymes, Busta 31
Robinson, Patrick 19
Rochon, Lela 16
Rowell, Victoria 13
Sims, Naomi 29
Smaltz, Audrey 12
Smith, B(arbara) 11
Smith, Willi 8
Steele, Lawrence 28
Taylor, Karin 34
Walker, T. J. 7
Webb, Veronica 10
Wek, Alek 18

Film

Aaliyah 30
Akomfrah, John 37
Alexander, Khandi 43
Allen, Debbie 13, 42
Amos, John 8
Anderson, Eddie "Rochester" 30
Awoonor, Kofi 37
Babatunde, Obba 35
Baker, Josephine 3
Banks, Tyra 11
Barclay, Paris 37
Bassett, Angela 6, 23
Beach, Michael 26
Beals, Jennifer 12
Belafonte, Harry 4
Bellamy, Bill 12
Berry, Fred "Rerun" 48
Berry, Halle 4, 19
Blackwood, Maureen 37
Bogle, Donald 34
Braugher, Andre 13
Breeze, Jean "Binta" 37
Brooks, Hadda 40
Brown, Jim 11
Brown, Tony 3
Burnett, Charles 16
Byrd, Michelle 19
Byrd, Robert 11
Calloway, Cab 14

Campbell, Naomi **1, 31**
Campbell Martin, Tisha **8, 42**
Cannon, Nick **47**
Carroll, Diahann **9**
Carson, Lisa Nicole **21**
Cash, Rosalind **28**
Cedric the Entertainer **29**
Cheadle, Don **19**
Chestnut, Morris **31**
Clash, Kevin **14**
Cliff, Jimmy **28**
Combs, Sean "Puffy" **17, 43**
Cortez, Jayne **43**
Cosby, Bill **7, 26**
Crothers, Scatman **19**
Curry, Mark **17**
Curtis-Hall, Vondie **17**
Dandridge, Dorothy **3**
Daniels, Lee Louis **36**
Dash, Julie **4**
David, Keith **27**
Davidson, Jaye **5**
Davidson, Tommy **21**
Davis, Guy **36**
Davis, Ossie **5**
Davis, Sammy, Jr. **18**
de Passe, Suzanne **25**
Dee, Ruby **8**
Devine, Loretta **24**
Dickerson, Ernest **6, 17**
Diesel, Vin **29**
Diggs, Taye **25**
DMX **28**
Dourdan, Gary **37**
Dr. Dre **10**
Driskell, David C. **7**
Duke, Bill **3**
Duncan, Michael Clarke **26**
Dunham, Katherine **4**
Dutton, Charles S. **4, 22**
Edmonds, Kenneth "Babyface" **10, 31**
Elder, Lonne, III **38**
Elise, Kimberly **32**
Emmanuel, Alphonsia **38**
Epps, Omar **23**
Esposito, Giancarlo **9**
Evans, Darryl **22**
Everett, Francine **23**
Fetchit, Stepin **32**
Fishburne, Larry **4, 22**
Fisher, Antwone **40**
Fox, Rick **27**
Fox, Vivica A. **15**
Foxx, Jamie **15, 48**
Foxx, Redd **2**
Franklin, Carl **11**
Freeman, Al, Jr. **11**
Freeman, Morgan **2, 20**
Freeman, Yvette **27**
Friday, Jeff **24**
Fuller, Charles **8**
Fuqua, Antoine **35**
George, Nelson **12**
Gerima, Haile **38**
Givens, Robin **4, 25**
Glover, Danny **1, 24**
Glover, Savion **14**
Goldberg, Whoopi **4, 33**
Gooding, Cuba, Jr. **16**
Gordon, Dexter **25**
Gordy, Berry, Jr. **1**
Gossett, Louis, Jr. **7**

Gray, F. Gary **14**
Greaves, William **38**
Grier, David Alan **28**
Grier, Pam **9, 31**
Guillaume, Robert **3, 48**
Gunn, Moses **10**
Guy, Jasmine **2**
Hampton, Henry **6**
Hardison, Kadeem **22**
Harper, Hill **32**
Harris, Leslie **6**
Harris, Robin **7**
Hawkins, Screamin' Jay **30**
Hayes, Isaac **20**
Hayes, Teddy **40**
Haysbert, Dennis **42**
Hemsley, Sherman **19**
Henriques, Julian **37**
Henry, Lenny **9**
Henson, Darrin **33**
Hill, Dulé **29**
Hill, Lauryn **20**
Hines, Gregory **1, 42**
Horne, Lena **5**
Hounsou, Djimon **19, 45**
Houston, Whitney **7, 28**
Howard, Sherri **36**
Hudlin, Reginald **9**
Hudlin, Warrington **9**
Hughes, Albert **7**
Hughes, Allen **7**
Ice Cube **8, 30**
Ice-T **6, 31**
Iman **4, 33**
Ingram, Rex **5**
Jackson, George **19**
Jackson, Janet **6, 30**
Jackson, Samuel L. **8, 19**
Jean-Baptiste, Marianne **17, 46**
Johnson, Beverly **2**
Johnson, Dwayne "The Rock" **29**
Jones, James Earl **3**
Jones, Orlando **30**
Jones, Quincy **8, 30**
Julien, Isaac **3**
King, Regina **22, 45**
King, Woodie, Jr. **27**
Kirby, George **14**
Kitt, Eartha **16**
Knowles, Beyoncé **39**
Kool Moe Dee **37**
Kotto, Yaphet **7**
Kunjufu, Jawanza **3**
L. L. Cool J **16**
La Salle, Eriq **12**
LaBelle, Patti **13, 30**
Lane, Charles **3**
Lathan, Sanaa **27**
Lawrence, Martin **6, 27**
Lee, Joie **1**
Lee, Spike **5, 19**
Lemmons, Kasi **20**
LeNoire, Rosetta **37**
Lester, Adrian **46**
Lewis, Samella **25**
Lil' Kim **28**
Lincoln, Abbey **3**
Lindo, Delroy **18, 45**
LisaRaye **27**
Long, Nia **17**
Love, Darlene **23**
Lover, Ed **10**
Mabley, Jackie "Moms" **15**

Mac, Bernie **29**
Marsalis, Branford **34**
Martin, Darnell **43**
Martin, Helen **31**
Master P **21**
McDaniel, Hattie **5**
McKee, Lonette **12**
McKinney, Nina Mae **40**
McQueen, Butterfly **6**
Meadows, Tim **30**
Micheaux, Oscar **7**
Michele, Michael **31**
Mo'Nique **35**
Mooney, Paul **37**
Moore, Chante **26**
Moore, Melba **21**
Moore, Shemar **21**
Morris, Garrett **31**
Morris, Greg **28**
Morton, Joe **18**
Mos Def **30**
Moses, Gilbert **12**
Moss, Carlton **17**
Murphy, Eddie **4, 20**
Muse, Clarence Edouard **21**
Nas **33**
Nash, Johnny **40**
Neal, Elise **29**
Newton, Thandie **26**
Nicholas, Fayard **20**
Nicholas, Harold **20**
Nichols, Nichelle **11**
Norman, Maidie **20**
Odetta **37**
O'Neal, Ron **46**
Onwurah, Ngozi **38**
Parks, Gordon **1, 35**
Payne, Allen **13**
Peck, Raoul **32**
Phifer, Mekhi **25**
Pinkett Smith, Jada **10, 41**
Poitier, Sidney **11, 36**
Prince **18**
Prince-Bythewood, Gina **31**
Pryor, Richard **3**
Queen Latifah **1, 16**
Ralph, Sheryl Lee **18**
Randle, Theresa **16**
Reese, Della **6, 20**
Reuben, Gloria **15**
Rhames, Ving **14**
Rhymes, Busta **31**
Richards, Beah **30**
Riggs, Marlon **5, 44**
Robinson, Shaun **36**
Rochon, Lela **16**
Rock, Chris **3, 22**
Rolle, Esther **13, 21**
Rollins, Howard E., Jr. **16**
Ross, Diana **8, 27**
Roundtree, Richard **27**
Rowell, Victoria **13**
Rupaul **17**
Schultz, Michael A. **6**
Seal **14**
Sembène, Ousmane **13**
Shakur, Tupac **14**
Simpson, O. J. **15**
Sinbad **1, 16**
Singleton, John **2, 30**
Sisqo **30**
Smith, Anjela Lauren **44**
Smith, Anna Deavere **6, 44**

Smith, Roger Guenveur **12**
Smith, Will **8, 18**
Snipes, Wesley **3, 24**
St. Jacques, Raymond **8**
St. John, Kristoff **25**
Sullivan, Maxine **37**
Tate, Larenz **15**
Taylor, Meshach **4**
Taylor, Regina **9, 46**
Thigpen, Lynne **17, 41**
Thomas, Sean Patrick **35**
Thurman, Wallace **16**
Tillman, George, Jr. **20**
Torry, Guy **31**
Toussaint, Lorraine **32**
Townsend, Robert **4, 23**
Tucker, Chris **13, 23**
Turner, Tina **6, 27**
Tyler, Aisha N. **36**
Tyrese **27**
Tyson, Cicely **7**
Uggams, Leslie **23**
Underwood, Blair **7, 27**
Union, Gabrielle **31**
Usher **23**
Van Peebles, Mario **2**
Van Peebles, Melvin **7**
Vance, Courtney B. **15**
Vereen, Ben **4**
Walker, Eamonn **37**
Ward, Douglas Turner **42**
Warfield, Marsha **2**
Warner, Malcolm-Jamal **22, 36**
Warren, Michael **27**
Warwick, Dionne **18**
Washington, Denzel **1, 16**
Washington, Fredi **10**
Washington, Kerry **46**
Waters, Ethel **7**
Wayans, Damon **8, 41**
Wayans, Keenen Ivory **18**
Wayans, Marlon **29**
Wayans, Shawn **29**
Weathers, Carl **10**
Webb, Veronica **10**
Whitaker, Forest **2**
Whitfield, Lynn **18**
Williams, Billy Dee **8**
Williams, Clarence, III **26**
Williams, Samm-Art **21**
Williams, Saul **31**
Williams, Vanessa **32**
Williams, Vanessa L. **4, 17**
Williamson, Mykelti **22**
Wilson, Debra **38**
Winfield, Paul **2, 45**
Winfrey, Oprah **2, 15**
Witherspoon, John **38**
Woodard, Alfre **9**
Yoba, Malik **11**

Government and politics--international
Abacha, Sani **11**
Abbott, Diane **9**
Achebe, Chinua **6**
Ali Mahdi Mohamed **5**
Amadi, Elechi **40**
Amin, Idi **42**
Amos, Valerie **41**
Annan, Kofi Atta **15, 48**
Aristide, Jean-Bertrand **6, 45**
Arthur, Owen **33**

Awoonor, Kofi 37
Azikiwe, Nnamdi 13
Babangida, Ibrahim 4
Baker, Gwendolyn Calvert 9
Banda, Hastings Kamuzu 6
Bedie, Henri Konan 21
Berry, Mary Frances 7
Biko, Steven 4
Bishop, Maurice 39
Biya, Paul 28
Bizimungu, Pasteur 19
Bongo, Omar 1
Boye, Madior 30
Bunche, Ralph J. 5
Buthelezi, Mangosuthu Gatsha 9
Césaire, Aimé 48
Charlemagne, Manno 11
Charles, Mary Eugenia 10
Chissano, Joaquim 7
Christophe, Henri 9
Conté, Lansana 7
Curling, Alvin 34
da Silva, Benedita 5
Dadié, Bernard 34
Davis, Ruth 37
Déby, Idriss 30
Diop, Cheikh Anta 4
Diouf, Abdou 3
dos Santos, José Eduardo 43
Ekwensi, Cyprian 37
Eyadéma, Gnassingbé 7
Fela 1, 42
Gbagbo, Laurent 43
Gordon, Pamela 17
Habré, Hissène 6
Habyarimana, Juvenal 8
Haile Selassie 7
Haley, George Williford Boyce 21
Hani, Chris 6
Houphouët-Boigny, Félix 4
Ifill, Gwen 28
Ingraham, Hubert A. 19
Isaac, Julius 34
Jagan, Cheddi 16
Jammeh, Yahya 23
Jawara, Sir Dawda Kairaba 11
Ka Dinizulu, Mcwayizeni 29
Kabbah, Ahmad Tejan 23
Kabila, Joseph 30
Kabila, Laurent 20
Kabunda, Kenneth 2
Kenyatta, Jomo 5
Kerekou, Ahmed (Mathieu) 1
King, Oona 27
Liberia-Peters, Maria Philomena 12
Lumumba, Patrice 33
Luthuli, Albert 13
Maathai, Wangari 43
Mabuza, Lindiwe 18
Machel, Samora Moises 8
Mamadou, Tandja 33
Mandela, Nelson 1, 14
Mandela, Winnie 2, 35
Masekela, Barbara 18
Masire, Quett 5
Mbeki, Thabo Mvuyelwa 14
Mbuende, Kaire 12
Meles Zenawi 3
Mkapa, Benjamin 16
Mobutu Sese Seko 1
Mogae, Festus Gontebanye 19
Moi, Daniel 1, 35
Mongella, Gertrude 11

Mugabe, Robert Gabriel 10
Muluzi, Bakili 14
Museveni, Yoweri 4
Mutebi, Ronald 25
Mwinyi, Ali Hassan 1
Ndadaye, Melchior 7
Neto, António Agostinho 43
Ngubane, Ben 33
Nkomo, Joshua 4
Nkrumah, Kwame 3
Ntaryamira, Cyprien 8
Nujoma, Samuel 10
Nyanda, Siphiwe 21
Nyerere, Julius 5
Nzo, Alfred 15
Obasanjo, Olusegun 5, 22
Obasanjo, Stella 32
Okara, Gabriel 37
Oyono, Ferdinand 38
Pascal-Trouillot, Ertha 3
Patterson, P. J. 6, 20
Pereira, Aristides 30
Perkins, Edward 5
Perry, Ruth 15
Pitt, David Thomas 10
Pitta, Celso 17
Poitier, Sidney 36
Ramaphosa, Cyril 3
Rawlings, Jerry 9
Rawlings, Nana Konadu Agyeman 13
Rice, Condoleezza 3, 28
Robinson, Randall 7, 46
Sampson, Edith S. 4
Sankara, Thomas 17
Savimbi, Jonas 2, 34
Sawyer, Amos 2
Senghor, Léopold Sédar 12
Sisulu, Walter 47
Smith, Jennifer 21
Soglo, Nicephore 15
Soyinka, Wole 4
Taylor, Charles 20
Taylor, John (David Beckett) 16
Touré, Sekou 6
Toure, Amadou Toumani 18
Tsvangirai, Morgan 26
Tutu, Desmond (Mpilo) 6, 44
Vieira, Joao 14
Wharton, Clifton Reginald, Sr. 36
Wharton, Clifton R., Jr. 7
Zuma, Jacob G. 33
Zuma, Nkosazana Dlamini 34

Government and politics--U.S.
Adams, Floyd, Jr. 12
Alexander, Archie Alphonso 14
Alexander, Clifford 26
Ali, Muhammad 2, 16
Allen, Ethel D. 13
Archer, Dennis 7, 36
Arrington, Richard 24
Avant, Clarence 19
Baker, Thurbert 22
Ballance, Frank W. 41
Barden, Don H. 9, 20
Barrett, Andrew C. 12
Barrett, Jacqueline 28
Barry, Marion S(hepilov, Jr.) 7, 44
Bell, Michael 40
Belton, Sharon Sayles 9, 16
Berry, Mary Frances 7
Berry, Theodore M. 31

Bethune, Mary McLeod 4
Blackwell, Unita 17
Bond, Julian 2, 35
Bosley, Freeman, Jr. 7
Boykin, Keith 14
Bradley, Jennette B. 40
Bradley, Thomas 2
Braun, Carol Moseley 4, 42
Brazile, Donna 25
Brimmer, Andrew F. 2, 48
Brooke, Edward 8
Brown, Cora 33
Brown, Corrine 24
Brown, Elaine 8
Brown, Jesse 6, 41
Brown, Lee Patrick 24
Brown, Les 5
Brown, Ron 5
Brown, Willie L., Jr. 7
Bruce, Blanche K. 33
Bryant, Wayne R. 6
Buckley, Victoria (Vicki) 24
Bunche, Ralph J. 5
Burke, Yvonne Braithwaite 42
Burris, Chuck 21
Burris, Roland W. 25
Butler, Jerry 26
Caesar, Shirley 19
Campbell, Bill 9
Cardozo, Francis L. 33
Carson, Julia 23
Chavis, Benjamin 6
Chisholm, Shirley 2
Christian-Green, Donna M. 17
Clay, William Lacy 8
Clayton, Eva M. 20
Cleaver, Eldridge 5
Cleaver, Emanuel 4, 45
Clyburn, James 21
Coleman, Michael B. 28
Collins, Barbara-Rose 7
Collins, Cardiss 10
Coleman, Mary 46
Colter, Cyrus J. 36
Connerly, Ward 14
Conyers, John, Jr. 4, 45
Cook, Mercer 40
Cose, Ellis 5
Craig-Jones, Ellen Walker 44
Crockett, George, Jr. 10
Cummings, Elijah E. 24
Cunningham, Evelyn 23
Currie, Betty 21
Davis, Angela 5
Davis, Artur 41
Davis, Benjamin O., Sr. 4
Davis, Benjamin O., Jr. 2, 43
Davis, Danny K. 24
Days, Drew S., III 10
Delany, Martin R. 27
Delco, Wilhemina R. 33
Dellums, Ronald 2
Diggs, Charles R. 21
Dinkins, David 4
Dixon, Julian C. 24
Dixon, Sharon Pratt 1
Dougherty, Mary Pearl 47
Du Bois, W. E. B. 3
Dunbar-Nelson, Alice Ruth Moore 44
Dymally, Mervyn 42
Edmonds, Terry 17
Elders, Joycelyn 6

Espy, Mike 6
Farmer, James 2
Farrakhan, Louis 2
Fattah, Chaka 11
Fauntroy, Walter E. 11
Ferguson, Roger W. 25
Fields, C. Virginia 25
Fields, Cleo 13
Flake, Floyd H. 18
Flipper, Henry O. 3
Ford, Harold Eugene 42
Ford, Jack 39
Fortune, T. Thomas 6
Foster, Ezola 28
Franklin, Shirley 34
Franks, Gary 2
Fulani, Lenora 11
Gantt, Harvey 1
Garvey, Marcus 1
Gibson, Johnnie Mae 23
Gibson, Kenneth Allen 6
Gibson, William F. 6
Goode, W. Wilson 4
Gravely, Samuel L., Jr. 5
Gray, William H., III 3
Grimké, Archibald H. 9
Guinier, Lani 7, 30
Haley, George Williford Boyce 21
Hamer, Fannie Lou 6
Harmon, Clarence 26
Harris, Alice 7
Harris, Patricia Roberts 2
Harvard, Beverly 11
Hastie, William H. 8
Hastings, Alcee L. 16
Hayes, James C. 10
Henry, Aaron 19
Herenton, Willie W. 24
Herman, Alexis M. 15
Hernandez, Aileen Clarke 13
Hill, Bonnie Guiton 20
Hilliard, Earl F. 24
Hobson, Julius W. 44
Holder, Eric H., Jr. 9
Ifill, Gwen, 28
Irving, Larry, Jr. 12
Jackson, Alphonso R. 48
Jackson, George 14
Jackson, Jesse 1
Jackson, Jesse, Jr. 14, 27, 45
Jackson Lee, Sheila 20
Jackson, Maynard 2, 41
Jackson, Shirley Ann 12
Jacob, John E. 2
James, Sharpe 23
Jarvis, Charlene Drew 21
Jefferson, William J. 25
Johnson, Eddie Bernice 8
Johnson, Harvey Jr. 24
Johnson, James Weldon 5
Johnson, Norma L. Holloway 17
Johnson, Robert T. 17
Jones, Elaine R. 7, 45
Jordan, Barbara 4
Jordan, Vernon 3, 35
Kennard, William Earl 18
Keyes, Alan L. 11
Kidd, Mae Street 39
Kilpatrick, Carolyn Cheeks 16
Kilpatrick, Kwame 34
Kincaid, Bernard 28
King, Martin Luther, III 20
Kirk, Ron 11

Lafontant, Jewel Stradford **3**
Lee, Barbara **25**
Leland, Mickey **2**
Lewis, Delano **7**
Lewis, John **2**, **46**
Majette, Denise **41**
Mallett, Conrad, Jr. **16**
Marsh, Henry, III **32**
Marshall, Bella **22**
Marshall, Thurgood **1**, 44
Martin, Louis E. **16**
McCall, H. Carl **27**
McGee, James Madison **46**
McKinney, Cynthia Ann **11**
McKissick, Floyd B. **3**
Meek, Carrie **6**, **36**
Meek, Kendrick **41**
Meeks, Gregory **25**
Meredith, James H. **11**
Metcalfe, Ralph **26**
Mfume, Kweisi **6**, **41**
Millender-McDonald, Juanita **21**
Mitchell, Parren J. **42**
Moore, Minyon **45**
Morial, Ernest "Dutch" **26**
Morial, Marc **20**
Morton, Azie Taylor **48**
Moses, Robert Parris **11**
Nagin, Ray **42**
Norton, Eleanor Holmes **7**
O'Leary, Hazel **6**
Owens, Major **6**
Page, Alan **7**
Paige, Rod **29**
Patrick, Deval **12**
Patterson, Louise **25**
Payne, Donald M. **2**
Perez, Anna **1**
Perkins, Edward **5**
Perry, Lowell **30**
Pinchback, P. B. S. **9**
Powell, Adam Clayton, Jr. **3**
Powell, Colin **1**, **28**
Powell, Debra A. **23**
Powell, Michael **32**
Raines, Franklin Delano **14**
Randolph, A. Philip **3**
Rangel, Charles **3**
Reeves, Triette Lipsey **27**
Rice, Condoleezza **3**, **28**
Rice, Norm **8**
Robinson, Randall **7**, **46**
Rogers, Joe **27**
Ross, Don **27**
Rush, Bobby **26**
Rustin, Bayard **4**
Sampson, Edith S. **4**
Sanders, Malika **48**
Satcher, David **7**
Sayles Belton, Sharon **9**
Schmoke, Kurt **1**, **48**
Scott, David **41**
Scott, Robert C. **23**
Sears-Collins, Leah J. **5**
Shakur, Assata **6**
Shavers, Cheryl **31**
Sharpton, Al **21**
Simpson, Carole **6**, **30**
Sisulu, Sheila Violet Makate **24**
Slater, Rodney E. **15**
Stanton, Robert **20**
Staupers, Mabel K. **7**
Steele, Michael **38**
Stokes, Carl B. **10**
Stokes, Louis **3**
Stone, Chuck **9**
Street, John F. **24**
Sullivan, Louis **8**
Sutton, Percy E. **42**
Terry, Clark **39**
Thomas, Clarence **2**, **39**
Thompson, Bennie G. **26**
Thompson, Larry D. **39**
Thompson, William C. **35**
Towns, Edolphus **19**
Tribble, Israel, Jr. **8**
Trotter, Donne E. **28**
Tubbs Jones, Stephanie **24**
Tucker, C. DeLores **12**
Turner, Henry McNeal **5**
Usry, James L. **23**
Vaughn, Gladys Gary **47**
Von Lipsey, Roderick K. **11**
Wallace, Phyllis A. **9**
Washington, Harold **6**
Washington, Val **12**
Washington, Walter **45**
Waters, Maxine **3**
Watkins, Shirley R. **17**
Watson, Diane **41**
Watt, Melvin **26**
Watts, J. C., Jr. **14**, **38**
Weaver, Robert C. **8**, **46**
Webb, Wellington **3**
Wharton, Clifton Reginald, Sr. **36**
Wharton, Clifton R., Jr. **7**
Wheat, Alan **14**
White, Jesse **22**
White, Michael R. **5**
Wilder, L. Douglas **3**, **48**
Wilkins, Roger **2**
Williams, Anthony **21**
Williams, Eddie N. **44**
Williams, George Washington **18**
Williams, Hosea Lorenzo **15**, **31**
Williams, Maggie **7**
Wilson, Sunnie **7**
Wynn, Albert **25**
Young, Andrew **3**, **48**

Law

Alexander, Clifford **26**
Alexander, Joyce London **18**
Alexander, Sadie Tanner Mossell **22**
Allen, Samuel W. **38**
Archer, Dennis **7**, **36**
Arnwine, Barbara **28**
Bailey, Clyde **45**
Banks, William **11**
Barrett, Andrew C. **12**
Barrett, Jacqueline **28**
Baugh, David **23**
Bell, Derrick **6**
Berry, Mary Frances **7**
Berry, Theodore M. **31**
Bishop Jr., Sanford D. **24**
Bolin, Jane **22**
Bolton, Terrell D. **25**
Bosley, Freeman, Jr. **7**
Boykin, Keith **14**
Bradley, Thomas **2**
Braun, Carol Moseley **4**, **42**
Brooke, Edward **8**
Brown, Cora **33**
Brown, Homer S. **47**
Brown, Janice Rogers **43**
Brown, Joe **29**
Brown, Lee Patrick **1**, **24**
Brown, Ron **5**
Brown, Willie L., Jr. **7**
Bryant, Wayne R. **6**
Bully-Cummings, Ella **48**
Burke, Yvonne Braithwaite **42**
Burris, Roland W. **25**
Butler, Paul D. **17**
Bynoe, Peter C.B. **40**
Campbell, Bill **9**
Carter, Stephen L. **4**
Chambers, Julius **3**
Cleaver, Kathleen Neal **29**
Clendenon, Donn **26**
Cochran, Johnnie L., Jr. **11**, **39**
Colter, Cyrus J. **36**
Conyers, John, Jr. **4**, **45**
Crockett, George, Jr. **10**
Darden, Christopher **13**
Davis, Artur **41**
Days, Drew S., III **10**
DeFrantz, Anita **37**
Diggs-Taylor, Anna **20**
Dillard, Godfrey J. **45**
Dinkins, David **4**
Dixon, Sharon Pratt **1**
Edelman, Marian Wright **5**, **42**
Edley, Christopher **2**, **48**
Edley, Christopher F., Jr. **48**
Ellington, E. David **11**
Ephriam, Mablean **29**
Espy, Mike **6**
Farmer-Paellmann, Deadria **43**
Fields, Cleo **13**
Frazier-Lyde, Jacqui **31**
Freeman, Charles **19**
Gary, Willie E. **12**
Gibson, Johnnie Mae **23**
Glover, Nathaniel, Jr. **12**
Gomez-Preston, Cheryl **9**
Graham, Lawrence Otis **12**
Gray, Fred **37**
Gray, Willie **46**
Grimké, Archibald H. **9**
Guinier, Lani **7**, **30**
Haley, George Williford Boyce **21**
Hall, Elliott S. **24**
Harris, Patricia Roberts **2**
Harvard, Beverly **11**
Hassell, Leroy Rountree, Sr. **41**
Hastie, William H. **8**
Hastings, Alcee L. **16**
Hatchett, Glenda **32**
Hawkins, Steven **14**
Haywood, Margaret A. **24**
Higginbotham, A. Leon, Jr. **13**, **25**
Hill, Anita **5**
Hillard, Terry **25**
Hills, Oliver W. **24**
Holder, Eric H., Jr. **9**
Holton, Hugh, Jr. **39**
Hooks, Benjamin L. **2**
Houston, Charles Hamilton **4**
Hubbard, Arnette Rhinehart **38**
Hunter, Billy **22**
Hurtt, Harold **46**
Isaac, Julius **34**
Jackson Lee, Sheila **20**
Jackson, Maynard **2**, **41**
Johnson, James Weldon **5**
Johnson, Norma L. Holloway **17**
Jones, Elaine R. **7**, **45**
Jones, Star **10**, **27**
Jordan, Vernon E. **3**, **35**
Kearse, Amalya Lyle **12**
Keith, Damon J. **16**
Kennard, William Earl **18**
Kennedy, Florynce **12**, **33**
Kennedy, Randall **40**
King, Bernice **4**
Kirk, Ron **11**
Lafontant, Jewel Stradford **3**
Lewis, Delano **7**
Lewis, Reginald F. **6**
Majette, Denise **41**
Mallett, Conrad, Jr. **16**
Mandela, Nelson **1**, **14**
Marsh, Henry, III **32**
Marshall, Thurgood **1**, **44**
Mathis, Greg **26**
McDonald, Gabrielle Kirk **20**
McDougall, Gay J. **11**, **43**
McKinnon, Isaiah **9**
McKissick, Floyd B. **3**
McPhail, Sharon **2**
Meek, Kendrick **41**
Meeks, Gregory **25**
Moose, Charles **40**
Morial, Ernest "Dutch" **26**
Motley, Constance Baker **10**
Muhammad, Ava **31**
Murray, Pauli **38**
Napoleon, Benny N. **23**
Noble, Ronald **46**
Norton, Eleanor Holmes **7**
Nunn, Annetta **43**
O'Leary, Hazel **6**
Ogletree, Jr., Charles **12**, **47**
Ogunlesi, Adebayo O. **37**
Oliver, Jerry **37**
Page, Alan **7**
Paker, Kellis E. **30**
Parks, Bernard C. **17**
Parsons, James **14**
Parsons, Richard Dean **11**, **33**
Pascal-Trouillot, Ertha **3**
Patrick, Deval **12**
Payne, Ulice **42**
Payton, John **48**
Perry, Lowell **30**
Philip, Marlene Nourbese **32**
Powell, Michael **32**
Ramsey, Charles H. **21**
Redding, Louis L. **26**
Richie, Leroy C. **18**
Robinson, Malcolm S. **44**
Robinson, Randall **7**, **46**
Russell-McCloud, Patricia **17**
Sampson, Edith S. **4**
Schmoke, Kurt **1**, **48**
Sears-Collins, Leah J. **5**
Solomon, Jimmie Lee **38**
Steele, Michael **38**
Stokes, Carl B. **10**
Stokes, Louis **3**
Stout, Juanita Kidd **24**
Sutton, Percy E. **42**
Taylor, John (David Beckett) **16**
Thomas, Clarence **2**, **39**
Thomas, Franklin A. **5**
Thompson, Larry D. **39**
Tubbs Jones, Stephanie **24**
Vanzant, Iyanla **17**, **47**
Wagner, Annice **22**

Wainwright, Joscelyn **46**
Wallace, Perry E. **47**
Washington, Harold **6**
Watkins, Donald **35**
Watt, Melvin **26**
Wharton, Clifton Reginald, Sr. **36**
Wilder, L. Douglas **3, 48**
Wilkins, Roger **2**
Williams, Evelyn **10**
Williams, Gregory **11**
Williams, Patricia J. **11**
Williams, Willie L. **4**
Wilson, Jimmy **45**
Wright, Bruce McMarion **3**
Wynn, Albert **25**

Military

Abacha, Sani **11**
Adams Early, Charity **13, 34**
Adams-Ender, Clara **40**
Alexander, Margaret Walker **22**
Amin, Idi **42**
Babangida, Ibrahim **4**
Black, Barry C. **47**
Bolden, Charles F., Jr. **7**
Brashear, Carl **29**
Brown, Erroll M. **23**
Brown, Jesse **6, 41**
Brown, Jesse Leroy **31**
Brown, Willa **40**
Bullard, Eugene **12**
Cadoria, Sherian Grace **14**
Chissano, Joaquim **7**
Christophe, Henri **9**
Clemmons, Reginal G. **41**
Conté, Lansana **7**
Davis, Benjamin O., Jr. **2, 43**
Davis, Benjamin O., Sr. **4**
Europe, James Reese **10**
Eyadéma, Gnassingbé **7**
Fields, Evelyn J. **27**
Flipper, Henry O. **3**
Gravely, Samuel L., Jr. **5**
Gregory, Frederick D. **8**
Habré, Hissène **6**
Habyarimana, Juvenal **8**
Harris, Marcelite Jordan **16**
Howard, Michelle **28**
Jackson, Fred James **25**
James, Daniel, Jr. **16**
Johnson, Hazel **22**
Johnson, Shoshana **47**
Kerekou, Ahmed (Mathieu) **1**
Lawrence, Robert H., Jr. **16**
Lyles, Lester **31**
Miller, Dorie **29**
Nyanda, Siphiwe **21**
Obasanjo, Olusegun **5, 22**
Petersen, Frank E. **31**
Powell, Colin **1, 28**
Pratt, Geronimo **18**
Rawlings, Jerry **9**
Reason, J. Paul **19**
Scantlebury, Janna **47**
Stanford, John **20**
Staupers, Mabel K. **7**
Stokes, Louis **3**
Touré, Amadou Toumani **18**
Vieira, Joao **14**
Von Lipsey, Roderick K. **11**
Watkins, Perry **12**
West, Togo, D., Jr. **16**
Wilson, Jimmy **45**

Wright, Lewin **43**

Music

Aaliyah **30**
Ace, Johnny **36**
Adams, Johnny **39**
Adams, Leslie **39**
Adams, Oleta **18**
Adams, Yolanda **17**
Adderley, Julian "Cannonball" **30**
Adderley, Nat **29**
Ade, King Sunny **41**
Albright, Gerald **23**
Alert, Kool DJ **33**
Anderson, Carl **48**
Anderson, Marian **2, 33**
Armatrading, Joan **32**
Armstrong, Louis **2**
Armstrong, Vanessa Bell **24**
Arroyo, Marina **30**
Ashanti **37**
Ashford, Nickolas **21**
Austin, Lovie **40**
Austin, Patti **24**
Avant, Clarence **19**
Ayers, Roy **16**
Badu, Erykah **22**
Bailey, Buster **38**
Bailey, DeFord **33**
Baiocchi, Regina Harris **41**
Baker, Anita **21, 48**
Baker, Josephine **3**
Baker, LaVern **26**
Ballard, Hank **41**
Bambaataa, Afrika **34**
Barker, Danny **32**
Barnes, Roosevelt "Booba" **33**
Basie, Count **23**
Bassey, Shirley **25**
Baylor, Helen **36**
Bebey, Francis **45**
Bechet, Sidney **18**
Beenie Man **32**
Belafonte, Harry **4**
Belle, Regina **1**
Benét, Eric **28**
Benjamin, Andre **45**
Berry, Chuck **29**
Beverly, Frankie **25**
Blake, Eubie **29**
Blakey, Art **37**
Blanchard, Terence **43**
Bland, Bobby "Blue" **36**
Blige, Mary J. **20, 34**
Blondy, Alpha **30**
Blow, Kurtis **31**
Bolden, Buddy **39**
Bonds, Margaret **39**
Bonga, Kuenda **13**
(Lil') Bow Wow **35**
Brandy **14, 34**
Braxton, Toni **15**
Bridgewater, Dee Dee **32**
Brooks, Avery **9**
Brooks, Hadda **40**
Brown, Charles **23**
Brown, Foxy **25**
Brown, Uzee **42**
Bumbry, Grace **5**
Burke, Solomon **31**
Burns, Eddie **44**
Busby, Jheryl **3**
Butler, Jerry **26**

Butler, Jonathan **28**
Caesar, Shirley **19**
Calloway, Cab **1**
Campbell Martin, Tisha **8, 42**
Cannon, Nick **47**
Carey, Mariah **32**
Carroll, Diahann **9**
Cartíer, Xam Wilson **41**
Carter, Benny **46**
Carter, Betty **19**
Carter, Nell **39**
Carter, Regina **23**
Carter, Warrick L. **27**
Chapman, Tracy **26**
Charlemagne, Manno **11**
Charles, Ray **16, 48**
Cheatham, Doc **17**
Checker, Chubby **28**
Chenault, John **40**
Christie, Angella **36**
Chuck D **9**
Clarke, Kenny **27**
Clark-Sheard, Karen **22**
Clemons, Clarence **41**
Cleveland, James **19**
Cliff, Jimmy **28**
Clinton, George **9**
Cole, Nat King **17**
Cole, Natalie Maria **17**
Coleman, Ornette **39**
Collins, Albert **12**
Collins, Bootsy **31**
Coltrane, John **19**
Combs, Sean "Puffy" **17, 43**
Common **31**
Cook, Charles "Doc" **44**
Cook, Will Marion **40**
Cooke, Sam **17**
Cortez, Jayne **43**
Count Basie **23**
Cox, Deborah **28**
Cox, Ida **42**
Craig, Carl **31**
Crawford, Randy **19**
Cray, Robert **30**
Creagh, Milton **27**
Crocker, Frankie **29**
Crothers, Scatman **19**
Crouch, Andraé **27**
Crouch, Stanley **11**
Crowder, Henry **16**
D'Angelo **27**
Dash, Damon **31**
Dash, Darien **29**
David, Craig **31**
Davis, Anthony **11**
Davis, Gary **41**
Davis, Guy **36**
Davis, Miles **4**
Davis, Sammy, Jr. **18**
Dawson, William Levi **39**
de Passe, Suzanne **25**
Dennard, Brazeal **37**
Dickenson, Vic **38**
Diddley, Bo **39**
Dixon, Willie **4**
DJ Jazzy Jeff **32**
DMX **28**
Dobbs, Mattiwilda **34**
Donegan, Dorothy **19**
Dorsey, Thomas **15**
Downing, Will **19**
Dr. Dre **10**

Dre, Dr. **14, 30**
Duke, George **21**
Dumas, Henry **41**
Dunner, Leslie B. **45**
Dupri, Jermaine **13, 46**
Dupri, Jermaine **13**
Eckstine, Billy **28**
Edmonds, Kenneth "Babyface" **10, 31**
Edmonds, Tracey **16**
Edwards, Esther Gordy **43**
Eldridge, Roy **37**
Ellington, Duke **5**
Elliott, Missy "Misdemeanor" **31**
Estes, Simon **28**
Estes, Sleepy John **33**
Eubanks, Kevin **15**
Europe, James Reese **10**
Evans, Faith **22**
Eve **29**
Evora, Cesaria **12**
Falana, Lola **42**
Farmer, Art **38**
Fats Domino **20**
Fela **1, 42**
Ferrell, Rachelle **29**
Ferrer, Ibrahim **41**
50 Cent **46**
Fitzgerald, Ella **8, 18**
Flack, Roberta **19**
Flash, Grandmaster **33**
Foster, George "Pops" **40**
Foxx, Jamie **15, 48**
Franklin, Aretha **11, 44**
Franklin, Kirk **15**
Freelon, Nnenna **32**
Freeman, Paul **39**
Freeman, Yvette **27**
Fuqua, Antoine **35**
Gaines, Grady **38**
Gaye, Marvin **2**
Gaynor, Gloria **36**
George, Zelma Watson **42**
Gibson, Althea **8, 43**
Gillespie, Dizzy **1**
Ginuwine **35**
Glover, Corey **34**
Golson, Benny **37**
Gordon, Dexter **25**
Gordy, Berry, Jr. **1**
Gotti, Irv **39**
Graves, Denyce **19**
Gray, F. Gary **14**
Gray, Macy **29**
Greaves, William **38**
Greely, M. Gasby **27**
Green, Al **13, 47**
Griffiths, Marcia **29**
Guy, Buddy **31**
Hailey, JoJo **22**
Hailey, K-Ci **22**
Hammer, M. C. **20**
Hammond, Fred **23**
Hammond, Lenn **34**
Hampton, Lionel **17, 41**
Hancock, Herbie **20**
Handy, W. C. **8**
Hardin Armstrong, Lil **39**
Harper, Ben **34**
Harrell, Andre **9, 30**
Harris, Corey **39**
Hathaway, Donny **18**
Hawkins, Coleman **9**

Hawkins, Erskine **14**
Hawkins, Screamin' Jay **30**
Hawkins, Tramaine **16**
Hayes, Isaac **20**
Hayes, Roland **4**
Hayes, Teddy **40**
Hemphill, Jessie Mae **33**
Henderson, Fletcher **32**
Hendricks, Barbara **3**
Hendrix, Jimi **10**
Henry, Clarence "Frogman" **46**
Higginbotham, J. C. **37**
Hill, Lauryn **20**
Hinderas, Natalie **5**
Hines, Earl "Fatha" **39**
Hinton, Milt **30**
Holiday, Billie **1**
Holland-Dozier-Holland **36**
Holt, Nora **38**
Hooker, John Lee **30**
Horn, Shirley **32**
Horne, Lena **5**
House, Son **8**
Houston, Cissy **20**
Houston, Whitney **7, 28**
Howlin' Wolf **9**
Humphrey, Bobbi **20**
Hunter, Alberta **42**
Hyman, Phyllis **19**
Ice Cube **8, 30**
Ice-T **6, 31**
India.Arie **34**
Isley, Ronald **25**
Ja Rule **35**
Jackson, Fred James **25**
Jackson, George **19**
Jackson, Hal **41**
Jackson, Isaiah **3**
Jackson, Janet **6, 30**
Jackson, John **36**
Jackson, Mahalia **5**
Jackson, Michael **19**
Jackson, Millie **25**
Jackson, Milt **26**
Jackson, Randy **40**
James, Etta **13**
James, Rick **17**
James, Skip **38**
Jarreau, Al **21**
Jay-Z **27**
Jean, Wyclef **20**
Jean-Baptiste, Marianne **17, 46**
Jenkins, Ella **15**
Jerkins, Rodney **31**
Jimmy Jam **13**
Johnson, Beverly **2**
Johnson, Buddy **36**
Johnson, J. J. **37**
Johnson, James Weldon **5**
Johnson, Robert **2**
Jones, Bobby **20**
Jones, Donell **29**
Jones, Elvin **14**
Jones, Etta **35**
Jones, Jonah **39**
Jones, Quincy **8, 30**
Joplin, Scott **6**
Jordan, Montell **23**
Jordan, Ronny **26**
Joyner, Matilda Sissieretta **15**
Joyner, Tom **19**
Kay, Ulysses **37**
Kee, John P. **43**

Kelly, R(obert) **18, 44**
Kem **47**
Kendricks, Eddie **22**
Kenoly, Ron **45**
Keys, Alicia **32**
Khan, Chaka **12**
King, B. B. **7**
King, Coretta Scott **3**
Kitt, Eartha **16**
Knight, Gladys **16**
Knight, Suge **11, 30**
Knowles, Beyoncé **39**
Knuckles, Frankie **42**
Kool Moe Dee **37**
Kravitz, Lenny **10, 34**
KRS-One **34**
Kuti, Femi **47**
L.L. Cool J **16**
LaBelle, Patti **13, 30**
Lattimore, Kenny **35**
Lefel, Edith **41**
León, Tania **13**
Lester, Julius **9**
Levert, Gerald **22**
Lewis, Ananda **28**
Lewis, Henry **38**
Lewis, Ramsey **35**
Lewis, Terry **13**
Lil' Kim **28**
Liles, Kevin **42**
Lincoln, Abbey **3**
Little Milton **36**
Little Richard **15**
Little Walter **36**
Locke, Eddie **44**
Lopes, Lisa "Left Eye" **36**
Love, Darlene **23**
Lover, Ed **10**
Ludacris **37**
Lymon, Frankie **22**
Madhubuti, Haki R. **7**
Mahal, Taj **39**
Majors, Jeff **41**
Makeba, Miriam **2**
Marley, Bob **5**
Marley, Rita **32**
Marley, Ziggy **41**
Marrow, Queen Esther **24**
Marsalis, Branford **34**
Marsalis, Delfeayo **41**
Marsalis, Wynton **16**
Martin, Sara **38**
Mary Mary **34**
Mase **24**
Masekela, Hugh **1**
Massenburg, Kedar **23**
Master P **21**
Mathis, Johnny **20**
Maxwell **20**
May, Derrick **41**
Mayfield, Curtis **2, 43**
Maynor, Dorothy **19**
MC Lyte **34**
McBride, James **35**
McClurkin, Donnie **25**
McDaniel, Hattie **5**
McKee, Lonette **12**
McKinney, Nina Mae **40**
McKnight, Brian **18, 34**
McPherson, David **32**
Memphis Minnie **33**
Mills, Stephanie **36**
Mingus, Charles **15**

Mitchell, Leona **42**
Mo', Keb' **36**
Monica **21**
Monk, Thelonious **1**
Moore, Chante **26**
Moore, Dorothy Rudd **46**
Moore, Johnny B. **38**
Moore, Melba **21**
Moore, Undine Smith **28**
Morton, Jelly Roll **29**
Mos Def **30**
Moses, Gilbert **12**
Moten, Etta **18**
Mowatt, Judy **38**
Mullen, Nicole C. **45**
Mumba, Samantha **29**
Murphy, Eddie **4, 20**
Murray, Tai **47**
Muse, Clarence Edouard **21**
Musiq **37**
Mya **35**
N'Dour, Youssou **1**
Nas **33**
Nascimento, Milton **2**
Nash, Johnny **40**
Ndegéocello, Me'Shell **15**
Neal, Raful **44**
Nelly **32**
Neville, Aaron **21**
Nicholas, Fayard **20**
Nicholas, Harold **20**
Norman, Jessye **5**
Notorious B.I.G. **20**
Odetta **37**
Olatunji, Babatunde **36**
Oliver, Joe "King" **42**
O'Neal, Shaquille **8, 30**
Ongala, Remmy **9**
Osborne, Jeffrey **26**
OutKast **35**
Owens, Jack **38**
Parker, Charlie **20**
Parks, Gordon **1, 35**
Patton, Antwan **45**
Pendergrass, Teddy **22**
Peoples, Dottie **22**
Perry, Ruth **19**
Peterson, James **38**
Peterson, Marvin "Hannibal" **27**
Powell, Maxine **8**
Powell, Bud **24**
Pratt, Awadagin **31**
Premice, Josephine **41**
Preston, Billy **39**
Price, Florence **37**
Price, Kelly **23**
Price, Leontyne **1**
Pride, Charley **26**
Prince **18**
Pritchard, Robert Starling **21**
Queen Latifah **1, 16**
Rainey, Ma **33**
Ralph, Sheryl Lee **18**
Randall, Alice **38**
Razaf, Andy **19**
Reagon, Bernice Johnson **7**
Redman, Joshua **30**
Reed, A. C. **36**
Reed, Jimmy **38**
Reese, Della **6, 20**
Reeves, Dianne **32**
Reid, Antonio "L.A." **28**
Reid, Vernon **34**

Rhone, Sylvia **2**
Rhymes, Busta **31**
Richie, Lionel **27**
Riperton, Minnie **32**
Roach, Max **21**
Roberts, Marcus **19**
Robeson, Paul **2**
Robinson, Fenton **38**
Robinson, Smokey **3**
Rogers, Jimmy **38**
Rollins, Sonny **37**
Ross, Diana **8, 27**
Ross, Isaiah "Doc" **40**
Roxanne Shante **33**
Rucker, Darius **34**
Run-DMC **31**
Rupaul **17**
Rush, Otis **38**
Rushen, Patrice **12**
Rushing, Jimmy **37**
Sade **15**
Sangare, Oumou **18**
Scott, Jill **29**
Scott, "Little" Jimmy **48**
Seal **14**
Shaggy **31**
Shakur, Tupac **14**
Shirley, George **33**
Shorty I, Ras **47**
Silver, Horace **26**
Simmons, Russell **1, 30**
Simone, Nina **15, 41**
Simpson, Valerie **21**
Sisqo **30**
Sissle, Noble **29**
Sister Souljah **11**
Sledge, Percy **39**
Sly & Robbie **34**
Smith, Bessie **3**
Smith, Cladys "Jabbo" **32**
Smith, Mamie **32**
Smith, Stuff **37**
Smith, Trixie **34**
Smith, Will **8, 18**
Snoop Dogg **35**
Sowande, Fela **39**
Staples, "Pops" **32**
Staton, Candi **27**
Steinberg, Martha Jean "The Queen" **28**
Still, William Grant **37**
Stone, Angie **31**
Stoute, Steve **38**
Strayhorn, Billy **31**
Streeter, Sarah **45**
Studdard, Ruben **46**
Sullivan, Maxine **37**
Summer, Donna **25**
Sweat, Keith **19**
Sykes, Roosevelt **20**
Tamia **24**
Tatum, Art **28**
Taylor, Billy **23**
Taylor, Koko **40**
Terrell, Tammi **32**
Terry, Clark **39**
The Supremes **33**
The Tempations **33**
Thomas, Irma **29**
Thomas, Rufus **20**
Thornton, Big Mama **33**
Three Mo' Tenors **35**
Tillis, Frederick **40**

Timbaland 32
TLC 34
Tosh, Peter 9
Turnbull, Walter 13
Turner, Tina 6, 27
Tyrese 27
Uggams, Leslie 23
Usher 23
Vandross, Luther 13, 48
Vaughan, Sarah 13
Vereen, Ben 4
Walker, Albertina 10
Walker, Cedric "Ricky" 19
Walker, George 37
Walker, Hezekiah 34
Wallace, Sippie 1
Waller, Fats 29
Warwick, Dionne 18
Washington, Dinah 22
Washington, Grover, Jr. 17, 44
Waters, Benny 26
Waters, Ethel 7
Waters, Muddy 34
Watson, Johnny "Guitar" 18
Webster, Katie 29
Wells, Mary 28
Whalum, Kirk 37
White, Barry 13, 41
White, Maurice 29
Williams, Bert 18
Williams, Clarence 33
Williams, Deniece 36
Williams, Denise 40
Williams, Joe 5, 25
Williams, Mary Lou 15
Williams, Pharrell 47
Williams, Saul 31
Williams, Vanessa L. 4, 17
Wilson, Cassandra 16
Wilson, Charlie 31
Wilson, Mary 28
Wilson, Nancy 10
Wilson, Natalie 38
Wilson, Sunnie 7
Winans, Angie 36
Winans, BeBe 14
Winans, CeCe 14, 43
Winans, Debbie 36
Winans, Marvin L. 17
Winans, Vickie 24
Wonder, Stevie 11
Yarbrough, Camille 40
Yoba, Malik 11
York, Vincent 40
Young, Lester 37

Religion
Abernathy, Ralph David 1
Adams, Yolanda 17
Agyeman, Jaramogi Abebe 10
Al-Amin, Jamil Abdullah 6
Anthony, Wendell 25
Arinze, Francis Cardinal 19
Aristide, Jean-Bertrand 6, 45
Armstrong, Vanessa Bell 24
Austin, Junius C. 44
Banks, William 11
Baylor, Helen 36
Bell, Ralph S. 5
Ben-Israel, Ben Ami 11
Black, Barry C. 47
Boyd, T. B., III 6
Bryant, John R. 45

Burgess, John 46
Butts, Calvin O., III 9
Bynum, Juanita 31
Cardozo, Francis L. 33
Caesar, Shirley 19
Cannon, Katie 10
Chavis, Benjamin 6
Cleaver, Emanuel 4, 45
Clements, George 2
Cleveland, James 19
Colemon, Johnnie 11
Collins, Janet 33
Cone, James H. 3
Cook, Suzan D. Johnson 22
Crouch, Andraé 27
DeLille, Henriette 30
Divine, Father 7
Dyson, Michael Eric 11, 40
Elmore, Ronn 21
Farrakhan, Louis 2, 15
Fauntroy, Walter E. 11
Flake, Floyd H. 18
Foreman, George 15
Franklin, Kirk 15
Franklin, Robert M. 13
Gilmore, Marshall 46
Gomes, Peter J. 15
Gray, William H., III 3
Green, Al 13, 47
Gregory, Wilton 37
Grier, Roosevelt 13
Haile Selassie 7
Harris, Barbara 12
Hawkins, Tramaine 16
Hayes, James C. 10
Healy, James Augustine 30
Hooks, Benjamin L. 2
Howard, M. William, Jr. 26
Jackson, Jesse 1, 27
Jakes, Thomas "T.D." 17, 43
Jemison, Major L. 48
Johns, Vernon 38
Jones, Bobby 20
Jones, E. Edward, Sr. 45
Kelly, Leontine 33
King, Barbara 22
King, Bernice 4
King, Martin Luther, Jr. 1
Kobia, Rev. Dr. Samuel 43
Lester, Julius 9
Lewis-Thornton, Rae 32
Lincoln, C. Eric 38
Little Richard 15
Long, Eddie L. 29
Lowery, Joseph 2
Lyons, Henry 12
Majors, Jeff 41
Marino, Eugene Antonio 30
Mays, Benjamin E. 7
McClurkin, Donnie 25
McKenzie, Vashti M. 29
Muhammad, Ava 31
Muhammad, Elijah 4
Muhammad, Khallid Abdul 10, 31
Muhammed, W. Deen 27
Murray, Cecil 12, 47
Patterson, Gilbert Earl 41
Pierre, Andre 17
Powell, Adam Clayton, Jr. 3
Price, Frederick K.C. 21
Reems, Ernestine Cleveland 27
Reese, Della 6, 20
Riley, Helen Caldwell Day 13

Rugambwa, Laurean 20
Shabazz, Betty 7, 26
Sharpton, Al 21
Shaw, William J. 30
Shuttlesworth, Fred 47
Somé, Malidoma Patrice 10
Stallings, George A., Jr. 6
Steinberg, Martha Jean "The Queen" 28
Sullivan, Leon H. 3, 30
Tillard, Conrad 29
Thurman, Howard 3
Turner, Henry McNeal 5
Tutu, Desmond (Mpilo) 6, 44
Vanzant, Iyanla 17, 47
Waddles, Charleszetta (Mother) 10
Walker, Hezekiah 34
Waters, Ethel 7
Weems, Renita J. 44
West, Cornel 5, 33
White, Reggie 6
Williams, Hosea Lorenzo 15, 31
Wilson, Natalie 38
Winans, BeBe 14
Winans, CeCe 14, 43
Winans, Marvin L. 17
Wright, Jeremiah A., Jr. 45
X, Malcolm 1
Youngblood, Johnny Ray 8

Science and technology
Adkins, Rod 41
Adkins, Rutherford H. 21
Alexander, Archie Alphonso 14
Allen, Ethel D. 13
Anderson, Charles Edward 37
Anderson, Michael P. 40
Anderson, Norman B. 45
Auguste, Donna 29
Auguste, Rose-Anne 13
Bacon-Bercey, June 38
Banda, Hastings Kamuzu 6
Bath, Patricia E. 37
Benjamin, Regina 20
Benson, Angela 34
Black, Keith Lanier 18
Bluford, Guy 2, 35
Bluitt, Juliann S. 14
Bolden, Charles F., Jr. 7
Brown, Willa 40
Brown, Vivian 27
Bullard, Eugene 12
Callender, Clive O. 3
Canady, Alexa 28
Cargill, Victoria A. 43
Carroll, L. Natalie 44
Carruthers, George R. 40
Carson, Benjamin 1, 35
Carter, Joye Maureen 41
Carver, George Washington 4
CasSelle, Malcolm 11
Chatard, Peter 44
Chinn, May Edward 26
Christian, Spencer 15
Cobb, W. Montague 39
Cobbs, Price M. 9
Cole, Rebecca 38
Coleman, Bessie 9
Comer, James P. 6
Coney, PonJola 48
Cooper, Edward S. 6
Daly, Marie Maynard 37
Davis, Allison 12

Dean, Mark 35
Delany, Bessie 12
Delany, Martin R. 27
Dickens, Helen Octavia 14
Diop, Cheikh Anta 4
Drew, Charles Richard 7
Dunham, Katherine 4
Dunston, Georgia Mae 48
Elders, Joycelyn 6
Ellington, E. David 11
Ellis, Clarence A. 38
Emeagwali, Dale 31
Emeagwali, Philip 30
Ericsson-Jackson, Aprille 28
Fields, Evelyn J. 27
Fisher, Rudolph 17
Flipper, Henry O. 3
Foster, Henry W., Jr. 26
Freeman, Harold P. 23
Fulani, Lenora 11
Fuller, A. Oveta 43
Fuller, Arthur 27
Fuller, Solomon Carter, Jr. 15
Gates, Sylvester James, Jr. 15
Gayle, Helene D. 3, 46
Gibson, Kenneth Allen 6
Gibson, William F. 6
Gourdine, Meredith 33
Granville, Evelyn Boyd 36
Gray, Ida 41
Gregory, Frederick D. 8
Griffin, Bessie Blout 43
Hall, Lloyd A. 8
Hannah, Marc 10
Harris, Mary Styles 31
Henderson, Cornelius Langston 26
Henson, Matthew 2
Hinton, William Augustus 8
Imes, Elmer Samuel 39
Irving, Larry, Jr. 12
Jackson, Shirley Ann 12
Jawara, Sir Dawda Kairaba 11
Jemison, Mae C. 1, 35
Jenifer, Franklyn G. 2
Johnson, Eddie Bernice 8
Johnson, Lonnie G. 32
Jones, Randy 35
Julian, Percy Lavon 6
Just, Ernest Everett 3
Kenney, John A., Jr. 48
Knowling, Robert E., Jr. 38
Kountz, Samuel L. 10
Latimer, Lewis H. 4
Lavizzo-Mourey, Risa 48
Lawless, Theodore K. 8
Lawrence, Robert H., Jr. 16
Leevy, Carrol M. 42
Leffall, LaSalle, Jr. 3
Lewis, Delano 7
Logan, Onnie Lee 14
Lyttle, Hulda Margaret 14
Madison, Romell 45
Manley, Audrey Forbes 16
Massey, Walter E. 5, 45
Massie, Samuel P., Jr. 29
Maxey, Randall 46
Mays, William G. 34
Mboup, Souleymane 10
McCoy, Elijah 8
McNair, Ronald 3
Mensah, Thomas 48
Millines Dziko, Trish 28
Morgan, Garrett 1

Murray, Pauli 38
Nabrit, Samuel Milton 47
Neto, António Agostinho 43
O'Leary, Hazel 6
Person, Waverly 9
Peters, Lenrie 43
Pickett, Cecil 39
Pierre, Percy Anthony 46
Pitt, David Thomas 10
Poussaint, Alvin F. 5
Prothrow-Stith, Deborah 10
Quarterman, Lloyd Albert 4
Riley, Helen Caldwell Day 13
Robeson, Eslanda Goode 13
Robinson, Rachel 16
Roker, Al 12
Samara, Noah 15
Satcher, David 7
Shabazz, Betty 7, 26
Shavers, Cheryl 31
Sigur, Wanda 44
Sinkford, Jeanne C. 13
Staples, Brent 8
Staupers, Mabel K. 7
Stewart, Ella 39
Sullivan, Louis 8
Terrell, Dorothy A. 24
Thomas, Vivien 9
Tyson, Neil de Grasse 15
Wambugu, Florence 42
Washington, Patrice Clarke 12
Watkins, Levi, Jr. 9
Welsing, Frances Cress 5
Wilkens, J. Ernest, Jr. 43
Williams, Daniel Hale 2
Williams, O. S. 13
Witt, Edwin T. 26
Woods, Granville T. 5
Wright, Louis Tompkins 4
Young, Roger Arliner 29

Social issues
Aaron, Hank 5
Abbot, Robert Sengstacke 27
Abbott, Diane 9
Abdul-Jabbar, Kareem 8
Abernathy, Ralph David 1
Abu-Jamal, Mumia 15
Achebe, Chinua 6
Adams, Sheila J. 25
Agyeman, Jaramogi Abebe 10
Ake, Claude 30
Al-Amin, Jamil Abdullah 6
Alexander, Clifford 26
Alexander, Sadie Tanner Mossell 22
Ali, Muhammad, 2, 16
Allen, Ethel D. 13
Andrews, Benny 22
Angelou, Maya 1, 15
Annan, Kofi Atta 15, 48
Anthony, Wendell 25
Archer, Dennis 7
Aristide, Jean-Bertrand 6, 45
Arnwine, Barbara 28
Asante, Molefi Kete 3
Ashe, Arthur 1, 18
Auguste, Rose-Anne 13
Azikiwe, Nnamdi 13
Ba, Mariama 30
Baisden, Michael 25
Baker, Ella 5
Baker, Gwendolyn Calvert 9

Baker, Houston A., Jr. 6
Baker, Josephine 3
Baker, Thurbert 22
Baldwin, James 1
Baraka, Amiri 1, 38
Bass, Charlotta Spears 40
Bates, Daisy 13
Beals, Melba Patillo 15
Belafonte, Harry 4
Bell, Derrick 6
Bell, Ralph S. 5
Bennett, Lerone, Jr. 5
Berry, Bertice 8
Berry, Mary Frances 7
Bethune, Mary McLeod 4
Betsch, MaVynee 28
Biko, Steven 4
Blackwell, Unita 17
Bolin, Jane 22
Bond, Julian 2, 35
Bonga, Kuenda 13
Bosley, Freeman, Jr. 7
Boyd, John W., Jr. 20
Boyd, T. B., III 6
Boykin, Keith 14
Bradley, David Henry, Jr. 39
Braun, Carol Moseley 4, 42
Broadbent, Hydeia 36
Brown, Cora 33
Brown, Eddie C. 35
Brooke, Edward 8
Brown, Elaine 8
Brown, Homer S. 47
Brown, Jesse 6, 41
Brown, Jim 11
Brown, Lee P. 1
Brown, Les 5
Brown, Llyod Louis 42
Brown, Tony 3
Brown, Willa 40
Brown, Zora Kramer 12
Brutus, Dennis 38
Bryant, Wayne R. 6
Bullock, Steve 22
Bunche, Ralph J. 5
Burks, Mary Fair 40
Burroughs, Margaret Taylor 9
Butler, Paul D. 17
Butts, Calvin O., III 9
Campbell, Bebe Moore 6, 24
Canada, Geoffrey 23
Carby, Hazel 27
Carmichael, Stokely 5, 26
Carter, Mandy 11
Carter, Rubin 26
Carter, Stephen L. 4
Cary, Lorene 3
Cary, Mary Ann Shadd 30
Cayton, Horace 26
Chavis, Benjamin 6
Chideya, Farai 14
Childress, Alice 15
Chissano, Joaquim 7
Christophe, Henri 9
Chuck D 9
Clark, Joe 1
Clark, Kenneth B. 5
Clark, Septima 7
Clay, William Lacy 8
Claytor, Helen 14
Cleaver, Eldridge 5
Cleaver, Kathleen Neal 29
Clements, George 2

Cobbs, Price M. 9
Cole, Johnnetta B. 5, 43
Cole, Lorraine 48
Collins, Barbara-Rose 7
Comer, James P. 6
Cone, James H. 3
Connerly, Ward 14
Conté, Lansana 7
Conyers, John, Jr. 4, 45
Cook, Toni 23
Cooper, Margaret J. 46
Cooke, Marvel 31
Cooper, Anna Julia 20
Cooper, Edward S. 6
Cosby, Bill 7
Cosby, Camille 14
Cose, Ellis 5
Creagh, Milton 27
Crockett, George, Jr. 10
Crouch, Stanley 11
Cummings, Elijah E. 24
Cunningham, Evelyn 23
da Silva, Benedita 5
Dash, Julie 4
Davis, Angela 5
Davis, Artur 41
Davis, Danny K. 24
Davis, Ossie 5
Dawson, Matel "Mat," Jr. 39
DeBaptiste, George 32
Dee, Ruby 8
Delany, Martin R. 27
Dellums, Ronald 2
Diallo, Amadou 27
Dickerson, Ernest 6
Diop, Cheikh Anta 4
Divine, Father 7
Dixon, Margaret 14
Dodson, Howard, Jr. 7
Dortch, Thomas W., Jr. 45
Dove, Rita 6
Drew, Charles Richard 7
Du Bois, W. E. B. 3
DuBois, Shirley Graham 21
Dumas, Henry 41
Dunham, Katherine 4
Early, Gerald 15
Edelin, Ramona Hoage 19
Edelman, Marian Wright 5, 42
Edley, Christopher 2, 48
Edwards, Harry 2
Elder, Larry 25
Elder, Lee 6
Elders, Joycelyn 6
Ellison, Ralph 7
Esposito, Giancarlo 9
Espy, Mike 6
Europe, James Reese 10
Evers, Medgar 3
Evers, Myrlie 8
Farmer, James 2
Farrakhan, Louis 15
Fauntroy, Walter E. 11
Fauset, Jessie 7
Fela 1, 42
Fields, C. Virginia 25
Fletcher, Bill, Jr. 41
Foreman, George 15
Forman, James 7
Fortune, T. Thomas 6
Foster, Marie 48
Franklin, Hardy R. 9
Franklin, John Hope 5

Franklin, Robert M. 13
Frazier, E. Franklin 10
Fulani, Lenora 11
Fuller, Arthur 27
Fuller, Charles 8
Gaines, Ernest J. 7
Garvey, Marcus 1
Gates, Henry Louis, Jr. 3, 38
Gayle, Helene D. 3
George, Zelma Watson 42
Gibson, Kenneth Allen 6
Gibson, William F. 6
Gist, Carole 1
Goldberg, Whoopi 4, 33
Golden, Marita 19
Gomez, Jewelle 30
Gomez-Preston, Cheryl 9
Gossett, Louis, Jr. 7
Graham, Lawrence Otis 12
Gray, Fred 37
Gregory, Dick 1
Gregory, Wilton 37
Grier, Roosevelt 13
Griffith, Mark Winston 8
Grimké, Archibald H. 9
Guinier, Lani 7, 30
Guy, Rosa 5
Guy-Sheftall, Beverly 13
Hale, Lorraine 8
Haley, Alex 4
Hall, Elliott S. 24
Hamblin, Ken 10
Hamer, Fannie Lou 6
Hampton, Fred 18
Hampton, Henry 6
Hani, Chris 6
Hansberry, Lorraine 6
Hansberry, William Leo 11
Harper, Frances Ellen Watkins 11
Harrington, Oliver W. 9
Harris, Alice 7
Harris, Leslie 6
Harris, Marcelite Jordan 16
Harris, Patricia Roberts 2
Hastings, Alcee L. 16
Hawkins, Steven 14
Haynes, George Edmund 8
Hedgeman, Anna Arnold 22
Height, Dorothy I. 2, 23
Henderson, Wade J. 14
Henry, Aaron 19
Henry, Lenny 9
Hernandez, Aileen Clarke 13
Hill, Anita 5
Hill, Jessie, Jr. 13
Hill, Lauryn 20
Hill, Oliver W. 24
Hilliard, David 7
Holland, Endesha Ida Mae 3
Hooks, Benjamin L. 2
hooks, bell 5
Horne, Lena 5
Houston, Charles Hamilton 4
Howard, M. William, Jr. 26
Hubbard, Arnette Rhinehart 38
Hughes, Albert 7
Hughes, Allen 7
Hughes, Langston 4
Hunter-Gault, Charlayne 6, 31
Hutchinson, Earl Ofari 24
Hutson, Jean Blackwell 16
Ice-T 6, 31
Iceberg Slim 11

Iman 4, 33
Ingram, Rex 5
Innis, Roy 5
Jackson, Fred James 25
Jackson, George 14
Jackson, Janet 6, 30
Jackson, Jesse 1, 27
Jackson, Mahalia 5
Jacob, John E. 2
Jagan, Cheddi 16
James, Daniel, Jr. 16
Jean, Wyclef 20
Jeffries, Leonard 8
Johnson, Charles S. 12
Johnson, Earvin "Magic" 3, 39
Johnson, James Weldon 5
Jolley, Willie 28
Jones, Elaine R. 7, 45
Jordan, Barbara 4
Jordan, June 7, 35
Jordan, Vernon E. 3, 35
Josey, E. J. 10
Joyner, Marjorie Stewart 26
Joyner, Tom 19
Julian, Percy Lavon 6
Kaunda, Kenneth 2
Keith, Damon J. 16
Kennedy, Florynce 12, 33
Khanga, Yelena 6
Kidd, Mae Street 39
King, B. B. 7
King, Bernice 4
King, Coretta Scott 3
King, Dexter 10
King, Martin Luther, III 20
King, Martin Luther, Jr. 1
King, Preston 28
King, Yolanda 6
Kitt, Eartha 16
Ladner, Joyce A. 42
LaGuma, Alex 30
Lampkin, Daisy 19
Lane, Charles 3
Lane, Vincent 5
Lee, Canada 8
Lee, Spike 5, 19
Leland, Mickey 2
Lester, Julius 9
Lewis, Ananda 28
Lewis, Delano 7
Lewis, John 2, 46
Lewis, Thomas 19
Lewis-Thornton, Rae 32
Little, Robert L. 2
Logan, Rayford W. 40
Long, Eddie L. 29
Lorde, Audre 6
Louis, Errol T. 8
Lowery, Joseph 2
Lucas, John 7
Lucy Foster, Autherine 35
Maathai, Wangari 43
Mabuza-Suttle, Felicia 43
Madhubuti, Haki R. 7
Madison, Joseph E. 17
Makeba, Miriam 2
Malveaux, Julianne 32
Mandela, Nelson 1, 14
Mandela, Winnie 2, 35
Manley, Audrey Forbes 16
Marable, Manning 10
Marley, Bob 5
Marshall, Paule 7

Marshall, Thurgood 1, 44
Martin, Louis E. 16
Masekela, Barbara 18
Masekela, Hugh 1
Mason, Ronald 27
Mathabane, Mark 5
Maynard, Robert C. 7
Mays, Benjamin E. 7
McCabe, Jewell Jackson 10
McCarty, Osceola 16
McDaniel, Hattie 5
McDougall, Gay J. 11, 43
McKay, Claude 6
McKenzie, Vashti M. 29
McKissick, Floyd B. 3
McMurray, Georgia L. 36
McQueen, Butterfly 6
McWhorter, John 35
Meek, Carrie 6, 36
Meredith, James H. 11
Mfume, Kweisi 6, 41
Micheaux, Oscar 7
Millines Dziko, Trish 28
Millender-McDonald, Juanita 21
Mkapa, Benjamin 16
Mongella, Gertrude 11
Moore, Harry T. 29
Morial, Ernest "Dutch" 26
Morrison, Toni 2
Moses, Robert Parris 11
Mosley, Walter 5, 25
Mossell, Gertrude Bustill 40
Motley, Constance Baker 10
Moutoussamy-Ashe, Jeanne 7
Mowry, Jess 7
Muhammad, Elijah 4
Muhammad, Khallid Abdul 10, 31
Murphy, Laura M. 43
Murray, Pauli 38
Ndadaye, Melchior 7
Nelson, Jill 6
Newton, Huey 2
Nkrumah, Kwame 3
Norman, Pat 10
Norton, Eleanor Holmes 7
Nzo, Alfred 15
O'Leary, Hazel 6
Obasanjo, Olusegun 5
Oglesby, Zena 12
Owens, Major 6
Page, Alan 7
Page, Clarence 4
Paige, Satchel 7
Parker, Kellis E. 30
Parker, Pat 19
Parks, Rosa 1, 35
Patterson, Frederick Douglass 12
Patterson, Louise 25
Patterson, Orlando 4
Patterson, P. J. 6, 20
Perkins, Edward 5
Pitt, David Thomas 10
Pleasant, Mary Ellen 9
Plessy, Homer Adolph 31
Poussaint, Alvin F. 5
Powell, Adam Clayton, Jr. 3
Powell, Kevin 31
Pratt, Geronimo 18
Pressley, Condace L. 41
Price, Hugh B. 9
Primus, Pearl 6
Pritchard, Robert Starling 21
Prothrow-Stith, Deborah 10

Quarles, Benjamin Arthur 18
Ramaphosa, Cyril 3
Ramphele, Mamphela 29
Ramsey, Charles H. 21
Rand, A. Barry 6
Randolph, A. Philip 3
Rangel, Charles 3
Rawlings, Nana Konadu Agyeman 13
Reagon, Bernice Johnson 7
Reed, Ishmael 8
Rice, Norm 8
Riggs, Marlon 5
Riley, Helen Caldwell Day 13
Ringgold, Faith 4
Robeson, Eslanda Goode 13
Robeson, Paul 2
Robinson, Jackie 6
Robinson, Rachel 16
Robinson, Randall 7, 46
Robinson, Sharon 22
Robinson, Spottswood 22
Rowan, Carl T. 1, 30
Rustin, Bayard 4
Sampson, Edith S. 4
Sanders, Malika 48
Sané, Pierre Gabriel 21
Sapphire 14
Saro-Wiwa, Kenule 39
Satcher, David 7
Savimbi, Jonas 2, 34
Sawyer, Amos 2
Sayles Belton, Sharon 9, 16
Schomburg, Arthur Alfonso 9
Seale, Bobby 3
Seele, Pernessa 46
Senghor, Léopold Sédar 12
Shabazz, Attallah 6
Shabazz, Betty 7, 26
Shakur, Assata 6
Shinhoster, Earl 32
Shuttlesworth, Fred 47
Sifford, Charlie 4
Simone, Nina 15, 41
Simpson, Carole 6, 30
Sister Souljah 11
Sisulu, Sheila Violet Makate 24
Sleet, Moneta, Jr. 5
Smith, Anna Deavere 6
Smith, Barbara 28
Smith, Greg 28
Soyinka, Wole 4
Stallings, George A., Jr. 6
Staupers, Mabel K. 7
Steele, Claude Mason 13
Steele, Shelby 13
Stewart, Alison 13
Stewart, Ella 39
Stewart, Maria W. Miller 19
Stone, Chuck 9
Sullivan, Leon H. 3, 30
Sutton, Percy E. 42
Tate, Eleanora E. 20
Taulbert, Clifton Lemoure 19
Taylor, Mildred D. 26
Taylor, Susan L. 10
Terrell, Mary Church 9
Thomas, Franklin A. 5
Thomas, Isiah 7, 26
Thompson, Bennie G. 26
Thurman, Howard 3
Thurman, Wallace 16
Till, Emmett 7

Toomer, Jean 6
Tosh, Peter 9
Touré, Askia (Muhammad Abu Bakr el) 47
Tribble, Israel, Jr. 8
Trotter, Donne E. 28
Trotter, Monroe 9
Tsvangirai, Morgan 26
Tubman, Harriet 9
Tucker, C. DeLores 12
Tucker, Cynthia 15
Tucker, Rosina 14
Tutu, Desmond 6
Tyree, Omar Rashad 21
Underwood, Blair 7, 27
Van Peebles, Melvin 7
Vanzant, Iyanla 17, 47
Vincent, Marjorie Judith 2
Waddles, Charleszetta (Mother) 10
Walcott, Derek 5
Walker, A'lelia 14
Walker, Alice 1, 43
Walker, Cedric "Ricky" 19
Walker, Madame C. J. 7
Wallace, Michele Faith 13
Wallace, Phyllis A. 9
Washington, Booker T. 4
Washington, Fredi 10
Washington, Harold 6
Waters, Maxine 3
Wattleton, Faye 9
Wells-Barnett, Ida B. 8
Wells, James Lesesne 10
Welsing, Frances Cress 5
West, Cornel 5, 33
White, Michael R. 5
White, Reggie 6
White, Walter F. 4
Wideman, John Edgar 5
Wilkins, Roger 2
Wilkins, Roy 4
Williams, Armstrong 29
Williams, Evelyn 10
Williams, Fannie Barrier 27
Williams, George Washington 18
Williams, Hosea Lorenzo 15, 31
Williams, Maggie 7
Williams, Montel 4
Williams, Patricia J. 11
Williams, Robert F. 11
Williams, Stanley "Tookie" 29
Williams, Walter E. 4
Williams, Willie L. 4
Wilson, August 7, 33
Wilson, Phill 9
Wilson, Sunnie 7
Wilson, William Julius 22
Winfield, Paul 2, 45
Winfrey, Oprah 2, 15
Wolfe, George C. 6, 43
Woodson, Robert L. 10
Worrill, Conrad 12
Wright, Charles H. 35
Wright, Louis Tompkins 4
Wright, Richard 5
X, Malcolm 1
Yancy, Dorothy Cowser 42
Yarbrough, Camille 40
Yoba, Malik 11
Young, Andrew 3, 48
Young, Jean Childs 14
Young, Whitney M., Jr. 4

Youngblood, Johnny Ray **8**

Sports
Aaron, Hank **5**
Abdul-Jabbar, Kareem **8**
Abdur-Rahim, Shareef **28**
Ali, Laila **27**
Ali, Muhammad **2, 16**
Allen, Marcus **20**
Amos, John **8**
Anderson, Elmer **25**
Anderson, Jamal **22**
Anthony, Carmelo **46**
Ashe, Arthur **1, 18**
Ashford, Emmett **22**
Ashley, Maurice **15, 47**
Baines, Harold **32**
Baker, Dusty **8, 43**
Banks, Ernie **33**
Barber, Ronde **41**
Barkley, Charles **5**
Barnes, Ernie **16**
Barney, Lem **26**
Barnhill, David **30**
Baylor, Don **6**
Beamon, Bob **30**
Beasley, Jamar **29**
Bell, James "Cool Papa" **36**
Belle, Albert **10**
Bickerstaff, Bernie **21**
Bing, Dave **3**
Briscoe, Marlin **37**
Blair, Paul **36**
Blake, James **43**
Blanks, Billy **22**
Blanton, Dain **29**
Bol, Manute **1**
Bolton-Holifield, Ruthie **28**
Bonaly, Surya **7**
Bonds, Barry **6, 34**
Bonds, Bobby **43**
Bowe, Riddick **6**
Brand, Elton **31**
Brandon, Terrell **16**
Brashear, Donald **39**
Brathwaite, Fred **35**
Brock, Lou **18**
Brooks, Aaron **33**
Brooks, Derrick **43**
Brown, James **22**
Brown, Jim **11**
Brown, Willard **36**
Bruce, Isaac **26**
Bryant, Kobe **15, 31**
Buchanan, Ray **32**
Butler, Leroy, III **17**
Bynoe, Peter C.B. **40**
Campanella, Roy **25**
Carew, Rod **20**
Carnegie, Herbert **25**
Carter, Anson **24**
Carter, Butch **27**
Carter, Cris **21**
Carter, Joe **30**
Carter, Rubin **26**
Carter, Vince **26**
Catchings, Tamika **43**
Chamberlain, Wilt **18, 47**
Charleston, Oscar **39**
Cheeks, Maurice **47**
Cherry, Deron **40**
Christie, Linford **8**
Claiborne, Loretta **34**

Clendenon, Donn **26**
Clifton, Nathaniel "Sweetwater" **47**
Coachman, Alice **18**
Coleman, Leonard S., Jr. **12**
Cooper, Charles "Chuck" **47**
Cooper, Michael **31**
Cooper, Cynthia **17**
Copeland, Michael **47**
Cottrell, Comer **11**
Culpepper, Daunte **32**
Cunningham, Randall **23**
Dandridge, Ray **36**
Davis, Ernie **48**
Davis, Mike **41**
Davis, Piper **19**
Davis, Terrell **20**
Dawes, Dominique **11**
Day, Leon **39**
DeFrantz, Anita **37**
Devers, Gail **7**
Dickerson, Eric **27**
Doby, Lawrence Eugene Sr. **16, 41**
Doig, Jason **45**
Drew, Charles Richard **7**
Drexler, Clyde **4**
Dumars, Joe **16**
Duncan, Tim **20**
Dungy, Tony **17, 42**
Dunn, Jerry **27**
Edwards, Harry **2**
Edwards, Teresa **14**
Elder, Lee **6**
Ellerbe, Brian **22**
Elliott, Sean **26**
Ellis, Jimmy **44**
Erving, Julius **18, 47**
Ewing, Patrick A. **17**
Farr, Mel **24**
Faulk, Marshall **35**
Felix, Allyson **48**
Fielder, Cecil **2**
Flood, Curt **10**
Flowers, Vonetta **35**
Ford, Cheryl **45**
Foreman, George **1, 15**
Fox, Rick **27**
Frazier, Joe **19**
Frazier-Lyde, Jacqui **31**
Freeman, Cathy **29**
Freeman, Marianna **23**
Fuhr, Grant **1**
Fuller, Vivian **33**
Futch, Eddie **33**
Gaither, Alonzo Smith (Jake) **14**
Garnett, Kevin **14**
Garrison, Zina **2**
Gentry, Alvin **23**
Gibson, Althea **8, 43**
Gibson, Bob **33**
Gibson, Josh **22**
Gilliam, Frank **23**
Gilliam, Joe **31**
Gooden, Dwight **20**
Goss, Tom **23**
Gourdine, Meredith **33**
Gourdine, Simon **11**
Grand-Pierre, Jean-Luc **46**
Green, A. C. **32**
Green, Darrell **39**
Green, Dennis **5, 45**
Greene, Joe **10**
Greene, Maurice **27**
Gregg, Eric **16**

Grier, Mike **43**
Grier, Roosevelt **1**
Griffey, Ken, Jr. **12**
Griffith, Yolanda **25**
Griffith-Joyner, Florence **28**
Gumbel, Bryant **14**
Gumbel, Greg **8**
Gwynn, Tony **18**
Hardaway, Anfernee (Penny) **13**
Hardaway, Tim **35**
Harrison, Alvin **28**
Harrison, Calvin **28**
Haskins, Clem **23**
Heard, Gar **25**
Hearns, Thomas **29**
Henderson, Rickey **28**
Hickman, Fred **11**
Hill, Calvin **19**
Hill, Grant **13**
Hines, Garrett **35**
Holdsclaw, Chamique **24**
Holmes, Kelly **47**
Holmes, Larry **20**
Holyfield, Evander **6**
Hopkins, Bernard **35**
Horton, Andre **33**
Horton, Suki **33**
Howard, Desmond **16**
Howard, Juwan **15**
Howard, Sherri **36**
Hunter, Billy **22**
Hunter, Torii **43**
Hyde, Cowan F. "Bubba" **47**
Iginla, Jarome **35**
Irvin, Monte **31**
Iverson, Allen **24, 46**
Jackson, Mannie **14**
Jackson, Reggie **15**
Jacobs, Regina **38**
James, LeBron **46**
Jenkins, Fergie **46**
Jeter, Derek **27**
Johnson, Ben **1**
Johnson, Dwayne "The Rock" **29**
Johnson, Earvin "Magic" **3, 39**
Johnson, Jack **8**
Johnson, Larry **28**
Johnson, Levi **48**
Johnson, Mamie "Peanut" **40**
Johnson, Michael **13**
Johnson, Rafer **33**
Johnson, Rodney Van **28**
Jones, Cobi N'Gai **18**
Jones, Ed "Too Tall" **46**
Jones, Marion **21**
Jones, Merlakia **34**
Jones, Randy **35**
Jones, Roy Jr. **22**
Jordan, Michael **6, 21**
Joyner-Kersee, Jackie **5**
Justice, David **18**
Kaiser, Cecil **42**
Kennedy-Overton, Jayne Harris **46**
Kerry, Leon G. **46**
Kimbro, Henry A. **25**
King, Don **14**
Lacy, Sam **30, 46**
Lanier, Bob **47**
Lanier, Willie **33**
Lankford, Ray **23**
Laraque, Georges **48**
Larkin, Barry **24**
Lassiter, Roy **24**

Lee, Canada **8**
Lennox, Betty **31**
Leonard, Sugar Ray **15**
Leslie, Lisa **16**
Lester, Bill **42**
Lewis, Carl **4**
Lewis, Denise **33**
Lewis, Lennox **27**
Lewis, Ray **33**
Liston, Sonny **33**
Littlepage, Craig **35**
Lloyd, Earl **26**
Lloyd, John Henry "Pop" **30**
Lofton, James **42**
Lofton, Kenny **12**
Lott, Ronnie **9**
Louis, Joe **5**
Love, Nat **9**
Lucas, John **7**
Malone, Karl A. **18**
Manigault, Earl "The Goat" **15**
Mariner, Jonathan **41**
Master P **21**
Mayers, Jamal **39**
Mays, Willie **3**
McBride, Bryant **18**
McCray, Nikki **18**
McGriff, Fred **24**
McKegney, Tony **3**
McNabb, Donovan **29**
McNair, Steve **22, 47**
McNeil, Lori **1**
Metcalfe, Ralph **26**
Milla, Roger **2**
Miller, Cheryl **10**
Miller, Reggie **33**
Milton, DeLisha **31**
Mills, Sam **33**
Minor, DeWayne **32**
Monk, Art **38**
Montgomery, Tim **41**
Moon, Warren **8**
Moorer, Michael **19**
Morgan, Joe Leonard **9**
Moses, Edwin **8**
Mosley, Shane **32**
Moss, Randy **23**
Motley, Marion **26**
Mourning, Alonzo **17, 44**
Murray, Eddie **12**
Murray, Lenda **10**
Mutola, Maria **12**
Mutombo, Dikembe **7**
Nakhid, David **25**
Newcombe, Don **24**
Newsome, Ozzie **26**
Noah, Yannick **4**
O'Neal, Shaquille **8, 30**
O'Neil, Buck **19**
O'Ree, Willie **5**
Olajuwon, Hakeem **2**
Owens, Jesse **2**
Pace, Orlando **21**
Page, Alan **7**
Paige, Satchel **7**
Parish, Robert **43**
Patterson, Floyd **19**
Payne, Ulice **42**
Payton, Walter **11, 25**
Peck, Carolyn **23**
Peete, Calvin **11**
Pelé **7**
Perrot, Kim **23**

Perry, Lowell **30**
Peters, Margaret and Matilda **43**
Phillips, Teresa L. **42**
Pickett, Bill **11**
Pippen, Scottie **15**
Powell, Mike **7**
Powell, Renee **34**
Pride, Charley **26**
Puckett, Kirby **4**
Quirot, Ana **13**
Rashad, Ahmad **18**
Ready, Stephanie **33**
Reese, Pokey **28**
Rhodes, Ray **14**
Ribbs, Willy T. **2**
Rice, Jerry **5**
Richardson, Donna **39**
Richardson, Nolan **9**
Richmond, Mitch **19**
Rivers, Glenn "Doc" **25**
Robertson, Oscar **26**
Robinson, David **24**
Robinson, Eddie G. **10**
Robinson, Frank **9**
Robinson, Jackie **6**
Robinson, Sugar Ray **18**
Rodman, Dennis **12, 44**
Rudolph, Wilma **4**
Rubin, Chanda **37**
Russell, Bill **8**
Sampson, Charles **13**
Sanders, Barry **1**
Sanders, Deion **4, 31**
Sapp, Warren **38**
Sayers, Gale **28**
Scott, Stuart **34**
Scott, Wendell Oliver, Sr. **19**
Scurry, Briana **27**
Sharper, Darren **32**
Sheffield, Gary **16**
Shell, Art **1**
Shippen, John **43**
Showers, Reggie **30**
Sifford, Charlie **4**
Silas, Paul **24**
Simmons, Bob **29**
Simpson, O. J. **15**
Singletary, Mike **4**
Smith, Emmitt **7**
Smith, Hilton **29**
Smith, Tubby **18**
Solomon, Jimmie Lee **38**
Sosa, Sammy **21, 44**
Sprewell, Latrell **23**
St. Julien, Marlon **29**
Stackhouse, Jerry **30**
Stargell, Willie **29**
Stearns, Norman "Turkey" **31**
Steward, Emanuel **18**
Stewart, Kordell **21**
Stone, Toni **15**
Strahan, Michael **35**
Strawberry, Darryl **22**
Stringer, C. Vivian **13**
Stringer, Korey **35**
Swann, Lynn **28**
Swoopes, Sheryl **12**
Taylor, Lawrence **25**
Thomas, Debi **26**
Thomas, Derrick **25**
Thomas, Frank **12**
Thomas, Isiah **7, 26**
Thompson, Tina **25**
Thrower, Willie **35**
Thugwane, Josia **21**
Tyson, Mike **28, 44**
Unseld, Wes **23**
Upshaw, Gene **18, 47**
Ussery, Terdema, II **29**
Vick, Michael **39**
Virgil, Ozzie **48**
Walker, Herschel **1**
Wallace, Perry E. **47**
Ware, Andre **37**
Washington, MaliVai **8**
Watson, Bob **25**
Watts, J. C., Jr. **14, 38**
Weathers, Carl **10**
Webber, Chris **15, 30**
Westbrook, Peter **20**
Whitaker, Pernell **10**
White, Bill **1, 48**
White, Jesse **22**
White, Reggie **6**
Whitfield, Fred **23**
Wilkens, Lenny **11**
Williams, Doug **22**
Williams, Serena **20, 41**
Williams, Natalie **31**
Williams, Venus Ebone **17, 34**
Willingham, Tyrone **43**
Wilson, Sunnie **7**
Winfield, Dave **5**
Winkfield, Jimmy **42**
Woods, Tiger **14, 31**

Television
Alexander, Khandi **43**
Allen, Byron **3**
Allen, Debbie **13, 42**
Allen, Marcus **20**
Amos, John **8**
Anderson, Eddie "Rochester" **30**
Arkadie, Kevin **17**
Babatunde, Obba **35**
Banks, William **11**
Barclay, Paris **37**
Barden, Don H. **9**
Bassett, Angela **6, 23**
Beach, Michael **26**
Beaton, Norman **14**
Beauvais, Garcelle **29**
Belafonte, Harry **4**
Bellamy, Bill **12**
Berry, Bertice **8**
Berry, Fred "Rerun" **48**
Berry, Halle **4, 19**
Blackwood, Maureen **37**
Blake, Asha **26**
Boston, Kelvin E. **25**
Bowser, Yvette Lee **17**
Bradley, Ed **2**
Brady, Wayne **32**
Brandy **14, 34**
Braugher, Andre **13**
Bridges, Todd **37**
Brooks, Avery **9**
Brooks, Hadda **40**
Brown, James **22**
Brown, Joe **29**
Brown, Les **5**
Brown, Tony **3**
Brown, Vivian **27**
Burnett, Charles **16**
Burton, LeVar **8**
Byrd, Robert **11**
Caldwell, Benjamin **46**
Cameron, Earl **44**
Campbell, Naomi **1, 31**
Campbell Martin, Tisha **8, 42**
Cannon, Nick **47**
Carroll, Diahann **9**
Carson, Lisa Nicole **21**
Carter, Nell **39**
Cash, Rosalind **28**
Cedric the Entertainer **29**
Cheadle, Don **19**
Chestnut, Morris **31**
Chideya, Farai **14**
Christian, Spencer **15**
Clash, Kevin **14**
Clayton, Xernona **3, 45**
Cole, Nat King **17**
Cole, Natalie Maria **17**
Coleman, Gary **35**
Corbi, Lana **42**
Cornelius, Don **4**
Cosby, Bill **7, 26**
Crothers, Scatman **19**
Curry, Mark **17**
Curtis-Hall, Vondie **17**
Davidson, Tommy **21**
Davis, Ossie **5**
Davis, Viola **34**
de Passe, Suzanne **25**
Dee, Ruby **8**
Devine, Loretta **24**
Dickerson, Eric **27**
Dickerson, Ernest **6**
Diggs, Taye **25**
Dourdan, Gary **37**
Dr. Dre **10**
Duke, Bill **3**
Dutton, Charles S. **4, 22**
Elder, Larry **25**
Elise, Kimberly **32**
Emmanuel, Alphonsia **38**
Ephriam, Mablean **29**
Erving, Julius **18, 47**
Esposito, Giancarlo **9**
Eubanks, Kevin **15**
Evans, Harry **25**
Falana, Lola **42**
Fields, Kim **36**
Fishburne, Larry **4, 22**
Fox, Rick **27**
Foxx, Jamie **15, 48**
Foxx, Redd **2**
Freeman, Al, Jr. **11**
Freeman, Morgan **2**
Freeman, Yvette **27**
Gaines, Ernest J. **7**
Givens, Robin **4, 25**
Glover, Danny **3, 24**
Glover, Savion **14**
Goldberg, Whoopi **4, 33**
Goode, Mal **13**
Gooding, Cuba, Jr. **16**
Gordon, Ed **10**
Gossett, Louis, Jr. **7**
Greely, M. Gasby **27**
Grier, David Alan **28**
Grier, Pam **9, 31**
Guillaume, Robert **3, 48**
Gumbel, Bryant **14**
Gumbel, Greg **25**
Gunn, Moses **10**
Guy, Jasmine **2**
Haley, Alex **4**
Hampton, Henry **6**
Hardison, Kadeem **22**
Harper, Hill **32**
Harrell, Andre **9, 30**
Harris, Robin **7**
Harvey, Steve **18**
Hatchett, Glenda **32**
Hayes, Isaac **20**
Haynes, Trudy **44**
Haysbert, Dennis **42**
Hemsley, Sherman **19**
Henriques, Julian **37**
Henry, Lenny **9**
Henson, Darrin **33**
Hickman, Fred **11**
Hill, Dulé **29**
Hill, Lauryn **20**
Hinderas, Natalie **5**
Hines, Gregory **1, 42**
Horne, Lena **5**
Hounsou, Djimon **19, 45**
Houston, Whitney **7, 28**
Howard, Sherri **36**
Hughley, D.L. **23**
Hunter-Gault, Charlayne **6, 31**
Hyman, Earle **25**
Ice-T **6, 31**
Ifill, Gwen **28**
Iman **4, 33**
Ingram, Rex **5**
Jackson, George **19**
Jackson, Janet **6, 30**
Jackson, Jesse **1**
Jackson, Randy **40**
Jarret, Vernon D. **42**
Joe, Yolanda **21**
Johnson, Beverly **2**
Johnson, Dwayne "The Rock" **29**
Johnson, Linton Kwesi **37**
Johnson, Robert L. **3, 39**
Johnson, Rodney Van **28**
Jones, Bobby **20**
Jones, James Earl **3**
Jones, Orlando **30**
Jones, Quincy **8, 30**
Jones, Star **10, 27**
Kennedy-Overton, Jayne Harris **46**
King, Gayle **19**
King, Regina **22, 45**
King, Woodie, Jr. **27**
Kirby, George **14**
Kitt, Eartha **16**
Knight, Gladys **16**
Kodjoe, Boris **34**
Kotto, Yaphet **7**
L.L. Cool J **16**
La Salle, Eriq **12**
LaBelle, Patti **13, 30**
Langhart, Janet **19**
Lathan, Sanaa **27**
Lawrence, Martin **6, 27**
Lawson, Jennifer **1**
Lemmons, Kasi **20**
Lewis, Ananda **28**
Lewis, Byron E. **13**
Lewis, Emmanuel **36**
Lil' Kim **28**
Lindo, Delroy **18, 45**
LisaRaye **27**
Lofton, James **42**
Long, Nia **17**
Lover, Ed **10**
Lumbly, Carl **47**

Mabrey, Vicki 26
Mabuza-Suttle, Felicia 43
Mac, Bernie 29
Madison, Paula 37
Martin, Helen 31
Martin, Jesse L. 31
Mathis, Greg 26
Mayo, Whitman 32
McDaniel, Hattie 5
McEwen, Mark 5
McKee, Lonette 12
McKenzie, Vashti M. 29
McKinney, Nina Mae 40
McQueen, Butterfly 6
Meadows, Tim 30
Mercado-Valdes, Frank 43
Merkerson, S. Epatha 47
Michele, Michael 31
Mickelbury, Penny 28
Miller, Cheryl 10
Mitchell, Brian Stokes 21
Mitchell, Russ 21
Mo'Nique 35
Mooney, Paul 37
Moore, Chante 26
Moore, Melba 21
Moore, Shemar 21
Morgan, Joe Leonard 9
Morris, Garrett 31
Morris, Greg 28
Morton, Joe 18
Mos Def 30
Moses, Gilbert 12
Moss, Carlton 17
Murphy, Eddie 4, 20
Muse, Clarence Edouard 21
Nash, Johnny 40
Neal, Elise 29
Nichols, Nichelle 11
Nissel, Angela 42
Norman, Christina 47
Norman, Maidie 20
Odetta 37
Onwurah, Ngozi 38
Payne, Allen 13
Peete, Holly Robinson 20
Perkins, Tony 24
Perry, Lowell 30
Perry, Tyler 40
Phifer, Mekhi 25
Pinkett Smith, Jada 10, 41
Pinkston, W. Randall 24
Price, Frederick K.C. 21
Price, Hugh B. 9
Quarles, Norma 25
Queen Latifah 1, 16
Ralph, Sheryl Lee 18
Randle, Theresa 16
Rashad, Ahmad 18
Rashad, Phylicia 21
Raven, 44
Ray, Gene Anthony 47
Reese, Della 6, 20
Reuben, Gloria 15
Ribeiro, Alfonso 17
Richards, Beah 30
Richardson, Donna 39
Roberts, Deborah 35
Roberts, Robin 16
Robinson, Max 3
Robinson, Shaun 36
Rochon, Lela 16
Rock, Chris 3, 22

Rodgers, Johnathan 6
Roker, Al 12
Rolle, Esther 13, 21
Rollins, Howard E., Jr. 16
Ross, Diana 8, 27
Ross, Tracee Ellis 35
Roundtree, Richard 27
Rowan, Carl T. 1, 30
Rowell, Victoria 13
Rudolph, Maya 46
Rupaul 17
Russell, Bill 8
Schultz, Michael A. 6
Scott, Stuart 34
Shaw, Bernard 2, 28
Simpson, Carole 6, 30
Simpson, O. J. 15
Sinbad 1, 16
Smiley, Tavis 20
Smith, Anjela Lauren 44
Smith, B(arbara) 11
Smith, Roger Guenveur 12
Smith, Will 8, 18
St. Jacques, Raymond 8
St. John, Kristoff 25
St. Patrick, Mathew 48
Stewart, Alison 13
Stokes, Carl B. 10
Stone, Chuck 9
Sykes, Wanda 48
Swann, Lynn 28
Tate, Larenz 15
Taylor, Karin 34
Taylor, Meshach 4
Taylor, Regina 9, 46
Thigpen, Lynne 17, 41
Thomas-Graham, Pamela 29
Thomason, Marsha 47
Torry, Guy 31
Toussaint, Lorraine 32
Townsend, Robert 4, 23
Tucker, Chris 13, 23
Tyler, Aisha N. 36
Tyrese 27
Tyson, Cicely 7
Uggams, Leslie 23
Underwood, Blair 7, 27
Union, Gabrielle 31
Usher 23
Van Peebles, Mario 2
Van Peebles, Melvin 7
Vereen, Ben 4
Walker, Eamonn 37
Ware, Andre 37
Warfield, Marsha 2
Warner, Malcolm-Jamal 22, 36
Warren, Michael 27
Warwick, Dionne 18
Washington, Denzel 1, 16
Wattleton, Faye 9
Watts, Rolonda 9
Wayans, Damon 8, 41
Wayans, Keenen Ivory 18
Wayans, Marlon 29
Wayans, Shawn 29
Weathers, Carl 10
Whack, Rita Coburn 36
Whitfield, Lynn 1, 18
Wilkins, Roger 2
Williams, Armstrong 29
Williams, Billy Dee 8
Williams, Clarence, III 26
Williams, Juan 35

Williams, Montel 4
Williams, Samm-Art 21
Williams, Vanessa 32
Williams, Vanessa L. 4, 17
Williamson, Mykelti 22
Wilson, Debra 38
Wilson, Flip 21
Winfield, Paul 2, 45
Winfrey, Oprah 2, 15
Witherspoon, John 38
Yoba, Malik 11

Theater
Adams, Osceola Macarthy 31
Ailey, Alvin 8
Alexander, Khandi 43
Allen, Debbie 13, 42
Amos, John 8
Anderson, Carl 48
Andrews, Bert 13
Angelou, Maya 1, 15
Arkadie, Kevin 17
Armstrong, Vanessa Bell 24
Babatunde, Obba 35
Baraka, Amiri 1, 38
Barrett, Lindsay 43
Bassett, Angela 6, 23
Beach, Michael 26
Beaton, Norman 14
Belafonte, Harry 4
Borders, James 9
Branch, William Blackwell 39
Brooks, Avery 9
Caldwell, Benjamin 46
Calloway, Cab 14
Cameron, Earl 44
Campbell, Naomi 1
Campbell, Tisha 8
Carroll, Diahann 9
Carroll, Vinnette 29
Carter, Nell 39
Cash, Rosalind 28
Cheadle, Don 19
Chenault, John 40
Childress, Alice 15
Clarke, Hope 14
Cleage, Pearl 17
Cook, Will Marion 40
Corthron, Kia 43
Curtis-Hall, Vondie 17
Dadié, Bernard 34
David, Keith 27
Davis, Ossie 5
Davis, Sammy, Jr. 18
Davis, Viola 34
Dee, Ruby 8
Devine, Loretta 24
Diggs, Taye 25
Dodson, Owen Vincent 38
Dourdan, Gary 37
Duke, Bill 3
Dunham, Katherine 4
Dutton, Charles S. 4, 22
Elder, Lonne, III 38
Emmanuel, Alphonsia 38
Esposito, Giancarlo 9
Europe, James Reese 10
Falana, Lola 42
Fishburne, Larry 4, 22
Franklin, J.E. 44
Freeman, Al, Jr. 11
Freeman, Morgan 2, 20
Freeman, Yvette 27

Fuller, Charles 8
Glover, Danny 1, 24
Glover, Savion 14
Goldberg, Whoopi 4, 33
Gordone, Charles 15
Gossett, Louis, Jr. 7
Graves, Denyce 19
Greaves, William 38
Grier, Pam 9, 31
Guillaume, Robert 3, 48
Gunn, Moses 10
Guy, Jasmine 2
Hansberry, Lorraine 6
Harris, Robin 7
Hayes, Teddy 40
Hemsley, Sherman 19
Hill, Dulé 29
Hill, Errol 40
Hines, Gregory 1, 42
Holder, Laurence 34
Holland, Endesha Ida Mae 3
Horne, Lena 5
Hyman, Earle 25
Hyman, Phyllis 19
Ingram, Rex 5
Jackson, Millie 25
Jackson, Samuel L. 8, 19
Jamison, Judith 7
Jean-Baptiste, Marianne 17, 46
Jones, James Earl 3
Jones, Sarah 39
Joyner, Matilda Sissieretta 15
King, Woodie, Jr. 27
King, Yolanda 6
Kitt, Eartha 16
Kotto, Yaphet 7
Lampley, Oni Faida 43
Lathan, Sanaa 27
La Salle, Eriq 12
Lee, Canada 8
Lemmons, Kasi 20
LeNoire, Rosetta 37
Leon, Kenny 10
Lester, Adrian 46
Letson, Al 39
Lincoln, Abbey 3
Lindo, Delroy 18, 45
Mabley, Jackie "Moms" 15
Marrow, Queen Esther 24
Martin, Helen 31
Martin, Jesse L. 31
McDaniel, Hattie 5
McDonald, Audra 20
McKee, Lonette 12
McQueen, Butterfly 6
Mickelbury, Penny 28
Mills, Florence 22
Milner, Ron 39
Mitchell, Brian Stokes 21
Mollel, Tololwa 38
Moore, Melba 21
Moses, Gilbert 12
Moss, Carlton 17
Moten, Etta 18
Muse, Clarence Edouard 21
Nicholas, Fayard 20
Nicholas, Harold 20
Norman, Maidie 20
Orlandersmith, Dael 42
Parks, Suzan-Lori 34
Payne, Allen 13
Perry, Tyler 40
Powell, Maxine 8

Premice, Josephine **41**
Primus, Pearl **6**
Ralph, Sheryl Lee **18**
Randle, Theresa **16**
Rashad, Phylicia **21**
Raven, **44**
Reese, Della **6, 20**
Rhames, Ving **14**
Richards, Beah **30**
Richards, Lloyd **2**
Richardson, Desmond **39**
Robeson, Paul **2**
Rolle, Esther **13, 21**
Rollins, Howard E., Jr. **16**
Rotimi, Ola **1**
Schultz, Michael A. **6**
Shabazz, Attallah **6**
Shange, Ntozake **8**
Smith, Anjela Lauren **44**
Smith, Anna Deavere **6, 44**
Smith, Roger Guenveur **12**
Snipes, Wesley **3, 24**
Soyinka, Wole **4**
St. Jacques, Raymond **8**
Talbert, David **34**
Taylor, Meshach **4**
Taylor, Regina **9, 46**
Taylor, Ron **35**
Thigpen, Lynne **17, 41**
Thompson, Tazewell **13**
Thurman, Wallace **16**
Toussaint, Lorraine **32**
Townsend, Robert **4, 23**
Tyson, Cicely **7**
Uggams, Leslie **23**
Underwood, Blair **7, 27**
Van Peebles, Melvin **7**
Vance, Courtney B. **15**
Vereen, Ben **4**
Walcott, Derek **5**
Walker, Eamonn **37**
Ward, Douglas Turner **42**
Washington, Denzel **1, 16**
Washington, Fredi **10**
Waters, Ethel **7**
Whitaker, Forest **2**
Whitfield, Lynn **18**
Williams, Bert **18**
Williams, Billy Dee **8**
Williams, Clarence, III **26**
Williams, Samm-Art **21**
Williams, Vanessa L. **4, 17**
Williamson, Mykelti **22**
Wilson, August **7, 33**
Winfield, Paul **2, 45**
Wolfe, George C. **6, 43**
Woodard, Alfre **9**

Writing
Abrahams, Peter **39**
Abu-Jamal, Mumia **15**
Achebe, Chinua **6**
Adams-Ender, Clara **40**
Aidoo, Ama Ata **38**
Ake, Claude **30**
Al-Amin, Jamil Abdullah **6**
Alexander, Margaret Walker **22**
Allen, Debbie **13, 42**
Allen, Robert L. **38**
Allen, Samuel W. **38**
Amadi, Elechi **40**
Ames, Wilmer **27**
Andrews, Raymond **4**

Angelou, Maya **1, 15**
Ansa, Tina McElroy **14**
Anthony, Michael **29**
Aristide, Jean-Bertrand **6, 45**
Arkadie, Kevin **17**
Asante, Molefi Kete **3**
Ashe, Arthur **1, 18**
Ashley-Ward, Amelia **23**
Atkins, Cholly **40**
Atkins, Russell **45**
Aubert, Alvin **41**
Auguste, Arnold A. **47**
Awoonor, Kofi **37**
Azikiwe, Nnamdi **13**
Ba, Mariama **30**
Baiocchi, Regina Harris **41**
Baisden, Michael **25**
Baker, Augusta **38**
Baker, Houston A., Jr. **6**
Baldwin, James **1**
Ballard, Allen Butler, Jr. **40**
Bambara, Toni Cade **10**
Bandele, Asha **36**
Baraka, Amiri **1, 38**
Barnett, Amy Du Bois **46**
Barrax, Gerald William **45**
Barrett, Lindsay **43**
Bass, Charlotta Spears **40**
Bates, Karen Grigsby **40**
Beals, Melba Patillo **15**
Bebey, Francis **45**
Beckham, Barry **41**
Bell, Derrick **6**
Bell, James Madison **40**
Bennett, George Harold "Hal" **45**
Bennett, Lerone, Jr. **5**
Benson, Angela **34**
Berry, James **41**
Berry, Mary Frances **7**
Beti, Mongo **36**
Bishop, Maurice **39**
Bland, Eleanor Taylor **39**
Blassingame, John Wesley **40**
Blockson, Charles L. **42**
Bluitt, Juliann S. **14**
Bolden, Tonya **32**
Bontemps, Arna **8**
Booker, Simeon **23**
Borders, James **9**
Boston, Lloyd **24**
Boyd, Gerald M. **32**
Bradley, David Henry, Jr. **39**
Bradley, Ed **2**
Branch, William Blackwell **39**
Brand, Dionne **32**
Brathwaite, Kamau **36**
Brawley, Benjamin **44**
Breeze, Jean "Binta" **37**
Bridges, Sheila **36**
Brimmer, Andrew F. **2, 48**
Briscoe, Connie **15**
Britt, Donna **28**
Brooks, Gwendolyn **1, 28**
Brown, Cecil M. **46**
Brown, Claude **38**
Brown, Elaine **8**
Brown, Les **5**
Brown, Llyod Louis **42**
Brown, Marie Dutton **12**
Brown, Sterling **10**
Brown, Tony **3**
Brown, Wesley **23**
Brutus, Dennis **38**

Bryan, Ashley F. **41**
Buckley, Gail Lumet **39**
Bullins, Ed **25**
Bunche, Ralph J. **5**
Bunkley, Anita Richmond **39**
Burroughs, Margaret Taylor **9**
Butler, Octavia **8, 43**
Bynum, Juanita **31**
Campbell, Bebe Moore **6, 24**
Carby, Hazel **27**
Carmichael, Stokely **5, 26**
Carroll, Vinnette **29**
Cartíer, Xam Wilson **41**
Carter, Joye Maureen **41**
Carter, Stephen L. **4**
Cartey, Wilfred **47**
Cary, Lorene **3**
Cary, Mary Ann Shadd **30**
Cayton, Horace **26**
Césaire, Aimé **48**
Chamberlain, Wilt **18, 47**
Channer, Colin **36**
Chase-Riboud, Barbara **20, 46**
Chenault, John **40**
Cheney-Coker, Syl **43**
Chesnutt, Charles **29**
Chideya, Farai **14**
Childress, Alice **15**
Christian, Barbara T. **44**
Clark, Kenneth B. **5**
Clark, Septima **7**
Clark-Bekedermo, J. P. **44**
Clarke, Austin C. **32**
Clarke, Cheryl **32**
Clarke, George **32**
Cleage, Pearl **17**
Cleaver, Eldridge **5**
Cliff, Michelle **42**
Clifton, Lucille **14**
Cobbs, Price M. **9**
Cohen, Anthony **15**
Cole, Johnnetta B. **5, 43**
Coleman, Wanda **48**
Colter, Cyrus J. **36**
Comer, James P. **6**
Cone, James H. **3**
Cook, Suzan D. Johnson **22**
Cooke, Marvel **31**
Coombs, Orde M. **44**
Cooper, Andrew W. **36**
Cooper, Anna Julia **20**
Cooper, J. California **12**
Cortez, Jayne **43**
Cosby, Bill **7, 26**
Cosby, Camille **14**
Cose, Ellis **5**
Cotter, Joseph Seamon, Sr. **40**
Couto, Mia **45**
Creagh, Milton **27**
Crouch, Stanley **11**
Cullen, Countee **8**
Cuney, William Waring **44**
Cunningham, Evelyn **23**
Curry, George E. **23**
Curtis, Christopher Paul **26**
Curtis-Hall, Vondie **17**
Dabydeen, David **48**
Dadié, Bernard **34**
Damas, Léon-Gontran **46**
Dandridge, Raymond Garfield **45**
Danticat, Edwidge **15**
Dash, Leon **47**
Davis, Allison **12**

Davis, Angela **5**
Davis, Charles T. **48**
Davis, Frank Marshall **47**
Davis, George **36**
Davis, Miles **4**
Davis, Nolan **45**
Davis, Ossie **5**
Dawkins, Wayne **20**
de Passe, Suzanne **25**
De Veaux, Alexis **44**
Delany, Martin R. **27**
Delany, Samuel R., Jr. **9**
DeLoach, Nora **30**
Dickey, Eric Jerome **21**
Diesel, Vin **29**
Diop, Cheikh Anta **4**
Dodson, Howard, Jr. **7**
Dodson, Owen Vincent **38**
Dove, Rita **6**
Draper, Sharon Mills **16, 43**
Driskell, David C. **7**
Driver, David E. **11**
Drummond, William J. **40**
Du Bois, David Graham **45**
Du Bois, W. E. B. **3**
DuBois, Shirley Graham **21**
Due, Tananarive **30**
Dumas, Henry **41**
Dunbar, Paul Laurence **8**
Dunbar-Nelson, Alice Ruth Moore **44**
Dunham, Katherine **4**
Dunnigan, Alice Allison **41**
Dyson, Michael Eric **11, 40**
Early, Gerald **15**
Edmonds, Terry **17**
Ekwensi, Cyprian **37**
Elder, Lonne, III **38**
Elliot, Lorris **37**
Ellison, Ralph **7**
Elmore, Ronn **21**
Emanuel, James A. **46**
Emecheta, Buchi **30**
Estes, Rufus **29**
Evans, Mari **26**
Fabio, Sarah Webster **48**
Fair, Ronald L. **47**
Fanon, Frantz **44**
Farah, Nuruddin **27**
Farrakhan, Louis **15**
Fauset, Jessie **7**
Feelings, Muriel **44**
Feelings, Tom **11, 47**
Fields, Julia **45**
Figueroa, John J. **40**
Files, Lolita **35**
Fisher, Antwone **40**
Fisher, Rudolph **17**
Fleming, Raymond **48**
Fletcher, Bill, Jr. **41**
Forbes, Calvin **46**
Ford, Clyde W. **40**
Ford, Nick Aaron **44**
Forman, James **7**
Forrest, Leon **44**
Fortune, T. Thomas **6**
Foster, Cecil **32**
Foster, Jylla Moore **45**
Franklin, John Hope **5**
Franklin, Robert M. **13**
Frazier, E. Franklin **10**
French, Albert **18**
Fuller, Charles **8**

Fuller, Hoyt 44
Gaines, Ernest J. 7
Gates, Henry Louis, Jr. 3, 38
Gayle, Addison, Jr. 41
Gaynor, Gloria 36
George, Nelson 12
Gibson, Althea 8, 43
Gibson, Donald Bernard 40
Giddings, Paula 11
Giovanni, Nikki 9, 39
Goines, Donald 19
Golden, Marita 19
Gomez, Jewelle 30
Graham, Lawrence Otis 12
Graham, Lorenz 48
Grant, Gwendolyn Goldsby 28
Greaves, William 38
Greenfield, Eloise 9
Greenlee, Sam 48
Greenwood, Monique 38
Griffith, Mark Winston 8
Grimké, Archibald H. 9
Guinier, Lani 7, 30
Guy, Rosa 5
Guy-Sheftall, Beverly 13
Haley, Alex 4
Hamblin, Ken 10
Hamilton, Virginia 10
Hansberry, Lorraine 6
Hare, Nathan 44
Harkless, Necia Desiree 19
Harper, Frances Ellen Watkins 11
Harper, Michael S. 34
Harrington, Oliver W. 9
Harris, Claire 34
Harris, Eddy L. 18
Harris, Jay 19
Harris, Leslie 6
Harris, Monica 18
Harrison, Alvin 28
Harrison, Calvin 28
Haskins, James 36
Hayden, Robert 12
Hayes, Teddy 40
Haywood, Gar Anthony 43
Head, Bessie 28
Heard, Nathan C. 45
Hearne, John Edgar Caulwell 45
Hemphill, Essex 10
Henderson, Stephen E. 45
Henries, A. Doris Banks 44
Henriques, Julian 37
Henry, Lenny 9
Henson, Matthew 2
Hercules, Frank 44
Hill, Donna 32
Hill, Errol 40
Hill, Leslie Pinckney 44
Hilliard, David 7
Hoagland, Everett H. 45
Hobson, Julius W. 44
Holland, Endesha Ida Mae 3
Holt, Nora 38
Holton, Hugh, Jr. 39
Hooks, Bell 5
Horne, Frank 44
Hrabowski, Freeman A. III 22
Hudson, Cheryl 15
Hudson, Wade 15
Hughes, Langston 4
Hull, Akasha Gloria 45
Hunter-Gault, Charlayne 6, 31
Hurston, Zora Neale 3

Iceberg Slim 11
Ifill, Gwen 28
Jackson, Fred James 25
Jackson, George 14
Jackson, Sheneska 18
Jarret, Vernon D. 42
Jasper, Kenji 39
Jenkins, Beverly 14
Joachim, Paulin 34
Joe, Yolanda 21
Johnson, Charles 1
Johnson, Charles S. 12
Johnson, Dwayne "The Rock" 29
Johnson, Georgia Douglas 41
Johnson, James Weldon 5
Johnson, John H. 3
Johnson, Linton Kwesi 37
Johnson, Mat 31
Johnson, R. M. 36
Jolley, Willie 28
Jones, Edward P. 43
Jones, Gayl 37
Jones, Orlando 30
Jones, Sarah 39
Jordan, June 7, 35
Josey, E. J. 10
July, William 27
Just, Ernest Everett 3
Kamau, Kwadwo Agymah 28
Karenga, Maulana 10
Kay, Jackie 37
Kayira, Legson 40
Kennedy, Adrienne 11
Kennedy, Florynce 12, 33
Kennedy, Randall 40
Khanga, Yelena 6
Kimbro, Dennis 10
Kincaid, Jamaica 4
King, Coretta Scott 3
King, Preston 28
King, Woodie, Jr. 27
King, Yolanda 6
Kitt, Sandra 23
Knight, Etheridge 37
Kobia, Rev. Dr. Samuel 43
Kotto, Yaphet 7
Kunjufu, Jawanza 3
Lacy, Sam 30, 46
Ladner, Joyce A. 42
Laferriere, Dany 33
LaGuma, Alex 30
Lamming, George 35
Lampley, Oni Faida 43
Larsen, Nella 10
Lawrence, Martin 6, 27
Lawrence-Lightfoot, Sara 10
Lemmons, Kasi 20
Lester, Julius 9
Letson, Al 39
Lewis, David Levering 9
Lewis, Samella 25
Lincoln, C. Eric 38
Little, Benilde 21
Locke, Alain 10
Lorde, Audre 6
Louis, Errol T. 8
Loury, Glenn 36
Mabuza-Suttle, Felicia 43
Madhubuti, Haki R. 7
Madison, Paula 37
Major, Clarence 9
Makeba, Miriam 2

Malveaux, Julianne 32
Manley, Ruth 34
Marechera, Dambudzo 39
Markham, E.A. 37
Marshall, Paule 7
Mason, Felicia 31
Massaquoi, Hans J. 30
Mathabane, Mark 5
Maynard, Robert C. 7
Mays, Benjamin E. 7
Mbaye, Mariétou 31
McBride, James 35
McCall, Nathan 8
McFadden, Bernice L. 39
McGruder, Robert 22, 35
McKay, Claude 6
McKinney-Whetstone, Diane 27
McMillan, Rosalynn A. 36
McMillan, Terry 4, 17
Memmi, Albert 37
Meredith, James H. 11
Mfume, Kweisi 6, 41
Micheaux, Oscar 7
Mickelbury, Penny 28
Milner, Ron 39
Mitchell, Loften 31
Mitchell, Russ 21
Mitchell, Sharon 36
Mofolo, Thomas Mokopu 37
Mollel, Tololwa 38
Monroe, Mary 35
Moore, Jessica Care 30
Morrison, Toni 2, 15
Mosley, Walter 5, 25
Moss, Carlton 17
Mossell, Gertrude Bustill 40
Moutoussamy-Ashe, Jeanne 7
Mowry, Jess 7
Mphalele, Es'kia (Ezekiel) 40
Mugo, Micere Githae 32
Mullen, Harryette 34
Murphy, John H. 42
Murray, Albert L. 33
Murray, Pauli 38
Mwangi, Meja 40
Myers, Walter Dean 8
Naylor, Gloria 10, 42
Neal, Larry 38
Nelson, Jill 6
Neto, António Agostinho 43
Newton, Huey 2
Nissel, Angela 42
Nkosi, Lewis 46
Nkrumah, Kwame 3
Nugent, Richard Bruce 39
Okara, Gabriel 37
Oliver, John J., Jr. 48
Onwueme, Tess Osonye 23
Orlandersmith, Dael 42
Owens, Major 6
Oyono, Ferdinand 38
Page, Clarence 4
Painter, Nell Irvin 24
Palmer, Everard 37
Parker, Pat 19
Parks, Suzan-Lori 34
Patterson, Orlando 4
Payne, Ethel L. 28
Peters, Lenrie 43
Petry, Ann 19
Philip, Marlene Nourbese 32
Poitier, Sidney 36
Poussaint, Alvin F. 5

Powell, Adam Clayton, Jr. 3
Powell, Kevin 31
Pressley, Condace L. 41
Prince-Bythewood, Gina 31
Pryor, Richard 3
Quarles, Benjamin Arthur 18
Rahman, Aishah 37
Randall, Alice 38
Randall, Dudley 8
Raspberry, William 2
Reagon, Bernice Johnson 7
Reddick, Lawrence Dunbar 20
Redding, J. Saunders 26
Redmond, Eugene 23
Reed, Ishmael 8
Rice, Condoleezza 3, 28
Richards, Beah 30
Riggs, Marlon 5
Ringgold, Faith 4
Robeson, Eslanda Goode 13
Rodman, Dennis 12
Rogers, Joel Augustus 30
Rotimi, Ola 1
Rowan, Carl T. 1, 30
Saint James, Synthia 12
Salih, Al-Tayyib 37
Sanchez, Sonia 17
Sanders, Dori 8
Sapphire 14
Saro-Wiwa, Kenule 39
Schomburg, Arthur Alfonso 9
Schuyler, George Samuel 40
Seale, Bobby 3
Sembène, Ousmane 13
Senghor, Léopold Sédar 12
Sengstacke, John 18
Senior, Olive 37
Shabazz, Attallah 6
Shabazz, Ilyasah 36
Shakur, Assata 6
Shange, Ntozake 8
Shaw, Bernard 2, 28
Shipp, E. R. 15
Simone, Nina 15, 41
Simpson, Carole 6, 30
Singleton, John 2, 30
Sister Souljah 11
Smiley, Tavis 20
Smith, Anna Deavere 6
Smith, B(arbara) 11
Smith, Barbara 28
Smith, Danyel 40
Smith, Jessie Carney 35
Smith, Mary Carter 26
Somé, Malidoma Patrice 10
Sowell, Thomas 2
Soyinka, Wole 4
Spencer, Anne 27
St. John, Kristoff 25
Staples, Brent 8
Stewart, Alison 13
Stone, Chuck 9
Tademy, Lalita 36
Talbert, David 34
Tate, Eleanora E. 20
Taulbert, Clifton Lemoure 19
Taylor, Kristin Clark 8
Taylor, Mildred D. 26
Taylor, Susan L. 10
Thomas-Graham, Pamela 29
Thurman, Howard 3
Tillis, Frederick 40
Tolson, Melvin 37

Toomer, Jean **6**
Touré, Askia (Muhammad Abu Bakr el) **47**
Townsend, Robert **4**
Trotter, Monroe **9**
Tucker, Cynthia **15**
Turner, Henry McNeal **5**
Turner, Tina **6, 27**
Tutu, Desmond **6**
Tutuola, Amos **30**
Tyree, Omar Rashad **21**
Tyson, Asha **39**
Tyson, Neil de Grasse **15**
Van Peebles, Melvin **7**
van Sertima, Ivan **25**
Vera, Yvonne **32**
Verdelle, A. J. **26**
wa Thiong'o, Ngugi **29**

Wade-Gayles, Gloria Jean **41**
Walcott, Derek **5**
Walker, Alice **1, 43**
Walker, Margaret **29**
Wallace, Michele Faith **13**
Wallace, Phyllis A. **9**
Ward, Douglas Turner **42**
Washington, Booker T. **4**
Washington, James, Jr. **38**
Washington, Laura S. **18**
Waters, Ethel **7**
Wattleton, Faye **9**
Wayans, Damon **8, 41**
Weaver, Afaa Michael **37**
Webb, Veronica **10**
Weems, Renita J. **44**
Wells-Barnett, Ida B. **8**
Wesley, Dorothy Porter **19**

Wesley, Valerie Wilson **18**
West, Cornel **5, 33**
West, Dorothy **12**
Whack, Rita Coburn **36**
Wharton, Clifton R., Jr. **7**
Whitaker, Mark **21, 47**
White, Walter F. **4**
Whitfield, Van **34**
Wideman, John Edgar **5**
Wiley, Ralph **8**
Wilkins, Roger **2**
Wilkins, Roy **4**
Williams, Armstrong **29**
Williams, Fannie Barrier **27**
Williams, George Washington **18**
Williams, John A. **27**
Williams, Juan **35**
Williams, Patricia J. **11**

Williams, Robert F. **11**
Williams, Samm-Art **21**
Williams, Saul **31**
Williams, Sherley Anne **25**
Williams, Stanley "Tookie" **29**
Wilson, August **7, 33**
Wilson, Mary **28**
Wilson, William Julius **22**
Winans, Marvin L. **17**
Wolfe, George C. **6, 43**
Woodson, Carter G. **2**
Worrill, Conrad **12**
Wright, Bruce McMarion **3**
Wright, Richard **5**
X, Marvin **45**
Yarbrough, Camille **40**
Young, Whitney M., Jr., **4**
Youngblood, Shay **32**

Cumulative Subject Index

A Better Chance
Lewis, William M., Jr. **40**

A Harvest Biotech Foundation International
Wambugu, Florence **42**

AA
See Alcoholics Anonymous

AAAS
See American Association for the Advancement of Science

Aaron Gunner series
Haywood, Gar Anthony **43**

AARP
Dixon, Margaret **14**

ABC
See American Broadcasting Company

Abstract expressionism
Lewis, Norman **39**

A. C. Green Youth Foundation
Green, A. C. **32**

Academy awards
Austin, Patti **24**
Freeman, Morgan **2, 20**
Goldberg, Whoopi **4, 33**
Gooding, Cuba, Jr. **16**
Gossett, Louis, Jr. **7**
Jean-Baptiste, Marianne **17, 46**
McDaniel, Hattie **5**
Poitier, Sidney **11, 36**
Prince **18**
Richie, Lionel **27**
Washington, Denzel **1, 16**
Wonder, Stevie **11**

Academy of Praise
Kenoly, Ron **45**

A cappella
Cooke, Sam **17**
Reagon, Bernice Johnson **7**

Access Hollywood
Robinson, Shaun **36**

ACDL
See Association for Constitutional Democracy in Liberia

ACLU
See American Civil Liberties Union

Acquired Immune Deficiency Syndrome (AIDS)
Ashe, Arthur **1, 18**
Broadbent, Hydeia **36**
Cargill, Victoria A. **43**
Gayle, Helene D. **3, 46**
Hale, Lorraine **8**
Johnson, Earvin "Magic" **3, 39**
Lewis-Thornton, Rae **32**
Mboup, Souleymane **10**
Moutoussamy-Ashe, Jeanne **7**
Norman, Pat **10**
Pickett, Cecil **39**
Riggs, Marlon **5, 44**
Satcher, David **7**
Seele, Pernessa **46**
Wilson, Phill **9**

Act*1 Personnel Services
Howroyd, Janice Bryant **42**

ACT-SO
See Afro-Academic Cultural, Technological, and Scientific Olympics

Acting
Aaliyah **30**
Adams, Osceola Macarthy **31**
Ailey, Alvin **8**
Alexander, Khandi **43**
Allen, Debbie **13, 42**
Amos, John **8**
Anderson, Carl **48**
Anderson, Eddie "Rochester" **30**
Angelou, Maya **1, 15**
Armstrong, Vanessa Bell **24**
Ashanti **37**
Babatunde, Obba **35**
Baker, Josephine **3**
Banks, Tyra **11**
Bassett, Angela **6, 23**
Beach, Michael **26**
Beals, Jennifer **12**
Beaton, Norman **14**
Beauvais, Garcelle **29**
Berry, Fred "Rerun" **48**
Berry, Halle **4, 19**
Blanks, Billy **22**
Blige, Mary J. **20, 34**
Borders, James **9**
Brady, Wayne **32**
Branch, William Blackwell **39**
Braugher, Andre **13**
Bridges, Todd **37**
Brooks, Avery **9**
Brown, Jim **11**
Caesar, Shirley **19**
Calloway, Cab **14**
Cameron, Earl **44**
Campbell, Naomi **1, 31**
Campbell-Martin, Tisha **8, 42**
Cannon, Nick **47**
Carroll, Diahann **9**
Carson, Lisa Nicole **21**
Carey, Mariah **32**
Cash, Rosalind **28**
Cedric the Entertainer **29**
Cheadle, Don **19**
Chestnut, Morris **31**
Childress, Alice **15**
Clarke, Hope **14**
Cliff, Jimmy **28**
Cole, Nat King **17**
Cole, Natalie Maria **17**
Coleman, Gary **35**
Combs, Sean "Puffy" **17, 43**
Cosby, Bill **7, 26**
Crothers, Scatman **19**
Curry, Mark **17**
Curtis-Hall, Vondie **17**
Dandridge, Dorothy **3**
David, Keith **27**
Davidson, Jaye **5**
Davis, Guy **36**
Davis, Ossie **5**
Davis, Sammy Jr. **18**
Davis, Viola **34**
Dee, Ruby **8**
Devine, Loretta **24**
Diesel, Vin **29**
Diggs, Taye **25**
DMX **28**
Dourdan, Gary **37**
Duke, Bill **3**
Duncan, Michael Clarke **26**
Dutton, Charles S. **4, 22**
Elise, Kimberly **32**
Emmanuel, Alphonsia **38**
Epps, Omar **23**
Esposito, Giancarlo **9**
Everett, Francine **23**
Falana, Lola **42**
Fields, Kim **36**
Fetchit, Stepin **32**
Fishburne, Larry **4, 22**
Fox, Rick **27**
Fox, Vivica A. **15**
Foxx, Jamie **15, 48**
Foxx, Redd **2**
Freeman, Al, Jr. **11**
Freeman, Morgan **2, 20**
Freeman, Yvette **27**
Gibson, Althea **8, 43**
Ginuwine **35**
Givens, Robin **4, 25**
Glover, Danny **1, 24**
Goldberg, Whoopi **4, 33**
Gooding, Cuba, Jr. **16**
Gordon, Dexter **25**
Gossett, Louis, Jr. **7**
Greaves, William **38**
Grier, David Alan **28**
Grier, Pam **9, 31**
Guillaume, Robert **3, 48**
Gunn, Moses **10**
Guy, Jasmine **2**
Hammer, M. C. **20**
Hammond, Fred **23**
Hardison, Kadeem **22**
Harper, Hill **32**
Harris, Robin **7**
Harvey, Steve **18**
Hawkins, Screamin' Jay **30**
Hayes, Isaac **20**
Haysbert, Dennis **42**
Hemsley, Sherman **19**
Henry, Lenny **9**
Hill, Dulé **29**
Hill, Lauryn **20**
Hines, Gregory **1, 42**
Horne, Lena **5**
Hounsou, Djimon **19, 45**
Houston, Whitney **7, 28**
Howard, Sherri **36**
Hughley, D.L. **23**
Hyman, Earle **25**
Ice Cube **8, 30**
Iman **4, 33**
Ingram, Rex **5**
Ja Rule **35**
Jackson, Janet **6, 30**
Jackson, Michael **19**
Jackson, Millie **25**
Jackson, Samuel L. **8, 19**
Jean-Baptiste, Marianne **17, 46**
Johnson, Dwayne "The Rock" **29**
Johnson, Rafer **33**
Johnson, Rodney Van **28**

205

Jones, James Earl 3
Jones, Orlando 30
Kennedy-Overton, Jayne Harris 46
King, Regina 22, 45
King, Woodie, Jr. 27
Kirby, George 14
Kitt, Eartha 16
Knight, Gladys 16
Knowles, Beyoncé 39
Kodhoe, Boris 34
Kotto, Yaphet 7
L. L. Cool J 16
LaBelle, Patti 13, 30
La Salle, Eriq 12
Lampley, Oni Faida 43
Lane, Charles 3
Lassiter, Roy 24
Lathan, Sanaa 27
Lawrence, Martin 6, 27
Lee, Canada 8
Lee, Joie 1
Lee, Spike 5, 19
Lemmons, Kasi 20
LeNoire, Rosetta 37
Lester, Adrian 46
Lewis, Emmanuel 36
(Lil') Bow Wow 35
Lil' Kim 28
Lincoln, Abbey 3
Lindo, Delroy 18, 45
LisaRaye 27
Love, Darlene 23
Lumbly, Carl 47
Mabley, Jackie "Moms" 15
Mac, Bernie 29
Marrow, Queen Esther 24
Martin, Helen 31
Martin, Jesse L. 31
Master P 21
Mayo, Whitman 32
McDaniel, Hattie 5
McDonald, Audra 20
Mckee, Lonette 12
McKinney, Nina Mae 40
McQueen, Butterfly 6
Meadows, Tim 30
Merkerson, S. Epatha 47
Michele, Michael 31
Mitchell, Brian Stokes 21
Mo'Nique 35
Moore, Chante 26
Moore, Melba 21
Moore, Shemar 21
Morris, Garrett 31
Morris, Greg 28
Morton, Joe 18
Mos Def 30
Moten, Etta 18
Murphy, Eddie 4, 20
Muse, Clarence Edouard 21
Nash, Johnny 40
Neal, Elise 29
Newton, Thandie 26
Nicholas, Fayard 20
Nicholas, Harold 20
Nichols, Nichelle 11
Norman, Maidie 20
Notorious B.I.G. 20
O'Neal, Ron 46
Orlandersmith, Dael 42
Payne, Allen 13
Peete, Holly Robinson 20
Perry, Tyler 40

Phifer, Mekhi 25
Pinkett Smith, Jada 10, 41
Poitier, Sidney 11, 36
Premice, Josephine 41
Prince 18
Pryor, Richard 3, 24
Queen Latifah 1, 16
Randle, Theresa 16
Rashad, Phylicia 21
Raven, 44
Ray, Gene Anthony 47
Reese, Della 6, 20
Reuben, Gloria 15
Rhames, Ving 14
Rhymes, Busta 31
Ribeiro, Alfonso 17
Richards, Beah 30
Richards, Lloyd 2
Robeson, Paul 2
Robinson, Shaun 36
Rock, Chris 3, 22
Rodgers, Rod 36
Rolle, Esther 13, 21
Ross, Diana 8, 27
Ross, Tracee Ellis 35
Roundtree, Richard 27
Rowell, Victoria 13
Rudolph, Maya 46
Shakur, Tupac 14
Sinbad 1, 16
Sisqo 30
Smith, Anjela Lauren 44
Smith, Anna Deavere 6, 44
Smith, Barbara 11
Smith, Roger Guenveur 12
Smith, Will 8, 18
Snipes, Wesley 3, 24
Snoop Dogg 35
St. Jacques, Raymond 8
St. John, Kristoff 25
St. Patrick, Mathew 48
Tamia 24
Tate, Larenz 15
Taylor, Meshach 4
Taylor, Regina 9, 46
Taylor, Ron 35
Thomas, Sean Patrick 35
Thomason, Marsha 47
Thompson, Tazewell 13
Torry, Guy 31
Toussaint, Lorraine 32
Townsend, Robert 4, 23
Tucker, Chris 13, 23
Turner, Tina 6, 27
Tyler, Aisha N. 36
Tyrese 27
Tyson, Cicely 7
Uggams, Leslie 23
Underwood, Blair 7, 27
Union, Gabrielle 31
Usher 23
Van Peebles, Mario 2
Van Peebles, Melvin 7
Vance, Courtney B. 15
Vereen, Ben 4
Walker, Eamonn 37
Ward, Douglas Turner 42
Warfield, Marsha 2
Warner, Malcolm-Jamal 22, 36
Warren, Michael 27
Washington, Denzel 1, 16
Washington, Fredi 10
Washington, Kerry 46

Waters, Ethel 7
Wayans, Damon 8, 41
Wayans, Keenen Ivory 18
Wayans, Marlon 29
Wayans, Shawn 29
Weathers, Carl 10
Webb, Veronica 10
Whitaker, Forest 2
Whitfield, Lynn 18
Williams, Bert 18
Williams, Billy Dee 8
Williams, Clarence, III 26
Williams, Joe 5, 25
Williams, Samm-Art 21
Williams, Saul 31
Williams, Vanessa 32
Williams, Vanessa L. 4, 17
Williamson, Mykelti 22
Wilson, Debra 38
Wilson, Flip 21
Winfield, Paul 2, 45
Winfrey, Oprah 2, 15
Witherspoon, John 38
Woodard, Alfre 9
Yoba, Malik 11

Active Ministers Engaged in Nurturance (AMEN)
King, Bernice 4

Actors Equity Association
Lewis, Emmanuel 36

Actuarial science
Hill, Jessie, Jr. 13

ACT UP
See AIDS Coalition to Unleash Power

Acustar, Inc.
Farmer, Forest 1

ADC
See Agricultural Development Council

Addiction Research and Treatment Corporation
Cooper, Andrew W. 36

Adoption and foster care
Baker, Josephine 3
Clements, George 2
Gossett, Louis, Jr. 7
Hale, Clara 16
Hale, Lorraine 8
Oglesby, Zena 12

Adventures in Movement (AIM)
Morgan, Joe Leonard 9

Advertising
Barboza, Anthony 10
Burrell, Thomas J. 21
Campbell, E. Simms 13
Chisholm, Samuel J. 32
Coleman, Donald A. 24
Johnson, Beverly 2
Jones, Caroline R. 29
Jordan, Montell 23
Lewis, Byron E. 13
Mingo, Frank 32
Olden, Georg(e) 44
Pinderhughes, John 47

Roche, Joyce M. 17

Advocates Scene
Seale, Bobby 3

AFCEA
See Armed Forces Communications and Electronics Associations

Affirmative action
Arnwine, Barbara 28
Berry, Mary Frances 7
Carter, Stephen L. 4
Edley, Christopher F., Jr. 48
Higginbotham, A. Leon Jr. 13, 25
Maynard, Robert C. 7
Norton, Eleanor Holmes 7
Rand, A. Barry 6
Thompson, Bennie G. 26
Waters, Maxine 3

AFL-CIO
See American Federation of Labor and Congress of Industrial Organizations

African/African-American Summit
Sullivan, Leon H. 3, 30

African American Catholic Congregation
Stallings, George A., Jr. 6

African American Dance Ensemble
Davis, Chuck 33

African American folklore
Bailey, Xenobia 11
Brown, Sterling 10
Driskell, David C. 7
Ellison, Ralph 7
Gaines, Ernest J. 7
Hamilton, Virginia 10
Hughes, Langston 4
Hurston, Zora Neale 3
Lester, Julius 9
Morrison, Toni 2, 15
Primus, Pearl 6
Tillman, George, Jr. 20
Williams, Bert 18
Yarbrough, Camille 40

African American folk music
Cuney, William Waring 44
Handy, W. C. 8
House, Son 8
Johnson, James Weldon 5
Lester, Julius 9

African American history
Angelou, Maya 1, 15
Ashe, Arthur 1, 18
Bennett, Lerone, Jr. 5
Berry, Mary Frances 7
Blockson, Charles L. 42
Burroughs, Margaret Taylor 9
Camp, Kimberly 19
Chase-Riboud, Barbara 20, 46
Cheadle, Don 19
Clarke, John Henrik 20
Coombs, Orde M. 44
Cooper, Anna Julia 20
Dodson, Howard, Jr. 7
Douglas, Aaron 7

Du Bois, W. E. B. **3**
DuBois, Shirley Graham **21**
Dyson, Michael Eric **11, 40**
Feelings, Tom **11, 47**
Franklin, John Hope **5**
Gaines, Ernest J. **7**
Gates, Henry Louis, Jr. **3, 38**
Haley, Alex **4**
Harkless, Necia Desiree **19**
Hine, Darlene Clark **24**
Hughes, Langston **4**
Johnson, James Weldon **5**
Jones, Edward P. **43**
Lewis, David Levering **9**
Madhubuti, Haki R. **7**
Marable, Manning **10**
Morrison, Toni **2**
Painter, Nell Irvin **24**
Pritchard, Robert Starling **21**
Quarles, Benjamin Arthur **18**
Reagon, Bernice Johnson **7**
Ringgold, Faith **4**
Schomburg, Arthur Alfonso **9**
Wilson, August **7, 33**
Woodson, Carter G. **2**
Yarbrough, Camille **40**

African American Images
Kunjufu, Jawanza **3**

African American literature
Andrews, Raymond **4**
Angelou, Maya **1, 15**
Baisden, Michael **25**
Baker, Houston A., Jr. **6**
Baldwin, James **1**
Bambara, Toni Cade **1**
Baraka, Amiri **1, 38**
Bennett, George Harold "Hal" **45**
Bontemps, Arna **8**
Briscoe, Connie **15**
Brooks, Gwendolyn **1, 28**
Brown, Claude **38**
Brown, Wesley **23**
Burroughs, Margaret Taylor **9**
Campbell, Bebe Moore **6, 24**
Cary, Lorene **3**
Childress, Alice **15**
Cleage, Pearl **17**
Cullen, Countee **8**
Curtis, Christopher Paul **26**
Davis, Arthur P. **41**
Davis, Nolan **45**
Dickey, Eric Jerome **21**
Dove, Rita **6**
Du Bois, W. E. B. **3**
Dunbar, Paul Laurence **8**
Ellison, Ralph **7**
Evans, Mari **26**
Fair, Ronald L. **47**
Fauset, Jessie **7**
Feelings, Tom **11, 47**
Fisher, Rudolph **17**
Ford, Nick Aaron **44**
Fuller, Charles **8**
Gaines, Ernest J. **7**
Gates, Henry Louis, Jr. **3, 38**
Gayle, Addison, Jr. **41**
Gibson, Donald Bernard **40**
Giddings, Paula **11**
Giovanni, Nikki **9, 39**
Goines, Donald **19**
Golden, Marita **19**
Guy, Rosa **5**
Haley, Alex **4**
Hansberry, Lorraine **6**
Harper, Frances Ellen Watkins **11**
Heard, Nathan C. **45**
Himes, Chester **8**
Holland, Endesha Ida Mae **3**
Hughes, Langston **4**
Hull, Akasha Gloria **45**
Hurston, Zora Neale **3**
Iceberg Slim **11**
Joe, Yolanda **21**
Johnson, Charles **1**
Johnson, James Weldon **5**
Jones, Gayl **37**
Jordan, June **7, 35**
July, William **27**
Kitt, Sandra **23**
Larsen, Nella **10**
Lester, Julius **9**
Little, Benilde **21**
Lorde, Audre **6**
Madhubuti, Haki R. **7**
Major, Clarence **9**
Marshall, Paule **7**
McKay, Claude **6**
McKay, Nellie Yvonne **17**
McKinney-Whetstone, Diane **27**
McMillan, Terry **4, 17**
Morrison, Toni **2, 15**
Mowry, Jess **7**
Naylor, Gloria **10, 42**
Painter, Nell Irvin **24**
Petry, Ann **19**
Pinkney, Jerry **15**
Rahman, Aishah **37**
Randall, Dudley **8**
Redding, J. Saunders **26**
Redmond, Eugene **23**
Reed, Ishmael **8**
Ringgold, Faith **4**
Sanchez, Sonia **17**
Schomburg, Arthur Alfonso **9**
Schuyler, George Samuel **40**
Shange, Ntozake **8**
Smith, Mary Carter **26**
Taylor, Mildred D. **26**
Thurman, Wallace **16**
Toomer, Jean **6**
Tyree, Omar Rashad **21**
Van Peebles, Melvin **7**
Verdelle, A. J. **26**
Walker, Alice **1, 43**
Wesley, Valerie Wilson **18**
Wideman, John Edgar **5**
Williams, John A. **27**
Williams, Sherley Anne **25**
Wilson, August **7, 33**
Wolfe, George C. **6, 43**
Wright, Richard **5**
Yarbrough, Camille **40**

African American studies
Brawley, Benjamin **44**
Carby, Hazel **27**
Christian, Barbara T. **44**
De Veaux, Alexis **44**
Ford, Nick Aaron **44**
Hare, Nathan **44**
Henderson, Stephen E. **45**

African Canadian literature
Elliott, Lorris **37**
Foster, Cecil **32**
Senior, Olive **37**

African Continental Telecommunications Ltd.
Sutton, Percy E. **42**

African dance
Ailey, Alvin **8**
Davis, Chuck **33**
Fagan, Garth **18**
Primus, Pearl **6**

African music
Ade, King Sunny **41**
Fela **1, 42**
Kuti, Femi **47**
Makeba, Miriam **2**
Nascimento, Milton **2**

African Heritage Network
See The Heritage Network

African history
Chase-Riboud, Barbara **20, 46**
Clarke, John Henrik **20**
Diop, Cheikh Anta **4**
Dodson, Howard, Jr. **7**
DuBois, Shirley Graham **21**
Feelings, Muriel **44**
Hansberry, William Leo **11**
Harkless, Necia Desiree **19**
Henries, A. Doris Banks **44**
Jawara, Sir Dawda Kairaba **11**
Madhubuti, Haki R. **7**
Marshall, Paule **7**
van Sertima, Ivan **25**

African literature
Aidoo, Ama Ata **38**
Awoonor, Kofi **37**
Cartey, Wilfred 1992 **47**
Cheney-Coker, Syl **43**
Couto, Mia **45**
Dadié, Bernard **34**
Ekwensi, Cyprian **37**
Farah, Nuruddin **27**
Head, Bessie **28**
Kayira, Legson **40**
Memmi, Albert **37**
Mphalele, Es'kia (Ezekiel) **40**
Mwangi, Meja **40**
Oyono, Ferdinand **38**
Peters, Lenrie **43**
Salih, Al-Tayyib **37**

African Methodist Episcopal Church (AME)
Bryant, John R. **45**
Flake, Floyd H. **18**
McKenzie, Vashti M. **29**
Murray, Cecil **12, 47**
Shuttlesworth, Fred **47**
Turner, Henry McNeal **5**
Youngblood, Johnny Ray **8**

African National Congress (ANC)
Baker, Ella **5**
Hani, Chris **6**
Ka Dinizulu, Mcwayizeni **29**
Kaunda, Kenneth **2**
Luthuli, Albert **13**
Mandela, Nelson **1, 14**
Mandela, Winnie **2, 35**
Masekela, Barbara **18**
Mbeki, Thabo Mvuyelwa **14**
Nkomo, Joshua **4**
Nyanda, Siphiwe **21**
Nzo, Alfred **15**
Ramaphosa, Cyril **3**
Sisulu, Walter **47**
Tutu, Desmond Mpilo **6, 44**
Weems, Renita J. **44**
Zuma, Nkosazana Dlamini **34**

African Party for the Independence of Guinea and Cape Verde
Pereira, Aristides **30**

African Women on Tour conference
Taylor, Susan L. **10**

Afro-Academic Cultural, Technological, and Scientific Olympics
Jarret, Vernon D. **42**

Afro-American Dance Ensemble
Hall, Arthur **39**

Afro-American League
Fortune, T. Thomas **6**

Afro-American Newspaper Company
Murphy, John H. **42**

Afro-Beat music
Fela **1, 42**

Afrocentricity
Asante, Molefi Kete **3**
Biggers, John **20, 33**
Diop, Cheikh Anta **4**
Hansberry, Lorraine **6**
Hansberry, William Leo **11**
Sanchez, Sonia **17**
Turner, Henry McNeal **5**

Afro-Cuban music
Lefel, Edith **41**

Aftermath Entertainment
Dre, Dr. **14, 30**

Agency for International Development (AID)
Gayle, Helene D. **3, 46**
Perkins, Edward **5**
Wilkins, Roger **2**

A. G. Gaston Boys and Girls Club
Gaston, Arthur G. **4**

A. G. Gaston Motel
Gaston, Arthur G. **4**

Agricultural Development Council (ADC)
Wharton, Clifton R., Jr. **7**

Agriculture
Boyd, John W., Jr. **20**
Carver, George Washington **4**
Espy, Mike **6**
Hall, Lloyd A. **8**
Masire, Quett **5**
Obasanjo, Olusegun **5**

Sanders, Dori **8**
Wambugu, Florence **42**

AHA
See American Heart Association

AID
See Agency for International Development

AIDS
See Acquired Immune Deficiency Syndrome

AIDS Coalition to Unleash Power (ACT UP)
Norman, Pat **10**

AIDS Health Care Foundation
Wilson, Phill **9**

AIDS Prevention Team
Wilson, Phill **9**

AIDS research
Mboup, Souleymane **10**

AIM
See Adventures in Movement

Akwaaba Mansion Bed & Breakfast
Greenwood, Monique **38**

ALA
See American Library Association

Alabama state government
Davis, Artur **41**
Gray, Fred **37**

Alamerica Bank
Watkins, Donald **35**

Alcoholics Anonymous (AA)
Hilliard, David **7**
Lucas, John **7**

All Afrikan People's Revolutionary Party
Carmichael, Stokely **5, 26**
Moses, Robert Parris **11**

Alliance for Children
McMurray, Georgia L. **36**

Alliance Theatre
Leon, Kenny **10**

Allied Arts Academy
Bonds, Margaret **39**

Alligator Records
Harris, Corey **39**

Alpha Kappa Alpha Sorority
White, Linda M. **45**

Alpha & Omega Ministry
White, Reggie **6**

Alvin Ailey American Dance Theater
Ailey, Alvin **8**
Clarke, Hope **14**
Dove, Ulysses **5**
Faison, George **16**
Jamison, Judith **7**
Primus, Pearl **6**
Rhoden, Dwight **40**
Richardson, Desmond **39**
Tyson, Andre **40**

Alvin Ailey Repertory Ensemble
Ailey, Alvin **8**
Miller, Bebe **3**

Amadou Diallo Foundation
Diallo, Amadou **27**

AMAS Repertory Theater
LeNoire, Rosetta **37**

Ambassadors
Braun, Carol Moseley **4, 42**
Cook, Mercer **40**
Dymally, Mervyn **42**
Watson, Diane **41**

AME
See African Methodist Episcopal Church

AMEN
See Active Ministers Engaged in Nurturance

American Academy of Arts and Sciences
Loury, Glenn **36**

American Art Award
Simpson, Lorna **4, 36**

American Association for the Advancement of Science (AAAS)
Cobb, W. Montague **39**
Massey, Walter E. **5, 45**
Pickett, Cecil **39**

American Association of University Women
Granville, Evelyn Boyd **36**

American Ballet Theatre
Dove, Ulysses **5**
Richardson, Desmond **39**

American Bar Association
Archer, Dennis **7, 36**
Thompson, Larry D. **39**

American Basketball Association (ABA)
Chamberlain, Wilt **18, 47**
Erving, Julius **18, 47**

American Beach
Betsch, MaVynee **28**

American Book Award
Baraka, Amiri **1, 38**
Bates, Daisy **13**
Bradley, David Henry, Jr. **39**
Clark, Septima **7**
Gates, Henry Louis, Jr. **3, 38**
Lorde, Audre **6**
Loury, Glenn **36**
Marshall, Paule **7**
Sanchez, Sonia **17**
Walker, Alice **1, 43**

American Broadcasting Company (ABC)
Christian, Spencer **15**
Goode, Mal **13**
Jackson, Michael **19**
Jones, Star **10, 27**
Joyner, Tom **19**
Mickebury, Penny **28**
Roberts, Robin **16**
Robinson, Max **3**
Simpson, Carole **6, 30**
Winfrey, Oprah **2, 15**

American Postal Worker's Union
Burrus, William Henry "Bill" **45**

American Cancer Society
Ashe, Arthur **1, 18**
Leffall, LaSalle, Jr. **3**
Riperton, Minnie **32**

American Choral Directors Association
Adams, Leslie **39**

American Civil Liberties Union (ACLU)
Baugh, David **23**
Murphy, Laura M. **43**
Murray, Pauli **38**
Norton, Eleanor Holmes **7**

American Composers Alliance
Tillis, Frederick **40**

American Communist Party
Patterson, Louise **25**

American Community Housing Associates, Inc.
Lane, Vincent **5**

American Counseling Association
Mitchell, Sharon **36**

American Dance Guild
Hall, Arthur **39**

American Economic Association
Loury Glenn **36**

American Enterprise Institute
Woodson, Robert L. **10**

American Express Company
Adams, Eula L. **39**
Chenault, Kenneth I. **4, 36**

American Express Consumer Card Group, USA
Chenault, Kenneth I. **4, 36**

American Federation of Labor and Congress of Industrial Organizations (AFL-CIO)
Fletcher, Bill, Jr. **41**
Randolph, A. Philip **3**

American Federation of Television and Radio Artists
Falana, Lola **42**
Fields, Kim **36**
Lewis, Emmanuel **36**
Daniels, Lee Louis **36**

American Guild of Organists
Adams, Leslie **39**

American Heart Association (AHA)
Cooper, Edward S. **6**
Richardson, Donna **39**

American Idol
Jackson, Randy **40**

American Institute for the Prevention of Blindness
Bath, Patricia E. **37**

American Library Association (ALA)
Franklin, Hardy R. **9**
Hayden, Carla D. **47**
Josey, E. J. **10**
McFadden, Bernice L. **39**
Rollins, Charlamae Hill **27**
Wedgeworth, Robert W. **42**

American Management Association
Cooper, Andrew W. **36**

American Negro Academy
Grimké, Archibald H. **9**
Schomburg, Arthur Alfonso **9**

American Negro Theater
Martin, Helen **31**

American Nuclear Society
Wilkens, J. Ernest, Jr. **43**

American Nurses' Association (ANA)
Kennedy, Adrienne **11**
Staupers, Mabel K. **7**

American Psychological Association
Anderson, Norman B. **45**
Mitchell, Sharon **36**

American Red Cross
Bullock, Steve **22**

American Red Cross blood banks
Drew, Charles Richard **7**

American Society of Magazine Editors
Curry, George E. **23**

American Tennis Association
Gibson, Althea **8, 43**
Peters, Margaret and Matilda **43**

American Writers Association
Schuyler, George Samuel **40**

America's Promise
Powell, Colin **1, 28**

Amistad Freedom Schooner
Pinckney, Bill **42**

Amos Fraser Bernard Consultants
Amos, Valerie **41**

Amsterdam News
Cooper, Andrew W. **36**
Holt, Nora **38**

ANA
See American Nurses' Association

ANC
See African National Congress

Angella Christie Sound Ministries
Christie, Angella **36**

Anglican church hierarchy
Tutu, Desmond Mpilo **6, 44**

Angolan government
dos Santos, José Eduardo **43**
Neto, António Agostinho **43**

Anheuser-Busch distribution
Cherry, Deron **40**

Anthropology
Asante, Molefi Kete **3**
Bunche, Ralph J. **5**
Cole, Johnnetta B. **5, 43**
Davis, Allison **12**
Diop, Cheikh Anta **4**
Dunham, Katherine **4**
Hansberry, William Leo **11**
Morrison, Toni **2, 15**
Primus, Pearl **6**
Robeson, Eslanda Goode **13**

Antoinette Perry awards
See Tony awards

APA
See American Psychological Association

Apartheid
Abrahams, Peter **39**
Ashe, Arthur **18**
Berry, Mary Frances **7**
Biko, Steven **4**
Brutus, Dennis **38**
Butler, Jonathan **28**
Howard, M. William, Jr. **26**
Ka Dinizulu, Mcwayizeni **29**
LaGuma, Alex **30**
Luthuli, Albert **13**
Makeba, Miriam **2**
Mandela, Nelson **1, 14**
Mandela, Winnie **2, 35**
Masekela, Hugh **1**
Mathabane, Mark **5**
Mbeki, Thabo Mvuyelwa **14**
Mbuende, Kaire **12**
McDougall, Gay J. **11, 43**
Mphalele, Es'kia (Ezekiel) **40**
Nyanda, Siphiwe **21**
Nzo, Alfred **15**
Ramaphosa, Cyril **3**
Ramphele, Maphela **29**
Robinson, Randall **7, 46**
Sisulu, Walter **47**
Sullivan, Leon H. **13, 30**
Tutu, Desmond Mpilo **6, 44**

Apollo Theater
Sims, Howard "Sandman" **48**
Sutton, Percy E. **42**

Apollo 13
Williams, O. S. **13**

APWU
American Postal Worker's Union

Arab-Israeli conflict
Bunche, Ralph J. **5**

ARCH
See Argonne National Laboratory-University of Chicago Development Corporation

Architecture
Adjaye, David **38**
Gantt, Harvey **1**
Johnson, Jeh Vincent **44**
Sklarek, Norma Merrick **25**
Williams, Paul R. **9**

Argonne National Laboratory
Massey, Walter E. **5, 45**
Quarterman, Lloyd Albert **4**

Argonne National Laboratory-University of Chicago Development Corporation (ARCH)
Massey, Walter E. **5, 45**

Ariel Capital Management
Rogers, John W., Jr. **5**
Hobson, Mellody **40**

Arista Records
Lattimore, Kenny **35**
Reid, Antonio "L.A." **28**

Arkansas Department of Health
Elders, Joycelyn **6**

Armed Forces Communications and Electronics Associations (AFCEA)
Gravely, Samuel L., Jr. **5**

Art history
Campbell, Mary Schmidt **43**

Arthritis treatment
Julian, Percy Lavon **6**

Artists for a Free South Africa
Woodard, Alfre **9**

ASALH
See Association for the Study of Afro-American Life and History

ASH
See Association for the Sexually Harassed

Assocation of Tennis Professionals (ATP)
Blake, James **43**

Association for Constitutional Democracy in Liberia (ACDL)
Sawyer, Amos **2**

Association for the Sexually Harassed (ASH)
Gomez-Preston, Cheryl **9**

Association for the Study of Afro-American Life and History (ASALH)
Dodson, Howard, Jr. **7**
Woodson, Carter G. **2**

Association of Volleyball Professionals (AVP)
Blanton, Dain **29**

Astronauts
Anderson, Michael P. **40**
Bluford, Guy **2, 35**
Bolden, Charles F., Jr. **7**
Gregory, Frederick D. **8**
Jemison, Mae C. **1, 35**
Lawrence, Robert H., Jr. **16**
McNair, Ronald **3**

Astrophysics
Carruthers, George R. **40**

Atco-EastWest
Rhone, Sylvia **2**

ATD Publishing
Tyson, Asha **39**

Athletic administration
Goss, Tom **23**
Littlpage, Craig **35**

Atlanta Association of Black Journalists
Pressley, Condace L. **41**

Atlanta Baptist College
See Morehouse College

Atlanta Beat
Scurry, Briana **27**

Atlanta Board of Education
Mays, Benjamin E. **7**

Atlanta Braves baseball team
Aaron, Hank **5**
Baker, Dusty **8, 43**
Justice, David **18**
McGriff, Fred **24**
Sanders, Deion **4, 31**

Atlanta Chamber of Commerce
Hill, Jessie, Jr. **13**

Atlanta City Council
Campbell, Bill **9**
Williams, Hosea Lorenzo **15, 31**

Atlanta city government
Campbell, Bill **9**
Franklin, Shirley **34**
Jackson, Maynard **2, 41**
Williams, Hosea Lorenzo **15, 31**
Young, Andrew **3, 48**

Atlanta Falcons football team
Anderson, Jamal **22**
Buchanan, Ray **32**
Sanders, Deion **4, 31**
Vick, Michael **39**

Atlanta Hawks basketball team
Silas, Paul **24**
Wilkens, Lenny **11**

Atlanta Life Insurance Company
Hill, Jessie, Jr. **13**

Atlanta Negro Voters League
Hill, Jessie, Jr. **13**

Atlanta Police Department
Brown, Lee Patrick **1, 24**
Harvard, Beverly **11**

Atlantic City city government
Usry, James L. **23**

Atlantic Records
Franklin, Aretha **11, 44**
Lil' Kim **28**
Rhone, Sylvia **2**

Atlanta World
Scott, C. A. **29**

ATP
See Association of Tennis Professionals

Audelco awards
Holder, Laurence **34**
Rodgers, Rod **36**

Aurelian Honor Society Award
Lewis, William M., Jr. **40**

Authors Guild
Davis, George **36**
Gayle, Addison, Jr. **41**
Schuyler, George Samuel **40**

Authors League of America
Abrahams, Peter **39**
Cotter, Joseph Seamon, Sr. **40**
Davis, George **36**
Gayle, Addison, Jr. **41**

Aviation
Brown, Jesse Leroy **31**
Brown, Willa **40**
Bullard, Eugene **12**
Coleman, Bessie **9**
McLeod, Gus **27**
Petersen, Frank E. **31**

AVP
See Association of Volleyball Professionals

"Back to Africa" movement
Turner, Henry McNeal **5**

Bad Boy Entertainment
Combs, Sean "Puffy" **17, 43**
Harrell, Andre **9, 30**
Notorious B.I.G. **20**

Ballet
Ailey, Alvin **8**
Allen, Debbie **13, 42**
Collins, Janet **33**
Dove, Ulysses **5**
Faison, George **16**
Johnson, Virginia **9**
Mitchell, Arthur **2, 47**
Nichols, Nichelle **11**
Parks, Gordon **1, 35**
Rhoden, Dwight **40**
Richardson, Desmond **39**
Tyson, Andre **40**

Balm in Gilead, The
Seele, Pernessa **46**

Baltimore city government
Schmoke, Kurt **1, 48**

Baltimore Black Sox baseball team
Day, Leon **39**

Baltimore Colts football team
Barnes, Ernie 16

Baltimore Elite Giants baseball team
Campanella, Roy 25
Day, Leon 39
Kimbro, Henry A. 25

Baltimore Orioles baseball team
Baylor, Don 6
Blair, Paul 36
Carter, Joe 30
Jackson, Reggie 15
Robinson, Frank 9

Banking
Boyd, T. B., III 6
Bradley, Jennette B. 40
Bridgforth, Glinda 36
Brimmer, Andrew F. 2, 48
Bryant, John 26
Chapman, Nathan A. Jr. 21
Chappell, Emma 18
Ferguson, Roger W. 25
Funderburg, I. Owen 38
Griffith, Mark Winston 8
Lawless, Theodore K. 8
Louis, Errol T. 8
Morgan, Rose 11
Parsons, Richard Dean 11
Utendahl, John 23
Walker, Maggie Lena 17
Watkins, Walter C. 24
Wright, Deborah C. 25

Baptist World Alliance Assembly
Mays, Benjamin E. 7

Baptist
Austin, Rev. Junius C. 44
Davis, Gary 41
Gomes, Peter J. 15
Jemison, Major L. 48
Jones, E. Edward, Sr. 45
Long, Eddie L. 29
Meek, Carrie 6
Meek, Kendrick 41

Barnett-Ader Gallery
Thomas, Alma 14

Baseball
Aaron, Hank 5
Anderson, Elmer 25
Ashford, Emmett 22
Baines, Harold 32
Baker, Dusty 8, 43
Banks, Ernie 33
Barnhill, David 30
Baylor, Don 6
Bell, James "Cool Papa" 36
Belle, Albert 10
Blair, Paul 36
Bonds, Barry 6, 34
Bonds, Bobby 43
Brock, Lou 18
Brown, Willard 36
Campanella, Roy 25
Carew, Rod 20
Carter, Joe 30
Charleston, Oscar 39
Clendenon, Donn 26
Coleman, Leonard S., Jr. 12
Cottrell, Comer 11
Dandridge, Ray 36
Davis, Piper 19
Doby, Lawrence Eugene 16
Day, Leon 39
Edwards, Harry 2
Fielder, Cecil 2
Flood, Curt 10
Gibson, Bob 33
Gibson, Josh 22
Gooden, Dwight 20
Gregg, Eric 16
Griffey, Ken, Jr. 12
Hammer, M. C. 20
Henderson, Rickey 28
Hunter, Torii 43
Hyde, Cowan F. "Bubba" 47
Irvin, Monte 31
Jackson, Reggie 15
Jenkins, Fergie 46
Jeter, Derek 27
Johnson, Mamie "Peanut" 40
Justice, David 18
Kaiser, Cecil 42
Kimbro, Henry A. 25
Lacy, Sam 30, 46
Lankford, Ray 23
Larkin, Barry 24
Lloyd, John Henry "Pop" 30
Lofton, Kenny 12
Mariner, Jonathan 41
Mays, Willie 3
McGriff, Fred 24
Morgan, Joe Leonard 9
Murray, Eddie 12
Newcombe, Don 24
O'Neil, Buck 19
Paige, Satchel 7
Payne, Ulice 42
Pride, Charley 26
Puckett, Kirby 4
Reese, Pokey 28
Robinson, Frank 9
Robinson, Jackie 6
Robinson, Sharon 22
Sanders, Deion 4, 31
Sheffield, Gary 16
Smith, Hilton 29
Sosa, Sammy 21, 44
Stargell, Willie 29
Stearnes, Norman "Turkey" 31
Stone, Toni 15
Strawberry, Darryl 22
Thomas, Frank 12
Vaughn, Mo 16
Virgil, Ozzie 48
Watson, Bob 25
White, Bill 1, 48
Winfield, Dave 5

Baseball Hall of Fame
Bell, James "Cool Papa" 36
Charleston, Oscar 39
Day, Leon 39
Doby, Lawrence Eugene Sr. 16, 41

Barbadian government
Arthur, Owen 33

Basketball
Abdul-Jabbar, Kareem 8
Abdur-Rahim, Shareef 28
Anthony, Carmelo 46
Barkley, Charles 5
Bing, Dave 3
Bol, Manute 1
Bolton-Holifield, Ruthie 28
Brand, Elton 31
Brandon, Terrell 16
Bryant, Kobe 15, 31
Carter, Butch 27
Carter, Vince 26
Catchings, Tamika 43
Chamberlain, Wilt 18, 47
Cheeks, Maurice 47
Clifton, Nathaniel "Sweetwater" 47
Cooper, Charles "Chuck" 47
Cooper, Cynthia 17
Cooper, Michael 31
Davis, Mike 41
Drexler, Clyde 4
Dumars, Joe 16
Duncan, Tim 20
Dunn, Jerry 27
Edwards, Harry 2
Edwards, Teresa 14
Ellerbe, Brian 22
Elliott, Sean 26
Ewing, Patrick A. 17
Fox, Rick 27
Freeman, Marianna 23
Garnett, Kevin 14
Gentry, Alvin 23
Gossett, Louis, Jr. 7
Green, A. C. 32
Griffith, Yolanda 25
Hardaway, Anfernee (Penny) 13
Hardaway, Tim 35
Haskins, Clem 23
Haynes, Marques 22
Heard, Gar 25
Hill, Grant 13
Holdsclaw, Chamique 24
Howard, Juwan 15
Hunter, Billy 22
Iverson, Allen 24, 46
James, LeBron 46
Johnson, Earvin "Magic" 3, 39
Johnson, Larry 28
Jones, Merlakia 34
Jones, Roy Jr. 22
Jordan, Michael 6, 21
Justice, David 18
Kelly, R. 18, 44
Lanier, Bob 47
Lennox, Betty 31
Leslie, Lisa 16
Lloyd, Earl 26
Lofton, Kenny 12
Lucas, John 7
Malone, Karl A. 18
Manigault, Earl "The Goat" 15
Master P 21
Miller, Cheryl 10
Miton, DeLisha 31
Mourning, Alonzo 17, 44
Mutombo, Dikembe 7
O'Neal, Shaquille 8, 30
Olajuwon, Hakeem 2
Parish, Robert 43
Peck, Carolyn 23
Phillips, Teresa L. 42
Pippen, Scottie 15
Richardson, Nolan 9
Richmond, Mitch 19
Rivers, Glenn "Doc" 25
Robertson, Oscar 26
Robinson, David 24
Russell, Bill 8
Silas, Paul 24
Smith, Tubby 18
Sprewell, Latrell 23
Stackhouse, Jerry 30
Stringer, C. Vivian 13
Swoopes, Sheryl 12
Thomas, Isiah 7, 26
Thompson, Tina 25
Unseld, Wes 23
Wallace, Perry E. 47
Webber, Chris 15, 30
Wilkens, Lenny 11
Williams, Natalie 31

Basketball Hall of Fame
Parish, Robert 43

Bass
Foster, George "Pops" 40

BBC
See British Broadcasting Company

BCALA
See Black Caucus of the American Library Association

BDP
See Botswana Democratic Party

Beach Volleyball America (BVA)
Blanton, Dain 29

Beale Streeters
Ace, Johnny 36
Bland, Bobby "Blue" 36
King, B.B. 7

Bear, Stearns & Co.
Fletcher, Alphonso, Jr. 16

Beatrice International
See TLC Beatrice International Holdings, Inc.

Bebop
Carter, Betty 19
Clarke, Kenny 27
Coltrane, John 19
Davis, Miles 4
Eckstine, Billy 28
Fitzgerald, Ella 8, 18
Gillespie, Dizzy 1
Gordon, Dexter 25
Hancock, Herbie 20
Hawkins, Coleman 9
Jackson, Milt 26
Parker, Charlie 20
Powell, Bud 24
Roach, Max 21
Vaughan, Sarah 13

Bechuanaland Protectorate Legislative Council
Masire, Quett 5

Beckham Publications Group Inc.
Beckham, Barry 41

Bedford-Stuyvesant Restoration Corporation
Thomas, Franklin A. 5

Bell of Pennsylvania
Gordon, Bruce S. **41**

Ben & Jerry's Homemade Ice Cream, Inc.
Holland, Robert, Jr. **11**

Bennett College
Cole, Johnnetta B. **5, 43**
Player, Willa B. **43**

Bessie award
Richardson, Desmond **39**

BET
See Black Entertainment Television

Bethann Management, Inc.
Hardison, Bethann **12**

Bethune-Cookman College
Bethune, Mary McLeod **4**
Joyner, Marjorie Stewart **26**

BFF
See Black Filmmaker Foundation

BGLLF
See Black Gay and Lesbian Leadership Forum

Big Easy Award
Adams, Johnny **39**

Billy Graham Evangelistic Association
Bell, Ralph S. **5**
Waters, Ethel **7**

Bing Steel, Inc.
Bing, Dave **3**
Lloyd, Earl **26**

Biology
Cobb, Jewel Plummer **42**
Pickett, Cecil **39**
Emeagwali, Dale **31**
Just, Ernest Everett **3**

Biotechnology
Wambugu, Florence **42**

Birmingham city government
Kincaid, Bernard **28**
Nunn, Annetta **43**

Birmingham police department
Nunn, Annetta **43**

Birth control
Elders, Joycelyn **6**
Williams, Maggie **7**

Bishop College
Cottrell, Comer **11**

Bismark Bisons baseball team
Dandridge, Ray **36**

BLA
See Black Liberation Army

Black Aesthetic
Baker, Houston A., Jr. **6**

Black Alliance for Educational Options
Fuller, Howard L. **37**

Black American West Museum
Stewart, Paul Wilbur **12**

Black Americans for Family Values
Foster, Ezola **28**

Black Academy of Arts & Letters
White, Charles **39**

Black and White Minstrel Show
Henry, Lenny **9**

Black arts movement
Barrett, Lindsay **43**
Caldwell, Benjamin **46**
Cortez, Jayne **43**
Donaldson, Jeff **46**
Dumas, Henry **41**
Gayle, Addison, Jr. **41**
Giovanni, Nikki **9, 39**
Hoagland, Everett H. **45**
Neal, Larry **38**
Smith, Vincent D. **48**
Touré, Askia (Muhammad Abu Bakr el) **47**
X, Marvin **45**

Black Cabinet
Hastie, William H. **8**

Black Caucus of the American Library Association (BCALA)
Josey, E. J. **10**

Black Christian Nationalist movement
Agyeman, Jaramogi Abebe **10**

Black Coaches Association (BCA)
Freeman, Marianna **23**

Black Consciousness movement
Biko, Steven **4**
Fanon, Frantz **44**
Fuller, Hoyt **44**
Muhammad, Elijah **4**
Ramaphosa, Cyril **3**
Ramphele, Maphela **29**
Tutu, Desmond Mpilo **6, 44**

Black culturalism
Karenga, Maulana **10**

Black Economic Union (BEU)
Brown, Jim **11**

Black Enterprise **magazine**
Brimmer, Andrew F. **2, 48**
Graves, Earl G. **1, 35**
Wallace, Phyllis A. **9**

Black Enterprise **Corporate Executive of the Year**
Chenault, Kenneth I. **5, 36**
Steward, David L. **36**

Black Entertainment Television (BET)
Ames, Wilmer **27**
Gordon, Ed **10**
Greely, M. Gasby **27**
Johnson, Robert L. **3, 39**
Johnson, Sheila Crump **48**
Jones, Bobby **20**
Smiley, Tavis **20**

Black Filmmaker Foundation (BFF)
Hudlin, Reginald **9**
Hudlin, Warrington **9**
Jackson, George **19**
Williams, Terrie **35**

Black Filmmakers Hall of Fame
McKinney, Nina Mae **40**

Black Gay and Lesbian Leadership Forum (BGLLF)
Wilson, Phill **9**

Black Guerrilla Family (BGF)
Jackson, George **14**

Black History Month
Woodson, Carter G. **2**

Black Horizons on the Hill
Wilson, August **7, 33**

Black Liberation Army (BLA)
Shakur, Assata **6**
Williams, Evelyn **10**

Black literary theory
Gates, Henry Louis, Jr. **3, 38**

Black Manifesto
Forman, James **7**

Black Music Center
Moore, Undine Smith **28**

Black Muslims
Abdul-Jabbar, Kareem **8**
Ali, Muhammad **2, 16**
Farrakhan, Louis **2**
Muhammad, Elijah **4**
Muhammed, W. Deen **27**
X, Malcolm **1**

Black nationalism
Baker, Houston A., Jr. **6**
Baraka, Amiri **1, 38**
Caldwell, Benjamin **46**
Carmichael, Stokely **5, 26**
Donaldson, Jeff **46**
Farrakhan, Louis **2**
Forman, James **7**
Garvey, Marcus **1**
Heard, Nathan C. **45**
Innis, Roy **5**
Muhammad, Elijah **4**
Turner, Henry McNeal **5**
X, Malcolm **1**

Black Oscar Awards
Daniels, Lee Louis **36**

Black Panther Party (BPP)
Abu-Jamal, Mumia **15**
Al-Amin, Jamil Abdullah **6**
Brown, Elaine **8**
Carmichael, Stokely **5**
Cleaver, Eldridge **5**
Cleaver, Kathleen Neal **29**
Davis, Angela **5**
Forman, James **7**
Hampton, Fred **18**
Hilliard, David **7**
Jackson, George **14**
Neal, Larry **38**
Newton, Huey **2**
Pratt, Geronimo **18**
Rush, Bobby **26**
Seale, Bobby **3**
Shakur, Assata **6**

Black Power movement
Al-Amin, Jamil Abdullah **6**
Baker, Houston A., Jr. **6**
Brown, Elaine **8**
Carmichael, Stokely **5, 26**
Dodson, Howard, Jr. **7**
Donaldson, Jeff **46**
Dumas, Henry **41**
Giovanni, Nikki **9, 39**
Hare, Nathan **44**
McKissick, Floyd B. **3**
Stone, Chuck **9**

Blackside, Inc.
Hampton, Henry **6**

Black theology
Cone, James H. **3**

Black Think Tank
Hare, Nathan **44**

Blackvoices.com
Cooper, Barry **33**

Black World **magazine**
See *Negro Digest* magazine

Black Writers Conference
McMillan, Rosalynn A. **36**

"Blood for Britain"
Drew, Charles Richard **7**

Blessed Martin House
Riley, Helen Caldwell Day **13**

Blood plasma research/preservation
Drew, Charles Richard **7**

Blues
Ace, Johnny **36**
Austin, Lovie **40**
Barnes, Roosevelt "Booba" **33**
Bland, Bobby "Blue" **36**
Brown, Charles **23**
Burns, Eddie **44**
Clarke, Kenny **27**
Collins, Albert **12**
Cox, Ida **42**
Cray, Robert **30**
Davis, Gary **41**
Davis, Guy **36**
Dixon, Willie **4**
Dorsey, Thomas **15**
Estes, Sleepy John **33**
Evora, Cesaria **12**
Freeman, Yvette **27**
Gaines, Grady **38**
Guy, Buddy **31**
Handy, W. C. **8**
Harris, Corey **39**
Hemphill, Jessie Mae **33**
Holiday, Billie **1**
Hooker, John Lee **30**
House, Son **8**

Howlin' Wolf **9**
Hunter, Alberta **42**
Jean-Baptiste, Marianne **17, 46**
Jackson, John **36**
James, Skip **38**
Johnson, Buddy **36**
King, B. B. **7**
Little Mitlon **36**
Little Walton **36**
Mahal, Taj **39**
Martin, Sara **38**
Mo', Keb' **36**
Moore, Johnny B. **38**
Muse, Clarence Edouard **21**
Neal, Raful **44**
Odetta **37**
Owens, Jack **38**
Parker, Charlie **20**
Peterson, James **38**
Reed, A. C. **36**
Reed, Jimmy **38**
Reese, Della **6, 20**
Robinson, Fenton **38**
Rogers, Jimmy **38**
Ross, Isaiah "Doc" **40**
Rush, Otis **38**
Smith, Bessie **3**
Smith, Mamie **32**
Smith, Trixie **34**
Staples, "Pops" **32**
Streeter, Sarah **45**
Sykes, Roosevelt **20**
Taylor, Koko **40**
Wallace, Sippie **1**
Washington, Dinah **22**
Waters, Ethel **7**
Waters, Muddy **34**
Watson, Johnny "Guitar" **18**
Webster, Katie **29**
Williams, Joe **5, 25**
Wilson, August **7, 33**

Blues Hall of Fame
Little Mitlon **36**

Blues Heaven Foundation
Dixon, Willie **4**

Blues vernacular
Baker, Houston A., Jr. **6**

Bobsledding
Flowers, Vonetta **35**
Hines, Garrett **35**
Jones, Randy **35**
Moses, Edwin **8**

Bodybuilding
Murray, Lenda **10**

Bola Press
Cortez, Jayne **43**

Bolero music
Ferrer, Ibrahim **41**

Boogie music
Brooks, Hadda **40**

Booker T. Washington Business College
Gaston, Arthur G. **4**

Booker T. Washington Insurance Company
Gaston, Arthur G. **4**

The Boondocks
McGruder, Aaron **28**

Boston Bruins hockey team
O'Ree, Willie **5**

Boston Celtics basketball team
Cooper, Charles "Chuck" **47**
Fox, Rick **27**
Parish, Robert **43**
Russell, Bill **8**
Silas, Paul **24**

Boston Collective
Crite, Alan Rohan **29**

Boston Red Sox baseball team
Baylor, Don **6**
Vaughn, Mo **16**

Boston University
Loury, Glenn **36**
Mitchell, Sharon **36**

Botany
Carver, George Washington **4**

Botswana Democratic Party (BDP)
Masire, Quett **5**
Mogae, Festus Gontebanye **19**

Bountiful Blessings magazine
Patterson, Gilbert Earl **41**

Boxing
Ali, Laila **27**
Ali, Muhammad **2, 16**
Bowe, Riddick **6**
Carter, Rubin **26**
Ellis, Jimmy **44**
Foreman, George **1, 15**
Frazier, Joe **19**
Frazier-Lyde, Jacqui **31**
Futch, Eddie **33**
Hearns, Thomas **29**
Holmes, Larry **20**
Holyfield, Evander **6**
Hopkins, Bernard **35**
Johnson, Jack **8**
Jones, Roy Jr. **22**
King, Don **14**
Lee, Canada **8**
Leonard, Sugar Ray **15**
Lewis, Lennox **27**
Louis, Joe **5**
Moorer, Michael **19**
Mosley, Shane **32**
Patterson, Floyd **19**
Robinson, Sugar Ray **18**
Steward, Emanuel **18**
Tyson, Mike **28, 44**
Whitaker, Pernell **10**

Boys Choir of Harlem
Turnbull, Walter **13**

BPP
See Black Panther Party

Brazeal Dennard Chorale
Dennard, Brazeal **37**

Brazilian Congress
da Silva, Benedita **5**

Breast Cancer awareness
Riperton, Minnie **32**

Breast Cancer Resource Committee
Brown, Zora Kramer **12**

Bridgforth Financial Management Group
Bridgeforth, Glinda **36**

Bristol Myers Squibb Inc.
Potter, Myrtle **40**

British Broadcasting Company (BBC)
Figueroa, John J. **40**

British Film Institute
Akomfrah, John **37**

British House of Commons
Abbott, Diane **9**
King, Oona **27**
Pitt, David Thomas **10**

British House of Lords
Amos, Valerie **41**
Pitt, David Thomas **10**

British Open golf tournament
Woods, Tiger **14, 31**

British Parliament
See British House of Commons

Broadcasting
Allen, Byron **3, 24**
Ashley, Maurice **15, 47**
Banks, William **11**
Barden, Don H. **9, 20**
Bradley, Ed **2**
Branch, William Blackwell **39**
Brown, Les **5**
Brown, Tony **3**
Brown, Vivian **27**
Brunson, Dorothy **1**
Clayton, Xernona **3, 45**
Cornelius, Don **4**
Davis, Ossie **5**
Elder, Larry **25**
Evans, Harry **25**
Figueroa, John J. **40**
Goode, Mal **13**
Gumbel, Bryant **14**
Gumbel, Greg **8**
Hamblin, Ken **10**
Hickman, Fred **11**
Hunter-Gault, Charlayne **6, 31**
Jackson, Hal **41**
Johnson, Rafer **33**
Johnson, Robert L. **3, 39**
Jones, Bobby **20**
Jones, Star **10, 27**
Joyner, Tom **19**
Kennedy-Overton, Jayne Harris **46**
Langhart, Janet **19**
Lawson, Jennifer **1**
Lewis, Delano **7**
Lofton, James **42**
Long, Eddie L. **29**
Mabrey, Vicki **26**
Madison, Joseph E. **17**
Madison, Paula **37**
McEwen, Mark **5**
Mickelbury, Penny **28**

Miller, Cheryl **10**
Mitchell, Russ **21**
Morgan, Joe Leonard **9**
Pinkston, W. Randall **24**
Quarles, Norma **25**
Roberts, Deborah **35**
Roberts, Robin **16**
Robinson, Max **3**
Rodgers, Johnathan **6**
Russell, Bill **8**
Shaw, Bernard **2, 28**
Simpson, Carole **6, 30**
Simpson, O. J. **15**
Smiley, Tavis **20**
Stewart, Alison **13**
Stokes, Carl B. **10**
Swann, Lynn **28**
Watts, Rolonda **9**
White, Bill **1, 48**
Williams, Armstrong **29**
Williams, Juan **35**
Williams, Montel **4**
Winfrey, Oprah **2, 15**

Broadside Press
Hoagland, Everett H. **45**
Randall, Dudley **8**

Bronner Brothers
Bronner, Nathaniel H., Sr. **32**

Brookings Institute
Ladner, Joyce A. **42**

Brooklyn Academy of Music
Miller, Bebe **3**

Brooklyn Dodgers baseball team
Campanella, Roy **25**
Newcombe, Don **24**
Robinson, Jackie **6**

Brooklyn Eagles baseball team
Day, Leon **39**

Brooks Bunch
Brooks, Derrick **43**

Brotherhood of Sleeping Car Porters
Randolph, A. Philip **3**
Tucker, Rosina **14**

Brown Capital Management
Brown, Eddie C. **35**

Brown University
Beckham, Barry **41**
Gibson, Donald Bernard **40**
Simmons, Ruth **13, 38**

Brown v. Board of Education of Topeka
Bell, Derrick **6**
Clark, Kenneth B. **5**
Franklin, John Hope **5**
Hill, Oliver W. **24**
Houston, Charles Hamilton **4**
Marshall, Thurgood **1, 44**
Motley, Constance Baker **10**
Redding, Louis L. **26**

Robinson, Spottswood W., III **22**

Buena Vista Social Club
Ferrer, Ibrahim **41**

Buffalo Bills football team
Lofton, James **42**
Simpson, O. J. **15**

Bull-riding
Sampson, Charles **13**

Bushi Designs
Rhymes, Busta **31**

Busing (anti-busing legislation)
Bosley, Freeman, Jr. **7**

BVA
See Beach Volleyball America

Cabinet
See U.S. Cabinet

Cable News Network (CNN)
Chideya, Farai **14**
Hickman, Fred **11**
Quarles, Norma **25**
Shaw, Bernard **2, 28**

Calabash International Literary Festival
Channer, Colin **36**

Calgary Flames hockey team
Iginla, Jarome **35**

California Angels baseball team
Baylor, Don **6**
Bonds, Bobby **43**
Carew, Rod **20**
Robinson, Frank **9**
Winfield, Dave **5**

California Eagle newspaper
Bass, Charlotta Spears **40**
Jackson, Vera **40**

California State Assembly
Brown, Willie L., Jr. **7**
Dixon, Julian C. **24**
Dymally, Mervyn **42**
Lee, Barbara **25**
Millender-McDonald, Juanita **21**
Waters, Maxine **3**

California state government
Brown, Janice Rogers **43**
Dymally, Mervyn **42**
Watson, Diane **41**

California State-Fullerton College
Cobb, Jewel Plummer **42**

California State University
Granville, Evelyn Boyd **36**

California Supreme Court
Brown, Janice Rogers **43**

Calypso
Belafonte, Harry **4**
Jean, Wyclef **20**

Premice, Josephine **41**

Camac Holdings, Inc.
Lawal, Kase L. **45**

Cameroon National Union (CNU)
Biya, Paul **28**

Cameroon People's Democratic Movement (CPDM)
Biya, Paul **28**

Cameroonian government
Oyono, Ferdinand **38**

Canadian Argicultural Chemistry Association
Donald, Arnold Wayne **36**

Canadian Football League (CFL)
Gilliam, Frank **23**
Moon, Warren **8**
Thrower, Willie **35**
Weathers, Carl **10**

Canadian Provincial baseball league
Kaiser, Cecil **42**

Cancer research
Chinn, May Edward **26**
Clark, Celeste **15**
Daly, Marie Maynard **37**
Dunston, Georgia Mae **48**
Freeman, Harold P. **23**
Leffall, LaSalle, Jr. **3**

Capital punishment
Hawkins, Steven **14**

Cardiac research
Watkins, Levi, Jr. **9**

CARE
Gossett, Louis, Jr. **7**
Stone, Chuck **9**

Caribbean Artists' Movement
Brathwaite, Kamau **36**

Caribbean dance
Ailey, Alvin **8**
Dunham, Katherine **4**
Fagan, Garth **18**
Nichols, Nichelle **11**
Primus, Pearl **6**

Caribbean literature
Breeze, Jean "Binta" **37**
Cartey, Wilfred 1992 **47**
Dabydeen, David **48**
Hearne, John Edgar Caulwell **45**

Caroline Jones Advertising, Inc
Jones, Caroline R. **29**

Catalyst Award (American Express)
Chenault, Kenneth I. **5, 36**

Cartoonists
Armstrong, Robb **15**
Brandon, Barbara **3**
Campbell, E. Simms **13**
Fax, Elton **48**

Harrington, Oliver W. **9**
McGruder, Aaron **28**

Catholicism
See Roman Catholic Church

CBEA
See Council for a Black Economic Agenda

CBC
See Congressional Black Caucus

CBS
See Columbia Broadcasting System

CBS Television Stations Division
Rodgers, Johnathan **6**

CDC
See Centers for Disease Control and Prevention

CDF
See Children's Defense Fund

CEDBA
See Council for the Economic Development of Black Americans

Celebrities for a Drug-Free America
Vereen, Ben **4**

Censorship
Butts, Calvin O., III **9**
Ice-T **6, 31**

Center of Hope Church
Reems, Ernestine Cleveland **27**

Centers for Disease Control and Prevention (CDC)
Gayle, Helene D. **3**
Satcher, David **7**

Central Intercollegiate Athletic Association (CIAA)
Kerry, Leon G. **46**
Yancy, Dorothy Cowser **42**

Certified Public Accountant
Jones, Thomas W. **41**

CFL
See Canadian Football League

CHA
See Chicago Housing Authority

Challenger
McNair, Ronald **3**

Challenger Air Pilot's Association
Brown, Willa **40**

Chama cha Mapinduzi (Tanzania; Revolutionary Party)
Mkapa, Benjamin **16**
Mongella, Gertrude **11**
Nyerere, Julius **5**

Chamber of Deputies (Brazil)
da Silva, Benedita **5**

Chanteuses
Baker, Josephine **3**
Dandridge, Dorothy **3**

Horne, Lena **5**
Kitt, Eartha **16**
Lefel, Edith **41**
Moore, Melba **21**
Moten, Etta **18**
Reese, Della **6, 20**

Charles H. Wright Museum of African American History (CWMAAH)
Wright, Charles H. **35**

Charles R. Drew University
Bath, Patricia E. **37**

Charlotte Hornets basketball team
Bryant, Kobe **15, 31**
Parish, Robert **43**

Charter Schools USA
Mariner, Jonathan **41**

Che-Lumumba Club
Davis, Angela **5**

Chemistry
Daly, Marie Maynard **37**
Hall, Lloyd A. **8**
Humphries, Frederick **20**
Julian, Percy Lavon **6**
Massie, Samuel Proctor Jr. **29**
Mays, William G. **34**
Mensah, Thomas **48**

Chemurgy
Carver, George Washington **4**

Chesapeake and Potomac Telephone Company
Lewis, Delano **7**

Chess
Ashley, Maurice **15, 47**

Chess Records
Taylor, Koko **40**

Chicago American Giants baseball team
Charleston, Oscar **39**

Chicago Art League
Wilson, Ellis **39**

Chicago Bears football team
Page, Alan **7**
Payton, Walter **11, 25**
Sayers, Gale **28**
Singletary, Mike **4**
Thrower, Willie **35**

Chicago Black Arts Movement
Cortor, Eldzier **42**
Sebree, Charles **40**

Chicago Blaze basketball team
Catchings, Tamika **43**

Chicago Bulls basketball team
Brand, Elton **31**
Jordan, Michael **6, 21**
Parish, Robert **43**
Pippen, Scottie **15**

Rodman, Dennis **12**, **44**

Chicago city government
Metcalfe, Ralph **26**
Washington, Harold **6**

Chicago Cubs baseball team
Baker, Dusty **8**, **43**
Banks, Ernie **33**
Bonds, Bobby **43**
Carter, Joe **30**
Sosa, Sammy **21**, **44**

Chicago Defender
Abbott, Robert Sengstacke **27**
Holt, Nora **38**
Payne, Ethel L. **28**

Chicago Defender Charities
Joyner, Marjorie Stewart **26**

Chicago Eight
Seale, Bobby **3**

Chicago American Giants baseball team
Bell, James "Cool Papa" **36**

Chicago Housing Authority (CHA)
Lane, Vincent **5**

Chicago Library Board
Williams, Fannie Barrier **27**

Chicago Negro Chamber of Commerce
Fuller, S. B. **13**

Chicago Police Department
Hillard, Terry **25**
Holton, Hugh, Jr. **39**

Chicago Reporter
Washington, Laura S. **18**

Chicago Tribune
Page, Clarence **4**

Chicago White Sox baseball team
Baines, Harold **32**
Bonds, Bobby **43**
Doby, Lawrence Eugene Sr. **16**, **41**
Thomas, Frank **12**

Chicago Women's Club
Williams, Fannie Barrier **27**

Child abuse prevention
Waters, Maxine **3**

Child Care Trust
Obasanjo, Stella **32**

Child psychiatry
Comer, James P. **6**

Child psychology
Hale, Lorraine **8**

Child Welfare Administration
Little, Robert L. **2**

Children's Defense Fund (CDF)
Edelman, Marian Wright **5**, **42**
Williams, Maggie **7**

Children's literature
Berry, James **41**
Bryan, Ashley F. **41**
De Veaux, Alexis **44**
Feelings, Muriel **44**
Graham, Lorenz **48**
Mollel, Tololwa **38**
Okara, Gabriel **37**
Palmer, Everard **37**
Yarbrough, Camille **40**

Chiropractics
Ford, Clyde W. **40**

Chisholm-Mingo Group, Inc.
Chisholm, Samuel J. **32**
Mingo, Frank **32**

Choreography
Ailey, Alvin **8**
Alexander, Khandi **43**
Allen, Debbie **13**, **42**
Atkins, Cholly **40**
Babatunde, Obba **35**
Beatty, Talley **35**
Brooks, Avery **9**
Byrd, Donald **10**
Campbell-Martin, Tisha **8**, **42**
Collins, Janet **33**
Davis, Chuck **33**
de Passe, Suzanne **25**
Dove, Ulysses **5**
Dunham, Katherine **4**
Ellington, Mercedes **34**
Fagan, Garth **18**
Faison, George **16**
Glover, Savion **14**
Hall, Arthur **39**
Henson, Darrin **33**
Jamison, Judith **7**
Johnson, Virginia **9**
Jones, Bill T. **1**
King, Alonzo **38**
Miller, Bebe **3**
Mitchell, Arthur **2**, **47**
Nicholas, Fayard **20**
Nicholas, Harold **20**
Primus, Pearl **6**
Rhoden, Dwight **40**
Richardson, Desmond **39**
Robinson, Cleo Parker **38**
Robinson, Fatima **34**
Rodgers, Rod **36**
Tyson, Andre **40**
Zollar, Jawole **28**

Christian Financial Ministries, Inc.
Ross, Charles **27**

Christian Science Monitor
Khanga, Yelena **6**

Chrysler Corporation
Colbert, Virgis William **17**
Farmer, Forest **1**
Richie, Leroy C. **18**

Church for the Fellowship of All Peoples
Thurman, Howard **3**

Church of God in Christ
Franklin, Robert M. **13**
Hayes, James C. **10**

Patterson, Gilbert Earl **41**

CIAA
See Central Intercollegiate Athletic Association

Cincinnati city government
Berry, Theodore M. **31**

Cincinnati Reds baseball team
Blair, Paul **36**
Larkin, Barry **24**
Morgan, Joe Leonard **9**
Reese, Pokey **28**
Robinson, Frank **9**
Sanders, Deion **4**, **31**

Cinematography
Dickerson, Ernest **6**, **17**

Citadel Press
Achebe, Chinua **6**

Citigroup
Gaines, Brenda **41**
Jones, Thomas W. **41**

Citizens Federal Savings and Loan Association
Gaston, Arthur G. **4**

Citizens for Affirmative Action's Preservation
Dillard, Godfrey J. **45**

City government--U.S.
Archer, Dennis **7**, **36**
Barden, Don H. **9**, **20**
Barry, Marion S. **7**, **44**
Berry, Theodore M. **31**
Bosley, Freeman, Jr. **7**
Bradley, Thomas **2**, **20**
Brown, Lee P. **1**, **24**
Burris, Chuck **21**
Caesar, Shirley **19**
Campbell, Bill **9**
Clayton, Constance **1**
Cleaver, Emanuel **4**, **45**
Craig-Jones, Ellen Walker **44**
Dinkins, David **4**
Dixon, Sharon Pratt **1**
Evers, Myrlie **8**
Fauntroy, Walter E. **11**
Fields, C. Virginia **25**
Ford, Jack **39**
Gibson, Kenneth Allen **6**
Goode, W. Wilson **4**
Harmon, Clarence **26**
Hayes, James C. **10**
Jackson, Maynard **2**, **41**
James, Sharpe **23**
Jarvis, Charlene Drew **21**
Johnson, Eddie Bernice **8**
Johnson, Harvey Jr. **24**
Kirk, Ron **11**
Mallett, Conrad, Jr. **16**
McPhail, Sharon **2**
Metcalfe, Ralph **26**
Millender-McDonald, Juanita **21**
Morial, Ernest "Dutch" **26**
Morial, Marc **20**
Powell, Adam Clayton, Jr. **3**
Powell, Debra A. **23**
Rice, Norm **8**
Sayles Belton, Sharon **9**, **16**
Schmoke, Kurt **1**, **48**

Stokes, Carl B. **10**
Street, John F. **24**
Usry, James L. **23**
Washington, Harold **6**
Webb, Wellington **3**
White, Michael R. **5**
Williams, Anthony **21**
Young, Andrew **3**, **48**
Young, Coleman **1**, **20**

City Sun newspaper
Cooper, Andrew W. **36**

City University of New York
Ballard, Allen Butler, Jr. **40**
Davis, George **36**
Gayle, Addison, Jr. **41**
Shabazz, Ilyasah **36**

Civic Progress
Steward, David L. **36**

Civil rights
Abbott, Diane **9**
Abernathy, Ralph **1**
Agyeman, Jaramogi Abebe **10**
Al-Amin, Jamil Abdullah **6**
Alexander, Clifford **26**
Ali, Muhammad **2**, **16**
Angelou, Maya **1**, **15**
Anthony, Wendell **25**
Aristide, Jean-Bertrand **6**, **45**
Arnwine, Barbara **28**
Baker, Ella **5**
Baker, Houston A., Jr. **6**
Baker, Josephine **3**
Ballance, Frank W. **41**
Bass, Charlotta Spears **40**
Bates, Daisy **13**
Baugh, David **23**
Beals, Melba Patillo **15**
Belafonte, Harry **4**
Bell, Derrick **6**
Bell, James Madison **40**
Bennett, Lerone, Jr. **5**
Berry, Mary Frances **7**
Berry, Theodore M. **31**
Biko, Steven **4**
Bishop, Sanford D. Jr. **24**
Bond, Julian **2**, **35**
Booker, Simeon **23**
Boyd, John W., Jr. **20**
Bradley, David Henry, Jr. **39**
Brown, Elaine **8**
Brown, Homer S. **47**
Brown, Tony **3**
Brown, Wesley **23**
Brown, Willa **40**
Burks, Mary Fair **40**
Campbell, Bebe Moore **6**, **24**
Carmichael, Stokely **5**, **26**
Carter, Mandy **11**
Carter, Rubin **26**
Carter, Stephen L. **4**
Cary, Mary Ann Shadd **30**
Cayton, Horace **26**
Chambers, Julius **3**
Chavis, Benjamin **6**
Clark, Septima **7**
Clay, William Lacy **8**
Cleaver, Eldridge **5**
Cleaver, Kathleen Neal **29**
Clyburn, James **21**
Cobb, W. Montague **39**

Cobbs, Price M. 9
Cooper, Anna Julia 20
Cosby, Bill 7, 26
Crockett, George, Jr. 10
Cunningham, Evelyn 23
Davis, Angela 5
Davis, Artur 41
Days, Drew S., III 10
Dee, Ruby 8
Diallo, Amadou 27
Diggs, Charles C. 21
Diggs-Taylor, Anna 20
Divine, Father 7
Dodson, Howard, Jr. 7
Du Bois, W. E. B. 3
Dumas, Henry 41
Edelman, Marian Wright 5, 42
Ellison, Ralph 7
Evers, Medgar 3
Evers, Myrlie 8
Farmer, James 2
Farmer-Paellmann, Deadria 43
Fauntroy, Walter E. 11
Fletcher, Bill, Jr. 41
Forman, James 7
Fortune, T. Thomas 6
Foster, Marie 48
Franklin, John Hope 5
Gaines, Ernest J. 7
George, Zelma Watson 42
Gibson, William F. 6
Gray, Fred 37
Gregory, Dick 1
Grimké, Archibald H. 9
Guinier, Lani 7, 30
Haley, Alex 4
Haley, George Williford Boyce 21
Hall, Elliott S. 24
Hamer, Fannie Lou 6
Hampton, Fred 18
Hampton, Henry 6
Hansberry, Lorraine 6
Harper, Frances Ellen Watkins 11
Harris, Patricia Roberts 2
Hastie, William H. 8
Hawkins, Steven 14
Hedgeman, Anna Arnold 22
Height, Dorothy I. 2, 23
Henderson, Wade J. 14
Henry, Aaron 19
Higginbotham, A. Leon Jr. 13, 25
Hill, Jessie, Jr. 13
Hill, Oliver W. 24
Hilliard, David 7
Hobson, Julius W. 44
Holland, Endesha Ida Mae 3
Hooks, Benjamin L. 2
Hooks, bell 5
Horne, Lena 5
Houston, Charles Hamilton 4
Howard, M. William, Jr. 26
Hughes, Langston 4
Innis, Roy 5
Jackson, Alexine Clement 22
Jackson, Jesse 1, 27
James, Daniel, Jr. 16
Jarret, Vernon D. 42
Johnson, Eddie Bernice 8
Johnson, Georgia Douglas 41
Johnson, James Weldon 5
Johnson, Norma L. Holloway 17
Johns, Vernon 38
Jones, Elaine R. 7, 45

Jordan, Barbara 4
Jordan, June 7, 35
Jordan, Vernon E. 3, 35
Julian, Percy Lavon 6
Kennedy, Florynce 12, 33
Kenyatta, Jomo 5
Kidd, Mae Street 39
King, Bernice 4
King, Coretta Scott 3
King, Martin Luther, Jr. 1
King, Martin Luther, III 20
King, Preston 28
King, Yolanda 6
Ladner, Joyce A. 42
Lampkin, Daisy 19
Lee, Spike 5, 19
Lester, Julius 9
Lewis, John 2, 46
Logan, Rayford W. 40
Lorde, Audre 6
Lowery, Joseph 2
Lucy Foster, Autherine 35
Makeba, Miriam 2
Mandela, Nelson 1, 14
Mandela, Winnie 2, 35
Martin, Louis E. 16
Mayfield, Curtis 2, 43
Mays, Benjamin E. 7
Mbeki, Thabo Mvuyelwa 14
McDonald, Gabrielle Kirk 20
McDougall, Gay J. 11, 43
McKissick, Floyd B. 3
Meek, Carrie 6
Meredith, James H. 11
Metcalfe, Ralph 26
Moore, Harry T. 29
Morial, Ernest "Dutch" 26
Morrison, Toni 2, 15
Moses, Robert Parris 11
Motley, Constance Baker 10
Mowry, Jess 7
Murphy, Laura M. 43
Murray, Pauli 38
Ndadaye, Melchior 7
Nelson, Jill 6
Newton, Huey 2
Nkomo, Joshua 4
Norman, Pat 10
Norton, Eleanor Holmes 7
Nunn, Annetta 43
Nzo, Alfred 15
Parker, Kellis E. 30
Parks, Rosa 1, 35
Patrick, Deval 12
Patterson, Louise 25
Patterson, Orlando 4
Perkins, Edward 5
Pinchback, P. B. S. 9
Player, Willa B. 43
Pleasant, Mary Ellen 9
Plessy, Homer Adolph 31
Poitier, Sidney 11, 36
Powell, Adam Clayton, Jr. 3
Price, Hugh B. 9
Ramaphosa, Cyril 3
Randolph, A. Philip 3
Reagon, Bernice Johnson 7
Redding, Louis L. 26
Riggs, Marlon 5, 44
Robeson, Paul 2
Robinson, Jackie 6
Robinson, Rachel 16
Robinson, Randall 7, 46

Robinson, Sharon 22
Robinson, Spottswood W. III 22
Rowan, Carl T. 1, 30
Rush, Bobby 26
Rustin, Bayard 4
Sané, Pierre Gabriel 21
Sanders, Malika 48
Saro-Wiwa, Kenule 39
Seale, Bobby 3
Shabazz, Attallah 6
Shabazz, Betty 7, 26
Shakur, Assata 6
Shinhoster, Earl 32
Shuttlesworth, Fred 47
Simone, Nina 15, 41
Sisulu, Sheila Violet Makate 24
Sleet, Moneta, Jr. 5
Smith, Barbara 28
Staupers, Mabel K. 7
Sullivan, Leon H. 3, 30
Sutton, Percy E. 42
Thompson, Bennie G. 26
Thurman, Howard 3
Till, Emmett 7
Trotter, Monroe 9
Tsvangirai, Morgan 26
Turner, Henry McNeal 5
Tutu, Desmond Mpilo 6, 44
Underwood, Blair 7
Washington, Booker T. 4
Washington, Fredi 10
Watt, Melvin 26
Weaver, Robert C. 8, 46
Wells-Barnett, Ida B. 8
Wells, James Lesesne 10
West, Cornel 5
White, Walter F. 4
Wideman, John Edgar 5
Wilkins, Roy 4
Williams, Evelyn 10
Williams, Fannie Barrier 27
Williams, Hosea Lorenzo 15, 31
Williams, Robert F. 11
Williams, Walter E. 4
Wilson, August 7, 33
Wilson, Sunnie 7
Wilson, William Julius 22
Woodson, Robert L. 10
X, Malcolm 1
Yoba, Malik 11
Young, Andrew 3, 48
Young, Jean Childs 14
Young, Whitney M., Jr. 4

Civilian Pilots Training Program
Brown, Willa 40

Classical music
Adams, Leslie 39
Baiocchi, Regina Harris 41
Bonds, Margaret 39
Brown, Uzee 42
Cook, Will Marion 40
Dawson, William Levi 39
DePriest, James 37
Dunner, Leslie B. 45
Freeman, Paul 39
Kay, Ulysses 37
Lewis, Henry 38
Moore, Dorothy Rudd 46
Murray, Tai 47
Pratt, Awadagin 31

Price, Florence 37
Sowande, Fela 39
Still, William Grant 37
Tillis, Frederick 40
Walker, George 37
Williams, Denise 40

Classical singers
Anderson, Marian 2, 33
Bumbry, Grace 5
Hayes, Roland 4
Hendricks, Barbara 3
Norman, Jessye 5
Price, Leontyne 1
Three Mo' Tenors 35
Williams, Denise 40

Clearview Golf Club
Powell, Renee 34

Cleo Parker Robinson Dance Ensemble
Robinson, Cleo Parker 38

Clergy
Anthony, Wendell 25
Austin, Junius C. 44
Black, Barry C. 47
Burgess, John 46
Caesar, Shirley 19
Cleveland, James 19
Cook, Suzan D. Johnson 22
Dyson, Michael Eric 11, 40
Gilmore, Marshall 46
Gomes, Peter J. 15
Gregory, Wilton 37
Howard, M. William, Jr. 26
Jakes, Thomas "T.D." 17, 43
James, Skip 38
Jemison, Major L. 48
Johns, Vernon 38
Kelly, Leontine 33
King, Barbara 22
Kobia, Rev. Dr. Samuel 43
Lincoln, C. Eric 38
Long, Eddie L. 29
McClurkin, Donnie 25
McKenzie, Vashti M. 29
Reese, Della 6, 20
Shuttlesworth, Fred 47
Tillard, Conrad 47
Weems, Renita J. 44
Winans, Marvin L. 17

Cleveland Browns football team
Brown, Jim 11
Hill, Calvin 19
Motley, Marion 26
Newsome, Ozzie 26

Cleveland Cavaliers basketball team
Brandon, Terrell 16
Wilkens, Lenny 11

Cleveland city government
Stokes, Carl B. 10
White, Michael R. 5

Cleveland Foundation
Adams, Leslie 39

Cleveland Indians baseball team
Belle, Albert 10
Bonds, Bobby 43

Carter, Joe 30
Doby, Lawrence Eugene Sr. 16, 41
Justice, David 18
Lofton, Kenny 12
Murray, Eddie 12
Paige, Satchel 7
Robinson, Frank 9

Cleveland Rockers basketball team
Jones, Merlakia 34

CLIO Awards
Lewis, Emmanuel 36

Clothing design
Bailey, Xenobia 11
Burrows, Stephen 31
Henderson, Gordon 5
John, Daymond 23
Jones, Carl 7
Kani, Karl 10
Kelly, Patrick 3
Lars, Byron 32
Malone, Maurice 32
Pinkett Smith, Jada 10, 41
Robinson, Patrick 19
Smith, Willi 8
Walker, T. J. 7

CNBC
Thomas-Graham, Pamela 29

CNN
See Cable News Network

CNU
See Cameroon National Union

Coaching
Ashley, Maurice 15, 47
Baker, Dusty 8, 43
Baylor, Don 6
Bickerstaff, Bernie 21
Bonds, Bobby 43
Campanella, Roy 25
Carew, Rod 20
Carter, Butch 27
Cheeks, Maurice 47
Cooper, Michael 31
Davis, Mike 41
Dungy, Tony 17, 42
Dunn, Jerry 27
Ellerbe, Brian 22
Freeman, Marianna 23
Gaither, Alonzo Smith (Jake) 14
Gentry, Alvin 23
Gibson, Althea 8, 43
Gibson, Bob 33
Green, Dennis 5, 45
Greene, Joe 10
Haskins, Clem 23
Heard, Gar 25
Lofton, James 42
Miller, Cheryl 10
O'Neil, Buck 19
Parish, Robert 43
Phillips, Teresa L. 42
Rhodes, Ray 14
Richardson, Nolan 9
Rivers, Glenn "Doc" 25
Robinson, Eddie G. 10
Russell, Bill 8
Shell, Art 1
Silas, Paul 24

Simmons, Bob 29
Smith, Tubby 18
Stringer, C. Vivian 13
White, Jesse 22
Williams, Doug 22
Willingham, Tyrone 43

Coca-Cola Company
Ware, Carl T. 30

Coca-Cola Foundation
Jones, Ingrid Saunders 18

COHAR
See Committee on Appeal for Human Rights

Collage
Andrews, Benny 22
Bearden, Romare 2
Driskell, David C. 7

College and University Administration
Archie-Hudson, Marguerite 44
Barnett, Marguerite 46
Burnim, Mickey L. 48
Christian, Barbara T. 44
Ford, Nick Aaron 44
Hill, Leslie Pinckney 44
Horne, Frank 44
Lee, Joe A. 45
Massey, Walter E. 5, 45

Colorado Rockies baseball team
Baylor, Don 6

Colorado state government
Rogers, Joe 27

Columbia Broadcasting System (CBS)
Bradley, Ed 2
Dourdan, Gary 37
Mabrey, Vicki 26
McEwen, Mark 5
Mitchell, Russ 21
Olden, Georg(e) 44
Pinkston, W. Randall 24
Rashad, Phylicia 21
Rodgers, Johnathan 6
Taylor, Meshach 4
Ware, Andre 37

Columbia Records
Carey, Mariah 32
Jackson, Randy 40
Olatunji, Babatunde 36
Williams, Deniece 36

Columbia Space Shuttle
Anderson, Michael P. 40

Columbus city government
Bradley, Jennette B. 40
Coleman, Michael 28

Comedy
Allen, Byron 3, 24
Amos, John 8
Anderson, Eddie "Rochester" 30
Beaton, Norman 14
Bellamy, Bill 12
Berry, Bertice 8
Brady, Wayne 32
Campbell-Martin, Tisha 8, 42

Cannon, Nick 47
Cedric the Entertainer 29
Cosby, Bill 7, 26
Curry, Mark 17
Davidson, Tommy 21
Davis, Sammy Jr. 18
Foxx, Jamie 15, 48
Foxx, Redd 2
Goldberg, Whoopi 4, 33
Gregory, Dick 1
Harris, Robin 7
Harvey, Steve 18
Henry, Lenny 9
Hughley, D.L. 23
Kirby, George 14
Lawrence, Martin 6, 27
Mabley, Jackie "Moms" 15
Mac, Bernie 29
Mayo, Whitman 32
McEwen, Mark 5
Meadows, Tim 30
Mo'Nique 35
Mooney, Paul 37
Moore, Melba 21
Morris, Garrett 31
Murphy, Eddie 4, 20
Pryor, Richard 3, 24
Rashad, Phylicia 21
Reese, Della 6, 20
Rock, Chris 3, 22
Schultz, Michael A. 6
Sinbad 1, 16
Smith, Will 8, 18
Sykes, Wanda 48
Taylor, Meshach 4
Torry, Guy 31
Townsend, Robert 4, 23
Tucker, Chris 13, 23
Tyler, Aisha N. 36
Warfield, Marsha 2
Wayans, Damon 8, 41
Wayans, Keenen Ivory 18
Wayans, Marlon 29
Wayans, Shawn 29
Wilson, Debra 38
Wilson, Flip 21
Witherspoon, John 38

Comer Method
Comer, James P. 6

Comic Relief
Goldberg, Whoopi 4, 33

Commercial art
Freeman, Leonard 27

Commission for Racial Justice
Chavis, Benjamin 6

Committee on Appeal for Human Rights (COHAR)
Bond, Julian 2, 35

Communist party
Brown, Llyod Louis 42
Davis, Angela 5
Du Bois, W. E. B. 3
Jagan, Cheddi 16
Wright, Richard 5

Complexions dance troupe
Rhoden, Dwight 40
Richardson, Desmond 39

Tyson, Andre 40

Computer graphics
Hannah, Marc 10

Computer science
Adkins, Rod 41
Auguste, Donna 29
Dean, Mark 35
Ellis, Clarence 38
Emeagwali, Philip 30
Hannah, Marc 10
Mensah, Thomas 48
Millines Dziko, Trish 28
Zollar, Alfred 40

Conceptual art
Allen, Tina 22
Bailey, Xenobia 11
Simpson, Lorna 4, 36

Concerned Black Men
Holder, Eric H., Jr. 9

Conductors
Cook, Will Marion 40
Dawson, William Levi 39
DePriest, James 37
Dunner, Leslie B. 45
Freeman, Paul 39
Jackson, Isaiah 3
Calloway, Cab 14
León, Tania 13
Lewis, Henry 38

Co-nect Schools
Fuller, Arthur 27

Congressional Black Caucus (CBC)
Christian-Green, Donna M. 17
Clay, William Lacy 8
Clyburn, James 21
Collins, Cardiss 10
Conyers, John, Jr. 4, 45
Dellums, Ronald 2
Diggs, Charles C. 21
Fauntroy, Walter E. 11
Gray, William H. III 3
Hastings, Alcee L. 16
Johnson, Eddie Bernice 8
Mfume, Kweisi 6, 41
Owens, Major 6
Payton, John 48
Rangel, Charles 3
Scott, Robert C. 23
Stokes, Louis 3
Thompson, Bennie G. 26
Towns, Edolphus 19

Congressional Black Caucus Higher Education Braintrust
Owens, Major 6

Congress of Racial Equality (CORE)
Dee, Ruby 8
Farmer, James 2
Hobson, Julius W. 44
Innis, Roy 5
Jackson, Jesse 1, 27
McKissick, Floyd B. 3
Rustin, Bayard 4

Connerly & Associates, Inc.
Connerly, Ward 14

Continental Basketball Association (CBA)
Davis, Mike 41
Thomas, Isiah 7, 26
Ussery, Terdema II 29

Convention People's Party (Ghana; CPP)
Nkrumah, Kwame 3

Cook County Circuit Court
Sampson, Edith S. 4

Cooking
Clark, Patrick 14
Estes, Rufus 29
Evans, Darryl 22

Coppin State College
Blair, Paul 36

Corbico
Corbi, Lana 42

CORE
See Congress of Racial Equality

Corporation for Public Broadcasting (CPB)
Brown, Tony 3

Coretta Scott King Awards
Haskins, James 36

Coronet
Oliver, Joe "King" 42

Cosmetology
Cottrell, Comer 11
Fuller, S. B. 13
Morgan, Rose 11
Powell, Maxine 8
Roche, Joyce M. 17
Walker, A'lelia 14
Walker, Madame C. J. 7

Cotton Club Revue
Johnson, Buddy 36

Council for a Black Economic Agenda (CBEA)
Woodson, Robert L. 10

Council for Social Action of the Congregational Christian Churches
Julian, Percy Lavon 6

Council for the Economic Development of Black Americans (CEDBA)
Brown, Tony 3

Council on Legal Education Opportunities (CLEO)
Henderson, Wade J. 14
Henry, Aaron 19

Count Basie Orchestra
Eldridge, Roy 37
Johnson, J.J. 37
Rushing, Jimmy 37
Williams, Joe 5, 25
Young, Lester 37

Country music
Bailey, DeFord 33
Pride, Charley 26

Randall, Alice 38

Covad Communications
Knowling, Robert 38

Cowboy
Love, Nat 9
Pickett, Bill 11

CPB
See Corporation for Public Broadcasting

CPDM
See Cameroon People's Democratic Movement

CPP
See Convention People's Party

Creative Artists Agency
Nelson Meigs, Andrea 48

Credit Suisse First Boston, Inc.
Ogunlesi, Adebayo 37

Cress Theory of Color-Confrontation and Racism
Welsing, Frances Cress 5

Crisis
Du Bois, W. E. B. 3
Fauset, Jessie 7
Wilkins, Roy 4

Critic's Choice Award
Channer, Colin 36

Crown Media
Corbi, Lana 42

Cross Colours
Jones, Carl 7
Kani, Karl 10
Walker, T. J. 7

Crucial Films
Henry, Lenny 9

Crusader
Williams, Robert F. 11

CTRN
See Transitional Committee for National Recovery (Guinea)

Cuban League
Charleston, Oscar 39
Day, Leon 39

Cuban music
Ferrer, Ibrahim 41

CubeVision
Ice Cube 8, 30

Cubism
Bearden, Romare 2

Culinary arts
Clark, Patrick 14

Cultural pluralism
Locke, Alain 10

Cumulative voting
Guinier, Lani 7, 30

Curator/exhibition designer
Camp, Kimberly 19
Campbell, Mary Schmidt 43

Golden, Thelma 10
Hutson, Jean Blackwell 16
Sanders, Joseph R., Jr. 11
Sims, Lowery Stokes 27
Stewart, Paul Wilbur 12

Cytogenetics
Satcher, David 7

Dallas city government
Johnson, Eddie Bernice 8
Kirk, Ron 11

Dallas Cowboys football team
Hill, Calvin 19
Jones, Ed "Too Tall" 46
Sanders, Deion 4, 31
Smith, Emmitt 7

Dallas Mavericks basketball team
Ussery, Terdema 29

Dallas Police Department
Bolton, Terrell D. 25

DanceAfrica
Davis, Chuck 33

Dance Theatre of Harlem
Johnson, Virginia 9
King, Alonzo 38
Mitchell, Arthur 2, 47
Nicholas, Fayard 20
Nicholas, Harold 20
Tyson, Cicely 7

Darell Green Youth Life Foundation
Green, Darrell 39

Darkchild Records
Jerkins, Rodney 31

DAV
See Disabled American Veterans

David M. Winfield Foundation
Winfield, Dave 5

Daytona Institute
See Bethune-Cookman College

Dayton Philharmonic Orchestra
Jackson, Isaiah 3

D.C. Black Repertory Theater
Reagon, Bernice Johnson 7

D.C. Sniper
Moose, Charles 40

Death Row Records
Dre, Dr. 14, 30
Hammer, M. C. 20
Knight, Suge 11, 30
Shakur, Tupac 14

De Beers Botswana
See Debswana
Allen, Debbie 13, 42

Debswana
Masire, Quett 5

Decca Records
Hardin Armstrong, Lil 39

Defense Communications Agency
Gravely, Samuel L., Jr. 5

Def Jam Records
Brown, Foxy 25
DMX 28
Gotti, Irv 39
Jay-Z 27
Jordan, Montell 23
L.L. Cool J 16
Liles, Kevin 42
Simmons, Russell 1, 30

Def Jam South Records
Ludacris 37

Def Poetry Jam
Letson, Al 39

Democratic National Committee (DNC)
Brown, Ron 5
Brown, Willie L., Jr. 7
Dixon, Sharon Pratt 1
Fattah, Chaka 11
Hamer, Fannie Lou 6
Jackson, Maynard 2, 41
Jordan, Barbara 4
Joyner, Marjorie Stewart 26
Mallett, Conrad, Jr. 16
Martin, Louis E. 16
Moore, Minyon 45
Waters, Maxine 3
Williams, Maggie 7

Democratic National Convention
Allen, Ethel D. 13
Brown, Ron 5
Brown, Willie L., Jr. 7
Dixon, Sharon Pratt 1
Hamer, Fannie Lou 6
Herman, Alexis M. 15
Jordan, Barbara 4
Millender-McDonald, Juanita 21
Waters, Maxine 3
Williams, Maggie 7

Democratic Socialists of America (DSA)
West, Cornel 5
Marable, Manning 10

Dentistry
Bluitt, Juliann S. 14
Delany, Bessie 12
Gray, Ida 41
Madison, Romell 45
Sinkford, Jeanne C. 13

Denver Broncos football team
Barnes, Ernie 16
Briscoe, Marlin 37
Davis, Terrell 20

Denver city government
Webb, Wellington 3

Denver Nuggets basketball team
Bickerstaff, Bernie 21
Bynoe, Peter C.B. 40
Hardaway, Tim 35
Lee, Sr., Bertram M. 46

Mutombo, Dikembe **7**

DePaul University
Braun, Carol Moseley **4, 42**
Sizemore, Barbara A. **26**

Depression/The Great Depression
Hampton, Henry **6**

Deputy attorney general
Thompson, Larry D. **39**

Desert Shield
See Operation Desert Shield

Desert Storm
See Operation Desert Storm

Destiny's Child
Knowles, Beyoncé **39**

Detective fiction
Bates, Karen Grigsby **40**
Bland, Eleanor Taylor **39**
DeLoach, Nora **30**
Hayes, Teddy **40**
Haywood, Gar Anthony **43**
Himes, Chester **8**
Holton, Hugh Jr. **39**
Mosley, Walter **5, 25**
Wesley, Valerie Wilson **18**

Detroit Bible Institute
Patterson, Gilbert Earl **41**

Detroit City Council
Collins, Barbara-Rose **7**

Detroit city government
Archer, Dennis **7, 36**
Crockett, George, Jr. **10**
Kilpatrick, Kwame **34**
Marshall, Bella **22**
Young, Coleman **1, 20**

Detroit College of Law
Archer, Dennis **7, 36**

Detroit entertainment
Wilson, Sunnie **7**

Detroit Golden Gloves
Wilson, Sunnie **7**

Detroit Lions football team
Barney, Lem **26**
Farr, Mel **24**
Johnson, Levi **48**
Sanders, Barry **1**
Ware, Andre **37**

Detroit Pistons basketball team
Bing, Dave **3**
Dumars, Joe **16**
Gentry, Alvin **23**
Hill, Grant **13**
Lanier, Bob **47**
Lloyd, Earl **26**
Stackhouse, Jerry **30**
Thomas, Isiah **7, 26**

Detroit Police Department
Bully-Cummings, Ella **48**
Gomez-Preston, Cheryl **9**
McKinnon, Isaiah **9**

Napoleon, Benny N. **23**

Detroit Stars baseball team
Kaiser, Cecil **42**

Detroit Tigers baseball team
Fielder, Cecil **2**
Virgil, Ozzie **48**

Detroit Wolves baseball team
Dandridge, Ray **36**

Diamond mining
Masire, Quett **5**

Dictators
Amin, Idi **42**

Digital Divide
Adkins, Rod **41**

Dillard University
Cook, Samuel DuBois **14**

Dime Savings Bank
Parsons, Richard Dean **11**

Diner's Club
Gaines, Brenda **41**

Diplomatic Corps
See U.S. Diplomatic Corps

Directing
Akomfrah, John **37**
Barclay, Paris **37**
Branch, William Blackwell **39**
Hines, Gregory **1, 42**
Milner, Ron **39**
Perry, Tyler **40**
Thompson, Tazewell **13**
Ward, Douglas Turner **42**
Warner, Malcolm-Jamal **22, 36**
Whack, Rita Coburn **36**
Wolfe, George C. **6, 43**

Director's Guild of America
Barclay, Paris **37**

Disabled American Veterans (DAV)
Brown, Jesse **6, 41**

Disco
Gaynor, Gloria **36**
Staton, Candi **27**
Summer, Donna **25**

Diving
Brashear, Carl **29**

DJ
Alert, Kool DJ Red **32**
DJ Jazzy Jeff **32**
Grandmaster Flash **33**

Djing
Knuckles, Frankie **42**

DNC
See Democratic National Committee

Documentary film
Blackwood, Maureen **37**
Branch, William Blackwell **39**
Byrd, Robert **11**
Dash, Julie **4**
Davis, Ossie **5**

Greaves, William **38**
Hampton, Henry **6**
Henry, Lenny **9**
Hudlin, Reginald **9**
Hudlin, Warrington **9**
Julien, Isaac **3**
Lee, Spike **5, 19**
Peck, Raoul **32**
Riggs, Marlon **5, 44**
Whack, Rita Coburn **36**

Dollmaking
El Wilson, Barbara **35**

Donald Byrd/The Group
Byrd, Donald **10**

Donnaerobics
Richardson, Donna **39**

Down Beat Jazz Hall of Fame
Terry, Clark **39**

Dove Award
Baylor, Helen **36**
Winans, CeCe **14, 43**

Dr. Martin Luther King Boys and Girls Club
Gaines, Brenda **41**

Drama Desk Awards
Carter, Nell **39**
Taylor, Ron **35**

Dreamland Orchestra
Cook, Charles "Doc" **44**

Drug abuse prevention
Brown, Les **5**
Clements, George **2**
Creagh, Milton **27**
Hale, Lorraine **8**
Harris, Alice **7**
Lucas, John **7**
Rangel, Charles **3**

Drug synthesis
Julian, Percy Lavon **6**
Pickett, Cecil **39**

Drums
Blakey, Art **37**
Locke, Eddie **44**

DSA
See Democratic Socialists of America

Dub poetry
Breeze, Jean "Binta" **37**
Johnson, Linton Kwesi **37**

Duke Ellington School of Arts
Cooper Cafritz, Peggy **43**

Duke Records
Bland, Bobby "Blue" **36**

Dunham Dance Company
Dunham, Katherine **4**

DuSable Museum of African American History
Burroughs, Margaret Taylor **9**

E Street Band
Clemons, Clarence **41**

Earthquake Early Alerting Service
Person, Waverly **9**

East Harlem School at Exodus House
Hageman, Hans **36**
Hageman, Ivan **36**

East St. Louis city government
Powell, Debra A. **23**

Ebenezer Baptist Church
King, Bernice **4**

Ebonics
Cook, Toni **23**

Ebony magazine
Bennett, Lerone, Jr. **5**
Branch, William Blackwell **39**
Fuller, Hoyt **44**
Johnson, John H. **3**
Massaquoi, Hans J. **30**
Rice, Linda Johnson **9, 41**
Sleet, Moneta, Jr. **5**

Ebony Museum of African American History
See DuSable Museum of African American History

E.C. Reems Women's International Ministries
Reems, Ernestine Cleveland **27**

Economic Community of West African States (ECOWAS)
Sawyer, Amos **2**

Economic Regulatory Administration
O'Leary, Hazel **6**

Economics
Ake, Claude **30**
Arthur, Owen **33**
Boyd, T. B. III **6**
Brimmer, Andrew F. **2, 48**
Brown, Tony **3**
Divine, Father **7**
Dodson, Howard, Jr. **7**
Gibson, William F. **6**
Hamer, Fannie Lou **6**
Hampton, Henry **6**
Machel, Graca Simbine **16**
Malveaux, Julianne **32**
Masire, Quett **5**
Raines, Franklin Delano **14**
Robinson, Randall **7, 46**
Sowell, Thomas **2**
Sullivan, Leon H. **3, 30**
Van Peebles, Melvin **7**
Wallace, Phyllis A. **9**
Wharton, Clifton R., Jr. **7**
White, Michael R. **5**
Williams, Walter E. **4**

ECOWAS
See Economic Community of West African States

Edelman Public Relations
Barrett, Andrew C. **12**

Editing
Aubert, Alvin **41**
Bass, Charlotta Spears **40**

Brown, Llyod Louis **42**
Curry, George E. **23**
Delany, Martin R. **27**
Dumas, Henry **41**
Murphy, John H. **42**
Schuyler, George Samuel **40**

Edmonds Entertainment
Edmonds, Kenneth "Babyface" **10, 31**
Edmonds, Tracey **16**
Tillman, George, Jr. **20**

Edmonton Oilers hockey team
Fuhr, Grant **1**
Grier, Mike **43**
Laraque, Georges **48**

Educational Testing Service
Stone, Chuck **9**

EEC
See European Economic Community

EEOC
See Equal Employment Opportunity Commission

Egyptology
Diop, Cheikh Anta **4**

Elder Foundation
Elder, Lee **6**

Electronic music
Craig, Carl **31**

Elektra Records
McPherson, David **32**

Emerge (Savoy) magazine
Ames, Wilmer **27**
Curry, George E. **23**

Emmy awards
Allen, Debbie **13, 42**
Amos, John **8**
Ashe, Arthur **1, 18**
Barclay, Paris **37**
Belafonte, Harry **4**
Bradley, Ed **2**
Branch, William Blackwell **39**
Brown, James **22**
Brown, Les **5**
Carter, Nell **39**
Clayton, Xernona **3, 45**
Cosby, Bill **7, 26**
Curtis-Hall, Vondie **17**
Dee, Ruby **8**
Foxx, Redd **2**
Freeman, Al, Jr. **11**
Goldberg, Whoopi **4, 33**
Gossett, Louis, Jr. **7**
Guillaume, Robert **3, 48**
Gumbel, Greg **8**
Hunter-Gault, Charlayne **6, 31**
Jones, James Earl **3**
La Salle, Eriq **12**
Mabrey, Vicki **26**
McQueen, Butterfly **6**
Moore, Shemar **21**
Parks, Gordon **1, 35**
Pinkston, W. Randall **24**
Quarles, Norma **25**
Richards, Beah **30**

Robinson, Max **3**
Rock, Chris **3, 22**
Rolle, Esther **13, 21**
St. John, Kristoff **25**
Stokes, Carl B. **10**
Taylor, Billy **23**
Thigpen, Lynne **17, 41**
Tyson, Cicely **7**
Uggams, Leslie **23**
Wayans, Damon **8, 41**
Whack, Rita Coburn **36**
Whitfield, Lynn **18**
Williams, Montel **4**
Williams, Sherley Anne **25**
Winfrey, Oprah **2, 15**
Woodard, Alfre **9**

Emory University
Cole, Johnnetta B. **5, 43**

Endocrinology
Elders, Joycelyn **6**

Energy studies
Cose, Ellis **5**
O'Leary, Hazel **6**

Engineering
Alexander, Archie Alphonso **14**
Anderson, Charles Edward **37**
Auguste, Donna **29**
Benson, Angela **34**
Emeagwali, Philip **30**
Ericsson-Jackson, Aprille **28**
Gibson, Kenneth Allen **6**
Gourdine, Meredith **33**
Hannah, Marc **10**
Henderson, Cornelius Langston **26**
McCoy, Elijah **8**
Pierre, Percy Anthony **46**
Sigur, Wanda **44**
Wilkens, J. Ernest, Jr. **43**
Williams, O. S. **13**

Environmental issues
Chavis, Benjamin **6**
Hill, Bonnie Guiton **20**

Epic Records
McPherson, David **32**
Mo', Keb' **36**

Epidemiology
Gayle, Helene D. **3**

Episcopal Diocese of Massachusetts
Harris, Barbara **12**

Episcopalian
Burgess, John **46**

EPRDF
See Ethiopian People's Revolutionary Democratic Front

Equal Employment Opportunity Commission (EEOC)
Alexander, Clifford **26**
Hill, Anita **5**
Lewis, Delano **7**
Norton, Eleanor Holmes **7**
Thomas, Clarence **2, 39**

Wallace, Phyllis A. **9**

Equality Now
Jones, Sarah **39**

ESPN
Roberts, Robin **16**
Scott, Stuart **34**

Essence magazine
Bandele, Asha **36**
Channer, Colin **36**
De Veaux, Alexis **44**
Grant, Gwendolyn Goldsby **28**
Greenwood, Monique **38**
Lewis, Edward T. **21**
Parks, Gordon **1, 35**
Smith, Clarence O. **21**
Taylor, Susan L. **10**
Wesley, Valerie Wilson **18**

Essence Award
Broadbent, Hydeia **36**
McMurray, Georgia L. **36**

Essence Communications
Lewis, Edward T. **21**
Smith, Clarence O. **21**
Taylor, Susan L. **10**

Essence, the Television Program
Taylor, Susan L. **10**

Esalen Institute
Olatunji, Babatunde **36**

Ethiopian People's Revolutionary Democratic Front (EPRDF)
Meles Zenawi **3**

Etiquette
Bates, Karen Grigsby **40**

Eugene O'Neill Theater
Richards, Lloyd **2**

European Economic Community (EEC)
Diouf, Abdou **3**

Executive Leadership Council
Jackson, Mannie **14**

Exiled heads of state
Aristide, Jean-Bertrand **6, 45**

Exploration
Henson, Matthew **2**

Eyes on the Prize series
Hampton, Henry **6**

F & M Schaefer Brewing Co.
Cooper, Andrew W. **36**

Fairbanks city government
Hayes, James C. **10**

FAIRR
See Foundation for the Advancement of Inmate Rehabilitation and Recreation

Fair Share Agreements
Gibson, William F. **6**

Famine relief
See World hunger

Famous Amos Cookie Corporation
Amos, Wally **9**

FAN
See Forces Armées du Nord (Chad)

Fannie Mae
Jackson, Maynard **2, 41**

FANT
See Forces Amrées Nationales Tchadiennes

Fashion
Boateng, Ozwald **35**
Delice, Ronald **48**
Delice, Rony **48**
Hendy, Francis **47**
Lars, Byron **32**
Malone, Maurice **32**
Sade **15**
Smaltz, Audrey **12**
Steele, Lawrence **28**

Fashion Institute of Technology (FIT)
Brown, Joyce F. **25**

Fast 50 Awards
Steward, David L. **36**

FCC
See Federal Communications Commission

Federal Bureau of Investigation (FBI)
Gibson, Johnnie Mae **23**
Harvard, Beverly **11**

Federal Communications Commission (FCC)
Barrett, Andrew C. **12**
Hooks, Benjamin L. **2**
Hughes, Cathy **27**
Kennard, William Earl **18**
Powell, Michael **32**
Russell-McCloud, Patricia A. **17**

Federal Court of Canada
Isaac, Julius **34**

Federal Energy Administration
O'Leary, Hazel **6**

Federal Reserve Bank
Brimmer, Andrew F. **2, 48**
Ferguson, Roger W. **25**

Federal Set-Aside Program
Mitchell, Parren J. **42**

Federation of Nigeria
Sowande, Fela **39**

Feed the Hungry program
Williams, Hosea Lorenzo **15, 31**

Fellowship of Reconciliation (FOR)
Farmer, James **2**
Rustin, Bayard **4**

Feminist studies
Carby, Hazel 27
Christian, Barbara T. 44
De Veaux, Alexis 44
Hull, Akasha Gloria 45
Smith, Barbara 28

Fencing
Westbrook, Peter 20

Fiction
Alexander, Margaret Walker 22
Amadi, Elechi 40
Anthony, Michael 29
Ansa, Tina McElroy 14
Ba, Mariama 30
Baiocchi, Regina Harris 41
Baisden, Michael 25
Ballard, Allen Butler, Jr. 40
Barrett, Lindsay 43
Bates, Karen Grigsby 40
Beckham, Barry 41
Benson, Angela 34
Berry, James 41
Bland, Eleanor Taylor 39
Bolden, Tonya 32
Bradley, David Henry, Jr. 39
Brand, Dionne 32
Briscoe, Connie 15
Brown, Cecil M. 46
Brown, Llyod Louis 42
Bunkley, Anita Richmond 39
Butler, Octavia 8, 43
Campbell, Bebe Moore 6, 24
Cartíer, Xam Wilson 41
Chase-Riboud, Barbara 20, 46
Cheney-Coker, Syl 43
Chesnutt, Charles 29
Clarke, Austin 32
Cleage, Pearl 17
Cliff, Michelle 42
Creagh, Milton 27
Curtis, Christopher Paul 26
Danticat, Edwidge 15
Draper, Sharon Mills 16, 43
Due, Tananarive 30
Dumas, Henry 41
Dunbar-Nelson, Alice Ruth Moore 44
Emecheta, Buchi 30
Fair, Ronald L. 47
Farah, Nuruddin 27
Files, Lolita 35
Ford, Nick Aaron 44
Forrest, Leon 44
Gomez, Jewelle 30
Greenlee, Sam 48
Harris, E. Lynn 12, 33
Haywood, Gar Anthony 43
Hercules, Frank 44
Hill, Donna 32
Holton, Hugh, Jr. 39
Horne, Frank 44
Jackson, Sheneska 18
Jakes, Thomas "T.D." 17, 43
Jasper, Kenji 39
Jenkins, Beverly 14
Johnson, Georgia Douglas 41
Johnson, Mat 31
Jones, Edward P. 43
Jones, Gayl 37
Kamau, Kwadwo Agymah 28
Kay, Jackie 37
Kayira, Legson 40
Laferriere, Dany 33
LaGuma, Alex 30
Lamming, George 35
Marechera, Dambudzo 39
Markham, E.A. 37
Mason, Felicia 31
Mbaye, Mariétou 31
McFadden, Bernice L. 39
McKinney-Whetstone, Diane 27
McMillan, Terry 4, 17
Memmi, Albert 37
Monroe, Mary 35
Mosley, Walter 5, 25
Mossell, Gertrude Bustill 40
Mphalele, Es'kia (Ezekiel) 40
Mwangi, Meja 40
Naylor, Gloria 10, 42
Nkosi, Lewis 46
Nugent, Richard Bruce 39
Okara, Gabriel 37
Peters, Lenrie 43
Philip, Marlene Nourbese 32
Randall, Alice 38
Saro-Wiwa, Kenule 39
Schuyler, George Samuel 40
Senior, Olive 37
Smith, Danyel 40
Tate, Eleanora E. 20
Taylor, Mildred D. 26
Thomas-Graham, Pamela 29
Tutuola, Amos 30
Vera, Yvonne 32
Verdelle, A. J. 26
wa Thiong'o, Ngugi 29
Walker, Margaret 29
Weaver, Afaa Michael 37
Whitfield, Van 34
Williams, Sherley Anne 25
Williams, Stanley "Tookie" 29
Yarbrough, Camille 40
Youngblood, Shay 32

Figure skating
Bonaly, Surya 7
Thomas, Debi 26

Film direction
Akomfrah, John 37
Allen, Debbie 13, 42
Blackwood, Maureen 37
Burnett, Charles 16
Byrd, Robert 11
Campbell-Martin, Tisha 8, 42
Cortez, Jayne 43
Curtis-Hall, Vondie 17
Dash, Julie 4
Davis, Ossie 5
Dickerson, Ernest 6, 17
Diesel, Vin 29
Duke, Bill 3
Franklin, Carl 11
Freeman, Al, Jr. 11
Fuqua, Antoine 35
Gerima, Haile 38
Gray, F. Gary 14
Greaves, William 38
Harris, Leslie 6
Hayes, Teddy 40
Henriques, Julian 37
Hines, Gregory 1, 42
Hudlin, Reginald 9
Hudlin, Warrington 9
Hughes, Albert 7
Hughes, Allen 7
Jackson, George 19
Julien, Isaac 3
Lane, Charles 3
Lee, Spike 5, 19
Lemmons, Kasi 20
Lewis, Samella 25
Martin, Darnell 43
Micheaux, Oscar 7
Morton, Joe 18
Moses, Gilbert 12
Moss, Carlton 17
Mwangi, Meja 40
Onwurah, Ngozi 38
Peck, Raoul 32
Poitier, Sidney 11, 36
Prince-Bythewood, Gina 31
Riggs, Marlon 5, 44
Schultz, Michael A. 6
Sembène, Ousmane 13
Singleton, John 2, 30
Smith, Roger Guenveur 12
St. Jacques, Raymond 8
Tillman, George, Jr. 20
Townsend, Robert 4, 23
Tyler, Aisha N. 36
Underwood, Blair 7
Van Peebles, Mario 2
Van Peebles, Melvin 7
Ward, Douglas Turner 42
Wayans, Damon 8, 41
Wayans, Keenen Ivory 18

Film production
Daniels, Lee Louis 36
Gerima, Haile 38
Greaves, William 38
Hines, Gregory 1, 42
Lewis, Emmanuel 36
Martin, Darnell 43
Onwurah, Ngozi 38
Poitier, Sidney 11, 36
Randall, Alice 38
Tyler, Aisha N. 36
Ward, Douglas Turner 42

Film scores
Blanchard, Terence 43
Crouch, Andraé 27
Hancock, Herbie 20
Jean-Baptiste, Marianne 17, 46
Jones, Quincy 8, 30
Prince 18

Finance
Adams, Eula L. 39
Banks, Jeffrey 17
Boston, Kelvin E. 25
Bryant, John 26
Chapman, Nathan A. Jr. 21
Doley, Harold, Jr. 26
Ferguson, Roger W. 25
Fletcher, Alphonse, Jr. 16
Funderburg, I. Owen 38
Gaines, Brenda 41
Griffith, Mark Winston 8
Hobson, Mellody 40
Jones, Thomas W. 41
Lawless, Theodore K. 8
Lewis, William M., Jr. 40
Louis, Errol T. 8
Marshall, Bella 22
Rogers, John W., Jr. 5
Ross, Charles 27
Thompson, William C. 35

Firefighters
Bell, Michael 40

First Data Corporation
Adams, Eula L. 39

Fisk University
Harvey, William R. 42
Imes, Elmer Samuel 39
Johnson, Charles S. 12
Phillips, Teresa L. 42
Smith, John L. 22

Fitness
Richardson, Donna 39

FlipMode Entertainment
Rhymes, Busta 31

Florida A & M University
Gaither, Alonzo Smith (Jake) 14
Humphries, Frederick 20
Meek, Kendrick 41

Florida International baseball league
Kaiser, Cecil 42

Florida Marlins baseball team
Mariner, Jonathan 41
Sheffield, Gary 16

Florida state government
Brown, Corrine 24
Meek, Carrie 6
Meek, Kendrick 41
Tribble, Isreal, Jr. 8

Flouride chemistry
Quarterman, Lloyd Albert 4

Focus Detroit Electronic Music Festival
May, Derrick 41

Folk music
Bailey, DeFord 33
Chapman, Tracy 26
Charlemagne, Manno 11
Cuney, William Waring 44
Davis, Gary 41
Dawson, William Levi 39
Harper, Ben 34
Jenkins, Ella 15
Odetta 37
Williams, Denise 40
Wilson, Cassandra 16

Football
Allen, Marcus 20
Amos, John 8
Anderson, Jamal 22
Barber, Ronde 41
Barney, Lem 26
Briscoe, Marlin 37
Brooks, Aaron 33
Brooks, Derrick 43
Brown, James 22
Brown, Jim 11
Bruce, Isaac 26
Buchanan, Ray 32
Butler, LeRoy III 17
Carter, Cris 21
Cherry, Deron 40

Culpepper, Daunte 32
Cunningham, Randall 23
Davis, Ernie 48
Davis, Terrell 20
Dickerson, Eric 27
Dungy, Tony 17, 42
Edwards, Harry 2
Farr, Mel Sr. 24
Faulk, Marshall 35
Gaither, Alonzo Smith (Jake) 14
Gilliam, Frank 23
Gilliam, Joe 31
Green, Darrell 39
Green, Dennis 5, 45
Greene, Joe 10
Grier, Roosevelt 13
Hill, Calvin 19
Johnson, Levi 48
Jones, Ed "Too Tall" 46
Lanier, Willie 33
Lofton, James 42
Lott, Ronnie 9
McNair, Steve 22, 47
McNabb, Donovan 29
Monk, Art 38
Moon, Warren 8
Moss, Randy 23
Motley, Marion 26
Newsome, Ozzie 26
Pace, Orlando 21
Page, Alan 7
Payton, Walter 11, 25
Perry, Lowell 30
Rashad, Ahmad 18
Rice, Jerry 5
Robinson, Eddie G. 10
Sanders, Barry 1
Sanders, Deion 4, 31
Sapp, Warren 38
Sayers, Gale 28
Sharper, Darren 32
Shell, Art 1
Simmons, Bob 29
Simpson, O. J. 15
Singletary, Mike 4
Smith, Emmitt 7
Stewart, Kordell 21
Strahan, Michael 35
Stringer, Korey 35
Swann, Lynn 28
Taylor, Lawrence 25
Thomas, Derrick 25
Thrower, Willie 35
Upshaw, Gene 18, 47
Vick, Michael 39
Walker, Herschel 1
Ware, Andre 37
Watts, J. C., Jr. 14, 38
Weathers, Carl 10
White, Reggie 6
Williams, Doug 22
Willingham, Tyrone 43

Football Hall of Fame
Lofton, James 42

FOR
See Fellowship of Reconciliation

Forces Armées du Nord (Chad; FAN)
Déby, Idriss 30
Habré, Hissène 6

Ford Foundation
Thomas, Franklin A. 5
Franklin, Robert M. 13

Ford Motor Company
Cherry, Deron 40
Dawson, Matel "Mat," Jr. 39
Goldsberry, Ronald 18
McMillan, Rosalynn A. 36

Fordham University
Blair, Paul 36
McMurray, Georgia L. 36

Foreign policy
Bunche, Ralph J. 5
Rice, Condoleezza 3, 28
Robinson, Randall 7, 46

Foreign Service Office
Wharton, Clifton Reginald, Sr. 36

Forensic science
Griffin, Bessie Blout 43

Forest Club
Wilson, Sunnie 7

40 Acres and a Mule Filmworks
Dickerson, Ernest 6, 17
Lee, Spike 5, 19

Foster care
Hale, Clara 16
Hale, Lorraine 8

Foundation for the Advancement of Inmate Rehabilitation and Recreation (FAIRR)
King, B. B. 7

Fox Broadcasting Company
Corbi, Lana 42

FPI
See Ivorian Popular Front

Freddie Mac Corporation
Baker, Maxine 28

Freddie Mac Foundation
Baker, Maxine 28

Frederick Douglass Caring Award
Broadbent, Hydeia 36

Frederick Douglass Memorial Hospital
Mossell, Gertrude Bustill 40

Freedom Farm Cooperative
Hamer, Fannie Lou 6

Free Southern Theater (FST)
Borders, James 9

FRELIMO
See Front for the Liberation of Mozambique

French Order of Arts and Letters
Coleman, Ornette 39

French West Africa
Diouf, Abdou 3

FRODEBU
See Front for Democracy in Burundi

FROLINAT
See Front de la Libération Nationale du Tchad (Chad)

FRONASA
See Front for National Salvation (Uganda)

Front de la Libération Nationale du Tchad (Chad; FROLINAT)
Habré, Hissène 6

Front for Democracy in Burundi (FRODEBU)
Ndadaye, Melchior 7
Ntaryamira, Cyprien 8

Front for National Salvation (Uganda; FRONASA)
Museveni, Yoweri 4

Front for the Liberation of Mozambique (FRELIMO)
Chissano, Joaquim 7
Machel, Graca Simbine 16
Machel, Samora Moises 8

FST
See Free Southern Theater

Full Gospel Baptist
Long, Eddie L. 29

FullerMusic
Fuller, Arthur 27

Fulton County Juvenile Court
Hatchett, Glenda 32

Funk music
Ayers, Roy 16
Clinton, George 9
Collins, Bootsy 31
Richie, Lionel 27
Watson, Johnny "Guitar" 18

Fusion
Davis, Miles 4
Jones, Quincy 8, 30

FWP Union
Nugent, Richard Bruce 39

Gangs
Williams, Stanley "Tookie" 29

Gary, Williams, Parenti, Finney, Lewis & McManus
Gary, Willie E. 12

Gary Enterprises
Gary, Willie E. 12

Gary Post-Tribune
Ross, Don 27

Gassaway, Crosson, Turner & Parsons
Parsons, James 14

Gay Men of Color Consortium
Wilson, Phill 9

Gay and Lesbian Activism
De Veaux, Alexis 44

Genealogy
Blockson, Charles L. 42
Dash, Julie 4
Haley, Alex 4

General Hospital TV series
Cash, Rosalind 28

General Motors Corporation
O'Neal, Stanley 38
Roberts, Roy S. 14

Genetech
Potter, Myrtle 40

Genetics
Dunston, Georgia Mae 48
Harris, Mary Styles 31

Geometric symbolism
Douglas, Aaron 7

Geophysics
Person, Waverly 9

George Foster Peabody Broadcasting Award
Bradley, Ed 2
Hunter-Gault, Charlayne 6, 31
Shaw, Bernard 2

George Mason University
Dunn, Jerry 27

George Washington University
Carter, Joye Maureen 41

Georgia state government
Baker, Thurbert 22
Bishop, Sanford D. Jr. 24
Bond, Julian 2, 35
Majette, Denise 41
Scott, David 41
Williams, Hosea Lorenzo 15, 31

Georgia State Supreme Court
Sears-Collins, Leah J. 5

Ghanian government
Awoonor, Kofi 37

Glaucoma treatment
Julian, Percy Lavon 6

GLM Group
McMurray, Georgia L. 36

Glidden Company
Julian, Percy Lavon 6

Goddard Space Flight Center
Ericsson-Jackson, Aprille 28

Gold Mind, Inc.
Elliott, Missy "Misdemeanor" 31

Golden Globe awards
Allen, Debbie 13, 42
Bassett, Angela 23
Carroll, Diahann 9
Freeman, Morgan 2, 20
Ross, Diana 8, 27

Taylor, Regina 9, 46

Golden Pen award
McFadden, Bernice L. 39

Golden State Warriors basketball team
Edwards, Harry 2
Lucas, John 7
Parish, Robert 43
Sprewell, Latrell 23

Golf
Elder, Lee 6
Gibson, Althea 8, 43
Jackson, Fred James 25
Peete, Calvin 11
Richmond, Mitch 19
Shippen, John 43
Sifford, Charlie 4
Webber, Chris 15, 30
Woods, Tiger 14, 31

Goodwill ambassador
Terry, Clark 39

Goodwill Games
Swoopes, Sheryl 12

Gospel music
Adams, Oleta 18
Adams, Yolanda 17
Armstrong, Vanessa Bell 24
Baylor Helen 36
Bonds, Margaret 39
Caesar, Shirley 19
Clark-Sheard, Karen 22
Cleveland, James 19
Christie, Angella 36
Cooke, Sam 17
Crouch, Andraé 27
Davis, Gary 41
Dorsey, Thomas 15
Franklin, Aretha 11, 44
Franklin, Kirk 15
Gaynor, Gloria 36
Green, Al 13, 47
Hammond, Fred 23
Hawkins, Tramaine 16
Houston, Cissy 20
Jackson, Mahalia 5
Jakes, Thomas "T.D." 17, 43
Jones, Bobby 20
Kee, John P. 43
Kenoly, Ron 45
Lassiter, Roy 24
Little Richard 15
Majors, Jeff 41
Marrow, Queen Esther 24
Mary Mary 34
Mayfield, Curtis 2, 43
McClurkin, Donnie 25
Mills, Stephanie 36
Monica 21
Mullen, Nicole C. 45
Peoples, Dottie 22
Preston, Billy 39
Reagon, Bernice Johnson 7
Reese, Della 6, 20
Staples, "Pops" 32
Staton, Candi 27
Steinberg, Martha Jean "The Queen" 28
Walker, Albertina 10
Walker, Hezekiah 34

Washington, Dinah 22
Whalum, Kirk 37
Williams, Deniece 36
Wilson, Natalie 38
Winans, Angie 36
Winans, BeBe 14
Winans, CeCe 14, 43
Winans, Debbie 36
Winans, Marvin L. 17
Winans, Vickie 24

Gospel theater
Perry, Tyler 40

Graffiti art
White, Dondi 34

Grambling State University
Favors, Steve 23

Grammy awards
Adams, Oleta 18
Adderley, Nat 29
Badu, Erykah 22
Belafonte, Harry 4
Blige, Mary J. 20, 34
Brandy 14, 34
Caesar, Shirley 19
Chapman, Tracy 26
Cleveland, James 19
Cole, Natalie Maria 17
Combs, Sean "Puffy" 17, 43
Cosby, Bill 7, 26
Cray, Robert 30
Crouch, Andraé 27
Davis, Miles 4
Edmonds, Kenneth "Babyface" 10, 31
Ellington, Duke 5
Ferrer, Ibrahim 41
Fitzgerald, Ella 8
Franklin, Aretha 11, 44
Gaye, Marvin 2
Gaynor, Gloria 36
Glover, Corey 34
Goldberg, Whoopi 4, 33
Gray, Macy 29
Guy, Buddy 31
Hammer, M. C. 20
Hathaway, Donny 18
Hawkins, Tramaine 16
Hill, Lauryn 20
Holland-Dozier-Holland 36
Hooker, John Lee 30
Houston, Cissy 20
Houston, Whitney 7, 28
Isley, Ronald 25
Jackson, Michael 19
Jackon, Janet 6, 30
James, Etta 13
Jay-Z 27
Jean, Wyclef 20
Jimmy Jam 13
Jones, Bobby 20
Jones, Quincy 8, 30
Kee, John P. 43
Kelly, R. 18, 44
Knowles, Beyoncé 39
Knuckles, Frankie 42
LaBelle, Patti 13, 30
Lewis, Terry 13
Lopes, Lisa "Left Eye" 36
Mahal, Taj 39
Makeba, Miriam 2

Marley, Ziggy 41
Marsalis, Branford 34
Mills, Stephanie 36
Mo', Keb' 36
Murphy, Eddie 4, 20
Norman, Jessye 5
Olatunji, Babatunde 36
Poitier, Sidney 11, 36
Price, Leontyne 1
Pride, Charley 26
Prince 18
Queen Latifah 1, 16
Reagon, Bernice Johnson 7
Redding, Otis 16
Reid, Vernon 34
Richie, Lionel 27
Robinson, Smokey 3
Ross, Isaiah "Doc" 40
Rucker, Darius 34
Sade 15
Shaggy 31
Smith, Will 8, 18
Summer, Donna 25
Turner, Tina 6, 27
Tyrese 27
Walker, Hezekiah 34
Warwick, Dionne 18
White, Barry 13, 41
White, Maurice 29
Williams, Deniece 36
Williams, Joe 5, 25
Wilson, Nancy 10
Winans, CeCe 14, 43
Winans, Marvin L. 17
Wonder, Stevie 11

Grand Ole Opry
Bailey, DeFord 33

Greater Emmanuel Temple of Faith
Jakes, Thomas "T.D." 17, 43

Green Bay Packers football team
Brooks, Aaron 33
Butler, Leroy III 17
Howard, Desmond 16
Lofton, James 42
Sharper, Darren 32
White, Reggie 6

Green Belt Movement
Maathai, Wangari 43

Grenadian government
Bishop, Maurice 39

Groupe de Recherche Choréographique de
Dove, Ulysses 5

Guardian
Trotter, Monroe 9

Guggenheim fellowship
Rollins, Sonny 37
Wilson, Ellis 39

Guitar
Ade, King Sunny 41
Barker, Danny 32
Barnes, Roosevelt "Booba" 33
Butler, Jonathan 28
Burns, Eddie 44

Collins, Bootsy 31
Cray, Robert 30
Davis, Gary 41
Diddley, Bo 39
Estes, Sleepy John 33
Guy, Buddy 31
Harris, Corey 39
Hemphill, Jessie Mae 33
Hendrix, Jimi 10
House, Son 8
Hooker, John Lee 30
Howlin' Wolf 9
Jean, Wyclef 20
Johnson, Robert 2
Jordan, Ronny 26
King, B. B. 7
Kravitz, Lenny 10, 34
Marley, Bob 5
Mayfield, Curtis 2, 43
Ndegéocello, Me'Shell 15
Ongala, Remmy 9
Staples, "Pops" 32
Watson, Johnny "Guitar" 18
Wilson, Cassandra 16

Gulf War
Powell, Colin 1, 28
Shaw, Bernard 2
Von Lipsey, Roderick K. 11

Gurdjieff Institute
Toomer, Jean 6

Gymnastics
Dawes, Dominique 11
White, Jesse 22

Hair care
Cottrell, Comer 11
Fuller, S. B. 13
Johnson, George E. 29
Joyner, Marjorie Stewart 26
Malone, Annie 13
Roche, Joyce M. 17
Walker, Madame C. J. 7

Haitian refugees
Ashe, Arthur 1, 18
Dunham, Katherine 4
Jean, Wyclef 20
Robinson, Randall 7, 46

Hal Jackson's Talented Teens International
Jackson, Hal 41

Hale House
Hale, Clara 16
Hale, Lorraine 8

Handy Award
Hunter, Alberta 42

Harlem Artist Guild
Nugent, Richard Bruce 39
Wilson, Ellis 39

Harlem Cultural Council
Nugent, Richard Bruce 39

Harlem Junior Tennis League
Blake, James 43

Harlem Globetrotters
Chamberlain, Wilt 18, 47
Haynes, Marques 22

Jackson, Mannie 14

Harlem Renaissance
Alexander, Margaret Walker 22
Christian, Barbara T. 44
Cullen, Countee 8
Cuney, William Waring 44
Dandridge, Raymond Garfield 45
Davis, Arthur P. 41
Delaney, Beauford 19
Ellington, Duke 5
Fauset, Jessie 7
Fisher, Rudolph 17
Frazier, E. Franklin 10
Horne, Frank 44
Hughes, Langston 4
Hurston, Zora Neale 3
Imes, Elmer Samuel 39
Johnson, Georgia Douglas 41
Johnson, James Weldon 5
Johnson, William Henry 3
Larsen, Nella 10
Locke, Alain 10
McKay, Claude 6
Mills, Florence 22
Nugent, Richard Bruce 39
Petry, Ann 19
Thurman, Wallace 16
Toomer, Jean 6
VanDerZee, James 6
West, Dorothy 12
Wilson, Ellis 39

Harlem Writers Guild
Guy, Rosa 5
Wesley, Valerie Wilson 18

Harlem Youth Opportunities Unlimited (HARYOU)
Clark, Kenneth B. 5

Harvard University
Epps, Archie C., III 45

Hallmark Channel
Corbi, Lana 42

Hampton University
Harvey, William R. 42

Harmolodics Records
Coleman, Ornette 39

Harmonica
Bailey, DeFord 33
Barnes, Roosevelt "Booba" 33
Burns, Eddie 44
Howlin' Wolf 9
Neal, Raful 44
Ross, Isaiah "Doc" 40

Harness racing
Minor, DeWayne 32

Harp
Majors, Jeff 41

Harriet Tubman Home for Aged and Indigent Colored People
Tubman, Harriet 9

Harrisburg Giants baseball team
Charleston, Oscar 39

Harvard Law School
Bell, Derrick 6
Ogletree, Charles, Jr. 12, 47

Harvard University
Loury, Glenn 36

HARYOU
See Harlem Youth Opportunities Unlimited

Hazelitt Award for Excellence in Arts
Bradley, David Henry, Jr. 39

Head Start
Edelman, Marian Wright 5, 42
Taylor, Helen (Lavon Hollingshed) 30

Health care reform
Brown, Jesse 6, 41
Carroll, L. Natalie 44
Cole, Lorraine 48
Cooper, Edward S. 6
Davis, Angela 5
Gibson, Kenneth A. 6
Lavizzo-Mourey, Risa 48
Norman, Pat 10
Potter, Myrtle 40
Satcher, David 7
Williams, Daniel Hale 2

Heart disease
Cooper, Edward S. 6

Heidelberg Project
Guyton, Tyree 9

Heisman Trophy
Ware, Andre 37

The Heritage Network
Mercado-Valdes, Frank 43

HEW
See U.S. Department of Health, Education, and Welfare

HHS
See U.S. Department of Health and Human Services

Hip-hop music
Ashanti 37
Benjamin, Andre 45
Patton, Antwan 45
Smith, Danyel 40
Williams, Pharrell 47

Historians
Ballard, Allen Butler, Jr. 40
Berry, Mary Frances 7
Blassingame, John Wesley 40
Blockson, Charles L. 42
Bogle, Donald 34
Chase-Riboud, Barbara 20, 46
Cooper, Anna Julia 20
Diop, Cheikh Anta 4
Dodson, Howard, Jr. 7
Du Bois, W. E. B. 3
Franklin, John Hope 5
Gates, Henry Louis, Jr. 3, 38
Giddings, Paula 11
Logan, Rayford W. 40
Hansberry, William Leo 11
Harkless, Necia Desiree 19

Hine, Darlene Clark 24
Marable, Manning 10
Painter, Nell Irvin 24
Patterson, Orlando 4
Quarles, Benjamin Arthur 18
Reagon, Bernice Johnson 7
Reddick, Lawrence Dunbar 20
Rogers, Joel Augustus 30
Schomburg, Arthur Alfonso 9
van Sertima, Ivan 25
Williams, George Washington 18
Woodson, Carter G. 2

Hockey
Brashear, Donald 39
Brathwaite, Fred 35
Brown, James 22
Carnegie, Herbert 25
Doig, Jason 45
Fuhr, Grant 1
Grand-Pierre, Jean-Luc 46
Grier, Mike 43
Iginla, Jarome 35
Mayers, Jamal 39
McBride, Bryant 18
McKegney, Tony 3
O'Ree, Willie 5

Homestead Grays baseball team
Charleston, Oscar 39
Day, Leon 39

Homosexuality
Carter, Mandy 11
Clarke, Cheryl 32
Delany, Samuel R., Jr. 9
Gomes, Peter J. 15
Harris, E. Lynn 12, 33
Hemphill, Essex 10
Julien, Isaac 3
Lorde, Audre 6
Norman, Pat 10
Nugent, Richard Bruce 39
Parker, Pat 19
Riggs, Marlon 5, 44
Rupaul 17
Wilson, Phill 9

Honeywell Corporation
Jackson, Mannie 14

Horse racing
St. Julien, Marlon 29
Winkfield, Jimmy 42

House music
Knuckles, Frankie 42

House of Representatives
See U.S. House of Representatives

Housing Authority of New Orleans
Mason, Ronald 27

Houston Astros baseball team
Morgan, Joe Leonard 9
Watson, Bob 25

Houston Comets basketball team
Perrot, Kim 23
Thompson, Tina 25

Houston Oilers football team
McNair, Steve 22, 47
Moon, Warren 8

Houston Rockets basketball team
Lucas, John 7
Olajuwon, Hakeem 2

Howard University
Cardozo, Francis L. 33
Carter, Joye Maureen 41
Cobb, W. Montague 39
Davis, Arthur P. 41
Dodson, Owen 38
Gerima, Haile 38
Jenifer, Franklyn G. 2
Ladner, Joyce A. 42
Locke, Alain 10
Logan, Rayford W. 40
Mays, Benjamin E. 7
Neal, Larry 38
Payton, Benjamin F. 23
Porter, James A. 11
Reid, Irvin D. 20
Robinson, Spottswood W. III 22
Sowande, Fela 39
Swygert, H. Patrick 22
Wells, James Lesesne 10
Wesley, Dorothy Porter 19
White, Charles 39
Young, Roger Arliner 29

HRCF
See Human Rights Campaign Fund

Hubbard Hospital
Lyttle, Hulda Margaret 14

HUD
See U.S. Department of Housing and Urban Development

Hugo awards
Butler, Octavia 8, 43
Delany, Samuel R., Jr. 9

Hull-Ottawa Canadiens hockey team
O'Ree, Willie 5

Human Resources
Howroyd, Janice Bryant 42

Human Rights Campaign Fund (HRCF)
Carter, Mandy 11

Hunter College
DeCarava, Roy 42
Mayhew, Richard 39

Hurdle
Devers, Gail 7

IBF
See International Boxing Federation

IBM
Adkins, Rod 41
Chenault, Kenneth I. 5, 36
Dean, Mark 35
Foster, Jylla Moore 45
Thompson, John W. 26

Zollar, Alfred **40**

IBM's National Black Family Technology Awareness
Adkins, Rod **41**

Ice Hockey in Harlem
Mayers, Jamal **39**

Ice skating
See Figure skating

Igbo people/traditions
Achebe, Chinua **6**

IHRLG
See International Human Rights Law Group

I-Iman Cosmetics
Iman, **4, 33**

Ile Ife Films
Hall, Arthur **39**

Illinois state government
Braun, Carol Moseley **4, 42**
Burris, Roland W. **25**
Colter, Cyrus J. **36**
Trotter, Donne E. **28**
Washington, Harold **6**
White, Jesse **22**

Illustrations
Biggers, John **20, 33**
Bryan, Ashley F. **41**
Campbell, E. Simms **13**
Fax, Elton **48**
Hudson, Cheryl **15**
Kitt, Sandra **23**
Pinkney, Jerry **15**
Saint James, Synthia **12**

Imani Temple
Stallings, George A., Jr. **6**

IMF
See International Monetary Fund

Imhotep National Conference on Hospital Integration
Cobb, W. Montague **39**

Indecorp, Inc.
Johnson, George E. **29**

Indiana Fever basketball team
Catchings, Tamika **43**

Indiana state government
Carson, Julia **23**

Indianapolis 500
Ribbs, Willy T. **2**

Indianapolis ABCs baseball team
Charleston, Oscar **39**

Indianapolis Clowns baseball team
Charleston, Oscar **39**
Johnson, Mamie "Peanut" **40**

Indianapolis Colts football team
Dickerson, Eric **27**
Dungy, Tony **17, 42**

Indianapolis Crawfords baseball team
Charleston, Oscar **39**
Kaiser, Cecil **42**

Information technology
Smith, Joshua **10**
Zollar, Alfred **40**

In Friendship
Baker, Ella **5**

Inkatha
Buthelezi, Mangosuthu Gatsha **9**

Inner City Broadcasting Corporation
Jackson, Hal **41**
Sutton, Percy E. **42**

Institute for Black Parenting
Oglesby, Zena **12**

Institute for Journalism Education
Harris, Jay T. **19**
Maynard, Robert C. **7**

Institute for Research in African American Studies
Marable, Manning **10**

Institute of Positive Education
Madhubuti, Haki R. **7**

Institute of Social and Religious Research
Mays, Benjamin E. **7**

Institute of the Black World
Dodson, Howard, Jr. **7**
Ford, Clyde W. **40**

Insurance
Hill, Jessie, Jr. **13**
Kidd, Mae Street **39**
Procope, Ernesta **23**
Spaulding, Charles Clinton **9**
Vaughns, Cleopatra **46**

Interior design
Bridges, Sheila **36**
Hayes, Cecil N. **46**
Taylor, Karin **34**

Internal Revenue Service
Colter, Cyrus J. **36**

International ambassadors
Davis, Ruth **37**
Poitier, Sidney **11, 36**
Wharton, Clifton Reginald, Sr. **36**

International Association of Fire Chiefs
Bell, Michael **40**
Day, Leon **39**

International Boxing Federation (IBF)
Ali, Muhammad **2, 16**
Hearns, Thomas **29**
Hopkins, Bernard **35**
Lewis, Lennox **27**
Moorer, Michael **19**
Mosley, Shane **32**
Tyson, Mike **28, 44**
Whitaker, Pernell **10**

International Federation of Library Associations and Institutions
Wedgeworth, Robert W. **42**

International Free and Accepted Masons and Eastern Star
Banks, William **11**

International Human Rights Law Group (IHRLG)
McDougall, Gay J. **11, 43**

International Ladies' Auxiliary
Tucker, Rosina **14**

International Law
Payne, Ulice **42**

International Monetary Fund (IMF)
Babangida, Ibrahim **4**
Chissano, Joaquim **7**
Conté, Lansana **7**
Diouf, Abdou **3**
Patterson, P. J. **6, 20**

International Olympic Committee (IOC)
DeFrantz, Anita **37**

International Workers Organization (IWO)
Patterson, Louise **25**

Internet
Cooper, Barry **33**
Knowling, Robert **38**
Thomas-Graham, Pamela **29**

Internet security
Thompson, John W. **26**

Interpol
Noble, Ronald **46**

Interscope Geffen A & M Records
Stoute, Steve **38**

In the Black television show
Jones, Caroline R. **29**

Inventions
Johnson, Lonnie **32**
Julian, Percy Lavon **6**
Latimer, Lewis H. **4**
McCoy, Elijah **8**
Morgan, Garrett **1**
Woods, Granville T. **5**

Investment management
Beal, Bernard B. **46**
Bryant, John **26**
Procope, Ernesta **23**
Rogers, John W., Jr. **5**
Utendahl, John **23**

Island Def Jam Music Group
Liles, Kevin **42**

Island Records
Ade, King Sunny **41**

Ivorian Popular Front (FPI)
Gbagbo, Laurent **43**

Ivory Coast Government
Gbagbo, Laurent **43**

Jackie Robinson Foundation
Robinson, Rachel **16**

Jackson Securities, Inc.
Jackson, Maynard **2, 41**

Jackson University
Mason, Ronald **27**

Jacksonville Jaguars football team
Cherry, Deron **40**

Jamison Project
Jamison, Judith **7**

Jazz
Adderley, Julian "Cannonball" **30**
Adderley, Nat **29**
Albright, Gerald **23**
Anderson, Carl **48**
Armstrong, Louis **2**
Austin, Lovie **40**
Austin, Patti **24**
Ayers, Roy **16**
Barker, Danny **32**
Bailey, Buster **38**
Basie, Count **23**
Bechet, Sidney **18**
Belle, Regina **1**
Blakey, Art **37**
Blanchard, Terence **43**
Bolden, Buddy **39**
Bridgewater, Dee Dee **32**
Brooks, Avery **9**
Butler, Jonathan **28**
Calloway, Cab **14**
Carter, Benny **46**
Carter, Betty **19**
Carter, Regina **23**
Carter, Warrick L. **27**
Cartíer, Xam Wilson **41**
Charles, Ray **16, 48**
Cheatham, Doc **17**
Clarke, Kenny **27**
Cole, Nat King **17**
Coleman, Ornette **39**
Coltrane, John **19**
Cook, Charles "Doc" **44**
Count Basie **23**
Crawford, Randy **19**
Crothers, Scatman **19**
Crouch, Stanley **11**
Crowder, Henry **16**
Davis, Anthony **11**
Davis, Frank Marshall **47**
Davis, Miles **4**
Dickenson, Vic **38**
Donegan, Dorothy **19**
Downing, Will **19**
Duke, George **21**
Dumas, Henry **41**
Eckstine, Billy **28**
Eldridge, Roy **37**
Ellington, Duke **5**
Ellison, Ralph **7**
Eubanks, Kevin **15**
Farmer, Art **38**
Ferrell, Rachelle **29**

Fitzgerald, Ella **8, 18**
Foster, George "Pops" **40**
Freelon, Nnenna **32**
Freeman, Yvette **27**
Fuller, Arthur **27**
Gillespie, Dizzy **1**
Golson, Benny **37**
Gordon, Dexter **25**
Hampton, Lionel **17, 41**
Hancock, Herbie **20**
Hardin Armstrong, Lil **39**
Hawkins, Coleman **9**
Henderson, Fletcher **32**
Higginbotham, J. C. **37**
Hines, Earl "Fatha" **39**
Hinton, Milt **30**
Holiday, Billie **1**
Horn, Shirley **32**
Hyman, Phyllis **19**
Jackson, Milt **26**
James, Etta **13**
Jarreau, Al **21**
Johnson, Buddy **36**
Johnson, J.J. **37**
Jones, Elvin **14**
Jones, Etta **35**
Jones, Jonah **39**
Jones, Quincy **8, 30**
Jordan, Ronny **26**
Lewis, Ramsey **35**
Lincoln, Abbey **3**
Locke, Eddie **44**
Madhubuti, Haki R. **7**
Marsalis, Branford **34**
Marsalis, Delfeayo **41**
Marsalis, Wynton **16**
McBride, James **35**
Mills, Florence **22**
Mingus, Charles **15**
Monk, Thelonious **1**
Moore, Melba **21**
Morton, Jelly Roll **29**
Muse, Clarence Edouard **21**
Nascimento, Milton **2**
Oliver, Joe "King" **42**
Parker, Charlie **20**
Peterson, Marvin "Hannibal" **27**
Powell, Bud **24**
Redman, Joshua **30**
Reese, Della **6, 20**
Reeves, Dianne **32**
Roach, Max **21**
Roberts, Marcus **19**
Rollins, Sonny **37**
Ross, Diana **8, 27**
Rushing, Jimmy **37**
Scott, "Little" Jimmy **48**
Silver, Horace **26**
Sissle, Noble **29**
Smith, Bessie **3**
Smith, Cladys "Jabbo" **32**
Smith, Stuff **37**
Strayhorn, Billy **31**
Sullivan, Maxine **37**
Swann, Lynn **28**
Taylor, Billy **23**
Terry, Clark **39**
Vaughan, Sarah **13**
Waller, Fats **29**
Washington, Dinah **22**
Washington, Grover, Jr. **17, 44**
Waters, Benny **26**
Watson, Johnny "Guitar" **18**

Webster, Katie **29**
Whalum, Kirk **37**
White, Maurice **29**
Williams, Joe **5, 25**
Williams, Mary Lou **15**
Wilson, Cassandra **16**
Wilson, Nancy **10**
York, Vincent **40**
Young, Lester **37**

Jazzistry
York, Vincent **40**

***Jet* magazine**
Bennett, Lerone, Jr. **5**
Johnson, John H. **3**
Massaquoi, Hans J. **30**
Sleet, Moneta, Jr. **5**

Jive Records
McPherson, David **32**

Jockeys
Winkfield, Jimmy **42**

John Lucas Enterprises
Lucas, John **7**

Johnny Ace with the New Blues Sound
Ace, Johnny **36**

Johnson C. Smith University
Yancy, Dorothy Cowser **42**

Johnson Products
Johnson, George E. **29**

Johnson Publishing Company, Inc.
Bennett, Lerone, Jr. **5**
Booker, Simeon **23**
Johnson, John H. **3**
Rice, Linda Johnson **9, 41**
Sleet, Moneta, Jr. **5**

Joint Center for Political Studies
Williams, Eddie N. **44**

Joint Chiefs of Staff
See U.S. Joint Chiefs of Staff

Joint Regional Terrorism Task Force
Bell, Michael **40**

Journalism
Abbott, Robert Sengstacke **27**
Abrahams, Peter **39**
Abu-Jamal, Mumia **15**
Ansa, Tina McElroy **14**
Ashley-Ward, Amelia **23**
Auguste, Arnold A. **47**
Azikiwe, Nnamdi **13**
Barden, Don H. **9, 20**
Barnett, Amy Du Bois **46**
Barrett, Lindsay **43**
Bass, Charlotta Spears **40**
Bates, Karen Grigsby **40**
Bennett, Lerone, Jr. **5**
Blake, Asha **26**
Bolden, Frank E. **44**
Booker, Simeon **23**
Borders, James **9**
Boyd, Gerald M. **32**
Bradley, Ed **2**

Britt, Donna **28**
Brown, Llyod Louis **42**
Brown, Tony **3**
Buckley, Gail Lumet **39**
Campbell, Bebe Moore **6, 24**
Cary, Mary Ann Shadd **30**
Cayton, Horace **26**
Chideya, Farai **14**
Cooke, Marvel **31**
Cooper, Barry **33**
Cose, Ellis **5**
Crouch, Stanley **11**
Cullen, Countee **8**
Cunningham, Evelyn **23**
Dash, Leon **47**
Davis, Frank Marshall **47**
Dawkins, Wayne **20**
Drummond, William J. **40**
Due, Tananarive **30**
Dunbar, Paul Laurence **8**
Dunnigan, Alice Allison **41**
Edmonds, Terry **17**
Forman, James **7**
Fortune, T. Thomas **6**
Fuller, Hoyt **44**
Giddings, Paula **11**
Goode, Mal **13**
Gordon, Ed **10**
Grimké, Archibald H. **9**
Gumbel, Bryant **14**
Gumbel, Greg **8**
Hansberry, Lorraine **6**
Hare, Nathan **44**
Harrington, Oliver W. **9**
Harris, Claire **34**
Harris, Jay **19**
Haynes, Trudy **44**
Henriques, Julian **37**
Hickman, Fred **11**
Hunter-Gault, Charlayne **6, 31**
Ifill, Gwen **28**
Jarret, Vernon D. **42**
Jasper, Kenji **39**
Joachim, Paulin **34**
Johnson, Georgia Douglas **41**
Johnson, James Weldon **5**
Khanga, Yelena **6**
Knight, Etheridge **37**
LaGuma, Alex **30**
Lacy, Sam **30, 46**
Lampkin, Daisy **19**
Leavell, Dorothy R. **17**
Lewis, Edward T. **21**
Mabrey, Vicki **26**
Mabuza-Suttle, Felicia **43**
Madison, Paula **37**
Martin, Louis E. **16**
Mason, Felicia **31**
Maynard, Robert C. **7**
McBride, James **35**
McCall, Nathan **8**
McGruder, Robert **22, 35**
McKay, Claude **6**
Mickelbury, Penny **28**
Mitchell, Russ **21**
Mkapa, Benjamin **16**
Mossell, Gertrude Bustill **40**
Murphy, John H. **42**
Murray, Pauli **38**
Nelson, Jill **6**
Nkosi, Lewis **46**
Page, Clarence **4**
Palmer, Everard **37**

Parks, Gordon **1, 35**
Payne, Ethel L. **28**
Perez, Anna **1**
Perkins, Tony **24**
Pinkston, W. Randall **24**
Pressley, Condace L. **41**
Price, Hugh B. **9**
Quarles, Norma **25**
Raspberry, William **2**
Reed, Ishmael **8**
Reeves, Rachel J. **23**
Roberts, Robin **16**
Robinson, Max **3**
Rodgers, Johnathan **6**
Rowan, Carl T. **1, 30**
Salih, Al-Tayyib **37**
Schuyler, George Samuel **40**
Senior, Olive **37**
Shaw, Bernard **2, 28**
Shipp, E. R. **15**
Simpson, Carole **6, 30**
Smith, Clarence O. **21**
Smith, Danyel **40**
Sowell, Thomas **2**
Staples, Brent **8**
Stewart, Alison **13**
Stokes, Carl B. **10**
Stone, Chuck **9**
Tate, Eleanora E. **20**
Taylor, Kristin Clark **8**
Taylor, Susan L. **10**
Thurman, Wallace **16**
Tolson, Melvin B. **37**
Trotter, Monroe **9**
Tucker, Cynthia **15**
Wallace, Michele Faith **13**
Watts, Rolonda **9**
Webb, Veronica **10**
Wells-Barnett, Ida B. **8**
Wesley, Valerie Wilson **18**
Whitaker, Mark **21, 47**
Wiley, Ralph **8**
Wilkins, Roger **2**
Williams, Armstrong **29**
Williams, Juan **35**
Williams, Patricia J. **11**

Journal of Negro History
Woodson, Carter G. **2**

Juanita Bynum Ministries
Bynum, Juanita **31**

Juju music
Ade, King Sunny **41**

Just Us Books
Hudson, Cheryl **15**
Hudson, Wade **15**

Kansas City Athletics baseball team
Paige, Satchel **7**

Kansas City Chiefs football team
Allen, Marcus **20**
Cherry, Deron **40**
Dungy, Tony **17, 42**
Thomas, Derrick **25**

Kansas City government
Cleaver, Emanuel **4, 45**

Kansas City Monarchs baseball team
Bell, James "Cool Papa" 36
Brown, Willard 36

KANU
See Kenya African National Union

Kappa Alpha Psi
Hamilton, Samuel C. 47

Karl Kani Infinity
Kani, Karl 10

KAU
See Kenya African Union

KCA
See Kikuyu Central Association

Kentucky Derby
Winkfield, Jimmy 42

Kentucky state government
Kidd, Mae Street 39

Kentucky Negro Educational Association
Cotter, Joseph Seamon, Sr. 40

Kenya African National Union (KANU)
Kenyatta, Jomo 5
Moi, Daniel arap 1, 35

Kenya African Union (KAU)
Kenyatta, Jomo 5

Kenya National Council of Churchs (NCCK)
Kobia, Rev. Dr. Samuel 43

Keyan government
Maathai, Wangari 43

Kikuyu Central Association (KCA)
Kenyatta, Jomo 5

King Center
See Martin Luther King Jr. Center for Nonviolent Social Change

King Oliver's Creole Band
Armstrong, (Daniel) Louis 2
Hardin Armstrong, Lil 39
Oliver, Joe "King" 42

King's Troop of the Royal Horse Artillery
Scantlebury, Janna 47

King Sunny Ade Foundation
Ade, King Sunny 41

Kitchen Table: Women of Color Press
Smith, Barbara 28

Koko Taylor's Celebrity
Taylor, Koko 40

Kraft General Foods
Fudge, Ann 11
Sneed, Paula A. 18

Kwanzaa
Karenga, Maulana 10

Kwazulu Territorial Authority
Buthelezi, Mangosuthu Gatsha 9

Labour Party
Amos, Valerie 41

Ladies Professional Golfers' Association (LPGA)
Gibson, Althea 8, 43
Powell, Renee 34

LaFace Records
Benjamin, Andre 45
Edmonds, Kenneth "Babyface" 10, 31
Patton, Antwan 45
Reid, Antonio "L.A." 28
OutKast 35

Lamb of God Ministry
Falana, Lola 42

Langston (OK) city government
Tolson, Melvin B. 37

LAPD
See Los Angeles Police Department

Latin American folk music
Nascimento, Milton 2

Latin baseball leagues
Kaiser, Cecil 42

Law enforcement
Alexander, Joyce London 18
Barrett, Jacquelyn 28
Bolton, Terrell D. 25
Bradley, Thomas 2, 20
Brown, Lee P. 1, 24
Freeman, Charles 19
Gibson, Johnnie Mae 23
Glover, Nathaniel, Jr. 12
Gomez-Preston, Cheryl 9
Harvard, Beverly 11
Hillard, Terry 25
Holton, Hugh, Jr. 39
Hurtt, Harold 46
Johnson, Norma L. Holloway 17
Johnson, Robert T. 17
Keith, Damon J. 16
McKinnon, Isaiah 9
Moose, Charles 40
Napoleon, Benny N. 23
Noble, Ronald 46
Oliver, Jerry 37
Parks, Bernard C. 17
Ramsey, Charles H. 21
Schmoke, Kurt 1, 48
Thomas, Franklin A. 5
Wainwright, Joscelyn 46
Williams, Willie L. 4
Wilson, Jimmy 45

Lawrence Steele Design
Steele, Lawrence 28

Lawyers' Committee for Civil Rights Under Law
Arnwine, Barbara 28
Hubbard, Arnette 38

McDougall, Gay J. 11, 43

LDF
See NAACP Legal Defense and Educational Fund

Leadership Conference on Civil Rights (LCCR)
Henderson, Wade J. 14

League of Nations
Haile Selassie 7

League of Women Voters
Meek, Carrie 36

Leary Group Inc.
Leary, Kathryn D. 10

"Leave No Child Behind"
Edelman, Marian Wright 5, 42

Lee Elder Scholarship Fund
Elder, Lee 6

Legal Defense Fund
See NAACP Legal Defense and Educational Fund

Les Brown Unlimited, Inc.
Brown, Les 5

Lexicography
Major, Clarence 9

Liberian government
Henries, A. Doris Banks 44

Liberation theology
West, Cornel 5

Librettist
Chenault, John 40

Library science
Bontemps, Arna 8
Franklin, Hardy R. 9
Harsh, Vivian Gordon 14
Hutson, Jean Blackwell 16
Josey, E. J. 10
Kitt, Sandra 23
Larsen, Nella 10
Owens, Major 6
Rollins, Charlemae Hill 27
Schomburg, Arthur Alfonso 9
Smith, Jessie Carney 35
Spencer, Anne 27
Wedgeworth, Robert W. 42
Wesley, Dorothy Porter 19

Lincoln University
Cuney, William Waring 44
Randall, Dudley 8
Sudarkasa, Niara 4

LISC
See Local Initiative Support Corporation

Listen Up Foundation
Jones, Quincy 8, 30

Literacy Volunteers of America
Amos, Wally 9

Literary criticism
Baker, Houston A., Jr. 6
Brown, Sterling 10

Cartey, Wilfred 1992 47
Christian, Barbara T. 44
Cook, Mercer 40
De Veaux, Alexis 44
Emanuel, James A. 46
Fleming, Raymond 48
Ford, Nick Aaron 44
Fuller, Hoyt 44
Joachim, Paulin 34
Mugo, Micere Githae 32
Redding, J. Saunders 26
Reed, Ishmael 8
Smith, Barbara 28
wa Thiong'o, Ngugi 29
Wesley, Valerie Wilson 18
West, Cornel 5

Literary Hall of Fame for Writers of African Descent
Colter, Cyrus J. 36

Lithography
White, Charles 39

Little Junior Project
Fuller, Arthur 27

"Little Paris" group
Thomas, Alma 14

"Little Rock Nine"
Bates, Daisy 13

Liver research
Leevy, Carrol M. 42

Lobbying
Brooke, Edward 8
Brown, Elaine 8
Brown, Jesse 6, 41
Brown, Ron 5
Edelman, Marian Wright 5, 42
Lee, Canada 8
Mallett, Conrad, Jr. 16
Robinson, Randall 7, 46

Local Initiative Support Corporation (LISC)
Thomas, Franklin A. 5

Long jump
Lewis, Carl 4
Powell, Mike 7

Los Angeles city government
Bradley, Thomas 2, 20
Evers, Myrlie 8

Los Angeles Clippers basketball team
Brand, Elton 31

Los Angeles Dodgers baseball team
Baker, Dusty 8, 43
Newcombe, Don 24
Robinson, Frank 9
Strawberry, Darryl 22

Los Angeles Galaxy soccer team
Jones, Cobi N'Gai 18

Los Angeles Lakers basketball team
Abdul-Jabbar, Kareem 8
Bryant, Kobe 15, 31

Chamberlain, Wilt **18, 47**
Fox, Rick **27**
Green, A. C. **32**
Johnson, Earvin "Magic" **3, 39**
O'Neal, Shaquille **8, 30**

Los Angeles Philharmonic
Lewis, Henry **39**

Los Angeles Police Department (LAPD)
Parks, Bernard C. **17**
Williams, Willie L. **4**

Los Angeles Raiders football team
Allen, Marcus **20**
Lofton, James **42**
Lott, Ronnie **9**
Shell, Art **1**

Los Angeles Rams football team
Dickerson, Eric **27**

Los Angeles Times newspaper
Drummond, William J. **40**

Los Angeles Sparks basketball team
Leslie, Lisa **16**

Lost-Found Nation of Islam
Ali, Muhammad **2, 16**
Farrakhan, Louis **2, 15**
Heard, Nathan C. **45**
Muhammad, Ava **31**
Muhammad, Elijah **4**
Muhammad, Khallid Abdul **10, 31**
Muhammed, W. Deen **27**
Sutton, Percy E. **42**
Tillard, Conrad **47**
X, Malcolm **1**
X, Marvin **45**

Louisiana state government
Fields, Cleo **13**
Morial, Ernest "Dutch" **26**
Pinchback, P. B. S. **9**

Louisiana State Senate
Fields, Cleo **13**
Jefferson, William J. **25**
Pinchback, P. B. S. **9**

LPGA
See Ladies Professional Golfers' Association

Lunar Surface Ultraviolet Camera
See Ultraviolet Camera/Spectrograph (UVC)

Lynching (anti-lynching legislation)
Johnson, James Weldon **5**
Moore, Harry T. **29**
Till, Emmett **7**

Lyricist
Crouch, Andraé **27**
D'Angelo **27**
Dunbar, Paul Laurence **8**
Fitzgerald, Ella **8**
Jean, Wyclef **20**
Johnson, James Weldon **5**
KRS-One **34**
Lil' Kim **28**
MC Lyte **34**
Randall, Alice **38**
Run-DMC **31**

MacArthur Genius Grant
Parks, Suzan-Lori **34**

MacNeil/Lehrer NewsHour
Hunter-Gault, Charlayne **6, 31**

Mad TV
Jones, Orlando **30**
Wilson, Debra **38**

Madame C. J. Walker Manufacturing Company
Joyner, Marjorie Stewart **26**
Walker, A'lelia **14**
Walker, Madame C. J. **7**

Major League Baseball
Mariner, Jonathan **41**
Solomon, Jimmie Lee **38**

Major League Baseball Players Association
Blair, Paul **36**

Major League Baseball Properties
Doby, Lawrence Eugene Sr. **16, 41**

Malawi Congress Party (MCP)
Banda, Hastings Kamuzu **6**

Malaco Records
Bland, Bobby "Blue" **36**

Manhattan Project
Quarterman, Lloyd Albert **4**
Wilkens, J. Ernest, Jr. **43**

MARC Corp.
See Metropolitan Applied Research Center

March on Washington/Freedom March
Baker, Josephine **3**
Belafonte, Harry **4**
Bunche, Ralph J. **5**
Davis, Ossie **5**
Fauntroy, Walter E. **11**
Forman, James **7**
Franklin, John Hope **5**
Hedgeman, Anna Arnold **22**
Horne, Lena **5**
Jackson, Mahalia **5**
King, Coretta Scott **3**
King, Martin Luther, Jr. **1**
Lewis, John **2, 46**
Meredith, James H. **11**
Randolph, A. Philip **3**
Rustin, Bayard **4**
Sleet, Moneta, Jr. **5**
Wilkins, Roy **4**
Young, Whitney M., Jr. **4**

Marie Brown Associates
Brown, Marie Dutton **12**

Martial Arts
Copeland, Michael **47**

Martin Luther King Jr. Center for Nonviolent Social Change
Dodson, Howard, Jr. **7**
King, Bernice **4**
King, Coretta Scott **3**
King, Dexter **10**
King, Martin Luther, Jr. **1**
King, Yolanda **6**

Martin Luther King Jr. Drum Major Award
Broadbent, Hydeia **36**
Mfume, Kweisi **6, 41**

Marxism
Baraka, Amiri **1, 38**
Bishop, Maurice **39**
Jagan, Cheddi **16**
Machel, Samora Moises **8**
Nkrumah, Kwame **3**
Sankara, Thomas **17**

Maryland Mustangs basketball team
Parish, Robert **43**

Maryland state government
Steele, Michael **38**

Massachusetts state government
Brooke, Edward **8**

Masters Tournament
Elder, Lee **6**
Woods, Tiger **14, 31**

Mathematics
Emeagwali, Philip **30**
Gates, Sylvester James, Jr. **15**
Wilkens, J. Ernest, Jr. **43**

Maurice Malone Design
Malone, Maurice **32**

MAXIMA Corporation
Smith, Joshua **10**

Maxwell House Coffee Company
Fudge, Ann **11**

Mays Chemical Co.
Mays, William G. **34**

McArthur Foundation Fellowship
Butler, Octavia **8, 43**

McCall Pattern Company
Lewis, Reginald F. **6**

McGill University (Canada)
Elliott, Lorris **37**

MCP
See Malawi Congress Party

Medical examiners
Carter, Joye Maureen **41**

Medicine
Banda, Hastings Kamuzu **6**
Benjamin, Regina **20**
Black, Keith Lanier **18**
Callender, Clive O. **3**
Canady, Alexa **28**
Carroll, L. Natalie **44**
Carson, Benjamin **1, 35**
Carter, Joye Maureen **41**
Chatard, Peter **44**
Chinn, May Edward **26**
Christian-Green, Donna M. **17**
Cobb, W. Montague **39**
Cole, Rebecca **38**
Comer, James P. **6**
Coney, PonJola **48**
Cooper, Edward S. **6**
Dickens, Helen Octavia **14**
Drew, Charles Richard **7**
Elders, Joycelyn **6**
Fisher, Rudolph **17**
Foster, Henry W., Jr. **26**
Freeman, Harold P. **23**
Fuller, Solomon Carter, Jr. **15**
Gayle, Helene D. **3**
Gibson, William F. **6**
Hinton, William Augustus **8**
Jemison, Mae C. **1, 35**
Johnson, R.M. **36**
Kenney, John A., Jr. **48**
Kountz, Samuel L. **10**
Lawless, Theodore K. **8**
Lavizzo-Mourey, Risa **48**
Leffall, LaSalle, Jr. **3**
Logan, Onnie Lee **14**
Maxey, Randall **46**
Pitt, David Thomas **10**
Poussaint, Alvin F. **5**
Satcher, David **7**
Stewart, Ella **39**
Sullivan, Louis **8**
Thomas, Vivien **9**
Watkins, Levi, Jr. **9**
Welsing, Frances Cress **5**
Williams, Daniel Hale **2**
Witt, Edwin T. **26**
Wright, Charles H. **35**
Wright, Louis Tompkins **4**

Meharry Medical College
Coney, PonJola **48**
Foster, Henry W., Jr. **26**
Lyttle, Hulda Margaret **14**

Melanin theory of racism
See also Cress Theory of Color Confrontation and Racism

Melody Makers
Marley, Ziggy **41**

Men's movement
Somé, Malidoma Patrice **10**

Merce Cunningham Dance Company
Dove, Ulysses **5**

Merrill Lynch & Co., Inc.
O'Neal, Stanley **38**

MESBICs
See Minority Enterprise Small Business Investment Corporations

Meteorology
Anderson, Charles Edward **37**
Bacon-Bercey, June **38**

Metropolitan Applied Research Center (MARC Corp.)
Clark, Kenneth B. **5**
Anderson, Marian **2, 33**

Collins, Janet 33
Dobbs, Mattiwilda 34
Bell, James "Cool Papa" 36
Dandridge, Ray 36

MFDP
See Mississippi Freedom Democratic Party

Miami Dolphins football team
Greene, Joe 10

Michael Jordan Foundation
Jordan, Michael 6, 21

Michigan House of Representatives
Collins, Barbara-Rose 7
Kilpatrick, Carolyn Cheeks 16
Kilpatrick, Kwame 34
Reeves, Triette Lipsey 27

Michigan state government
Brown, Cora 33

Michigan State Supreme Court
Archer, Dennis 7, 36
Mallett, Conrad, Jr. 16

Michigan State University
Wharton, Clifton R., Jr. 7
Willingham, Tyrone 43

Microsoft Corporation
Millines Dziko, Trish 28

Midwifery
Logan, Onnie Lee 14
Robinson, Sharon 22

Military police
Cadoria, Sherian Grace 14

Miller Brewing Company
Colbert, Virgis William 17

Millinery
Bailey, Xenobia 11

Million Man March
Farrakhan, Louis 2, 15
Hawkins, La-Van 17
Worrill, Conrad 12

Milwaukee Braves baseball team
Aaron, Hank 5

Milwaukee Brewers baseball team
Aaron, Hank 5
Baylor, Don 6
Payne, Ulice 42
Sheffield, Gary 16

Milwaukee Bucks basketball team
Abdul-Jabbar, Kareem 8
Lucas, John 7
Robertson, Oscar 26

Mingo-Jones Advertising
Chisholm, Samuel J. 32
Jones, Caroline R. 29

Mingo, Frank 32

Minneapolis City Council
Sayles Belton, Sharon 9, 16

Minneapolis city government
Sayles Belton, Sharon 9, 16

Minneapolis Millers baseball team
Dandridge, Ray 36

Minnesota State Supreme Court
Page, Alan 7

Minnesota Timberwolves basketball team
Garnett, Kevin 14

Minnesota Twins baseball team
Baylor, Don 6
Carew, Rod 20
Hunter, Torii 43
Puckett, Kirby 4
Winfield, Dave 5

Minnesota Vikings football team
Carter, Cris 21
Culpepper, Daunte 32
Cunningham, Randall 23
Dungy, Tony 17, 42
Gilliam, Frank 23
Green, Dennis 5, 45
Moon, Warren 8
Moss, Randy 23
Page, Alan 7
Rashad, Ahmad 18
Stringer, Korey 35
Walker, Herschel 1

Minority Business Enterprise Legal Defense and Education Fund
Mitchell, Parren J. 42

Minority Business Resource Center
Hill, Jessie, Jr. 13

Minority Enterprise Small Business Investment Corporations (MESBICs)
Lewis, Reginald F. 6

Minstrel shows
McDaniel, Hattie 5

Miracle Network Telethon
Warner, Malcolm-Jamal 22, 36

Miss America
Vincent, Marjorie Judith 2
Williams, Vanessa L. 4, 17

Miss Collegiate African-American Pageant
Mercado-Valdes, Frank 43

Miss USA
Gist, Carole 1

Mississippi Freedom Democratic Party (MFDP)
Baker, Ella 5
Blackwell, Unita 17

Hamer, Fannie Lou 6
Henry, Aaron 19
Norton, Eleanor Holmes 7

Mississippi state government
Hamer, Fannie Lou 6

MLA
See Modern Language Association of America

Model Inner City Community Organization (MICCO)
Fauntroy, Walter E. 11

Modeling
Banks, Tyra 11
Beckford, Tyson 11
Berry, Halle 4, 19
Campbell, Naomi 1, 31
Hardison, Bethann 12
Hounsou, Djimon 19, 45
Houston, Whitney 7, 28
Iman 4, 33
Johnson, Beverly 2
Kodjoe, Boris 34
Langhart, Janet 19
Leslie, Lisa 16
LisaRaye 27
Michele, Michael 31
Onwurah, Ngozi 38
Powell, Maxine 8
Rochon, Lela 16
Sims, Naomi 29
Smith, Barbara 11
Tamia 24
Taylor, Karin 34
Tyrese 27
Tyson, Cicely 7
Webb, Veronica 10
Wek, Alek 18

Modern dance
Ailey, Alvin 8
Allen, Debbie 13, 42
Byrd, Donald 10
Collins, Janet 33
Davis, Chuck 33
Dove, Ulysses 5
Fagan, Garth 18
Faison, George 16
Henson, Darrin 33
Jamison, Judith 7
Jones, Bill T. 1, 46
King, Alonzo 38
Kitt, Eartha 16
Miller, Bebe 3
Primus, Pearl 6
Vereen, Ben 4

Modern Language Association of America (MLA)
Baker, Houston A., Jr. 6

Modern Records
Brooks, Hadda 40

Montgomery bus boycott
Abernathy, Ralph David 1
Baker, Ella 5
Burks, Mary Fair 40
Jackson, Mahalia 5
King, Martin Luther, Jr. 1
Parks, Rosa 1, 35

Rustin, Bayard 4

Montgomery County Police Department
Moose, Charles 40

Montreal Canadians hockey team
Brashear, Donald 39

Montreal Expos baseball team
Doby, Lawrence Eugene Sr. 16, 41

Moore Black Press
Moore, Jessica Care 30

Morehouse College
Brown, Uzee 42
Hope, John 8
Mays, Benjamin E. 7

Morgan Stanley
Lewis, William M., Jr. 40

Morna
Evora, Cesaria 12

Morris Brown College
Cross, Dolores E. 23

Moscow World News
Khanga, Yelena 6
Sullivan, Louis 8

Mother Waddles Perpetual Mission, Inc.
Waddles, Charleszetta (Mother) 10

Motivational speaking
Brown, Les 5
Bunkley, Anita Richmond 39
Creagh, Milton 27
Grant, Gwendolyn Goldsby 28
Jolley, Willie 28
July, William 27
Kimbro, Dennis 10
Russell-McCloud, Patricia 17
Tyson, Asha 39

Motor City Giants baseball team
Kaiser, Cecil 42

Motorcycle racing
Showers, Reggie 30

Motown Historical Museum
Edwards, Esther Gordy 43

Motown Records
Atkins, Cholly 40
Bizimungu, Pasteur 19
Busby, Jheryl 3
de Passe, Suzanne 25
Edwards, Esther Gordy 43
Gaye, Marvin 2
Gordy, Berry, Jr. 1
Harrell, Andre 9, 30
Holland-Dozier-Holland 36
Jackson, George 19
Jackson, Michael 19
Kendricks, Eddie 22
Massenburg, Kedar 23
Powell, Maxine 8
Richie, Lionel 27
Robinson, Smokey 3
Ross, Diana 8, 27

Terrell, Tammi **32**
Wells, Mary **28**
Wilson, Mary **28**
Wonder, Stevie **11**

Mt. Holyoke College
Tatum, Beverly Daniel **42**

Mouvement Revolutionnaire National pour la Developpement (Rwanda; MRND)
Habyarimana, Juvenal **8**

MOVE
Goode, W. Wilson **4**
Wideman, John Edgar **5**

Movement for Assemblies of the People
Bishop, Maurice **39**

Movement for Democratic Change (MDC)
Tsvangirai, Morgan **26**

Movement for the Survival of the Ogoni People
Saro-Wiwa, Kenule **39**

Moviement Popular de Libertação de Angola (MPLA)
dos Santos, José Eduardo **43**
Neto, António Agostinho **43**

MPLA
See Moviement Popular de Libertação de Angola

MPS
See Patriotic Movement of Salvation

MRND
See Mouvement Revolutionnaire National pour la Developpement

MTV Jams
Bellamy, Bill **12**

Muddy Waters
Little Walter **36**

Multimedia art
Bailey, Xenobia **11**
Simpson, Lorna **4, 36**

Multiple Sclerosis
Falana, Lola **42**

Muppets, The
Clash, Kevin **14**

Murals
Alston, Charles **33**
Biggers, John **20, 33**
Douglas, Aaron **7**
Lee-Smith, Hughie **5**
Walker, Kara **16**

Murder Inc.
Ashanti **37**
Gotti, Irv **39**
Ja Rule **35**

Music Critics Circle
Holt, Nora **38**

Music One, Inc.
Majors, Jeff **41**

Music publishing
Combs, Sean "Puffy" **17, 43**
Cooke, Sam **17**
Edmonds, Tracey **16**
Gordy, Berry, Jr. **1**
Handy, W. C. **8**
Holland-Dozier-Holland **36**
Humphrey, Bobbi **20**
Ice Cube **8, 30**
Jackson, George **19**
Jackson, Michael **19**
James, Rick **17**
Knight, Suge **11, 30**
Lewis, Emmanuel **36**
Master P **21**
Mayfield, Curtis **2, 43**
Prince **18**
Redding, Otis **16**
Ross, Diana **8, 27**
Shorty I, Ras **47**

Music Television (MTV)
Bellamy, Bill **12**
Chideya, Farai **14**
Norman, Christina **47**
Powell, Kevin **31**

Musical composition
Armatrading, Joan **32**
Ashford, Nickolas **21**
Baiocchi, Regina Harris **41**
Ballard, Hank **41**
Bebey, Francis **45**
Blanchard, Terence **43**
Blige, Mary J **20, 34**
Bonds, Margaret **39**
Bonga, Kuenda **13**
Braxton, Toni **15**
Brown, Uzee **42**
Burke, Solomon **31**
Caesar, Shirley **19**
Carter, Warrick L. **27**
Chapman, Tracy **26**
Charlemagne, Manno **11**
Charles, Ray **16, 48**
Cleveland, James **19**
Cole, Natalie Maria **17**
Coleman, Ornette **39**
Collins, Bootsy **31**
Combs, Sean "Puffy" **17, 43**
Cook, Will Marion **40**
Davis, Anthony **11**
Davis, Miles **4**
Davis, Sammy Jr. **18**
Dawson, William Levi **39**
Diddley, Bo **39**
Ellington, Duke **5**
Elliott, Missy "Misdemeanor" **31**
Europe, James Reese **10**
Evans, Faith **22**
Fats Domino **20**
Freeman, Paul **39**
Fuller, Arthur **27**
Gaynor, Gloria **36**
George, Nelson **12**
Gillespie, Dizzy **1**
Golson, Benny **37**
Gordy, Berry, Jr. **1**
Green, Al **13, 47**
Hailey, JoJo **22**
Hailey, K-Ci **22**
Hammer, M. C. **20**
Handy, W. C. **8**

Harris, Corey **39**
Hathaway, Donny **18**
Hayes, Isaac **20**
Hayes, Teddy **40**
Hill, Lauryn **20**
Holland-Dozier-Holland **36**
Holt, Nora **38**
Humphrey, Bobbi **20**
Isley, Ronald **25**
Jackson, Fred James **25**
Jackson, Michael **19**
Jackson, Randy **40**
James, Rick **17**
Jean-Baptiste, Marianne **17, 46**
Jean, Wyclef **20**
Jerkins, Rodney **31**
Jones, Jonah **39**
Jones, Quincy **8, 30**
Johnson, Buddy **36**
Johnson, Georgia Douglas **41**
Joplin, Scott **6**
Jordan, Montell **23**
Jordan, Ronny **26**
Kay, Ulysses **37**
Kee, John P. **43**
Kelly, R. **18, 44**
Keys, Alicia **32**
King, B. B. **7**
León, Tania **13**
Lincoln, Abbey **3**
Little Milton **36**
Little Walter **36**
Lopes, Lisa "Left Eye" **36**
Majors, Jeff **41**
Marsalis, Delfeayo **41**
Marsalis, Wynton **16**
Master P **21**
Maxwell **20**
Mayfield, Curtis **2, 43**
McClurkin, Donnie **25**
Mills, Stephanie **36**
Mitchell, Brian Stokes **21**
Mo', Keb' **36**
Monica **21**
Moore, Chante **26**
Moore, Dorothy Rudd **46**
Moore, Undine Smith **28**
Muse, Clarence Edouard **21**
Nash, Johnny **40**
Ndegéocello, Me'Shell **15**
Osborne, Jeffrey **26**
Pratt, Awadagin **31**
Price, Florence **37**
Prince **18**
Pritchard, Robert Starling **21**
Reagon, Bernice Johnson **7**
Redding, Otis **16**
Reed, A. C. **36**
Reid, Antonio "L.A." **28**
Roach, Max **21**
Run-DMC **31**
Rushen, Patrice **12**
Sangare, Oumou **18**
Shorty I, Ras **47**
Silver, Horace **26**
Simone, Nina **15, 41**
Simpson, Valerie **21**
Sowande, Fela **39**
Still, William Grant **37**
Strayhorn, Billy **31**
Sweat, Keith **19**
Tillis, Frederick **40**
Usher **23**

Van Peebles, Melvin **7**
Walker, George **37**
Warwick, Dionne **18**
Washington, Grover, Jr. **17, 44**
Williams, Deniece **36**
Winans, Angie **36**
Winans, Debbie **36**

Musicology
George, Zelma Watson **42**

Muslim Mosque, Inc.
X, Malcolm **1**

The Mystery
Delany, Martin R. **27**

Mysteries
Bland, Eleanor Taylor **39**
Creagh, Milton **27**
DeLoach, Nora **30**
Himes, Chester **8**
Holton, Hugh, Jr. **39**
Mickelbury, Penny **28**
Mosley, Walter **5, 25**
Thomas-Graham **29**
Wesley, Valerie Wilson **18**

Mystic Seaport Museum
Pinckney, Bill **42**

NAACP
See National Association for the Advancement of Colored People

NAACP Image Awards
Fields, Kim **36**
Lawrence, Martin **6, 27**
Warner, Malcolm-Jamal **22, 36**

NAACP Legal Defense and Educational Fund (LDF)
Bell, Derrick **6**
Chambers, Julius **3**
Edelman, Marian Wright **5, 42**
Guinier, Lani **7, 30**
Jones, Elaine R. **7, 45**
Julian, Percy Lavon **6**
Marshall, Thurgood **1, 44**
Motley, Constance Baker **10**

NABJ
See National Association of Black Journalists

NAC
See Nyasaland African Congress

NACGN
See National Association of Colored Graduate Nurses

NACW
See National Association of Colored Women

NAG
See Nonviolent Action Group

NASA
See National Aeronautics and Space Administration

NASCAR
See National Association of Stock Car Auto Racing

NASCAR Craftsman Truck series
Lester, Bill 42

NASCAR Diversity Council
Lester, Bill 42

Nation
Wilkins, Roger 2

Nation of Islam
See Lost-Found Nation of Islam

National Action Council for Minorities in Engineering
Pierre, Percy Anthony 46

National Action Network
Sharpton, Al 21

National Academy of Design
White, Charles 39

National Aeronautics and Space Administration (NASA)
Anderson, Michael P. 40
Bluford, Guy 2, 35
Bolden, Charles F., Jr. 7
Carruthers, George R. 40
Gregory, Frederick D. 8
Jemison, Mae C. 1, 35
McNair, Ronald 3
Nichols, Nichelle 11
Sigur, Wanda 44

National Afro-American Council
Fortune, T. Thomas 6
Mossell, Gertrude Bustill 40

National Airmen's Association of America
Brown, Willa 40

National Alliance of Postal and Federal Employees
McGee, James Madison 46

National Alliance Party (NAP)
Fulani, Lenora 11

National Association for the Advancement of Colored People (NAACP)
Anthony, Wendell 25
Austin, Junius C. 44
Baker, Ella 5
Ballance, Frank W. 41
Bates, Daisy 13
Bell, Derrick 6
Bond, Julian 2, 35
Bontemps, Arna 8
Brooks, Gwendolyn 1
Brown, Homer S. 47
Bunche, Ralph J. 5
Chambers, Julius 3
Chavis, Benjamin 6
Clark, Kenneth B. 5
Clark, Septima 7
Cobb, W. Montague 39
Colter, Cyrus, J. 36
Cotter, Joseph Seamon, Sr. 40
Creagh, Milton 27
Days, Drew S., III 10
Dee, Ruby 8
DuBois, Shirley Graham 21
Du Bois, W. E. B. 3
Edelman, Marian Wright 5, 42
Evers, Medgar 3
Evers, Myrlie 8
Farmer, James 2
Ford, Clyde W. 40
Fuller, S. B. 13
Gibson, William F. 6
Grimké, Archibald H. 9
Hampton, Fred 18
Harrington, Oliver W. 9
Henderson, Wade 14
Hobson, Julius W. 44
Hooks, Benjamin L. 2
Horne, Lena 5
Houston, Charles Hamilton 4
Jackson, Vera 40
Johnson, James Weldon 5
Jordan, Vernon E. 3, 35
Kidd, Mae Street 39
Lampkin, Daisy 19
Madison, Joseph E. 17
Marshall, Thurgood 1, 44
McKissick, Floyd B. 3
McPhail, Sharon 2
Meek, Carrie 36
Meredith, James H. 11
Mfume, Kweisi 6, 41
Mitchell, Sharon 36
Moore, Harry T. 29
Moses, Robert Parris 11
Motley, Constance Baker 10
Moyo, Yvette Jackson 36
Owens, Major 6
Payton, John 48
Rustin, Bayard 4
Sutton, Percy E. 42
Terrell, Mary Church 9
Tucker, C. DeLores 12
White, Walter F. 4
Wilkins, Roger 2
Wilkins, Roy 4
Williams, Hosea Lorenzo 15, 31
Williams, Robert F. 11
Wright, Louis Tompkins 4

National Association of Black Journalists (NABJ)
Curry, George E. 23
Dawkins, Wayne 20
Harris, Jay T. 19
Jarret, Vernon D. 42
Madison, Paula 37
Rice, Linda Johnson 9, 41
Shipp, E. R. 15
Stone, Chuck 9
Washington, Laura S. 18

National Association of Colored Graduate Nurses (NACGN)
Staupers, Mabel K. 7

National Association of Colored Women (NACW)
Bethune, Mary McLeod 4
Cooper, Margaret J. 46
Harper, Frances Ellen Watkins 11
Lampkin, Daisy 19
Stewart, Ella 39
Terrell, Mary Church 9

National Association of Negro Business and Professional Women's Clubs
Vaughns, Cleopatra 46

National Association of Negro Musicians
Bonds, Margaret 39
Brown, Uzee 42

National Association of Regulatory Utility Commissioners
Colter, Cyrus, J. 36

National Association of Social Workers
McMurray, Georgia L. 36

National Association of Stock Car Auto Racing
Lester, Bill 42

National Baptist Convention USA
Jones, E. Edward, Sr. 45
Lyons, Henry 12
Shaw, William J. 30

National Baptist Publishing Board
Boyd, T. B., III 6

National Baptist Sunday Church School and Baptist Training Union Congress
Boyd, T. B., III 6

National Bar Association
Alexander, Joyce London 18
Alexander, Sadie Tanner Mossell 22
Archer, Dennis 7, 36
Bailey, Clyde 45
Hubbard, Arnette 38
McPhail, Sharon 2
Robinson, Malcolm S. 44
Thompson, Larry D. 39

National Basketball Association (NBA)
Abdul-Jabbar, Kareem 8
Abdur-Rahim, Shareef 28
Anthony, Carmelo 46
Barkley, Charles 5
Bing, Dave 3
Bol, Manute 1
Brandon, Terrell 16
Bryant, Kobe 15, 31
Bynoe, Peter C.B. 40
Carter, Vince 26
Chamberlain, Wilt 18, 47
Cheeks, Maurice 47
Clifton, Nathaniel "Sweetwater" 47
Cooper, Charles "Chuck" 47
Drexler, Clyde 4
Duncan, Tim 20
Elliott, Sean 26
Erving, Julius 18, 47
Ewing, Patrick A. 17
Garnett, Kevin 14
Gourdine, Simon 11
Green, A. C. 32
Hardaway, Anfernee (Penny) 13
Hardaway, Tim 35
Heard, Gar 25
Hill, Grant 13
Howard, Juwan 15
Hunter, Billy 22
Johnson, Earvin "Magic" 3, 39
Johnson, Larry 28
Jordan, Michael 6, 21
Lanier, Bob 47
Lucas, John 7
Mourning, Alonzo 17, 44
Mutombo, Dikembe 7
O'Neal, Shaquille 8, 30
Olajuwon, Hakeem 2
Parish, Robert 43
Pippen, Scottie 15
Rivers, Glenn "Doc" 25
Robertson, Oscar 26
Robinson, David 24
Rodman, Dennis 12, 44
Russell, Bill 8
Silas, Paul 24
Sprewell, Latrell 23
Thomas, Isiah 7, 26
Webber, Chris 15, 30
Wilkens, Lenny 11

National Basketball Players Association
Erving, Julius 18, 47
Ewing, Patrick A. 17
Gourdine, Simon 11
Hunter, Billy 22

National Black Arts Festival (NBAF)
Borders, James 9
Brooks, Avery 9

National Black Association of Journalist
Pressley, Condace L. 41

National Black College Hall of Fame
Dortch, Thomas W., Jr. 45

National Black Farmers Association (NBFA)
Boyd, John W., Jr. 20

National Black Fine Art Show
Wainwright, Joscelyn 46

National Black Gay and Lesbian Conference
Wilson, Phill 9

National Black Gay and Lesbian Leadership Forum (NBGLLF)
Boykin, Keith 14
Carter, Mandy 11

National Book Award
Ellison, Ralph 7
Haley, Alex 4
Johnson, Charles 1
Patterson, Orlando 4

National Broadcasting Company (NBC)
Allen, Byron 3, 24
Cosby, Bill 7, 26
Grier, David Alan 28
Gumbel, Bryant 14
Hinderas, Natalie 5
Ifill, Gwen 28
Johnson, Rodney Van 28
Jones, Star 10, 27

Madison, Paula 37
Rashad, Phylicia 21
Reuben, Gloria 15
Roker, Al 12
Simpson, Carole 6, 30
Stokes, Carl B. 10
Thomas-Graham, Pamela 29
Williams, Montel 4
Wilson, Flip 21

National Brotherhood of Skiers (NBS)
Horton, Andre 33
Horton, Suki 33

National Center for Neighborhood Enterprise (NCNE)
Woodson, Robert L. 10

National Coalition of 100 Black Women (NCBW)
Mays, Leslie A. 41
McCabe, Jewell Jackson 10

National Coalition to Abolish the Death Penalty (NCADP)
Hawkins, Steven 14

National Commission for Democracy (Ghana; NCD)
Rawlings, Jerry 9

National Conference on Black Lawyers (NCBL)
McDougall, Gay J. 11, 43

National Council of Churches
Howard, M. William, Jr. 26

National Council of Negro Women (NCNW)
Bethune, Mary McLeod 4
Blackwell, Unita 17
Cole, Johnnetta B. 5, 43
Hamer, Fannie Lou 6
Height, Dorothy I. 2, 23
Horne, Lena 5
Lampkin, Daisy 19
Sampson, Edith S. 4
Smith, Jane E. 24
Staupers, Mabel K. 7

National Council of Nigeria and the Cameroons (NCNC)
Azikiwe, Nnamdi 13

National Council of Teachers of Mathematics
Granville, Evelyn Boyd 36

National Council on the Arts
Robinson, Cleo Parker 38

National Defence Council (Ghana; NDC)
Rawlings, Jerry 9

National Democratic Party (Rhodesia)
Mugabe, Robert Gabriel 10

National Dental Association
Madison, Romell 45

National Earthquake Information Center (NEIC)
Person, Waverly 9

National Endowment for the Arts (NEA)
Bradley, David Henry, Jr. 39
Hall, Arthur 39
Hemphill, Essex 10
Serrano, Andres 3
Williams, John A. 27
Williams, William T. 11

National Endowment for the Arts Jazz Hall of Fame
Terry, Clark 39

National Endowment for the Humanities
Gibson, Donald Bernard 40

National Education Association (NEA)
Futrell, Mary Hatwood 33

National Equal Rights League (NERL)
Trotter, Monroe 9

National Football League (NFL)
Allen, Marcus 20
Barney, Lem 26
Briscoe, Marlin 37
Brooks, Aaron 33
Brooks, Derrick 43
Brown, Jim 11
Bruce, Isaac 26
Butler, Leroy III 17
Cherry, Deron 40
Culpepper, Daunte 32
Cunningham, Randall 23
Davis, Terrell 20
Dickerson, Eric 27
Farr, Mel Sr. 24
Faulk, Marshall 35
Gilliam, Frank 23
Gilliam, Joe 31
Green, Darrell 39
Green, Dennis 5, 45
Greene, Joe 10
Hill, Calvin 19
Howard, Desmond 16
Johnson, Levi 48
Lofton, James 42
Lott, Ronnie 9
Monk, Art 38
Moon, Warren 8
Moss, Randy 23
Motley, Marion 26
Newsome, Ozzie 26
Pace, Orlando 21
Page, Alan 7
Payton, Walter 11, 25
Rhodes, Ray 14
Rice, Jerry 5
Sanders, Barry 1
Sanders, Deion 4, 31
Sapp, Warren 38
Sayers, Gale 28
Sharper, Darren 32
Shell, Art 1
Simpson, O.J. 15
Singletary, Mike 4
Smith, Emmitt 7
Stewart, Kordell 21
Strahan, Michael 35
Stringer, Korey 35
Swann, Lynn 28
Taylor, Lawrence 25
Thomas, Derrick 25
Thrower, Willie 35
Upshaw, Gene 18, 47
Vick, Michael 39
Walker, Herschel 1
Ware, Andre 37
White, Reggie 6
Williams, Doug 22

NFL Hall of Fame
Sayers, Gale 28
Swann, Lynn 28

National Heritage "Living Treasure" Fellowship
Jackson, John 36

National Hockey League (NHL)
Brashear, Donald 39
Brathwaite, Fred 35
Mayers, Jamal 39
McBride, Bryant 18
Fuhr, Grant 1
Grier, Mike 43
Iginla, Jarome 35
Laraque, Georges 48
McKegney, Tony 3
O'Ree, Willie 5

National Inventors Hall of Fame
Carruthers, George R. 40

National Immigration Forum
Jones, Sarah 39

National Information Infrastructure (NII)
Lewis, Delano 7

National Institute of Arts & Letters
Lewis, Norman 39
White, Charles 39

National Institute of Education
Baker, Gwendolyn Calvert 9

National Institute of Health (NIH)
Cargill, Victoria A. 43
Dunston, Georgia Mae 48

National League
Coleman, Leonard S., Jr. 12

National Lawn & Garden Distributor Association
Donald, Arnold Wayne 36

National Medical Association
Cole, Lorraine 48
Maxey, Randall 46

National Minority Business Council
Leary, Kathryn D. 10

National Museum of American History
Reagon, Bernice Johnson 7

National Negro Congress
Bunche, Ralph J. 5

National Negro Suffrage League
Trotter, Monroe 9

National Network for African American Women and the Law
Arnwine, Barbara 28

National Newspaper Publishers' Association
Cooper, Andrew W. 36
Oliver, John J., Jr. 48
Bacon-Bercey, June 38
Fields, Evelyn J. 27

National Organization for Women (NOW)
Kennedy, Florynce 12, 33
Hernandez, Aileen Clarke 13
Meek, Carrie 6, 36
Murray, Pauli 38
Letson, Al 39

National Political Congress of Black Women
Chisholm, Shirley 2
Tucker, C. DeLores 12
Waters, Maxine 3

National Public Radio (NPR)
Bates, Karen Grigsby 40
Drummond, William J. 40
Early, Gerald 15
Lewis, Delano 7
Abu-Jamal, Mumia 15

National Resistance Army (Uganda; NRA)
Museveni, Yoweri 4

National Resistance Movement
Museveni, Yoweri 4

National Revolutionary Movement for Development
See Mouvement Revolutionnaire National pour la Developpment

National Rifle Association (NRA)
Williams, Robert F. 11

National Science Foundation (NSF)
Massey, Walter E. 5, 45

National Security Advisor
Rice, Condoleezza 3, 28

National Security Council
Powell, Colin 1, 28
Rice, Condoleezza 3, 28

National Society of Black Engineers
Donald, Arnold Wayne 36

National Union for the Total Independence of Angola (UNITA)
Savimbi, Jonas 2, 34

National Union of Mineworkers (South Africa; NUM)
Ramaphosa, Cyril 3

National Urban Affairs Council
Cooper, Andrew W. **36**

National Urban Coalition (NUC)
Edelin, Ramona Hoage **19**

National Urban League
Brown, Ron **5**
Gordon, Bruce S. **41**
Greely, M. Gasby **27**
Haynes, George Edmund **8**
Jacob, John E. **2**
Jordan, Vernon E. **3, 35**
Price, Hugh B. **9**
Young, Whitney M., Jr. **4**

National War College
Clemmons, Reginal G. **41**

National Women's Basketball League (NWBL)
Catchings, Tamika **43**

National Women's Hall of Fame
Kelly, Leontine **33**

National Women's Political Caucus
Hamer, Fannie Lou **6**

National Youth Administration (NYA)
Bethune, Mary McLeod **4**
Primus, Pearl **6**

Nature Boy Enterprises
Yoba, Malik **11**

Naval Research Laboratory (NRL)
Carruthers, George R. **40**

NBA
See National Basketball Association

NBAF
See National Black Arts Festival

NBC
See National Broadcasting Company

NBGLLF
See National Black Gay and Lesbian Leadership Forum

NCBL
See National Conference on Black Lawyers

NCBW
See National Coalition of 100 Black Women

NCCK
See Kenya National Council of Churches

NCD
See National Commission for Democracy

NCNE
See National Center for Neighborhood Enterprise

NCNW
See National Council of Negro Women

NDC
See National Defence Council

NEA
See National Endowment for the Arts

Nebula awards
Butler, Octavia **8, 43**
Delany, Samuel R. Jr. **9**

Négritude
Césaire, Aimé **48**
Damas, Léon-Gontran **46**

Negro American Labor Council
Randolph, A. Philip **3**

Negro American Political League
Trotter, Monroe **9**

Negro Digest magazine
Johnson, John H. **3**
Fuller, Hoyt **44**

Negro Ensemble Company
Cash, Rosalind **28**
Schultz, Michael A. **6**
Taylor, Susan L. **10**
Ward, Douglas Turner **42**

Negro History Bulletin
Woodson, Carter G. **2**

Negro Leagues
Banks, Ernie **33**
Barnhill, David **30**
Bell, James "Cool Papa" **36**
Brown, Willard **36**
Campanella, Roy **25**
Charleston, Oscar **39**
Dandridge, Ray **36**
Davis, Piper **19**
Day, Leon **39**
Gibson, Josh **22**
Hyde, Cowan F. "Bubba" **47**
Irvin, Monte **31**
Johnson, Mamie "Peanut" **40**
Kaiser, Cecil **42**
Kimbro, Henry A. **25**
Lloyd, John Henry "Pop" **30**
O'Neil, Buck **19**
Paige, Satchel **7**
Pride, Charley **26**
Smith, Hilton **29**
Stearnes, Norman "Turkey" **31**
Stone, Toni **15**

Negro Theater Ensemble
Rolle, Esther **13, 21**

Negro World
Fortune, T. Thomas **6**

NEIC
See National Earthquake Information Center

Neo-hoodoo
Reed, Ishmael **8**

Nequai Cosmetics
Taylor, Susan L. **10**

NERL
See National Equal Rights League

Netherlands Antilles
Liberia-Peters, Maria Philomena **12**

NetNoir Inc.
CasSelle, Malcolm **11**
Ellington, E. David **11**

Neurosurgery
Black, Keith Lanier **18**
Carson, Benjamin **1, 35**
Canady, Alexa **28**

Neustadt International Prize for Literature
Brathwaite, Kamau **36**

New Birth Missionary Baptist Church
Long, Eddie L. **29**

New Black Muslims
Muhammad, Khallid Abdul **10, 31**

New Black Panther Party
Muhammad, Khallid, Abdul **10, 31**

New Concept Development Center
Madhubuti, Haki R. **7**

New Dance Group
Primus, Pearl **6**

New Jewel Movement
Bishop, Maurice **39**

New Jersey Family Development Act
Bryant, Wayne R. **6**

New Jersey General Assembly
Bryant, Wayne R. **6**

New Jersey Nets
Doby, Lawrence Eugene Sr. **16, 41**

New Jersey Symphony Orchestra
Lewis, Henry **38**

New Life Community Choir
Kee, John P. **43**

New Life Fellowship Church
Kee, John P. **43**

New Orleans city government
Nagin, Ray **42**

New Orleans Saints football team
Brooks, Aaron **33**
Mills, Sam **33**

New Negro movement
See Harlem Renaissance

New York Age
Fortune, T. Thomas **6**

New York City government
Campbell, Mary Schmidt **43**
Crew, Rudolph F. **16**
Dinkins, David **4**
Fields, C. Virginia **25**
Hageman, Hans **36**
Sutton, Percy E. **42**
Thompson, William **35**

New York Daily News
Cose, Ellis **5**

New York Drama Critics Circle Award
Hansberry, Lorraine **6**

New York Freeman
Fortune, T. Thomas **6**

New York Giants baseball team
Dandridge, Ray **36**
Mays, Willie **3**

New York Giants football team
Strahan, Michael **35**
Taylor, Lawrence **25**

New York Globe
Fortune, T. Thomas **6**

New York Hip Hop Theater Festival
Jones, Sarah **39**

New York Institute for Social Therapy and Research
Fulani, Lenora **11**

New York Jets football team
Lott, Ronnie **9**

New York Knicks basketball team
Ewing, Patrick A. **17**
Johnson, Larry **28**
Sprewell, Latrell **23**

New York Mets baseball team
Clendenon, Donn **26**

New York Philharmonic
DePriest, James **37**

New York Public Library
Baker, Augusta **38**
Dodson, Howard, Jr. **7**
Schomburg, Arthur Alfonso **9**

New York Shakespeare Festival
Gunn, Moses **10**
Wolfe, George C. **6, 43**

New York state government
McCall, H. Carl **27**

New York State Senate
McCall, H. Carl **27**
Motley, Constance Baker **10**
Owens, Major **6**

New York State Supreme Court
Wright, Bruce McMarion **3**

New York Stock Exchange
Doley, Harold, Jr. **26**

New York Sun
Fortune, T. Thomas **6**

New York Times
Boyd, Gerald M. **32**
Davis, George **36**

Hunter-Gault, Charlayne **6**, **31**
Ifill, Gwen **28**
Price, Hugh B. **9**
Wilkins, Roger **2**

New York University
Brathwaite, Kamau **36**
Campbell, Mary Schmidt **43**

New York Yankees baseball team
Baylor, Don **6**
Bonds, Bobby **43**
Jackson, Reggie **15**
Jeter, Derek **27**
Strawberry, Darryl **22**
Watson, Bob **25**
Winfield, Dave **5**

Newark city government
Gibson, Kenneth Allen **6**
James, Sharpe **23**

Newark Dodgers baseball team
Dandridge, Ray **36**

Newark Eagles baseball team
Dandridge, Ray **36**
Doby, Lawrence Eugene Sr. **16**, **41**

Newark Housing Authority
Gibson, Kenneth Allen **6**

The News Hour with Jim Lehrer TV series
Ifill, Gwen **28**

NFL
See National Football League

Nguzo Saba
Karenga, Maulana **10**

NHL
See National Hockey League

Niagara movement
Du Bois, W. E. B. **3**
Hope, John **8**
Trotter, Monroe **9**

Nigerian Armed Forces
Abacha, Sani **11**
Babangida, Ibrahim **4**
Obasanjo, Olusegun **5**, **22**

Nigerian Association of Patriotic Writers and Artists
Barrett, Lindsay **43**

Nigerian literature
Achebe, Chinua **6**
Amadi, Elechi **40**
Barrett, Lindsay **43**
Ekwensi, Cyprian **37**
Onwueme, Tess Osonye **23**
Rotimi, Ola **1**
Saro-Wiwa, Kenule **39**
Soyinka, Wole **4**

NIH
See National Institute of Health

NII
See National Information Infrastructure

1960 Masks
Soyinka, Wole **4**

Nobel Peace Prize
Annan, Kofi Atta **15**, **48**
Bunche, Ralph J. **5**
King, Martin Luther, Jr. **1**
Luthuli, Albert **13**
Tutu, Desmond Mpilo **6**, **44**

Nobel Prize for literature
Soyinka, Wole **4**
Morrison, Toni **2**, **15**
Walcott, Derek **5**

Noma Award for Publishing in African
Ba, Mariama **30**

Nonfiction
Abrahams, Peter **39**
Adams-Ender, Clara **40**
Allen, Debbie **13**, **42**
Allen, Robert L. **38**
Atkins, Cholly **40**
Ballard, Allen Butler, Jr. **40**
Blassingame, John Wesley **40**
Blockson, Charles L. **42**
Bogle, Donald **34**
Brown, Cecil M. **46**
Brown, Llyod Louis **42**
Buckley, Gail Lumet **39**
Carby, Hazel **27**
Carter, Joye Maureen **41**
Cole, Johnnetta B. **5**, **43**
Cook, Mercer **40**
Davis, Arthur P. **41**
Dunnigan, Alice Allison **41**
Edelman, Marian Wright **5**, **42**
Elliott, Lorris **37**
Fax, Elton **48**
Fisher, Antwone **40**
Fletcher, Bill, Jr. **41**
Ford, Clyde W. **40**
Foster, Cecil **32**
Gayle, Addison, Jr. **41**
Gibson, Donald Bernard **40**
Greenwood, Monique **38**
Harrison, Alvin **28**
Harrison, Calvin **28**
Henries, A. Doris Banks **44**
Henriques, Julian **37**
Hercules, Frank **44**
Hill, Errol **40**
Hobson, Julius W. **44**
Horne, Frank **44**
Jakes, Thomas "T.D." **17**, **43**
Jolley, Willie **28**
Jordan, Vernon E. **7**, **35**
Kayira, Legson **40**
Kennedy, Randall **40**
Knight, Etheridge **37**
Kobia, Rev. Dr. Samuel **43**
Ladner, Joyce A. **42**
Lampley, Oni Faida **43**
Lincoln, C. Eric **38**
Long, Eddie L. **29**
Mabuza-Suttle, Felicia **43**
Malveaux, Julianne **32**
Manley, Ruth **34**
McBride, James **35**
McKenzie, Vashti M. **29**
McWhorter, John **35**
Mossell, Gertrude Bustill **40**

Murray, Pauli **38**
Naylor, Gloria **10**, **42**
Nissel, Angela **42**
Parks, Rosa **1**, **35**
Smith, Jessie Carney **35**
Tillis, Frederick **40**
Wade-Gayles, Gloria Jean **41**
Wambugu, Florence **42**
Wilkens, J. Ernest, Jr. **43**
Williams, Terrie **35**

Nonviolent Action Group (NAG)
Al-Amin, Jamil Abdullah **6**

North Carolina Mutual Life Insurance
Spaulding, Charles Clinton **9**

North Carolina state government
Ballance, Frank W. **41**

North Pole
Henson, Matthew **2**
McLeod, Gus **27**
Delany, Martin R. **27**

Notre Dame Univeristy
Willingham, Tyrone **43**

NOW
See National Organization for Women

NPR
See National Public Radio

NRA
See National Resistance Army (Uganda)

NRA
See National Rifle Association

NRL
See Naval Research Laboratory

NSF
See National Science Foundation

Nuclear energy
O'Leary, Hazel **6**
Quarterman, Lloyd Albert **4**

Nuclear Regulatory Commission
Jackson, Shirley Ann **12**

Nucleus
King, Yolanda **6**
Shabazz, Attallah **6**

NUM
See National Union of Mineworkers (South Africa)

Nursing
Adams-Ender, Clara **40**
Auguste, Rose-Anne **13**
Hunter, Alberta **42**
Johnson, Eddie Bernice **8**
Johnson, Hazel **22**
Johnson, Mamie "Peanut" **40**
Larsen, Nella **10**
Lyttle, Hulda Margaret **14**
Riley, Helen Caldwell Day **13**
Robinson, Rachel **16**

Robinson, Sharon **22**
Shabazz, Betty **7**, **26**
Staupers, Mabel K. **7**
Taylor, Susie King **13**

Nursing agency
Daniels, Lee Louis **36**

Nutrition
Clark, Celeste **15**
Gregory, Dick **1**
Watkins, Shirley R. **17**

NWBL
See National Women's Basketball League

NYA
See National Youth Administration

Nyasaland African Congress (NAC)
Banda, Hastings Kamuzu **6**

Oakland Athletics baseball team
Baker, Dusty **8**, **43**
Baylor, Don **6**
Henderson, Rickey **28**
Jackson, Reggie **15**
Morgan, Joe Leonard **9**

Oakland Oaks baseball team
Dandridge, Ray **36**

Oakland Raiders football team
Howard, Desmond **16**
Upshaw, Gene **18**, **47**

Oakland Tribune
Maynard, Robert C. **7**

OAR
See Office of AIDS Research

OAU
See Organization of African Unity

Obie awards
Carter, Nell **39**
Freeman, Yvette **27**
Orlandersmith, Dael **42**
Thigpen, Lynne **17**, **41**

OBSSR
See Office of Behavioral and Social Sciences Research

OECS
See Organization of Eastern Caribbean States

Office of AIDS Research (OAR)
Cargill, Victoria A. **43**

Office of Behavioral and Social Science Research
Anderson, Norman B. **45**

Office of Civil Rights
See U.S. Department of Education

Office of Management and Budget
Raines, Franklin Delano **14**

Office of Public Liaison
Herman, Alexis M. **15**

Ohio House of Representatives
Stokes, Carl B. 10

Ohio state government
Brown, Les 5
Ford, Jack 39
Stokes, Carl B. 10
Williams, George Washington 18

Ohio State Senate
White, Michael R. 5

Ohio Women's Hall of Fame
Craig-Jones, Ellen Walker 44
Stewart, Ella 39

OIC
See Opportunities Industrialization Centers of America, Inc.

OKeh record label
Brooks, Hadda 40
Mo', Keb' 36

Oklahoma Hall of Fame
Mitchell, Leona 42

Oklahoma House of Representatives
Ross, Don 27

Oklahoma Eagle
Ross, Don 27

Olatunji Center for African Culture
Olatunji, Babatunde 36

Olympics
Abdur-Rahim, Shareef 28
Ali, Muhammad 2, 16
Beamon, Bob 30
Bonaly, Surya 7
Bowe, Riddick 6
Carter, Vince 26
Christie, Linford 8
Coachman, Alice 18
Dawes, Dominique 11
DeFrantz, Anita 37
Devers, Gail 7
Edwards, Harry 2
Edwards, Teresa 14
Ewing, Patrick A. 17
Felix, Allyson 48
Flowers, Vonetta 35
Ford, Cheryl 45
Freeman, Cathy 29
Garrison, Zina 2
Gourdine, Meredith 33
Greene, Maurice 27
Griffith, Yolanda 25
Griffith-Joyner, Florence 28
Hardaway, Anfernee (Penny) 13
Hardaway, Tim 35
Harrison, Alvin 28
Harrison, Calvin 28
Hill, Grant 13
Hines, Garrett 35
Holmes, Kelly 47
Holyfield, Evander 6
Howard, Sherri 36
Iginla, Jarome 35
Johnson, Ben 1
Johnson, Michael 13
Johnson, Rafer 33
Jones, Randy 35
Joyner-Kersee, Jackie 5
Leslie, Lisa 16
Lewis, Carl 4
Malone, Karl A. 18
Metcalfe, Ralph 26
Miller, Cheryl 10
Montgomery, Tim 41
Moses, Edwin 8
Mutola, Maria 12
Owens, Jesse 2
Pippen, Scottie 15
Powell, Mike 7
Quirot, Ana 13
Robertson, Oscar 26
Rudolph, Wilma 4
Russell, Bill 8
Scurry, Briana 27
Swoopes, Sheryl 12
Thomas, Debi 26
Thugwane, Josia 21
Ward, Lloyd 21, 46
Westbrook, Peter 20
Whitaker, Pernell 10
Wilkens, Lenny 11

On A Roll Radio
Smith, Greg 28

Oncology
Leffall, LaSalle, Jr. 3

One Church, One Child
Clements, George 2

100 Black Men of America
Dortch, Thomas W., Jr. 45

One Way-Productions
Naylor, Gloria 10, 42

Ontario Legislature
Curling, Alvin 34

Onyx Opera
Brown, Uzee 42

OPC
See Ovambo People's Congress

Opera
Adams, Leslie 39
Anderson, Marian 2, 33
Arroyo, Martina 30
Brooks, Avery 9
Brown, Uzee 42
Bumbry, Grace 5
Davis, Anthony 11
Dobbs, Mattiwilda 34
Estes, Simon 28
Freeman, Paul 39
Graves, Denyce 19
Greely, M. Gasby 27
Hendricks, Barbara 3
Joplin, Scott 6
Joyner, Matilda Sissieretta 15
Maynor, Dorothy 19
McDonald, Audra 20
Mitchell, Leona 42
Norman, Jessye 5
Price, Leontyne 1
Still, William Grant 37
Three Mo' Tenors 35

Operation Desert Shield
Powell, Colin 1, 28

Operation Desert Storm
Powell, Colin 1, 28

Operation HOPE
Bryant, John 26

Ophthalmology
Bath, Patricia E. 37

OPO
See Ovamboland People's Organization

Opportunities Industrialization Centers of America, Inc. (OIC)
Sullivan, Leon H. 3, 30

Ora Nelle Records
Little Walter 36

Oregon Symphony
DePriest, James 37

Organization of African States
Museveni, Yoweri 4

Organization of African Unity (OAU)
Diouf, Abdou 3
Haile Selassie 7
Kaunda, Kenneth 2
Kenyatta, Jomo 5
Nkrumah, Kwame 3
Nujoma, Samuel 10
Nyerere, Julius 5
Touré, Sekou 6

Organization of Afro-American Unity
Feelings, Muriel 44
X, Malcolm 1

Organization of Eastern Caribbean States (OECS)
Charles, Mary Eugenia 10

Organization of Women Writers of African Descent
Cortez, Jayne 43

Orisun Repertory
Soyinka, Wole 4

Orlando Magic basketball team
Erving, Julius 18, 47
O'Neal, Shaquille 8, 30
Rivers, Glenn "Doc" 25

Orlando Miracle basketball team
Peck, Carolyn 23

Osteopathy
Allen, Ethel D. 13

Ovambo People's Congress (South Africa; OPC)
Nujoma, Samuel 10

Ovamboland People's Organization (South Africa; OPO)
Nujoma, Samuel 10

Overbrook Entertainment
Pinkett Smith, Jada 10, 41

Page Education Foundation
Page, Alan 7

PAIGC
See African Party for the Independence of Guinea and Cape Verde

Paine College
Lewis, Shirley A. R. 14

Painting
Alston, Charles 33
Andrews, Benny 22
Bailey, Radcliffe 19
Barthe, Richmond 15
Basquiat, Jean-Michel 5
Bearden, Romare 2
Beasley, Phoebe 34
Biggers, John 20, 33
Campbell, E. Simms 13
Cortor, Eldzier 42
Cowans, Adger W. 20
Crite, Alan Rohan 29
Delaney, Beauford 19
Delaney, Joseph 30
Delsarte, Louis 34
Douglas, Aaron 7
Driskell, David C. 7
Ewing, Patrick A. 17
Flood, Curt 10
Freeman, Leonard 27
Gilliam, Sam 16
Goodnight, Paul 32
Guyton, Tyree 9
Harkless, Necia Desiree 19
Hayden, Palmer 13
Hunter, Clementine 45
Jackson, Earl 31
Johnson, William Henry 3
Jones, Lois Mailou 13
Lawrence, Jacob 4, 28
Lee, Annie Francis 22
Lee-Smith, Hughie 5, 22
Lewis, Norman 39
Lewis, Samella 25
Loving, Alvin 35
Mayhew, Richard 39
Major, Clarence 9
McGee, Charles 10
Mitchell, Corinne 8
Motley, Archibald Jr. 30
Mutu, Wangechi 19(?) 44
Nugent, Richard Bruce 39
Ouattara 43
Pierre, Andre 17
Pippin, Horace 9
Porter, James A. 11
Ringgold, Faith 4
Ruley, Ellis 38
Sallee, Charles 38
Sebree, Charles 40
Smith, Vincent D. 48
Tanksley, Ann 37
Tanner, Henry Ossawa 1
Thomas, Alma 14
Tolliver, William 9
Washington, James Jr. 38
Wells, James Lesesne 10
White, Charles 39
Williams, Billy Dee 8
Williams, William T. 11
Wilson, Ellis 39
Woodruff, Hale 9

Pan-Africanism
Carmichael, Stokely 5, 26
Clarke, John Henrik 20

Du Bois, David Graham 45
Du Bois, W. E. B. 3
Garvey, Marcus 1
Haile Selassie 7
Kenyatta, Jomo 5
Madhubuti, Haki R. 7
Marshall, Paule 7
Nkrumah, Kwame 3
Nyerere, Julius 5
Touré, Sekou 6
Turner, Henry McNeal 5

Pan African Congress
Logan, Rayford W. 40

Pan African Orthodox Christian Church
Agyeman, Jaramogi Abebe 10

Papal Medal
Hampton, Lionel 17, 41

Parents of Watts (POW)
Harris, Alice 7

Parti Démocratique de Guinée (Guinea Democratic Party; PDG)
Touré, Sekou 6

Parti Démocratique de la Côte d'Ivoire (Democratic Party of the Ivory Coast; PDCI)
Houphouët-Boigny, Félix 4
Bedie, Henri Konan 21

Partido Africano da Independencia da Guine e Cabo Verde (PAIGC)
Vieira, Joao 14

Party for Unity and Progress (Guinea; PUP)
Conté, Lansana 7

PATC
See Performing Arts Training Center

Pathology
Fuller, Solomon Carter, Jr. 15

Patriot Party
Fulani, Lenora 11

Patriotic Alliance for Reconstruction and Construction (PARC)
Jammeh, Yahya 23

Patriotic Movement of Salvation (MPS)
Déby, Idriss 30

PBS
See Public Broadcasting Service

PDCI
See Parti Démocratique de la Côte d'Ivoire (Democratic Party of the Ivory Coast)

PDG
See Parti Démocratique de Guinée (Guinea Democratic Party)

PDP
See People's Democratic Party

Peace and Freedom Party
Cleaver, Eldridge 5

Peace Corps
See U.S. Peace Corps

Peace Mission
Divine, Father 7

Peck School of the Fine Arts
Tyson, Andre 40

Pediatrics
Carson, Benjamin 1, 35
Elders, Joycelyn 6
Witt, Edwin T. 26
Zuma, Nkosazana Dlamini 34

Peg Leg Bates Country Club
Bates, Peg Leg 14

PEN/Faulkner award
Bradley, David Henry, Jr. 39

Penn State University
Dunn, Jerry 27
Mayhew, Richard 39

Pennsylvania state government
Allen, Ethel D. 13
Brown, Homer S. 47

People Organized and Working for Economic Rebirth (POWER)
Farrakhan, Louis 2

People United to Serve Humanity (PUSH)
Jackson, Jesse 1, 27
Jackson, Jesse, Jr. 14, 45

People's Association Human Rights
Williams, Robert F. 11

People's Choice Awards
Lewis, Emmanuel 36

People's Democratic Party (Nigeria; PDP)
Obasanjo, Stella 32

People's Liberation Army of Namibia (PLAN)
Nujoma, Samuel 10

People's National Party (Jamaica; PNP)
Patterson, P. J. 6, 20

People's Progressive Party (PPP)
Jagan, Cheddi 16
Jawara, Sir Dawda Kairaba 11

People's Revolutionary Government
Bishop, Maurice 39

PepsiCo Inc.
Harvey, William R. 42

Performing Arts Training Center (PATC)
Dunham, Katherine 4

Perkins Prize
Jones, Thomas W. 41

PGA
See Professional Golfers' Association

Pharmaceuticals
Potter, Myrtle 40

Pharmaceutical research
Pickett, Cecil 39

Pharmacist
Pickett, Cecil 39
Stewart, Ella 39

Phelps Stokes Fund
Patterson, Frederick Douglass 12

Philadelphia City Council
Allen, Ethel D. 13

Philadelphia city government
Goode, W. Wilson 4
Street, John F. 24

Philadelphia Eagles football team
Cunningham, Randall 23
McNabb, Donovan 29
Rhodes, Ray 14
White, Reggie 6

Philadelphia Flyers hockey team
Brashear, Donald 39
Charleston, Oscar 39

Philadelphia Phillies baseball team
Morgan, Joe Leonard 9

Philadelphia public schools
Clayton, Constance 1

Philadelphia 76ers basketball team
Barkley, Charles 5
Bol, Manute 1
Chamberlain, Wilt 18, 47
Erving, Julius 18, 47
Iverson, Allen 24, 46
Lucas, John 7
Stackhouse, Jerry 30

Philadelphia Stars baseball team
Charleston, Oscar 39

Philadelphia Warriors
Chamberlain, Wilt 18, 47

Philanthropy
Brown, Eddie C. 35
Cooper, Evern 40
Cosby, Bill 7, 26
Cosby, Camille 14
Dawson, Matel "Mat," Jr. 39
Edley, Christopher 2, 48
Golden, Marita 19
Gray, Willie 46
Johnson, Sheila Crump 48
Lavizzo-Mourey, Risa 48
Malone, Annie 13
McCarty, Osceola 16
Millines Dziko, Trish 28

Pleasant, Mary Ellen 9
Reeves, Rachel J. 23
Thomas, Franklin A. 5
Waddles, Charleszetta (Mother) 10
Walker, Madame C. J. 7
White, Reggie 6
Williams, Fannie Barrier 27
Wonder, Stevie 11

Philosophy
Baker, Houston A., Jr. 6
Davis, Angela 5
Toomer, Jean 6
West, Cornel 5

Phoenix Suns basketball team
Barkley, Charles 5
Heard, Gar 25

Photography
Andrews, Bert 13
Barboza, Anthony 10
Cowans, Adger W. 20
DeCarava, Roy 42
Hinton, Milt 30
Jackson, Vera 40
Lester, Julius 9
Moutoussamy-Ashe, Jeanne 7
Parks, Gordon 1, 35
Pinderhughes, John 47
Robeson, Eslanda Goode 13
Serrano, Andres 3
Simpson, Lorna 4, 36
Sleet, Moneta, Jr. 5
Smith, Marvin 46
Smith, Morgan 46
Tanner, Henry Ossawa 1
VanDerZee, James 6
White, John H. 27

Photojournalism
Ashley-Ward, Amelia 23
DeCarava, Roy 42
Jackson, Vera 40
Moutoussamy-Ashe, Jeanne 7
Parks, Gordon 1, 35
Sleet, Moneta, Jr. 5
White, John H. 27

Physical therapy
Elders, Joycelyn 6
Griffin, Bessie Blout 43

Physics
Adkins, Rutherford H. 21
Carruthers, George R. 40
Gates, Sylvester James, Jr. 15
Gourdine, Meredith 33
Imes, Elmer Samuel 39
Jackson, Shirley Ann 12
Massey, Walter E. 5, 45
Tyson, Neil de Grasse 15

Piano
Adams, Leslie 39
Austin, Lovie 40
Basie, Count 23
Bonds, Margaret 39
Brooks, Hadda 40
Cartíer, Xam Wilson 41
Cole, Nat King 17
Cook, Charles "Doc" 44
Donegan, Dorothy 19
Duke, George 21
Ellington, Duke 5

Fats Domino 20
Hancock, Herbie 20
Hardin Armstrong, Lil 39
Hayes, Isaac 20
Hinderas, Natalie 5
Hines, Earl "Fatha" 39
Horn, Shirley 32
Joplin, Scott 6
Keys, Alicia 32
Monk, Thelonious 1
Powell, Bud 24
Pratt, Awadagin 31
Preston, Billy 39
Price, Florence 37
Pritchard, Robert Starling 21
Roberts, Marcus 19
Silver, Horace 26
Simone, Nina 15, 41
Swann, Lynn 28
Sykes, Roosevelt 20
Taylor, Billy 23
Vaughan, Sarah 13
Walker, George 37
Waller, Fats 29
Webster, Katie 29
Williams, Mary Lou 15

Pittsburgh Crawfords
See Indianapolis Crawfords

Pittsburgh Homestead Grays baseball team
Charleston, Oscar 39
Kaiser, Cecil 42

Pittsburgh Pirates baseball team
Bonds, Barry 6, 34
Clendenon, Donn 26
Stargell, Willie 29

Pittsburgh Steelers football team
Dungy, Tony 17, 42
Gilliam, Joe 31
Greene, Joe 10
Perry, Lowell 30
Stargell, Willie 29
Stewart, Kordell 21
Swann, Lynn 28

PLAN
See People's Liberation Army of Namibia

Planet E Communications
Craig, Carl 31

Planned Parenthood Federation of America Inc.
Wattleton, Faye 9

Playboy
Taylor, Karin 34

Playwright
Allen, Debbie 13, 42
Arkadie, Kevin 17
Baldwin, James 1
Barrett, Lindsay 43
Beckham, Barry 41
Branch, William Blackwell 39
Brown, Cecil M. 46
Bullins, Ed 25
Caldwell, Benjamin 46
Carroll, Vinnette 29

Césaire, Aimé 48
Cheadle, Don 19
Chenault, John 40
Childress, Alice 15
Clark-Bekedermo, J. P. 44
Clarke, George 32
Cleage, Pearl 17
Corthron, Kia 43
Cotter, Joseph Seamon, Sr. 40
Dadié, Bernard 34
De Veaux, Alexis 44
Dodson, Owen 38
Elder, Larry III 38
Evans, Mari 26
Farah, Nuruddin 27
Franklin, J.E. 44
Gordone, Charles 15
Hansberry, Lorraine 6
Hayes, Teddy 40
Hill, Errol 40
Hill, Leslie Pinckney 44
Holder, Laurence 34
Hughes, Langston 4
Jean-Baptiste, Marianne 17, 46
Johnson, Georgia Douglas 41
Jones, Sarah 39
Kennedy, Adrienne 11
King, Woodie, Jr. 27
Lampley, Oni Faida 43
Marechera, Dambudzo 39
Milner, Ron 39
Mitchell, Loften 31
Moss, Carlton 17
Mugo, Micere Githae 32
Onwueme, Tess Osonye 23
Orlandersmith, Dael 42
Parks, Suzan-Lori 34
Perry, Tyler 40
Rahman, Aishah 37
Richards, Beah 30
Sanchez, Sonia 17
Schuyler, George Samuel 40
Sebree, Charles 40
Smith, Anna Deavere 6, 44
Talbert, David 34
Taylor, Regina 9, 46
Thurman, Wallace 17
Tolson, Melvin B. 37
Walcott, Derek 5
Ward, Douglas Turner 42
Williams, Samm-Art 21
Wilson, August 7, 33
Wolfe, George C. 6, 43
Youngblood, Shay 32

PNP
See People's National Party (Jamaica)

Podium Records
Patterson, Gilbert Earl 41

Poet laureate (U.S.)
Dove, Rita 6

Poetry
Alexander, Margaret Walker 22
Allen, Samuel L. 38
Angelou, Maya 1, 15
Atkins, Russell 45
Aubert, Alvin 41
Baiocchi, Regina Harris 41
Bandele, Asha 36
Barrax, Gerald William 45

Barrett, Lindsay 43
Bell, James Madison 40
Berry, James 41
Bontemps, Arna 8
Brand, Dionne 32
Breeze, Jean "Binta" 37
Brooks, Gwendolyn 1, 28
Brown, Cecil M. 46
Brutus, Dennis 38
Cartey, Wilfred 1992 47
Césaire, Aimé 48
Chenault, John 40
Cheney-Coker, Syl 43
Clark-Bekedermo, J. P. 44
Clarke, Cheryl 32
Clarke, George 32
Cleage, Pearl 17
Cliff, Michelle 42
Clifton, Lucille 14
Coleman, Wanda 48
Cortez, Jayne 43
Cotter, Joseph Seamon, Sr. 40
Cuney, William Waring 44
Dabydeen, David 48
Dadié, Bernard 34
Damas, Léon-Gontran 46
Dandridge, Raymond Garfield 45
Davis, Charles T. 48
Davis, Frank Marshall 47
De Veaux, Alexis 44
Dodson, Owen 38
Dove, Rita 6
Draper, Sharon Mills 16, 43
Dumas, Henry 41
Dunbar-Nelson, Alice Ruth Moore 44
Emanuel, James A. 46
Evans, Mari 26
Fabio, Sarah Webster 48
Fair, Ronald L. 47
Figueroa, John J. 40
Fisher, Antwone 40
Fleming, Raymond 48
Forbes, Calvin 46
Ford, Nick Aaron 44
Harkless, Necia Desiree 19
Harper, Frances Ellen Watkins 11
Harper, Michael S. 34
Harris, Claire 34
Hayden, Robert 12
Hill, Leslie Pinckney 44
Hoagland, Everett H. 45
Horne, Frank 44
Hughes, Langston 7
Jackson, Fred James 25
Joachim, Paulin 34
Johnson, Georgia Douglas 41
Johnson, Linton Kwesi 37
Jones, Sarah 39
Kay, Jackie 37
Knight, Etheridge 37
Letson, Al 39
Lorde, Audre 6
Manley, Ruth 34
Marechera, Dambudzo 39
Moore, Jessica Care 30
Mugo, Micere Githae 32
Mullen, Harryette 34
Naylor, Gloria 10, 42
Neto, António Agostinho 43
Nugent, Richard Bruce 39
Okara, Gabriel 37
Parker, Pat 19

Peters, Lenrie 43
Philip, Marlene Nourbese 32
Powell, Kevin 31
Randall, Dudley 8
Redmond, Eugene 23
Richards, Beah 30
Sanchez, Sonia 17
Sapphire 14
Senghor, Léopold Sédar 12
Senior, Olive 37
Smith, Mary Carter 26
Spencer, Anne 27
Tillis, Frederick 40
Tolson, Melvin B. 37
Touré, Askia (Muhammad Abu Bakr el) 47
van Sertima, Ivan 25
Walker, Margaret 29
Washington, James Jr. 38
Weaver, Afaa Michael 37
Williams, Saul 31
Williams, Sherley Anne 25

Political science
Ake, Claude 30

Politics
Alexander, Archie Alphonso 14
Arthur, Owen 33
Austin, Junius C. 44
Baker, Thurbert 22
Ballance, Frank W. 41
Bass, Charlotta Spears 40
Belton, Sharon Sayles 9, 16
Bishop, Sanford D. Jr. 24
Blackwell, Unita 17
Boye, Madior 30
Brazile, Donna 25
Brown, Corrine 24
Buckley, Victoria (Vikki) 24
Burris, Chuck 21
Burris, Roland W. 25
Butler, Jerry 26
Césaire, Aimé 48
Chideya, Farai 14
Christian-Green, Donna M. 17
Clayton, Eva M. 20
Coleman, Mary 46
Connerly, Ward 14
Cummings, Elijah E. 24
Curling, Alvin 34
Currie, Betty 21
Davis, Artur 41
dos Santos, José Eduardo 43
Dixon, Julian C. 24
Dymally, Mervyn 42
Edmonds, Terry 17
Fields, C. Virginia 25
Fields, Julia 45
Ford, Harold Eugene 42
Ford, Harold Eugene, Jr. 16
Ford, Jack 39
Gbagbo, Laurent 43
Gordon, Pamela 17
Greenlee, Sam 48
Henry, Aaron 19
Herenton, Willie W. 24
Hilliard, Earl F. 24
Hobson, Julius W. 44
Ingraham, Hubert A. 19
Isaac, Julius 34
Jackson Lee, Sheila 20
James, Sharpe 23

Jammeh, Yahya 23
Jarvis, Charlene Drew 21
Jefferson, William J. 25
Johnson, Harvey Jr. 24
Kabbah, Ahmad Tejan 23
Kabila, Joseph 30
Kidd, Mae Street 39
Kilpatrick, Kwame 34
Lee, Barbara 25
Maathai, Wangari 43
Majette, Denise 41
Meek, Carrie 6, 36
Meek, Kendrick 41
Meeks, Gregory 25
Metcalfe, Ralph 26
Millender-McDonald, Juanita 21
Moore, Harry T. 29
Morial, Ernest "Dutch" 26
Morial, Marc 20
Nagin, Ray 42
Obasanjo, Olusegun 22
Pereira, Aristides 30
Perry, Ruth 15
Powell, Debra A. 23
Rice, Condoleezza 3, 28
Rush, Bobby 26
Saro-Wiwa, Kenule 39
Scott, David 41
Scott, Robert C. 23
Sisulu, Sheila Violet Makate 24
Smith, Jennifer 21
Thompson, Bennie G. 26
Touré, Amadou Toumani 18
Tsvangirai, Morgan 26
Watson, Diane 41
Watt, Melvin 26
Watts, J. C., Jr. 14, 38
Wheat, Alan 14
White, Jesse 22
Williams, Anthony 21
Williams, Eddie N. 44
Williams, George Washington 18
Wynn, Albert R. 25

Pop music
Ashanti 37
Ashford, Nickolas 21
Bassey, Shirley 25
Blige, Mary J. 20, 34
Butler, Jonathan 28
Carey, Mariah 32
Checker, Chubby 28
Cole, Nat King 17
Combs, Sean "Puffy" 17, 43
Cox, Deborah 28
Duke, George 21
Edmonds, Kenneth "Babyface" 10, 31
Ferrell, Rachelle 29
Franklin, Aretha 11, 44
Franklin, Kirk 15
Gray, Macy 29
Hailey, JoJo 22
Hailey, K-Ci 22
Hammer, M. C. 20
Hawkins, Screamin' Jay 30
Hayes, Isaac 20
Hill, Lauryn 20
Houston, Cissy 20
Houston, Whitney 7, 28
Humphrey, Bobbi 20
Isley, Ronald 25
Ja Rule 35
Jackson, Janet 6, 30
Jackson, Michael 19
James, Rick 17
Jarreau, Al 21
Jean, Wyclef 20
Jones, Quincy 8, 30
Jordan, Montell 23
Kelly, R. 18, 44
Kendricks, Eddie 22
Keys, Alicia 32
Khan, Chaka 12
LaBelle, Patti 13, 30
Love, Darlene 23
Massenburg, Kedar 23
Mathis, Johnny 20
Monica 21
Moore, Chante 26
Mumba, Samantha 29
Mya 35
Neville, Aaron 21
Osborne, Jeffrey 26
Preston, Billy 39
Prince 18
Reid, Antonio "L.A." 28
Reid, Vernon 34
Richie, Lionel 27
Robinson, Smokey 3
Rucker, Darius 34
Rupaul 17
Sade 15
Seal 14
Senghor, Léopold Sédar 12
Simpson, Valerie 21
Sisqo 30
Staton, Candi 27
Summer, Donna 25
The Supremes 33
Sweat, Keith 19
The Temptations 33
Thomas, Irma 29
TLC 34
Turner, Tina 6, 27
Usher 23
Washington, Dinah 22
Washington, Grover, Jr. 17, 44
Washington, Val 12
White, Barry 13, 41
White, Maurice 29
Williams, Vanessa L. 4, 17
Wilson, Mary 28
Wilson, Nancy 10
Wonder, Stevie 11

Portland Police Department
Moose, Charles 40

Portland Trail Blazers basketball team
Drexler, Clyde 4
Wilkens, Lenny 11

Potters' House
Jakes, Thomas "T.D." 17, 43

POW
See Parents of Watts

POWER
See People Organized and Working for Economic Rebirth

PPP
See People's Progressive Party (Gambia)

Pratt Institute
Mayhew, Richard 39

Presbyterianism
Cannon, Katie 10

Pride Economic Enterprises
Barry, Marion S. 7, 44

Princeton University
Simmons, Ruth 13, 38

Printmaking
Blackburn, Robert 28
Tanksley, Ann 37
Thrash, Dox 35
Wells, James Lesesne 10

Printmaking Workshop
Blackburn, Robert 28
Tanksley, Ann 37

Prison ministry
Bell, Ralph S. 5

Pro-Line Corp.
Cottrell, Comer 11

Professional Golfers' Association (PGA)
Elder, Lee 6
Powell, Renee 34
Sifford, Charlie 4
Woods, Tiger 14, 31

Professional Women's Club of Chicago
Gray, Ida 41

Progressive Party
Bass, Charlotta Spears 40

Progressive Labour Party
Smith, Jennifer 21

Project Teen Aid
McMurray, Georgia L. 36

Proposition 209
Connerly, Ward 14

Provincial Freeman
Cary, Mary Ann Shadd 30

Psychiatry
Cobbs, Price M. 9
Comer, James P. 6
Fanon, Frantz 44
Fuller, Solomon Carter, Jr. 15
Poussaint, Alvin F. 5
Welsing, Frances Cress 5

Psychic health
Ford, Clyde W. 40

Psychology
Anderson, Norman B. 45
Archie-Hudson, Marguerite 44
Brown, Joyce F. 25
Fulani, Lenora 11
Hare, Nathan 44
Staples, Brent 8
Steele, Claude Mason 13
Tatum, Beverly Daniel 42

Psychotheraphy
Ford, Clyde W. 40

Public Broadcasting Service (PBS)
Brown, Les 5
Davis, Ossie 5
Duke, Bill 3
Hampton, Henry 6
Hunter-Gault, Charlayne 6, 31
Lawson, Jennifer 1
Riggs, Marlon 5, 44
Wilkins, Roger 2

Public housing
Hamer, Fannie Lou 6
Lane, Vincent 5
Reems, Ernestine Cleveland 27

Public relations
Barden, Don H. 9, 20
Edmonds, Terry 17
Graham, Stedman 13
Hedgeman, Anna Arnold 22
McCabe, Jewell Jackson 10
Perez, Anna 1
Pritchard, Robert Starling 21
Rowan, Carl T. 1, 30
Taylor, Kristin Clark 8
Williams, Maggie 7

Public speaking
Bell, James Madison 40
Kennedy, Randall 40

Public television
Brown, Tony 3
Creagh, Milton 27
Ifill, Gwen 28

Publishing
Abbott, Robert Sengstacke 27
Achebe, Chinua 6
Ames, Wilmer 27
Ashley-Ward, Amelia 23
Aubert, Alvin 41
Auguste, Arnold A. 47
Baisden, Michael 25
Barden, Don H. 9, 20
Bass, Charlotta Spears 40
Bates, Daisy 13
Boston, Lloyd 24
Boyd, T. B. III 6
Brown, Marie Dutton 12
Cary, Mary Ann Shadd 30
Coombs, Orde M. 44
Dawkins, Wayne 20
Driver, David E. 11
Ducksworth, Marilyn 12
Dumas, Henry 41
Fuller, Hoyt 44
Giddings, Paula 11
Graves, Earl G. 1, 35
Harris, Jay 19
Harris, Monica 18
Hill, Bonnie Guiton 20
Hudson, Cheryl 15
Hudson, Wade 15
James, Juanita 13
Johnson, John H. 3
Jones, Quincy 8, 30
Kunjufu, Jawanza 3
Lawson, Jennifer 1
Leavell, Dorothy R. 17
Lewis, Edward T. 21
Lorde, Audre 6
Madhubuti, Haki R. 7

Maynard, Robert C. 7
McDonald, Erroll 1
Moore, Jessica Care 30
Morgan, Garrett 1
Murphy, John H. 42
Myers, Walter Dean 8
Parks, Gordon 1, 35
Perez, Anna 1
Randall, Dudley 8
Scott, C. A. 29
Sengstacke, John 18
Smith, Clarence O. 21
Tyree, Omar Rashad 21
Vanzant, Iyanla 17, 47
Walker, Alice 1, 43
Washington, Alonzo 29
Washington, Laura S. 18
Wells-Barnett, Ida B. 8
Williams, Armstrong 29
Williams, Patricia J. 11

Pulitzer prize
Brooks, Gwendolyn 1, 28
Dove, Rita 6
Fuller, Charles 8
Gordone, Charles 15
Haley, Alex 4
Komunyakaa, Yusef 9
Lewis, David Levering 9
Morrison, Toni 2, 15
Page, Clarence 4
Parks, Suzan-Lori 34
Shipp, E. R. 15
Sleet, Moneta, Jr. 5
Walker, Alice 1, 43
Walker, George 37
White, John H. 27
Wilkins, Roger 2
Wilson, August 7, 33

PUP
See Party for Unity and Progress (Guinea)

Puppeteer
Clash, Kevin 14

PUSH
See People United to Serve Humanity

Quiltmaking
Ringgold, Faith 4

Quincy Jones Media Group
Jones, Quincy 8, 30

Qwest Records
Jones, Quincy 8, 30

Race car driving
Lester, Bill 42
Ribbs, Willy T. 2
Scott, Wendell Oliver Sr. 19

Race relations
Abbott, Diane 9
Achebe, Chinua 6
Alexander, Clifford 26
Anthony, Wendell 25
Asante, Molefi Kete 3
Baker, Ella 5
Baker, Houston A., Jr. 6
Baldwin, James 1
Beals, Melba Patillo 15
Bell, Derrick 6
Bennett, Lerone, Jr. 5
Bethune, Mary McLeod 4
Booker, Simeon 23
Bosley, Freeman, Jr. 7
Boyd, T. B. III 6
Bradley, David Henry, Jr. 39
Branch, William Blackwell 39
Brown, Elaine 8
Bunche, Ralph J. 5
Butler, Paul D. 17
Butts, Calvin O., III 9
Carter, Stephen L. 4
Cary, Lorene 3
Cayton, Horace 26
Chavis, Benjamin 6
Clark, Kenneth B. 5
Clark, Septima 7
Cobbs, Price M. 9
Cochran, Johnnie L., Jr. 11, 39
Cole, Johnnetta B. 5, 43
Comer, James P. 6
Cone, James H. 3
Conyers, John, Jr. 4, 45
Cook, Suzan D. Johnson 22
Cook, Toni 23
Cosby, Bill 7, 26
Cunningham, Evelyn 23
Darden, Christopher 13
Davis, Angela 5
Davis, Benjamin O., Sr. 4
Davis, Benjamin O., Jr. 2, 43
Dee, Ruby 8
Delany, Martin R. 27
Dellums, Ronald 2
Diallo, Amadou 27
Divine, Father 7
DuBois, Shirley Graham 21
Dunbar, Paul Laurence 8
Dunbar-Nelson, Alice Ruth Moore 44
Dyson, Michael Eric 11, 40
Edelman, Marian Wright 5, 42
Elder, Lee 6
Ellison, Ralph 7
Esposito, Giancarlo 9
Farmer, James 2
Farmer-Paellmann, Deadria 43
Farrakhan, Louis 2
Fauset, Jessie 7
Franklin, John Hope 5
Fuller, Charles 8
Gaines, Ernest J. 7
Gibson, William F. 6
Goode, W. Wilson 4
Graham, Lawrence Otis 12
Gregory, Dick 1
Grimké, Archibald H. 9
Guinier, Lani 7, 30
Guy, Rosa 5
Haley, Alex 4
Hall, Elliott S. 24
Hampton, Henry 6
Hansberry, Lorraine 6
Harris, Alice 7
Hastie, William H. 8
Haynes, George Edmund 8
Hedgeman, Anna Arnold 22
Henry, Aaron 19
Henry, Lenny 9
Hill, Oliver W. 24
Hooks, Benjamin L. 2
hooks, bell 5
Hope, John 8
Howard, M. William, Jr. 26
Ingram, Rex 5
Innis, Roy 5
Jeffries, Leonard 8
Johnson, James Weldon 5
Jones, Elaine R. 7, 45
Jordan, Vernon E. 3, 35
Khanga, Yelena 6
King, Bernice 4
King, Coretta Scott 3
King, Martin Luther, Jr. 1
King, Yolanda 6
Lane, Charles 3
Lee-Smith, Hughie 5, 22
Lee, Spike 5, 19
Lorde, Audre 6
Mabuza-Suttle, Felicia 43
Mandela, Nelson 1, 14
Martin, Louis E. 16
Mathabane, Mark 5
Maynard, Robert C. 7
Mays, Benjamin E. 7
McDougall, Gay J. 11, 43
McKay, Claude 6
Meredith, James H. 11
Micheaux, Oscar 7
Moore, Harry T. 29
Mosley, Walter 5, 25
Muhammad, Khallid Abdul 10, 31
Norton, Eleanor Holmes 7
Page, Clarence 4
Perkins, Edward 5
Pitt, David Thomas 10
Poussaint, Alvin F. 5
Price, Frederick K.C. 21
Price, Hugh B. 9
Robeson, Paul 2
Robinson, Spottswood W. III 22
Sampson, Edith S. 4
Shabazz, Attallah 6
Sifford, Charlie 4
Simpson, Carole 6, 30
Sister Souljah 11
Sisulu, Sheila Violet Makate 24
Smith, Anna Deavere 6, 44
Sowell, Thomas 2
Spaulding, Charles Clinton 9
Staples, Brent 8
Steele, Claude Mason 13
Taulbert, Clifton Lemoure 19
Till, Emmett 7
Tutu, Desmond Mpilo 6, 44
Tyree, Omar Rashad 21
Walcott, Derek 5
Walker, Maggie 17
Washington, Booker T. 4
Washington, Harold 6
Wells-Barnett, Ida B. 8
Welsing, Frances Cress 5
West, Cornel 5
Wideman, John Edgar 5
Wiley, Ralph 8
Wilkins, Roger 2
Wilkins, Roy 4
Williams, Fannie Barrier 27
Williams, Gregory 11
Williams, Hosea Lorenzo 15, 31
Williams, Patricia J. 11
Williams, Walter E. 4
Wilson, Sunnie 7
Wright, Richard 5
Young, Whitney M., Jr. 4

Radio
Abrahams, Peter 39
Abu-Jamal, Mumia 15
Alert, Kool DJ Red 33
Anderson, Eddie "Rochester" 30
Banks, William 11
Bates, Karen Grigsby 40
Beasley, Phoebe 34
Booker, Simeon 23
Branch, William Blackwell 39
Crocker, Frankie 29
Dee, Ruby 8
Dr. Dre 10
Elder, Larry 25
Fuller, Charles 8
Goode, Mal 13
Gumbel, Greg 8
Hamblin, Ken 10
Haynes, Trudy 44
Holt, Nora 38
Hughes, Cathy 27
Jackson, Hal 41
Jarret, Vernon D. 42
Joe, Yolanda 21
Joyner, Tom 19
Keyes, Alan L. 11
Lewis, Delano 7
Lewis, Ramsey 35
Ligging, Alfred III 43
Lover, Ed 10
Ludacris 37
Madison, Joseph E. 17
Majors, Jeff 41
Mickelbury, Penny 28
Moss, Carlton 17
Pressley, Condace L. 41
Samara, Noah 15
Smiley, Tavis 20
Smith, Greg 28
Steinberg, Martha Jean "The Queen" 28
Taylor, Billy 23
Whack, Rita Coburn 36
Williams, Armstrong 29
Williams, Juan 35
Yarbrough, Camille 40

Radio Jamaica
Abrahams, Peter 39

Radio One Inc.
Hughes, Cathy 27
Ligging, Alfred III 43
Majors, Jeff 41

Radio-Television News Directors Association
Pressley, Condace L. 41

Ragtime
Blake, Eubie 29
Europe, James Reese 10
Joplin, Scott 6
Sissle, Noble 29

Rainbow Coalition
Chappell, Emma 18
Jackson, Jesse 1, 27
Jackson, Jesse, Jr. 14, 45
Moore, Minyon 45

Rap music
50 Cent 46
Alert, Kool DJ Red 33

Baker, Houston A., Jr. **6**
Bambaataa, Afrika **34**
Benjamin, Andre **45**
Blow, Kurtis **31**
Brown, Foxy **25**
Butts, Calvin O., III **9**
Chuck D. **9**
Combs, Sean "Puffy" **17**, **43**
Common **31**
DJ Jazzy Jeff **32**
DMX **28**
Dr. Dre **10**
Dre, Dr. **14**, **30**
Dupri, Jermaine **13**, **46**
Dyson, Michael Eric **11**, **40**
Elliott, Missy "Misdemeanor" **31**
Eve **29**
Gotti, Irv **39**
Grandmaster Flash **33**
Gray, F. Gary **14**
Hammer, M. C. **20**
Harrell, Andre **9**, **30**
Hill, Lauryn **20**
Ice Cube **8**, **30**
Ice-T **6**, **31**
Ja Rule **35**
Jay-Z **27**
Jean, Wyclef **20**
Jones, Quincy **8**, **30**
Knight, Suge **11**, **30**
KRS-One **34**
(Lil') Bow Wow **35**
Lil' Kim **28**
Liles, Kevin **42**
Lopes, Lisa "Left Eye" **36**
Lover, Ed **10**
Ludacris **37**
Mase **24**
Master P **21**
MC Lyte **34**
Mos Def **30**
Nelly **32**
Notorious B.I.G. **20**
O'Neal, Shaquille **8**, **30**
OutKast **35**
Queen Latifah **1**, **16**
Rhymes, Busta **31**
Run-DMC **31**
Shakur, Tupac **14**
Simmons, Russell **1**, **30**
Sister Souljah **11**
Smith, Will **8**, **18**
Snoop Dogg **35**
Timbaland **32**
Tucker, C. DeLores **12**
Yarbrough, Camille **40**

Rassemblement Démocratique Africain (African Democratic Rally; RDA)
Houphouët-Boigny, Félix **4**
Touré, Sekou **6**

Rastafarianism
Haile Selassie **7**
Marley, Bob **5**
Marley, Rita **32**
Tosh, Peter **9**

RDA
See Rassemblement Démocratique Africain (African Democratic Rally)

Reader's Choice Award
Holton, Hugh, Jr. **39**

Real estate development
Barden, Don H. **9**, **20**
Brooke, Edward **8**
Lane, Vincent **5**
Marshall, Bella **22**
Russell, Herman Jerome **17**

"Real Men Cook"
Moyo, Karega Kofi **36**

Recording executives
Avant, Clarence **19**
Busby, Jheryl **3**
Combs, Sean "Puffy" **17**, **43**
de Passe, Suzanne **25**
Dupri, Jermaine **13**, **46**
Gordy, Berry, Jr. **1**
Gotti, Irv **39**
Harrell, Andre **9**, **30**
Jackson, George **19**
Jackson, Randy **40**
Jimmy Jam **13**
Jones, Quincy **8**, **30**
Knight, Suge **11**, **30**
Lewis, Terry **13**
Liles, Kevin **42**
Massenburg, Kedar **23**
Master P **21**
Mayfield, Curtis **2**, **43**
Queen Latifah **1**, **16**
Reid, Antonio "L.A." **28**
Rhone, Sylvia **2**
Robinson, Smokey **3**
Simmons, Russell **1**, **30**

Record producer
Albright, Gerald **23**
Ayers, Roy **16**
Bambaataa, Afrika **34**
Blige, Mary J. **20**, **34**
Coleman, Ornette **39**
Combs, Sean "Puffy" **17**, **43**
de Passe, Suzanne **25**
DJ Jazzy Jeff **32**
Dre, Dr. **14**, **30**
Duke, George **21**
Dupri, Jermaine **13**, **46**
Edmonds, Kenneth "Babyface" **10**, **31**
Elliott, Missy "Misdemeanor" **31**
Gotti, Irv **39**
Hailey, JoJo **22**
Hailey, K-Ci **22**
Hammond, Fred **23**
Hill, Lauryn **20**
Ice Cube **8**, **30**
Ja Rule **35**
Jackson, George **19**
Jackson, Michael **19**
Jackson, Randy **40**
Jean, Wyclef **20**
Jerkins, Rodney **31**
Jimmy Jam **13**
Jones, Quincy **8**, **30**
Kelly, R. **18**, **44**
Lewis, Terry **13**
Liles, Kevin **42**
Master P **21**
Mayfield, Curtis **2**, **43**
Timbaland **32**
Osborne, Jeffrey **26**
Prince **18**
Queen Latifah **1**, **16**
Reid, Antonio "L.A." **28**
Sweat, Keith **19**
Vandross, Luther **13**, **48**
White, Barry **13**, **41**
Williams, Pharrell **47**

Reform Party
Foster, Ezola **28**

Reggae
Beenie Man **32**
Blondy, Alpha **30**
Cliff, Jimmy **28**
Griffiths, Marcia **29**
Hammond, Lenn **34**
Johnson, Linton Kwesi **37**
Marley, Bob **5**
Marley, Rita **32**
Marley, Ziggy **41**
Mowatt, Judy **38**
Perry, Ruth **19**
Shaggy **31**
Sly & Robbie **34**
Tosh, Peter **9**

Republican National Convention
Allen, Ethel D. **13**

Republic of New Africa (RNA)
Williams, Robert F. **11**

Resource Associates International
Moyo, Karega Kofi **36**
Moyo, Yvette Jackson **36**

Restaurants
Cain, Herman **15**
Daniels-Carter, Valerie **23**
Hawkins, La-Van **17**
Rodriguez, Jimmy **47**
Smith, Barbara **11**
Washington, Regynald G. **44**

Restitution Study Group, Inc.
Farmer-Paellmann, Deadria **43**

Revolutionary Party of Tanzania
See Chama cha Mapinduzi

Revolutionary People's Communication Network
Cleaver, Kathleen Neal **29**

Rheedlen Centers for Children and Families
Canada, Geoffrey **23**

Rhode Island School of Design
Prophet, Nancy Elizabeth **42**

Rhodes scholar
Kennedy, Randall **40**

Rhythm and blues/soul music
Ace, Johnny **36**
Aaliyah **30**
Adams, Johnny **39**
Adams, Oleta **18**
Ashanti **37**
Ashford, Nickolas **21**
Austin, Patti **24**
Ayers, Roy **16**
Badu, Erykah **22**
Baker, Anita **21**, **48**
Baker, LaVern **26**
Ballard, Hank **41**
Baylor, Helen **36**
Belle, Regina **1**
Benét, Eric **28**
Berry, Chuck **29**
Beverly, Frankie **25**
Blige, Mary J. **20**, **34**
Brandy **14**, **34**
Braxton, Toni **15**
Brooks, Hadda **40**
Brown, Charles **23**
Burke, Solomon **31**
Busby, Jheryl **3**
Butler, Jerry **26**
Campbell-Martin, Tisha **8**, **42**
Carey, Mariah **32**
Charles, Ray **16**, **48**
Clinton, George **9**
Combs, Sean "Puffy" **17**, **43**
Cooke, Sam **17**
Cox, Deborah **28**
D'Angelo **27**
David, Craig **31**
Diddley, Bo **39**
Downing, Will **19**
Dre, Dr. **14**, **30**
Dupri, Jermaine **13**, **46**
Edmonds, Kenneth "Babyface" **10**, **31**
Elliott, Missy "Misdemeanor" **31**
Evans, Faith **22**
Fats Domino **20**
Foxx, Jamie **15**, **48**
Franklin, Aretha **11**, **44**
Gaye, Marvin **2**
Gaynor, Gloria **36**
Ginuwine **35**
Gotti, Irv **39**
Gray, Macy **29**
Green, Al **13**, **47**
Hailey, JoJo **22**
Hailey, K-Ci **22**
Hammer, M. C. **20**
Harris, Corey **39**
Hathaway, Donny **18**
Hayes, Isaac **20**
Henry, Clarence "Frogman" **46**
Hill, Lauryn **20**
Houston, Cissy **20**
Houston, Whitney **7**
Hyman, Phyllis **19**
India.Arie **34**
Isley, Ronald **25**
Ja Rule **35**
Jackson, Janet **6**, **30**
Jackson, Michael **19**
Jackson, Millie **25**
James, Etta **13**
James, Rick **17**
Jarreau, Al **21**
Jean, Wyclef **20**
Johnson, Robert **2**
Jones, Donell **29**
Jones, Quincy **8**, **30**
Jordan, Montell **23**
Kelly, R. **18**, **44**
Kem **47**

Kendricks, Eddie 22
Keys, Alicia 32
Knight, Gladys 16
Knowles, Beyoncé 39
LaBelle, Patti 13, 30
Lattimore, Kenny 35
Levert, Gerald 22
Little Richard 15
Lopes, Lisa "Left Eye" 36
Massenburg, Kedar 23
Master P 21
Maxwell 20
Mayfield, Curtis 2, 43
McKnight, Brian 18, 34
Monica 21
Moore, Chante 26
Moore, Melba 21
Musiq 37
Mya 35
Nash, Johnny 40
Ndegéocello, Me'Shell 15
Neville, Aaron 21
Notorious B.I.G. 20
Pendergrass, Teddy 22
Preston, Billy 39
Price, Kelly 23
Prince 18
Redding, Otis 16
Reed, A. C. 36
Richie, Lionel 27
Riperton, Minnie 32
Robinson, Smokey 3
Ross, Diana 8, 27
Sade 15
Scott, Jill 29
Scott, "Little" Jimmy 48
Simpson, Valerie 21
Sisqo 30
Sledge, Percy 39
Staples, "Pops" 32
Staton, Candi 27
Steinberg, Martha Jean "The Queen" 28
Stone, Angie 31
Studdard, Ruben 46
The Supremes 33
Sweat, Keith 19
Tamia 24
The Temptations 33
Terrell, Tammi 32
Thomas, Irma 29
Thomas, Rufus 20
TLC 34
Turner, Tina 6, 27
Tyrese 27
Usher 23
Vandross, Luther 13, 48
Wells, Mary 28
White, Barry 13, 41
Williams, Vanessa L. 4, 17
Wilson, Cassandra 16
Wilson, Mary 28
Wilson, Charlie 31
Wilson, Nancy 10
Wonder, Stevie 11

Richmond city government
Marsh, Henry 32

RNA
See Republic of New Africa

Roc-A-Fella Films
Dash, Damon 31

Roc-A-Fella Records
Dash, Damon 31
Jay-Z 27

Roc-A-Wear
Dash, Damon 31
Jay-Z 27

Rock and Roll Hall of Fame
Ballard, Hank 41
Bland, Bobby "Blue" 36
Brown, Charles 23
Diddley, Bo 39
Franklin, Aretha 11, 44
Holland-Dozier-Holland 36
Hooker, John Lee 30
Isley, Ronald 25
James, Etta 13
Mayfield, Curtis 2, 43
Steinberg, Martha Jean "The Queen" 28
Turner, Tina 6, 27
Wilson, Mary 28
Wonder, Stevie 11

Rockefeller Foundation
Price, Hugh B. 9

Rock music
Ballard, Hank 41
Berry, Chuck 29
Clemons, Clarence 41
Clinton, George 9
Diddley, Bo 39
Edwards, Esther Gordy 43
Fats Domino 20
Glover, Corey 34
Hendrix, Jimi 10
Ice-T 6, 31
Kravitz, Lenny 10, 34
Little Richard 15
Lymon, Frankie 22
Mayfield, Curtis 2, 43
Preston, Billy 39
Prince 18
Reid, Vernon 34
Run-DMC 31
Turner, Tina 6, 27

Rockets
Williams, O. S. 13

Rodeo
Nash, Johnny 40
Pickett, Bill 11
Sampson, Charles 13
Whitfield, Fred 23

Romance fiction
Bunkley, Anita Richmond 39
Hill, Donna 32

Roman Catholic Church
Arinze, Francis Cardinal 19
Aristide, Jean-Bertrand 6, 45
Clements, George 2
DeLille, Henriette 30
Gregory, Wilton D. 37
Guy, Rosa 5
Healy, James Augustine 30
Marino, Eugene Antonio 30
Rugambwa, Laurean 20

Stallings, George A., Jr. 6

Rounder Records
Harris, Corey 39

Royal Ballet
Jackson, Isaiah 3

Royalty
Christophe, Henri 9
Ka Dinizulu, Mcwayizeni 29
Mutebi, Ronald 25

RPT
See Togolese People's Rally

Ruff Ryders Records
Eve 29

Rush Artists Management Co.
Simmons, Russell 1, 30

Russell-McCloud and Associates
Russell-McCloud, Patricia A. 17

Rutgers University
Davis, George 36
Gibson, Donald Bernard 40

SAA
See Syndicat Agricole Africain

SACC
See South African Council of Churches

Sacramento Kings basketball team
Russell, Bill 8
Webber, Chris 15, 30

Sacramento Monarchs basketball team
Griffith, Yolanda 25

SADCC
See Southern African Development Coordination Conference

Sailing
Pinckney, Bill 42

St. Louis Browns baseball team
Brown, Willard 36

St. Louis Blues hockey team
Brathwaite, Fred 35
Mayers, Jamal 39

St. Louis Browns baseball team
Paige, Satchel 7

St. Louis Cardinals baseball team
Baylor, Don 6
Bonds, Bobby 43
Brock, Lou 18
Flood, Curt 10
Gibson, Bob 33
Lankford, Ray 23

St. Louis city government
Bosley, Freeman, Jr. 7
Harmon, Clarence 26

St. Louis Giants baseball team
Charleston, Oscar 39

St. Louis Hawks basketball team
See Atlanta Hawks basketball team

St. Louis Rams football team
Bruce, Isaac 26
Faulk, Marshall 35
Pace, Orlando 21

St. Louis Stars baseball team
Bell, James "Cool Papa" 36

Sainte Beuve Prize
Beti, Mongo 36

SAMM
See Stopping AIDS Is My Mission

Sammy Davis Jr. National Liver Institute University Hospital
Leevy, Carrol M. 42

San Antonio Spurs basketball team
Duncan, Tim 20
Elliott, Sean 26
Lucas, John 7
Robinson, David 24

San Diego Chargers football team
Barnes, Ernie 16
Lofton, James 42

San Diego Conquistadors
Chamberlain, Wilt 18, 47

San Diego Gulls hockey team
O'Ree, Willie 5

San Diego Hawks hockey team
O'Ree, Willie 5

San Diego Padres baseball team
Carter, Joe 30
Gwynn, Tony 18
McGriff, Fred 24
Sheffield, Gary 16
Winfield, Dave 5

San Francisco 49ers football team
Edwards, Harry 2
Green, Dennis 5, 45
Lott, Ronnie 9
Rice, Jerry 5
Simpson, O. J. 15

San Francisco Giants baseball team
Baker, Dusty 8
Bonds, Barry 6, 34
Bonds, Bobby 43
Carter, Joe 30
Mays, Willie 3
Morgan, Joe Leonard 9
Robinson, Frank 9

Strawberry, Darryl 22

San Francisco Opera
Mitchell, Leona 42

Sankofa Film and Video
Blackwood, Maureen 37
Julien, Isaac 3

Sankofa Video and Bookstore
Gerima, Haile 38

Saturday Night Live
Meadows, Tim 30
Morris, Garrett 31
Murphy, Eddie 4, 20
Rock, Chris 3, 22
Rudolph, Maya 46

Savoy Ballroom
Johnson, Buddy 36

Saxophone
Adderley, Julian "Cannonball" 30
Albright, Gerald 23
Bechet, Sidney 18
Clemons, Clarence 41
Coltrane, John 19
Golson, Benny 37
Gordon, Dexter 25
Hawkins, Coleman 9
Kay, Ulyssess 37
Parker, Charlie 20
Redman, Joshua 30
Rollins, Sonny 37
Washington, Grover, Jr. 17, 44
Waters, Benny 26
Whalum, Kirk 37
York, Vincent 40
Young, Lester 37

Schomburg Center for Research in Black Culture
Andrews, Bert 13
Dodson, Howard, Jr. 7
Hutson, Jean Blackwell 16
Reddick, Lawrence Dunbar 20
Schomburg, Arthur Alfonso 9

School desegregation
Fortune, T. Thomas 6
Hamer, Fannie Lou 6
Hobson, Julius W. 44

Scotland Yard
Griffin, Bessie Blout 43

Science fiction
Bell, Derrick 6
Butler, Octavia 8, 43
Delany, Samuel R., Jr. 9

SCLC
See Southern Christian Leadership Conference

Score One for Kids
Cherry, Deron 40

Screen Actors Guild
Fields, Kim 36
Howard, Sherri 36
Lewis, Emmanuel 36
Poitier, Sidney 11, 36

Screenplay writing
Brown, Cecil M. 46
Campbell-Martin, Tisha 8, 42
Elder, Lonne III 38
Fisher, Antwone 40
Greaves, William 38
Ice Cube 8, 30
Jones, Orlando 30
Martin, Darnell 43
Nissel, Angela 42
Prince-Bythewood, Gina 31
Singleton, John 2, 30

Sculpture
Allen, Tina 22
Bailey, Radcliffe 19
Barthe, Richmond 15
Biggers, John 20, 33
Brown, Donald 19
Burke, Selma 16
Catlett, Elizabeth 2
Chase-Riboud, Barbara 20, 46
Cortor, Eldzier 42
Edwards, Melvin 22
Fuller, Meta Vaux Warrick 27
Guyton, Tyree 9
Hathaway, Isaac Scott 33
Hunt, Richard 6
Lewis, Edmonia 10
Lewis, Samella 25
Manley, Edna 26
McGee, Charles 10
Moody, Ronald 30
Perkins, Marion 38
Prophet, Nancy Elizabeth 42
Puryear, Martin 42
Ringgold, Faith 4
Saar, Alison 16
Savage, Augusta 12
Shabazz, Attallah 6
Washington, James Jr. 38

Sean John clothing line
Combs, Sean "Puffy" 17, 43

Seattle city government
Rice, Norm 8

Seattle Mariners baseball team
Griffey, Ken, Jr. 12

Seattle Supersonics basketball team
Bickerstaff, Bernie 21
Lucas, John 7
Russell, Bill 8
Silas, Paul 24
Wilkens, Lenny 11

Second District Education and Policy Foundation
Burke, Yvonne Braithwaite 42

Second Republic (Nigeria)
Obasanjo, Olusegun 5

Seismology
Person, Waverly 9

Senate Confirmation Hearings
Ogletree, Charles, Jr. 12, 47

Senate Judiciary Subcommittee on the Consitution
Hageman, Hans 36

Sesame Street
Clash, Kevin 14
Glover, Savion 14

Sexual harassment
Gomez-Preston, Cheryl 9
Hill, Anita 5
Thomas, Clarence 2, 39

Share
Auguste, Arnold A. 47

Sheila Bridges Design Inc.
Bridges, Sheila 36

Shell Oil Company
Mays, Leslie A. 41

Shrine of the Black Madonna
Agyeman, Jaramogi Abebe 10

Sickle cell anemia
Satcher, David 7

Sierra Leone People's Party (SLPP)
Kabbah, Ahmad Tejan 23

Silicon Graphics Incorporated
Hannah, Marc 10

Siméus Foods International
Siméus, Dumas M. 25

Sisters of the Holy Family
DeLille, Henriette 30

Sketches
Crite, Alan Rohan 29
Sallee, Charles 38

Skiing
Horton, Andre 33
Horton, Suki 33

Slavery
Asante, Molefi Kete 3
Bennett, Lerone, Jr. 5
Blassingame, John Wesley 40
Chase-Riboud, Barbara 20, 46
Cooper, Anna Julia 20
Douglas, Aaron 7
Du Bois, W. E. B. 3
Dunbar, Paul Laurence 8
Farmer-Paellmann, Deadria 43
Gaines, Ernest J. 7
Haley, Alex 4
Harper, Frances Ellen Watkins 11
Johnson, Charles 1
Jones, Edward P. 43
Morrison, Toni 2, 15
Muhammad, Elijah 4
Patterson, Orlando 4
Pleasant, Mary Ellen 9
Stephens, Charlotte Andrews 14
Stewart, Maria W. Miller 19
Taylor, Susie King 13
Tubman, Harriet 9
X, Malcolm 1

Small Business Association Hall of Fame
Steward, David L. 36

Smart Books
Pinkett Smith, Jada 10, 41

Smith College
Mayhew, Richard 39
Simmons, Ruth 13, 38

SNCC
See Student Nonviolent Coordinating Committee

Soccer
Beasley, Jamar 29
Jones, Cobi N'Gai 18
Milla, Roger 2
Nakhid, David 25
Pelé 7
Scurry, Briana 27

Social disorganization theory
Frazier, E. Franklin 10

Social science
Berry, Mary Frances 7
Bunche, Ralph J. 5
Cayton, Horace 26
Clark, Kenneth B. 5
Cobbs, Price M. 9
Frazier, E. Franklin 10
George, Zelma Watson 42
Hare, Nathan 44
Harris, Eddy L. 18
Haynes, George Edmund 8
Ladner, Joyce A. 42
Lawrence-Lightfoot, Sara 10
Marable, Manning 10
Steele, Claude Mason 13
Woodson, Robert L. 10

Social Service Auxiliary
Mossell, Gertrude Bustill 40

Social work
Auguste, Rose-Anne 13
Berry, Bertice 8
Brown, Cora 33
Canada, Geoffrey 23
Dunham, Katherine 4
Fields, C. Virginia 25
Hale, Clara 16
Hale, Lorraine 8
Harris, Alice 7
Haynes, George Edmund 8
King, Barbara 22
Lewis, Thomas 19
Little, Robert L. 2
Robinson, Rachel 16
Waddles, Charleszetta (Mother) 10
Williams, Fannie Barrier 27
Thrower, Willie 35
Young, Whitney M., Jr. 4

Socialist Party of Senegal
Diouf, Abdou 3

Soft Sheen Products
Gardner, Edward G. 45

Soledad Brothers
Jackson, George 14

Soul City, NC
McKissick, Floyd B. 3

Soul Train
Baylor, Helen 36
Cornelius, Don 4
D'Angelo 27
Knowles, Beyoncé 39

Lil' Kim 28
Winans, CeCe 14, 43

Source music awards
Nelly 32

South African Communist Party
Hani, Chris 6

South African Council of Churches (SACC)
Tutu, Desmond Mpilo 6, 44

South African Defence Force (SADF)
Nujoma, Samuel 10

South African government
Sisulu, Walter 47
Zuma, Nkosazana Dlamini 34

South African literature
Abrahams, Peter 39
Brutus, Dennis 38
Head, Bessie 28
Mathabane, Mark 5
Mofolo, Thomas 37
Mphalele, Es'kia (Ezekiel) 40

South African Students' Organization
Biko, Steven 4

South Carolina state government
Cardozo, Francis L. 33

South West African People's Organization (SWAPO)
Nujoma, Samuel 10

Southeastern University
Jarvis, Charlene Drew 21

Southern African Development Community (SADC)
Mbuende, Kaire 12

Southern African Development Coordination Conference (SADCC)
Masire, Quett 5
Numjoma, Samuel 10

Southern African Project
McDougall, Gay J. 11, 43

Southern Christian Leadership Conference (SCLC)
Abernathy, Ralph 1
Angelou, Maya 1, 15
Baker, Ella 5
Chavis, Benjamin 6
Dee, Ruby 8
Fauntroy, Walter E. 11
Hooks, Benjamin L. 2
Jackson, Jesse 1, 27
King, Martin Luther, Jr. 1
King, Martin Luther, III 20
Lowery, Joseph 2
Moses, Robert Parris 11
Rustin, Bayard 4
Shuttlesworth, Fred 47
Williams, Hosea Lorenzo 15, 31

Young, Andrew 3, 48

Southern Syncopated Orchestra
Cook, Will Marion 40

Space Shuttle
Anderson, Michael 40
Bluford, Guy 2, 35
Bolden, Charles F., Jr. 7
Gregory, Frederick D. 8
Jemison, Mae C. 1, 35
McNair, Ronald 3

Special Olympics
Clairborne, Loretta 34

Spectroscopy
Quarterman, Lloyd Albert 4

Spelman College
Cole, Johnnetta B. 5, 43
Price, Glenda 22
Simmons, Ruth 13, 38
Tatum, Beverly Daniel 42
Wade-Gayles, Gloria Jean 41

Spingarn medal
Aaron, Hank 5
Ailey, Alvin 8
Anderson, Marian 2, 33
Angelou, Maya 1, 15
Bates, Daisy 13
Bethune, Mary McLeod 4
Bradley, Thomas 2, 20
Brooke, Edward 8
Bunche, Ralph J. 5
Carver, George Washington 4
Chesnutt, Charles 29
Clark, Kenneth B. 5
Cosby, Bill 7, 26
Davis, Sammy Jr. 18
Drew, Charles Richard 7
Du Bois, W. E. B. 3
Ellington, Duke 5
Evers, Medgar 3
Franklin, John Hope 5
Grimké, Archibald H. 9
Haley, Alex 4
Hastie, William H. 8
Hayes, Roland 4
Height, Dorothy I. 2, 23
Higginbotham, A. Leon Jr. 13, 25
Hinton, William Augustus 8
Hooks, Benjamin L. 2
Horne, Lena 5
Houston, Charles Hamilton 4
Hughes, Langston 4
Jackson, Jesse 1, 27
Johnson, James Weldon 5
Johnson, John H. 3
Jordan, Barbara 4
Julian, Percy Lavon 6
Just, Ernest Everett 3
Keith, Damon 16
King, Martin Luther, Jr. 1
Lawless, Theodore K. 8
Lawrence, Jacob 4
Logan, Rayford 40
Marshall, Thurgood 1, 44
Mays, Benjamin E. 7
Moore, Harry T. 29
Parks, Gordon 1, 35
Parks, Rosa 1, 35
Powell, Colin 1, 28

Price, Leontyne 1
Randolph, A. Philip 3
Robeson, Paul 2
Robinson, Jackie 6
Staupers, Mabel K. 7
Sullivan, Leon H. 3, 30
Weaver, Robert C. 8, 46
White, Walter F. 4
Wilder, L. Douglas 3, 48
Wilkins, Roy 4
Williams, Paul R. 9
Woodson, Carter 2
Wright, Louis Tompkins 4
Wright, Richard 5
Young, Andrew 3, 48
Young, Coleman 1, 20

Spiral Group
Mayhew, Richard 39

Spirituals
Anderson, Marian 2, 33
Hayes, Roland 4
Jackson, Mahalia 5
Joyner, Matilda Sissieretta 15
Norman, Jessye 5
Reese, Della 6, 20
Robeson, Paul 2
Williams, Denise 40

Sports administration
Fuller, Vivian 33
Kerry, Leon G. 46
Lee, Sr., Bertram M. 46
Mills, Steve 47
Phillips, Teresa L. 42

Sports psychology
Edwards, Harry 2

Stanford University
Rice, Condoleezza 3, 28
Willingham, Tyrone 43

Starcom
McCann, Renetta 44

State University of New York System
Ballard, Allen Butler, Jr. 40
Baraka, Amiri 1, 38
Wharton, Clifton R., Jr. 7

Stay Fit Plus
Richardson, Donna 39

Stellar Awards
Baylor, Helen 36

Stonewall 25
Norman, Pat 10

Stop The Violence Movement
KRS-One 34
MC Lyte 34

Stopping AIDS Is My Mission (SAMM)
Cargill, Victoria A. 43

Storytelling
Baker, Augusta 38

Structural Readjustment Program
Babangida, Ibrahim 4

Student Nonviolent Coordinating Committee (SNCC)
Al-Amin, Jamil Abdullah 6
Baker, Ella 5
Barry, Marion S. 7, 44
Blackwell, Unita 17
Bond, Julian 2, 35
Carmichael, Stokely 5, 26
Clark, Septima 7
Crouch, Stanley 11
Davis, Angela 5
Forman, James 7
Hamer, Fannie Lou 6
Holland, Endesha Ida Mae 3
Lester, Julius 9
Lewis, John 2, 46
Moses, Robert Parris 11
Norton, Eleanor Holmes 7
Poussaint, Alvin F. 5
Reagon, Bernice Johnson 7
Touré, Askia (Muhammad Abu Bakr el) 47

Sugarfoots
El Wilson, Barbara 35

Sun Microsystems
Tademy, Lalita 36

Sundance Film Festival
Harris, Leslie 6

Sunni Muslim
Muhammed, W. Deen 27

Sunny Alade Records
Ade, King Sunny 41

Supreme Court
See U.S. Supreme Court

Supreme Court of Haiti
Pascal-Trouillot, Ertha 3

Surrealism
Ellison, Ralph 7
Lee-Smith, Hughie 5, 22

SWAPO
See South West African People's Organization

Sweet Honey in the Rock
Reagon, Bernice Johnson 7

Syndicat Agricole Africain (SAA)
Houphouët-Boigny, Félix 4

Sylvia's restaurant
Washington, Regynald G. 44
Woods, Sylvia 34

Synthetic chemistry
Julian, Percy Lavon 6

Talk Soup
Tyler, Aisha N. 36

T. D. Jakes Ministry
Jakes, Thomas "T.D." 17, 43

Talladega College
Archie-Hudson, Marguerite 44

Tampa Bay Buccaneers football team
Barber, Ronde 41
Brooks, Derrick 43

Dungy, Tony 17, 42
Sapp, Warren 38
Williams, Doug 22

Tanga Consultative Congress (Tanzania)
Nujoma, Samuel 10

Tanganyikan African National Union (TANU)
Nyerere, Julius 5

TANU
See Tanganyikan African National Union

Tanzanian African National Union (TANU)
See Tanganyikan African National Union

Tap dancing
Atkins, Cholly 40
Bates, Peg Leg 14
Glover, Savion 14
Hines, Gregory 1, 42
Sims, Howard "Sandman" 48

TBS
See Turner Broadcasting System

Teacher of the Year Award
Draper, Sharon Mills 16, 43

Teachers Insurance and Annuity Association and the College Retirement Equities Fund (TIAA-CREF)
Wharton, Clifton R., Jr. 7

Teaching
Adams-Ender, Clara 40
Alexander, Margaret Walker 22
Amadi, Elechi 40
Archie-Hudson, Marguerite 44
Aubert, Alvin 41
Baiocchi, Regina Harris 41
Ballard, Allen Butler, Jr. 40
Blassingame, John Wesley 40
Branch, William Blackwell 39
Brawley, Benjamin 44
Brown, Uzee 42
Brown, Willa 40
Bryan, Ashley F. 41
Campbell, Mary Schmidt 43
Cardozo, Francis L. 33
Carruthers, George R. 40
Carter, Joye Maureen 41
Chenault, John 40
Cheney-Coker, Syl 43
Clarke, John Henrik 20
Clemmons, Reginal G. 41
Cobb, Jewel Plummer 42
Cobb, W. Montague 39
Cole, Johnnetta B. 5, 43
Cook, Mercer 40
Cooper Cafritz, Peggy 43
Cortez, Jayne 43
Cortor, Eldzier 42
Cotter, Joseph Seamon, Sr. 40
Davis, Arthur P. 41
Davis, Gary 41
Dennard, Brazeal 37
De Veaux, Alexis 44
Draper, Sharon Mills 16, 43
Drummond, William J. 40

Dumas, Henry 41
Dunnigan, Alice Allison 41
Dymally, Mervyn 42
Early, Gerald 15
Feelings, Muriel 44
Figueroa, John J. 40
Fletcher, Bill, Jr. 41
Ford, Nick Aaron 44
Forrest, Leon 44
Fuller, A. Oveta 43
Fuller, Arthur 27
Fuller, Howard L. 37
Gates, Sylvester James, Jr. 15
Gayle, Addison, Jr. 41
George, Zelma Watson 42
Gibson, Donald Bernard 40
Hall, Arthur 39
Hare, Nathan 44
Harvey, William R. 42
Henries, A. Doris Banks 44
Hill, Errol 40
Hill, Leslie Pinckney 44
Horne, Frank 44
Humphries, Frederick 20
Imes, Elmer Samuel 39
Jackson, Fred James 25
Jarret, Vernon D. 42
Kennedy, Randall 40
Ladner, Joyce A. 42
Leevy, Carrol M. 42
Lewis, Norman 39
Logan, Rayford W. 40
Maathai, Wangari 43
Mitchell, Parren J. 42
Moore, Harry T. 29
Mphalele, Es'kia (Ezekiel) 40
Naylor, Gloria 10, 42
Norman, Maidie 20
Owens, Helen 48
Palmer, Everard 37
Peters, Margaret and Matilda 43
Player, Willa B. 43
Prophet, Nancy Elizabeth 42
Puryear, Martin 42
Redmond, Eugene 23
Smith, Anna Deavere 6, 44
Smith, John L. 22
Tatum, Beverly Daniel 42
Tillis, Frederick 40
Tyson, Andre 40
Wambugu, Florence 42
Watson, Diane 41
Wilkens, J. Ernest, Jr. 43
Yancy, Dorothy Cowser 42
Yarbrough, Camille 40
York, Vincent 40

Techno music
Craig, Carl 31
May, Derrick 41

Technology Access Foundation
Millines Dziko, Trish 28

TEF
See Theological Education Fund

Telecommunications
Gordon, Bruce S. 41
Wilkins, Ray 47

Telemat Incorporated
Bynoe, Peter C.B. 40

Television
Alexander, Khandi 43
Anderson, Eddie "Rochester" 30
Arkadie, Kevin 17
Barclay, Paris 37
Beach, Michael 26
Blake, Asha 26
Bowser, Yvette Lee 17
Brady, Wayne 32
Branch, William Blackwell 39
Bridges, Todd 37
Brooks, Hadda 40
Brown, Joe 29
Brown, Vivian 27
Burnett, Charles 16
Carson, Lisa Nicole 21
Carter, Nell 39
Cash, Rosalind 28
Cedric the Entertainer 29
Cheadle, Don 19
Coleman, Gary 35
Corbi, Lana 42
Cosby, Bill 7, 26
Creagh, Milton 27
Curtis-Hall, Vondie 17
Davis, Viola 34
de Passe, Suzanne 25
Diggs, Taye 25
Dourdan, Gary 37
Elder, Larry 25
Ephriam, Mablean 29
Eubanks, Kevin 15
Evans, Harry 25
Falana, Lola 42
Fields, Kim 36
Fox, Rick 27
Freeman, Yvette 27
Givens, Robin 4, 25
Gray, Willie 46
Greely, M. Gasby 27
Grier, David Alan 28
Hardison, Kadeem 22
Hatchett, Glenda 32
Haynes, Trudy 44
Haysbert, Dennis 42
Hemsley, Sherman 19
Henriques, Julian 37
Hill, Lauryn 20
Houston, Whitney 7, 28
Hughley, D.L. 23
Hyman, Earle 25
Jackson, George 19
Jackson, Randy 40
Jarret, Vernon D. 42
Joe, Yolanda 21
Jones, Bobby 20
Johnson, Rodney Van 28
Jones, Star 10, 27
Kodjoe, Boris 34
Lathan, Sanaa 27
Lewis, Emmanuel 36
Lumbly, Carl 47
Mabuza-Suttle, Felicia 43
Mac, Bernie 29
Marsalis, Branford 34
Martin, Helen 31
Martin, Jesse L. 31
Mathis, Greg 26
McKenzie, Vashti M. 29
McKinney, Nina Mae 40
Meadows, Tim 30
Mercado-Valdes, Frank 43
Merkerson, S. Epatha 47

Michele, Michael 31
Mitchell, Brian Stokes 21
Mitchell, Russ 21
Moss, Carlton 16
Nash, Johnny 40
Neal, Elise 29
Nissel, Angela 42
Norman, Christina 47
Perry, Tyler 40
Phifer, Mekhi 25
Premice, Josephine 41
Price, Frederick K. C. 21
Quarles, Norma 25
Ray, Gene Anthony 47
Richards, Beah 30
Roberts, Deborah 35
Robinson, Shaun 36
Rock, Chris 3, 22
Rollins, Howard E. Jr., 17
Smiley, Tavis 20
Snipes, Wesley 3, 24
St. Patrick, Mathew 48
Sykes, Wanda 48
Taylor, Karin 34
Taylor, Regina 9, 46
Thigpen, Lynne 17, 41
Tyler, Aisha N. 36
Union, Gabrielle 31
Usher 23
Wainwright, Joscelyn 46
Warner, Malcolm-Jamal 22, 36
Warren, Michael 27
Wayans, Damon 8, 41
Wayans, Marlon 29
Wayans, Shawn 29
Williams, Armstrong 29
Williams, Clarence, III 26
Williams, Serena 20
Williams, Vanessa 32
Williamson, Mykelti 22

Temple of Hip-Hop
KRS-One 34

Tennessee state government
Ford, Harold Eugene 42

Tennessee State University
Phillips, Teresa L. 42

Tennessee Titans football team
McNair, Steve 22, 47

Tennis
Ashe, Arthur 1, 18
Blake, James 43
Garrison, Zina 2
Gibson, Althea 8, 43
Lucas, John 7
McNeil, Lori 1
Noah, Yannick 4
Peters, Margaret and Matilda 43
Rubin, Chanda 37
Washington, MaliVai 8
Williams, Samm-Art 21
Williams, Serena 20, 41
Williams, Venus 17, 34

Terrie Williams Agency
Williams, Terrie 35

Texas House of Representatives
Delco, Wilhemina 33
Johnson, Eddie Bernice 8

Wilson, Flip 21

Texas Rangers baseball team
Bonds, Bobby 43
Cottrell, Comer 11

Texas State Senate
Johnson, Eddie Bernice 8
Jordan, Barbara 4

Theatre Owner's Booking Association (TOBA)
Austin, Lovie 40
Cox, Ida 42

Theatrical direction
Hayes, Teddy 40

Theatrical production
Hayes, Teddy 40
Perry, Tyler 40

Thelonius Monk Institute of Jazz Performance
Blanchard, Terence 43

Theological Education Fund (TEF)
Gordon, Pamela 17
Tutu, Desmond Mpilo 6, 44

Theology
Franklin, Robert M. 13

They All Played Baseball Foundation
Johnson, Mamie "Peanut" 40

Third World Press
Madhubuti, Haki R. 7
Moyo, Karega Kofi 36

Threads 4 Life
Jones, Carl 7
Kani, Karl 10
Walker, T. J. 7

Three Fifths Productions
Marsalis, Delfeayo 41

TIAA-CREF
See Teachers Insurance and Annuity Association and the College Retirement Equities Fund

Tiger Woods Foundation
Woods, Tiger 14, 31

Time-Warner Inc.
Ames, Wilmer 27
Parsons, Richard Dean 11, 33

TLC Beatrice International Holdings, Inc.
Lewis, Reginald F. 6

TLC Group L.P.
Lewis, Reginald F. 6

TOBA
See Theatre Owner's Booking Association

Today show
Gumbel, Bryant 14

Togolese Army
Eyadéma, Gnassingbé 7

Togolese People's Rally (RPT)
Eyadéma, Gnassingbé 7

Toledo city government
Bell, Michael 40

Toledo Civic Hall of Fame
Stewart, Ella 39

The Tonight Show
Eubanks, Kevin 15

Tony awards
Allen, Debbie 13, 42
Belafonte, Harry 4
Carroll, Diahann 9
Carter, Nell 39
Clarke, Hope 14
Davis, Viola 34
Faison, George 16
Falana, Lola 42
Fishburne, Larry 4, 22
Horne, Lena 5
Hyman, Phyllis 19
Jones, James Earl 3
McDonald, Audra 20
Moore, Melba 21
Premice, Josephine 41
Richards, Lloyd 2
Thigpen, Lynne 17, 41
Uggams, Leslie 23
Vereen, Ben 4
Wilson, August 7, 33
Wolfe, George C. 6, 43

Top Dawg Productions
Gotti, Irv 39

Toronto Blue Jays baseball team
Carter, Joe 30
McGriff, Fred 24
Winfield, Dave 5

Toronto Raptors basketball team
Carter, Butch 27
Carter, Vince 26
Thomas, Isiah 7, 26

Toronto Symphony Orchestra
Williams, Denise 40

Tourism
Edmunds, Gladys 48

Track and field
Beamon, Bob 30
Christie, Linford 8
Devers, Gail 7
Felix, Allyson 48
Freeman, Cathy 29
Greene, Maurice 27
Griffith-Joyner, Florence 28
Harrison, Alvin 28
Harrison, Calvin 28
Holmes, Kelly 47
Jacobs, Regina 38
Johnson, Michael 13
Johnson, Rodney Van 28
Jones, Marion 21
Joyner-Kersee, Jackie 5
Lewis, Carl 4
Metcalfe, Ralph 26
Montgomery, Tim 41
Moses, Edwin 8

Mutola, Maria 12
Owens, Jesse 2
Powell, Mike 7
Quirot, Ana 13
Rudolph, Wilma 4
Thugwane, Josia 21

Trans-Urban News Service
Cooper, Andrew W. 36

TransAfrica Forum, Inc.
Fletcher, Bill, Jr. 41
Robinson, Randall 7, 46

Transition
Soyinka, Wole 4

Transitional Committee for National Recovery (Guinea; CTRN)
Conté, Lansana 7

Transplant surgery
Callender, Clive O. 3
Kountz, Samuel L. 10

Transportation Administration Services
Steward, David L. 36

Transporation Business Services
Steward, David L. 36

Treasurer of the United States
Morton, Azie Taylor 48

"Trial of the Century"
Cochran, Johnnie L., Jr. 11, 39
Darden, Christopher 13
Simpson, O.J. 15

Trinidad Theatre Workshop
Walcott, Derek 5

Trinity United Church of Christ
Wright, Jeremiah A., Jr. 45

Trombone
Marsalis, Delfeayo 41

Trumpet
Adderley, Nat 29
Armstrong, Louis 2
Blanchard, Terence 43
Davis, Miles 4
Eldridge, Roy 37
Ellison, Ralph 7
Farmer, Art 38
Gillespie, Dizzy 1
Jones, Jonah 39
Smith, Cladys "Jabbo" 32
Terry, Clark 39

Tulane University
Mason, Ronald 27

Turner Broadcasting System (TBS)
Clayton, Xernona 3, 45

Tuskegee Airmen
Brown, Willa 40
Davis, Benjamin O., Jr. 2, 43
James, Daniel, Jr. 16

Patterson, Frederick Douglass 12

Tuskegee Experiment Station
Carver, George Washington 4

Tuskegee Institute School of Music
Dawson, William Levi 39

Tuskegee University
Harvey, William R. 42
Payton, Benjamin F. 23

TV One
Ligging, Alfred III 43

UAW
See United Auto Workers

UCC
See United Church of Christ

UFBL
See Universal Foundation for Better Living

UGA
See United Golf Association

Ugandan government
Amin, Idi 42

Ultraviolet Camera/Spectrograph (UVC)
Carruthers, George R. 40

Umkhonto we Sizwe
Hani, Chris 6
Mandela, Nelson 1, 14
Zuma, Jacob 33

UN
See United Nations

UNCF
See United Negro College Fund

Uncle Nonamé Cookie Company
Amos, Wally 9

Underground Railroad
Blockson, Charles L. 42
Cohen, Anthony 15
DeBaptiste, George 32

Unemployment and Poverty Action Committee
Forman, James 7

UNESCO
See United Nations Educational, Scientific, and Cultural Organization

UNIA
See Universal Negro Improvement Association

UNICEF
See United Nations Children's Fund

Unions
Brown, Llyod Louis 42
Clay, William Lacy 8
Crockett, George, Jr. 10
Europe, James Reese 10
Farmer, James 2
Fletcher, Bill, Jr. 41

Hilliard, David **7**
Ramaphosa, Cyril **3**
Randolph, A. Philip **3**
Touré, Sekou **6**

UNIP
See United National Independence Party

UNITA
See National Union for the Total Independence of Angola

United Auto Workers (UAW)
Dawson, Matel "Mat," Jr. **39**
Fletcher, Bill, Jr. **41**

United Bermuda Party
Gordon, Pamela **17**

United Church of Christ (UCC)
Chavis, Benjamin **6**

United Democratic Front (UDF)
Muluzi, Bakili **14**

United Golf Association (UGA)
Elder, Lee **6**
Sifford, Charlie **4**

United Methodist Church
Lewis, Shirley A. R. **14**

United National Independence Party (UNIP)
Kaunda, Kenneth **2**

United Nations (UN)
Annan, Kofi Atta **15, 48**
Bunche, Ralph J. **5**
Diouf, Abdou **3**
Lafontant, Jewel Stradford **3**
McDonald, Gabrielle Kirk **20**
Mongella, Gertrude **11**
Perkins, Edward **5**
Sampson, Edith S. **4**
Young, Andrew **3, 48**

United Nations Children's Fund (UNICEF)
Baker, Gwendolyn Calvert **9**
Belafonte, Harry **4**
Machel, Graca Simbine **16**

United Nations Educational, Scientific, and Cultural Organization (UNESCO)
Diop, Cheikh Anta **4**
Frazier, E. Franklin **10**
Machel, Graca Simbine **16**

UNESCO Medals
Dadié, Bernard **34**

United Negro College Fund (UNCF)
Boyd, T. B. III **6**
Bunkley, Anita Richmond **39**
Creagh, Milton **27**
Dawson, Matel "Mat," Jr. **39**
Edley, Christopher **2, 48**
Gray, William H. III **3**
Jordan, Vernon E. **3, 35**
Mays, Benjamin E. **7**
Patterson, Frederick Douglass **12**

Tillis, Frederick **40**

Universal Negro Improvement Association (UNIA)
Garvey, Marcus **1**
Austin, Rev. Junius C. **44**

United Parcel Service
Coopor, Evorn **40**
Darden, Calvin **38**
Washington, Patrice Clarke **12**

United Parcel Service Foundation
Cooper, Evern **40**

United Somali Congress (USC)
Ali Mahdi Mohamed **5**

United States Delegations
Shabazz, Ilyasah **36**

United States Football (USFL)
White, Reggie **6**
Williams, Doug **22**

United Way
Donald, Arnold Wayne **36**
Steward, David L. **36**

United Workers Union of South Africa (UWUSA)
Buthelezi, Mangosuthu Gatsha **9**

Universal Foundation for Better Living (UFBL)
Colemon, Johnnie **11**
Reese, Della **6, 20**

University of Alabama
Davis, Mike **41**
Lucy Foster, Autherine **35**

University of California Berkeley
Drummond, William J. **40**
Edley, Christopher F., Jr. **48**

Univeristy of Cape Town
Ramphele, Maphela **29**

University of Colorado administration
Berry, Mary Frances **7**

University of Delaware's Center for Counseling and Student Development
Mitchell, Sharon **36**

University of Florida
Haskins, James **36**

University of Michigan
Dillard, Godfrey J. **45**
Goss, Tom **23**
Gray, Ida **41**
Imes, Elmer Samuel **39**

University of Missouri
Floyd, Elson S. **41**

University of Michigan
Fuller, A. Oveta **43**

University of North Carolina
Floyd, Elson S. **41**

University of Texas
Granville, Evelyn Boyd **36**

University of the West Indies
Brathwaite, Kamau **36**
Hill, Errol **40**

University of Virginia
Littlepage, Craig **35**

UniverSoul Circus
Walker, Cedric "Ricky" **19**

Upscale magazine
Bronner, Nathaniel H., Sr. **32**

Uptown Music Theater
Marsalis, Delfeayo **41**

Urban Bush Women
Zollar, Jawole **28**

Urbancrest, Ohio, government
Craig-Jones, Ellen Walker **44**

Urban League (regional)
Adams, Sheila J. **25**
Clayton, Xernona **3, 45**
Jacob, John E. **2**
Mays, Benjamin E. **7**
Young, Whitney M., Jr. **4**

Urban renewal
Archer, Dennis **7, 36**
Barry, Marion S. **7, 44**
Bosley, Freeman, Jr. **7**
Collins, Barbara-Rose **7**
Harris, Alice **7**
Lane, Vincent **5**
Waters, Maxine **3**

Urban theater
Perry, Tyler **40**

US
Karenga, Maulana **10**

U.S. Air Force
Anderson, Michael P. **40**
Carter, Joye Maureen **41**
Davis, Benjamin O., Jr. **2, 43**
Gregory, Frederick D. **8**
Harris, Marcelite Jordan **16**
James, Daniel, Jr. **16**
Johnson, Lonnie **32**
Lyles, Lester **31**

U.S. Armed Forces Nurse Corps
Staupers, Mabel K. **7**

U.S. Army
Adams-Ender, Clara **40**
Cadoria, Sherian Grace **14**
Clemmons, Reginal G. **41**
Davis, Benjamin O., Sr. **4**
Delany, Martin R. **27**
Flipper, Henry O. **3**
Jackson, Fred James **25**
Johnson, Hazel **22**
Johnson, Shoshana **47**
Powell, Colin **1, 28**
Stanford, John **20**
Watkins, Perry **12**

West, Togo D., Jr. **16**

U.S. Army Air Corps
Anderson, Charles Edward **37**

U.S. Atomic Energy Commission
Nabrit, Samuel Milton **47**

U.S. Attorney's Office
Lafontant, Jewel Stradford **3**

U.S. Basketball League (USBL)
Lucas, John **7**

USBL
See U.S. Basketball League

USC
See United Somali Congress

U.S. Cabinet
Brown, Ron **5**
Elders, Joycelyn **6**
Espy, Mike **6**
Harris, Patricia Roberts **2**
Herman, Alexis M. **15**
O'Leary, Hazel **6**
Powell, Colin **1, 28**
Rice, Condoleezza **3, 28**
Slater, Rodney E. **15**
Sullivan, Louis **8**
Weaver, Robert C. **8, 46**

U.S. Circuit Court of Appeals
Hastie, William H. **8**
Keith, Damon J. **16**

U.S. Coast Guard
Brown, Erroll M. **23**

U.S. Commission on Civil Rights
Berry, Mary Frances **7**
Edley, Christopher **2, 48**

U.S. Conference of Catholic Bishops
Gregory, Wilton D. **37**

U.S. Court of Appeals
Higginbotham, A. Leon, Jr. **13, 25**
Kearse, Amalya Lyle **12**
Ogunlesi, Adebayo **37**

USDA
See U.S. Department of Agriculture

U.S. Department of Agriculture (USDA)
Espy, Mike **6**
Vaughn, Gladys Gary **47**
Watkins, Shirley R. **17**
Williams, Hosea Lorenzo **15, 31**

U.S. Department of Commerce
Brown, Ron **5**
Irving, Larry, Jr. **12**
Person, Waverly **9**
Shavers, Cheryl **31**
Wilkins, Roger **2**

U.S. Department of Defense
Tribble, Israel, Jr. **8**

U.S. Department of Education
Hill, Anita **5**
Hill, Bonnie Guiton **20**

Paige, Rod 29
Thomas, Clarence 2, 39
Tribble, Israel, Jr. 8

U.S. Department of Energy
O'Leary, Hazel 6

U.S. Department of Health and Human Services (HHS)
See also U.S. Department of Health, Education, and Welfare

U.S. Department of Health, Education, and Welfare (HEW)
Bell, Derrick 6
Berry, Mary Frances 7
Harris, Patricia Roberts 2
Johnson, Eddie Bernice 8
Sullivan, Louis 8

U.S. Department of Housing and Urban Development (HUD)
Gaines, Brenda 41
Harris, Patricia Roberts 2
Jackson, Alphonso R. 48
Weaver, Robert C. 8, 46

U.S. Department of Justice
Bell, Derrick 6
Campbell, Bill 9
Days, Drew S., III 10
Guinier, Lani 7, 30
Holder, Eric H., Jr. 9
Lafontant, Jewel Stradford 3
Lewis, Delano 7
Patrick, Deval 12
Payton, John 48
Thompson, Larry D. 39
Wilkins, Roger 2

U.S. Department of Labor
Crockett, George, Jr. 10
Herman, Alexis M. 15

U.S. Department of Social Services
Little, Robert L. 2

U.S. Department of State
Bethune, Mary McLeod 4
Bunche, Ralph J. 5
Keyes, Alan L. 11
Lafontant, Jewel Stradford 3
Perkins, Edward 5
Powell, Colin 1, 28
Rice, Condoleezza 3, 28
Wharton, Clifton Reginald, Sr. 36
Wharton, Clifton R., Jr. 7

U.S. Department of the Interior
Person, Waverly 9

U.S. Department of Transportation
Davis, Benjamin O., Jr. 2, 43

U.S. Department of Veterans Affairs
Brown, Jesse 6, 41

U.S. Diplomatic Corps
Grimké, Archibald H. 9
Haley, George Williford Boyce 21
Harris, Patricia Roberts 2

Stokes, Carl B. 10

U.S. District Court judge
Diggs-Taylor, Anna 20
Keith, Damon J. 16
Parsons, James 14

USFL
See United States Football League

U.S. Foreign Service
Davis, Ruth 37
Dougherty, Mary Pearl 47

U.S. Geological Survey
Person, Waverly 9

U.S. House of Representatives
Archie-Hudson, Marguerite 44
Ballance, Frank W. 41
Bishop, Sanford D., Jr. 24
Brown, Corrine 24
Burke, Yvonne Braithwaite 42
Carson, Julia 23
Chisholm, Shirley 2
Clay, William Lacy 8
Clayton, Eva M. 20
Clyburn, James 21
Collins, Barbara-Rose 7
Collins, Cardiss 10
Conyers, John, Jr. 4, 45
Crockett, George, Jr. 10
Cummings, Elijah E. 24
Davis, Artur 41
Dellums, Ronald 2
Diggs, Charles C. 21
Dixon, Julian C. 24
Dymally, Mervyn 42
Espy, Mike 6
Fauntroy, Walter E. 11
Fields, Cleo 13
Flake, Floyd H. 18
Ford, Harold Eugene 42
Ford, Harold E., Jr., 16
Franks, Gary 2
Gray, William H. III 3
Hastings, Alcee L. 16
Hilliard, Earl F. 24
Jackson, Jesse, Jr. 14, 45
Jackson Lee, Sheila 20
Jefferson, William J. 25
Jordan, Barbara 4
Kilpatrick, Carolyn Cheeks 16
Lee, Barbara 25
Leland, Mickey 2
Lewis, John 2, 46
Majette, Denise 41
Meek, Carrie 6
Meek, Kendrick 41
Meeks, Gregory 25
Metcalfe, Ralph 26
Mfume, Kweisi 6, 41
Millender-McDonald, Juanita 21
Mitchell, Parren J. 42
Norton, Eleanor Holmes 7
Owens, Major 6
Payne, Donald M. 2
Pinchback, P. B. S. 9
Powell, Adam Clayton, Jr. 3
Rangel, Charles 3
Rush, Bobby 26
Scott, David 41
Scott, Robert C. 23

Stokes, Louis 3
Towns, Edolphus 19
Tubbs Jones, Stephanie 24
Washington, Harold 6
Waters, Maxine 3
Watson, Diane 41
Watt, Melvin 26
Watts, J.C. 14, 38
Wheat, Alan 14
Wynn, Albert R. 25
Young, Andrew 3, 48

U.S. Information Agency
Allen, Samuel 38

U.S. Joint Chiefs of Staff
Howard, Michelle 28
Powell, Colin 1, 28
Rice, Condoleezza 3, 28

U.S. Marines
Bolden, Charles F., Jr. 7
Brown, Jesse 6, 41
Petersen, Franke E. 31
Von Lipsey, Roderick K. 11

U.S. Navy
Black, Barry C. 47
Brashear, Carl 29
Brown, Jesse Leroy 31
Doby, Lawrence Eugene Sr. 16, 41
Fields, Evelyn J. 27
Gravely, Samuel L., Jr. 5
Howard, Michelle 28
Miller, Dorie 29
Pinckney, Bill 42
Reason, J. Paul 19
Wright, Lewin 43

U.S. Olympic Committee (USOC)
DeFrantz, Anita 37

U.S. Open golf tournament
Shippen, John 43
Woods, Tiger 14, 31

U.S. Open tennis tournament
Williams, Venus 17, 34

U.S. Peace Corps
Days, Drew S., III 10
Johnson, Rafer 33
Lewis, Delano 7

U.S. Register of the Treasury
Bruce, Blanche Kelso 33

U.S. Senate
Black, Barry C. 47
Braun, Carol Moseley 4, 42
Brooke, Edward 8
Bruce, Blanche Kelso 33
Dodson, Howard, Jr. 7
Johnson, Eddie Bernice 8
Pinchback, P. B. S. 9

U.S. Supreme Court
Marshall, Thurgood 1, 44
Thomas, Clarence 2, 39

U.S. Surgeon General
Elders, Joycelyn 6

U.S. Virgin Islands government
Hastie, William H. 8

U.S.S. Constitution
Wright, Lewin 43

UVC
See Ultraviolent Camera/Spectrograph

UWUSA
See United Workers Union of South Africa

Vancouver Canucks hockey team
Brashear, Donald 39

Vancouver Grizzlies basketball team
Abdur-Rahim, Shareef 28

Vaudeville
Anderson, Eddie "Rochester" 30
Austin, Lovie 40
Bates, Peg Leg 14
Cox, Ida 42
Davis, Sammy Jr. 18
Johnson, Jack 8
Martin, Sara 38
McDaniel, Hattie 5
Mills, Florence 22
Robinson, Bill "Bojangles" 11
Waters, Ethel 7

Verizon Communication
Gordon, Bruce S. 41

Veterinary science
Jawara, Sir Dawda Kairaba 11
Maathai, Wangari 43
Patterson, Frederick Douglass 12
Thomas, Vivien 9

Video direction
Barclay, Paris 37
Fuqua, Antoine 35
Pinkett Smith, Jada 10, 41

Vibe
Jones, Quincy 8, 30
Smith, Danyel 40

Vibraphone
Hampton, Lionel 17, 41

Village Voice
Cooper, Andrew W. 36
Crouch, Stanley 11

Violin
Murray, Tai 47
Smith, Stuff 37

VIP Memphis magazine
McMillan, Rosalynn A. 36

Virginia state government
Marsh, Henry 32
Wilder, L. Douglas 3, 48

Virgin Records
Brooks, Hadda 40
Carey, Mariah 32
Sledge, Percy 39

Virginia State Supreme Court
Hassell, Leroy Rountree, Sr. 41

Virginia Tech University
Vick, Michael 39

Virology
Fuller, A. Oveta 43

Volleyball
Blanton, Dain 29

Voodoo
Dunham, Katherine 4
Guy, Rosa 5
Hurston, Zora Neale 3
Pierre, Andre 17

Voting rights
Clark, Septima 7
Cary, Mary Ann Shadd 30
Forman, James 7
Guinier, Lani 7, 30
Hamer, Fannie Lou 6
Harper, Frances Ellen Watkins 11
Hill, Jessie, Jr. 13
Johnson, Eddie Bernice 8
Lampkin, Daisy 19
Mandela, Nelson 1, 14
Moore, Harry T. 29
Moses, Robert Parris 11
Terrell, Mary Church 9
Trotter, Monroe 9
Tubman, Harriet 9
Wells-Barnett, Ida B. 8
Williams, Fannie Barrier 27
Williams, Hosea Lorenzo 15, 31
Woodard, Alfre 9

Vulcan Realty and Investment Company
Gaston, Arthur G. 4

WAAC
See Women's Auxiliary Army Corp

WAC
See Women's Army Corp

Wall Street
Lewis, William M., Jr. 40

Wall Street Project
Jackson, Jesse 1, 27

Walter Payton Inc.
Payton, Walter 11, 25

War Resister's League (WRL)
Carter, Mandy 11

Washington Capitols basketball team
Lloyd, Earl 26

Washington Capitols hockey team
Grier, Mike 43

Washington Color Field group
Thomas, Alma 14

Washington, D.C., city government
Barry, Marion S. 7, 44
Cooper Cafritz, Peggy 43
Dixon, Sharon Pratt 1
Fauntroy, Walter E. 11
Hobson, Julius W. 44
Jarvis, Charlene Drew 21
Norton, Eleanor Holmes 7
Washington, Walter 45

Williams, Anthony 21

Washington, D.C., Commission on the Arts and Humanities
Neal, Larry 38

Washington Mystics basketball team
McCray, Nikki 18

Washington Post
Britt, Donna 28
Davis, George 36
Ifill, Gwen 28
Maynard, Robert C. 7
McCall, Nathan 8
Nelson, Jill 6
Raspberry, William 2
Wilkins, Roger 2
Green, Darrell 39
Monk, Art 38
Sanders, Deion 4, 31

Washington State Higher Education Coordinating Board
Floyd, Elson S. 41

Washington Week in Review
TV Series
Ifill, Gwen 28

Washington Wizards basketball team
Bickerstaff, Bernie 21
Heard, Gar 25
Howard, Juwan 15
Lucas, John 7
Unseld, Wes 23
Webber, Chris 15, 30

Watts Repetory Theater Company
Cortez, Jayne 43

WBA
See World Boxing Association

WBC
See World Boxing Council

WCC
See World Council of Churches

Weather
Brown, Vivian 27
Christian, Spencer 15
McEwen, Mark 5

Welfare reform
Bryant, Wayne R. 6
Carson, Julia 23
Williams, Walter E. 4

Wellspring Gospel
Winans, CeCe 14, 43

West Indian folklore
Walcott, Derek 5

West Indian folk songs
Belafonte, Harry 4

West Indian literature
Coombs, Orde M. 44
Guy, Rosa 5
Kincaid, Jamaica 4
Markham, E.A. 37

Marshall, Paule 7
McKay, Claude 6
Walcott, Derek 5

West Point
Davis, Benjamin O., Jr. 2, 43
Flipper, Henry O. 3

West Side Preparatory School
Collins, Marva 3

Western Michigan University
Floyd, Elson S. 41

White House Conference on Civil Rights
Randolph, A. Philip 3

Whitney Museum of American Art
Golden, Thelma 10
Simpson, Lorna 4, 36

WHO
See Women Helping Offenders

"Why Are You on This Planet?"
Yoba, Malik 11

William Morris Talent Agency
Amos, Wally 9

WillieWear Ltd.
Smith, Willi 8

Wilmington 10
Chavis, Benjamin 6

Wimbledon
Williams, Venus 17, 34

Winery production
Rideau, Iris 46

WOMAD
See World of Music, Arts, and Dance

Women Helping Offenders (WHO)
Holland, Endesha Ida Mae 3

Women's Auxiliary Army Corps
See Women's Army Corp

Women's Army Corps (WAC)
Adams Earley, Charity 13, 34
Cadoria, Sherian Grace 14

Women's issues
Allen, Ethel D. 13
Angelou, Maya 1, 15
Ba, Mariama 30
Baker, Ella 5
Berry, Mary Frances 7
Brown, Elaine 8
Campbell, Bebe Moore 6, 24
Cannon, Katie 10
Cary, Mary Ann Shadd 30
Charles, Mary Eugenia 10
Chinn, May Edward 26
Christian, Barbara T. 44
Christian-Green, Donna M. 17
Clark, Septima 7
Cole, Johnnetta B. 5, 43
Cooper, Anna Julia 20

Cunningham, Evelyn 23
Dash, Julie 4
Davis, Angela 5
Edelman, Marian Wright 5, 42
Elders, Joycelyn 6
Fauset, Jessie 7
Giddings, Paula 11
Goldberg, Whoopi 4, 33
Gomez, Jewelle 30
Grimké, Archibald H. 9
Guy-Sheftall, Beverly 13
Hale, Clara 16
Hale, Lorraine 8
Hamer, Fannie Lou 6
Harper, Frances Ellen Watkins 11
Harris, Alice 7
Harris, Leslie 6
Harris, Patricia Roberts 2
Height, Dorothy I. 2, 23
Hernandez, Aileen Clarke 13
Hill, Anita 5
Hine, Darlene Clark 24
Holland, Endesha Ida Mae 3
hooks, bell 5
Jackson, Alexine Clement 22
Joe, Yolanda 21
Jordan, Barbara 4
Jordan, June 7, 35
Lampkin, Daisy 19
Larsen, Nella 10
Lorde, Audre 6
Maathai, Wangari 43
Marshall, Paule 7
Mbaye, Mariétou 31
McCabe, Jewell Jackson 10
McKenzie, Vashti M. 29
McMillan, Terry 4, 17
Meek, Carrie 6
Millender-McDonald, Juanita 21
Mongella, Gertrude 11
Morrison, Toni 2, 15
Mossell, Gertrude Bustill 40
Naylor, Gloria 10, 42
Nelson, Jill 6
Nichols, Nichelle 11
Norman, Pat 10
Norton, Eleanor Holmes 7
Painter, Nell Irvin 24
Parker, Pat 19
Rawlings, Nana Konadu Agyeman 13
Ringgold, Faith 4
Shange, Ntozake 8
Simpson, Carole 6, 30
Smith, Jane E. 24
Terrell, Mary Church 9
Tubman, Harriet 9
Vanzant, Iyanla 17, 47
Walker, Alice 1, 43
Walker, Maggie Lena 17
Wallace, Michele Faith 13
Waters, Maxine 3
Wattleton, Faye 9
Williams, Fannie Barrier 27
Winfrey, Oprah 2, 15

Women's Leadership Forum
Shabazz, Ilyasah 36

Women's National Basketball Association (WNBA)
Burks, Mary Fair 40
Bolton-Holifield, Ruthie 28

Catchings, Tamika 43
Cooper, Cynthia 17
Edwards, Teresa 14
Ford, Cheryl 45
Griffith, Yolanda 25
Holdsclaw, Chamique 24
Jones, Merlakia 34
Lennox, Betty 31
Leslie, Lisa 16
McCray, Nikki 18
Milton, DeLisha 31
Peck, Carolyn 23
Perrot, Kim 23
Swoopes, Sheryl 12
Thompson, Tina 25
Williams, Natalie 31

Women's Political Council
Burks, Mary Fair 40

Women's Strike for Peace
King, Coretta Scott 3

Worker's Party (Brazil)
da Silva, Benedita 5

Women's United Soccer Association (WUSA)
Scurry, Briana 27

Workplace equity
Hill, Anita 5
Clark, Septima 7
Nelson, Jill 6
Simpson, Carole 6, 30

Works Progress (Projects) Administration (WPA)
Alexander, Margaret Walker 22
Baker, Ella 5
Blackburn, Robert 28
DeCarava, Roy 42
Douglas, Aaron 7
Dunham, Katherine 4
Lawrence, Jacob 4, 28
Lee-Smith, Hughie 5, 22
Murray, Pauli 38
Sallee, Charles 38
Sebree, Charles 40
Winkfield, Jimmy 42
Wright, Richard 5

World African Hebrew Israelite Community
Ben-Israel, Ben Ami 11

World beat
Belafonte, Harry 4
Fela 1, 42
N'Dour, Youssou 1
Ongala, Remmy 9

World Bank
Soglo, Nicéphore 15

World Boxing Association (WBA)
Ellis, Jimmy 44
Hearns, Thomas 29
Hopkins, Bernard 35
Lewis, Lennox 27
Tyson, Mike 28, 44
Whitaker, Pernell 10

World Boxing Council (WBC)
Mosley, Shane 32
Tyson, Mike 28, 44
Whitaker, Pernell 10

World Council of Churches (WCC)
Kobia, Rev. Dr. Samuel 43
Mays, Benjamin E. 7
Tutu, Desmond Mpilo 6, 44

World Cup
Milla, Roger 2
Pelé 7
Scurry, Briana 27

World hunger
Belafonte, Harry 4
Iman 4, 33
Jones, Quincy 8, 30
Leland, Mickey 2
Masire, Quett 5
Obasanjo, Olusegun 5

World of Music, Arts, and Dance (WOMAD)
Ongala, Remmy 9

World Wide Technology
Steward, David L. 36

World Wrestling Federation (WWF)
Johnson, Dwayne "The Rock" 29

WPA
See Works Progress Administration

Wrestling
Johnson, Dwayne "The Rock" 29

WRL
See War Resister's League

WSB Radio
Pressley, Condace L. 41

WWF
See World Wrestling Federation

Xerox Corp.
Rand, A. Barry 6

Yab Yum Entertainment
Edmonds, Tracey 16

Yale Child Study Center
Comer, James P. 6

Yale Repertory Theater
Dutton, Charles S. 4, 22
Richards, Lloyd 2
Wilson, August 7, 33

Yale School of Drama
Dutton, Charles S. 4, 22
Richards, Lloyd 2

Yale University
Blassingame, John Wesley 40
Carby, Hazel 27
Davis, Charles T. 48
Hill, Errol 40
Neal, Larry 38

Ybor City Boys and Girls Club
Brooks, Derrick 43

YMCA
See Young Men's Christian Associations

Yoruban folklore
Soyinka, Wole 4
Vanzant, Iyanla 17, 47

Young adult literature
Bolden, Tonya 32
Ekwensi, Cyprian 37

Young Men's Christian Association (YMCA)
Butts, Calvin O., III 9
Goode, Mal 13
Hope, John 8
Mays, Benjamin E. 7

Young Negroes' Cooperative League
Baker, Ella 5

Young Women's Christian Association (YWCA)
Baker, Ella 5
Baker, Gwendolyn Calvert 9
Clark, Septima 7
Hedgeman, Anna Arnold 22
Height, Dorothy I. 2, 23
Jackson, Alexine Clement 22
Jenkins, Ella 15
Sampson, Edith S. 4
Stewart, Ella 39

Youth Pride Inc.
Barry, Marion S. 7, 44

Youth Services Administration
Little, Robert L. 2

YWCA
See Young Women's Christian Association

ZANLA
See Zimbabwe African National Liberation Army

ZAPU
See Zimbabwe African People's Union

Zimbabwe African National Liberation Army (ZANLA)
Mugabe, Robert Gabriel 10

Zimbabwe African People's Union (ZAPU)
Mugabe, Robert Gabriel 10
Nkomo, Joshua 4

Zimbabwe Congress of Trade Unions (ZCTU)
Tsvangirai, Morgan 26
Young, Roger Arliner 29

Zouk music
Lefel, Edith 41

ZTA
See Zululand Territorial Authority

Zululand Territorial Authority (ZTA)
Buthelezi, Mangosuthu Gatsha 9

Cumulative Name Index

Aaliyah 1979-2001 **30**
Aaron, Hank 1934— **5**
Aaron, Henry Louis *See Aaron, Hank*
Abacha, Sani 1943— **11**
Abbott, Diane (Julie) 1953— **9**
Abbott, Robert Sengstacke 1868-1940 **27**
Abdul-Jabbar, Kareem 1947— **8**
Abdulmajid, Iman Mohamed *See Iman*
Abdur-Rahim, Shareef 1976— **28**
Abernathy, Ralph David 1926-1990 **1**
Abrahams, Peter 1919— **39**
Abu-Jamal, Mumia 1954— **15**
Ace, Johnny 1929-1954 **36**
Achebe, (Albert) Chinua(lumogu) 1930— **6**
Adams Earley, Charity (Edna) 1918— **13, 34**
Adams, Eula L. 1950— **39**
Adams, Floyd, Jr. 1945— **12**
Adams, H. Leslie *See Adams, Leslie*
Adams, Johnny 1932-1998 **39**
Adams, Leslie 1932— **39**
Adams, Oleta 19(?)(?)— **18**
Adams, Osceola Macarthy 1890-1983 **31**
Adams, Sheila J. 1943— **25**
Adams, Yolanda 1961— **17**
Adams-Ender, Clara 1939— **40**
Adderley, Julian "Cannonball" 1928-1975 **30**
Adderley, Nat 1931-2000 **29**
Adderley, Nathaniel *See Adderley, Nat*
Ade, Sunny King 1946— **41**
Adeniyi, Sunday *See Ade, Sunny King*
Adjaye, David 1966— **38**
Adkins, Rod 1958— **41**
Adkins, Rutherford H. 1924-1998 **21**
Adu, Helen Folasade *See Sade*
Agyeman Rawlings, Nana Konadu 1948— **13**
Agyeman, Jaramogi Abebe 1911— **10**
Aidoo, Ama Ata 1942— **38**
Aiken, Loretta Mary *See Mabley, Jackie "Moms"*
Ailey, Alvin 1931-1989 **8**
Ake, Claude 1939-1996 **30**
Akomfrah, John 1957— **37**
Al-Amin, Jamil Abdullah 1943— **6**
Albright, Gerald 1947— **23**
Alcindor, Ferdinand Lewis *See Abdul-Jabbar, Kareem*
Alert, Kool DJ Red 19(?)(?)— **33**
Alexander, Archie Alphonso 1888-1958 **14**
Alexander, Clifford 1933— **26**
Alexander, John Marshall *See Ace, Johnny*
Alexander, Joyce London 1949— **18**
Alexander, Khandi 1957— **43**
Alexander, Margaret Walker 1915-1998 **22**
Alexander, Sadie Tanner Mossell 1898-1989 **22**
Ali Mahdi Mohamed 1940— **5**
Ali, Laila 1978— **27**
Ali, Muhammad 1942— **2, 16**
Allen, Byron 1961— **3, 24**
Allen, Debbie 1950— **13, 42**
Allen, Ethel D. 1929-1981 **13**
Allen, Marcus 1960— **20**
Allen, Richard 1760-1831 **14**
Allen, Robert L. 1942— **38**
Allen, Samuel W. 1917— **38**
Allen, Tina 1955— **22**
Alston, Charles Henry 1907-1997 **33**
Amadi, Elechi 1934— **40**
Ames, Wilmer 1950-1993 **27**
Amin, Idi 1925-2003 **42**
Amos, John 1941— **8**
Amos, Valerie 1954— **41**
Amos, Wally 1937— **9**
Anderson, Carl 1945-2004 **48**
Anderson, Charles Edward 1919-1994 **37**
Anderson, Eddie "Rochester" 1905-1977 **30**
Anderson, Elmer 1941— **25**
Anderson, Jamal 1972— **22**
Anderson, Marian 1902— **2, 33**
Anderson, Michael P. 1959-2003 **40**
Anderson, Norman B. 1955— **45**
Andre 3000 *See Benjamin, Andre*
Andrews, Benny 1930— **22**
Andrews, Bert 1929-1993 **13**
Andrews, Mark *See Sisqo*
Andrews, Raymond 1934-1991 **4**
Angelou, Maya 1928— **1, 15**
Anna Marie *See Lincoln, Abbey*
Annan, Kofi Atta 1938— **15, 48**
Ansa, Tina McElroy 1949— **14**
Anthony, Carmelo 1984— **46**
Anthony, Michael 1930(?)— **29**
Anthony, Wendell 1950— **25**
Archer, Dennis (Wayne) 1942— **7, 36**
Archer, Michael D'Angelo *See D'Angelo*
Archer, Osceola *See Adams, Osceola Macarthy*
Archie-Hudson, Marguerite 1937— **44**
Arinze, Francis Cardinal 1932— **19**
Aristide, Jean-Bertrand 1953— **6, 45**
Arkadie, Kevin 1957— **17**
Armatrading, Joan 1950— **32**
Armstrong, (Daniel) Louis 1900-1971 **2**
Armstrong, Robb 1962— **15**
Armstrong, Vanessa Bell 1953— **24**
Arnold, Monica *See Monica*
Arnwine, Barbara 1951(?)— **28**
Arrington, Richard 1934— **24**
Arroyo, Martina 1936— **30**
Arthur, Owen 1949— **33**
Asante, Molefi Kete 1942— **3**
Ashanti 1980— **37**
Ashe, Arthur Robert, Jr. 1943-1993 **1, 18**
Ashford, Emmett 1914-1980 **22**
Ashford, Nickolas 1942— **21**
Ashley, Maurice 1966— **15, 47**
Ashley-Ward, Amelia 1957— **23**
Atkins, Cholly 1930-2003 **40**
Atkins, David *See Sinbad*
Atkins, Erica 1972(?)— *See Mary Mary*
Atkins, Jeffrey *See Ja Rule*
Atkins, Russell 1926— **45**
Atkins, Tina 1975(?)— *See Mary Mary*
Aubert, Alvin 1930— **41**
Auguste, (Marie Carmele) Rose-Anne 1963— **13**
Auguste, Arnold A. 1946— **47**
Auguste, Donna 1958— **29**
Austin, Junius C. 1887-1968 **44**
Austin, Lovie 1887-1972 **40**
Austin, Patti 1948— **24**
Avant, Clarence 19(?)(?)— **19**
Awoonor, Kofi 1935— **37**
Awoonor-Williams, George *See Awoonor, Kofi*
Ayers, Roy 1940— **16**
Azikiwe, Nnamdi 1904-1996 **13**
Ba, Mariama 1929-1981 **30**
Babangida, Ibrahim (Badamasi) 1941— **4**
Babatunde, Obba 19(?)(?)— **35**
Babyface *See Edmonds, Kenneth "Babyface"*
Bacon-Bercey, June 1942— **38**
Badu, Erykah 1971(?)— **22**
Bailey, Buster 1902-1967 **38**
Bailey, Clyde 1946— **45**
Bailey, DeFord 1899-1982 **33**
Bailey, Pearl Mae 1918-1990 **14**
Bailey, Radcliffe 1968— **19**
Bailey, William C. *See Bailey, Buster*
Bailey, Xenobia 1955(?)— **11**
Baines, Harold 1959— **32**
Baiocchi, Regina Harris 1956— **41**
Baisden, Michael 1963— **25**
Baker, Anita 1957— **21, 48**
Baker, Augusta 1911-1998 **38**
Baker, Constance *See Motley, Constance Baker*
Baker, Dusty 1949— **8, 43**
Baker, Ella 1903-1986 **5**
Baker, George *See Divine, Father*
Baker, Gwendolyn Calvert 1931— **9**
Baker, Houston A(lfred), Jr. 1943— **6**
Baker, Johnnie B., Jr. *See Baker, Dusty*
Baker, Josephine 1906-1975 **3**
Baker, LaVern 1929-1997 **26**
Baker, Maxine 1952— **28**
Baker, Thurbert 1952— **22**
Balance, Frank W. 1942— **41**
Baldwin, James 1924-1987 **1**
Ballard, Allen B(utler), Jr. 1930— **40**
Ballard, Hank 1927-2003 **41**
Bambaataa, Afrika 1958— **34**
Bambara, Toni Cade 1939— **10**
Banda, (Ngwazi) Hastings Kamuzu 1898(?)— **6**
Bandele, Asha 1970(?)— **36**
Banks, A. Doris *See Henries, A. Doris Banks*
Banks, Ernie 1931— **33**
Banks, Jeffrey 1953— **17**
Banks, Tyra 1973— **11**

Banks, William (Venoid) 1903-1985 **11**
Baraka, Amiri 1934— **1, 38**
Barber, Ronde 1975— **41**
Barboza, Anthony 1944— **10**
Barclay, Paris 1957— **37**
Barden, Don H. 1943— **9, 20**
Barker, Danny 1909-1994 **32**
Barkley, Charles (Wade) 1963— **5**
Barnes, Ernie 1938— **16**
Barnes, Roosevelt "Booba" 1936-1996 **33**
Barnett, Amy Du Bois 1969— **46**
Barnett, Marguerite 1942-1992 **46**
Barney, Lem 1945— **26**
Barnhill, David 1914-1983 **30**
Barrax, Gerald William 1933- **45**
Barrett, Andrew C. 1942(?)— **12**
Barrett, Jacqueline 1950— **28**
Barrett, Lindsay 1941— **43**
Barrow, Joseph Louis See Louis, Joe
Barry, Marion S(hepilov, Jr.) 1936— **7, 44**
Barthe, Richmond 1901-1989 **15**
Basie, William James See Count Basie
Basquiat, Jean-Michel 1960-1988 **5**
Bass, Charlotta Amanda Spears 1874-1969 **40**
Bassett, Angela 1959(?)— **6, 23**
Bassey, Shirley 1937— **25**
Bates, Clayton See Bates, Peg Leg
Bates, Daisy (Lee Gatson) 1914(?)— **13**
Bates, Karen Grigsby 19(?)(?)— **40**
Bates, Peg Leg 1907— **14**
Bath, Patricia E. 1942— **37**
Baugh, David 1947— **23**
Baylor, Don(ald Edward) 1949— **6**
Baylor, Helen 1953— **36**
Beach, Michael 1963— **26**
Beal, Bernard B. 1954(?)— **46**
Beals, Jennifer 1963— **12**
Beals, Melba Patillo 1941— **15**
Beamon, Bob 1946— **30**
Bearden, Romare (Howard) 1912-1988 **2**
Beasley, Jamar 1979— **29**
Beasley, Myrlie See Evers, Myrlie
Beasley, Phoebe 1943— **34**
Beaton, Norman Lugard 1934-1994 **14**
Beatty, Talley 1923(?)-1995 **35**
Beauvais, Garcelle 1966— **29**
Bebey, Francis 1929-2001 **45**
Bechet, Sidney 1897-1959 **18**
Beck, Robert See Iceberg Slim
Beckford, Tyson 1970— **11**
Beckham, Barry 1944— **41**
Bedie, Henri Konan 1934— **21**
Beenie Man 1973— **32**
Belafonte, Harold George, Jr. See Belafonte, Harry
Belafonte, Harry 1927— **4**
Bell, Derrick (Albert, Jr.) 1930— **6**
Bell, James "Cool Papa" 1901-1991 **36**
Bell, James Madison 1826-1902 **40**
Bell, Michael 1955— **40**
Bell, Ralph S. 1934— **5**
Bell, Robert Mack 1943— **22**
Bellamy, Bill 1967— **12**

Belle, Albert (Jojuan) 1966— **10**
Belle, Regina 1963— **1**
Belton, Sharon Sayles 1951— **9, 16**
Benét, Eric 1970— **28**
Ben-Israel, Ben Ami 1940(?)— **11**
Benjamin, Andre 1975— **45**
Benjamin, Andre (3000) 1975(?)— See OutKast
Benjamin, Regina 1956— **20**
Bennett, George Harold "Hal" 1930— **45**
Bennett, Lerone, Jr. 1928— **5**
Benson, Angela 19(?)(?)— **34**
Berry, Bertice 1960— **8**
Berry, Charles Edward Anderson See Berry, Chuck
Berry, Chuck 1926— **29**
Berry, Fred "Rerun" 1951-2003 **48**
Berry, Halle 1967(?)— **4, 19**
Berry, James 1925— **41**
Berry, Mary Frances 1938— **7**
Berry, Theodore M. 1905-2000 **31**
Betha, Mason Durrell 1977(?)— **24**
Bethune, Mary (Jane) McLeod 1875-1955 **4**
Beti, Mongo 1932-2001 **36**
Betsch, MaVynee 1935— **28**
Beverly, Frankie 1946— **25**
Beze, Dante Terrell See Mos Def
Bickerstaff, Bernard Tyrone 1944— **21**
Big Boi See Patton, Antwan
Biggers, John 1924-2001 **20, 33**
Biko, Stephen See Biko, Steven (Bantu)
Biko, Steven (Bantu) 1946-1977 **4**
Bing, Dave 1943— **3**
Bishop, Eric See Foxx, Jamie
Bishop, Maurice 1944-1983 **39**
Bishop, Sanford D. Jr. 1947— **24**
Biya, Paul 1933-**28**
Biyidi-Awala, Alexandre See Beti, Mongo
Bizimungu, Pasteur 1951— **19**
Black, Barry C. 1948— **47**
Black, Keith Lanier 1955— **18**
Blackburn, Robert 1920— **28**
Blackwell, Unita 1933— **17**
Blackwood, Maureen 1960— **37**
Blair, Maxine See Powell, Maxine
Blair, Paul 1944— **36**
Blake, Asha 1961(?)— **26**
Blake, Eubie 1883-1983 **29**
Blake, James 1979— **43**
Blake, James Hubert See Blake, Eubie
Blakey, Art(hur) 1919-1990 **37**
Blanchard, Terence 1962— **43**
Bland, Bobby "Blue" 1930— **36**
Bland, Eleanor Taylor 1944— **39**
Bland, Robert Calvin See Bland, Bobby "Blue"
Blanks, Billy 1955(?)— **22**
Blanton, Dain 1971— **29**
Blassingame, John Wesley 1940-2000 **40**
Blige, Mary J(ane) 1971— **20, 34**
Blockson, Charles L. 1933— **42**
Blondy, Alpha 1953— **30**
Blow, Kurtis 1959— **31**
Bluford, Guion Stewart, Jr. See Bluford, Guy

Bluford, Guy 1942— **2, 35**
Bluitt, Juliann Stephanie 1938— **14**
Boateng, Ozwald 1968— **35**
Bogle, Donald 19(?)(?)— **34**
Bol, Manute 1963— **1**
Bolden, Buddy 1877-1931 **39**
Bolden, Charles F(rank), Jr. 1946— **7**
Bolden, Charles Joseph See Bolden, Buddy
Bolden, Frank E. 1913-2003 **44**
Bolden, Tonya 1959— **32**
Bolin, Jane 1908— **22**
Bolton, Terrell D. 1959(?)— **25**
Bolton-Holifield, Ruthie 1967— **28**
Bonaly, Surya 1973— **7**
Bond, (Horace) Julian 1940— **2, 35**
Bonds, Barry (Lamar) 1964— **6, 34**
Bonds, Bobby 1946— **43**
Bonds, Margaret 1913-1972 **39**
Bonga, Kuenda 1942— **13**
Bongo, (El Hadj) Omar 1935— **1**
Bongo, Albert-Bernard See Bongo, (El Hadj) Omar
Bontemps, Arna(ud Wendell) 1902-1973 **8**
Booker, Simeon 1918— **23**
Borders, James (Buchanan, IV) 1949— **9**
Bosley, Freeman (Robertson), Jr. 1954— **7**
Boston, Kelvin E. 1955(?)— **25**
Boston, Lloyd 1970(?)— **24**
Bowe, Riddick (Lamont) 1967— **6**
Bowser, Yvette Lee 1965(?)— **17**
Boyd, Gerald M. 1950— **32**
Boyd, John W., Jr. 1965— **20**
Boyd, T(heophilus) B(artholomew), III 1947— **6**
Boye, Madior 1940— **30**
Boykin, Keith 1965— **14**
Bradley, David Henry, Jr. 1950— **39**
Bradley, Ed(ward R.) 1941— **2**
Bradley, Jennette B. 1952— **40**
Bradley, Thomas 1917— **2, 20**
Brady, Wayne 1972— **32**
Branch, William Blackwell 1927— **39**
Brand, Dionne 1953— **32**
Brand, Elton 1979— **31**
Brandon, Barbara 1960(?)— **3**
Brandon, Thomas Terrell 1970— **16**
Brandy 1979— **14, 34**
Brashear, Carl Maxie 1931— **29**
Brashear, Donald 1972— **39**
Brathwaite, Fred 1972— **35**
Brathwaite, Kamau 1930— **36**
Brathwaite, Lawson Edward See Kamau Brathwaite
Braugher, Andre 1962(?)— **13**
Braun, Carol (Elizabeth) Moseley 1947— **4, 42**
Brawley, Benjamin 1882-1939 **44**
Braxton, Toni 1968(?)— **15**
Brazile, Donna 1959— **25**
Breedlove, Sarah See Walker, Madame C. J.
Breeze, Jean "Binta" 1956— **37**
Bridges, Christopher See Ludacris
Bridges, Sheila 1964— **36**
Bridges, Todd 1965— **37**
Bridgewater, Dee Dee 1950— **32**
Bridgforth, Glinda 1952— **36**
Brimmer, Andrew F. 1926— **2, 48**

Briscoe, Connie 1952— **15**
Briscoe, Marlin 1946(?)— **37**
Britt, Donna 1954(?)— **28**
Broadbent, Hydeia 1984— **36**
Brock, Louis Clark 1939— **18**
Bronner, Nathaniel H., Sr. 1914-1993 **32**
Brooke, Edward (William, III) 1919— **8**
Brooks, Aaron 1976— **33**
Brooks, Avery 1949— **9**
Brooks, Derrick 1973— **43**
Brooks, Gwendolyn 1917-2000 **1, 28**
Brooks, Hadda 1916-2002 **40**
Brown Bomber, The See Louis, Joe
Brown, Andre See Dr. Dre
Brown, Cecil M. 1943— **46**
Brown, Charles 1922-1999 **23**
Brown, Claude 1937-2002 **38**
Brown, Cora 1914-1972 **33**
Brown, Corrine 1946— **24**
Brown, Donald 1963— **19**
Brown, Eddie C. 1940— **35**
Brown, Elaine 1943— **8**
Brown, Erroll M. 1950(?)— **23**
Brown, Foxy 1979— **25**
Brown, H. Rap See Al-Amin, Jamil Abdullah
Brown, Homer S. 1896-1977 **47**
Brown, Hubert Gerold See Al-Amin, Jamil Abdullah
Brown, James 1933— **15**
Brown, James 1951— **22**
Brown, James Nathaniel See Brown, Jim
Brown, James Willie, Jr. See Komunyakaa, Yusef
Brown, Janice Rogers 1949— **43**
Brown, Jesse 1944-2003 **6, 41**
Brown, Jesse Leroy 1926-1950 **31**
Brown, Jim 1936— **11**
Brown, Joe 19(?)(?)— **29**
Brown, Joyce F. 1946— **25**
Brown, Lee P(atrick) 1937— **1, 24**
Brown, Les(lie Calvin) 1945— **5**
Brown, Lloyd Louis 1913-2003 **42**
Brown, Ron(ald Harmon) 1941— **5**
Brown, Sterling (Allen) 1901— **10**
Brown, Tony 1933— **3**
Brown, Uzee 1950— **42**
Brown, Vivian 1964— **27**
Brown, Wesley 1945— **23**
Brown, Willa Beatrice 1906-1992 **40**
Brown, Willard 1911(?)-1996 **36**
Brown, William Anthony See Brown, Tony
Brown, Willie L., Jr. 1934— **7**
Brown, Zora Kramer 1949— **12**
Bruce, Blanche Kelso 1849-1898 **33**
Bruce, Isaac 1972— **26**
Brunson, Dorothy 1938— **1**
Brutus, Dennis 1924— **38**
Bryan, Ashley F. 1923— **41**
Bryant, John 1966— **26**
Bryant, John R. 1943— **45**
Bryant, Kobe 1978— **15, 31**
Bryant, Wayne R(ichard) 1947— **6**
Buchanan, Ray 1971— **32**
Buckley, Gail Lumet 1937— **39**

Buckley, Victoria (Vikki) 1947-1999 **24**
Bullard, Eugene Jacques 1894-1961 **12**
Bullins, Ed 1935— **25**
Bullock, Anna Mae *See Turner, Tina*
Bullock, Steve 1936— **22**
Bully-Cummings, Ella 1957(?)— **48**
Bumbry, Grace (Ann) 1937— **5**
Bunche, Ralph J(ohnson) 1904-1971 **5**
Bunkley, Anita Richmond 19(?)(?)— **39**
Burgess, John 1909-2003 **46**
Burke, Selma Hortense 1900-1995 **16**
Burke, Solomon 1936— **31**
Burke, Yvonne Braithwaite 1932— **42**
Burks, Mary Fair 1920-1991 **40**
Burley, Mary Lou *See Williams, Mary Lou*
Burnett, Charles 1944— **16**
Burnett, Chester Arthur *See Howlin' Wolf*
Burnett, Dorothy 1905-1995 **19**
Burnim, Mickey L. 1949— **48**
Burns, Eddie 1928— **44**
Burrell, Orville Richard *See Shaggy*
Burrell, Stanley Kirk *See Hammer, M. C.*
Burrell, Thomas J. 1939— **21**
Burris, Chuck 1951— **21**
Burris, Roland W. 1937— **25**
Burroughs, Margaret Taylor 1917— **9**
Burrows, Stephen 1943— **31**
Burrus, William Henry "Bill" 1936— **45**
Burton, LeVar(dis Robert Martyn) 1957— **8**
Busby, Jheryl 1949(?)— **3**
Buthelezi, Mangosuthu Gatsha 1928— **9**
Butler, Jerry 1939— **26**
Butler, Jonathan 1961— **28**
Butler, Leroy, III 1968— **17**
Butler, Octavia (Estelle) 1947— **8**, **43**
Butler, Paul D. 1961— **17**
Butts, Calvin O(tis), III 1950— **9**
Bynoe, Peter C.B. 1951— **40**
Bynum, Juanita 1959— **31**
Byrd, Donald 1949— **10**
Byrd, Michelle 1965— **19**
Byrd, Robert (Oliver Daniel, III) 1952— **11**
Byron, JoAnne Deborah *See Shakur, Assata*
Cade, Toni *See Bambara, Toni Cade*
Cadoria, Sherian Grace 1940— **14**
Caesar, Shirley 1938— **19**
Cain, Herman 1945— **15**
Caldwell, Benjamin 1937— **46**
Calhoun, Cora *See Austin, Lovie*
Callender, Clive O(rville) 1936— **3**
Calloway, Cabell, III 1907-1994 **14**
Cameron, Earl 1917— **44**
Camp, Georgia Blanche Douglas *See Johnson, Georgia Douglas*
Camp, Kimberly 1956— **19**
Campanella, Roy 1921-1993 **25**

Campbell, Bebe Moore 1950— **6**, **24**
Campbell, Bill 1954— **9**
Campbell, Charleszetta Lena *See Waddles, Charleszetta (Mother)*
Campbell, E(lmer) Simms 1906-1971 **13**
Campbell, Mary Schmidt 1947— **43**
Campbell, Milton *Little Milton*
Campbell, Naomi 1970— **1**, **31**
Campbell, Tisha *See Campbell-Martin, Tisha*
Campbell-Martin, Tisha 1969— **8**, **42**
Canada, Geoffrey 1954— **23**
Canady, Alexa 1950— **28**
Canegata, Leonard Lionel Cornelius *See Lee, Canada*
Cannon, Katie 1950— **10**
Cannon, Nick 1980— **47**
Carby, Hazel 1948— **27**
Cardozo, Francis L. 1837-1903 **33**
Carew, Rod 1945— **20**
Carey, Mariah 1970— **32**
Cargill, Victoria A. 19(?)(?)— **43**
Carmichael, Stokely 1941-1998 **5**, **26**
Carnegie, Herbert 1919— **25**
Carroll, Diahann 1935— **9**
Carroll, L. Natalie 1950— **44**
Carroll, Vinnette 1922— **29**
Carruthers, George R. 1939— **40**
Carson, Benjamin 1951— **1**, **35**
Carson, Josephine *See Baker, Josephine*
Carson, Julia 1938— **23**
Carson, Lisa Nicole 1969— **21**
Carter, Anson 1974— **24**
Carter, Ben *See Ben-Israel, Ben Ami*
Carter, Benny 1907-2003 **46**
Carter, Betty 1930— **19**
Carter, Butch 1958— **27**
Carter, Cris 1965— **21**
Carter, Joe 1960— **30**
Carter, Joye Maureen 1957— **41**
Carter, Mandy 1946— **11**
Carter, Nell 1948-2003 **39**
Carter, Regina 1966(?)— **23**
Carter, Rubin 1937— **26**
Carter, Shawn *See Jay-Z*
Carter, Stephen L(isle) 1954— **4**
Carter, Vince 1977— **26**
Carter, Warrick L. 1942— **27**
Cartey, Wilfred 1931-1992 **47**
Cartiér, Xam Wilson 1949— **41**
Carver, George Washington 1861(?)-1943 **4**
Cary, Lorene 1956— **3**
Cary, Mary Ann Shadd 1823-1893 **30**
Cash, Rosalind 1938-1995 **28**
CasSelle, Malcolm 1970— **11**
Catchings, Tamika 1979— **43**
Catlett, Elizabeth 1919— **2**
Cayton, Horace 1903-1970 **26**
Cedric the Entertainer 1964(?)— **29**
Césaire, Aimé 1913— **48**
Chamberlain, Wilt 1936-1999 **18**, **47**
Chambers, James *See Cliff, Jimmy*
Chambers, Julius (LeVonne) 1936— **3**

Channer, Colin 1963— **36**
Chapman, Nathan A. Jr. 1957— **21**
Chapman, Tracy 1964— **26**
Chappell, Emma C. 1941— **18**
Charlemagne, Emmanuel *See Charlemagne, Manno*
Charlemagne, Manno 1948— **11**
Charles, Mary Eugenia 1919— **10**
Charles, Ray 1930-2004 **16**, **48**
Charleston, Oscar 1896-1954 **39**
Chase-Riboud, Barbara 1939— **20**, **46**
Chatard, Peter 1936— **44**
Chavis, Benjamin (Franklin, Jr.) 1948— **6**
Cheadle, Don 1964— **19**
Cheatham, Doc 1905-1997 **17**
Checker, Chubby 1941— **28**
Cheeks, Maurice 1956— **47**
Chenault, John 1952— **40**
Chenault, Kenneth I. 1952— **4**, **36**
Cheney-Coker, Syl 1945— **43**
Cherry, Deron 1959— **40**
Chesimard, JoAnne (Deborah) *See Shakur, Assata*
Chesnutt, Charles 1858-1932 **29**
Chestnut, Morris 1969— **31**
Chideya, Farai 1969— **14**
Childress, Alice 1920-1994 **15**
Chinn, May Edward 1896-1980 **26**
Chisholm, Samuel J. 1942— **32**
Chisholm, Shirley (Anita St. Hill) 1924— **2**
Chissano, Joaquim (Alberto) 1939— **7**
Christian, Barbara T. 1946-2000 **44**
Christian, Spencer 1947— **15**
Christian-Green, Donna M. 1945— **17**
Christie, Angella **36**
Christie, Linford 1960— **8**
Christophe, Henri 1767-1820 **9**
Chuck D 1960— **9**
Claiborne, Loretta 1953— **34**
Clark, Celeste (Clesteen) Abraham 1953— **15**
Clark, Joe 1939— **1**
Clark, John Pepper *See Clark-Bekedermo, J. P.*
Clark, Kenneth B(ancroft) 1914— **5**
Clark, Kristin *See Taylor, Kristin Clark*
Clark, Patrick 1955— **14**
Clark, Septima (Poinsette) 1898-1987 **7**
Clark-Bekedermo, J. P. 1935— **44**
Clarke, Austin C. 1934— **32**
Clarke, Cheryl 1947— **32**
Clarke, George Elliott 1960— **32**
Clarke, Hope 1943(?)— **14**
Clarke, John Henrik 1915-1998 **20**
Clarke, Kenny 1914-1985 **27**
Clarke, Patrice Francise *See Washington, Patrice Clarke*
Clark-Sheard, Karen 19(?)(?)— **22**
Clash, Kevin 1961(?)— **14**
Clay, Cassius Marcellus, Jr. *See Ali, Muhammad*
Clay, William Lacy 1931— **8**
Clayton, Constance 1937— **1**
Clayton, Eva M. 1934— **20**
Clayton, Xernona 1930— **3**, **45**
Claytor, Helen 1907— **14**

Cleage, Albert Buford *See Agyeman, Jaramogi Abebe*
Cleage, Pearl Michelle 1934— **17**
Cleaver, (Leroy) Eldridge 1935— **5**, **45**
Cleaver, Emanuel (II) 1944— **4**
Cleaver, Kathleen Neal 1945— **29**
Clements, George (Harold) 1932— **2**
Clemmons, Reginal G. 19(?)(?)— **41**
Clemons, Clarence 1942— **41**
Clendenon, Donn 1935— **26**
Cleveland, James 1932(?)-1991 **19**
Cliff, Jimmy 1948— **28**
Cliff, Michelle 1946— **42**
Clifton, Lucille 1936— **14**
Clifton, Nathaniel "Sweetwater" 1922(?)-1990 **47**
Clinton, George (Edward) 1941— **9**
Clyburn, James 1940— **21**
Coachman, Alice 1923— **18**
Cobb, Jewel Plummer 1924— **42**
Cobb, Monty *See Cobb, W. Montague*
Cobb, W. Montague 1904-1990 **39**
Cobbs, Price M(ashaw) 1928— **9**
Cochran, Johnnie (L., Jr.) 1937— **11**, **39**
Cohen, Anthony 1963— **15**
Colbert, Virgis William 1939— **17**
Cole, Johnnetta B(etsch) 1936— **5**, **43**
Cole, Lorraine 195(?)— **48**
Cole, Nat King 1919-1965 **17**
Cole, Natalie Maria 1950— **17**
Cole, Rebecca 1846-1922 **38**
Coleman, Bessie 1892-1926 **9**
Coleman, Donald A. 1952— **24**
Coleman, Gary 1968— **35**
Coleman, Leonard S., Jr. 1949— **12**
Coleman, Mary 1946— **46**
Coleman, Michael B. 1955(?)— **28**
Coleman, Ornette 1930— **39**
Coleman, Wanda 1946— **48**
Colemon, Johnnie 1921(?)— **11**
Collins, Albert 1932-1993 **12**
Collins, Barbara-Rose 1939— **7**
Collins, Bootsy 1951— **31**
Collins, Cardiss 1931— **10**
Collins, Janet 1917— **33**
Collins, Marva 1936— **3**
Collins, William *See Collins, Bootsy*
Colter, Cyrus J. 1910-2002 **36**
Coltrane, John William 1926-1967 **19**
Combs, Sean "Puffy" 1969— **17**, **43**
Comer, James P(ierpont) 1934— **6**
Common 1972— **31**
Cone, James H. 1938— **3**
Coney, PonJola 1951— **48**
Connerly, Ward 1939— **14**
Conté, Lansana 1944(?)— **7**
Conyers, John, Jr. 1929— **4**, **45**
Conyers, Nathan G. 1932— **24**
Cook, (Will) Mercer 1903-1987 **40**
Cook, Charles "Doc" 1891-1958 **44**
Cook, Sam 1931-1964 **17**
Cook, Samuel DuBois 1928— **14**
Cook, Suzan D. Johnson 1957— **22**
Cook, Toni 1944— **23**

Cook, Victor Trent 19(?)(?)— See Three Mo' Tenors
Cook, Wesley See Abu-Jamal, Mumia
Cook, Will Marion 1869-1944 **40**
Cooke, Charles L. See Cook, Charles "Doc"
Cooke, Marvel 1901(?)-2000 **31**
Cooks, Patricia 1944-1989 **19**
Cool Papa Bell See Bell, James "Cool Papa"
Coombs, Orde M. 1939-1984 **44**
Cooper Cafritz, Peggy 1947— **43**
Cooper, Andrew W. 1928-2002 **36**
Cooper, Anna Julia 1858-1964 **20**
Cooper, Barry 1956— **33**
Cooper, Charles "Chuck" 1926-1984 **47**
Cooper, Cynthia 1963— **17**
Cooper, Edward S(awyer) 1926— **6**
Cooper, Evern 19(?)(?)— **40**
Cooper, J. California 19(?)(?)— **12**
Cooper, Margaret J. 194(?)— **46**
Cooper, Michael 1956— **31**
Copeland, Michael 1954— **47**
Corbi, Lana 1955— **42**
Cornelius, Don 1936— **4**
Cortez, Jayne 1936— **43**
Corthron, Kia 1961— **43**
Cortor, Eldzier 1916— **42**
Cosby, Bill 1937— **7, 26**
Cosby, Camille Olivia Hanks 1944— **14**
Cosby, William Henry, Jr. See Cosby, Bill
Cose, Ellis 1951— **5**
Cotter, Joseph Seamon, Sr. 1861-1949 **40**
Cottrell, Comer 1931— **11**
Count Basie 1904-1984 **23**
Couto, Mia 1955— **45**
Cowans, Adger W. 1936— **20**
Cox, Deborah 1974(?)— **28**
Cox, Ida 1896-1967 **42**
Craig, Carl 1969— **31**
Craig-Jones, Ellen Walker 1906-2000 **44**
Crawford, Randy 1952— **19**
Crawford, Veronica See Crawford, Randy
Cray, Robert 1953— **30**
Creagh, Milton 1957— **27**
Crew, Rudolph F. 1950(?)— **16**
Crite, Alan Rohan 1910— **29**
Crocker, Frankie 1937-2000 **29**
Crockett, George (William), Jr. 1909— **10**
Cross, Dolores E. 1938— **23**
Crothers, Benjamin Sherman See Crothers, Scatman
Crothers, Scatman 1910-1986 **19**
Crouch, Andraé 1942— **27**
Crouch, Stanley 1945— **11**
Crowder, Henry 1895-1954(?) **16**
Cullen, Countee 1903-1946 **8**
Culpepper, Daunte 1977— **32**
Cummings, Elijah E. 1951— **24**
Cuney, William Waring 1906-1976 **44**
Cunningham, Evelyn 1916— **23**
Cunningham, Randall 1963— **23**
Curling, Alvin 1939— **34**
Currie, Betty 1939(?)— **21**
Curry, George E. 1947— **23**

Curry, Mark 1964— **17**
Curtis, Christopher Paul 1954(?)— **26**
Curtis-Hall, Vondie 1956— **17**
D'Angelo 1974— **27**
Déby, Idriss 1952— **30**
da Silva, Benedita 1942— **5**
Dabydeen, David 1956— **48**
Dadié, Bernard 1916— **34**
Daly, Marie Maynard 1921— **37**
Damas, Léon-Gontran 1912-1978 **46**
Dandridge, Dorothy 1922-1965 **3**
Dandridge, Ray 1913-1994 **36**
Dandridge, Raymond Garfield 1882-1930 **45**
Daniels, Gertrude See Haynes, Trudy
Daniels, Lee Louis 1959— **36**
Daniels-Carter, Valerie 19(?)(?)— **23**
Danticat, Edwidge 1969— **15**
Darden, Calvin 1950— **38**
Darden, Christopher 1957— **13**
Dash, Damon 19(?)(?)— **31**
Dash, Darien 1972(?)— **29**
Dash, Julie 1952— **4**
Dash, Leon 1944— **47**
Davenport, Arthur See Fattah, Chaka
David, Craig 1981— **31**
David, Keith 1954— **27**
Davidson, Jaye 1967(?)— **5**
Davidson, Tommy— **21**
Davis, Allison 1902-1983 **12**
Davis, Angela (Yvonne) 1944— **5**
Davis, Anthony 1951— **11**
Davis, Anthony Moses See Beenie Man
Davis, Arthur P. 1904-1996 **41**
Davis, Artur 1967— **41**
Davis, Benjamin O(liver), Jr. 1912-2002 **2, 43**
Davis, Benjamin O(liver), Sr. 1877-1970 **4**
Davis, Charles T. 1918-1981 **48**
Davis, Chuck 1937— **33**
Davis, Danny K. 1941— **24**
Davis, Ed 1911-1999 **24**
Davis, Ernie 1939-1963 **48**
Davis, Frank Marshall 1905-1987 **47**
Davis, Gary 1896-1972 **41**
Davis, George 1939— **36**
Davis, Guy 1952— **36**
Davis, Lorenzo "Piper" 1917-1997 **19**
Davis, Mike 1960— **41**
Davis, Miles (Dewey, III) 1926-1991 **4**
Davis, Nolan 1942— **45**
Davis, Ossie 1917— **5**
Davis, Ruth 1943— **37**
Davis, Sammy, Jr. 1925-1990 **18**
Davis, Terrell 1972— **20**
Davis, Viola 1965— **34**
Dawes, Dominique (Margaux) 1976— **11**
Dawkins, Wayne 1955— **20**
Dawson, Matel "Mat," Jr. 1921-2002 **39**
Dawson, William Levi 1899-1900 **39**
Day, Leon 1916-1995 **39**

Days, Drew S(aunders, III) 1941— **10**
de Carvalho, Barcelo See Bonga, Kuenda
de Passe, Suzanne 1948(?)— **25**
De Veaux, Alexis 1948— **44**
"Deadwood Dick" See Love, Nat
Dean, Mark E. 1957— **35**
DeBaptiste, George 1814(?)-1875 **32**
DeCarava, Roy 1919— **42**
Dee, Ruby 1924— **8**
DeFrantz, Anita 1952— **37**
Delaney, Beauford 1901-1979 **19**
Delaney, Joseph 1904-1991 **30**
Delany, Annie Elizabeth 1891-1995 **12**
Delany, Martin R. 1812-1885 **27**
Delany, Samuel R(ay), Jr. 1942— **9**
Delany, Sarah (Sadie) 1889— **12**
Delco, Wilhemina R. 1929— **33**
Delice, Ronald 1966— **48**
Delice, Rony 1966— **48**
DeLille, Henriette 1813-1862 **30**
Dellums, Ronald (Vernie) 1935— **2**
DeLoach, Nora 1940-2001 **30**
Delsarte, Louis 1944— **34**
Dennard, Brazeal 1929— **37**
DePriest, James 1936— **37**
Devers, (Yolanda) Gail 1966— **7**
Devine, Loretta 1953— **24**
Devine, Major J. See Divine, Father
DeWese, Mohandas See Kool Moe Dee
Diallo, Amadou 1976-1999 **27**
Dickens, Helen Octavia 1909— **14**
Dickenson, Vic 1906-1984 **38**
Dickerson, Eric 1960— **27**
Dickerson, Ernest 1952(?)— **6, 17**
Dickey, Eric Jerome 19(?)(?)— **21**
Diddley, Bo 1928— **39**
Diesel, Vin 1967(?)— **29**
Diggs, Charles C. 1922-1998 **21**
Diggs, Taye 1972— **25**
Diggs-Taylor, Anna 1932— **20**
Dillard, Godfrey J. 1948— **45**
Dinkins, David (Norman) 1927— **4**
Diop, Cheikh Anta 1923-1986 **4**
Diouf, Abdou 1935— **3**
Divine, Father 1877(?)-1965 **7**
Dixon, Julian C. 1934— **24**
Dixon, Margaret 192(?)— **14**
Dixon, Rodrick 19(?)(?)— See Three Mo' Tenors
Dixon, Sharon Pratt 1944— **1**
Dixon, Willie (James) 1915-1992 **4**
DJ Jazzy Jeff 1965— **32**
DJ Red Alert See Alert, Kool DJ Red
DMC 1964— **31**
DMX 1970— **28**
do Nascimento, Edson Arantes See Pelé
Dobbs, Mattiwilda 1925— **34**
Doby, Larry See Doby, Lawrence Eugene, Sr.
Doby, Lawrence Eugene, Sr. 1924-2003 **16, 41**
Dodson, Howard, Jr. 1939— **7**
Dodson, Owen 1914-1983 **38**
Doig, Jason 1977— **45**
Doley, Harold, Jr. 1947— **26**

Domini, Rey See Lorde, Audre (Geraldine)
Donald, Arnold Wayne 1954— **36**
Donaldson, Jeff 1932-2004 **46**
Donegan, Dorothy 1922-1998 **19**
Donovan, Kevin See Bambaataa, Afrika
Dorsey, Thomas Andrew 1899-1993 **15**
Dortch, Thomas W., Jr. 1950— **45**
dos Santos, José Eduardo 1942— **43**
Dougherty, Mary Pearl 1915-2003 **47**
Douglas, Aaron 1899-1979 **7**
Douglas, Ashanti See Ashanti
Douglas, Lizzie See Memphis Minnie
Dourdan, Gary 1966— **37**
Dove, Rita (Frances) 1952— **6**
Dove, Ulysses 1947— **5**
Downing, Will 19(?)(?)— **19**
Dozier, Lamont See Holland-Dozier-Holland
Dr. Dre **10**
Dr. J See Erving, Julius
Draper, Sharon Mills 1952— **16, 43**
Dre, Dr. 1965(?)— **14, 30**
Drew, Charles Richard 1904-1950 **7**
Drexler, Clyde 1962— **4**
Driskell, David C(lyde) 1931— **7**
Driver, David E. 1955— **11**
Drummond, William J. 1944— **40**
Du Bois, David Graham 1925— **45**
Du Bois, W(illiam) E(dward) B(urghardt) 1868-1963 **3**
DuBois, Shirley Graham 1907-1977 **21**
Ducksworth, Marilyn 1957— **12**
Due, Tananarive 1966— **30**
Duke, Bill 1943— **3**
Duke, George 1946— **21**
Dumars, Joe 1963— **16**
Dumas, Henry 1934-1968 **41**
Dunbar, Alice See Dunbar-Nelson, Alice Ruth Moore
Dunbar, Paul Laurence 1872-1906 **8**
Dunbar, Sly 1952— See Sly & Robbie
Dunbar-Nelson, Alice Ruth Moore 1875-1935 **44**
Duncan, Michael Clarke 1957— **26**
Duncan, Tim 1976— **20**
Dungy, Tony 1955— **17, 42**
Dunham, Katherine (Mary) 1910(?)— **4**
Dunn, Jerry 1953— **27**
Dunner, Leslie B. 1956— **45**
Dunnigan, Alice Allison 1906-1983 **41**
Dunston, Georgia Mae 1944— **48**
Dupri, Jermaine 1972— **13, 46**
Dutton, Charles S. 1951— **4, 22**
Dutton, Marie Elizabeth 1940— **12**
Dymally, Mervyn 1926— **42**
Dyson, Michael Eric 1958— **11, 40**
Early, Deloreese Patricia See Reese, Della
Early, Gerald (Lyn) 1952— **15**
Eckstein, William Clarence See Eckstine, Billy
Eckstine, Billy 1914-1993 **28**
Edelin, Ramona Hoage 1945— **19**

Edelman, Marian Wright 1939— **5, 42**
Edley, Christopher 1928-2003 **2, 48**
Edley, Christopher F., Jr. 1953— **48**
Edmonds, Kenneth "Babyface" 1958(?)— **10, 31**
Edmonds, Terry 1950(?)— **17**
Edmonds, Tracey 1967(?)— **16**
Edmunds, Gladys 1951(?)— **48**
Edwards, Eli *See* McKay, Claude
Edwards, Esther Gordy 1920(?)— **43**
Edwards, Harry 1942— **2**
Edwards, Melvin 1937— **22**
Edwards, Teresa 1964— **14**
Ekwensi, Cyprian 1921— **37**
El Wilson, Barbara 1959— **35**
Elder, (Robert) Lee 1934— **6**
Elder, Larry 1952— **25**
Elder, Lonne III 1931-1996 **38**
Elders, Joycelyn (Minnie) 1933— **6**
Eldridge, Roy 1911-1989 **37**
El-Hajj Malik El-Shabazz *See* X, Malcolm
Elise, Kimberly 1967— **32**
Ellerbe, Brian 1963— **22**
Ellington, Duke 1899-1974 **5**
Ellington, E. David 1960— **11**
Ellington, Edward Kennedy *See* Ellington, Duke
Ellington, Mercedes 1939— **34**
Elliott, Lorris 1931-1999 **37**
Elliott, Missy "Misdemeanor" 1971— **31**
Elliott, Sean 1968— **26**
Ellis, Clarence A. 1943— **38**
Ellis, Jimmy 1940— **44**
Ellison, Ralph (Waldo) 1914-1994 **7**
Elmore, Ronn 1957— **21**
El-Shabazz, El-Hajj Malik *See* X, Malcolm
Emanuel, James A. 1921— **46**
Emeagwali, Dale 1954— **31**
Emeagwali, Philip 1954— **30**
Emecheta, Buchi 1944— **30**
Emmanuel, Alphonsia 1956— **38**
Ephriam, Mablean 1949(?)— **29**
Epps, Archie C., III 1937-2003 **45**
Epps, Omar 1973— **23**
Ericsson-Jackson, Aprille 19(?)(?)— **28**
Erving, Julius 1950— **18, 47**
Esposito, Giancarlo (Giusseppi Alessandro) 1958— **9**
Espy, Alphonso Michael *See* Espy, Mike
Espy, Mike 1953— **6**
Estes, Rufus 1857-19(?)(?) **29**
Estes, Simon 1938— **28**
Estes, Sleepy John 1899-1977 **33**
Eubanks, Kevin 1957— **15**
Europe, (William) James Reese 1880-1919 **10**
Evans, Darryl 1961— **22**
Evans, Ernest *See* Checker, Chubby
Evans, Faith 1973(?)— **22**
Evans, Harry 1956(?)— **25**
Evans, Mari 1923— **26**
Eve 1979— **29**
Everett, Francine 1917-1999 **23**
Everett, Ronald McKinley *See* Karenga, Maulana
Evers, Medgar (Riley) 1925-1963 **3**

Evers, Myrlie 1933— **8**
Evora, Cesaria 1941— **12**
Ewing, Patrick Aloysius 1962— **17**
Eyadéma, (Étienne) Gnassingbé 1937— **7**
Fabio, Sarah Webster 1928-1979 **48**
Fagan, Garth 1940— **18**
Fair, Ronald L. 1932— **47**
Faison, George William 1946— **16**
Falana, Lola 1942— **42**
Fanon, Frantz 1925-1961 **44**
Farah, Nuruddin 1945— **27**
Farmer, Art(hur Stewart) 1928-1999 **38**
Farmer, Forest J(ackson) 1941— **1**
Farmer, James 1920— **2**
Farmer-Paellmann, Deadria 1966— **43**
Farr, Mel 1944— **24**
Farrakhan, Louis 1933— **2, 15**
Fats Domino 1928— **20**
Fattah, Chaka 1956— **11**
Faulk, Marshall 1973— **35**
Fauntroy, Walter E(dward) 1933— **11**
Fauset, Jessie (Redmon) 1882-1961 **7**
Favors, Steve 1948— **23**
Fax, Elton 1909-1993 **48**
Feelings, Muriel 1938— **44**
Feelings, Tom 1933-2003 **11, 47**
Fela 1938-1997 **1, 42**
Felix, Allyson 1985— **48**
Ferguson, Roger W. 1951— **25**
Ferrell, Rachelle 1961— **29**
Ferrer, Ibrahim 1927— **41**
Fetchit, Stepin 1892-1985 **32**
Fielder, Cecil (Grant) 1963— **2**
Fields, C. Virginia 1946— **25**
Fields, Cleo 1962— **13**
Fields, Evelyn J. 1949— **27**
Fields, Julia 1938— **45**
Fields, Kim 1969— **36**
50 Cent 1976— **46**
Figueroa, John J. 1920-1999 **40**
Files, Lolita 1964(?)— **35**
Fishburne, Larry 1962— **4, 22**
Fishburne, Laurence, III *See* Fishburne, Larry
Fisher, Antwone Quenton 1959— **40**
Fisher, Rudolph John Chauncey 1897-1934 **17**
Fitzgerald, Ella 1918-1996 **8, 18**
Flack, Roberta 1940— **19**
Flake, Floyd H. 1945— **18**
Flash, Grandmaster *See* Grandmaster Flash
Fleming, Raymond 1945— **48**
Fletcher, Alphonse, Jr. 1965— **16**
Fletcher, Bill, Jr. 1954— **41**
Flipper, Henry O(ssian) 1856-1940 **3**
Flood, Curt(is) 1963— **10**
Flowers, Vonetta 1973— **35**
Floyd, Elson S. 1956— **41**
Folks, Byron *See* Allen, Byron
Forbes, Audrey Manley 1934— **16**
Forbes, Calvin 1945- **46**
Ford, Cheryl 1981— **45**
Ford, Clyde W. 1951— **40**
Ford, Harold Eugene 1945— **42**
Ford, Harold Eugene, Jr. 1970— **16**

Ford, Jack 1947— **39**
Ford, Nick Aaron 1904--1982 **44**
Foreman, George 1948— **1, 15**
Forman, James 1928— **7**
Forrest, Leon 1937--1997 **44**
Forrest, Vernon 1971— **40**
Fortune, T(imothy) Thomas 1856-1928 **6**
Foster, Cecil (A.) 1954— **32**
Foster, Ezola 1938— **28**
Foster, George "Pops" 1892-1969 **40**
Foster, Henry W., Jr. 1933— **26**
Foster, Jylla Moore 1954— **45**
Foster, Marie 1917-2003 **48**
Fowles, Gloria Gaynor, Gloria
Fox, Rick 1969— **27**
Fox, Ulrich Alexander *See* Fox, Rick
Fox, Vivica A. 1964— **15**
Foxx, Jamie 1967— **15, 48**
Foxx, Redd 1922-1991 **2**
Franklin, Aretha 1942— **11, 44**
Franklin, Carl 1949— **11**
Franklin, Hardy R. 1929— **9**
Franklin, J.E. 1937— **44**
Franklin, John Hope 1915— **5**
Franklin, Kirk 1970— **15**
Franklin, Robert M(ichael) 1954— **13**
Franklin, Shirley 1945— **34**
Franks, Gary 1954(?)— **2**
Frazier, Edward Franklin 1894-1962 **10**
Frazier, Joe 1944— **19**
Frazier-Lyde, Jacqui 1961— **31**
Fredericks, Henry Saint Claire *See* Mahal, Taj
Freelon, Nnenna 1954— **32**
Freeman, Al(bert Cornelius), Jr. 1934— **11**
Freeman, Cathy 1973— **29**
Freeman, Charles Eldridge 1933— **19**
Freeman, Harold P. 1933— **23**
Freeman, Leonard 1950— **27**
Freeman, Marianna 1957— **23**
Freeman, Morgan 1937— **2, 20**
Freeman, Paul 1936— **39**
Freeman, Yvette **27**
French, Albert 1943— **18**
Fresh Prince, The *See* Smith, Will
Friday, Jeff 1964(?)— **24**
Fudge, Ann (Marie) 1951(?)— **11**
Fuhr, Grant 1962— **1**
Fulani, Lenora (Branch) 1950— **11**
Fuller, A. Oveta 1955— **43**
Fuller, Arthur 1972— **27**
Fuller, Charles (Henry) 1939— **8**
Fuller, Howard L. 1941— **37**
Fuller, Hoyt 1923-1981 **44**
Fuller, Meta Vaux Warrick 1877-1968 **27**
Fuller, S. B. 1895-1988 **13**
Fuller, Solomon Carter, Jr. 1872-1953 **15**
Fuller, Vivian 1954— **33**
Funderburg, I. Owen 1924-2002 **38**
Fuqua, Antoine 1966— **35**
Futch, Eddie 1911-2001 **33**
Gaines, Brenda 19(?)(?)— **41**
Gaines, Ernest J(ames) 1933— **7**
Gaines, Grady 1934— **38**

Gaither, Jake 1903-1994 **14**
Gantt, Harvey (Bernard) 1943— **1**
Gardner, Edward G. 1925— **45**
Garnett, Kevin 1976— **14**
Garrison, Zina 1963— **2**
Garvey, Marcus 1887-1940 **1**
Gary, Willie Edward 1947— **12**
Gaston, Arthur G(eorge) 1892— **4**
Gates, Henry Louis, Jr. 1950— **3, 38**
Gates, Sylvester James, Jr. 1950— **15**
Gay, Marvin Pentz, Jr. *See* Gaye, Marvin
Gaye, Marvin 1939-1984 **2**
Gayle, Addison, Jr. 1932-1991 **41**
Gayle, Helene D. 1955— **3, 46**
Gaynor, Gloria 1947— **36**
Gbagbo, Laurent 1945— **43**
Gentry, Alvin 1954— **23**
George, Nelson 1957— **12**
George, Zelma Watson 1903-1994 **42**
Gerima, Haile 1946— **38**
Gibson, Althea 1927-2003 **8, 43**
Gibson, Bob 1935— **33**
Gibson, Donald Bernard 1933— **40**
Gibson, Johnnie Mae 1949— **23**
Gibson, Josh 1911-1947 **22**
Gibson, Kenneth Allen 1932— **6**
Gibson, Tyrese *See* Tyrese
Gibson, William F(rank) 1933— **6**
Giddings, Paula (Jane) 1947— **11**
Gillespie, Dizzy 1917-1993 **1**
Gillespie, John Birks *See* Gillespie, Dizzy
Gilliam, Frank 1934(?)— **23**
Gilliam, Joe, Jr. 1950-2000 **31**
Gilliam, Sam 1933— **16**
Gilmore, Marshall 1931— **46**
Ginuwine 1975(?)— **35**
Giovanni, Nikki 1943— **9, 39**
Giovanni, Yolande Cornelia, Jr. *See* Giovanni, Nikki
Gist, Carole 1970(?)— **1**
Givens, Robin 1965— **4, 25**
Glover, Corey 1964— **34**
Glover, Danny 1948— **1, 24**
Glover, Nathaniel, Jr. 1943— **12**
Glover, Savion 1974— **14**
"The Goat" *See* Manigault, Earl "The Goat"
Goines, Donald 1937(?)-1974 **19**
Goldberg, Whoopi 1955— **4, 33**
Golden, Marita 1950— **19**
Golden, Thelma 1965— **10**
Goldsberry, Ronald 1942— **18**
Golson, Benny 1929— **37**
Gomes, Peter J(ohn) 1942— **15**
Gomez, Jewelle 1948— **30**
Gomez-Preston, Cheryl 1954— **9**
Goode, Mal(vin Russell) 1908-1995 **13**
Goode, W(oodrow) Wilson 1938— **4**
Gooden, Dwight 1964— **20**
Gooden, Lolita *See* Roxanne Shante
Gooding, Cuba, Jr. 1968— **16**
Goodnight, Paul 1946— **32**
Gordon, Bruce S. 1946— **41**
Gordon, Dexter 1923-1990 **25**

Gordon, Ed(ward Lansing, III) 1960— **10**
Gordon, Pamela 1955— **17**
Gordone, Charles 1925-1995 **15**
Gordy, Berry, Jr. 1929— **1**
Goreed, Joseph *See* Williams, Joe
Goss, Tom 1946— **23**
Gossett, Louis, Jr. 1936— **7**
Gotti, Irv 1971— **39**
Gourdine, Meredith 1929-1998 **33**
Gourdine, Simon (Peter) 1940— **11**
Grace, George H. 1948— **48**
Graham, Lawrence Otis 1962— **12**
Graham, Lorenz 1902-1989 **48**
Graham, Stedman 1951(?)— **13**
Grandmaster Flash 1958— **33**
Grand-Pierre, Jean-Luc 1977— **46**
Grant, Gwendolyn Goldsby 19(?)(?)— **28**
Granville, Evelyn Boyd 1924— **36**
Gravely, Samuel L(ee), Jr. 1922— **5**
Graves, Denyce Antoinette 1964— **19**
Graves, Earl G(ilbert) 1935— **1, 35**
Gray (Nelson Rollins), Ida 1867-1953 **41**
Gray, F. Gary 1969— **14**
Gray, Fred Sr. 1930— **37**
Gray, Frizzell *See* Mfume, Kweisi
Gray, Macy 1970— **29**
Gray, William H., III 1941— **3**
Gray, Willie 1947— **46**
Greaves, William 1926— **38**
Greely, M. Gasby 1946— **27**
Greely, Margaret Gasby *See* Greely, M. Gasby
Green, A. C. 1963— **32**
Green, Al 1946— **13, 47**
Green, Darrell 1960— **39**
Green, Dennis 1949— **5, 45**
Greene, Joe 1946— **10**
Greene, Maurice 1974— **27**
Greenfield, Eloise 1929— **9**
Greenlee, Sam 1930— **48**
Greenwood, Monique 1959— **38**
Gregg, Eric 1951— **16**
Gregory, Dick 1932— **1**
Gregory, Frederick D(rew) 1941— **8**
Gregory, Wilton 1947— **37**
Grier, David Alan 1955— **28**
Grier, Mike 1975— **43**
Grier, Pam(ala Suzette) 1949— **9, 31**
Grier, Roosevelt (Rosey) 1932— **13**
Griffey, George Kenneth, Jr. 1969— **12**
Griffin, Bessie Blout 1914— **43**
Griffith, Mark Winston 1963— **8**
Griffith, Yolanda 1970— **25**
Griffith-Joyner, Florence 1959-1998 **28**
Griffiths, Marcia 1948(?)— **29**
Grimké, Archibald H(enry) 1849-1930 **9**
Guarionex *See* Schomburg, Arthur Alfonso
Guillaume, Robert 1927— **3, 48**
Guinier, (Carol) Lani 1950— **7, 30**
Gumbel, Bryant Charles 1948— **14**
Gumbel, Greg 1946— **8**
Gunn, Moses 1929-1993 **10**
Guy, (George) Buddy 1936— **31**
Guy, Jasmine 1964(?)— **2**

Guy, Rosa 1925(?)— **5**
Guy-Sheftall, Beverly 1946— **13**
Guyton, Tyree 1955— **9**
Gwynn, Anthony Keith 1960— **18**
Habré, Hissène 1942— **6**
Habyarimana, Juvenal 1937-1994 **8**
Hageman, Hans 19(?)(?)— **36**
Hageman, Ivan 19(?)(?)— **36**
Haile Selassie 1892-1975 **7**
Hailey, JoJo 1971— **22**
Hailey, K-Ci 1969— **22**
Hale, Clara 1902-1992 **16**
Hale, Lorraine 1926(?)— **8**
Haley, Alex (Palmer) 1921-1992 **4**
Haley, George Williford Boyce 1925— **21**
Hall, Arthur 1943-2000 **39**
Hall, Elliott S. 1938(?)— **24**
Hall, Lloyd A(ugustus) 1894-1971 **8**
Hamblin, Ken 1940— **10**
Hamer, Fannie Lou (Townsend) 1917-1977 **6**
Hamilton, Samuel C. 19(?)(?)— **47**
Hamilton, Virginia 1936— **10**
Hammer *See* Hammer, M. C.
Hammer, M. C. 1963— **20**
Hammond, Fred 1960— **23**
Hammond, Lenn 1970(?)— **34**
Hampton, Fred 1948-1969 **18**
Hampton, Henry (Eugene, Jr.) 1940— **6**
Hampton, Lionel 1908(?)-2002 **17, 41**
Hancock, Herbie Jeffrey 1940— **20**
Handy, W(illiam) C(hristopher) 1873-1937 **8**
Hani, Chris 1942-1993 **6**
Hani, Martin Thembisile *See* Hani, Chris
Hannah, Marc (Regis) 1956— **10**
Hansberry, Lorraine (Vivian) 1930-1965 **6**
Hansberry, William Leo 1894-1965 **11**
Hardaway, Anfernee (Deon) *See* Hardaway, Anfernee (Penny)
Hardaway, Anfernee (Penny) 1971— **13**
Hardaway, Penny *See* Hardaway, Anfernee (Penny)
Hardaway, Tim 1966— **35**
Hardin Armstrong, Lil 1898-1971 **39**
Hardin, Lillian Beatrice *See* Hardin Armstrong, Lil
Hardison, Bethann 19(?)(?)— **12**
Hardison, Kadeem 1966— **22**
Hardy, Nell *See* Carter, Nell
Hare, Nathan 1934— **44**
Harkless, Necia Desiree 1920— **19**
Harmon, Clarence 1940(?)— **26**
Harper, Ben 1969— **34**
Harper, Frances E(llen) W(atkins) 1825-1911 **11**
Harper, Frank *See* Harper, Hill
Harper, Hill 1973— **32**
Harper, Michael S. 1938— **34**
Harrell, Andre (O'Neal) 1962— **9, 30**
Harrington, Oliver W(endell) 1912— **9**
Harris, "Sweet" Alice *See* Harris, Alice
Harris, Alice 1934— **7**
Harris, Barbara 1930— **12**

Harris, Claire 1937— **34**
Harris, Corey 1969— **39**
Harris, E. Lynn 1957— **12, 33**
Harris, Eddy L. 1956— **18**
Harris, James, III *See* Jimmy Jam
Harris, Jay **19**
Harris, Leslie 1961— **6**
Harris, Marcelite Jordon 1943— **16**
Harris, Mary Styles 1949— **31**
Harris, Monica 1968— **18**
Harris, Patricia Roberts 1924-1985 **2**
Harris, Robin 1953-1990 **7**
Harrison, Alvin 1974— **28**
Harrison, Calvin 1974— **28**
Harrison, Mya *See* Mya
Harsh, Vivian Gordon 1890-1960 **14**
Harvard, Beverly (Joyce Bailey) 1950— **11**
Harvey, Steve 1957— **18**
Harvey, William R. 1941— **42**
Haskins, Clem 1943— **23**
Haskins, James 1941— **36**
Hassell, Leroy Rountree, Sr. 1955— **41**
Hastie, William H(enry) 1904-1976 **8**
Hastings, Alcee Lamar 1936— **16**
Hatchett, Glenda 1951(?)— **32**
Hathaway, Donny 1945-1979 **18**
Hathaway, Isaac Scott 1874-1967 **33**
Haughton, Aaliyah *See* Aaliyah
Hawkins, "Screamin'" Jay 1929-2000 **30**
Hawkins, Adrienne Lita *See* Kennedy, Adrienne
Hawkins, Coleman 1904-1969 **9**
Hawkins, Erskine Ramsey 1914-1993 **14**
Hawkins, Jamesetta *See* James, Etta
Hawkins, La-Van 1960(?)— **17**
Hawkins, Steven Wayne 1962— **14**
Hawkins, Tramaine Aunzola 1951— **16**
Hayden, Carla D. 1952— **47**
Hayden, Palmer 1890-1973 **13**
Hayden, Robert Earl 1913-1980 **12**
Hayes, Cecil N. 1945— **46**
Hayes, Isaac 1942— **20**
Hayes, James C. 1946— **10**
Hayes, Roland 1887-1977 **4**
Hayes, Teddy 1951— **40**
Haynes, Cornell, Jr. *See* Nelly
Haynes, George Edmund 1880-1960 **8**
Haynes, Marques 1926— **22**
Haynes, Trudy 1926— **44**
Haysbert, Dennis 1955— **42**
Haywood, Gar Anthony 1954— **43**
Haywood, Margaret A. 1912— **24**
Head, Bessie 1937-1986 **28**
Healy, James Augustine 1830-1900 **30**
Heard, Gar 1948— **25**
Heard, Nathan C. 1936-2004 **45**
Hearne, John Edgar Caulwell 1926-1994 **45**
Hearns, Thomas 1958— **29**
Hedgeman, Anna Arnold 1899-1990 **22**

Hedgeman, Peyton Cole *See* Hayden, Palmer
Height, Dorothy I(rene) 1912— **2, 23**
Hemphill, Essex 1957— **10**
Hemphill, Jessie Mae 1937— **33**
Hemsley, Sherman 1938— **19**
Henderson, Cornelius Langston 1888(?)-1976 **26**
Henderson, Fletcher 1897-1952 **32**
Henderson, Gordon 1957— **5**
Henderson, Natalie Leota *See* Hinderas, Natalie
Henderson, Rickey 1958— **28**
Henderson, Stephen E. 1925-1997 **45**
Henderson, Wade 1944(?)— **14**
Hendricks, Barbara 1948— **3**
Hendrix, James Marshall *See* Hendrix, Jimi
Hendrix, Jimi 1942-1970 **10**
Hendrix, Johnny Allen *See* Hendrix, Jimi
Hendy, Francis 195(?)— **47**
Henries, A. Doris Banks 1913-1981 **44**
Henriques, Julian 1955(?)— **37**
Henry, Aaron Edd 1922-1997 **19**
Henry, Clarence "Frogman" 1937— **46**
Henry, Lenny 1958— **9**
Henson, Darrin 1970(?)— **33**
Henson, Matthew (Alexander) 1866-1955 **2**
Hercules, Frank 1911-1996 **44**
Herenton, Willie W. 1940— **24**
Herman, Alexis Margaret 1947— **15**
Hernandez, Aileen Clarke 1926— **13**
Hickman, Fred(erick Douglass) 1951— **11**
Higginbotham, A(loyisus) Leon, Jr. 1928-1998 **13, 25**
Higginbotham, Jack *See* Higginbotham, Jay C.
Higginbotham, Jay C. 1906-1973 **37**
Hightower, Dennis F(owler) 1941— **13**
Hill, Anita (Faye) 1956— **5**
Hill, Beatrice *See* Moore, Melba
Hill, Bonnie Guiton 1941— **20**
Hill, Calvin 1947— **19**
Hill, Donna 1955— **32**
Hill, Dulé 1975(?)— **29**
Hill, Errol 1921— **40**
Hill, Grant (Henry) 1972— **13**
Hill, Janet 1947— **19**
Hill, Jesse, Jr. 1927— **13**
Hill, Lauryn 1975(?)— **20**
Hill, Leslie Pinckney 1880-1960 **44**
Hill, Oliver W. 1907— **24**
Hill, Tamia *See* Tamia
Hillard, Terry 1954— **25**
Hilliard, David 1942— **7**
Hilliard, Earl F. 1942— **24**
Himes, Chester 1909-1984 **8**
Hinderas, Natalie 1927-1987 **5**
Hine, Darlene Clark 1947— **24**
Hines, Earl "Fatha" 1905-1983 **39**
Hines, Garrett 1969— **35**
Hines, Gregory (Oliver) 1946-2003 **1, 42**
Hinton, Milt 1910-2000 **30**

Hinton, William Augustus 1883-1959 **8**
Hoagland, Everett H. 1942— **45**
Hobson, Julius W. 1919-1977 **44**
Hobson, Mellody 1969— **40**
Holder, Eric H., Jr. 1951(?)— **9**
Holder, Laurence 1939— **34**
Holdsclaw, Chamique 1977— **24**
Holiday, Billie 1915-1959 **1**
Holland, Brian *See Holland-Dozier-Holland*
Holland, Eddie *See Holland-Dozier-Holland*
Holland, Endesha Ida Mae 1944— **3**
Holland, Robert, Jr. 1940— **11**
Holland-Dozier-Holland **36**
Holmes, Kelly 1970— **47**
Holmes, Larry 1949— **20**
Holt, Nora 1885(?)-1974 **38**
Holte, Patricia Louise *See LaBelle, Patti*
Holton, Hugh, Jr. 1947-2001 **39**
Holyfield, Evander 1962— **6**
Hooker, John Lee 1917-2000 **30**
hooks, bell 1952— **5**
Hooks, Benjamin L(awson) 1925— **2**
Hope, John 1868-1936 **8**
Hopgood, Hadda *See Brooks, Hadda*
Hopkins, Bernard 1965— **35**
Horn, Shirley 1934— **32**
Horne, Frank 1899-1974 **44**
Horne, Lena (Mary Calhoun) 1917— **5**
Horton, (Andreana) "Suki" 1982— **33**
Horton, Andre 1979— **33**
Hounsou, Djimon 1964— **19, 45**
Houphouët, Dia *See Houphouët-Boigny, Félix*
Houphouët-Boigny, Félix 1905— **4**
House, Eddie James, Jr. *See House, Son*
House, Eugene *See House, Son*
House, Son 1902-1988 **8**
Houston, Charles Hamilton 1895-1950 **4**
Houston, Cissy 19(?)(?)— **20**
Houston, Whitney 1963— **7, 28**
Howard, Corinne *See Mitchell, Corinne*
Howard, Desmond Kevin 1970— **16**
Howard, Juwan Antonio 1973— **15**
Howard, M. William, Jr. 1946— **26**
Howard, Michelle 1960— **28**
Howard, Sherri 1962— **36**
Howlin' Wolf 1910-1976 **9**
Howroyd, Janice Bryant 1953— **42**
Hrabowski, Freeman A., III 1950— **22**
Hubbard, Arnette 19(?)(?)— **38**
Hudlin, Reginald 1962(?)— **9**
Hudlin, Warrington, Jr. 1953(?)— **9**
Hudson, Cheryl 19(?)(?)— **15**
Hudson, Wade 1946— **15**
Huggins, Larry 1950— **21**
Hughes, (James Mercer) Langston 1902-1967 **4**
Hughes, Albert 1972— **7**
Hughes, Allen 1972— **7**
Hughes, Cathy 1947(?)— **27**

Hughley, Darryl Lynn 1964— **23**
Hull, Akasha Gloria 1944— **45**
Humphrey, Bobbi 1950— **20**
Humphries, Frederick 1935— **20**
Hunt, Richard (Howard) 1935— **6**
Hunter, Alberta 1895-1984 **42**
Hunter, Billy 1943— **22**
Hunter, Charlayne *See Hunter-Gault, Charlayne*
Hunter, Clementine 1887-1988 **45**
Hunter, George William *See Hunter, Billy*
Hunter, Torii 1975— **43**
Hunter-Gault, Charlayne 1942— **6, 31**
Hurston, Zora Neale 1891-1960 **3**
Hurtt, Harold 1947(?)— **46**
Hutchinson, Earl Ofari 1945— **24**
Hutson, Jean Blackwell 1914— **16**
Hyde, Cowan F. "Bubba" 1908-2003 **47**
Hyman, Earle 1926— **25**
Hyman, Phyllis 1949(?)-1995 **19**
Ice Cube 1969(?)— **8, 30**
Iceberg Slim 1918-1992 **11**
Ice-T 1958(?)— **6, 31**
Ifill, Gwen 1955— **28**
Iginla, Jarome 1977— **35**
Iman 1955— **4, 33**
Imes, Elmer Samuel 1883-1941 **39**
India.Arie 1975— **34**
Ingraham, Hubert A. 1947— **19**
Ingram, Rex 1895-1969 **5**
Innis, Roy (Emile Alfredo) 1934— **5**
Irvin, (Monford Merrill) Monte 1919— **31**
Irving, Clarence (Larry) 1955— **12**
Isaac, Julius 1928— **34**
Isley, Ronald 1941— **25**
Iverson, Allen 1975— **24, 46**
Ja Rule 1976— **35**
Jackson Lee, Sheila 1950— **20**
Jackson, Alexine Clement 1936— **22**
Jackson, Alphonso R. 1946— **48**
Jackson, Earl 1948— **31**
Jackson, Fred James 1950— **25**
Jackson, George 1960(?)— **19**
Jackson, George Lester 1941-1971 **14**
Jackson, Hal 1915— **41**
Jackson, Isaiah (Allen) 1945— **3**
Jackson, Janet 1966— **6, 30**
Jackson, Jesse 1941— **1, 27**
Jackson, Jesse Louis, Jr. 1965— **14, 45**
Jackson, John 1924-2002 **36**
Jackson, Mahalia 1911-1972 **5**
Jackson, Mannie 1939— **14**
Jackson, Maynard (Holbrook, Jr.) 1938-2003 **2, 41**
Jackson, Michael Joseph 1958— **19**
Jackson, Millie 1944— **25**
Jackson, Milt 1923-1999 **26**
Jackson, O'Shea *See Ice Cube*
Jackson, Randy 1956— **40**
Jackson, Reginald Martinez 1946— **15**
Jackson, Samuel L. 1948— **8, 19**
Jackson, Sheneska 1970(?)— **18**
Jackson, Shirley Ann 1946— **12**
Jackson, Vera 1912— **40**
Jacob, John E(dward) 1934— **2**

Jacobs, Marion Walter *See Little Walter*
Jacobs, Regina 1963— **38**
Jagan, Cheddi 1918-1997 **16**
Jakes, Thomas "T.D." 1957— **17, 43**
Jam, Jimmy *See Jimmy Jam*
James, Daniel "Chappie", Jr. 1920-1978 **16**
James, Etta 1938— **13**
James, Juanita (Therese) 1952— **13**
James, LeBron 1984— **46**
James, Sharpe 1936— **23**
James, Skip 1902-1969 **38**
Jamison, Judith 1943— **7**
Jammeh, Yahya 1965— **23**
Jarreau, Al 1940— **21**
Jarret, Vernon D. 1921— **42**
Jarvis, Charlene Drew 1941— **21**
Jasper, Kenji 1976(?)— **39**
Jawara, Sir Dawda Kairaba 1924— **11**
Jay, Jam Master 1965— **31**
Jay-Z 1970— **27**
Jean, Wyclef 1970— **20**
Jean-Baptiste, Marianne 1967— **17, 46**
Jeffers, Eve Jihan *See Eve*
Jefferson, William J. 1947— **25**
Jeffries, Leonard 1937— **8**
Jemison, Mae C. 1957— **1, 35**
Jemison, Major L. 1955(?)— **48**
Jenifer, Franklyn G(reen) 1939— **2**
Jenkins, Beverly 1951— **14**
Jenkins, Ella (Louise) 1924— **15**
Jenkins, Fergie 1943— **46**
Jerkins, Rodney 1978(?)— **31**
Jeter, Derek 1974— **27**
Jimmy Jam 1959— **13**
Joachim, Paulin 1931— **34**
Joe, Yolanda 19(?)(?)— **21**
John, Daymond 1969(?)— **23**
Johns, Vernon 1892-1965 **38**
Johnson, "Magic" *See Johnson, Earvin "Magic"*
Johnson, Ben 1961— **1**
Johnson, Beverly 1952— **2**
Johnson, Buddy 1915-1977 **36**
Johnson, Carol Diann *See Carroll, Diahann*
Johnson, Caryn E. *See Goldberg, Whoopi*
Johnson, Charles 1948— **1**
Johnson, Charles Arthur *See St. Jacques, Raymond*
Johnson, Charles Spurgeon 1893-1956 **12**
Johnson, Dwayne "The Rock" 1972— **29**
Johnson, Earvin "Magic" 1959— **3, 39**
Johnson, Eddie Bernice 1935— **8**
Johnson, George E. 1927— **29**
Johnson, Georgia Douglas 1880-1966 **41**
Johnson, Harvey Jr. 1947(?)— **24**
Johnson, Hazel 1927— **22**
Johnson, J. J. 1924-2001 **37**
Johnson, Jack 1878-1946 **8**
Johnson, James Louis *See Johnson, J. J.*
Johnson, James Weldon 1871-1938 **5**

Johnson, James William *See Johnson, James Weldon*
Johnson, Jeh Vincent 1931— **44**
Johnson, John Arthur *See Johnson, Jack*
Johnson, John H(arold) 1918— **3**
Johnson, Larry 1969— **28**
Johnson, Levi 1950— **48**
Johnson, Linton Kwesi 1952— **37**
Johnson, Lonnie G. 1949— **32**
Johnson, Mamie "Peanut" 1932— **40**
Johnson, Marguerite *See Angelou, Maya*
Johnson, Mat 1971(?)— **31**
Johnson, Michael (Duane) 1967— **13**
Johnson, Norma L. Holloway 1932— **17**
Johnson, R. M. 1968— **36**
Johnson, Rafer 1934— **33**
Johnson, Robert 1911-1938 **2**
Johnson, Robert L. 1946(?)— **3, 39**
Johnson, Robert T. 1948— **17**
Johnson, Rodney Van 19(?)(?)— **28**
Johnson, Sheila Crump 1949(?)— **48**
Johnson, Shoshana 1973-— **47**
Johnson, Taalib *See Musiq*
Johnson, Virginia (Alma Fairfax) 1950— **9**
Johnson, William Henry 1901-1970 **3**
Johnson, Woodrow Wilson *See Johnson, Buddy*
Johnson-Brown, Hazel W. *See, Johnson, Hazel*
Jolley, Willie 1956— **28**
Jones, Bill T. 1952— **1, 46**
Jones, Bobby 1939(?)— **20**
Jones, Carl 1955(?)— **7**
Jones, Caroline R. 1942— **29**
Jones, Cobi N'Gai 1970— **18**
Jones, Donell 1973— **29**
Jones, E. Edward, Sr. 1931— **45**
Jones, Ed "Too Tall" 1951— **46**
Jones, Edward P. 1950— **43**
Jones, Elaine R. 1944— **7, 45**
Jones, Elvin 1927— **14**
Jones, Etta 1928-2001 **35**
Jones, Gayl 1949— **37**
Jones, Ingrid Saunders 1945— **18**
Jones, James Earl 1931— **3**
Jones, Jonah 1909-2000 **39**
Jones, Kimberly Denise *See Lil' Kim*
Jones, Le Roi *See Baraka, Amiri*
Jones, Lillie Mae *See Carter, Betty*
Jones, Lois Mailou 1905— **13**
Jones, Marion 1975— **21**
Jones, Merlakia 1973— **34**
Jones, Nasir *See Nas*
Jones, Orlando 1968— **30**
Jones, Quincy (Delight) 1933— **8, 30**
Jones, Randy 1969— **35**
Jones, Robert Elliott *See Jones, Jonah*
Jones, Roy Jr. 1969— **22**
Jones, Ruth Lee *See Washington, Dinah*
Jones, Sarah 1974— **39**

Jones, Sissieretta *See Joyner, Matilda Sissieretta*
Jones, Star(let Marie) 1962(?)— **10, 27**
Jones, Thomas W. 1949— **41**
Joplin, Scott 1868-1917 **6**
Jordan, Barbara (Charline) 1936— **4**
Jordan, Eric Benét *See Benét, Eric*
Jordan, June 1936— **7, 35**
Jordan, Michael (Jeffrey) 1963— **6, 21**
Jordan, Montell 1968(?)— **23**
Jordan, Ronny 1962— **26**
Jordan, Vernon E(ulion, Jr.) 1935— **3, 35**
Josey, E. J. 1924— **10**
Joyner, Jacqueline *See Joyner-Kersee, Jackie*
Joyner, Marjorie Stewart 1896-1994 **26**
Joyner, Matilda Sissieretta 1869(?)-1933 **15**
Joyner, Tom 1949(?)— **19**
Joyner-Kersee, Jackie 1962— **5**
Julian, Percy Lavon 1899-1975 **6**
Julien, Isaac 1960— **3**
July, William II 19(?)(?)— **27**
Just, Ernest Everett 1883-1941 **3**
Justice, David Christopher 1966— **18**
Ka Dinizulu, Israel *See Ka Dinizulu, Mcwayizeni*
Ka Dinizulu, Mcwayizeni 1932-1999 **29**
Kabbah, Ahmad Tejan 1932— **23**
Kabila, Joseph 1968(?)— **30**
Kabila, Laurent 1939— **20**
Kaiser, Cecil 1916— **42**
Kamau, Johnstone *See Kenyatta, Jomo*
Kamau, Kwadwo Agymah 1960(?)— **28**
Kani, Karl 1968(?)— **10**
Karenga, Maulana 1941— **10**
Kaunda, Kenneth (David) 1924— **2**
Kay, Jackie 1961— **37**
Kay, Ulysses 1917-1995 **37**
Kayira, Legson 1942— **40**
Kearse, Amalya Lyle 1937— **12**
Kee, John P. 1962— **43**
Keith, Damon Jerome 1922— **16**
Kelly, Leontine 1920— **33**
Kelly, Patrick 1954(?)-1990 **3**
Kelly, R(obert) 1969(?)— **18, 44**
Kelly, Sharon Pratt *See Dixon, Sharon Pratt*
Kem 196(?)— **47**
Kendricks, Eddie 1939-1992 **22**
Kennard, William Earl 1957— **18**
Kennedy, Adrienne 1931— **11**
Kennedy, Florynce Rae 1916-2000 **12, 33**
Kennedy, Lelia McWilliams Robinson 1885-1931 **14**
Kennedy, Randall 1954— **40**
Kennedy-Overton, Jayne Harris 1951— **46**
Kenney, John A., Jr. 1914-2003 **48**
Kenoly, Ron 1944— **45**
Kenyatta, Jomo 1891(?)-1978 **5**
Kerekou, Ahmed (Mathieu) 1933— **1**
Kerry, Leon G. 1949(?)— **46**

Keyes, Alan L(ee) 1950— **11**
Keys, Alicia 1981— **32**
Khan, Chaka 1953— **12**
Khanga, Yelena 1962— **6**
Kidd, Mae Street 1904-1995 **39**
Kilpatrick, Carolyn Cheeks 1945— **16**
Kilpatrick, Kwame 1970— **34**
Kimbro, Dennis (Paul) 1950— **10**
Kimbro, Henry A. 1912-1999 **25**
Kincaid, Bernard 1945— **28**
Kincaid, Jamaica 1949— **4**
King, Alonzo 19(?)(?)— **38**
King, B. B. 1925— **7**
King, Barbara 19(?)(?)— **22**
King, Bernice (Albertine) 1963— **4**
King, Coretta Scott 1929— **3**
King, Dexter (Scott) 1961— **10**
King, Don 1931— **14**
King, Gayle 1956— **19**
King, Martin Luther, III 1957— **20**
King, Martin Luther, Jr. 1929-1968 **1**
King, Oona 1967— **27**
King, Preston 1936— **28**
King, Regina 1971— **22, 45**
King, Riley B. *See King, B. B.*
King, Woodie Jr. 1937— **27**
King, Yolanda (Denise) 1955— **6**
Kirby, George 1924-1995 **14**
Kirk, Ron 1954— **11**
Kitt, Eartha Mae 1928(?)— **16**
Kitt, Sandra 1947— **23**
Knight, Etheridge 1931-1991 **37**
Knight, Gladys Maria 1944— **16**
Knight, Marion, Jr. *See Knight, Suge*
Knight, Suge 1966— **11, 30**
Knowles, Beyoncé 1981— **39**
Knowling, Robert Jr. 1955(?)— **38**
Knuckles, Frankie 1955— **42**
Kobia, Rev. Dr. Samuel 1947— **43**
Kodjoe, Boris 1973— **34**
Komunyakaa, Yusef 1941— **9**
Kone, Seydou *See Blondy, Alpha*
Kool DJ Red Alert *See Alert, Kool DJ Red*
Kool Moe Dee 1963— **37**
Kotto, Yaphet (Fredrick) 1944— **7**
Kountz, Samuel L(ee) 1930-1981 **10**
Kravitz, Lenny 1964— **10, 34**
Kravitz, Leonard *See Kravitz, Lenny*
KRS-One 1965— **34**
Krute, Fred *See Alert, Kool DJ Red*
Kunjufu, Jawanza 1953— **3**
Kuti, Fela Anikulapo *See Fela*
Kuti, Femi 1962— **47**
Kyles, Cedric *See Cedric the Entertainer*
L. L. Cool J 1968— **16**
La Menthe, Ferdinand Joseph *See Morton, Jelly Roll*
La Salle, Eriq 1962— **12**
LaBelle, Patti 1944— **13, 30**
Lacy, Sam 1903-2003 **30, 46**
Ladner, Joyce A. 1943— **42**
Laferriere, Dany 1953— **33**
Lafontant, Jewel Stradford 1922— **3**
LaGuma, Alex 1925-1985 **30**
Lamming, George 1927— **35**

Lampkin, Daisy 1883(?)-1965 **19**
Lampley, Oni Faida 1959— **43**
Lane, Charles 1953— **3**
Lane, Vincent 1942— **5**
Langhart, Janet 1941— **19**
Lanier, Bob 1948— **47**
Lanier, Willie 1945— **33**
Lankford, Raymond Lewis 1967— **23**
Laraque, Georges 1976— **48**
Larkin, Barry 1964— **24**
Lars, Byron 1965— **32**
Larsen, Nella 1891-1964 **10**
Lassiter, Roy 1969— **24**
Lathan, Sanaa 1971— **27**
Latimer, Lewis H(oward) 1848-1928 **4**
Lattimore, Kenny 1970(?)— **35**
Lavizzo-Mourey, Risa 1954— **48**
Lawal, Kase L. 19??— **45**
Lawless, Theodore K(enneth) 1892-1971 **8**
Lawrence, Jacob (Armstead) 1917-2000 **4, 28**
Lawrence, Martin 1965— **6, 27**
Lawrence, Robert Henry, Jr. 1935-1967 **16**
Lawrence-Lightfoot, Sara 1944— **10**
Lawson, Jennifer (Karen) 1946— **1**
León, Tania 1943— **13**
Leary, Kathryn D. 1952— **10**
Leavell, Dorothy R. 1944— **17**
Lee, Annie Francis 1935— **22**
Lee, Barbara 1946— **25**
Lee, Canada 1907-1952 **8**
Lee, Don L(uther) *See Madhubuti, Haki R.*
Lee, Gabby *See Lincoln, Abbey*
Lee, Joe A. 1946(?)— **45**
Lee, Joie 1962(?)— **1**
Lee, Shelton Jackson *See Lee, Spike*
Lee, Spike 1957— **5, 19**
Lee, Sr., Bertram M. 1939-2003 **46**
Lee-Smith, Hughie 1915— **5, 22**
Leevy, Carrol M. 1920— **42**
Lefel, Edith 1963-2003 **41**
Leffall, LaSalle (Doheny), Jr. 1930— **3**
Leland, George Thomas *See Leland, Mickey*
Leland, Mickey 1944-1989 **2**
Lemmons, Kasi 1961— **20**
Lennox, Betty 1976— **31**
LeNoire, Rosetta 1911-2002 **37**
Leon, Kenny 1957(?)— **10**
Leonard, Sugar Ray 1956— **15**
Leslie, Lisa Deshaun 1972— **16**
Lester, Adrian 1968— **46**
Lester, Bill 1961— **42**
Lester, Julius 1939— **9**
Letson, Al 1972— **39**
Levert, Gerald 1966— **22**
Lewellyn, J(ames) Bruce 1927— **13**
Lewis, (Frederick) Carl(ton) 1961— **4**
Lewis, (Mary) Edmonia 1845(?)-1911(?) **10**
Lewis, Byron E(ugene) 1931— **13**
Lewis, David Levering 1936— **9**
Lewis, Delano (Eugene) 1938— **7**
Lewis, Denise 1972— **33**
Lewis, Edward T. 1940— **21**

Lewis, Emmanuel 1971— **36**
Lewis, Henry 1932-1996 **38**
Lewis, John 1940— **2, 46**
Lewis, Lennox 1965— **27**
Lewis, Norman 1909-1979 **39**
Lewis, Ramsey 1935— **35**
Lewis, Ray 1975— **33**
Lewis, Reginald F. 1942-1993 **6**
Lewis, Samella 1924— **25**
Lewis, Shirley Ann Redd 1937— **14**
Lewis, Terry 1956— **13**
Lewis, Thomas 1939— **19**
Lewis, William M., Jr. 1956— **40**
Lewis-Thornton, Rae 1962— **32**
Ligging, Alfred III 1965— **43**
(Lil') Bow Wow 1987— **35**
Lil' Kim 1975— **28**
Liles, Kevin 1968— **42**
Lincoln, Abbey 1930— **3**
Lincoln, C(harles) Eric 1924-2000 **38**
Lindo, Delroy 1952— **18, 45**
LisaRaye 1967— **27**
Liston, (Charles) Sonny 1928(?)-1970 **33**
Little Milton 1934— **36**
Little Richard 1932— **15**
Little Walter 1930-1968 **36**
Little, Benilde 1958— **21**
Little, Malcolm *See X, Malcolm*
Little, Robert L(angdon) 1938— **2**
Littlepage, Craig 1951— **35**
Lloyd, Earl 1928(?)— **26**
Lloyd, John Henry "Pop" 1884-1965 **30**
Locke, Alain (LeRoy) 1886-1954 **10**
Locke, Eddie 1930— **44**
Lofton, James 1956— **42**
Lofton, Kenneth 1967— **12**
Lofton, Ramona 1950— **14**
Logan, Onnie Lee 1910(?)-1995 **14**
Logan, Rayford W. 1897-1982 **40**
Long, Eddie L. 19(?)(?)— **29**
Long, Nia 1970— **17**
Lopes, Lisa "Left Eye" 1971-2002 **36**
Lord Pitt of Hampstead *See Pitt, David Thomas*
Lorde, Audre (Geraldine) 1934-1992 **6**
Lorenzo, Irving *See Gotti, Irv*
Lott, Ronnie 1959— **9**
Louis, Errol T. 1962— **8**
Louis, Joe 1914-1981 **5**
Loury, Glenn 1948— **36**
Love, Darlene 1941— **23**
Love, Nat 1854-1921 **9**
Lover, Ed **10**
Loving, Alvin 1935— **35**
Lowery, Joseph E. 1924— **2**
Lucas, John 1953— **7**
Lucy Foster, Autherine 1929— **35**
Ludacris 1978(?)— **37**
Lumbly, Carl 1952— **47**
Lumpkin, Elgin Baylor *See Ginuwine*
Lumumba, Patrice 1925-1961 **33**
Luthuli, Albert (John Mvumbi) 1898(?)-1967 **13**
Lyle, Marcenia *See Stone, Toni*
Lyles, Lester Lawrence 1946— **31**
Lymon, Frankie 1942-1968 **22**
Lynn, Lonnie Rashid *See Common*

Lyons, Henry 1942(?)— **12**
Lyttle, Hulda Margaret 1889-1983 **14**
Maathai, Wangari 1940— **43**
Mabley, Jackie "Moms" 1897(?)-1975 **15**
Mabrey, Vicki 1957(?)— **26**
Mabuza, Lindiwe 1938— **18**
Mabuza-Suttle, Felicia 1950— **43**
Mac, Bernie 1957— **29**
Machel, Graca Simbine 1945— **16**
Machel, Samora Moises 1933-1986 **8**
Madhubuti, Haki R. 1942— **7**
Madikizela, Nkosikazi Nobandle Nomzamo Winifred *See* Mandela, Winnie
Madison, Joseph E. 1949— **17**
Madison, Paula 1952— **37**
Madison, Romell 1952— **45**
Mahal, Taj 1942— **39**
Mainor, Dorothy Leigh 1910(?)-1996 **19**
Majette, Denise 1955— **41**
Major, Clarence 1936— **9**
Majors, Jeff 1960(?)— **41**
Makeba, (Zensi) Miriam 1932— **2**
Malcolm X *See* X, Malcolm
Mallett, Conrad, Jr. 1953— **16**
Malone, Annie (Minerva Turnbo Pope) 1869-1957 **13**
Malone, Karl A. 1963— **18**
Malone, Maurice 1965— **32**
Malveaux, Julianne 1953— **32**
Mamdou, Tandja 1938— **33**
Mandela, Nelson (Rolihlahla) 1918— **1, 14**
Mandela, Winnie 1934— **2, 35**
Manigault, Earl "The Goat" 1943— **15**
Manley, Audrey Forbes 1934— **16**
Manley, Edna 1900-1987 **26**
Manley, Ruth 1947— **34**
Marable, Manning 1950— **10**
Marchand, Inga *See* Foxy Brown
Marechera, Charles William *See* Marechera, Dambudzo
Marechera, Dambudzo 1952-1987 **39**
Marechera, Tambudzai *See* Marechera, Dambudzo
Mariner, Jonathan 1954(?)— **41**
Marino, Eugene Antonio 1934-2000 **30**
Markham, E(dward) A(rchibald) 1939— **37**
Marley, Bob 1945-1981 **5**
Marley, David *See* Marley, Ziggy
Marley, Rita 1947— **32**
Marley, Robert Nesta *See* Marley, Bob
Marley, Ziggy 1968— **41**
Marrow, Queen Esther 1943(?)— **24**
Marrow, Tracey *See* Ice-T
Marsalis, Branford 1960— **34**
Marsalis, Delfeayo 1965— **41**
Marsalis, Wynton 1961— **16**
Marsh, Henry L., III 1934(?)— **32**
Marshall, Bella 1950— **22**
Marshall, Gloria *See* Sudarkasa, Niara
Marshall, Paule 1929— **7**

Marshall, Thurgood 1908-1993 **1, 44**
Marshall, Valenza Pauline Burke *See* Marshall, Paule
Martha Jean "The Queen" *See* Steinberg, Martha Jean
Martin, Darnell 1964— **43**
Martin, Helen 1909-2000 **31**
Martin, Jesse L. 19(?)(?)— **31**
Martin, Louis Emanuel 1912-1997 **16**
Martin, Sara 1884-1955 **38**
Marvin X *See* X, Marvin
Mary Mary **34**
Mase 1977(?)— **24**
Masekela, Barbara 1941— **18**
Masekela, Hugh (Ramopolo) 1939— **1**
Masire, Quett (Ketumile Joni) 1925— **5**
Mason, Felicia 1963(?)— **31**
Mason, Ronald 1949— **27**
Massaquoi, Hans J. 1926— **30**
Massenburg, Kedar 1964(?)— **23**
Massey, Brandon 1973— **40**
Massey, Walter E(ugene) 1938— **5, 45**
Massie, Samuel Proctor, Jr. 1919— **29**
Master P 1970— **21**
Mathabane, Johannes *See* Mathabane, Mark
Mathabane, Mark 1960— **5**
Mathis, Greg 1960— **26**
Mathis, Johnny 1935— **20**
Mauldin, Jermaine Dupri *See* Dupri, Jermaine
Maxey, Randall 1941— **46**
Maxwell 1973— **20**
May, Derrick 1963— **41**
Mayers, Jamal 1974— **39**
Mayfield, Curtis (Lee) 1942-1999 **2, 43**
Mayhew, Richard 1924— **39**
Maynard, Robert C(lyve) 1937-1993 **7**
Maynor, Dorothy 1910-1996 **19**
Mayo, Whitman 1930-2001 **32**
Mays, Benjamin E(lijah) 1894-1984 **7**
Mays, Leslie A. 19(?)(?)— **41**
Mays, William G. 1946— **34**
Mays, William Howard, Jr. *See* Mays, Willie
Mays, Willie 1931— **3**
Mazrui, Ali Al'Amin 1933— **12**
Mbaye, Mariétou 1948— **31**
Mbeki, Thabo Mvuyelwa 1942— **14**
Mboup, Souleymane 1951— **10**
Mbuende, Kaire Munionganda 1953— **12**
MC Lyte 1971— **34**
McBride, Bryant Scott 1965— **18**
McBride, James C. 1957— **35**
McCabe, Jewell Jackson 1945— **10**
McCall, H. Carl 1938(?)— **27**
McCall, Nathan 1955— **8**
McCann, Renetta 1957(?)— **44**
McCarty, Osceola 1908— **16**
McClurkin, Donnie 1961— **25**
McCoy, Elijah 1844-1929 **8**
McCray, Nikki 1972— **18**
McDaniel, Hattie 1895-1952 **5**
McDaniels, Darryl *See* DMC

McDonald, Audra 1970— **20**
McDonald, Erroll 1954(?)— **1**
McDonald, Gabrielle Kirk 1942— **20**
McDougall, Gay J. 1947— **11, 43**
McEwen, Mark 1954— **5**
McFadden, Bernice L. 1966— **39**
McGee, Charles 1924— **10**
McGee, James Madison 1940— **46**
McGriff, Fred 1963— **24**
McGruder, Aaron Vincent 1974— **28**
McGruder, Robert 1942— **22, 35**
McIntosh, Winston Hubert *See* Tosh, Peter
McIntyre, Natalie *See* Gary, Macy
McKay, Claude 1889-1948 **6**
McKay, Festus Claudius *See* McKay, Claude
McKay, Nellie Yvonne 194(?)— **17**
McKee, Lonette 1952— **12**
McKegney, Tony 1958— **3**
McKenzie, Vashti M. 1947— **29**
McKinney, Cynthia Ann 1955— **11**
McKinney, Nina Mae 1912-1967 **40**
McKinney-Whetstone, Diane 1954(?)— **27**
McKinnon, Ike *See* McKinnon, Isaiah
McKinnon, Isaiah 1943— **9**
McKissick, Floyd B(ixler) 1922-1981 **3**
McKnight, Brian 1969— **18, 34**
McLeod, Gus 1955(?)— **27**
McLeod, Gustavus *See* McLeod, Gus
McMillan, Rosalynn A. 1953— **36**
McMillan, Terry 1951— **4, 17**
McMurray, Georgia L. 1934-1992 **36**
McNabb, Donovan 1976— **29**
McNair, Steve 1973— **22, 47**
McNair, Steve 1973— **22**
McNeil, Lori 1964(?)— **1**
McPhail, Sharon 1948— **2**
McPherson, David 1968— **32**
McQueen, Butterfly 1911— **6**
McQueen, Thelma *See* McQueen, Butterfly
McWhorter, John 1965— **35**
Meadows, Tim 1961— **30**
Meek, Carrie (Pittman) 1926— **6, 36**
Meek, Kendrick 1966— **41**
Meeks, Gregory 1953— **25**
Meles Zenawi 1955(?)— **3**
Memmi, Albert 1920— **37**
Memphis Minnie 1897-1973 **33**
Mensah, Thomas 1950— **48**
Mercado-Valdes, Frank 1962— **43**
Meredith, James H(oward) 1933— **11**
Merkerson, S. Epatha 1952— **47**
Messenger, The *See* Divine, Father
Metcalfe, Ralph 1910-1978 **26**
Meyer, June *See* Jordan, June
Mfume, Kweisi 1948— **6, 41**
Micheaux, Oscar (Devereaux) 1884-1951 **7**
Michele, Michael 1966— **31**
Mickelbury, Penny 1948— **28**
Milla, Roger 1952— **2**
Millender-McDonald, Juanita 1938— **21**

Miller, Bebe 1950— **3**
Miller, Cheryl 1964— **10**
Miller, Dorie 1919-1943 **29**
Miller, Doris *See* Miller, Dorie
Miller, Maria 1803-1879 **19**
Miller, Percy *See* Master P
Miller, Reggie 1965— **33**
Millines Dziko, Trish 1957— **28**
Mills, Florence 1896-1927 **22**
Mills, Sam 1959— **33**
Mills, Stephanie 1957— **36**
Mills, Steve 1960(?)— **47**
Milner, Ron 1938— **39**
Milton, DeLisha 1974— **31**
Mingo, Frank L. 1939-1989 **32**
Mingus, Charles Jr. 1922-1979 **15**
Minor, DeWayne 1956— **32**
Mitchell, Arthur 1934— **2, 47**
Mitchell, Brian Stokes 1957— **21**
Mitchell, Corinne 1914-1993 **8**
Mitchell, Leona 1949— **42**
Mitchell, Loften 1919-2001 **31**
Mitchell, Parren J. 1922— **42**
Mitchell, Russ 1960— **21**
Mitchell, Sharon 1962— **36**
Mizell, Jason *See* Jay, Jam Master
Mkapa, Benjamin William 1938— **16**
Mo', Keb' 1952— **36**
Mo'Nique 1967— **35**
Mobutu Sese Seko (Nkuku wa za Banga) 1930— **1**
Mobutu, Joseph-Desire *See* Mobutu Sese Seko (Nkuku wa za Banga)
Mofolo, Thomas (Mokopu) 1876-1948 **37**
Mogae, Festus Gontebanye 1939— **19**
Mohamed, Ali Mahdi *See* Ali Mahdi Mohamed
Mohammed, W. Deen 1933— **27**
Mohammed, Warith Deen *See* Mohammed, W. Deen
Moi, Daniel (Arap) 1924— **1, 35**
Mollel, Tololwa 1952— **38**
Mongella, Gertrude 1945— **11**
Monica 1980— **21**
Monk, Art 1957— **38**
Monk, Thelonious (Sphere, Jr.) 1917-1982 **1**
Monroe, Mary 19(?)(?)— **35**
Montgomery, Tim 1975— **41**
Moody, Ronald 1900-1984 **30**
Moon, (Harold) Warren 1956— **8**
Mooney, Paul 19(?)(?)— **37**
Moore, Alice Ruth *See* Dunbar-Nelson, Alice Ruth Moore
Moore, Bobby *See* Rashad, Ahmad
Moore, Chante 1970(?)— **26**
Moore, Dorothy Rudd 1940— **46**
Moore, Harry T. 1905-1951 **29**
Moore, Jessica Care 1971— **30**
Moore, Johnny B. 1950— **38**
Moore, Kevin *See* Mo', Keb'
Moore, Melba 1945— **21**
Moore, Minyon 19??— **45**
Moore, Shemar 1970— **21**
Moore, Undine Smith 1904-1989 **28**
Moorer, Lana *See* MC Lyte
Moorer, Michael 1967— **19**
Moose, Charles 1953— **40**

Morgan, Garrett (Augustus) 1877-1963 **1**
Morgan, Joe Leonard 1943— **9**
Morgan, Rose (Meta) 1912(?)— **11**
Morganfield, McKinley *See Muddy Waters*
Morial, Ernest "Dutch" 1929-1989 **26**
Morial, Marc 1958— **20**
Morris, Garrett 1937— **31**
Morris, Greg 1934-1996 **28**
Morris, Stevland Judkins *See Wonder, Stevie*
Morrison, Keith 1942— **13**
Morrison, Toni 1931— **2, 15**
Morton, Azie Taylor 1936-2003 **48**
Morton, Jelly Roll 1885(?)-1941 **29**
Morton, Joe 1947— **18**
Mos Def 1973— **30**
Moseka, Aminata *See Lincoln, Abbey*
Moseley-Braun, Carol *See Braun, Carol (Elizabeth) Moseley*
Moses, Edwin 1955— **8**
Moses, Gilbert, III 1942-1995 **12**
Moses, Robert Parris 1935— **11**
Mosley, "Sugar" Shane 1971— **32**
Mosley, Tim *See Timbaland*
Mosley, Walter 1952— **5, 25**
Moss, Carlton 1909-1997 **17**
Moss, Randy 1977— **23**
Moss, Shad Gregory *See (Lil') Bow Wow*
Mossell, Gertrude Bustill 1855-1948 **40**
Moten, Emma Barnett 1901— **18**
Motley, Archibald, Jr. 1891-1981 **30**
Motley, Constance Baker 1921— **10**
Motley, Marion 1920-1999 **26**
Mourning, Alonzo 1970— **17, 44**
Moutoussamy-Ashe, Jeanne 1951— **7**
Mowatt, Judy 1952(?)— **38**
Mowry, Jess 1960— **7**
Moyo, Karega Kofi 19(?)(?)— **36**
Moyo, Yvette Jackson 1953— **36**
Mphalele, Es'kia (Ezekiel) 1919— **40**
Mugabe, Robert Gabriel 1928— **10**
Mugo, Madeleine *See Mugo, Micere Githae*
Mugo, Micere Githae 1942— **32**
Muhajir, El *See X, Marvin*
Muhammad, Ava 1951— **31**
Muhammad, Elijah 1897-1975 **4**
Muhammad, Khallid Abdul 1951(?)— **10, 31**
Mullen, Harryette 1953— **34**
Mullen, Nicole C. 1967— **45**
Muluzi, Elson Bakili 1943— **14**
Mumba, Samantha 1983— **29**
Murphy McKenzie, Vashti *See McKenzie, Vashti M.*
Murphy, Eddie 1961— **4, 20**
Murphy, Edward Regan *See Murphy, Eddie*
Murphy, John H. 1916— **42**
Murphy, Laura M. 1955— **43**
Murray, Albert L. 1916— **33**
Murray, Cecil 1929— **12, 47**
Murray, Eddie 1956— **12**
Murray, Lenda 1962— **10**
Murray, Pauli 1910-1985 **38**

Murray, Tai 1982— **47**
Muse, Clarence Edouard 1889-1979 **21**
Museveni, Yoweri (Kaguta) 1944(?)— **4**
Musiq 1977— **37**
Mutebi, Ronald 1956— **25**
Mutola, Maria de Lurdes 1972— **12**
Mutombo, Dikembe 1966— **7**
Mutu, Wangechi 19(?)(?)— **44**
Mwangi, Meja 1948— **40**
Mwinyi, Ali Hassan 1925— **1**
Mya 1979— **35**
Myers, Walter Dean 1937— **8**
Myers, Walter Milton *See Myers, Walter Dean*
N'Dour, Youssou 1959— **1**
N'Namdi, George R. 1946— **17**
Nabrit, Samuel Milton 1905-2003 **47**
Nagin, Ray 1956— **42**
Nakhid, David 1964— **25**
Nanula, Richard D. 1960— **20**
Napoleon, Benny N. 1956(?)— **23**
Nas 1973— **33**
Nascimento, Milton 1942— **2**
Nash, Johnny 1940— **40**
Naylor, Gloria 1950— **10, 42**
Ndadaye, Melchior 1953-1993 **7**
Ndegeocello, Me'Shell 1968— **15**
Ndungane, Winston Njongonkulu 1941— **16**
Neal, Elise 1970— **29**
Neal, Larry 1937-1981 **38**
Neal, Raful 1936— **44**
Nelly 1978— **32**
Nelson Meigs, Andrea 1968— **48**
Nelson, Jill 1952— **6**
Nelson, Prince Rogers *See Prince*
Neto, António Agostinho 1922— **43**
Nettles, Marva Deloise *See Collins, Marva*
Neville, Aaron 1941— **21**
Newcombe, Don 1926— **24**
Newsome, Ozzie 1956— **26**
Newton, Huey (Percy) 1942-1989 **2**
Newton, Thandie 1972— **26**
Ngengi, Kamau wa *See Kenyatta, Jomo*
Ngubane, (Baldwin Sipho) Ben 1941— **33**
Ngugi, James wa Thiong'o *See wa Thiong'o, Ngugi*
Nicholas, Fayard 1914— **20**
Nicholas, Harold 1921— **20**
Nichols, Grace *See Nichols, Nichelle*
Nichols, James Thomas *See Bell, James "Cool Papa"*
Nichols, Nichelle 1933(?)— **11**
Nissel, Angela 1974— **42**
Njongonkulu, Winston Ndungane 1941— **16**
Nkomo, Joshua (Mqabuko Nyongolo) 1917— **4**
Nkosi, Lewis 1936— **46**
Nkrumah, Kwame 1909-1972 **3**
Noah, Yannick (Simon Camille) 1960— **4**
Noble, Ronald 1957— **46**
Norman, Christina 1960(?)— **47**
Norman, Jessye 1945— **5**
Norman, Maidie 1912-1998 **20**
Norman, Pat 1939— **10**

Norton, Eleanor Holmes 1937— **7**
Norwood, Brandy *See, Brandy*
Notorious B.I.G. 1972-1997 **20**
Nottage, Cynthia DeLores *See Tucker, C. DeLores*
Ntaryamira, Cyprien 1955-1994 **8**
Nugent, Richard Bruce 1906-1987 **39**
Nujoma, Samuel 1929— **10**
Nunn, Annetta 1959— **43**
Nyanda, Siphiwe 1950— **21**
Nyerere, Julius (Kambarage) 1922— **5**
Nzo, Alfred (Baphethuxolo) 1925— **15**
O'Leary, Hazel (Rollins) 1937— **6**
O'Neal, Ron 1937-2004 **46**
O'Neal, Shaquille (Rashaun) 1972— **8, 30**
O'Neal, Stanley 1951— **38**
O'Neil, Buck 1911— **19**
O'Neil, John Jordan *See O'Neil, Buck*
O'Ree, William Eldon *See O'Ree, Willie*
O'Ree, Willie 1935— **5**
Obasanjo, Olusegun 1937— **5, 22**
Obasanjo, Stella 1945— **32**
Odetta 1939 **37**
Oglesby, Zena 1947— **12**
Ogletree, Charles, Jr. 1952— **12, 47**
Ogunlesi, Adebayo O. 19(?)(?)— **37**
Okara, Gabriel 1921— **37**
Olajuwon, Akeem *See Olajuwon, Hakeem (Abdul Ajibola)*
Olajuwon, Hakeem (Abdul Ajibola) 1963— **2**
Olatunji, Babatunde 1927— **36**
Olden, Georg(e) 1920-1975 **44**
Oliver, Jerry 1947— **37**
Oliver, Joe "King" 1885-1938 **42**
Oliver, John J., Jr. 1945— **48**
Ongala, Ramadhani Mtoro *See Ongala, Remmy*
Ongala, Remmy 1947— **9**
Onwueme, Tess Osonye 1955— **23**
Onwurah, Ngozi 1966(?)— **38**
Orlandersmith, Dael 1959— **42**
Osborne, Jeffrey 1948— **26**
Ouattara 1957— **43**
Ousmane, Sembène *See Sembène, Ousmane*
OutKast **35**
Owens, Dana *See Queen Latifah*
Owens, Helen 1937— **48**
Owens, J. C. *See Owens, Jesse*
Owens, Jack 1904-1997 **38**
Owens, James Cleveland *See Owens, Jesse*
Owens, Jesse 1913-1980 **2**
Owens, Major (Robert) 1936— **6**
Oyono, Ferdinand 1929— **38**
P. Diddy *See Combs, Sean "Puffy"*
Pace, Orlando 1975— **21**
Page, Alan (Cedric) 1945— **7**
Page, Clarence 1947— **4**
Paige, Leroy Robert *See Paige, Satchel*
Paige, Rod 1933— **29**
Paige, Satchel 1906-1982 **7**
Painter, Nell Irvin 1942— **24**
Palmer, Everard 1930— **37**

Parish, Robert 1953— **43**
Parker, (Lawrence) Kris(hna) *See KRS-One*
Parker, Charlie 1920-1955 **20**
Parker, Kellis E. 1942-2000 **30**
Parks, Bernard C. 1943— **17**
Parks, Gordon (Roger Alexander Buchanan) 1912— **1, 35**
Parks, Rosa 1913— **1, 35**
Parks, Suzan-Lori 1964— **34**
Parsons, James Benton 1911-1993 **14**
Parsons, Richard Dean 1948— **11, 33**
Pascal-Trouillot, Ertha 1943— **3**
Patillo, Melba Joy 1941— **15**
Patrick, Deval Laurdine 1956— **12**
Patterson, Floyd 1935— **19**
Patterson, Frederick Douglass 1901-1988 **12**
Patterson, Gilbert Earl 1939— **41**
Patterson, Louise 1901-1999 **25**
Patterson, Orlando 1940— **4**
Patterson, P(ercival) J(ames) 1936(?)— **6, 20**
Patton, Antwan 1975— **45**
Patton, Antwan "Big Boi" 1975(?)— *See OutKast*
Payne, Allen 1962(?)— **13**
Payne, Donald M(ilford) 1934— **2**
Payne, Ethel L. 1911-1991 **28**
Payne, Ulice 1955— **42**
Payton, Benjamin F. 1932— **23**
Payton, John 1946— **48**
Payton, Walter (Jerry) 1954--1999 **11, 25**
Pearman, Raven-Symone Christina *See Raven*
Peck, Carolyn 1966(?)— **23**
Peck, Raoul 1953— **32**
Peete, Calvin 1943— **11**
Peete, Holly Robinson 1965— **20**
Pelé 1940— **7**
Pendergrass, Teddy 1950— **22**
Penniman, Richard Wayne *See, Little Richard*
Peoples, Dottie 19(?)(?)— **22**
Pereira, Aristides 1923— **30**
Perez, Anna 1951— **1**
Perkins, Anthony 1959?— **24**
Perkins, Edward (Joseph) 1928— **5**
Perkins, Marion 1908-1961 **38**
Perrot, Kim 1967-1999 **23**
Perry, Emmitt, Jr. *See, Perry, Tyler*
Perry, Lee "Scratch" 1936— **19**
Perry, Lincoln *See Fetchit, Stepin*
Perry, Lowell 1931-2001 **30**
Perry, Rainford Hugh *See Perry, Lee "Scratch"*
Perry, Ruth 1936— **19**
Perry, Ruth Sando 1939— **15**
Perry, Tyler 1969— **40**
Person, Waverly (J.) 1927— **9**
Peters, Lenrie 1932— **43**
Peters, Margaret and Matilda **43**
Peters, Maria Philomena 1941— **12**
Petersen, Frank E. 1932— **31**
Peterson, Hannibal *See, Peterson, Marvin "Hannibal"*
Peterson, James 1937— **38**
Peterson, Marvin "Hannibal" 1948— **27**
Petry, Ann 1909-1997 **19**

Phifer, Mekhi 1975— **25**
Philip, M. Nourbese *See Philip, Marlene Nourbese*
Philip, Marlene Nourbese 1947— **32**
Phillips, Teresa L. 1958— **42**
Pickett, Bill 1870-1932 **11**
Pickett, Cecil 1945— **39**
Pierre, Andre 1915— **17**
Pierre, Percy Anthony 1939— **46**
Pinchback, P(inckney) B(enton) S(tewart) 1837-1921 **9**
Pinckney, Bill 1935— **42**
Pinderhughes, John 1946— **47**
Pinkett Smith, Jada 1971— **10, 41**
Pinkett, Jada *See Pinkett Smith, Jada*
Pinkney, Jerry 1939— **15**
Pinkston, W. Randall 1950— **24**
Pippen, Scottie 1965— **15**
Pippin, Horace 1888-1946 **9**
Pitt, David Thomas 1913-1994 **10**
Pitta, (do Nascimento), Celso (Roberto) 19(?)(?)— **17**
Player, Willa B. 1909-2003 **43**
Pleasant, Mary Ellen 1814-1904 **9**
Plessy, Homer Adolph 1862-1925 **31**
Poitier, Sidney 1927— **11, 36**
Poole, Elijah *See Muhammad, Elijah*
Porter, Countee Leroy *See, Cullin, Countee*
Porter, James A(mos) 1905-1970 **11**
Potter, Myrtle 1958— **40**
Poussaint, Alvin F(rancis) 1934— **5**
Powell, Adam Clayton, Jr. 1908-1972 **3**
Powell, Bud 1924-1966 **24**
Powell, Colin (Luther) 1937— **1, 28**
Powell, Debra A. 1964— **23**
Powell, Kevin 1966— **31**
Powell, Maxine 1924— **8**
Powell, Michael Anthony *See Powell, Mike*
Powell, Michael K. 1963— **32**
Powell, Mike 1963— **7**
Powell, Renee 1946— **34**
Pratt Dixon, Sharon *See Dixon, Sharon Pratt*
Pratt, Awadagin 1966— **31**
Pratt, Geronimo 1947— **18**
Premice, Josephine 1926-2001 **41**
Pressley, Condace L. 1964— **41**
Preston, Billy 1946— **39**
Preston, William Everett *See Preston, Billy*
Price, Florence 1887-1953 **37**
Price, Frederick K.C. 1932— **21**
Price, Glenda 1939— **22**
Price, Hugh B. 1941— **9**
Price, Kelly 1973(?)— **23**
Price, Leontyne 1927— **1**
Pride, Charley 1938(?)— **26**
Primus, Pearl 1919— **6**
Prince 1958— **18**
Prince-Bythewood, Gina 1968— **31**
Pritchard, Robert Starling 1927— **21**
Procope, Ernesta 19(?)(?)— **23**
Prophet, Nancy Elizabeth 1890-1960 **42**

Prothrow, Deborah Boutin *See Prothrow-Stith, Deborah*
Prothrow-Stith, Deborah 1954— **10**
Pryor, Richard (Franklin Lennox Thomas) 1940— **3, 24**
Puckett, Kirby 1961— **4**
Puff Daddy *See Combs, Sean "Puffy"*
Puryear, Martin 1941— **42**
Quarles, Benjamin Arthur 1904-1996 **18**
Quarles, Norma 1936— **25**
Quarterman, Lloyd Albert 1918-1982 **4**
Queen Latifah 1970(?)— **1, 16**
Quirot, Ana (Fidelia) 1963— **13**
Rahman, Aishah 1936— **37**
Raines, Franklin Delano 1949— **14**
Rainey, Ma 1886-1939 **33**
Ralph, Sheryl Lee 1956— **18**
Ramaphosa, (Matamela) Cyril 1952— **3**
Ramphele, Mamphela 1947— **29**
Ramsey, Charles H. 1948— **21**
Rand, A(ddison) Barry 1944— **6**
Randall, Alice 1959— **38**
Randall, Dudley (Felker) 1914— **8**
Randle, Theresa 1967— **16**
Randolph, A(sa) Philip 1889-1979 **3**
Rangel, Charles (Bernard) 1930— **3**
Ras Tafari *See Haile Selassie*
Rashad, Ahmad 1949— **18**
Rashad, Phylicia 1948— **21**
Raspberry, William 1935— **2**
Raven, 1985— **44**
Raven-Symone *See Raven*
Rawlings, Jerry (John) 1947— **9**
Rawls, Lou 1936— **17**
Ray, Gene Anthony 1962-2003 **47**
Raymond, Usher, IV, *See Usher*
Razaf, Andy 1895-1973 **19**
Razafkeriefo, Andreamentania Paul *See Razaf, Andy*
Ready, Stephanie 1975— **33**
Reagon, Bernice Johnson 1942— **7**
Reason, Joseph Paul 1943— **19**
Reddick, Lawrence Dunbar 1910-1995 **20**
Redding, J. Saunders 1906-1988 **26**
Redding, Louis L. 1901-1998 **26**
Redding, Otis, Jr. 1941— **16**
Redman, Joshua 1969— **30**
Redmond, Eugene 1937— **23**
Reed, A. C. 1926— **36**
Reed, Ishmael 1938— **8**
Reed, Jimmy 1925-1976 **38**
Reems, Ernestine Cleveland 1932— **27**
Reese, Calvin *See Reese, Pokey*
Reese, Della 1931— **6, 20**
Reese, Pokey 1973— **28**
Reeves, Dianne 1956— **32**
Reeves, Rachel J. 1950(?)— **23**
Reeves, Triette Lipsey 1963— **27**
Reid, Antonio "L.A." 1958(?)— **28**
Reid, Irvin D. 1941— **20**
Reid, L.A. *See Reid, Antonio "L.A."*
Reid, Vernon 1958— **34**
Reuben, Gloria 19(?)(?)— **15**
Rhames, Ving 1961— **14**
Rhoden, Dwight 1962— **40**

Rhodes, Ray 1950— **14**
Rhone, Sylvia 1952— **2**
Rhymes, Busta 1972— **31**
Ribbs, William Theodore, Jr. *See Ribbs, Willy T.*
Ribbs, Willy T. 1956— **2**
Ribeiro, Alfonso 1971— **17**
Rice, Condoleezza 1954— **3, 28**
Rice, Jerry 1962— **5**
Rice, Linda Johnson 1958— **9, 41**
Rice, Norm(an Blann) 1943— **8**
Richards, Beah 1926-2000 **30**
Richards, Lloyd 1923(?)— **2**
Richardson, Desmond 1969— **39**
Richardson, Donna 1962— **39**
Richardson, Elaine Potter *See Kincaid, Jamaica*
Richardson, Nolan 1941— **9**
Richardson, Pat *See Norman, Pat*
Richie, Leroy C. 1941— **18**
Richie, Lionel 1949— **27**
Richmond, Mitchell James 1965— **19**
Rideau, Iris 1940(?)— **46**
Ridenhour, Carlton *See Chuck D.*
Riggs, Marlon 1957-1994 **5, 44**
Riley, Helen Caldwell Day 1926— **13**
Ringgold, Faith 1930— **4**
Riperton, Minnie 1947-1979 **32**
Rivers, Glenn "Doc" 1961— **25**
Roach, Max 1924— **21**
Roberts, Deborah 1960— **35**
Roberts, James *See Lover, Ed*
Roberts, Marcus 1963— **19**
Roberts, Marthaniel *See Roberts, Marcus*
Roberts, Robin 1960— **16**
Roberts, Roy S. 1939(?)— **14**
Robertson, Oscar 1938— **26**
Robeson, Eslanda Goode 1896-1965 **13**
Robeson, Paul (Leroy Bustill) 1898-1976 **2**
Robinson, Bill "Bojangles" 1878-1949 **11**
Robinson, Cleo Parker 1948(?)— **38**
Robinson, David 1965— **24**
Robinson, Eddie G. 1919— **10**
Robinson, Fatima 19(?)(?)— **34**
Robinson, Fenton 1935-1997 **38**
Robinson, Frank 1935— **9**
Robinson, Jack Roosevelt *See Robinson, Jackie*
Robinson, Jackie 1919-1972 **6**
Robinson, Luther *See Robinson, Bill "Bojangles"*
Robinson, Malcolm S. 1948— **44**
Robinson, Max 1939-1988 **3**
Robinson, Rachel 1922— **16**
Robinson, Randall 1941— **7, 46**
Robinson, Sharon 1950— **22**
Robinson, Shaun 19(?)(?)— **36**
Robinson, Smokey 1940— **3**
Robinson, Spottswood W., III 1916-1998 **22**
Robinson, Sugar Ray 1921— **18**
Robinson, William, Jr. *See Robinson, Smokey*
Roche, Joyce M. 1947— **17**
Rochester *See Anderson, Eddie "Rochester"*
Rochon, Lela 1965(?)— **16**

Rock, Chris 1967(?)— **3, 22**
Rodgers, Johnathan (Arlin) 1946— **6**
Rodgers, Rod 1937-2002 **36**
Rodman, Dennis 1961— **12, 44**
Rodriguez, Jimmy 1963(?)— **47**
Rogers, Jimmy 1924-1997 **38**
Rogers, Joe 1964— **27**
Rogero, Joel Augustus 1883(?)-1996 **30**
Rogers, John W., Jr. 1958— **5**
Rojas, Don 1949— **33**
Roker, Albert Lincoln, Jr. 1954(?)— **12**
Rolle, Esther 1920-1998 **13, 21**
Rollins, Charlemae Hill 1897-1979 **27**
Rollins, Howard Ellsworth 1950-1996 **16**
Rollins, Ida Gray Nelson *See Gray (Nelson Rollins), Ida*
Rollins, Sonny 1930— **37**
Ross, Araminta *See Tubman, Harriet*
Ross, Charles 1957— **27**
Ross, Diana 1944— **8, 27**
Ross, Don 1941— **27**
Ross, Isaiah "Doc" 1925-1993 **40**
Ross, Tracee Ellis 1972— **35**
Rotimi, (Emmanuel Gladstone) Ola(wale) 1938— **1**
Roundtree, Richard 1942— **27**
Rowan, Carl T(homas) 1925— **1, 30**
Rowell, Victoria 1962(?)— **13**
Roxanne Shante 1969— **33**
Rubin, Chanda 1976— **37**
Rucker, Darius 1966(?)— **34**
Rudolph, Maya 1972— **46**
Rudolph, Wilma (Glodean) 1940— **4**
Rugambwa, Laurean 1912-1997 **20**
Ruley, Ellis 1882-1959 **38**
Run 1964— **31**
Rupaul 1960— **17**
Rush, Bobby 1946— **26**
Rush, Otis 1934— **38**
Rushen, Patrice 1954— **12**
Rushing, Jimmy 1903-1972 **37**
Russell, Bill 1934— **8**
Russell, Herman Jerome 1931(?)— **17**
Russell, William Felton *See Russell, Bill*
Russell-McCloud, Patricia 1946— **17**
Rustin, Bayard 1910-1987 **4**
Saar, Alison 1956— **16**
Sade 1959— **15**
Sadler, Joseph *See Grandmaster Flash*
Saint James, Synthia 1949— **12**
Salih, Al-Tayyib 1929— **37**
Sallee, Charles 1911— **38**
Samara, Noah 1956— **15**
SAMO *See Basquiat, Jean-Michel*
Sampson, Charles 1957— **13**
Sampson, Edith S(purlock) 1901-1979 **4**
Samuel, Sealhenry Olumide 1963— **14**
Sané, Pierre Gabriel 1948-1998 **21**
Sanchez, Sonia 1934— **17**
Sanders, Barry 1968— **1**

Sanders, Deion (Luwynn) 1967— **4**, **31**
Sanders, Dori(nda) 1935— **8**
Sanders, Joseph R(ichard, Jr.) 1954— **11**
Sanders, Malika 1973— **48**
Sanford, John Elroy *See* Foxx, Redd
Sangare, Oumou 1968— **18**
Sankara, Thomas 1949-1987 **17**
Sapp, Warren 1972— **38**
Saro-Wiwa, Kenule 1941-1995 **39**
Satcher, David 1941— **7**
Satchmo *See* Armstrong, (Daniel) Louis
Savage, Augusta Christine 1892(?)-1962 **12**
Savimbi, Jonas (Malheiro) 1934-2002 **2**, **34**
Sawyer, Amos 1945— **2**
Sayers, Gale 1943— **28**
Sayles Belton, Sharon 1952(?)— **9**, **16**
Scantlebury, Janna 1984(?)— **47**
Schmoke, Kurt 1949— **1**, **48**
Schomburg, Arthur Alfonso 1874-1938 **9**
Schomburg, Arturo Alfonso *See* Schomburg, Arthur Alfonso
Schultz, Michael A. 1938— **6**
Schuyler, George Samuel 1895-1977 **40**
Scott, "Little" Jimmy 1925— **48**
Scott, C. A. 1908-2000 **29**
Scott, Coretta *See* King, Coretta Scott
Scott, Cornelius Adolphus *See* Scott, C. A.
Scott, David 1946— **41**
Scott, Jill 1972— **29**
Scott, Robert C. 1947— **23**
Scott, Stuart 1965— **34**
Scott, Wendell Oliver, Sr. 1921-1990 **19**
Scruggs, Mary Elfrieda *See* Williams, Mary Lou
Scurry, Briana 1971— **27**
Seal **14**
Seale, Bobby 1936— **3**
Seale, Robert George *See* Seale, Bobby
Sears-Collins, Leah J(eanette) 1955— **5**
Sebree, Charles 1914-1985 **40**
Seele, Pernessa 1954— **46**
Selassie, Haile *See* Haile Selassie
Sembène, Ousmane 1923— **13**
Senghor, Léopold Sédar 1906— **12**
Sengstacke, John Herman Henry 1912-1997 **18**
Senior, Olive 1941— **37**
Serrano, Andres 1951(?)— **3**
Shabazz, Attallah 1958— **6**
Shabazz, Betty 1936-1997 **7, 26**
Shabazz, Ilyasah 1962— **36**
Shaggy 1968— **31**
Shakespeare, Robbie 1953— *See* Sly & Robbie
Shakur, Assata 1947— **6**
Shakur, Tupac Amaru 1971-1996 **14**
Shange, Ntozake 1948— **8**
Sharper, Darren 1975— **32**
Sharpton, Al 1954— **21**

Shavers, Cheryl 19(?)(?)— **31**
Shaw, Bernard 1940— **2, 28**
Shaw, William J. 1934— **30**
Sheffey, Asa Bundy *See* Hayden, Robert Earl
Sheffield, Gary Antonian 1968— **16**
Shell, Art(hur, Jr.) 1946— **1**
Sherrod, Clayton 1944— **17**
Shinhoster, Earl 1950(?)-2000 **32**
Shipp, E. R. 1955— **15**
Shippen, John 1879-1968 **43**
Shirley, George I. 1934— **33**
Shorty I, Ras 1941-2000 **47**
Showers, Reggie 1964— **30**
Shuttlesworth, Fred 1922— **47**
Sifford, Charlie (Luther) 1922— **4**
Sigur, Wanda 1958— **44**
Silas, Paul 1943— **24**
Silver, Horace 1928— **26**
Siméus, Dumas M. 1940— **25**
Simmons, Bob 1948— **29**
Simmons, Joseph *See* Run
Simmons, Russell 1957(?)— **1, 30**
Simmons, Ruth J. 1945-**13, 38**
Simone, Nina 1933-2003 **15, 41**
Simpson, Carole 1940— **6, 30**
Simpson, Lorna 1960— **4, 36**
Simpson, O. J. 1947— **15**
Simpson, Valerie 1946— **21**
Sims, Howard "Sandman" 1917-2003 **48**
Sims, Lowery Stokes 1949— **27**
Sims, Naomi 1949— **29**
Sinbad 1957(?)— **1, 16**
Singletary, Michael *See* Singletary, Mike
Singletary, Mike 1958— **4**
Singleton, John 1968— **2, 30**
Sinkford, Jeanne C. 1933— **13**
Sisqo 1976— **30**
Sissle, Noble 1889-1975 **29**
Sister Souljah 1964— **11**
Sisulu, Sheila Violet Makate 1948(?)— **24**
Sisulu, Walter 1912-2003 **47**
Sizemore, Barbara A. 1927— **26**
Sklarek, Norma Merrick 1928— **25**
Slater, Rodney Earl 1955— **15**
Sledge, Percy 1940— **39**
Sleet, Moneta (J.), Jr. 1926— **5**
Sly & Robbie **34**
Smaltz, Audrey 1937(?)— **12**
Smiley, Tavis 1964— **20**
Smith, Anjela Lauren 1973— **44**
Smith, Anna Deavere 1950— **6, 44**
Smith, Arthur Lee, *See* Asante, Molefi Kete
Smith, B(arbara) 1949(?)— **11**
Smith, B. *See* Smith, B(arbara)
Smith, Barbara 1946— **28**
Smith, Bessie 1894-1937 **3**
Smith, Cladys "Jabbo" 1908-1991 **32**
Smith, Clarence O. 1933— **21**
Smith, Danyel 1966(?)— **40**
Smith, Emmitt (III) 1969— **7**
Smith, Greg 1964— **28**
Smith, Hezekiah Leroy Gordon *See* Smith, Stuff
Smith, Hilton 1912-1983 **29**
Smith, Jabbo *See* Smith, Cladys "Jabbo"
Smith, Jane E. 1946— **24**

Smith, Jennifer 1947— **21**
Smith, Jessie Carney 1930— **35**
Smith, John L. 1938— **22**
Smith, Joshua (Isaac) 1941— **10**
Smith, Mamie 1883-1946 **32**
Smith, Marvin 1910-2003 **46**
Smith, Mary Carter 1919— **26**
Smith, Morgan 1910-1993 **46**
Smith, Orlando *See* Smith, Tubby
Smith, Roger Guenveur 1960— **12**
Smith, Stuff 1909-1967 **37**
Smith, Trevor, Jr. *See* Rhymes, Busta
Smith, Trixie 1895-1943 **34**
Smith, Tubby 1951— **18**
Smith, Vincent D. 1929-2003 **48**
Smith, Walker, Jr. *See* Robinson, Sugar Ray
Smith, Will 1968— **8, 18**
Smith, Willi (Donnell) 1948-1987 **8**
Sneed, Paula A. 1947— **18**
Snipes, Wesley 1962— **3, 24**
Snoop Dogg 1972— **35**
Soglo, Nicéphore 1935— **15**
Solomon, Jimmie Lee 1947(?)— **38**
Somé, Malidoma Patrice 1956— **10**
Sosa, Sammy 1968— **21, 44**
Soulchild, Musiq *See* Musiq
Sowande, Fela 1905-1987 **39**
Sowande, Olufela Obafunmilayo *See* Sowande, Fela
Sowell, Thomas 1930— **2**
Soyinka, (Akinwande Olu)Wole 1934— **4**
Spaulding, Charles Clinton 1874-1952 **9**
Spencer, Anne 1882-1975 **27**
Spikes, Dolores Margaret Richard 1936— **18**
Sprewell, Latrell 1970— **23**
St. Jacques, Raymond 1930-1990 **8**
St. John, Kristoff 1966— **25**
St. Julien, Marlon 1972— **29**
St. Patrick, Mathew 1969— **48**
Stackhouse, Jerry 1974— **30**
Stallings, George A(ugustus), Jr. 1948— **6**
Stanford, John 1938— **20**
Stanton, Robert 1940— **20**
Staples, "Pops" 1915-2000 **32**
Staples, Brent 1951— **8**
Staples, Roebuck *See* Staples, "Pops"
Stargell, Willie "Pops" 1940(?)-2001 **29**
Staton, Candi 1940(?)— **27**
Staupers, Mabel K(eaton) 1890-1989 **7**
Stearnes, Norman "Turkey" 1901-1979 **31**
Steele, Claude Mason 1946— **13**
Steele, Lawrence 1963— **28**
Steele, Michael 1958— **38**
Steele, Shelby 1946— **13**
Steinberg, Martha Jean 1930(?)-2000 **28**
Stephens, Charlotte Andrews 1854-1951 **14**
Stephens, Myrtle *See* Potter, Myrtle
Stevens, Yvette *See* Khan, Chaka
Steward, David L. 19(?)(?)— **36**
Steward, Emanuel 1944— **18**
Stewart, Alison 1966(?)— **13**

Stewart, Ella 1893-1987 **39**
Stewart, Kordell 1972— **21**
Stewart, Paul Wilbur 1925— **12**
Still, William Grant 1895-1978 **37**
Stokes, Carl B(urton) 1927— **10**
Stokes, Louis 1925— **3**
Stone, Angie 1965(?)— **31**
Stone, Charles Sumner, Jr. *See* Stone, Chuck
Stone, Chuck 1924— **9**
Stone, Toni 1921-1996 **15**
Stout, Juanita Kidd 1919-1998 **24**
Stoute, Steve 1971(?)— **38**
Strahan, Michael 1971— **35**
Strawberry, Darryl 1962— **22**
Strayhorn, Billy 1915-1967 **31**
Street, John F. 1943(?)— **24**
Streeter, Sarah 1953— **45**
Stringer, C. Vivian 1948— **13**
Stringer, Korey 1974-2001 **35**
Studdard, Ruben 1978— **46**
Sudarkasa, Niara 1938— **4**
Sullivan, Leon H(oward) 1922— **3, 30**
Sullivan, Louis (Wade) 1933— **8**
Sullivan, Maxine 1911-1987 **37**
Summer, Donna 1948— **25**
Supremes, The **33**
Sutton, Percy E. 1920— **42**
Swann, Lynn 1952— **28**
Sweat, Keith 1961(?)— **19**
Swoopes, Sheryl Denise 1971— **12**
Swygert, H. Patrick 1943— **22**
Sykes, Roosevelt 1906-1984 **20**
Sykes, Wanda 1964— **48**
Tademy, Lalita 1948— **36**
Tafari Makonnen *See* Haile Selassie
Talbert, David 1966(?)— **34**
Tamia 1975— **24**
Tanksley, Ann (Graves) 1934— **37**
Tanner, Henry Ossawa 1859-1937 **1**
Tate, Eleanora E. 1948— **20**
Tate, Larenz 1975— **15**
Tatum, Art 1909-1956 **28**
Tatum, Beverly Daniel 1954— **42**
Taulbert, Clifton Lemoure 1945— **19**
Taylor, Billy 1921— **23**
Taylor, Charles 1948— **20**
Taylor, Helen (Lavon Hollingshed) 1942-2000 **30**
Taylor, John (David Beckett) 1952— **16**
Taylor, Karin 1971— **34**
Taylor, Koko 1935— **40**
Taylor, Kristin Clark 1959— **8**
Taylor, Lawrence 1959— **25**
Taylor, Meshach 1947(?)— **4**
Taylor, Mildred D. 1943— **26**
Taylor, Natalie 1959— **47**
Taylor, Regina 1959(?)— **9, 46**
Taylor, Ron 1952-2002 **35**
Taylor, Susan L. 1946— **10**
Taylor, Susie King 1848-1912 **13**
Temptations, The **33**
Terrell, Dorothy A. 1945— **24**
Terrell, Mary (Elizabeth) Church 1863-1954 **9**
Terrell, Tammi 1945-1970 **32**
Terry, Clark 1920— **39**
The Artist *See* Prince

The Rock *See Johnson, Dwayne "The Rock"*
Thigpen, Lynne 1948-2003 **17, 41**
Thomas, Alma Woodsey 1891-1978 **14**
Thomas, Clarence 1948— **2, 39**
Thomas, Debi 1967— **26**
Thomas, Derrick 1967-2000 **25**
Thomas, Frank Edward, Jr. 1968— **12**
Thomas, Franklin A(ugustine) 1934— **5**
Thomas, Irma 1941— **29**
Thomas, Isiah (Lord III) 1961— **7, 26**
Thomas, Rozonda "Chilli" 1971— *See TLC*
Thomas, Rufus 1917— **20**
Thomas, Sean Patrick 1970— **35**
Thomas, Vivien (T.) 1910-1985 **9**
Thomas-Graham, Pamela 1963(?)— **29**
Thomason, Marsha 1976— **47**
Thompson, Bennie G. 1948— **26**
Thompson, John W. 1949— **26**
Thompson, Larry D. 1945— **39**
Thompson, Tazewell (Alfred, Jr.) 1954— **13**
Thompson, Tina 1975— **25**
Thompson, William C. 1953(?)— **35**
Thornton, Big Mama 1926-1984 **33**
Thrash, Dox 1893-1965 **35**
Three Mo' Tenors **35**
Thrower, Willie 1930-2002 **35**
Thugwane, Josia 1971— **21**
Thurman, Howard 1900-1981 **3**
Thurman, Wallace Henry 1902-1934 **16**
Till, Emmett (Louis) 1941-1955 **7**
Tillard, Conrad 1964— **47**
Tillis, Frederick 1930— **40**
Tillman, George, Jr. 1968— **20**
Timbaland 1971— **32**
TLC **34**
Tolliver, William (Mack) 1951— **9**
Tolson, Melvin B(eaunorus) 1898-1966 **37**
Toomer, Jean 1894-1967 **6**
Toomer, Nathan Pinchback *See Toomer, Jean*
Torry, Guy 19(?)(?)— **31**
Tosh, Peter 1944-1987 **9**
Touré, Amadou Toumani 1948(?)— **18**
Touré, Askia (Muhammad Abu Bakr el) 1938— **47**
Touré, Sekou 1922-1984 **6**
Toussaint, Lorraine 1960— **32**
Townes, Jeffrey Allan *See DJ Jazzy Jeff*
Towns, Edolphus 1934— **19**
Townsend, Robert 1957— **4, 23**
Tribble, Isreal, Jr. 1940— **8**
Trotter, (William) Monroe 1872-1934 **9**
Trotter, Donne E. 1950— **28**
Trouillot, Ertha Pascal *See Pascal-Trouillot, Ertha*
Tsvangirai, Morgan 1952(?)— **26**
Tubbs Jones, Stephanie 1949— **24**
Tubman, Harriet 1820(?)-1913 **9**
Tucker, C. DeLores 1927— **12**
Tucker, Chris 1973(?)— **13, 23**
Tucker, Cynthia (Anne) 1955— **15**

Tucker, Rosina Budd Harvey Corrothers 1881-1987 **14**
Ture, Kwame *See Carmichael, Stokely*
Turnbull, Walter 1944— **13**
Turner, Henry McNeal 1834-1915 **5**
Turner, Tina 1939— **6, 27**
Tutu, Desmond (Mpilo) 1931— **6, 44**
Tutuola, Amos 1920-1997 **30**
Tyler, Aisha N. 1970— **36**
Tyree, Omar Rashad 1969— **21**
Tyrese 1978— **27**
Tyson, Andre 1960— **40**
Tyson, Asha 1970— **39**
Tyson, Cicely 1933— **7**
Tyson, Mike 1966— **28, 44**
Tyson, Neil de Grasse 1958— **15**
Uggams, Leslie 1943— **23**
Underwood, Blair 1964— **7, 27**
Union, Gabrielle 1973— **31**
Unseld, Wes 1946— **23**
Upshaw, Gene 1945— **18, 47**
Usher 1978(?)— **23**
Usry, James L. 1922— **23**
Ussery, Terdema Lamar, II 1958— **29**
Utendahl, John 1956— **23**
Van Peebles, Mario (Cain) 1957(?)— **2**
Van Peebles, Melvin 1932— **7**
van Sertima, Ivan 1935— **25**
Vance, Courtney B. 1960— **15**
VanDerZee, James (Augustus Joseph) 1886-1983 **6**
Vandross, Luther 1951— **13, 48**
Vann, Harold Moore *See Muhammad, Khallid Abdul*
Vanzant, Iyanla 1953— **17, 47**
Vaughan, Sarah (Lois) 1924-1990 **13**
Vaughn, Gladys Gary 1942(?)— **47**
Vaughn, Mo 1967— **16**
Vaughns, Cleopatra 1940— **46**
Vera, Yvonne 1964— **32**
Verdelle, A. J. 1960— **26**
Vereen, Ben(jamin Augustus) 1946— **4**
Vick, Michael 1980— **39**
Vieira, Joao 1939— **14**
Vincent, Marjorie Judith 1965(?)— **2**
Vincent, Mark *See Diesel, Vin*
Virgil, Ozzie 1933— **48**
Von Lipsey, Roderick 1959— **11**
wa Ngengi, Kamau *See Kenyatta, Jomo*
wa Thiong'o, Ngugi 1938— **29**
Waddles, Charleszetta (Mother) 1912— **19**
Waddles, Mother *See Waddles, Charleszetta (Mother)*
Wade-Gayles, Gloria Jean 1937(?)— **41**
Wagner, Annice 1937— **22**
Wainwright, Joscelyn 1941— **46**
Walcott, Derek (Alton) 1930— **5**
Walcott, Louis Eugene 1933— **2, 15**
Walker, Albertina 1929— **10**
Walker, Alice 1944— **1, 43**
Walker, Cedric "Ricky" 1953— **19**
Walker, Eamonn 1961— **37**
Walker, George 1922— **37**

Walker, Herschel (Junior) 1962— **1**
Walker, Hezekiah 1962— **34**
Walker, Kara 1969— **16**
Walker, Kurt *See Blow, Kurtis*
Walker, Madame C. J. 1867-1919 **7**
Walker, Maggie Lena 1867(?)-1934 **17**
Walker, Margaret 1915-1998 **29**
Walker, Nellie Marian *See Larsen, Nella*
Walker, T. J. 1961(?)— **7**
Walker, Thomas "T. J." *See Walker, T. J.*
Wallace, Michele Faith 1952— **13**
Wallace, Perry E. 1948— **47**
Wallace, Phyllis A(nn) 1920(?)-1993 **9**
Wallace, Ruby Ann *See Dee, Ruby*
Wallace, Sippie 1898-1986 **1**
Waller, Fats 1904-1943 **29**
Waller, Thomas Wright *See Waller, Fats*
Walton, Cora *See Taylor, Koko*
Wambugu, Florence 1953— **42**
Wamutombo, Dikembe Mutombo Mpolondo Mukamba Jean Jacque *See Mutombo, Dikembe*
Ward, Douglas Turner 1930— **42**
Ward, Lloyd 1949— **21, 46**
Ware, Andre 1968— **37**
Ware, Carl H. 1943— **30**
Warfield, Marsha 1955— **2**
Warner, Malcolm-Jamal 1970— **22, 36**
Warren, Michael 1946— **27**
Warren, Mike *See Warren, Michael*
Warwick, Dionne 1940— **18**
Washington, Alonzo 1967— **29**
Washington, Booker T(aliaferro) 1856-1915 **4**
Washington, Denzel 1954— **1, 16**
Washington, Dinah 1924-1963 **22**
Washington, Fred(er)i(cka Carolyn) 1903-1994 **10**
Washington, Grover, Jr. 1943-1999 **17, 44**
Washington, Harold 1922-1987 **6**
Washington, James Jr. 1909(?)-2000 **38**
Washington, Kerry 1977— **46**
Washington, Laura S. 1956(?)— **18**
Washington, MaliVai 1969— **8**
Washington, Patrice Clarke 1961— **12**
Washington, Regynald G. 1954(?)— **44**
Washington, Valores James 1903-1995 **12**
Washington, Walter 1915-2003 **45**
Wasow, Omar 1970— **15**
Waters, Benny 1902-1998 **26**
Waters, Ethel 1895-1977 **7**
Waters, Maxine 1938— **3**
Waters, Muddy 1915-1983 **34**
Watkins, Donald 1948— **35**
Watkins, Frances Ellen *See Harper, Frances Ellen Watkins*
Watkins, Gloria Jean *See hooks, bell*
Watkins, Levi, Jr. 1945— **9**
Watkins, Perry James Henry 1948-1996 **12**
Watkins, Shirley R. 1938— **17**

Watkins, Tionne "T-Boz" 1970— *See TLC*
Watkins, Walter C. 1946— **24**
Watson, Bob 1946— **25**
Watson, Diane 1933— **41**
Watson, Johnny "Guitar" 1935-1996 **18**
Watt, Melvin 1945— **26**
Wattleton, (Alyce) Faye 1943— **9**
Watts, Julius Caesar, Jr. 1957— **14, 38**
Watts, Rolonda 1959— **9**
Wayans, Damon 1961— **8, 41**
Wayans, Keenen Ivory 1958— **18**
Wayans, Marlon 1972— **29**
Wayans, Shawn 1971— **29**
Waymon, Eunice Kathleen *See Simone, Nina*
Weathers, Carl 1948— **10**
Weaver, Afaa Michael 1951— **37**
Weaver, Michael S. *See Weaver, Afaa Michael*
Weaver, Robert C. 1907-1997 **8, 46**
Webb, Veronica 1965— **10**
Webb, Wellington, Jr. 1941— **3**
Webber, Chris 1973— **15, 30**
Webster, Katie 1936-1999 **29**
Wedgeworth, Robert W. 1937— **42**
Weems, Renita J. 1954— **44**
Wek, Alek 1977— **18**
Wells, James Lesesne 1902-1993 **10**
Wells, Mary 1943-1992 **28**
Wells-Barnett, Ida B(ell) 1862-1931 **8**
Welsing, Frances (Luella) Cress 1935— **5**
Wesley, Valerie Wilson 194(?)— **18**
West, Cornel (Ronald) 1953— **5, 33**
West, Dorothy 1907— **12**
West, Togo Dennis, Jr. 1942— **16**
Westbrook, Peter 1952— **20**
Whack, Rita Coburn 1958— **36**
Whalum, Kirk 1958— **37**
Wharton, Clifton R(eginald), Jr. 1926— **7**
Wharton, Clifton Reginald, Sr. 1899-1990 **36**
Wheat, Alan Dupree 1951— **14**
Whitaker, "Sweet Pea" *See Whitaker, Pernell*
Whitaker, Forest 1961— **2**
Whitaker, Mark 1957— **21, 47**
Whitaker, Pernell 1964— **10**
White, (Donald) Dondi 1961-1998 **34**
White, Barry 1944-2003 **13, 41**
White, Bill 1933(?)— **1, 48**
White, Charles 1918-1979 **39**
White, Jesse 1934— **22**
White, John H. 1945— **27**
White, Linda M. 1942— **45**
White, Lois Jean 1938— **20**
White, Maurice 1941— **29**
White, Michael R(eed) 1951— **5**
White, Reggie 1961— **6**
White, Reginald Howard *See White, Reggie*
White, Walter F(rancis) 1893-1955 **4**
White, William DeKova *See White, Bill*
Whitfield, Fred 1967— **23**

Whitfield, Lynn 1954— **18**
Whitfield, Van 1960(?)— **34**
Wideman, John Edgar 1941— **5**
Wilder, L. Douglas 1931— **3**, **48**
Wiley, Ralph 1952— **8**
Wilkens, J. Ernest, Jr. 1923— **43**
Wilkens, Lenny 1937— **11**
Wilkens, Leonard Randolph *See Wilkens, Lenny*
Wilkins, Ray 1951— **47**
Wilkins, Roger (Wood) 1932— **2**
Wilkins, Roy 1901-1981 **4**
Williams, Anthony 1951— **21**
Williams, Armstrong 1959— **29**
Williams, Bert 1874-1922 **18**
Williams, Billy Dee 1937— **8**
Williams, Carl *See Kani, Karl*
Williams, Clarence 1893(?)-1965 **33**
Williams, Clarence, III 1939— **26**
Williams, Daniel Hale (III) 1856-1931 **2**
Williams, Deniece 1951— **36**
Williams, Denise 1958— **40**
Williams, Doug 1955— **22**
Williams, Eddie N. 1932— **44**
Williams, Evelyn 1922(?)— **10**
Williams, Fannie Barrier 1855-1944 **27**
Williams, George Washington 1849-1891 **18**
Williams, Gregory (Howard) 1943— **11**
Williams, Hosea Lorenzo 1926— **15**, **31**
Williams, Joe 1918-1999 **5**, **25**
Williams, John A. 1925— **27**
Williams, Juan 1954— **35**
Williams, Maggie 1954— **7**
Williams, Margaret Ann *See Williams, Maggie*

Williams, Mary Lou 1910-1981 **15**
Williams, Montel (B.) 1956(?)— **4**
Williams, Natalie 1970— **31**
Williams, O(swald) S. 1921— **13**
Williams, Patricia J. 1951— **11**
Williams, Paul R(evere) 1894-1980 **9**
Williams, Paulette Linda *See Shange, Ntozake*
Williams, Pharrell 1973— **47**
Williams, Robert F(ranklin) 1925— **11**
Williams, Robert Peter *See Guillaume, Robert*
Williams, Samuel Arthur 1946— **21**
Williams, Saul 1972— **31**
Williams, Serena 1981— **20**, **41**
Williams, Sherley Anne 1944-1999 **25**
Williams, Stanley "Tookie" 1953— **29**
Williams, Terrie M. 1954— **35**
Williams, Vanessa 1969— **32**
Williams, Vanessa L. 1963— **4**, **17**
Williams, Venus Ebone Starr 1980— **17**, **34**
Williams, Walter E(dward) 1936— **4**
Williams, William December *See Williams, Billy Dee*
Williams, William T(homas) 1942— **11**
Williams, Willie L(awrence) 1943— **4**
Williamson, Lisa *See Sister Souljah*
Williamson, Mykelti 1957— **22**
Willingham, Tyrone 1953— **43**
Willis, Cheryl *See Hudson, Cheryl*
Wilson, August 1945— **7**, **33**

Wilson, Cassandra 1955— **16**
Wilson, Charlie 1953— **31**
Wilson, Debra 1970(?)— **38**
Wilson, Ellis 1899-1977 **39**
Wilson, Flip 1933-1998 **21**
Wilson, Jimmy 1946— **45**
Wilson, Mary 1944 **28**
Wilson, Nancy 1937— **10**
Wilson, Natalie 1972(?)— **38**
Wilson, Phill 1956— **9**
Wilson, Sunnie 1908— **7**
Wilson, William Julius 1935— **22**
Wilson, William Nathaniel *See Wilson, Sunnie*
Winans, Angie 1968— **36**
Winans, Benjamin 1962— **14**
Winans, CeCe 1964— **14**, **43**
Winans, Debbie 1972— **36**
Winans, Marvin L. 1958— **17**
Winans, Vickie 1953(?)— **24**
Winfield, Dave 1951— **5**
Winfield, David Mark *See Winfield, Dave*
Winfield, Paul (Edward) 1941-2004 **2**, **45**
Winfrey, Oprah (Gail) 1954— **2**, **15**
Winkfield, Jimmy 1882-1974 **42**
Witherspoon, John 1942— **38**
Witt, Edwin T. 1920— **26**
Wofford, Chloe Anthony *See Morrison, Toni*
Wolfe, George C. 1954— **6**, **43**
Wonder, Stevie 1950— **11**
Woodard, Alfre 1953— **9**
Woodruff, Hale (Aspacio) 1900-1980 **9**
Woods, Eldrick *See Woods, Tiger*
Woods, Granville T. 1856-1910 **5**
Woods, Sylvia 1926— **34**

Woods, Tiger 1975— **14**, **31**
Woodson, Carter G(odwin) 1875-1950 **2**
Woodson, Robert L. 1937— **10**
Wooldridge, Anna Marie *See Lincoln, Abbey*
Worrill, Conrad 1941— **12**
Wright, Bruce McMarion 1918— **3**
Wright, Charles H. 1918-2002 **35**
Wright, Deborah C. 1958— **25**
Wright, Jeremiah A., Jr. 1941— **45**
Wright, Lewin 1962— **43**
Wright, Louis Tompkins 1891-1952 **4**
Wright, Richard 1908-1960 **5**
Wynn, Albert R. 1951— **25**
X, Malcolm 1925-1965 **1**
X, Marvin 1944— **45**
Yancy, Dorothy Cowser 1944— **42**
Yarbrough, Camille 1938— **40**
Yoba, (Abdul-)Malik (Kashie) 1967— **11**
York, Vincent 1952— **40**
Young, Andre Ramelle *See Dre, Dr.*
Young, Andrew 1932— **3**, **48**
Young, Coleman 1918-1997 **1**, **20**
Young, Jean Childs 1933-1994 **14**
Young, Roger Arliner 1899-1964 **29**
Young, Thomas 194(?)— *See Three Mo' Tenors*
Young, Whitney M(oore), Jr. 1921-1971 **4**
Youngblood, Johnny Ray, 1948— **8**
Youngblood, Shay 1959— **32**
Zollar, Alfred 1955(?)— **40**
Zollar, Jawole Willa Jo 1950— **28**
Zuma, Jacob G. 1942— **33**
Zuma, Nkosazana Dlamini 1949— **34**

Ref.
E
185.96
.C66

2005
v.48